FREEDOM AND UNITY

FREEDOM AND UNITY

A History of Vermont

Michael Sherman
Gene Sessions
P. Jeffrey Potash

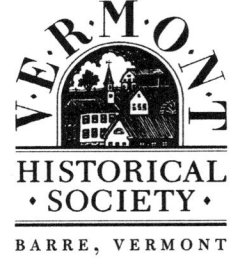

BARRE, VERMONT

Copyright © 2004 Michael Sherman, Gene Sessions, P. Jeffrey Potash

All rights reserved. No part of this book may be reproduced in any form or by any electronic or mechanical means including information storage and retrieval systems without permission in writing from the publisher, except by a reviewer who may quote brief passages in a review. Inquiries should be addressed to the Vermont Historical Society, 60 Washington St., Barre, Vermont, 05641

Book Design by Peter Holm, Sterling Hill Productions

LIBRARY OF CONGRESS CATALOGING-IN-PUBLICATION DATA
Sherman, Michael, 1944-
Freedom and unity: a history of Vermont/Michael Sherman, Gene Sessions, P. Jeffrey Potash
p. cm.
Includes bibliographical references and index
ISBN: 0-934720-48-7 (cloth : alk. paper) — ISBN: 0-934720-49-5 (pbk: alk. paper)
1. Vermont—History
F49 . S54 2004
974.3 22

2003064530

Printed in the United States of America
07 06 05 04   2 3 4 5

Second Printing, October 2004

Contents

Acknowledgments vii
Introduction xiii

Chapter 1
Footprints: Prehistory to 1609 1

Chapter 2
Struggle for Empire, the Vermont Crossroad: 1609–1763 33

Chapter 3
The Lure of the Land: 1763–1807 73

Chapter 4
Years of Optimism and Anxiety: 1807–1850 145

Chapter 5
Links to the Nation: 1850–1870 213

Chapter 6
The Reconfiguration of Vermont: 1870–1900 287

Chapter 7
"Behind the Times": 1900–1927 347

Chapter 8
Floods, Depression, and War: 1927–1945 421

Chapter 9
Vermont Transformed: 1945–1969 489

Chapter 10
"Another 250,000 People": 1969–2003 557

Appendices 625
Notes 643
Selected Bibliography 691
Index 703

Acknowledgments

This book has a long history and some who have followed its development and culmination have even suggested writing a history of the history. Rather than do that, we wish to acknowledge those who have contributed in one way or another to its coming to completion.

In 1976, H. Nicholas Muller III secured funding from the State Bicentennial Commission to coordinate and edit a collective work on the history of Vermont and assembled a group of scholars and writers to accomplish the task. Although that book did not come to completion, we inherited and read the drafts of many chapters and wish to acknowledge the work of those authors: T. D. Seymour Bassett, Deborah P. Clifford, J. Kevin Graffagnino, Samuel B. Hand, William Haviland, Richard M. Judd, J. Robert Maguire, H. Nicholas Muller III, Thomas Slayton, and Marshall True. We gratefully acknowledge the work of our predecessors in this task.

Many of those who contributed to the earlier effort read our work and we wish to acknowledge all who read and commented on drafts of chapters of our book in progress: T. D. Seymour Bassett, J. Kevin Graffagnino, William Haviland, Charles Johnson, Richard M. Judd, H. Nicholas Muller III, Randolph Roth, and Winn Taplin. Allen Davis and Hal Barron read and commented at length on the entire manuscript at an intermediary draft. Our special thanks to Samuel B. Hand and D. Gregory Sanford, who read and commented on the final draft.

Financial support for this book came from the unused portion of the 1976 Bicentennial Commission funding, which, as a designated portion of the Vermont Historical Society's publication fund, grew over a period of years to provide the resources necessary to complete and publish this volume. The Orton Family Foundation provided funds for one year to help restart the project. One of the authors received a Charles A. Dana Fellowship from Norwich University for a summer of research and writing. Vermont College of the Union Institute & University also provided some material and technological assistance.

The Vermont Historical Society Publications and Research Committee generously and patiently supported this project for the eight years it took to restart and complete it. We appreciate their comments as readers and overseers of the project. Our thanks also to Jan Westervelt (Acting Director 1995–1996), Gainor B. Davis (Director 1996–2002), and current Director J. Kevin Graffagnino, who as executive officers of the Society encouraged and managed its interest and investment in this book.

We received invaluable research and bibliographical assistance from Paul A. Carnahan, librarian, Marjorie Strong, assistant librarian, and Barney Bloom, former assistant librarian, at the Vermont Historical Society; Vermont State Archivist D. Gregory Sanford and Assistant State Archivist Christie Carter; the reference staff of the Reference and Law section of the Vermont Department of Libraries; the reference staff at Special Collections at the Bailey/Howe Library of the University of Vermont; and the staff of the Gary Library of Union Institute & University, located on the Vermont College campus in Montpelier. We owe enormous thanks to Mary Labate Rogstad, registrar of the Vermont Historical Society's museum, who spent many months locating illustrations for the book based on drafts of the chapters. Most of the images that appear in the volume are the result of her reading, searching, and inventive matching of text to illustrations. Syver Rogstad spent many hours scanning the images to prepare them for inclusion.

Alan Berolzheimer, book editor for the Vermont Historical Society, has been a patient, persistent, thoughtful, and encouraging editor, commentator, and guide through the processes of publication. He also served as the copyeditor for the final version, patiently following the text through its many versions to assure consistency of style and readability. Our thanks to designer, Peter Holm, who transformed the text into a book. Thanks to proofreader Rachael Cohen. And our special thanks to Reidun D. Nuquist who, calling upon her many years of experience as librarian for the Vermont Historical Society and indexer for its journals and books, assembled the index for this one.

We gratefully acknowledge the patient support and encouragement from our spouses, companions, family, friends, and colleagues who over the past several years have inquired about our progress and offered the encouragement to keep going. "Historians don't finish books," we heard one wag comment; "they abandon them." The encouragement we have received from many quarters has helped us not to fall into that particular trap. Of course, the omissions, errors, questionable interpretations, and other lapses that remain in our book are entirely our own responsibility.

Finally, we want to return to two individuals who have been our guides and models throughout the years we have worked on this book. Thomas

Day Seymour Bassett was for many years the curator of the Wilbur Collection in the Special Collections Department of the Bailey/Howe Library at the University of Vermont. Following his retirement, he continued as a major contributor to scholarship in Vermont history, through his own writing and his generous advice and sharing of information to all who consulted him. As noted, he read several of the chapters in draft and his critiques and recommendations helped improve our work. He died before he could see our final product, but his comment to one of us, "I know you are slow getting it done, but I'm sure you will finish it," was a statement of faith in this effort that helped see us through the long passage to the end.

Samuel B. Hand has been part of this project from its first form through the final reading of the final draft. Throughout he has been an encouraging, friendly, frank, and helpful critic, as well as an unfailing and unfailingly generous source of knowledge. We have relied heavily on his wide and deep knowledge of Vermont history and, despite his engagement in completing his own major study of Vermont political history and many other projects, he never failed to respond fully, patiently, and quickly to our requests for details, explanations, and elaborations on his own work. It is to him that we gratefully dedicate this book.

Dedicated To
Samuel B. Hand
Friend, Colleague, Mentor

Introduction

Tradition credits Ira Allen with the authorship of Vermont's state motto, "Freedom and Unity." Allen himself, who usually did not hesitate to take credit for his activities on behalf of the state of Vermont, is remarkably silent about this one. Aside from anecdotal evidence collected many years later by antiquarian and founder of the Vermont Historical Society, Henry Stevens, we are not even sure when Allen devised the motto, although it appears on the state seal, also said to have been designed by Ira Allen in 1778 and adopted by a resolution of the General Assembly in 1779.

Because he did not write about the motto, we do not know exactly what Allen had in mind when he devised it. The context in which it had its origin, however, suggests some possible interpretations.

Vermont faced two challenges in the years between 1777, when it declared itself an independent state, and 1791, when it became one of the United States. Internally it faced the challenge of balancing individual liberties, boldly proclaimed in the Declaration of Independence of 1776 and in Chapter I of the Vermont Constitution of 1777, with the claims and requirements of both the communities within which its citizens lived and the state government they had created. Externally, Vermonters in these years faced the dilemma of proclaiming their freedom from any other existing government or authority—in this case both New York and Great Britain—and at the same time their hope and expectation of being admitted as equal partners to the union of the former colonies, known as the United States of America. The motto, then, speaks of individual liberties and community identity, of freedom to act as a sovereign state and identity as one of the United States. Each of those identities—individual, local, state, national—carries implications for the breadth and boundaries of freedom, the advantages and obligations of unity.

The dilemmas implicit in the state motto adopted in 1779 are the dilemmas Vermonters have lived with for more than two centuries of their subsequent history. They constitute the underlying themes of this book.

In some respects, of course, these dilemmas are the ones faced by all citizens of all states in the nation. Vermonters in the past—as in the present—share with other Americans a history of creating institutions, making their livings, pursuing individual destinies and fortunes, and maintaining and acting on beliefs and principles by using the available natural, human, cultural, and historical resources. The task of this book, therefore, is to account for those resources and provide a coherent narrative of the events, movements, and people that have played some significant role in our journey as a society from a distant past to the present.

We have chosen to present our version of Vermont history chronologically. We also follow several topics that serve as narrative threads that emerge, disappear, and re-emerge as they seemed to command our attention and play their parts in shaping the times as well as the consciousness of the people who lived—and live—in Vermont. Among these persistent if sometimes discontinuous narrative threads are the shape and activities of state and local government; the influence and participation of individuals and groups in politics; the role of religion as a social and cultural force; the creation, reform, and support of public education; the changing nature and influence of agriculture, manufacturing, business, and recreation; and the development of infrastructures for transportation and communication. These are topics that most readers of a history of a place expect to find, and that writers of any place have an obligation to define and follow.

Another part of the task of this history is to identify and discuss those features, institutions, traditions, ideas, groups, and individuals that have taken root and flourished in the state, are closely associated with it, and contribute to its identity and character. Here we have reached beyond much of what we found in Vermont's earlier historiographical tradition, to include individuals, groups, and issues that only recently have begun to emerge from being invisible or in shadow in many earlier historical narratives. We therefore explore, among many other topics, the roles and history of women; the histories of several ethnic and racial groups, including the much-neglected and still controversial history of the Abenakis; the history of agricultural and industrial workers; and the effects of wars on those who remained at home. We examine the history of civil rights from our earliest days as a political entity to the present. We discuss the growing consciousness and importance of environmental issues in shaping communities and the state as a whole and planning for their future. Each of these topics, too, contains within it an echo of the dilemmas stated in the motto, "Freedom and Unity."

When we started this work a commentator wrote to one of us challenging us to "take the measure of Vermont." We have agreed that it is not a historian's task. We have agreed, instead, to write a history that can serve as a version of the collective memory of significant events, options, and choices. Our work therefore records a shared body of ideas, experiences, and values (what folklorists and some historians call "traditions" and what some anthropologists call "ethos"). We provide explanations for some of those events and choices; and we describe the endurance of those traditions and their function—or at least their influence—in the choices that individuals and groups make about their present and future.

We examined several possibilities along the way to arriving at "Freedom and Unity" as the unifying theme of our work. Vermont historiography itself has many models and myths to choose from. One of the most popular and enduring is the heroic story of the founding of Vermont as the determined effort of a few leaders—foremost among them, of course, Ethan Allen and the Green Mountain Boys—dedicated to forging an independent state in the political vacuum created successively by the collapse of New France and the rise of a New England, the questionable authority of colonial New Hampshire and the greedy oligarchy of New York, and the shaking off of royal authority to declare allegiance to the authority of the new United States of America. This model, whether we call it "rugged individualism," or "frontier rebel," or "revolutionary outlaw," continues to exercise enormous influence on Vermonters' self-image as independent and individualistic. It emphasizes freedom as personal liberty, perhaps at the expense of understanding the complex factors that contribute to political action and considering the compromises necessary to create and maintain "unity" among many diverse interests and needs at local, state, and national levels.

Another interpretive paradigm is the "frontier thesis" proposed in 1893 by Midwestern historian Frederick Jackson Turner, which sees the history of the United States as the continual recreation of political institutions and ideologies. In this interpretation, Vermont has been portrayed as continuously remote, continuously creating and recreating itself in relative isolation from other states and the nation as a whole.

Yet another explanatory framework, the inverse of the frontier thesis, is that Vermont has always been too small and too remote to have any effect on the world around it; its history is that of a small state where nothing important happened, or where everything has been tried and everything has failed.

None of these frameworks seemed to us to offer a rich or fruitful paradigm for describing or understanding the events, ideas, movements, continuities, and changes we encountered in our own journey through Vermont's remote and recent history.

Some models and metaphors do have powerful narrative and explanatory implications. Implicitly or explicitly, we have turned to those in our history, some to use, some to argue with, some to refute. The historian and bibliographer T. D. Seymour Bassett, in the introduction to his important and enduring *Vermont: A Bibliography of Its History*, published in 1981, reformulated the Turner thesis to discuss what he called "Vermont's kaleidoscopic diversity as a border area."[1]

Thinking of Vermont as a place of "kaleidoscopic diversity" may surprise many readers both within and outside the state who think of Vermont as the quintessential and enduring example of Yankee society. Our history presents several ways to think about diversity and demonstrates that Vermont has a long history of being racially, ethnically, socially, economically, and politically diverse.

Similarly, thinking of Vermont as a "border area" modifies in a productive way the old Turner frontier thesis that has led some writers to see Vermont as remote and immune from the influences, trends, ideas, and changes in the larger contexts of national and even global history. We have followed the implications of Bassett's phrase and analyzed Vermont history by thinking of Vermont as a place with a porous political, intellectual, and cultural environment. This perspective lets us see Vermont as a place where the concentric circles that include and surround it provide both opportunities and stimulus to adopt from neighbors' ideas and institutions and adapt them to local needs and conditions. It also allows us to see the state exerting some influence on its surrounding areas. This mental and geographical repositioning of Vermont allows us to think more constructively about one other important tradition in Vermont historical writing: Vermont exceptionalism.

Vermonters like to think of their state as a last bastion of independent thinking, rural living, and old-time American republican virtue—as a holdout, in short, against the downward drift of national culture and politics.

Vermont can make some good and valid claims to exceptionalism in the context of American history. We were the first state to write into its constitution a ban on adult slavery. The fact that Vermont made itself also set it apart from the first thirteen states, which had been colonies, and all the states that followed because, according to historian Peter Onuf, Vermont forced the hand of the Constitutional Convention of 1787 in drafting section 3 of Article IV (which prescribes how new states were to be admitted to the Union), then forced the hand of Congress in brokering an arrangement with New York State.² For a century Vermont was exceptional in its overwhelming loyalty to the Republican Party, exhibited most dramatically in the uninterrupted line of Republicans elected to statewide and national office. To the amusement and confusion of many, this trait even extended to Vermonters' refusal to succumb to the national popularity of Franklin Delano Roosevelt in any of his four elections for president of the United States.³ Vermont remains exceptional—or at least unusual—among the United States in its small population, its high proportion of rural population, its small proportion of non-white or self-defining ethnic and racial minority-group citizens, its direct democracy in town meetings, its close supervision of elected officials and representatives through the two-year term for all statewide officers and all legislators. Other states have some of these characteristics in different combinations; Vermont may claim exceptionalism—for what it's worth in this instance, and that is an important question—for having them all.

But is Vermont exceptional in some of the other qualities it claims for itself? In 1990, on the eve of the bicentennial anniversary of statehood, Vermonters enjoyed the spectacle of a series of debates over whether Vermont should exercise a supposed "escape clause": an agreement, according to folklore, that the state could exercise once every one hundred years an option to secede from the Union. This is part of the Vermont myth; part of its tradition. In all but one of the debates, Frank Bryan, professor of political science at the University of Vermont, argued for secession, and John Dooley, associate justice of the Vermont Supreme Court, argued for staying in the Union. For one debate they exchanged sides. And on that occasion Bryan argued that "Vermont has done more to create the United States than any other state." The idea of secession, he insisted, violates Vermont's culture, which includes the principle of having the courage to fix what is wrong. "Vermont nationalism is a nationalism of orneriness and that's the best kind of nationalism. . . . America needs us," he concluded, "because we are its conscience and its heart; we are its homeland."⁴ There is, perhaps, no better expression of Vermont exceptionalism and no more succinct distillation of the Vermont myth.

Claiming the distinction of exceptionalism for Vermont means remembering and emphasizing some details from the state's past and of its present, and forgetting or ignoring others. It means claiming isolation from and immunization against the deleterious influences of a wider national history, making Vermont a frontier territory in the Turnerian tradition rather than a porous border area as described by Bassett. It means using the small townscape of Peacham as the poster image for tourism rather than the city skyline of Burlington. It means celebrating stubborn, self-conscious resistance to change, as Dorothy Canfield Fisher did when she wrote in the 1937 Vermont volume of the American Guide Series, "if you will think of [Vermonters] as representing the American past, you may have a better understanding of what you see in Vermont,"[5] and ignoring the 1993 designation of the entire State of Vermont by the National Trust for Historic Preservation as one of the eleven most endangered historic places in the nation.

The exceptionalism theme is powerful and important for understanding Vermont's history because it challenges us to place what we know about our past in the larger context of American history and now, in global history, and because, as historian Joyce Appleby reminds us, "[w]hat we attend to in the past will form that restructured memory that we call history, the reservoir of knowledge about human experience that informs our ideas about suffering and crimes, virtues and vices, recordable accomplishments and unworthy happenings."[6]

Nonetheless, the history we have written largely rejects an exceptionalism model for explanation or for "taking the measure of Vermont." Instead we have adopted a way of thinking about state history that reflects the observation of Alexis de Tocqueville in his indispensable *Democracy in America*. "The great political principles which now rule American society were born and grew up in the state . . . So one must understand the state to gain the key to the rest."[7]

This dynamic relationship and creative tension between state and nation suggests why and how in an age of globalism it is still possible to write a history of Vermont; and, furthermore, why and how it is possible to write a history of Vermont and reject a theory of Vermont exceptionalism. Tocqueville's analysis also echoes one of the meanings we detect in the Vermont state motto. The choices Vermonters made and continue to make for themselves as individuals affect and are affected by the choices they make for their communities and their state. Those choices in turn affect and are affected by the choices Vermonters make in the context of their identities and participation in the life of their nation and beyond. These concentric circles of context, with their sometimes complementary, sometimes competing values and priorities, form the persistent background of our narrative and analysis of Vermont history.

Michael Sherman
Gene Sessions
P. Jeffrey Potash
Montpelier, Vermont
June 2003

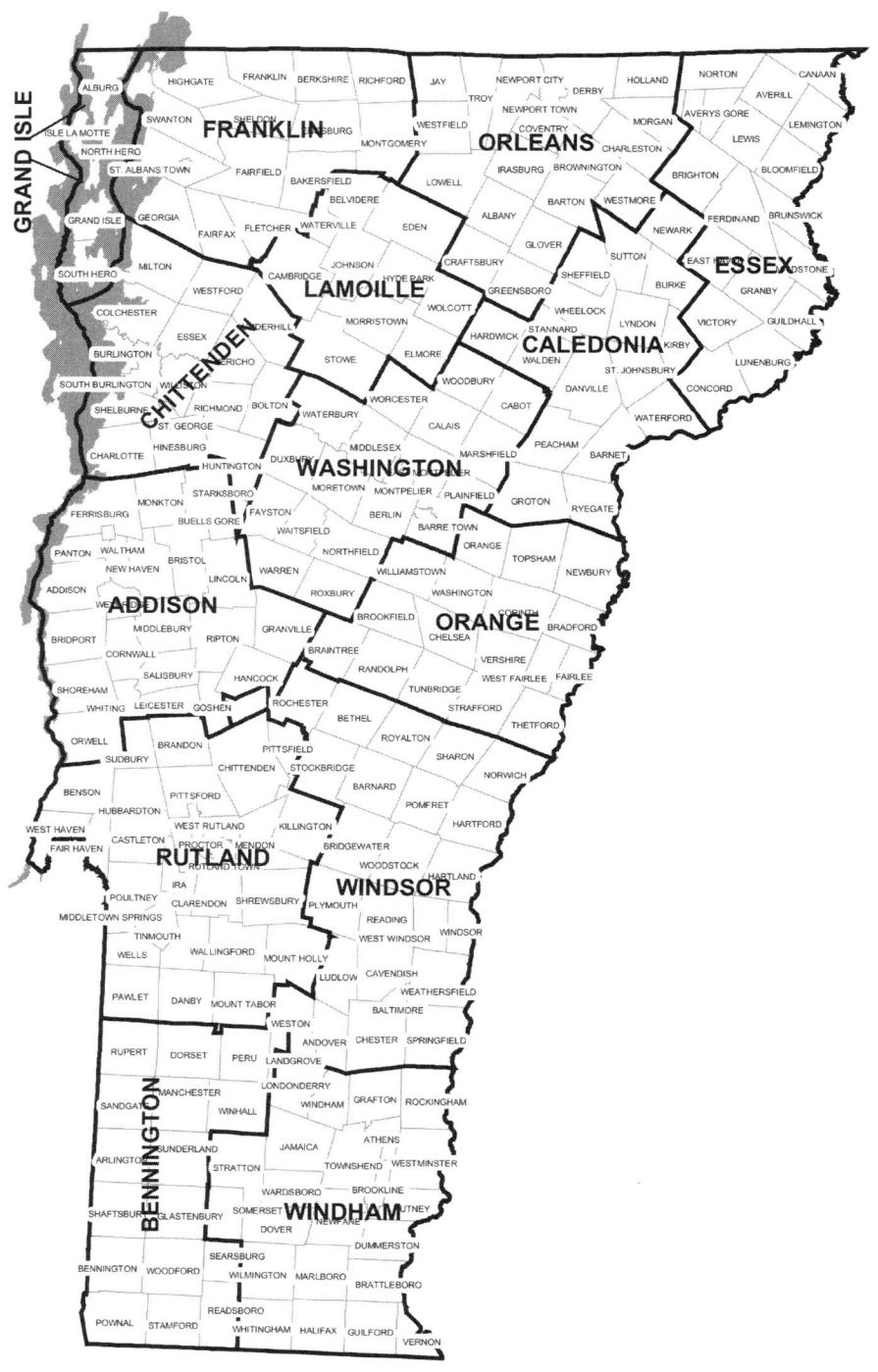

1
Footprints

PREHISTORY TO 1609

A Tumultuous Landscape

Every year, two hundred thousand people hike a portion of the Long Trail in Vermont. Begun in 1910, the trail took twenty-one years to complete. It runs 270 miles along the spine of the Green Mountains from the Massachusetts border to the Canadian frontier. Looking west from the highest point on the trail—"the chin" at Mt. Mansfield, 4,393 feet above sea level—today's hiker sees the broad valley of the Champlain Lowlands sloping down to Lake Champlain and, rising abruptly from the western shore of the lake, the Adirondack Mountains. To the east lie the mountains of the Worcester range, the relatively level northern uplands, and farther off (visible on a clear day), the White Mountains of New Hampshire. North and south, the hiker's eye follows the series of peaks, mostly covered with deciduous and conifer forests that give the Green Mountains their name.[1]

View from the "Chin," Mount Mansfield, looking south. Photograph by Harry W. Richardson. *Vermont Historical Society.*

A hiker at the southern end of the Long Trail looks west across the narrow Valley of Vermont to see the Taconic Range, while to the east the land ripples down through the Vermont Piedmont to the Connecticut River valley, revealing a few peaks and the isolated monadnock, Mount Ascutney. To the south the Green Mountains, now spread out to their maximum width of thirty-five miles, merge with the Hoosac Mountains and Berkshire Hills of Massachusetts. Beneath the hiker's feet in many places along the Long Trail lie what geologists believe are the oldest rocks in New England.

According to the current theory of plate tectonics, which describes the movement of continental land masses, the Green Mountains were formed out of a succession of continental plate collisions and recedings beginning 1.3 billion years ago. The first of these, the so-called Grenville event (about 1.3 to 1 billion years ago), took place late in the Precambrian era and produced the Adirondack Mountains, the oldest mountains on the continent. Following that first collision, the continental plates moved away from each other from about 1.1 billion years ago to 650 million years ago, opening a shallow sea, called the proto-Atlantic Ocean. Each year from January to early spring 180 Vermont legislators, the governor, lieutenant governor, scores of legislative and administrative staff, lobbyists, and hundreds of visitors of all ages crowd into Vermont's state house. As they scurry about their business these temporary residents routinely and casually tread on the remains of Vermont's oldest living creatures. Embedded in the "black marble" (in fact, a kind of limestone) from Isle La Motte are the fossils dating from approximately 470 million years ago that are constant reminders of this ancient ocean.

A second movement of continental plates, called the Taconian event, began 445 million years ago. This movement thrust up the Taconic Mountains at the foot of the Adirondacks, compressed the shale derived from the ancient Adirondacks into the slate that lies close to the surface near present-day Fair Haven, and transformed the limestone from the floor of the ancient Atlantic into the marble that runs from Dorset to Middlebury. Farther east, the African continental plate shoveled up from the ocean floor both the sediments from the earlier mountain-making event and more eroded rock from the ancient Adirondacks. When this motion ceased, 435 million years ago, the Atlantic Ocean lapped against the eastern slopes of the Green Mountains.

A third period of continental motion, called the Acadian Mountain Building Cycle, occurred between 375 and 355 million years ago. Part of

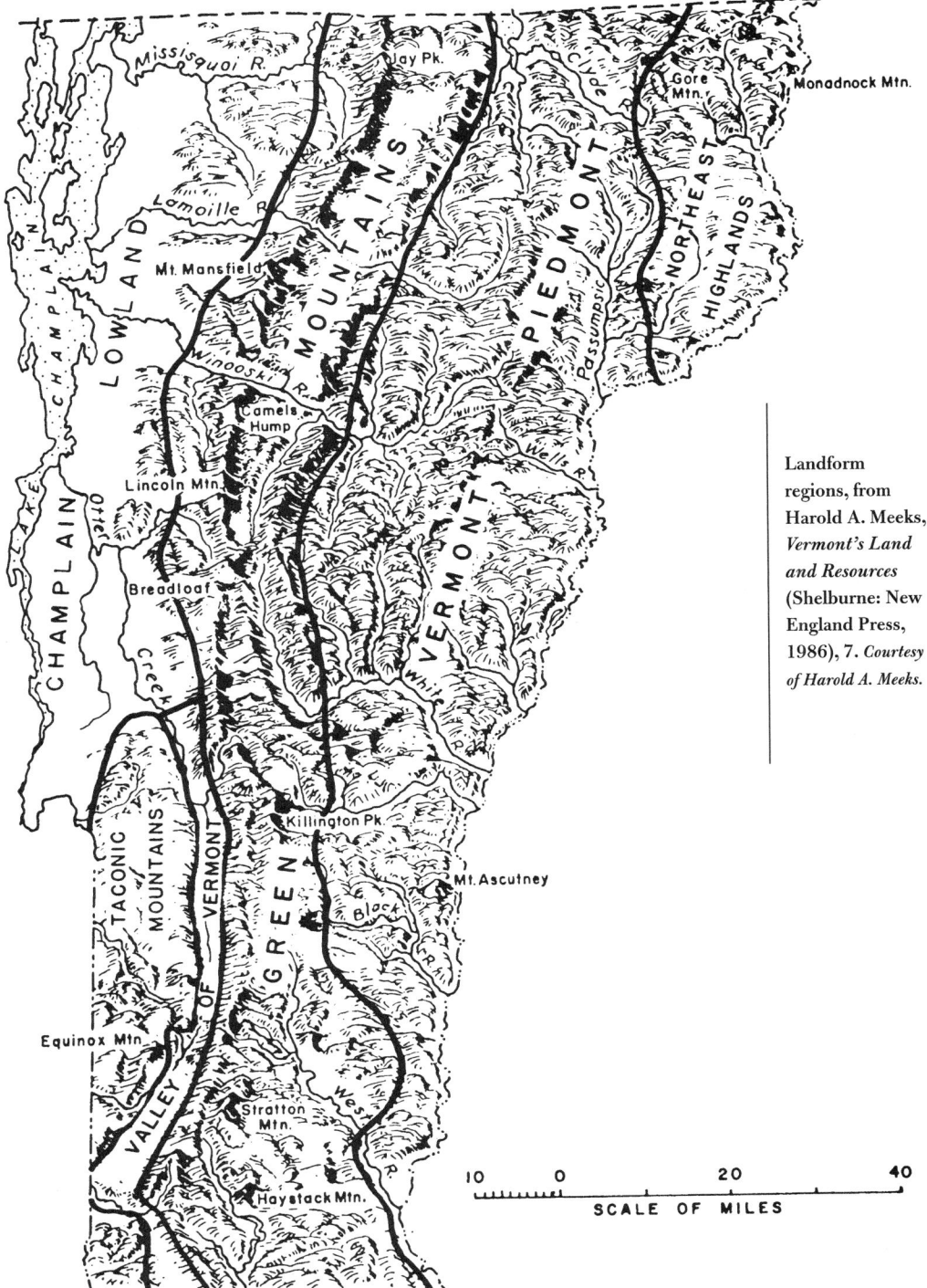

Landform regions, from Harold A. Meeks, *Vermont's Land and Resources* (Shelburne: New England Press, 1986), 7. *Courtesy of Harold A. Meeks.*

the worldwide motion that brought all the continental plates together to create a single land mass called Pangaea, this activity culminated in a collision of the North American and Eurasia-African plates. More rock and sediment bulldozed forward by the motion of the Eurasia-African plate crumpled and piled up behind mountains made in the Taconian event. The force of this collision caused the earth between the Adirondacks and the Green Mountains to snap along the fault line where Lake Champlain now lies and refolded the Green Mountains. Where melting occurred from the force of the collision, an enormous deposit of granite was created that is now quarried from a long strip of mountainous land stretching from Hardwick, through Barre, to Bethel. On the eastern side of the mountains, a portion of the Eurasia-African plate fused to North America to become the lowlands and coastal areas of present-day New England. This event left the Green Mountains landlocked. The continental plates again receded from each other, beginning around 200 million years ago, opening up the present-day Atlantic Ocean and leaving behind the outlines of the present-day North American continent.

The ancient geological events that created the land that hikers traverse along the Long Trail and see from its heights also helped shape the history of Vermont. Visible from almost every spot in Vermont, the Green Mountains, once barriers and obstacles to human passage and communication, often served as sources for exploitable and exportable raw materials, and increasingly over the past century and a half, as recreational resources. Running their relentless wall the entire length of the state, the mountains clearly separate the land between Lake Champlain and the Connecticut River into two north-south strips, connected in only a few places where ancient rivers cut valleys between two peaks to create a gap. From the earliest days of human habitation until the middle of the twentieth century, the mountains dictated the routes and limitations of settlement, transportation, communication, trade, cultural contact, and political and social continuity. A "Mountain Rule" for selecting candidates for U.S. senators, governors, and lieutenant governors transformed east-west geographical divisions into an informal political institution that operated for over a century. Only the coming of the automobile and especially the Interstate roads in the 1960s overcame the dominance of the mountains, and these significant developments have partially reconfigured Vermont politics, economy, society, and culture, emphasizing now the distance and differences between northern and southern communities in the state.

The mountains have also been the source of economic sustenance for Vermont. Marble, granite, slate, asbestos, talc, and copper have at various times and for varying amounts of time played important roles in the local and national economies. Other minerals, such as iron ore and gold, have contributed sporadically and mostly locally to individual prosperity. The heavily wooded mountains yielded lumber, potash and pearlash—Vermont's first industrial products—and charcoal for producing iron and lime. Today the mountains play a significant role in the state's economy as timber, tourism, and recreational resources.

Ice

The other great transforming event in Vermont's geography, from a more recent period of the geological past, was the ice age and postglacial reformation of the land. The Pleistocene, or Ice Age, in North America began two million years ago and ended about ten thousand years ago. During that time at least four glaciers descended on the land, with relatively long intervals between each glaciation. Evidence for only the last, the Wisconsin glaciation, exists in Vermont, the effects of earlier glaciers having been obliterated by each successive overrun of thick and heavy ice sheets.

The Wisconsin glaciation climaxed eighteen to twenty thousand years ago, when ice covered all of Canada, the areas around Seattle, Washington, the upper midwest states (hence its name), Ohio, most of Pennsylvania, and all of New York and New England. Over a mile thick in places, the glacier covered all of Vermont, including the highest peaks. As it advanced south, it stripped away soils and moved enormous amounts and weights of rock. The glacier's advance scraped a gentle slope on the north face of the mountains and pulled away rock from their south face (called "plucking") to create sheer cliffs. The distinctive outline of Camel's Hump is the best known example of this glacial effect. In the areas between the mountain ranges, the glacier scoured the land and broadened lowlands, sometimes cutting deeply into ancient outwashes, sometimes cutting new streams, north and south, between fingers of ice wall. As it retreated, the glacier left its footprint on the land. And this is what we see and live with today in Vermont.

As the glacier retreated for the last time, it deposited rocky, sandy debris over the reshaped landscape. Rocks carried from far in the north were dumped on the land, becoming many centuries later the raw material for

New England's famous stone walls, and the reason that many early New England farmers built "stone boats"—sturdy sledlike platforms used to help clear their fields of the ever-emerging boulders. Where ancient rivers carved tunnels under the ice sheet, the melting glacier left long, tall, sinuous mounds of debris known as eskers. The areas between fingers of the glacier filled with gravel and sand to become kames, used centuries later by Indians for burial sites, and even later by rail and automobile road builders for gravel. Where the melting glacier abutted a mountainside, the debris deposited between ice and land became a broad kame terrace. Isolated chunks of ice that broke off from the receding glacier created depressions, called kettles, in glacial till—the mix of clay, sand, gravel, and boulders. As the ice melted, the kettles formed ponds and lakes. And huge quantities of water from the melting, retreating glacier formed two enormous lakes on either side of the Green Mountains.

The Connecticut River, now the eastern boundary of Vermont separating it from New Hampshire, is an ancient relic of the collision of the North American and African continental plates. As the ice sheet crept down this narrow gap, it cleared away loose rock, deepening and widening the valley. Then, as the glacier receded, an ice dam on the lower Connecticut River held back the melting waters, forming a long, narrow lake, known in its successive stages as Lake Hitchcock and Upham Lake, that extended from Middletown, Connecticut to the Canadian border. A northern branch of the lake reached up the Passumpsic River valley beyond St. Johnsbury and a western branch moved out along the White River valley with fingers stretching up into Tunbridge, Randolph, and Bethel. Geologists now estimate that the glacier receded the two hundred miles from St. Johnsbury to Middletown in forty-three hundred years—a rate of about two hundred forty-five feet each year. The sudden break of the ice dam far downstream emptied Lake Hitchcock to the south and reduced the Connecticut River and its tributaries to approximately what we see today.

West of the mountains the story is more complicated. The weight of the mile-thick ice sheet depressed the land; but as the glacier retreated, the land began to "rebound"—faster in the south than in the north, still burdened under the ice, thus creating a tilt from south to north. With a northern exit blocked by the receding ice, the glacier's melting waters spread over the wide lowland area between the Adirondacks and Green Mountains, creating what geologists now call Lake Vermont. Some of the northern heights of the Taconics—Mount Philo and Snake Mountain in Addison County—stuck up as islands in this large body of water. At its maximum, the main body of Lake Vermont was about thirty-five miles wide from a point nearly five miles west of Plattsburgh, New York, to Richford, Vermont. In the major river valleys, such as the Lamoille and Winooski, branches of Lake Vermont extended as far east as Hardwick and Marshfield. Then, about ten thousand years ago, the ice dam in the north broke.

The land to the south had already begun to rebound from the weight of the glacier, so the waters of Lake Vermont flowed north. But because the land north of the outlet was still depressed under the burden of the ice sheet, salt water from the Atlantic Ocean ascended the St. Lawrence River and mixed with the fresh water of Lake Vermont, turning it brackish and creating what geologists now call the Champlain Sea. An abundance of marine life came with the sea water: salmon and other large saltwater fish; seals; possibly walrus; and another remarkable creature.

In 1849 workers building a railroad bed near Charlotte, Vermont, excavated an unrecognizable skeleton. First thought to be the remains of a horse, the bones were soon identified by Vermont naturalist Zadock Thompson as those of a whale, possibly a beluga. For years the precise identification remained a controversy and the skeleton lay badly mounted and largely forgotten in a dark corner of the University of Vermont's geology museum. In 1994, the Vermont legislature adopted the whale as the official state fossil, and the skeleton, reassembled to more exacting standards, gained new prominence in the university's museum as a vivid reminder of the era of the Champlain Sea.[2]

As the land to the north shed its burden of ice and rose above sea level, the waters between the Adirondack and Green Mountains turned fresh again. The transformation back to an inland lake was complete by about six thousand years ago. As Lake Champlain shrank to its present dimensions, a wide variety of life forms reestablished themselves in the area. Onto this renewed but somewhat changed landscape stepped Vermont's first human inhabitants.

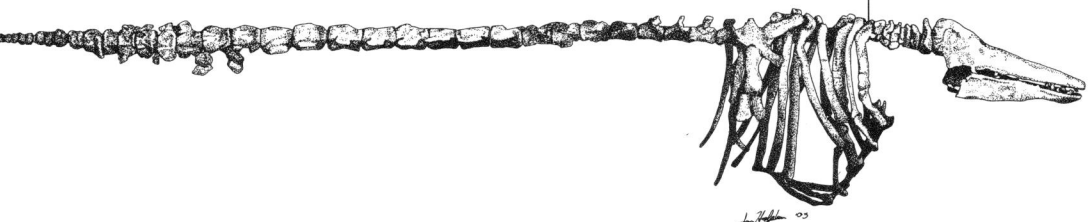

The "Charlotte Whale." Drawing by Ian Hodgdon (2003). The skeleton, dug up in 1849, now resides at the Perkins Geology Museum, University of Vermont, and has been designated as the State Fossil. The skeleton is 11 feet long, 13 inches wide. *Courtesy of Ian Hodgdon.*

Human Footprints

The glacier had not completely receded and Lake Champlain was still swollen and connected to the Atlantic when the first human inhabitants of Vermont walked onto the land. So much of the later history of North America was made by people migrating from east to west, that we too easily forget that for several thousands of years, movement from south and west to north and east first peopled the continent.

Recent archaeological finds and skeletal reconstructions suggest the possibility that some early inhabitants of North America may have arrived from the northeast. However, most archaeologists continue to believe that the people we call Paleoindians migrated across the land bridge from Asia to Alaska created during the Ice Age. They moved south and east, following the edge of the glacier, then spread out across the continent. The first inhabitants of Vermont arrived here about 11,300 years ago, moving along river valleys north from the Hudson and possibly up the Connecticut River, following the edge of the retreating glacier, which served as an important boundary for their "home" areas. These people were hunters and, to a far less degree, gatherers. They moved in seasonal cycles through large areas where they found edible plants and took the large game associated with a tundra environment that provided most of their food: caribou, moose-elk, musk ox, mastodons, and woolly mammoth like the one unearthed by railway workers at Mount Holly in 1849. Men hunted; women prepared meat, made clothing and other necessities from hides and skins, and gathered plants. This gender-based division of labor is typical of such societies. It persisted among Indian people even after the arrival of Europeans in the sixteenth century changed many other patterns of life. Until about ten thousand years ago, the men worked stone into fluted points, called by archaeologists Clovis points, first identified in the Southwest in the 1920s and now known to be ubiquitous throughout North America where there was large game. They attached these points to shafts to make spears for hunting. Relatively high concentrations of fluted points have been found along the boundaries of a late phase of what was once the Champlain Sea from Brandon and Orwell in the south to St. Albans, Swanton, and the important Reagan site near East Highgate—nearly ten miles from the present lake shore. The Paleoindians probably harvested marine life, such as clams and fish, and may have hunted from the shore some larger sea mammals, such as seals and the

Charlotte whale. It is unlikely that they ventured far out onto the water. Clovis points have also been found along Otter Creek, the Winooski and Connecticut rivers, and as far inland as Waterbury and Moretown. This distribution suggests the far-reaching movement of people along waterways in search of game.

The population appears to have been small, with an estimated density in lowland areas of ten people per 100 square kilometers, perhaps higher densities along the Champlain Valley. Mountain areas remained uninhabited and largely unhunted. We have very little direct evidence to give us details of the daily lives and social organization of these Paleoindians. Using information about recent hunting populations in the far north, however, anthropologists believe that they lived and moved in small bands of perhaps thirty to fifty people in two or more related family units that lived close together.

Radiocarbon dating has allowed archaeologists to date the continuity of Paleoindians in Vermont from about 9600 to around 7000 B.C.E. (before the common era).[3] What happened to these people then is a matter of conjecture. As the glacier receded, so did the tundra (now evident only in a few places, such as the summits of Mount Mansfield, Camel's Hump, and Mount Abraham). It was succeeded by evergreen forests—also called fir-spruce forests, boreal forests, and north woods—that supported smaller game and provided few food-bearing plants. The large game of the tundra moved north. At the same time, the Champlain Sea became an increasingly freshwater body, changing so rapidly that most species could not adapt and died off. As their sources and supplies of food changed, some Paleoindians moved on in pursuit of familiar game and plants. Others adapted to the new environment by altering some of their ways of life, changing their diets and patterns of hunting, gathering, and processing food, and exchanging goods with peoples to the south and west.

The next period of history, called by anthropologists the Archaic period, began in Vermont about 6000 B.C.E. and lasted until the second millennium B.C.E. The Archaic was a crucial period for Vermont's original inhabitants. The warming climate, freshening of Lake Champlain, and receding Connecticut River brought about significant transformations of plants and wildlife. Caribou, moose-elk, mammoth, and mastodon completely disappeared. As the boreal forest receded, a more varied forest of birch, maple, ash, and nut-bearing trees such as beech, hickory, and oak moved north, providing food and shelter for a wide variety of small and mid-size game. These conditions supported a more varied diet and a wider range of resources for human communities.

As the animal population changed during the Archaic period, hunting changed. Harder to find, quicker to escape, and providing less food with each kill, the smaller game required new hunting techniques and new tools. Lighter and smaller projectile points appear in late Archaic-era archaeological finds. Two important tools for hunting, the atlatl (a handheld platform for launching a spear) and bolas (stone weights tied to both ends of a length of thong), make their appearance at this time in Vermont. Both are known to have been used at earlier periods among people living south and west of Vermont.

The appearance of stone woodworking tools such as celts, adzes, and gouges suggests that Archaic people made dugout canoes for fishing and perhaps taking larger maritime game, such as seals, which still would have survived in the changing waters of Lake Champlain. Scrapers and awls are evidence of processing skins and furs for clothing and shelter. Archaeological findings at sites of human habitation include remains of deer, moose, bear, beaver, muskrat, fox, marten, otter, snakes, and birds, especially wild turkey, providing more evidence of variety in the diet of Archaic people.

Although hunting and fishing continued to be the main source of food, gathering now played a larger role in the diet. Several new grinding and cracking tools found at Archaic-period settlement sites provide evidence for a wide range of berries, nuts (especially butternuts, for which there is abundant evidence, and probably beechnuts, acorns, and chestnuts), and other wild plant foods gathered seasonally and processed by women. Close examination of teeth from human remains dated to this period show more cavities, another sign of more carbohydrates in the diet of Archaic-era people.

The types of projectile points recovered from Archaic-era sites is one bit of evidence suggesting the expansion of cultural contact over a wide area. Some designs can be traced to people living south and west of Vermont and to coastal people, as far south as Long Island, New York. The points were made of quartzite and chert from Vermont, which means that they were not brought here but were made by the people already on the land, using designs they learned in the expanding trade among native people. Other evidence of this widening cultural exchange are stone bowls (also coming from south of New England), copper from the western Great

Lakes area, shell from as far away as the Caribbean, and "exotic" mineral ornaments and tools that were found in one important burial site from Isle La Motte.

Elaborate burial rituals are thought to have been imported from the northeast and maritime areas of Canada during the Archaic period. Clusters of graves found in glacial kame (gravel and stone debris) and at the Ketchum Island site on Otter Creek near Rutland revealed to archaeologists some of the new rituals, including partial cremation, the use of red ocher (an oxide of iron mixed with sand or clay) sprinkled on one side of the human remains, and the burial with bodies of copper beads and tools along with stone, bone, and wood implements. The existence of similar burial practices farther west and south suggests that these ceremonial practices in Vermont were elements in cultural and material exchanges during the late Archaic period.

Above all else, the Archaic period is notable for the stability of life and habitation in the northeast. Archaic people continued to live and hunt in bands. Their movement was both seasonal and opportunistic, dictated by resources available at different times and places within a restricted area. Hunting, fishing, and gathering territories were defined by a central base settlement and generally stretched along river valleys. Some sites appear to have developed for specific purposes: fishing, food preparation, making projectile points. Some had repeated occupancy over the course of the hunting and gathering cycles; others appear to have been used once or a few times, then abandoned. One important consequence of that long period of stability was the gradual development of linguistic divisions and recognizably different patterns of life among subgroups who stayed closely in touch with each other but also established fixed if still fluid boundaries for their yearly cycles of hunting, fishing, and gathering.

Until about 2500 B.C.E. the area we identify as New York and New England was occupied by people speaking what anthropologists call proto-Algonquian dialects. While the language varied throughout the area, there was sufficient continuity along the chain of dialects to allow for communication among neighboring groups throughout the northeast. At around 2500 B.C.E., speakers of a proto-Iroquoian language moved into the New York area. As these people expanded their influence north to around Lake Ontario they drove a wedge between Algonquian-speaking peoples. Lake Champlain served as one boundary for the eastern and northern expansion of the Iroquoian people, but in the early colonial period it became a disputed territory and frontier for conflict, economic activity, and social as well as linguistic division between Iroquoian and Algonquian peoples for centuries thereafter.

The next and last period of distinctive change and development in Vermont before the arrival of Europeans (otherwise known as "precontact" history) is called the Woodland period. Evolving almost seamlessly from the Archaic at around 900 B.C.E., it lasted until after 1500 C.E., when sustained contact with Europeans dramatically and irreversibly altered the patterns of life of the native population.

In many respects, developments that occurred in the early (900–100 B.C.E.) and middle (100 B.C.E.–1000 C.E.) Woodland periods were extensions, elaborations, or variations of the developments that took place in the Archaic. Hunting, fishing, and gathering, wild edible plants continued to dominate both the diet and the energy of Woodland-period people. Burial rituals introduced toward the end of the Archaic continued to be elaborated by the use of a wider range of objects, some of which reflect the expanding trade associations of people during the early Woodland period: copper from the Great Lakes region, shells from the Atlantic and Gulf seacoasts, and stones from Indiana and northern Québec.

Initially, the social arrangements that appear to have dominated Archaic life continued into the Woodland period. Small bands of family groups, including perhaps as many as five families, lived together in a roughly egalitarian society. The men in the extended family fished and hunted together in well-known territories that were smaller than in Paleoindian times but large enough to allow for taking a variety of game and providing each nuclear family in the band with sufficient food.

An important early Woodland archaeological site, Boucher cemetery in Swanton, reveals the use of woven and vegetable materials for cordage, to supplement leather garments and thongs. Woodworking tools and the remains of wooden hafts for stone implements show that people from the early Woodland period expanded their range of skills and materials for accomplishing a wide variety of tasks.

A major cultural innovation of the Woodland period is revealed by the appearance of pottery vessels for cooking and storage. Like so many of the cultural changes noted before, production of pottery appears to have developed through cultural contact from societies south and west. An abundance of clay made Vermont soil suitable for making pottery, which is more durable than containers made of bark, animal skins, wood, or gourds and other vegetable material. Pottery is also lighter and more portable than stone vessels; it is better for storage because it does not disintegrate or react either with the contents or, if buried, with the earth; and can be more effectively sealed. Pottery is better than bark, stone, or skin for cooking because it conducts heat more uniformly, can be fashioned into a variety of shapes, and can be placed directly in the fire.

The "Colchester Jar," St. Lawrence Iroquois style, c. 1400–1550 AD, found in 1825 by a Burlington surveyor, known only as Captain Johnson. *Courtesy of the Robert Hull Fleming Museum, University of Vermont, gift of Luther Loomis.*

The earliest pottery found in Vermont has been dated using radiocarbon techniques to about 600 B.C.E. An elongated cone-shaped bowl, coming to a point at the bottom, with an incised triangular design, was recovered at the Boucher burial site near Swanton. Residue in the pot reveals that it was used for preparing food. Over the next thousand years pottery style changed slowly, culminating in the round-bottom, elaborately castellated style of the so-called Colchester jar. The changes in form and decoration suggest that in addition to cooking, storage, and conveyance, pottery came to be used as trade goods and for some ritual purposes.

The increasing use of pottery through the Woodland period is also an important clue to the growing stability of Indian life. Still a mobile society, Woodland people appear to have congregated for longer periods of time each year at base camps and villages, where they fished, hunted, gathered, stored, and prepared food. In winter they dispersed, moving in small bands to hunting areas. The Winooski site shows more or less continual use, probably on a seasonal basis, for four thousand years—with a hiatus between 300 and 600 C.E.—and was abandoned toward the end of the middle Woodland period (about 1000 C.E.).

The introduction of the bow and arrow for hunting was another important Woodland-era innovation. The primary evidence of this new approach to hunting comes from the growing abundance of a new kind of projectile point, called Jack's Reef points. Small, barbed, and thin, these points were not made to last but were especially effective for the longer-range hunting with bow and arrow. They exploded like shrapnel on impact with the prey, thereby more seriously wounding the animal and, as the bits of stone migrated within its body, finally incapacitating it. They could also be fashioned in a few minutes, giving the hunter an almost continuous supply of ammunition on short notice, especially if he could retrieve the shaft of his arrow from fallen game. Jack's Reef points appear and dominate the archaeological finds from 600 to 800 C.E.

Compared to spears, bows and arrows are easier to carry, have a longer range, with greater accuracy at short range, require less movement to launch a shot, and offer the possibility of getting off multiple shots before game detect and flee from the hunter. Although the spear and atlatl continued to have their uses, by about 1000 C.E. the bow and arrow had generally replaced them as the hunting weapon of choice. The abundance of hickory, increasing expertise in woodworking and cord making, and the ready supply of local cherts for the small Jack's Reef points made bows and arrows easier to fabricate and replace.

A third innovation of this era was the birch bark canoe, a refinement of the dug-out canoes from the Archaic period. Probably dating from the middle Woodland period, these water craft were quicker and easier to construct from local and abundantly available materials, and allowed greater flexibility for fishing and transporting foods and gear between seasonal camps along rivers and shallow waterways.

The fourth major innovation of Woodland-era life was the introduction of horticulture. Over many centuries, nuts, berries, and seeds or native grains had become increasingly important to the native diet, adding carbohydrates, fats, and other nutrients to the protein-rich foods of fish and game. Plants were also adapted to medicinal and utilitarian uses such as the fabrication of textiles, cordage, and dyestuffs. The frequent recovery of pipes from early and later Woodland burial sites suggests that smoking tobacco or some other plants had become part of Woodland-era ceremonial and spiritual life and possibly had nonceremonial uses. Because some of the wild vegetable foods that played important parts in the Woodland-era diet came into abundance in seasonal cycles but not necessarily annually, native people had to learn how to harvest and manage the supplies of nongame foods. Thus, anthropologists William Haviland and Marjory Power conclude that "whether intentionally or not, like historically known food foragers, [Woodland-era Abenakis] may have been effective plant managers, by for example, leaving seeds to propagate or manipulating these resources in other ways."[4]

Located on the Connecticut River in the town of Springfield, the Skitchewaug site, occupied more or less continuously from the late Archaic through the Woodland period to about 1370 C.E., was first investigated in 1987. When the eroding bank of the river threatened the site a few years later, archaeologists returned and in 1989 and 1990 found evidence of several layers of occupation, including seven storage and fire pits associated with two houses. All seven pits contained recognizable remains of corn (*Zea mays*). Further excavation, inventorying of plant remains, and radiocarbon dating of these sites confirm that Skitchewaug is the earliest known corn-, bean-, and squash-producing site in northern New England. Subsequent examination of several other Connecticut River sites suggests that corn, beans, and squash began to be cultivated in the New England interior, along river banks, by about 1100 C.E. On the other side of the Green Mountains, at the Donahue site on the Winooski River near Lake Champlain, similar evidence for horticulture appears in storage pits and hearths that have been dated at about 1440 to 1700 C.E. Here archaeologists found food-processing tools that provided further evidence of corn cultivation.

One important difference between the two sites that archaeological evidence reveals is that in the Connecticut River valley, corn, beans, and squash quickly became a dominant feature of the diet and farming became important in the cycle of food gathering. On the western side of the mountains, however, horticulture was adopted more slowly and supplemented rather than replaced the older pattern of hunting and gathering. Haviland and Power suggest that the steep uplands of the Connecticut Valley may have forced populations to focus more of their activity on the narrow floodplain, thus leading them sooner to horticulture, whereas inhabitants of the broad Champlain Valley continued to have more options in finding their food. This suggestion implies that horticulture was a reluctant second choice for Connecticut River people, a conclusion that may surprise contemporary readers, and a choice that certainly did call down on the Indians the disapproval of seventeenth-century European settlers, who regarded farming as a sign of civilization and stable society.

Scholars differ on the relative benefits and effects of hunter/gatherer versus agricultural food supply. Haviland and Power argue that hunting and gathering is far more enjoyable, less intensive, and a less time-consuming way of life, sending people to the forest and streams when depleted supplies dictate the need, and promoting a nonhierarchical, close-knit society that has a low impact on the land. Hunters-gatherers, moreover, had a wide range of foods for their diet, and could cure meats and dry fish, nuts, and some wild plants for long-term storage, giving them many options in an unpredictable climate.[5] Historian William Cronon, on the other hand, observes that a society dependent in large part on game may also go hungry, especially in late winter or if an extended winter season deprives game animals of sufficient nourishment. Horticulture, therefore, appears to give people an ability to store food over a longer period of time to assure adequate supplies as a contingency against unanticipated shortfalls in the hunt.[6] Ethnobiologist Jared Diamond argues that the introduction of agriculture has been a key aspect of cultural change worldwide, and that hunter-gatherer societies have uniformly suffered depredation and destruction at the hands of agricultural peoples who develop specialization, varied cultural production, and hierarchical social organization along with agriculture. Putting down roots, literally and figuratively, appears to be a major turning point in the history of all societies.[7] The argument may be unresolvable on a theoretical basis, so we must look at the experience and situation of the Abenakis themselves.

Vermont's Abenakis during the late Woodland era appear to have adopted horticulture as an extension of their management of resources such as nuts, berries, and seeds. Settlements were already located in areas that were suitable for horticulture, and horticulture allowed bands and families to remain longer on one site, rather than moving widely over territory in search of game or gathered foods. In other words, horticulture was similar to some of the food-managing activities already in place and could have been seen as simply a more intensified management of food resources. This was especially true in the Connecticut River valley, which had a much less varied animal and fish population and where, consequently, options were narrower.

A hunting culture persisted long after the Abenakis added horticulture to their food-gathering cycle. Many traditional tales still told by Abenaki storytellers focus on hunting. These stories inform us of the continuing importance of hunting in the yearly diet and cycle of life, and of the significance of the male in providing this resource for the family. In later years, when European settlements overran Indian hunting territories, Abenakis made their livings as guides and trappers. In the 1960s and 1970s, when present-day Abenakis reasserted their cultural and communal existence after a long period of invisibility among white communities, they chose to exercise traditional hunting and fishing rights in defiance of state fish and game laws, as both a symbolic and a political action to bring attention to their culture and their cause.

Adopting horticulture has important implications for a society. Groups can only benefit from their labor if they remain in one place through the growing season—in Vermont, late April through early October. This third element in the pattern of food gathering inserts a longer pause into seasonal cycles than previous generations of hunters and gatherers had experienced. Shelters become more permanent, including carefully and sturdily constructed underground storage pits. Territories used during the agricultural phases of the cycle become somewhat more centralized and constricted. The division of labor between the sexes takes on some new definitions: women plant, tend fields, and engage in more varied techniques of food preparation and storage. Pottery becomes more important for storage and thus becomes more common.

Horticulture also alters the landscape. If it was to be an adequate substitute for hunting, agriculture had to be conducted on a large enough scale to provide food to last through the winter and seed to replant the following spring. Indians therefore either opened areas in the forest that they could use for planting or developed open lowland areas along floodplains. Their staple crops of corn, beans, and squash— "the three sisters"—were planted in mounds placed two to three feet apart, both to minimize labor and to produce a high yield of food per acre under cultivation with minimal disturbance of the soil. When the soil was depleted, Indians did not hesitate to abandon a field and put their crops in a new place.

These horticultural practices confounded Europeans. Accustomed to working limited farm land to support a relatively large population, English and French farmers planted only one crop per field, used plows for deep cultivation in orderly rows, and adopted a crop-rotation system that allowed one field to lie fallow every three or four years to renew the productivity of the soil. Here are some of the roots of the discontinuity between ancient Indian culture and the ideologies and institutions that Europeans brought to North America at the end of the fifteenth century.[8]

On the eve of contact with Europeans, Woodland Indians had established a balanced and stable society built around the careful and effective use of resources, food-gathering techniques that coincided with the turning of the seasons, family and kinship cooperation, and spiritual connection to the earth. The petroglyphs at Bellows Falls, images of faces carved into two rock surfaces on the west bank of the Connecticut River, possibly as early as 1000 C.E., appear to have marked an especially sacred spot where Abenaki shamans returned year after year to interact with the spirit world and record their trances and visions.⁹ The cycle of seasonal food-producing activities had its cultural counterparts. Spring through early winter, the time of active food gathering, was also the time for teaching the next generation the skills necessary to sustain life. Midwinter, when food production was at its nadir, was the time of a community feast and storytelling, a way of creating community cohesion, passing on traditions, and keeping intact the world view of the people.¹⁰

This way of life placed heavy emphasis on the coordination of the family group. Nuclear families formed the core units within the larger unit of family bands. As a child reached adulthood and took a spouse, this new pair could choose to live with either the husband's or wife's family. Although the preference seems to have been to establish a fire with the husband's family, factors such as the size and status of the extended family group influenced this decision. Too many mouths to feed would put pressure on the family and the land it used for hunting and gathering. Indian families thus learned to restrict their populations to a number that could be fed using about one quarter of the food-supply capacity of their territories. This strategy allowed them to utilize approximately one quarter of their territory each year, preventing the exhaustion of food resources and without making game too timid or scarce.

Hunting territories lay along accessible waterways and were divided into quarters by paths running perpendicular to the river. Although these territories extended far into the interior, they tended to lie along river valleys and lower uplands, where game was easiest to hunt and carry back to camp. During the spring and summer, families converged on fishing and planting grounds to form macrobands at several village sites along the Champlain and Connecticut River valleys.

Archaeologists have ascertained the existence and continued use of several such sites. Some of these were also known to the first white settlers and are the basis for our earliest knowledge of Abenaki geography and place names. On the Connecticut River (from *Kwini-teguh-ack*, "long river place"), late-Woodland villages include Cowasuck at Newbury (from *Kowasek*, "the place of the white pines"), a site at Northfield, Massachusetts, and at Fort Hill near Hinsdale, New Hampshire (a Sokoki band site, from *Sohkwahkiak*, "the people who separated," corrupted to Squakheag). In western Vermont, near Lake Champlain (*Pe-ton-bowk*, "the waters that lie between"), villages were established near the mouths of Otter Creek and the Winooski, Lamoille, and Missisquoi rivers. *Winoskik* ("at wild onion land") gave its name to the Winooski River;

Mazipskoik ("at the flint," possibly referring to a chert quarry used for making tools and projectile points) was later corrupted to the present day Missisquoi.[11]

These villages consisted of several long houses, long rectangular structures of several rooms, with arched roofs of bark over pole frames. Each long house accommodated a single extended family. If the family became too big, a new shelter would be built nearby to accommodate the most recent arrivals. Other structures in the village included sweat lodges for hygienic and ritual purposes, and storage pits, which became refuse pits as their contents were used up. At Fort Hill, Sokokis constructed a log palisade around the village to protect themselves from attacks by rival Mohawks. The Europeans who saw this log wall called it a "castle." A similar palisaded retreat at Missisquoi appeared on maps as "Graylock's Castle."

Population estimates for Abenakis in Vermont at the time of contact vary. Haviland and Power emphasize that the people maintained a population size compatible with available resources and estimate that no more than four thousand Abenakis lived in the Champlain Valley and perhaps two thousand occupied the upper Connecticut Valley.[12] Average life expectancy was thirty-five to forty years, although those who survived beyond this age tended to live very long lives. Infant and child mortality was high, as was the death rate for women during childbirth.

Model of an Abenaki village (detail). *Courtesy of the Robert Hull Fleming Museum, University of Vermont.*

Families formed the basis for Abenaki political as well as social institutions. Within the macrobands—collections of families that came together in villages—decision making was a matter of consensus and families were recognized as sovereign units. No one could coerce another individual; resolution of conflict within a band was accomplished by persuasion. Because bands and macrobands were so closely tied to kinship relations, convergence of interests would be normal and more complicated political systems were therefore unnecessary. Villages chose leaders, usually a male and usually for life, but on the basis of ability in the hunt or wisdom, not heredity. If a leader lost the peoples' confidence, they ceased to pay him any attention. The leader acted in concert with a council comprised of family leaders. Women participated in these councils and enjoyed equal rights to speak. The leader's job was to secure the internal well-being of the macroband and represent it in dealings with other bands or people. When it became necessary to go to war, macrobands chose a separate war chief, always a male.

Warfare between western Abenakis and their Iroquois neighbors may have occurred occasionally before the arrival of white explorers and settlers. It became more frequent after that watershed event. Relations between the Iroquois, especially Mohawk—the easternmost tribe of the confederation—and Abenakis appear to have been tense for generations. Lake Champlain, however, served as an effective, if somewhat porous, natural boundary between the two peoples, providing opportunities for trade while presenting an obstacle to major sustained conflicts.

With the exception of these intervals of warfare, Abenaki culture and society appear to have had a sustained period of continuity and stability until the European explorations of North America began in the late fifteenth century. This stability was occasionally disrupted by climatic and biotic changes over many centuries and by occasional technological, cultural, and to some extent economic innovations transmitted from people living in far distant places (seacoast, the great inland lakes, and the Hudson and Mississippi river valleys). What the first Europeans saw and heard about the "People of the Dawnland," or as they called themselves, *Alnobak*, "the ordinary people" (to distinguish themselves from the giants, little people, and supernatural creatures that appear in their traditional tales and mythology, as well as all other non-Abenaki people), was largely a reflection of life as it had been lived for almost 1,500 years.

New Footprints on the Continent

Even before the Abenakis began to have frequent contact with Europeans in the 1620s, some changes in Indian life and culture near the Atlantic seacoast had begun to affect them, if not directly, then indirectly through other native people with whom they traded and maintained communication.

The Italian explorer John Cabot began sailing on behalf of England in 1497 to explore the northeast coast of what became known as North America. Even before his first voyage, however, during which he explored the east coast of Newfoundland, European sailors and fishing fleets, pursuing the abundance of cod and other large fish that could be taken off the Grand Banks, southeast of the island, had already made contact and initiated some informal trade with coastal Indians.[13] Although European explorers were determined to find a passage through North America to the Orient—the famous and illusive "Northwest Passage"—few voyages in the first generation of European exploration actually penetrated the interior of North America. Giovanni Verrazzano's long and productive voyage for France in 1524 resulted in the mapping of much of the northeast coast, Cape Breton, and Newfoundland. His maps established French claims for future economic exploitation of the northeast, and opened the way for more extensive exploration of the coastline by adventurers sailing under French, English, and Spanish flags. However, not until Jacques Cartier made his voyages in 1534, 1535, and 1541 did Europeans begin to penetrate the interior of northeast North America.

On his first voyage in 1534, Cartier sailed south through the Strait of Belle Isle along the northern and western coast of Newfoundland, crossed the Gulf of St. Lawrence, to Chaleur Bay and the Gaspé Peninsula, then headed north again across the mouth of the St. Lawrence River. He encountered Montagnais and Micmac fishing and seal-hunting parties who initiated an effort to trade furs for European knives and other tools, which suggests that they had already made previous contact with Europeans. Cartier himself reported encountering a fishing boat from the French city of La Rochelle on this voyage. Later, Cartier met another group of natives who, unlike the Micmacs, brought with them maize and dried plums and appeared to have come from far inland to fish and trade. In fact they were St. Lawrence Iroquois, from Stadacona (present-day Québec), sailing out of their summer camp at Tadoussac, at the mouth of the Saguenay River.[14] At one meeting, French sailors seized as captives the

Map of the "Land of Hochelaga." Drawn by Giovanni Battista Ramusio, based on Cartier's description in 1535 (G. B. Ramusio, *Navigationi et viaggi*, III, 1556, fol. 446v–447). *Courtesy of Dartmouth College Library.*

leader of the group and two young men, whom they assumed were his sons. Cartier bargained with the leader, Donnaconna, then released him but kept his sons, Taignoagny and Dom Agaya. Cartier hoped to teach his captives French and learn from them about the lands west of the Gulf of St. Lawrence, which he now assumed was the water passage to the Orient. The captives hinted at a kingdom called "Hochelaga" but offered no information about the gold or Oriental civilizations that the French expected to find on the other side of the land mass. What Cartier heard from his captives enticed him to propose a second voyage.

Returning in 1535, Cartier began his explorations of the St. Lawrence River, sailing as far as Tadoussac and the mouth of the Saguenay River, where he again encountered Donnaconna. Cartier planned to continue upstream, using his captives as guides. However, they refused to go further, perhaps, as some historians have suggested, because they were reluctant for the Europeans to make contact with interior groups and shift their attention and trade to them. Cartier proceeded on his own and on October 2, 1535, arrived at Hochelaga, a large settlement of another band of St.

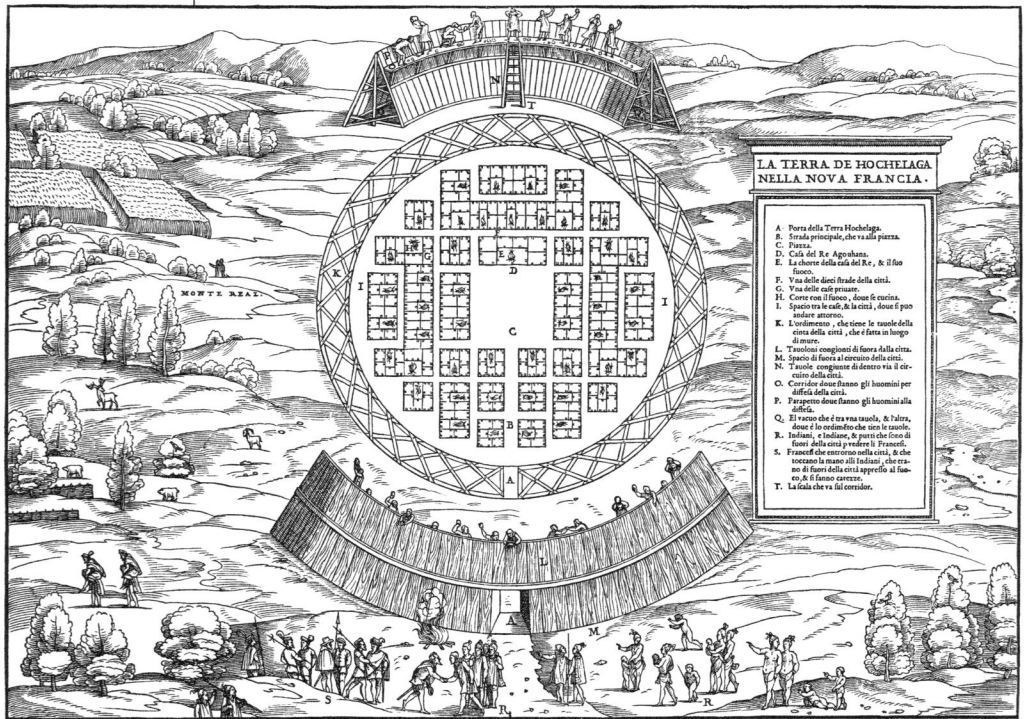

Lawrence Iroquois. Situated atop a high mountain overlooking the St. Lawrence, with corn fields, a triple-palisaded village containing fifty long houses, a large central square, and perhaps fifteen hundred inhabitants, Hochelaga offered long views in all directions. Cartier called the spot "Mont Royale." It is the present-day Montreal, and we may assume that from this height Cartier could look southeast into Vermont.

His interest was in the west, however, where his hosts told him of "the Kingdom of Saguenay," known only by reputation, which was the source of the copper they used for ornaments and which Cartier assumed would also yield the gold and gemstones he so desperately sought. The Hochelagans warned Cartier that great waterfalls barred the way to this land.

As several historians have suggested, the copper that Cartier saw probably came from the western Great Lakes, traded by Hurons, whose authority extended west to the far shore of Lake Superior. Because the route through the lakes is, indeed, barred by three sets of great falls, including Niagara, the Hurons conducted trade from the west by a northerly route through Georgian Bay to Lake Nipissing and down the Ottawa River to Montreal, where it joins the St. Lawrence. Some copper, apparently traded by portage, lake, and stream as far north and east as Lake St. Jean at the head of the Saguenay River, made its way downstream to villages such as the summer camp at Tadoussac. This roundabout route could account for the confusing fact that Donnaconna and his sons reported to Cartier that the Kingdom of Saguenay was both north on the Saguenay River, and west of Hochelaga. Cartier either did not learn about the Ottawa River route or deliberately chose not to take it, even though he could doubtless see it from Mont Royale, just as he chose not to go south from Hochelaga. His mind's eye was fixed on a western journey.

The story of gold, spices, and precious stones that Cartier heard may have arisen from unreliable translations. More likely, however, it was completely fabricated, a combination of politeness (the Indians replying agreeably to the anxious inquiries of their guests) and calculation. The Indians may have surmised quickly that in order to maintain access to the trade goods that the Europeans offered in exchange for information, they had to keep telling these strangers what they wanted to hear. Alternatively, the Indians may have decided that they were most interested in having the Europeans move on and so lured them further west with tales made up of the elements they heard in or surmised from their guests' inquiries. There is no evidence from archaeological sites in the northeast or Great Lakes area up through the Woodland period of the presence of gold in ornamental or burial goods. It would have been useless as material for tools because it is too soft to hold a sharp edge or withstand impact as a projectile point.

Cartier left Hochelaga on October 5, 1535, and wintered near the village of Stadacona at the present-day site of Québec City, where many of his men perished; he nearly did so as well. He returned to France in the spring of 1536, this time taking Donnaconna captive to join his sons, and immediately made plans for a third voyage. By 1540, King Francis I of France was ready to expand French claims in the New World to reap economic advantages and share in the symbolic glory of overseas exploration. He commissioned Cartier to sail west again, this time under the leadership of a protestant nobleman, Jean-François de La Rocque, Sieur de Roberval.

Cartier's third voyage, 1541–1542, took up where his second had left off. He returned to Stadacona determined to push on to the fabulous Kingdom of Saguenay. Donnaconna and his two sons had died in France but Cartier carefully kept this news from the Stadaconans. Relations between the Europeans and the Indians became increasingly tense—no doubt a result of the kidnappings perpetrated by the French—so Cartier decided to move his base camp further upstream from Stadacona, and launch from there an expedition in search of Saguenay. This time he got as far as the rapids at Lachine, where he may have learned about more rapids fifty miles upstream, at Long Sault, near present-day Massena, New York. Again, the fact that none of Cartier's guides showed him the way around this barrier by following the Ottawa River suggests that the Indians had become increasingly cautious in their relations with the Europeans and determined to prevent them from penetrating farther into the interior. During the winter of 1541–1542, Indians attacked Cartier's base camp. The Europeans escaped, briefly rejoined Roberval off the coast of Newfoundland, and returned to France in October 1542. Roberval stayed on in a futile effort to found a colony at Stadacona, then he too returned to France.

European exploration of the interior ceased for almost forty years after Cartier's third voyage. The French monarchy, which had financed early North American exploration, became entangled in a long, bitter civil and religious war. This tied up traditional royal tax revenues as well as whatever monetary resources the crown could extract from regional and local assemblies.

Although the king was stymied by a lack of resources, merchant companies and communities were free to act. Moreover, where royal aspirations for North American exploration continued to focus on gold, spices, and a northwest passage to the Orient, merchants of port towns such as St. Malo quickly recognized the commercial possibilities of the fur trade. Between 1545 and 1580, many traders and former fishermen, who saw greater prospects for riches in furs rather than in the increasingly competitive Atlantic cod fishery, maintained contact with Indians along the St. Lawrence River. They brought to the European market a modest but steady supply of *castor gras d'hiver* (beaver pelts that, having been worn by Indians for a year, had lost their long guard hairs to expose the more desirable short hairs required for felt hats). When news spread in France of a Rouen merchant's fruitful voyage in 1583 to the St. Lawrence, where he traded forty crowns worth of trinkets for four hundred crowns worth of furs, merchants of St. Malo sponsored a commercial expedition of five ships the following year and ten ships the next year. By 1587, rival traders competed in the frenzy to exploit the insatiable European market for furs.[15]

It was the fur trade most of all, therefore, that drove development of French overseas expansion during the sixty years between Cartier's voyages and Samuel de Champlain's establishment of a French colony at Québec in 1608. And the fur trade was the stimulus that began to change the lives of the Indians along the St. Lawrence valley from the middle of the sixteenth century.[16]

Contact, Confrontation, and Change

Writing of his journey in July 1609 up the Richelieu River, which he called the Iroquois River, Samuel de Champlain observed that "This region, although pleasant, is not inhabited by Indians, on account of their wars; for they withdraw from the rivers as far as they can into the interior, in order not to be surprised." At Montreal, Champlain found no trace of Hochelega or the people Cartier encountered a half-century earlier. Even more curious, the Europeans who had been trading on the St. Lawrence River in the 1580s made no mention of the village or its people. Between Cartier's last voyage and Champlain's expedition the St. Lawrence Iroquois had vanished.

Once in the lake, known to the French as "Iroquois Lake," and to the Indians as "the Waters Between," Champlain wrote, " I saw four beautiful islands about ten, twelve, and fifteen leagues in length, which, like the Iroquois river, were formerly inhabited by Indians: but they have been abandoned, since they have been at war with one another.... I enquired of the natives whether these parts were inhabited. They said they were, and by the Iroquois."[17]

These observations have caused historians a lot of trouble. We know from the rest of Champlain's account that he undertook his journey into the lake at the urging of his Montagnais and Algonquin allies, with the express purpose of helping them retain control of the St. Lawrence trade routes and giving a show of force to the Mohawk nation, which had already begun to acquire European tools and trade goods and was eager to expand its influence without having to trade through middlemen. Champlain encountered no resistance until he reached the area around Ticonderoga, where he had his famous engagement with a small group of Mohawks, described to him by his guides as a "war party," but by recent scholars as perhaps a diplomatic delegation.[18]

Who, then, were the "Iroquois" said to be living at the north end of the lake at this time? What happened to the people that Cartier encountered at Stadacona and Hochelaga seventy years earlier?[19] And where were the Abenakis, presumed by most archaeologists to be the descendants of the Woodland-era people living on the eastern shore of the Champlain valley?

Some historians and ethnologists now believe that the people at Hochelaga in 1535 were descendants of the Archaic-era "proto-Iroquoians." The archaeological evidence of Iroquoian pot sherds suggests that these people, called St. Lawrence Iroquoians, were widely dispersed through the St. Lawrence valley from Lake Ontario to Québec and in the Champlain valley. It is certain that they left Stadacona and Hochelega forty years before Champlain reached the area. Where they went is less certain. Reports of wars fought by the Five Nation Iroquois around 1570 to 1575, provide some hints that during a period of conflict among the Algonquins, Montagnais, and Iroquois the St. Lawrence Iroquois were defeated (but by whom is still a matter of conjecture), Hochelaga destroyed, and small refugee bands adopted into Iroquois, Abenaki, Huron, and Ottawa valley Algonquins.[20]

What were the wars about? Again we have no direct evidence, only the information passed along to Champlain by his native informants. Some scholars suggest that environmental degradation, which they attribute to Iroquois slash-and-burn horticulture, and the exhaustion of other natural resources around Iroquois villages that occurred in twelve-year cycles, may have forced the Iroquois south of the St. Lawrence and west of Lake Champlain to invade neighboring people's territory to obtain food and fertile land. Others argue by contrast that the success of Iroquois agriculture—work performed by women—freed young men to pursue warfare, which boosted their influence and prestige. In addition, the Great League of Peace and Power, established early in the sixteenth century to help maintain peace among five of the Iroquois nations, and the rituals of "mourning wars," by which Iroquois took prisoners from other peoples to replace men from their own populations lost in warfare, focused Iroquois attention more steadily on their neighbors as outlets for youthful energy and aggressiveness and as sources for a replacement population.[21]

Initial contact with Europeans may have added another factor. The Europeans' eager pursuit of trade and their introduction of devastating microbial diseases among native populations may have had the immediate effect of raising the level of enmity and rivalry between neighboring peoples. The intertribal warfare of the 1570s can therefore be interpreted as an early episode in the struggle of people along the St. Lawrence River both to control the emerging fur trade and to respond to the devastating population losses as new diseases tore through their villages. The St. Lawrence Iroquois may have been among the earliest victims of this new combination of disease and trade wars that eventually proved so destructive of native populations and cultures following contact with European explorers and traders.

From the beginning of their contact with the Europeans, the Indian people along the St. Lawrence learned that they could exchange furs for goods that had either practical uses—metal knives, hatchets, fish hooks, utensils, cloth—or symbolic value—glass beads and metal jewelry. By controlling the movement of furs from the interior to trading posts and controlling the movement of Europeans along the river, various Indian groups could exercise what amounted to the equivalent of European monopolies in the fur trade. It was in the interests of Indian trading partners to exclude possible rivals for the middleman role and to block the way of Europeans to the interior, where they could obtain furs directly. An early consequence of European-Indian contact, therefore, was the disruption of intertribal relations and trade, culminating in some truly cataclysmic struggles. Whole communities, such as Hochelaga, were destroyed, and entire peoples, such as the St. Lawrence Iroquois in 1570 and the Hurons in 1640, were wiped out or dispersed and adopted into other groups.[22]

These struggles for position in the fur trade point to some fundamental

Abenakis from one of the French mission villages on the St. Lawrence (Bécancour?). Middle of the eighteenth century. *Courtesy of the City of Montréal, Records Management and Archives.*

and wide-ranging changes taking place in Indian life as a result of the fur trade and the deepening European commitment to establish a presence in North America. The native concept of territory was an early casualty. In the Archaic and Woodland eras, family bands dispersed from autumn to mid-winter and again from late winter to early spring to traditional hunting territories, with well-known and generally respected boundaries marked by waterways and bisecting trails. Families were careful to stay within the boundaries and use only a quarter of the territory each year. As the demand for beaver increased, however, hunters had to use more of their total territory each year. And as the supply of beaver became exhausted in a territory, the boundaries themselves became points of dispute, either among families or between unrelated groups. In some cases, individual or family trading arrangements with Europeans even broke down the alliances between families that formed the basis for macrobands and villages. In some cases, witchcraft—a perversion of the traditional healing role of shamanism—became more prevalent within macrobands as individual families desperately sought ways to preserve or increase their hunting grounds.

The overwhelming focus on trapping beaver for fur also disrupted the well-established cycle of food gathering and consequently altered native diets. Men who formerly spent parts of their year hunting game, fishing, and helping plant food crops, now abandoned many of those activities to take beaver. The seminomadic lifestyle that had developed through the Archaic and Woodland periods broke down and hunting, fishing, and agriculture suffered, making Indians increasingly dependent on Europeans or raids on other native agricultural communities for food.

More subtle, but equally destructive of native life and culture, were changes in technology and materials. Historians and anthropologists map three stages of change in the appropriation of new cultural materials into traditional societies: first, the adaptation of new goods for symbolic use; second, the manufacture of traditional objects in traditional forms using new materials; and third, abandonment of traditional objects in favor of tools and objects introduced from the outside.

In their first trading contacts with Europeans, native people accepted objects such as glass beads, iron rings, and "trinkets" because they fit into a cultural framework that placed symbolic or spiritual value on similar objects already in the trade network: shells, copper beads, and exotic stones. By the 1620s, however, Indians were demanding clothing, cloth, and metal tools, such as knives, axes, hatchets, and mattock blades, and kettles. These objects were improvements in utility and durability over stone implements, fired clay pots, and bark containers. The metal utensils could be recycled into new tools such as needles, fish hooks, arrowheads, and spear points when they broke or wore out. Similarly, Indians easily and eagerly adapted wool and cotton cloth into their costume because it was more flexible and comfortable, even if less durable than deerskin or hide garments.

In the advanced stages of contact, some objects of traditional Indian life all but disappeared to be replaced by European objects. For example, bows and arrows steadily gave way to guns as tools for hunting and warfare. The exchange in technology ultimately had the effect of making Indians more dependent on Europeans for continuing supplies. Initially, however, exchange made hunting easier, allowing Indians to take game at even greater distances and without having to pursue wounded animals.[23]

If the long-term consequences of change were to the disadvantage of the native people, they were hard if not impossible to discern at the time. By contrast, the short-term advantages of pursuing contact with the Europeans, and admitting them into the web of trade that had existed in one form or another for many centuries, were clear to the native people and hard to resist. Indian groups, no better at seeing far into the future than any other people, made what appeared at the moment to be wise choices to cooperate with the Europeans, thinking that they could continue to control and limit the impact of the strangers on their individual and collective lives.

Finally, but most devastating, continuous contact with Europeans brought Europeans' diseases into Indian communities. Epidemics of smallpox and other new diseases brought to North America by Europeans began to decimate Indian populations early in the sixteenth century. "Many native groups," writes Eric Wolf, "were . . . broken up, or driven from their original habitats. Remnant populations sought refuge with allies or grouped together with other populations, often under new names and ethnic identities."[24] Food gathering, already disrupted by the fur trade, became increasingly difficult as large numbers of strong and healthy individuals became sick and died. Indians, struggling with diseases, became less visible on the land and were perceived by outsiders as less sturdy. Their declining numbers were ultimately no match for the endless waves of Europeans who descended on North America. Traditional healing techniques, of little use against microbial diseases, lost their authority within the community as French and English missionaries made inroads against native spiritual and religious systems.

Few of these changes brought about by contact with Europeans had taken place by the time Champlain ascended the "Iroquois River" and entered the "Lake Between," which he re-named for himself. But the process of rapid change in societies that had heretofore changed very slowly had begun.

The archaeological record does not show conclusively that the Western Abenakis occupying Vermont in 1609 had made direct contact with Europeans prior to Champlain's expedition. Nor do we know precisely when the Abenakis made such contact. Indeed, it is not entirely clear where the Abenakis were when Champlain entered the lake. However, we can be fairly confident that they had occupied the Champlain valley for many centuries, probably as descendants of the Archaic-era "Vergennes" people whose presence is well documented in the archaeological record. We know that in their own mythology the transformer figure Odziozo was credited with forming the lake that played so important a part in Abenaki life and subsistence. One story that has come down through tradition explains that when he finished creating the lake he sat in it and, reluctant to leave his masterpiece, turned himself into stone and sits there still.[25] Such a story would hardly form a central part of the mythology of a people who had only recently occupied the land or had no long-term attachment to it.

In 1609, however, the Abenakis appear to have retreated far inland, probably following the waterways that led them to traditional winter hunting grounds where they endeavored to avoid destruction at the hands of the Mohawk, as had befallen the St. Lawrence Iroquois thirty years earlier. Avoidance became an effective strategy that the Abenakis would be forced to use many times in the following centuries, although it contributed to the long-standing but erroneous assertion by white settlers that there were no Indians in Vermont, and that the land was merely a passageway for wandering groups.

Nonetheless, abundant evidence for Indian-European contact prior to 1609 in the Champlain Valley and across the mountains along the Connecticut River villages of Cowass (Cowasuck) near Newbury and Fort Hill near Hinsdale, New Hampshire, suggests that the Abenakis, wherever they were hiding to keep out of harm's way, had already begun to feel the effects of European presence. Their small numbers, light impact on the land, and decentralized political and social structures may have made them hard to see or recognize. But they were to play an important role in the competition for empire that brought almost continuous conflict into the area over the next 150 years.

"Odziozo's Rock," also known as "Rock Dunder," in Lake Champlain off Shelburne Point. *Vermont Historical Society.*

2
Struggle for Empire, The Vermont Crossroad
1609–1763

Voyages of Discovery

By the beginning of the seventeenth century, Europeans had begun to explore the interior of North America, slowly learning from their probing that the land mass was not the gateway to the Orient that they sought for trade, that it offered new, if challenging opportunities for trade, and that to extract any profit from this unexpected land mass, they would have to learn to deal effectively with its natives. Moreover, the commercial rivalries that had stimulated and supported the initial voyages of discovery by French, Dutch, and English mariners, adventurers, and traders soon translated into rivalries for control of the interior of North America. These only escalated over time, leading toward international warfare that drew the native population into a web of conflict, struggle for survival, and struggle for empire.

The area we know as Vermont, by virtue of its strategic location, provided throughout this period a focal point for the struggle. On an east-west axis, Vermont separated the Mohawks, members of the Iroquois Five Nations, from the Abenakis and Algonquins; on a north-south axis, it separated New France from New Netherlands and New England. In an increasingly lethal succession of campaigns, the three European colonial powers and their native allies struggled with each other to vanquish opponents from Vermont and, ultimately, from the entire continent. These efforts culminated in the clash of enormous European armies in the Champlain Valley. Concurrently, the Europeans' struggle for empire engulfed and finally eclipsed efforts by the far smaller numbers of native peoples to maintain their identity and control over the land. Vermont's location and landscape played a strategic role in these clashes and thereby established a number of stories about Vermont; set in motion the "New Hampshire Grants" crisis after 1763; and laid the foundation for subsequent patterns of settlement, diplomacy, warfare, and land use that dominated Vermont history for over a century.

On July 4, 1609, seventy-four years after Jacques Cartier gazed south upon the Green Mountains from the top of Mont Royale, Samuel de Champlain and two French compatriots, accompanied by sixty native allies, became the first Europeans to enter Vermont. They paddled south via what is now called the Richelieu River into the open lake, which so captivated Champlain by its extraordinary beauty that he named the place after himself, Lake Champlain. His journal described "many of the finest vines I had seen anywhere.... many chestnut trees ... [and] a great abundance of many species of fish." Reporting what he heard, or perhaps wanted to hear from his native guides, he transformed the benign lake gar into a ten-foot Chaosarou fish, with "scales ... so strong that a dagger could not pierce them" and cunningly capable of catching birds by tricking them into landing on its long snout as it hid amidst reeds and marshes. Here lay the origins of the present-day legend of "Champ," the oft-reported but not yet verified Lake Champlain "monster." Unfamiliar with the outcroppings of white limestone on the upper peaks of the Green Mountains, Champlain concluded that, even in the height of summer, he had seen "towards the east very high mountains on the tops of which there was snow."[1]

Champlain, at age forty-two when he entered Vermont, had already distinguished himself as a chronicler of the Americas, explorer, and, most ambitiously, as the "Father of New France." Beginning in 1599, sailing with a Spanish fleet, Champlain had traveled extensively throughout the Caribbean Islands, Panama, and Mexico, displaying his talent as an observer, chronicler, and geographer.

Champlain's experience in New Spain, with its vast riches, so impressed him that he turned his energies to creating a comparable colony in the Americas for France. He eventually received a court pension from the French King Henri IV and appointment to the post of royal geographer. In March 1603, Champlain joined an expedition to the St. Lawrence River organized by the merchant Aymar de Chastes, whom Henri IV had favored with capital resources and monopoly rights to the St. Lawrence fur trade. Champlain's talents for the role of chronicler are evident in his extraordinary diaries, which he later published as *Des Sauvages, ou, Voyage de Samuel Champlain, de Brouage*.[2] In the diaries he recorded vivid descriptions of his engagements with native peoples, concluding that, despite wide differences in behavior, if these "savages" could be taught to till the land and worship the true God, they could be made good French subjects.

The behavior of the people, however, remained secondary to Champlain's central concern for exploring and mapping the region. In June 1603, Champlain and his Montagnais guides reconnoitered up the St. Lawrence River from Tadoussac, passing by Québec and the ruined chimney that was the sole remaining evidence of Cartier's fort. They progressed as far as the abandoned site of Montreal. His guides described the lakes beyond the Lachine rapids, as far as Lake Ontario, the Ottawa River, and even Lake Erie and Niagara Falls, but he ventured no farther west at this time.

On his second trip to the region, in the spring of 1604, sponsored by Pierre du Gua, Sieur de Monts, to whom the king had redirected the Acadian fur monopoly, Champlain participated in establishing a small settlement at the entrance to the Bay of Fundy, strategically located to guard the river against competition from other European traders. Intended as a permanent settlement, it proved to be a poor location, with no fresh water, insufficient firewood, and an abundance of unproductive sandy soil. Thirty-five men died from scurvy in the blustery winds and frigid cold of winter. When spring arrived, the few survivors moved across the bay into the less exposed reaches of Port Royal in the Annapolis basin.

Champlain remained unconvinced of the benefits of even the new location. He therefore turned southward to continue his explorations. Over the next three years (1604–1607) he navigated along the Atlantic coast as far south as Stage Harbor on Cape Cod. Nowhere did he find a satisfactory site with a navigable harbor, nor for that matter, natives with substantial numbers of furs. In the fall of 1607 he sailed back to France.

In 1608, Champlain returned to Canada with a new plan of action. He supervised construction of a fortified *habitation* at Québec, deep inside the St. Lawrence, where the river narrowed. This allowed the French to intercept native fur traders before they reached the summer port of Tadoussac and gave them control of access to the interior of North America. By establishing a permanent settlement, Champlain acquired the honorific title, "Father of New France."

Champlain next turned his exploration attention westward. In June 1609, he began his momentous journey from Québec, up the St.

Lawrence, to the river now known as the Richelieu and into what would be identified thereafter as Lake Champlain. The lure of the land, however, contributed only a small element to the motivation that propelled him on this voyage. The Montagnais and Algonquin residents of the St. Lawrence had formed an alliance with the French in 1603. They had long sought French assistance in their struggle to maintain control of the St. Lawrence trade routes against challenges from the Five Nations of the Iroquois, the largest and most prominent of whom were the Mohawk. The French, however, had remained focused on finding the ideal site for profitable fur trading. Now joined by a third tribe, the Hurons, dominant traders in the Great Lakes region who promised to vastly expand the scope of the French fur empire, the native chorus grew more insistent that Champlain align with them against the Iroquois. Raiding parties of Iroquois had put the St. Lawrence valley in a state of perpetual warfare and Champlain's allies warned him that neutrality would have devastating effects on the tiny *habitation* at Québec. Thus, Champlain decided to cement his Huron and Algonquin allies' loyalties by honoring their request that he join them in an excursion against the Iroquois. In previous journeys, he had carried with him objects that signified friendship in his quest to expand French trade in furs. But this voyage had a fresh purpose. "I had no other intention than to

Samuel de Champlain's drawing of his battle with the Iroquois near Ticonderoga (?), July 30, 1609. Champlain portrayed himself in the middle foreground, discharging his arquebus. *From his Voyages (Paris, 1613)*

make war," Champlain wrote, "for we had with us only arms and not merchandise for barter."³

At the expedition's outset in Québec, it included two or three thousand Hurons and Algonquins, but by the time it reached the Richelieu in late June, the numbers had fallen to sixty Indians, Champlain, and two other Frenchmen. Once on the lake, Champlain and his party made a slow progression southward until July 29, when, according to the explorer's journal, the group came upon an assemblage of two hundred Mohawks in a temporary camp on a narrow meadow behind a beach, in the present-day vicinity of Fort Ticonderoga. Champlain's Indian allies portrayed the gathering as a "war party." The battle they had sought occurred the next day. During the incursion, Champlain stepped forward and discharged his arquebus (a small-caliber long gun fired by a slow-burning match), killing two chiefs and mortally wounding another. The deafening discharge of the unfamiliar French weapon caused the Mohawks to fall back in horror. A second shot fired by his French companions from the woods "astonished them again so much that, seeing their chiefs dead, they lost courage and took to flight, abandoning the field and their fort, and fleeing into the depth of the forest." Champlain then pursued the retreating Mohawks "and laid low still more of them." By the end of the engagement, Champlain and his allies had killed several, captured ten prisoners, and lost none of their own men.⁴ The party headed back to Canada the following day, its mission accomplished.

Champlain returned to France for the winter of 1609–1610, where he presented King Henri IV an account of his adventures, along with a Mohawk scalp, the skull of a garfish, a belt of porcupine quills, and two live scarlet tanagers. He made three more voyages to Canada. In June 1610 he fought another battle with Algonquin and Huron allies against Iroquois near the mouth of the Richelieu River. In 1613 he traveled up the Ottawa River as far as Allumette Lake. And in his final expedition in 1615 he traveled deep into the interior to Georgian Bay, then south to Lake Ontario and into present-day New York, where he fought with a party of Onondaga near Oneida Lake, just north of present-day Syracuse.

Champlain's dramatic effort to solidify the claims of the French and their native allies to valuable fur-laden territories turned out to be an early episode in the sequence of events that escalated into 150 years of French, Dutch, and British competition for native allegiances and economic gain.

The Competition for Furs and Hearts

Several historians have insisted that Champlain's shortsightedness in his military adventures in the summer of 1609 allowed him to win the skirmish yet lose the war. From this perspective, the enmity that Champlain planted in the Iroquois on that July morning and in his three subsequent skirmishes with Iroquois warriors drove them to seek out new strategies and new allies among the English and, a century and a half later, to join in the defeat of New France. Is it fair, however, to hold Champlain accountable, given that in 1609 the English had not yet entered the competition for North American empire? A more reasonable attribution of miscalculation on Champlain's part concerns his elusive plan to secure a regional monopoly on furs. He based his plan on the assumption that his explorations gave him control over the most vital passages into the interior. In this, he was mistaken. Three months after Champlain's venture into the lake known to natives as "the waters between," the Englishman Henry Hudson, in the employ of the Dutch East India Company, sailed his ship the *Half Moon* up the river that bears his name, and anchored it near modern-day Albany. There he exchanged "trifles" as well as knives and hatchets for food and furs with the Algonquian-speaking Mahicans. In doing so, he planted a Dutch presence in the interior of North America, and five years later, with the establishment of the trading post at Fort Orange, four Dutch companies vied for furs brought to them by Mahicans and Mohawks.

The arrival of the Dutch, as with the arrival of the French farther to the north, set in motion chain reactions. The Mahicans, with whom Hudson made his initial exchanges, were the first to respond to this new presence and the opportunities it presented. Numbering four thousand strong in 1610 and with settlements extending north to present-day Bennington and Pownal and south into the Hoosick and Housatonic regions, the Mahicans literally relocated along the Hudson to take advantage of Dutch trading posts. From the river shore opposite the fort, they levied tribute from Mohawks and others who sought to exchange furs for European cloth, axes, and other items increasingly integral to their survival.

The Mahicans' monopoly struck at the very core of Mohawk survival. Their subordinate position in relation to both the Mahicans and the Dutch, and their increasing reliance—like most native people—on the new economic conditions as well as the new materials introduced by Europeans forced the Mohawks to redirect energies away from their rich cornfields between the Hudson and the Genesee rivers. They increasingly hunted diminishing populations of beaver in order to bribe the Mahicans, and traded with the Dutch for hoes and axes (in addition to mouth harps, glass bottles, pottery, and multicolored glass beads) to preserve their autonomy and culture. Pressed between Mahicans to the south and the alliance of French, Algonquin, and Abenaki to the north and east, the Mohawks eventually realized their only option was to try to supplant the Mahicans as middlemen in the fur trade. In 1624, they initiated war. Within four years, the Mahicans had been defeated, and large numbers abandoned their villages in the Hudson valley to relocate in northwestern Massachusetts and southeastern Vermont. Those who remained were now obligated to pay tribute to the Mohawks.

The defeat of the Mahicans not only delivered the Dutch trade to the Mohawks but brought large numbers of native immigrants to bolster their ranks. Doubling their numbers from thirty years earlier to seventy-seven hundred, the emboldened Mohawks next turned northward to exact revenge for their 1609 humiliation. In 1629, they attacked and destroyed an Algonquin and Montagnais village at Three Rivers. Next, they began intercepting fur-laden canoes traveling from the Great Lakes areas and western New York bound for Albany and Montreal. With their own supplies of beaver dwindling, Mohawk raiding parties struck at rivals in the Connecticut River valley, Maine, and western Long Island.

Not merely the native allies of the French were now under fire, however. In the spring of 1628, New France itself became a target for extinction. The outbreak of war in Europe provided the occasion for an English expedition led by David Kirke to launch a direct attack on New France in a bid to steal away the lucrative St. Lawrence fur trade. With scarcely one hundred residents, Québec under Champlain nevertheless successfully rebuffed Kirke's initial call for capitulation. However, after Kirke defeated the French fleet opposite Tadoussac, as it sought to bring supplies to the beleaguered colony, the English initiated a year-long blockade of food and goods destined for Québec. Kirke demanded and received Champlain's surrender on July 19, 1629. The Englishmen maintained control of the land and a major portion of the fur trade during five years of postwar European political wrangling, before England finally returned Québec to French rule as part of the Treaty of St. Germain en Laye.

Kirke's departure, nevertheless, did not signal an end to the English presence. Rather, the English Crown's decision, beginning in 1620, to allow colonization by religious "dissenters," in stark contrast to France's policy of prohibiting Huguenots in New France, led to an explosion of English settlement in New England. Commencing with Plymouth in 1620, then Boston in 1630, and extending to a variety of surrounding towns, the archetypically compact, nucleated structure, replete with village "common" and obligatory Congregational church, replicated itself across New England with astounding speed. By 1630 the English population in Massachusetts had increased to nine thousand from its original thousand or less. The English emulated the French in following the trails of the trade, as in the settlement of New Haven and Providence, and in the planting of Thomas Pynchon's trading post in Springfield in 1636. The French settled into a few towns or along a thin line bordering the waterways connecting the frontier to the administrative and economic centers of their trade empire. By contrast, the English "moved massively and displaced Indian communities in order to occupy new territories with their own people."[5]

What were the consequences of these events in Vermont? For the native peoples who inhabited the region, the ever-expanding network of Europeans vying for furs shook the very foundations of their existence. The first indication took the form of disease. Coastal epidemics had ravaged native populations as early as Cartier's trips. An epidemic in 1617–1618 involving hepatic failure accounts for why the weary Pilgrims found an abundance of corn and food in the once settled but now deserted native village in Plymouth, a circumstance they readily attributed to "a spetiall providence of God."[6]

The interior of Vermont had been shielded from the spread of disease by the region's isolation from major trade routes. In 1633, however, the area's luck ran out. A smallpox epidemic that had broken out along the St. Lawrence and Connecticut Rivers blanketed the northeast, enveloping the Abenakis and others in the region, and causing an appalling number of deaths. Conversations between the French and natives two decades later indicated that, in the succeeding years, mortality rates exceeded ninety percent for the Abenaki and the Mahicans, probably a consequence of their compact settlements. The neighboring Mohawks experienced only slightly fewer deaths, losing between one-half and two-thirds of their populations.

The internal convulsions emanating from this extraordinary human tragedy are not known. The epidemic clearly did, however, set into motion a succession of events of unprecedented magnitude. First, Jesuit missionaries in the vicinity redoubled their efforts to minister to their native allies. Foremost among these allies were the Hurons, whose strategic location in the Great Lakes within large villages that served as commercial hubs, rendered them particularly attractive to missionaries for conversion. The number of Jesuits in the area increased from three in 1634 to ten in 1638 and eighteen in 1649. As disease, probably smallpox, carried unwittingly by traders and missionaries alike, took its toll, the population of thirty-two thousand plummeted to ten thousand by the early 1640s. The compassionate care delivered by the "Black Robes," however, yielded rewards in increased numbers of Huron baptisms. "I may say," Father Paul Ragueneau wrote back to his superiors, "that this country has never been in such deep affliction as we see it now, and that never has the Faith appeared to greater advantage."[7]

The alliance between Jesuits and Hurons did not escape the attention of the Iroquois. Determined to intimidate the French, the Iroquois preyed upon Jesuits in transit between Huronia and New France. Consequently, in August 1642, a band of Iroquois warriors at the mouth of the Richelieu River attacked and captured Father Isaac Jogues, a missionary to the Hurons, two lay brothers, and forty Huron guides. After subjecting Jogues to severe tortures, the Iroquois party and their captives traveled up Lake Champlain to Lake George, overland to the Hudson, and finally westward on the Mohawk River. Father Jogues remained a prisoner for thirteen months "as slave to an Indian family," until a Dutch merchant, Arendt van Corlaer, ransomed him in Schenectady and returned him to France by way of Manhattan and England.[8]

Jogues's retelling of his experiences bolstered rather than inhibited Jesuit endeavors. He received a Papal dispensation and returned to the area in 1646, this time bearing gifts for the Iroquois from the French government. Traveling deep into Mohawk territory, Jogues and his colleague La Lande were captured and charged with sorcery in relation to two recent disasters: an epidemic that had arisen among the Iroquois, and the loss of their grain, devoured by caterpillars. Their captors submitted the two men to much torture, and killed them on October 18, 1646, displaying their heads on the palisades of the village. Similar ends came to many other Jesuits, for whom martyrdom carried assurances "of eternal happiness in Heaven after our death."[9]

Jogues's harsh experience obscured a critical development associated with his initial capture in 1642: The Iroquois attack on Jogues and his party had involved firearms. He reported to the governor of New France that his captors' village contained "nearly three hundred arquebuses" and that the seven hundred Iroquois within the village were "skilled in handling them."[10] It was an ironic development for the French, who had adamantly followed Champlain's dictum not to provide firearms to their allies. As early as 1637, following a visit to Québec by a small band of eastern Abenaki from Maine, the French became aware that the British had placed a few guns in their allies' hands; now, in 1643, it was clear that the Dutch had done so as well. The escalating competition for furs dictated that native allies become more closely tutored in the European ways of trade and war. Firearms became increasingly important for hunting game and fur-bearing animals; inevitably, they became part of the conflict for territorial hegemony. The consequences in human losses would be devastating.

The first to be victimized were the Hurons. Devoid of a single arquebus, they drew repeated attacks from the Iroquois, determined "to make of them both but one people and only one land."[11] In March 1649, twelve hundred Iroquois warriors descended upon two Huron settlements. They tortured and slaughtered several natives and two Jesuit companions. Within a year, the Hurons, broken and panic stricken, abandoned their homes. A few hundred joined the Jesuits for relocation in Québec and the remainder scattered across the continent, bringing an ignominious end to a once flourishing nation.

Conquest and integration became the Iroquois' method for replenishing their strength and their numbers. They proved so effective in this practice that by 1650 most of those who claimed to be members of the Iroquois Five Nations had not been born Iroquois but rather adopted into the tribe. Their mounting victories emboldened the Iroquois to lash out forcefully also against their enemies to the east. While consolidating power in the Great Lakes, bands of Iroquois began traveling down Lake Champlain and the Richelieu River, repeatedly raiding the infant settlements at Montreal and Three Rivers, and killing and carrying off large numbers of French settlers and Indians. Sister Marie de l'Incarnation noted that Iroquois attacks on the outskirts of Québec evinced a brazenness "they had never before dared," and warned French officials that without help, "either we must die or we must return to France."[12]

As a more practical alternative to both these options, the French initiated a policy of arming and bolstering their native allies. In 1650, the Jesuit

Iroquois warrior, engraving by J. Larocque after Jacques Grasset St. Saveur. This unsympathetic French image includes traditional weapons and firearms, summertime dress, and snowshoes. *Courtesy of the National Archives of Canada, C-3165.*

missionary Father Gabriel Druillettes, accompanied by a Montagnais chief, traveled south to make overtures to the Sokokis and Abenakis to join in a French-led alliance "to check the insolence of these Iroquois Indians." The Sokokis responded positively, as Druillettes reported, "to deliver themselves from the annual tribute . . . which the Irocquois exact—nay, even, to revenge themselves for the death of many of their fellow-countrymen. . . . Besides that, they hope for the beaver hunt about quebecq, after the destruction of the Irocquois."[13] Following a meeting of Sokokis with the Mahicans, Pocumtucks, and Pennacooks, these tribes, too, agreed to join the French.

Still, the Iroquois juggernaut could not be stopped. Sporadic clashes between Mohawks and Sokokis on the Connecticut River and elsewhere finally exploded into open war in December 1663. In a massive attack on the Sokoki fort near Hinsdale, New Hampshire, the Mohawks lost more than one hundred warriors and failed to successfully storm the village itself. Yet, before withdrawing, they managed to empty the Sokokis' corn storage pits outside the walled fort. By early spring, the Sokokis, who had also taken many losses in the battle, abandoned their village and fled north to safety.

The French now undertook a reassessment of their entire colonial strategy. After a half century, New France, under siege from the Iroquois and captive to a fur trade economy, possessed a meager population of three thousand colonists, resident in three villages on the banks of the St. Lawrence River. In contrast, New England, continuing to lure religious dissidents and others with the promise of cheap, newly opened "vacant" lands, boasted more than thirty-three thousand residents, and enjoyed a doubling of its population every twenty years. King Louis XIV, recognizing that the Company of New France's St. Lawrence commercial monopoly had failed to provide adequately for the security or the growth of the colony, moved decisively: He transformed New France into a royal colony.

With that crucial step, France set out next to neutralize the Iroquois, an order of business rendered all the more urgent by an Iroquois alliance with the English following the latter's defeat of the Dutch. Previous French efforts to use native allies as surrogate warriors had failed, so the king now determined to deliver the help requested years earlier by Marie l'Incarnation. He dispatched to Canada four companies of regular French troops from the Regiment Carignan-Salières, totaling more than one thousand men. They accompanied the arrival there of the king's newly appointed viceroy, Alexandre de Prouville, Seigneur de Tracy.

Armies on the Warpath

The new French strategy called for constructing a line of forts to block the traditional Lake Champlain-Richelieu River invasion route. Thus, in

1665, the French built Forts Richelieu, St. Louis de Chambly, Ste. Therese, and St. Jean along the Richelieu River. The royal colony's new governor, Daniel de Rémy, Sieur de Courcelles, "breathed nothing but war" from the time he arrived in Canada. He wanted to use his army to punish the Mohawks for their brutal attacks, to impress them with French military strength, and to assuage French fears following raids they had absorbed in 1664 and 1665. He laid plans for an assault in early 1666 by way of the "Iroquois corridor," through Lake Champlain and Lake George, into the heart of Mohawk country.[14]

De Courcelles's expedition inaugurated a century of deadly warfare in which the Lake Champlain-Richelieu River route became a familiar warpath, involving the clash of native forces and European armies, supplemented by colonial recruits and Indian allies. The Lake Champlain corridor took its place as one of the theaters in which France, England, and to a lesser extent the Netherlands conducted the struggle for control of North America. Until one side or the other prevailed, this warfare discouraged new settlement by Europeans while simultaneously driving the native populations far from their habitual hunting, fishing, and planting grounds as they sought to avoid being drawn into the devastating armed conflict.

In January 1666, during the coldest winter in thirty years, de Courcelles launched the overland expedition that he had been planning against the Mohawks. "In all history," the Jesuit Francis Joseph Le Mercier later asserted, "there can scarcely be found a march of more difficulty or greater length than that of this little army" of six hundred men.[15] After six weeks of hardship in which they slept in the open in subzero temperatures, maneuvered on unfamiliar snowshoes, and inadvertently lost their way on snow-covered trails, de Courcelles and his troops walked into a Mohawk ambush outside the Dutch village of Schenectady. As a further setback, they learned that English military forces had seized New Amsterdam (now New York), effectively making the struggle for empire a two-party fight. With that news, de Courcelles and his expedition retraced their steps to Canada, bands of pursuing Mohawks skirmishing at their heels. Failing to find a cache of emergency provisions at Isle La Motte, sixty more men perished from cold and hunger on the return march, and many others lost their lives in the fighting along the Lake Champlain route.

Following this disastrous campaign, de Courcelles and de Tracy ordered three hundred troops to construct another fort, on the northwest shore of Isle La Motte, to guard against enemy movement between the lake and the

Richelieu River. It was the first European colonial settlement within the boundaries of Vermont. Strategically situated as the most advanced outpost in the chain of forts designed to sound an early warning against Iroquois attacks on Québec, the fort, dedicated to St. Anne in July 1666, became a critical rendezvous and staging point for French expeditions.

In September 1666, de Tracy gathered New France's largest army to date at Fort Ste. Anne to mount another campaign to subdue the Mohawks. A force of six hundred men from the Carignan regiment combined strength with six hundred colonial *habitants* and one hundred Algonquin and Huron allies. They traveled south along the lake in a flotilla of three hundred light boats and bark canoes. Marching to the loud pounding of their drums, the French forces arrived at a Mohawk village, but found it deserted. Likewise, they discovered abandoned each of the next four palisaded Indian towns they had planned to attack. The Mohawks, alerted by the advancing sound of the beating drums, had scattered into the forest. Before returning to Canada, de Tracy's troops burned all of the towns and destroyed the winter provisions. Hardly a brilliant military victory, the campaign nevertheless reduced the Mohawks' ranks to fewer than two thousand through starvation and disease during the ensuing winter.

The two sides then settled into a temporary and uneasy peace that lasted two decades. With a French mission planted among the Mohawks in 1668, Fort Ste. Anne's utility ended, and in 1671, the French abandoned the structure and temporarily withdrew from Lake Champlain. Concurrently, in the absence of an immediate threat of attack, New France experienced a steady in-migration of settlers, effectively doubling its population by 1673 to more than 6,700 residents.

With calm in the Champlain Valley, the king's first intendant in New France, Jean Baptist Talon, organized in 1670 a ceremonial gathering of fourteen Indian nations at the Mission of Sault St. Marie that proclaimed French sovereignty over the vast territory extending from the Atlantic Ocean and Hudson's Bay westward to Lakes Huron and Superior. The following year, the Jesuit Charles Albanel added Labrador and the lands surrounding Hudson Bay to France's claims, while Louis Joliet and the Jesuit Jacques Marquette descended the Mississippi River to within two hundred miles of its mouth. In these events, France signaled its ambition to encircle the seaboard English colonies and vigorously contest England for supremacy of North America.

The contest involved not only the French and British, however. Native

Americans pursued independent paths in the European power struggle, with results that became vividly apparent in King Philip's War in 1675. English settlements in southern New England had steadily encroached on tribal territories. Metacom (known to the English as King Philip), chief of the Wampanoag, called on his brethren to organize a confederation and rise up in rebellion. The rebellion split the native community itself, with Narragansetts, Nipmucks, Pocumtucks, and Wampanoags fighting not only the English settlers but also their allies: Mohegan, Pequot, and Christian Indians. According to historian Jill Lepore, the combatants on both sides "were fighting to protect their territory and to preserve their way of life."[16]

Squakheag, the Sokoki village in the pine woods at present-day South Vernon on the Connecticut River, became a center of Indian operations that involved several attacks on towns within twenty miles of Boston and the deaths of approximately two thousand white settlers. Participants often returned to Squakheag for sanctuary after these incursions. Metacom himself fled there in February 1676, and organized almost three thousand warriors from nine tribes in preparation for his next offensive.

In the course of Metacom's war, his allies destroyed twelve New England towns completely, inflicted damage on more than one half the remainder, and killed one in every sixteen men of military age, rendering it the costliest in lives of any American war (in proportion to population). The English, however, did not capitulate. Governor Edmund Andros of New York distributed arms to the Mohawks, who had enemies in Metacom's confederation, and encouraged them to scatter the Wampanoag chief's forces. Militia from Massachusetts followed in the Mohawks' wake, progressing up the Connecticut River, tracking the retreating bands, attacking and slaughtering hundreds as they slept. Many of Metacom's followers became demoralized and abandoned the rebellion. His confederation gradually dissolved, and in August 1676, vengeful militia forces hunted down and killed Metacom, and the active period of the war thus came to an end. The war was a turning point in colonial American history, "a defining moment, when any lingering, though slight, possibility for Algonquian political and cultural autonomy was lost" and when the English settlers of New England, fearful of losing their identity, determined that they could no longer live alongside the native people.[17]

Soon afterward, the English dispatched soldiers "to cut down the Indians' corn at Squakheag, etc., which [was] accordingly done and not any Indians seen thereabouts," an act of retribution that "constituted an

King Philip, engraved by Paul Revere (1772). *Courtesy of the American Antiquarian Society.*

ecological disaster for the Abenakis. It disrupted their agricultural, trapping, and trading activities and curtailed the seasonal mobility that was vital to their effective utilization of resources."[18] Moreover, it forced many New England tribes to migrate, blend, and form new identities on the frontier of white European settlement. Many Abenakis and Sokokis, formerly resident in the area, fled north to the security of French Canada. Others, however, remained or took refuge in the forests and around the lakes of northern Vermont and New Hampshire. In this way they could be close by French habitations and thus to the protection afforded by the French rivalry with England, but nonetheless temporarily independent of French or English domination. Within the Champlain Valley, Missisquoi, with its abundant resources, key location, and relative safety, became an important refuge for dislocated Sokokis, Abenakis, and other Algonquian tribe members. So, too, on the Connecticut River, Cowasuck, in the locality of Newbury, an area regarded by the English as a "foreboding wilderness," provided an important haven for displaced Pennacooks, Mahicans, and Sokokis.

Although scattered and weakened, natives refused to accept defeat. A year after King Philip's War ended, a party of refugee Indians returned from Canada to strike at their former neighbors in the frontier towns along the upper Connecticut River, in Hatfield, and later Deerfield, Massachusetts. Surprising the residents, they killed and wounded several and carried more than twenty captives to Canada. The route they took, which followed native paths through the Otter Creek and Winooski River valleys and the Wells, White, and Williams River valleys between Lake Champlain and the Connecticut River, received repeated similar use in the years that followed. The Indians launched raids on other Connecticut River settlements by way of this route innumerable times over the next century, and the phrase "carried captive to Canada whence they came not back" became a familiar refrain in the annals of colonial New England.

Those captives who did manage to return found a wide interest in their experiences among the captors. Puritan "captivity narratives" emerged as the first uniquely American literary form. More than seven hundred fifty such narratives appeared in print, beginning with Mary Rowlandson's 1682 report of her "captivity and restauration" following her capture in the frontier Massachusetts town of Lancaster during King Philip's War (which included a meeting with Metacom in Squakheag). These stories fulfilled a Puritan appetite for dramatic literature that was intensified by the "holy commonwealth's" rigid shunning of plays and fiction. Yet the accounts'

Frontispiece of *A Narrative of the Captivity, Suffering, and Removes of Mrs. Mary Rowlandson* (Boston: Z. Fowle, 1770). *Courtesy of the American Antiquarian Society.*

repetitive story line of misery and degradation, hardship and horror, resignation and, finally, unexpected release, underscored that the captivity narrative constituted more than merely literature to its Puritan readers. Captivity became not mere "military happenstance or secular accident. Captivity was God's punishment; redemption was His mercy; and New England must heed the lesson or suffer anew."[19]

The depiction of natives as other than human, and as instruments of the anti-Christ, emerged as a vital element within the stories. "None can imagine," wrote a contemporary commentator on Mary Rowlandson's ordeal, "what it is to be captivated, and enslaved to such atheisticall, proud, wild, cruel, barbarous, bruitish (in one word) diabolicall creatures as these, the worst of the heathen."[20] Small wonder, then, that narratives abounded with descriptions of unprovoked violence and butchery, the slaughter of small children, and prisoners weakened during the course of captivity. For the Puritans and their American successors, the captivity narrative planted a divine justification for retribution.

A scrupulous reading of the narratives, however, reveals that the natives were not primarily interested in physical revenge against their captives. William Hubbard, a contemporary chronicler of the New England Indian wars, noted that the Indians "how barbarous soever in their own Nature, yet civilly intreated their Prisoners." As well, Hubbard concluded, the Indians did not "offer an uncivil Carriage to any of the Females, nor ever attempted the Chastity of any of them."[21] Nowhere, among the brutal atrocities described, is recorded an instance involving the rape of a female prisoner.

In fact, a careful review of the literature reveals that Indians seized the bulk of captives either to pass along to French communities, where they were ransomed or converted and kept as servants, or to replace spouses and children lost to war or disease. Some captives chose to remain with their French or Indian captors when given the chance to go home. One recent study found that as many as 229 of 1,641 New England captives kidnapped between 1689 and 1763 chose to remain with their French or Indian captors—and most of them were females who created new networks of associations and in some cases enjoyed greater freedom and higher status among French or Indian families than among Puritan New Englanders.[22] Colonel John Schuyler, in Montreal in 1713, pleaded with Eunice Williams, the daughter of the Reverend John Williams of Deerfield, to return home after nine years of captivity. The sixteen-year-old girl, "looking very poor in body, bashfull in the face, but . . . harder than Steel in her breast," remained deaf to all entreaties that she leave her Indian husband.[23] Even as an adult, Eunice refused to return to her family in Massachusetts.

Echoes of Distant Wars

Natives repeatedly attacked settlers throughout the colonial era, yet the quantity and intensity of these attacks increased as their resentments became channeled into the revival of European warfare. In 1689, the accession of William and Mary to the English throne in the "Glorious Revolution" launched England into a war against France and Spain that spread to the American colonies as King William's War. In this struggle, promises of English support from colonial New York led the Iroquois to resume their assaults on New France.

A series of Iroquois raids on Montreal and its environs in August 1689 led New France's seventy-year-old governor, Louis de Baude, the Comte de Frontenac, to come out of retirement to reassure and avenge his beleaguered people. Frontenac recognized the virtual impossibility of making a successful surprise attack upon the Iroquois, so he planned a winter expedition via Lake Champlain against New York's frontier settlements around Albany. Convinced that by destroying these settlements he could halt the flow of English supplies to the Iroquois and force them to realign their fur trade with the French, he ordered his commanders to focus their attacks only on the English and spare the Iroquois. In January 1690, a party of 210 Canadians and Indians followed a customary line of travel along the frozen surfaces of Lake Champlain and Lake George and attacked Schenectady during a blinding snowstorm on February 9. "No pen can write, and no tongue express, the cruelties that were committed," Col. John Schuyler of Albany reported. Sixty men, women, and children in the garrison were killed, eighty prisoners taken, and all but two homes burned to the ground.[24]

In a series of retaliatory acts over the next several years, raiding parties from both sides continued to harass the exposed settlements at each end of the Champlain-Richelieu-Hudson route between Montreal and Albany.

In January 1693, the French tried again to drive a wedge between the English and their Mohawk allies. After another bitter winter march over the ice of Lake Champlain, they attacked three Mohawk villages south of Schenectady, destroying vital food supplies, killing several Mohawks, and taking three hundred prisoners. Later that year, the Indian allies of the French, mobilized by Frontenac's promise to boost payments for scalps and prisoners, launched the first of four raids on Deerfield, the most vulnerable of the Connecticut River frontier towns. In each year thereafter, until 1696, Indians killed Deerfield settlers and took captives.

The Treaty of Ryswick in 1697 brought an end to King William's War and its European counterpart. Five years later, however, fighting between England and France broke out again in Europe, in the War of the Spanish Succession, and ignited what in North America became Queen Anne's War. The Five Nations of the Iroquois, divided in their allegiances (the Mohawks and Oneidas leaned toward the English, the other three toward the French), remained neutral in the fighting, a stance accepted by both the French and the English. As a result, the Hudson and St. Lawrence valleys, both of which had experienced the devastation of the previous war, remained relatively quiet.

The brunt of Queen Anne's War fell upon the New England frontier, with Deerfield once again a major target. Early in 1704 a party of 200 French and 142 Abenaki and Caughnawaga Indians set out from Canada on snowshoes down Lake Champlain, across the Green Mountains via the Winooski River to the White River, then to the Connecticut River and down to Deerfield. On February 29, "not long before the break of day, the enemy came in like a flood upon us." Taking the community by surprise, the raiders killed 47 settlers and claimed 111 prisoners. Among the latter was the Reverend John Williams. In *The Redeemed Captive*, the record of his two and a half years in captivity, Williams described the raiding party's retreat. Captives and captors moved north along the frozen Connecticut River, traveled across the Green Mountains to the headwaters of the Winooski River, to Lake Champlain, and finally up to Canada. Twenty died during the twenty-five-day march to Montreal, some from wounds, and others, including Williams's wife, tomahawked when they became too weak to maintain the pace. On a Sunday morning, en route, Williams delivered the first Protestant sermon within Vermont, near Rockingham, choosing *Lamentations* as his text: "The Lord is righteous, for I have rebelled against his commandment. Hear, I pray you, all people, and behold my sorrow. My virgins and my young men are gone into captivity."[25]

After Deerfield, Queen Ann's War continued mainly as a series of skirmishes between frontiersmen of the English and French settlements as far north as the French settlement at Port Royal in Nova Scotia. By the terms of the 1713 Treaty of Utrecht that ended the war, France ceded Acadia "with its ancient boundaries," consisting of what is now Nova Scotia, New Brunswick, and part of Maine, to England. The French retained Cape Breton, however, and commenced construction of the great fortress at Louisbourg, to command the entrance to the Gulf of St. Lawrence.

For three decades after 1713, the French and British maintained a formal peace, although the region continued to experience numerous disputes and outbreaks of border hostility. It was during this period of uncertain peace that Vermont began to be settled by Europeans.

The Planting of English and French Settlements

Although the French established a short-lived community of soldiers, veterans, and their families near Fort Ste. Anne on Isle LaMotte in 1666, the English within New England were the first to plant permanent settlements in Vermont. On April 24 and 25, 1716, the colonial government of Connecticut held an auction in Hartford to dispose of 107,793 acres of prime frontier land. With New England's population rapidly expanding, and land speculation fever spiraling, land sales of this nature had become a common source of income for colonial governments. In this case, the rights to the auctioned land had been given to Connecticut by Massachusetts as "equivalent lands" for boundary tracts earlier sold by Massachusetts which, upon actual surveying, were found to have belonged to Connecticut. The plots included 43,943 acres situated north of the frontier township of Northfield, Massachusetts, west of the Connecticut River, within the limits of the present Vermont townships of Brattleboro, Dummerston, and Putney.

For the first time, English colonists owned land in Vermont. Four men received title to the Vermont tract: William Dummer, the newly commissioned lieutenant-governor of Massachusetts Bay; Anthony Stoddard, a prominent Boston merchant and judge; William Brattle, the distinguished minister from Cambridge; and John White, of which nothing more is known than that he commanded the title of "Gentleman," a formidable symbol of status. None of these men had any immediate plans to relocate; rather, their investment illustrated that anyone with money to spare and good social or political connections could participate in and in turn prosper from the speculative mania that enveloped New England.

Some investors, however, proved more resourceful than others. In October 1724, Dummer, now acting governor of Massachusetts, proposed constructing a line of early-warning forts across the Massachusetts frontier to prevent a recurrence of the Deerfield raids. The Massachusetts General Court balked, deeming the project too expensive. However, on December 27, the last day of the session, the Massachusetts House of Representatives voted to build a single fort "above Northfield, . . . and to post in it 40 able men, English and Western [Schagticoke] Indians, to be employed in scouting at a good distance up Connecticut river, West river, Otter creek . . . for the discovery of the enemy coming towards any of the frontier towns."[26]

In February 1724, Governor Dummer sent a party led by Captain John Stoddard and Captain Timothy Dwight of Northampton, Massachusetts, to find a suitable site for the fort. They chose a point on the west bank of the Connecticut River, in the southeast corner of the present town of Brattleboro—directly in the middle of Vermont's "equivalent lands." Completed in June 1724, Fort Dummer, 180 feet square, with block houses at each corner, four swivel guns for defense, and one cannon to sound an alarm in case of attack, became home to forty-three English soldiers and twelve Indians.

Immediately upon completion, the fort played an important role in the conflict known as Grey Lock's War (1723–1727). Grey Lock, a Waronoke from the Westfield River in Massachusetts, had fled north to Missisquoi as a refugee from King Philip's War. He attracted to his headquarters just south of the village a following of Abenaki warriors who shared his desire to engage in an undeclared war against residents on the Massachusetts frontier. Quietly supported by the French, who helped keep the Iroquois neutral and encouraged other native groups to cooperate with each other against the English, Grey Lock launched a series of successful guerrilla attacks on frontier settlements, beginning in August 1723, killing and capturing settlers in the Massachusetts border area around Northfield.

In response to Grey Lock's forays, Fort Dummer became the base for scouting parties and punitive expeditions into Abenaki country. For four years English search parties moved out from the fort and frontier towns, journeying as far as the Winooski River, destroying villages and crops, and searching for their elusive enemy. Yet Grey Lock eluded capture and struck with impunity, then quickly retreated into the wilderness of southern Vermont or to his "castle" near Otter Creek. Only with the death of his key supporter, New France Governor Vaudreuil, did Grey Lock and his allies finally tire in 1727 and virtually disappear from view. Despite the English efforts to find him—even to negotiate with him—Grey Lock and his allies from the Champlain basin and Connecticut River valley never yielded to diplomatic pressure, never risked destruction by full-scale confrontation, and successfully used guerrilla warfare to keep the English frontier settlements on edge and off balance. As historian Colin Calloway notes, "If Grey Lock did not win his war, neither did he lose it. He remained defiant and undefeated," the circumstances, place, and even the date of his death— sometime between 1744 and 1753—uncertain.[27] The conclusion of his

Fort Dummer at Brattleboro, the first permanent settlement in Vermont. From Walter Hill Crockett, *Vermont, The Green Mountain State*, vol. 1 (1921; reprinted 1938).

war against the settlements, however, opened an unusual seventeen-year period of "peace in the valley."

During this emergent era of stability, the Bay Colony hoped Fort Dummer could provide a base for improving relations with the area's native residents. In 1730, the Rev. Ebenezer Hinsdale received appointment to the post of chaplain at the fort, with responsibility to "instruct the Indian natives residing thereabouts in the true Christian religion."[28] A second strategy involved stocking the fort with critical items of trade. Fort personnel then distributed a portion of the supply of knives, pipes, tobacco, lead, shot, and flints to a few Iroquois chieftains whose allegiances were deemed particularly important. Traders visiting the fort distributed another share after letting it be known that they would pay more for the beaver and other pelts than the French. Within a short while, Fort Dummer developed the trappings of a frontier settlement. Crude agriculture and a few cabins emerged along the periphery. In May 1726, Timothy Dwight's wife gave birth to a son, the first recorded birth of a colonist in Vermont. By the late 1730s, several more tiny settlements began to take root around blockhouses between Fort Dummer and the Massachusetts border, and a gang of Connecticut men had cut waste timber in the Great Meadows in Putney.

The English settlers brought with them the open field method of agriculture. This involved clearing trees from a wide expanse of land surrounding the fort and devoting it exclusively to cultivation of life-sustaining crops. The approach served both an agricultural and a military strategy. It enabled English farmers to continue their traditional practice of devoting an entire field to a single crop and laying out adjacent fields in a way that allowed for three- or four-field rotation systems. It also resulted in a broad and clear landscape, which, from a military point of view, deprived enemies of ground cover and forest hiding places close to the garrison.

Not long after Massachusetts erected Fort Dummer, the French moved to solidify their position in the Champlain Valley. Pointe à la Chevelure, the location on Lake Champlain where Crown Point and Chimney Point reach toward each other to form a narrows that guards the passage on the lake, had long been recognized as an important strategic position. Over the years, the French, Dutch, and British had all based small scouting and trading operations there and probably had erected simple trading posts and even a blockhouse. In 1731, the French began constructing a major fort at Crown Point on the west side of the lake. Despite British protest that the land belonged to

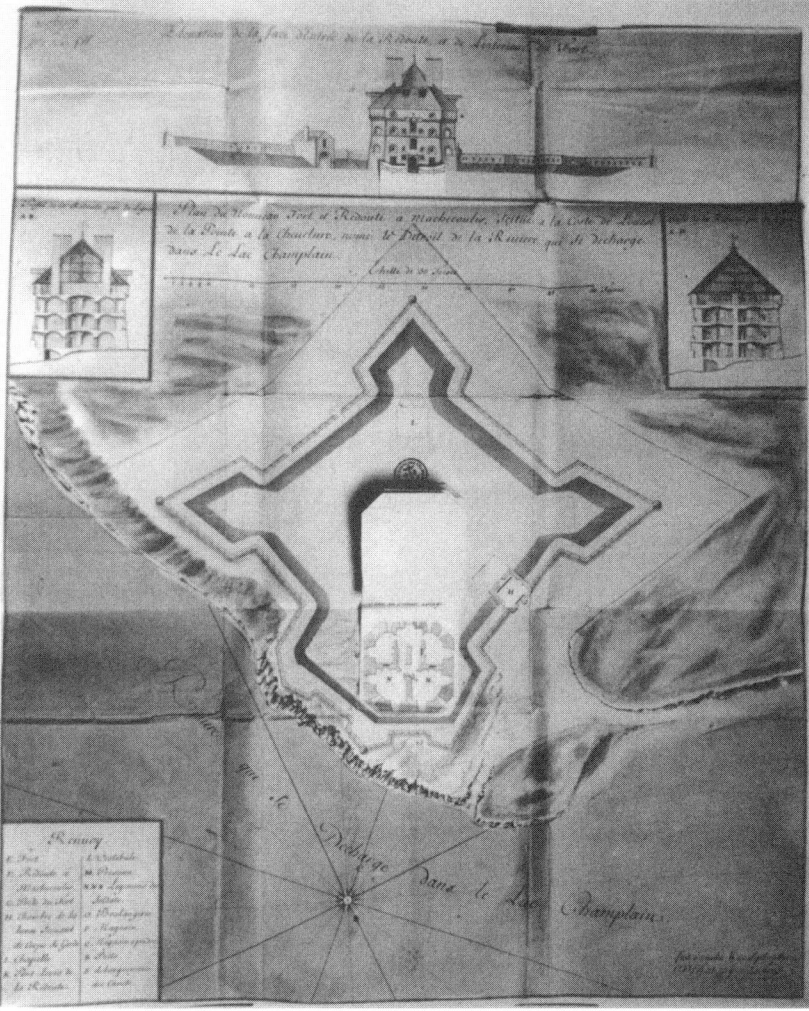

Plan of Fort St. Frédéric at Pointe à la Chevelure (Crown Point), Lake Champlain. *Vermont Historical Society (Map D 912.7430 C359co No. 7).*

New York, the French completed construction of the stone works, which they named Fort St. Frédéric, reinforced the fort with a major redoubt in 1735–1736, and added works on both sides of the lake in the early 1740s. By 1742, a garrison of 120 men and 25 cannon commanded the narrows.

Officially an enclave in the midst of the Seigneurie d'Hocquart, one of the grants of land and authority around Lake Champlain made by the King of France to members of the nobility, the fort occupied what was known as the "king's demesne" on the west side and included an area of forest to serve the fuel and construction needs of the military installation. Archival evidence uncovered by Canadian Studies scholar Joseph-André Senécal shows that the small fort housed fewer than fifty soldiers and officers of the garrison, plus some civilians, five or six slaves brought from the West Indies to serve the officers, and some Indian slaves, known as "panis."[29] The adjacent "seigneurie reserve"—lands owned by the seigneur under his royal grant—included a windmill, watermill, manor house, fields leased out to tenant farmers, and additional forests. The third area, the "censive," served as home for the *habitants*—by 1755 as many as two hundred to two hundred and fifty civilians, veterans, and active military personnel, living in fifty homes clustered around the fort on both sides of the lake.

The Swedish botanist Peter Kalm visited Fort St. Frédéric for more than two weeks on his tour of North America in 1747–1750. Although primarily interested in the plants and animals of North America, Kalm also recorded his observations of human habitations in his account published in 1750. He described the homes occupied by veterans of the garrison as "no more than wretched cottages," built of "boards standing perpendicularly close to each other . . . the crevices . . . stopped with clay to keep the room warm. The floor was usually clay, or black limestone, which is common here. The hearth was built of the same stone, except the place where the fire was to burn, which was made of gray stones. . . . Dampers had never been used here and the people had no glass in their windows."[30] The buildings that Kalm reported were one of only two types known to have stood in the settlement. These temporary structures, hastily built for new settlers with the aid of soldiers from the garrison, measured 18 by 22 feet, and only six or seven feet high, and were sparsely furnished—lacking even tables, chairs, and beds. They later served as sheds and barns when settlers built more permanent homes, constructed of squared logs, dovetailed to fit into corner posts, resting on stone foundations and with wood floors. According to Senécal, at least thirty of these would have been standing when Kalm visited the fort, although he fails to mention them at all.

The settlement always remained an adjunct to the garrison and many of the habitants were veterans, who upon leaving service received food for two years, farm animals, a plow and other agricultural tools, and assistance constructing their first house. A priest served the settlement and the parish records list 31 marriages, 243 baptisms, and 198 deaths occurring during its twenty-eight-year existence (1731–1759). The women at the habitation were recruited by the governor of Québec from its surrounding rural areas and sent as prospective wives for the soldier-settlers. Joseph-André

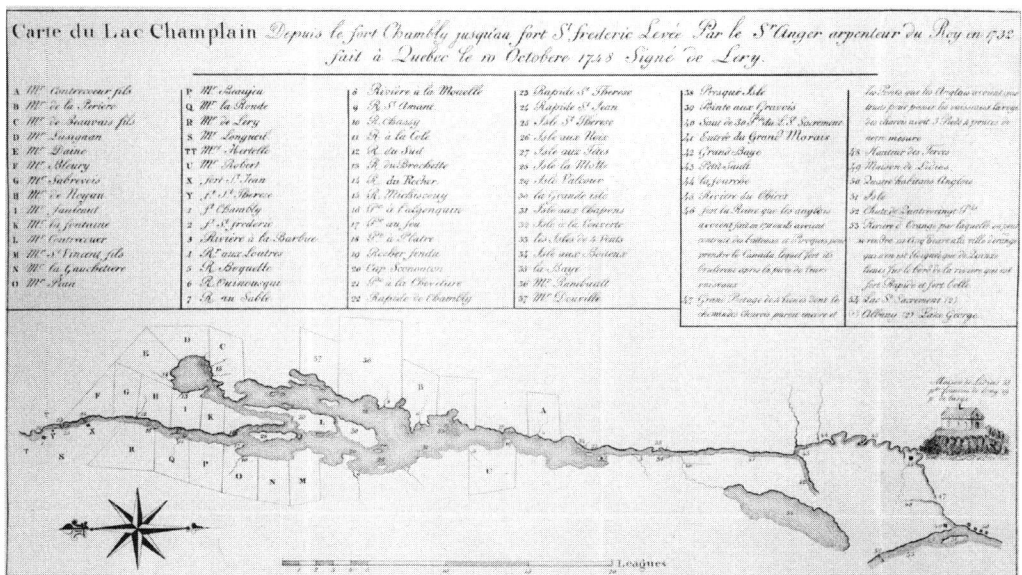

Map of Lake Champlain from Fort Chambly to Fort St. Frédéric, which shows and names the seigneuries as of 1732. The map was drawn in Québec in 1748. *Courtesy of Special Collections, Bailey/Howe Library, University of Vermont.*

Senecal's study of parish records suggests that in many cases these women were related to each other as sisters from families in which the mother had died and the father remarried. Kalm reported, however, that "the Canadians told me that they numbered four women to one man in Canada, because annually several Frenchmen were killed on their expeditions which they undertook for the sake of trading with the Indians."[31]

Conversely, the garrison depended on the *habitation* for "prompt aid to the fort in case of attack," and also for some essential food and supplies.[32] Although each soldier and officer was allowed a garden and permitted to plant whatever he wished, the *habitation* provided the essential staples of wheat, pork, beef, and fruit. Kalm was impressed by the abundance and variety of the diet of soldiers and *habitants*.

The mutual dependency of protection and economic exchange inextricably linked the fate of the community with the fort, and both would be abandoned by the French in 1759.

During the 1730s and 1740s, however, plans for French settlement in Vermont extended far beyond Crown Point. Between 1731 and 1737, King Louis XV of France granted a total of twenty seigneuries along Lake Champlain, with the condition that the seigneurs would locate settlers who would place the lands under cultivation, and thereby create a series of frontier outposts along the vital route.

The typical pattern of French agriculture fit easily into the military strategy of French colonial governors. Farmers worked long narrow strips of land rather than the broad fields of English agriculture. Consequently, along the St. Lawrence River and the Champlain basin a wall of narrow farmsteads stretched back only a mile or two from the water's edge to the interior. For farmers, the strip method gave each *habitant* some variety in land holdings, from alluvial soil near the water to woodlands farther back from the lake shore and river bank. With this variation in soil types and vegetation, the *habitant* farmer could grow a variety of crops, maintain a small stock of animals, and have an adequate supply of wood for fuel and construction. This pattern provided a long, thin line of population and productive land use adjacent to the connecting thread of waterway. It also enabled the French colonial government to maintain uninterrupted communication with the farthest reaches of its empire and safe passage of trade and military goods.

Despite the obligation to promote settlement, few of these seigneuries granted in the 1730s established *habitations*, underscoring the persistent problem the French had in populating New France (and which, a generation later, would contribute to their ultimate defeat by the British). In 1741 the king revoked most of his patents around the lake and started again. This time the obligation of settlement produced slightly better results. The grant to Nicolas-René Levasseur, Sieur de St. Armand, located in present-day Swanton, boasted the first sawmill built by the French in the Champlain Valley. By the mid-1750s, a community of about fifty families of lumberjacks and mill workers clustered around a stone church, with a village of about two hundred Abenakis nearby. Other small settlements emerged in the Seigneurie Foucault in Alburg, on Grand Isle, and around Malletts Bay. These settlements were wiped out in 1744, and their continued existence beyond that date is uncertain. Kalm reported seeing only an abandoned "wooden fort or redoubt on the eastern side of the lake, near the waterside . . . at present . . . quite overgrown with trees." He also saw a surviving windmill, "built of stone . . . on a projecting piece of ground. Some Frenchmen lived near it; but they left it when the war broke out, and have not yet come back to it. . . . The English, with their Indians, had burnt the houses here several times, but the mill remained unhurt."[33]

The Final Struggle for Empire

By 1743 the diversification of Vermont's human landscape was evident in the two markedly different European models of community, superimposed on a diminishing native village presence at selected sites along the Connecticut River and Lake Champlain. In 1744, when European hostilities between France and England broke out anew, the tenuous hold on the land by the parties to these models became imperiled once again.[34]

In fact, prospects for change had been brewing at Fort Dummer for several years. As the threat of frontier attacks abated during the 1730s, the government of Massachusetts grew increasingly aware of the high cost of maintaining the fort, including the expense of stocking items for trade with the Indians and, in the spirit of friendship, exchanging those goods at a lower rate than the French charged while concurrently offering a higher price for furs. An opportunity for Massachusetts to extricate itself from the financial drain of maintaining the trading post/fort presented itself in 1741, when the crown made New Hampshire a royal colony and redrew the boundary with Massachusetts, awarding additional lands to New Hampshire. Notwithstanding the New Hampshire Assembly's protests that the fort lay "fifty miles distant" from any settled New Hampshire towns (situated for the most part along the colony's eastern coast), the king accepted Massachusetts' petition obliging New Hampshire to bear responsibility for maintaining Fort Dummer. In contrast to his Assembly, New Hampshire's governor, Benning Wentworth, insisted that Fort Dummer did indeed fall within his colony's responsibility, and a decade later he seized on the Crown's decision to award New Hampshire title to this tiny speck of property on the west side of the Connecticut River as a precedent for issuing the "New Hampshire Grants."

The renewal of warfare in Europe in 1744 (known there as the War of Austrian Succession) led to new conflict between the British and French colonies on the New England frontier (referred to here as King George's War). This time, the French stood far better prepared than in the past. Fort St. Frédéric became the principal rendezvous for war parties that the French and their Indian allies unleashed on English settlements in the Connecticut River valley, including those established in the 1730s at present-day Westminster and Rockingham (known as Fort Number One and Fort Number Two) and another English blockhouse (Fort Number Four) at the present site of Charlestown, New Hampshire.

The Iroquois remained neutral during the initial hostilities and New York's frontier remained quiet until 1747, when the French and their allies struck settlements around Saratoga. At the urging of New York's governor, the Iroquois agreed to abandon their neutrality, and authorities dispatched two small war parties to retaliate with forays against Fort St. Frédéric and the garrison settlement at Crown Point as well as the St. Lawrence valley region around Montreal.

The renewed fighting revived the British grand design of a two-pronged expedition against Québec. The naval portion of the offensive, in June 1745, succeeded in capturing the great fortress of Louisbourg on Cape Breton Island, Nova Scotia, giving the British control of the sea lanes through to Québec. However, the expedition's second prong, an attack over the Champlain-Richelieu route, failed to materialize.

The Treaty of Aix-la-Chapelle in 1748, which terminated the war, restored the New Englanders' war conquests of Louisbourg and Cape Breton to the French. The settlement, however, left neither the French nor the British satisfied, and six years later their competing claims in the Ohio Valley formed the basis for the two rivals' next and final North American contest. In 1754, Virginia's governor sent an expedition led by twenty-two-year-old Colonel George Washington to assert its claim in western Pennsylvania near present-day Pittsburgh. The ensuing skirmishes with French forces ignited the entire American frontier, reawakening antagonisms not merely among the European powers but within the native populations as well. In 1754, two years before Europe officially erupted into a world war known as The Seven Years War, North America had begun "The English, French, and Indian War."

Within Vermont, the struggle initially pitted Abenakis against the English. In January 1753, responding to rumors of an English plan to cut a road from Fort Number Four to the Intervale at Cowass (near present-day Newbury), the location of a large Indian settlement, a band of Abenakis warned Captain Phineas Stevens at Fort Number Four that any attempt to dispossess "four hundred Indians now a hunting on this Side [of the] St. Francis River" would have dire consequences.[35] Nevertheless, the New Hampshire Assembly authorized a detachment of twenty men to begin blazing a trail to Cowass and construct a fort there.

Although "Fort Wentworth" (named for Governor Benning Wentworth) was never built, the expression of intentions presented sufficient impetus for Vermont's Abenakis to join with the French and promise to "beat all your enemies, who are our enemies, and drive them as the wind scatters the dust."[36] More than two hundred Abenaki warriors, drawn from their residences at Missisquoi and St. Francis in Québec (where many of the Connecticut River residents sought refuge during the war), joined in a 1754 defense of Fort St. Frédéric. They also fought their own war in the Connecticut Valley. In July 1754, a band of St. Francis Abenakis carried off James Johnson and his family along with others from Charlestown, New Hampshire. On the second day of the long return march to St. Francis, within the present limits of the town of Cavendish, Susannah Johnson gave birth to a daughter, whom the parents named Captive. Mrs. Johnson's dramatic narrative, published through ten editions, became one of the most popular of the New England captivity stories.

Subsequent Abenaki assaults in 1755 targeted Vernon, Hinsdale, and Walpole, New Hampshire. An attack on Fort Number Four in 1757 destroyed a mill and killed or captured seven people. The war thus became both the occasion for and the engine driving the escalating violence between exasperated English settlers who came to view Abenakis as the scourge of the frontier, and deeply resentful Indians struggling to retain their place on the land. Bitter and devastating to both sides, the "Indian" facet of the war in Vermont bore important cultural and political implications for the future of Indian and Euro-American relations. Nonetheless, it was but one facet of the contest pitting the English against the French in the Lake George–Lake Champlain theater. With large, well-equipped armies clashing head-on in a series of bloody battles in the European style of warfare, the "English and French War" became the final contest for colonial supremacy of North America.

The British and their colonial forces suffered some ignominious defeats early in the war, including the failure of Colonel Washington and his company of Virginia militiamen to dislodge the French from disputed territory in the Ohio River valley in 1754, and the rout of General Edward Braddock's army of three thousand British regulars in July 1755. However, the English held out and revised their strategy. The British colonies, now with more than 1.5 million residents, could draw not only upon their two hundred thousand white males of military age but also their dense patchwork of villages and towns to feed and sustain the war effort indefinitely. By contrast, New France, still only a string of fur-trading posts, with fewer than eighty thousand residents and twenty thousand males of military age, lacked that ability. The British thus decided to focus their naval strength on blockading Québec, then employing colonial troops and resources to fight alongside British regulars in a war of attrition. This strategy eventually succeeded, aided by poor harvests in Québec that necessitated imposing severe rationing upon an increasingly demoralized civilian population. With shortages of manpower and supplies continuing to reduce New France's military options, the contest for empire drew to a close.

At the same time, the English launched a campaign to dislodge the French from Fort St. Frédéric-Crown Point and push them out of the Champlain Valley. Temporarily stalemated following an indecisive battle at Lake George in August 1755, the two sides erected forts at opposite ends of the lake and dug in for a protracted and bloody conflict. The English immediately built Fort William Henry at the south end. Thirty-five miles to the north, the French began constructing Fort Carillon, which replaced Fort St. Frédéric as their most advanced position, guarding the southern entrance to Lake Champlain and serving as a base for raiding parties to continue inflicting terror on English frontier settlements. By the fall of 1756, the great fortress, with two thousand men and twenty artillery pieces, stood ready to resist attackers.

The British once again shifted their overall strategy, focusing on an effort to shut down French shipping to resupply New France. The diversion of British forces to Louisbourg allowed the French general Louis-Joseph Gozon de Véran, Marquis de Montcalm, to recapture territory in the Lake Champlain area. In 1757, his six thousand troops, reinforced by two thousand Indians representing nineteen nations, initiated a European-style siege against a weakened Fort William Henry. Montcalm methodically bombarded the fort, promising its commander generous terms of surrender and assuring all within the garrison safe conduct under a French escort to Fort Edward.

The English accepted Montcalm's terms. However, an orderly evacuation turned instead into a massacre when the French became unable to restrain the anger of their Indian allies, seeking revenge for English attacks on their villages. Montcalm and his officers restored order only minutes after the killing began, but the Indians slaughtered in excess of two hundred and carried off toward Canada another four hundred. Montcalm could only explain meekly that "what would be an infraction in Europe, cannot be so regarded in America."[37] Yet, for the English and more particularly New Englanders whose blood had been spilled, the massacre reinforced their hatred of the French and Indians and solidified their resolve to remove both from the St. Lawrence.

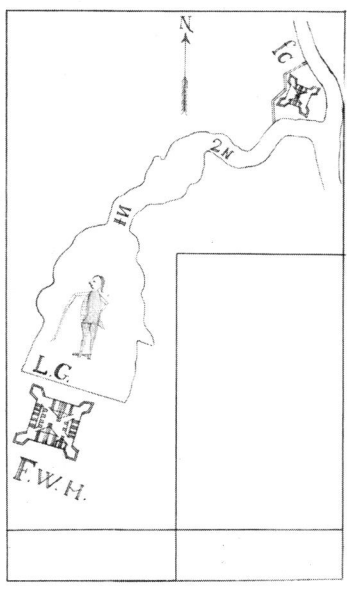
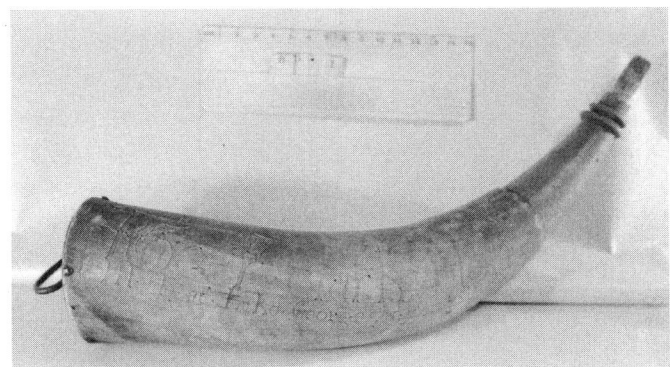

That determination led British Prime Minister William Pitt to focus his attention once again on Lake Champlain. In 1758, he ordered Major General James Abercromby to launch a full-scale attack on Carillon. On July 4, an army of sixteen thousand regulars and provincial troops began to move north on Lake George toward the great French fort. After two days' march, the British advance force under Lord George Howe, a thirty-four-year-old general described by Pitt as "a complete model of military virtue," unexpectedly confronted a French reconnaissance unit. The young general died in the engagement, robbing Abercromby of Howe's charismatic leadership. Nevertheless, with forces that outnumbered Montcalm almost five to one, Abercromby launched a bloody frontal assault on July 8 that failed to dislodge the French from Carillon.

The French triumph, however, did not alter the larger realities of this war of attrition. France's commitments across the globe, from the Great Lakes to India, spread thin the country's resources, and British naval superiority greatly restricted the French ability to supply reinforcements and much-needed foodstuffs to Canada. In contrast, seemingly inexhaustible supplies of colonial resources and manpower bolstered the British army.

Resolved now to bring the war to a close, Pitt's government devised yet another grand strategy for taking Canada. After Abercromby's defeat, command of the forces in the Lake Champlain area passed to General Jeffrey

Roger Clark's powder horn (1758), inscribed with "Roger Clark's horn made at Lake George July Ye 22 in the year 1758" and a map (see detail) showing the relative locations and plans of Fort William Henry and Fort Carillon. **Vermont Historical Society.**

Amherst. On July 23, he moved his army of ten thousand into position around Fort Carillon. On the 26th, French General Bourlamaque quietly withdrew most of his army, leaving behind four hundred troops to defend the fort. That evening the French, fearing a British charge, touched off the magazine and headed north to rejoin Bourlamaque at Fort St. Frédéric. The English occupied what was left of the fort, renamed it Ticonderoga, and set off in pursuit of their enemy. Four days later, Bourlamaque blew up Fort St. Frédéric and retired to Isle aux Noix, leaving the French defense of Lake Champlain to a schooner and three small gunboats.

With the French military in retreat, settlers in the communities around the forts abruptly gathered their belongings and abandoned or destroyed their homesteads. The advancing British and colonial troops thus found only the ruins of the French settlements in a few locations along the Lake Champlain shoreline. Later generations, referring to the architectural remnants, called the area on the east bank of Crown Point, "Chimney Point." Farther north, only the faint imprint on the land of the French strip fields remains to mark the presence of those settlements and *habitants*.

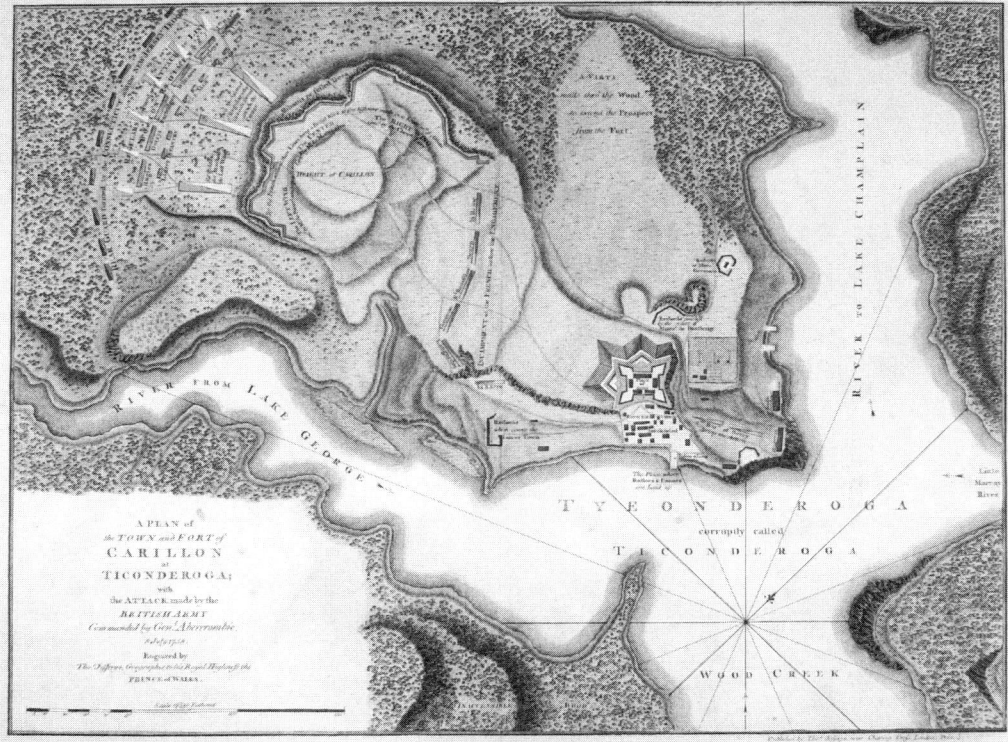

"A Plan of the Town and Fort of Carillon at Ticonderoga with the Attack made by the British Army Commanded by Gen'l Abercrombie, 8 July 1758." Engraved by Thomas Jeffreys. *Courtesy of Special Collections, Bailey/Howe Library, University of Vermont.*

Rather than pursue the retreating French, Amherst chose to rebuild the two French forts and commission the construction of an armed sloop and other smaller vessels. He also ordered construction of a road from Fort Number Four on the Connecticut River across the Green Mountains to Lake Champlain opposite Crown Point. In his October 25, 1759, letter to Major John Hawks commissioning the road, Amherst noted its military utility but also its potential contribution to "the wealth & prosperity" of the surrounding countryside. He therefore ordered the road cleared to a width of twenty feet and "wherever it may be necessary to lay any bridge across, you will lay them sufficiently strong to bear carriages. You will also at every fifteen miles distance cause log'd fences to be put up for harboring and keeping together the cattle that will be drove through that road for the use of the troops."[38]

The military road, keeping to higher ground, for the most part followed the old Indian trail up the Black River from Springfield. Progressing in the wilderness through what later would be the settled towns of Weathersfield, Ludlow, and Plymouth, it crossed the Green Mountains at Mt. Holly, then descended on the other side through Clarendon, Rutland, and Pittsford, to Brandon. There crossing the Otter Creek, the trail led through Sudbury, Whiting, and Shoreham, to Bridport and finally to Chimney Point.

Although poor even by contemporary standards, the Crown Point Road was built well enough to serve the needs of the military, transporting supplies, and later civilians carrying their meager practical needs into the frontier settlements. Colonel John Goffe of New Hampshire and his troops who completed the last stages of the construction graded some portions of the road, cut trees, removed stumps, built bridges and causeways, and in a few swamp areas, laid sections of corduroy over its seventy-seven-mile length.

In late July 1760, drovers marked the project's completion when they took the first herd of cattle from New Hampshire across the Crown Point military road to provision the troops heading for Canada. Completed too late to support more than the final operations against the French, this first road across the Green Mountains quickly became an important highway for the surge of settlers who poured into Vermont following the cessation of hostilities.

While Amherst, situated at Crown Point, built roads and rebuilt forts, the other two prongs of the British army successfully completed their charges. To the west, the British took Fort Niagara and gained control of Lake Ontario. At Québec, after a long summer of probing French defenses and futile skirmishes, Major General James Wolfe landed 4,500 troops above the town on the night of September 12, 1759, and led them up the narrow defile from the Anase au Foulon to the Plains of Abraham which spread west from the old citadel. The next morning, Montcalm launched an assault on Wolfe's lines. By the day's end, both generals lay dead, and the French had lost control of Québec.

On the same day the British scored their great victory on the Plains of Abraham, Amherst ordered Major Robert Rogers and two hundred twenty rangers to attack the Abenaki village at St. Francis, located on the St. Francis River south of where it meets the St. Lawrence. The settlement had long served as a base for Indian raids against the New England frontier. Rogers and his party, joined by Iroquois and Stockbridge scouts, traveled north from Crown Point to Missisquoi Bay, where they attempted to hide their boats for the return voyage. Then they moved overland to St. Francis. Arriving within three miles of the village on the evening of October 5, 1759, Rogers first took two of his soldiers with him to reconnoiter, then moved his force within five hundred yards of the settlement. At dawn the next day, Rogers's rangers torched the village, destroying forty houses and a church, seized whatever of value fell into their hands, and indiscriminately slaughtered men, women, and children. Indians taking refuge in the water were shot from the river bank. Rogers later boasted in his report to Amherst that "about seven o'clock in the morning the affair was completely over, in which time we had killed at least two hundred Indians and taken twenty of their women and children prisoners, fifteen of whom I let go their own way, and five I brought with me";[39] French accounts place the number of dead at thirty. Abenaki oral traditions recorded in the 1960s by anthropologist Gordon Day indicate that one of Rogers's Stockbridge guides probably gave warning during the night and suggest that the latter figure may be closer to the truth.[40]

Short of provisions and aware that the discovery of their boats precluded returning by Lake Champlain, Rogers led his men south, past Lake Memphremagog. The retreating rangers divided into three parties and agreed to meet at the great Coos oxbow in the upper Connecticut River at Newbury, where Rogers expected to receive supplies. On the retreat, the rangers suffered great hardships and near starvation. Moreover, forty-nine of their force died at the hands of the pursuing Abenakis. Rogers and the remaining rangers eventually returned to Crown Point by way of Fort Number Four.

Robert Rogers, "Commander in chief of the Indian troops in the service of the Americans."
Courtesy of the National Archives of Canada, C-6875.

The story of the raid and the destruction of the "nest of Barbarians" quickly became legend and New Englanders greeted the reports of the attack on "the enemy's Indian scoundrels" at St. Francis with as much enthusiasm as the news of the fall of Québec.[41] Although the raid itself had little military effect on the outcome of the war, the event took on mythic proportions when Rogers, seeking the best offer he could command to settle his debts, published his *Journals* in 1765, portraying himself as the liberator of the northern frontier from native attack.

Rogers's raid has been the subject of considerable controversy from the time he published his account of it to the present. Planned as an action to rid the New England frontier settlements of the continuous threat of raids by the Abenakis at St. Francis, the expedition clearly had as a goal the decimation of the native population. It accomplished neither. One year after Rogers's attack, a small party from St. Francis carried out a retaliatory attack against Charlestown, New Hampshire, seizing captives that they brought to Canada; and a force of two hundred Abenaki warriors who joined Bourlamaque's army at Isle aux Noix was one indication that the native population, though diminished and discouraged, had survived. For the native people, however, the raid further intensified their hatred and distrust for the English. It remains for contemporary Abenakis both a bitter memory and symbolic of the genocidal policies of Anglo-American settlers in their relationships to native people of northern New England.

When Amherst went into 1759–1760 winter quarters following a thrust at the French ships still plying Lake Champlain, the end of a century-long imperial rivalry between the masters of the St. Lawrence and the Hudson River valleys seemed close at hand. In May 1760, with the British fleet anchored off Québec, all hope of French reinforcements vanished. The fall of New France became a matter of time. The French army, undermanned and short on supplies, bravely prolonged the fighting until September 8, 1760, when Louis Antoine de Bougainville finally surrendered to Amherst at Montreal. With the French surrender, for the first time in its colonial history, the territory surrounding and including Vermont came under a single governing authority.

Amherst's New England troops quickly mustered out and left Canada. The Canadian campaign had introduced many of them to new territory. Some headed south to Crown Point and then east, via the Otter Creek to Brandon, across the mountains and over the new military road to the Connecticut River valley. Others headed to Crown Point and then south, through the great valley of Vermont into western Massachusetts and Connecticut. A few enterprising Yankees cut across country from St. John on the Richelieu River to Newbury on the great Coos oxbow. In the gentle New England autumn of 1760, they saw an inviting land cleared at last of the French and Indian menaces. Although the imperial war continued on other fronts for several more years, the New Englanders anticipated the peace. When the Treaty of Paris in 1763 confirmed the French loss of Canada, the Vermont forests already echoed to the clank of the surveyor's chain and the ring of the settlers' axes.

3
The Lure of the Land
1763–1807

The New Hampshire Grants

On January 3, 1749, New Hampshire's Royal Governor Benning Wentworth issued a charter establishing the town of Bennington, some forty miles west of the Connecticut River and just beyond New York's undisputed boundary, twenty miles east of the Hudson. This preemptive, and from the New York perspective presumptuous, action launched a flurry of activity in land grants by New Hampshire, with Wentworth issuing a total of 129 charters over the fourteen-year period to 1764, each of which brought him some profit. The grants affected the future ownership of approximately three million acres of land. His action thus launched an equally active period of land speculation by proprietors who, not necessarily interested in occupying the lands themselves, nonetheless saw opportunities for quick and substantial profits in land sales to eager settlers. Wentworth's rapid disposal of land, in fact, violated royal instructions providing for orderly settlement, which empowered colonial governors to charter new towns only when fifty males promised to settle immediately, confine their individual claims to fewer than fifteen hundred acres, and cultivate one of every five acres granted within five years. Yet Wentworth's grants resulted in fewer than one thousand residents actively cultivating fewer than thirty thousand acres.

The New Hampshire governor's grants also launched a legal battle with New York's colonial government, which believed itself to have sole authority to grant lands between the Hudson and Connecticut Rivers north of the Massachusetts border.

Distracted by the contest with France for hegemony in North America, the king's Board of Trade, which had oversight of the colonies, allowed the conflict to continue unresolved. After the defeat of France conclusively determined Britain's control of North America, however, the Board of

The antagonists in the land war over "The Grants." At the left, Governor Benning Wentworth of New Hampshire. *Courtesy of the New Hampshire Historical Society*. Right, Lieutenant Governor Cadwallader Colden of New York. *Vermont Historical Society*.

Trade issued its report reprimanding Wentworth for selling grants "with a view more to private interest than public advantage." On July 20, 1764, King George III issued a long-awaited Order in Council, following the recommendation of the board. The king's proclamation did "Order and Declare" the western banks of the Connecticut River "to be the Boundary Line" between New Hampshire and New York.[1] Although it settled the boundary dispute for the future, the proclamation failed either to recognize or invalidate the grants made by Wentworth, and thereby launched yet another period of confusion and conflict over jurisdiction.

The orphaning of hardy Yankee settlers who held New Hampshire titles to "the insidious intrigues of Yorker landjobbers" coincided with Ethan Allen's arrival upon the "New Hampshire Grants" and the commencement of his and his family's exploits, culminating in Vermont unilaterally declaring itself an independent state and eventually its union with the original thirteen colonies as one of the United States of America. Beginning with their own telling of the story highlighting their roles in the land grants controversy and the Revolution, the Allens have maintained what historian J. Kevin Graffagnino called "a remarkable tyranny"[2] over Vermont historiography that has persisted into the present. Recent biographies of Ethan Allen celebrating the "frontier rebel" and "revolutionary outlaw" continue to treat the story of Allen as indistinguishable from the story of frontier Vermont, one of them even insisting that "it is, in fact, very probable that without him Vermont would never have come into being."[3]

And yet, at least as many of Ethan Allen's contemporaries opposed his political leadership during the grants crisis as rallied around him. Many others in the flood of immigrants who trebled the state's population between the start of the Revolution and Vermont's 1791 entry into the Union were virtually oblivious of him. In addition, Allen's widely discussed deistical religious views represented merely one of many strains of belief in a diverse Vermont religious landscape that ran the gamut from Rhode Island "haters of religion" and "nothingarians," to orthodox "separatists." One such "separatist," Samuel Robinson, and his followers, first settled Bennington hoping to impose a greater purity than existed even in the Puritan reaches of southern New England. Many more settlers, in fact, exhibited characteristics of cautious and sedate farmers rather than of irrepressible "rebels" or "outlaws."

Vermont during this era began to assume its identity less from the bravado of a single individual than from the magnetic allure of the land for a diversity of people who sought to own it and who saw in it a promise of boundless opportunity. Within the tumultuous contest for ownership—which included speculators of varying allegiances, settlers, democrats, Tories, Whigs, religious refugees, and religious zealots—the most powerful unifying force remained the availability of land, as a commodity to be sold, a resource to own and develop as one saw fit.

For almost a half-century after the 1764 Order in Council, a continuing flow of immigrants joined Vermont's rapidly expanding population, certain that they could improve their personal fortunes by initiating residence and securing land. The struggle for political control became part of a larger contest to determine who should own land and how it should be divided up. Similarly, the diversity of economic experiences, from frontier adversity to agricultural self-sufficiency to large-scale wealth acquisition, present from the outset of settlement until virtually the start of the Embargo of 1807, suggests the importance of understanding Vermont as what historian T. D. Seymour Bassett called a "border area" with "kaleidoscopic diversity," and thus exhibiting a range of successes and failures.[4] All told, many "stories" converged to form the history of the Vermont frontier.

Two maps showing conflicting claims over the area known as Vermont. Right, detail of "A map of the most inhabited part of New England, containing the provinces of Massachusetts bay and New Hampshire, with the colonies of Conecticut and Rhode Island, divided into counties and townships," engraved by Thomas Jeffreys, 1777, (Cobb, #27) shows New Hampshire grants. Left, Gerard Bancker's Map (1775) shows the New York Patents (Cobb, #17). *Vermont Historical Society.*

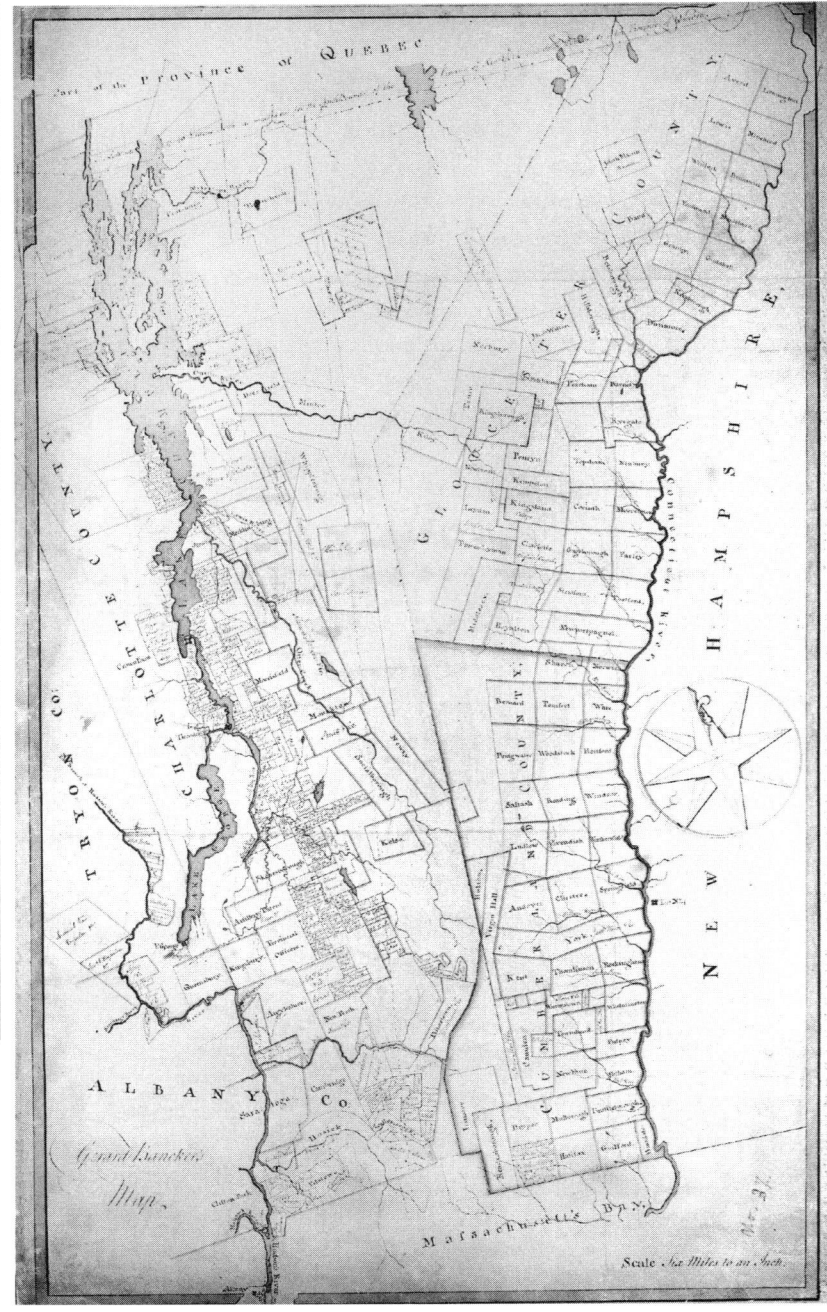

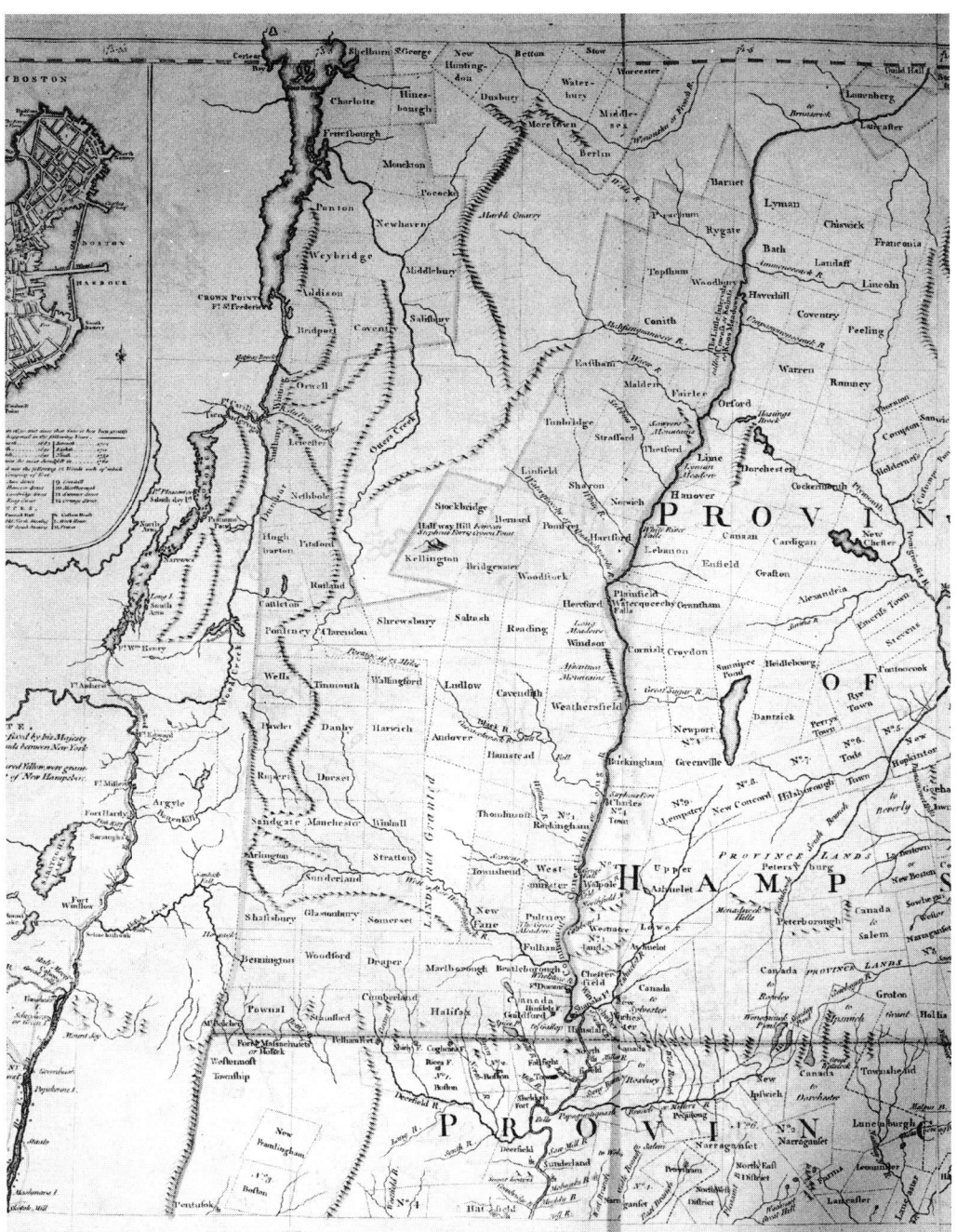

The image of Benning Wentworth as a schemer willing to dupe unsuspecting settlers for his own aggrandizement has been a powerful one for Vermont historians. There is little doubt that Wentworth used the grants to enrich himself by placing his own name on title to sixty-five thousand acres, and the names of members of his immediate family on other titles, including his father-in-law, Theodore Atkinson, who alone received three-hundred-acre grants in more than fifty-seven towns. Wentworth's remarkable twenty-five-year tenure as royal governor underscored his political genius for satisfying the seemingly incompatible allegiances involved in upholding the crown's interests while bolstering the political and economic power of resident New Hampshire elites. So it is not surprising that he also carefully distributed proprietary shares to those whose allegiances he needed to cultivate.

The lion's share of townships, however, went not to elites but rather to common people across New England, through sales intended largely to replenish the coffers of New Hampshire's treasury, depleted by the French and Indian War. New England's burgeoning population and its appetite for land delineated the fundamental reality. By drawing upon Connecticut's successful redrafting of its border with New York to within twenty miles of the Hudson River and the King's transfer of responsibility for Fort Dummer, on the west side of the Connecticut River, from Massachusetts to New Hampshire, Wentworth found a basis upon which—cautiously, at first—to test New Hampshire's claims to the vacant lands to its west. Between 1749 and 1753, Wentworth issued sixteen townships. All of them, with the exception of Bennington (situated in the southwestern tip of the "Grants"), lay along the western edge of the Connecticut River, adjacent to existing New Hampshire towns. He notified New York of his actions and agreed to submit the issue to the king, but after eight years passed with no decision rendered, Wentworth let it be known, following the final conquest of Canada in late 1760, that for twenty pounds he would issue charters in the territory. In two and a half years, he proceeded to issue one hundred and sixteen charters.

The speculative mania, which gave rise to the "New Hampshire Grants" as they subsequently became known, enveloped a cross section of New Englanders hoping to profit from the region's continuing population growth. The uncertainty of New Hampshire's claims was borne out in the price charged for New Hampshire titles, averaging one half-pence per acre, or less than one hundredth what a buyer could expect to pay for comparable wild lands in the interior of Maine and one four-hundredth of the price commanded by vacant lands in western Massachusetts. Although the investments might have been risky, purchasers knew that, given the territory's proximity to settled areas of New England, validation of their claims could provide quick and substantial monetary returns.

The sheer magnitude of Wentworth's venture led New York to act quickly after receiving the 1764 Order in Council. Within seven months, New York Lieutenant Governor Cadwallader Colden proceeded to issue patents amounting to 174,000 acres, nearly all of them on territory already granted by New Hampshire. While the vast majority of patents were military grants issued without fees on unsettled lands, Colden's issuance of the Princetown patent revealed his willingness to steal a page from Wentworth's book by advancing opportunism before strict adherence to the king's instructions. The patent covered twenty-six thousand acres of land within a twelve-mile-long by four-mile-wide tract embracing the whole of the rich Battenkill Valley, and including the towns of Shaftsbury, Glastenbury, Sunderland, and Arlington, which had already been settled and improved. It existed, however, as a "dummy grant" because shortly after Colden issued it to an official list of patentees in accordance with royal instructions, shares were conveyed to four of Colden's friends: Goldsbrow Banyar, who received over seven thousand acres; the former attorney general of New York, John Tabor Kemp; and fellow lawyers James Duane and Walter Rutherford. Similarly, Colden issued a grant of ten thousand acres to another of his associates, Crean Brush, covering considerable portions of southwest Bennington and northwest Pownal. For all these grants, the presence nearby of already settled lands obviously enhanced the prospect of realizing handsome returns on the speculative investment.

The drama that unfolded in the Grants after the 1764 Order in Council derived not only from competing land speculators but also from the differences that distinguished New England's way of life from that of New York. The intense prejudice New Yorkers held for New Englanders was evident in New York's Lewis Morris, himself a graduate of Yale, and a signer of the Declaration of Independence who, in his will, forbade his son Gouverneur from attending the college for fear that "he should imbibe in his youth that low craft and cunning so incident to the People of that Colony which is so interwoven in their Constitutions that all their art cannot disguise it from the World, though many of them under the sanctified garb of Religion, have endeavored to impose themselves on the World for honest men."[5]

The attitude of well-to-do New Yorkers such as Morris or Anne Grant, who dismissed New Englanders as "conceited . . . litigious . . . vulgar [and] insolent,"[6] reflected fundamental differences in the traditions of social structure, land ownership, and political participation.

From the initial Puritan settlements, New Englanders had emphasized widespread land ownership, attitudes of agricultural independence, and political participation through the town meeting, all of which were sustained through the steady migration of youth from established communities into the frontier reaches of New England. In contrast, New York's identity emerged under the formative influence of its relatively limited landmass situated in the Hudson Valley adjoining the Iroquois Confederacy, and the monopolization of this territory through the "manorial system." Manors created between 1680 and 1705 monopolized ownership of the choicest lands within the Hudson Valley. Owned by a few prominent families including the Delanceys, Livingstons, Van Rensselaers, Schuylers, and Van Cortlands, these manors had taken form through a combination of bribes delivered to corrupt colonial governors and conscious cheating of native Americans by altering boundary lines on titles. Rather than selling the lands outright, these "manorial lords" had developed an ingenious system of leases. These leases employed the use of "first refusal" in the purchase of produce, monopolies on mills and stores, and the threat of nonrenewal, to reinstitute—according to historian Irving Mark—the feudal "degradation of the peasant." Furthermore, to sustain control the manorial lords imposed high property requirements for suffrage (twenty times higher than in Connecticut), exploited power in New York's assembly and council to place prohibitive fees on land grants, and employed the courts to throw obstacles into efforts to openly sell lands. Even Cadwallader Colden was compelled to concede the genius of the system, in which "really poor industrious Farmers [were] not able to contend with rich & powerful Men."[7]

The prospect of New York's manorial system being transplanted by "Yorkers" into the disputed grants territory provoked a sense of indignation among Yankees holding New Hampshire titles. In fact, New York had no intention of replicating the manorial system. Its plan involved selling the land to all who could afford it and then collecting taxes on owned properties. However, the terms of land ownership proffered by those whom the New Englanders labeled "land jobbers," "land pirates," and "land thieves" bolstered both their deep-seated prejudices and their determination not to acquiesce.

In June 1766, New York's Council issued an order dictating that all New Hampshire grant holders must acquire confirmatory New York patents within three months. The payment of new fees, amounting to £14 per 1,000 acres or some £330 for an average-size township, still represented only one tenth the price of comparable frontier lands elsewhere for sale. The terms did not present an especially onerous burden for settlers holding only a few hundred acres and, in fact, by 1770, titleholders in seventy-nine towns had applied for new charters. However, for those who had acquired large speculative holdings at no cost or at one-tenth that now demanded by New York, the price became prohibitive.[8]

A gathering of dissident New Hampshire grant holders in Massachusetts, consisting of a majority of nonresident speculators, decided in 1767 to send one of the Bennington settlers, Samuel Robinson, to London to plead their case. Although he represented himself and those who sent him as poor settlers desirous only to retain the homesteads they had carved out for themselves, Robinson actually owned several proprietary shares throughout southwestern townships.

While in London, Robinson contracted smallpox and eventually died there. Before falling ill, however, he managed to enlist the aid of Connecticut's agent who, in turn, secured help from Lord Shelburne, secretary of state for the colonies, and from the Society for the Propagation of the Gospel (SPG). Impressed that New Hampshire townships set aside free lots for a Church of England glebe and one for the SPG itself to bolster the presence of the Church in the crucible of New England dissent, the SPG recommended to the Board of Trade the benefits that would accrue to the Anglican Church if Robinson's titles were validated. On July 24, 1767, the Privy Council issued a second Order in Council warning New York, "upon Pain of his Majesty's highest displeasure," not to issue any further grants "until his Majesty's further Pleasure shall be known."[9]

For two years following this decision, New York's government abided by the king's dictate, anxiously awaiting final verification of its rights. No verification came, however. In the meantime, New Hampshire titleholders, recognizing in the tenor of the dictate the strengthened possibility that settled claims would be honored, initiated a massive campaign to sell New Hampshire titles to prospective settlers. Their success became evident in the rapid increase in the Grants population. From fewer than one thousand in 1764, the population increased to just under four thousand in 1768 and, according to a New York census, to 7,000 in 1771.[10]

Those who ventured as settlers into the disputed reaches of the region presumably brought diverse motives and expectations. Most, however, shared the pioneer experience of detaching themselves from an established community and entering into the frontier. Aboriginal forest covered the vast majority of Vermont's lands, forcing migrants to follow paths of least resistance. They endured hard, frequently harrowing journeys, rendered even more difficult because they commonly transported field animals as well. They prized these animal possessions, knowing that a wooden plow attached to an ox could furrow an acre a day—three to four times as much work as could be expected from a human laboring alone.

After arriving at their claims, settlers set first priority on clearing and preparing lands for crops. Abandoned village sites, rich riverfront meadows, and beaver dams provided shortcuts for some travelers. The vast majority, however, took on the challenge of clearing, on average, one to three acres as quickly as possible to make way for a crop of corn. They typically adopted one of two methods: girdling, which involved stripping bark from the trunk of a tree to kill it; or the quicker process of burning, which provided the benefit of piles of ash. These ashes, first soaked in water to produce a lye and then boiled in big kettles, produced Vermont's first and most important early cash crop, potash, a commodity highly sought by the British to clean wool in preparation for carding and spinning. The settlers' survival, however, required cultivation of essential foodstuffs. Corn became the first staple, often planted among fields of stumps and rocks. Dried and pounded, it could be made into a pudding or baked as a bread into johnny-cake. And, with few mills available during the first decade of settlement, these frontier families did the hard work of grinding grain with a mortar and pestle.

When New York officials became aware of the growing number of settlers on the New Hampshire Grants, they abandoned their former caution and launched a charter campaign of their own. Within two years, they sold approximately one million acres, much of it conflicting with New Hampshire titles for the choice valley lands on either side of the Green Mountains. New England peddlers who offered New Hampshire rights now had their counterparts in New York landlords and agents seeking to lease or sell property. The contest had begun.

In October 1769, a band of sixty Bennington settlers challenged and drove off a New York surveying team on the farm of James Breakenridge, whose New Hampshire claim conflicted with a 1739 New York

Walloomsac patent. The confrontation dramatized the vulnerability of settlers who had undertaken substantial improvements of their land. Shortly thereafter, a group of New York titleholders sought writs of eviction from the New York Supreme Court against nine settlers living in the Bennington-Shaftsbury area on land held under New Hampshire titles.

The hearings on these lawsuits, known as the Ejectment Trials, took place in an Albany court in June 1770. They involved unprecedented stakes. If the court upheld the settlers' claims to ownership, it could validate all Wentworth titles; alternately, a ruling in favor of the plaintiffs could force all settlers without New York confirmatory patents to lose their lands.

With such high stakes, each side relied on talented legal representation. New York plaintiffs turned to James Duane and Attorney General John Tabor Kemp, both of whom owned large New York-chartered tracts. New Hampshire proprietors, most of whom remained nonresident, retained Jared Ingersoll of New Haven and Peter Sylvester of Albany as their counsel, and Ethan Allen as manager of their defense fund.

Allen's motivation appears easy to pinpoint. His father Joseph had moved his family to the Connecticut frontier community of Cornwall, where he carved out of the forest a large working farm, acquired land that identified him among the town's wealthiest residents, and gained election to the town selectboard, underscoring his wealth and political influence. He had arranged tutoring for Ethan, his seventeen-year-old first born, to prepare him to attend Yale. Joseph's sudden death, however, dictated that Ethan terminate his studies and take responsibility for his mother, five brothers, and one sister. Biographers have argued that Ethan's marriage at age twenty-four to the "dull, dreary, and far from pretty" Mary Brownson, six years his senior, provided Ethan the financial resources to pursue his own independence.[11] Difficulties dogged him, however. An investment in an ironworks in Salisbury yielded little in the way of profit, and Ethan displayed a persistent knack for running afoul of the law. He brawled with neighbors and violated a Connecticut statute forbidding the use of smallpox serum. A subsequent move to Northampton, Massachusetts, produced an unsuccessful investment effort in a lead mine, and, apparently, expulsion by the town fathers.

Thus, when Allen arrived on the New Hampshire frontier, the wealth and prestige he had been seeking since his father's untimely death still eluded him. At the time of the ejectment cases in Albany, Allen had acquired about one thousand acres of Grants land, and was maneuvering for more. Within three years he joined with his cousin Remember Baker and three of his brothers to form the Onion River Land Company, a loose partnership that acquired large land tracts in the northwestern portion of the Grants. Clearly, Allen had determined to stake his future on the viability of the New Hampshire Grants.

At the Albany courthouse in June 1770, the wait by Allen and the New Hampshire proprietors for a decision on the New York titleholders' claims proved anticlimactic. In the first of these cases, known as *Small* v. *Carpenter*, the New York court refused to allow copies of the New Hampshire land titles held by the defendant Isaiah Carpenter to be admitted as evidence, on the grounds that no satisfactory proof could be offered that Wentworth's jurisdiction ever extended west of the Connecticut River. The lawsuits were over before they had begun.

Ethan Allen and the Green Mountain Boys: Myths and Realities

Allen refused to concede victory to New York. Following the trial, the New York attorneys Duane and Kemp, accompanied by Goldsbrow Banyar, visited Allen, in an effort to urge him to cooperate with the New York government and to convince his followers and other New Hampshire patent holders to do the same. In reply, Allen issued his cryptic but obviously defiant warning that, should the New Yorkers venture to Bennington they would find that "the gods of the hills are not the gods of the valleys." He then retreated to the Grants and, in meetings held at the Catamount Tavern in Bennington, created the quasi-military unit known as the Green Mountain Boys. By the fall, a series of local companies in the southwestern Grants, with captains chosen by the settlers, had organized under the Green Mountain Boys' umbrella. Buoyed by Allen's powerful language emphasizing the rights of "the numerous families settled upon the land" to "defend themselves against this execrable Cunning of New York" or else "be by terms inslav'd," residents and nonresident speculators alike who took up the defense of the New Hampshire grants now cloaked their cause in the aura of righteousness.[12]

The Catamount Tavern, erected 1767-1769, Bennington, Vermont. Photographed c. 1869, probably by Calvin Dart. *Vermont Historical Society (VHS 119)*.

During the next five years, before the American colonies' revolution against the British redefined both their purpose and their organizational leadership, the Green Mountain Boys, with Allen at their head as colonel commandant, and his cousins Remember Baker and Seth Warner as company commanders, utilized an assortment of productive tactics. They preferred bluff, intimidation, and threats to outright violence or actual combat. House burnings, whippings, and luridly convincing death threats usually sufficed to cow their opponents into silence or cooperation.

An abundance of myths surround Allen and the Green Mountain Boys. Many of them Allen promulgated himself, for both personal and partisan advantage. The first and foremost of these myths involved his assertion that the Green Mountain Boys represented the vast majority of residents within the Grants. This was not the case. The region east of the Green Mountains, where more than three of every five settlers in the Grants resided in 1771, generally did not support Allen's extralegal activities. Evidence supporting this conclusion is extensive and varied. Settlers in the east had welcomed opportunities to acquire confirmation titles. Additionally, as early as 1766, they had agreed to form militia units under New York's jurisdiction. Two years later, with the formation of Cumberland County in the southeast, a county courthouse and jail were constructed in Chester, and two years after that, New York formed Gloucester County to the north. Both courts took active roles in maintaining order. Altogether, upwards of seventy-five percent of the adult male population in Gloucester County was involved as "active participants" within the court, acceding to its authority to issue tavern licenses and preside over civil and criminal matters.

On two occasions anticourt riots broke out involving eastside residents who rejected New York's authority, but the uprisings drew little support. On June 5, 1770, a contingent of thirty armed men, led by Nathan Stone of Windsor, disrupted the Cumberland County court sitting in Chester, intimidated the judges, and then, in an effort to prevent the court from functioning, kidnapped John Grout, the only practicing lawyer, and temporarily imprisoned him in Charlestown. In response, 421 adult male residents of Cumberland and Gloucester counties, comprising one-third of the entire population (based upon New York's 1771 census), forwarded a petition to the king decrying the "spirit of disorder and disobedience" evidenced by the "lawless transgressors" and asking that he resist any attempt to change the jurisdiction.[13] A petition sent to the king six weeks later asking that the area be reannexed to New Hampshire mustered only sixty-nine signatures.

Further evidence of eastside support of New York authority is a petition to the king, delivered on January 26, 1773, and signed by almost four hundred men of Cumberland and Gloucester Counties requesting permission to allow New York to proceed to issue confirmation titles to secure their properties. The petitioners noted that since the creation of the two New York counties under Letter Patent "the Course of Justice hath been duly established and the Inhabitants have enjoyed the Blessings and advantages of Peace, Order, and good Government," and claimed that they "are not desirous of any Change of Jurisdiction but are perfectly satisfied and earnestly wish to continue under the Government of New York."[14]

In the northeast, speculators such as Jacob Bayley also held views at odds with Ethan Allen. Bayley moved from "Ould" Newbury, Massachusetts, to Newbury, Vermont, where he boasted in a 1768 letter "tis but seven years since I struck the first stroke here, at which time there was not one inhabitant on the River for seventy miles down." Bayley's religious orthodoxy critically influenced his actions, leading him, at varying times between 1766 and 1776, to negotiate with New York and New Hampshire, but never with Allen and the Bennington party, "who I may particularly say are avowed enemies to the cause of Christ." Later circumstances obliged Bayley to soften this position, but his relations with Allen remained difficult.[15]

If Ethan Allen did not represent everyone in the Grants, neither did his own adherents, as has been widely assumed, consist of replicas of the man himself. The most dramatic finding in historian Donald Smith's study of 436 Green Mountain Boys revolves around religion.[16] Ethan Allen proclaimed himself a deist and hater of organized religion and in 1784 brought out the first diatribe against organized religion published in America, titled *Reason the Only Oracle of Man*. Smith found that approximately three quarters of Allen's Green Mountain Boys were evangelical Protestants. Far from rejecting the perceived constraints of orthodox Calvinism, many of these "New Lights" and "Separatists" actually sought refuge in Vermont to escape what they viewed as a lamentable decline into secularism throughout settled New England society and to impose stricter scriptural rules on behavior.

Foremost among this contingent stood the same Samuel Robinson who died in England as an envoy from Bennington, defending his land title. After hearing and embracing the message of the famed evangelist, Rev. George Whitefield, in 1741, then struggling with local officials in protest against a tax to support a church he no longer considered his own, Robinson led his followers from Hardwick, Massachusetts, together with members of two separatist churches in Sunderland and Newent, Connecticut, to become in 1761 the initial settlers in Bennington. They perceived Bennington as a haven wherein "true saints" could escape the corruption of sharing a church with unregenerate brethren. These separatists, who had already experienced persecution at the hands of neighbors demanding that they pay taxes to uphold the "standing order," emerged as vocal opponents of those who wielded political power in an obviously self-serving manner. These men could readily embrace the fiery rhetoric of Ethan Allen; yet, as time would show, the alliance grew from convenience, not deep-seated agreement.

New research on the Green Mountain Boys also identifies the routes by which they entered southwestern Vermont to settle and the consequent political orientation they likely brought with them. Allen migrated from the western frontier of New England to Vermont and historians traditionally assumed that also had been the pattern of most "westsiders," in contrast with their eastern cohorts. However, it now appears that more than one-third of the Green Mountain Boys arrived in the southwestern Grants via the disputed upper Hudson River region of New York, having experienced firsthand New York governance. Consequently, these men likely had been either active participants in, or immediate observers of the "New York Anti-Rent Wars" of the 1750s and 1760s, a watershed episode whose impact upon Vermont's grants dispute historians have generally overlooked. These Anti-Rent Wars had begun in the early 1750s after the Massachusetts government began issuing titles for disputed border areas in the vicinity of New York's northeast manor lands. The decision launched a "miniature border war."[17] Many settlers who had pushed west into New York had been accustomed to the Yankee land tenure practice of the freehold. Consequently they vigorously resisted the claims of New York's leasehold, quitrent tenure. Although the struggle stood in abeyance during the French and Indian War, it erupted again in the early 1760s. Mobs of between one hundred and five hundred men, armed with clubs, swords, and pistols, circulated throughout disputed areas, ejecting tenants, burning barns, and encouraging a general rebellion against landlords. Manorial lords, in response, hired private "blackguards" to protect their tenants and reciprocate in kind.

The Anti-Renters maintained the upper hand until June 26, 1766, when, after a bloody encounter, New York Governor Henry Moore called in British regulars armed with cannon and muskets. The soldiers quickly routed the farmers and arrested their leader, William Prendergast. The showcase trial that followed climaxed in Prendergast's conviction for "High Treason" and a sentence of death. However, sensing the popular mood, the governor waited for the uproar to subside and issued a pardon.

Many of the Anti-Rent veterans thereafter moved onto the New Hampshire Grants. Some historians speculate that Ethan Allen had actually participated on the side of the beleaguered farmers. It is more likely that Allen was one of a far larger group that, while not directly participating, resided within close enough proximity to comprehend clearly the course of events. New York sheriffs and posses had been unable on their own to quell a popular antirent movement, in which leaders had organized partisans into mobs charged with protecting and liberating their own interests while raising the stakes for their opponents to untenable heights. Only the British army had been able to put down the movement; yet, as revolutionary unrest continued to grow throughout the late 1760s, the king's royal representatives had become increasingly cautious in calling on the army to defuse popular movements.

The tactics of the Green Mountain Boys become far more comprehensible in light of the Anti-Rent War connection. As in the New York events, individuals sought protection against offensive efforts to dispossess them from the land. Thus, in July 1771, when Sheriff Henry Ten Eyck led a two-hundred-man posse from Albany to evict James Breakenridge from his Bennington farm, they were met by a welcoming party of 160 armed settlers already at Breakenridge's farm, distributed in the house, in the adjacent field, and above the farm on a ridge. Ten Eyck, as one New Yorker later observed, considered "the little probability of succeeding and the eminent Danger attending it," and chose to retreat.[18] During the same summer, when news arrived of the presence of Yorker surveyors in the Rutland area, a corps of Green Mountain Boys rudely chased them out.

Stymied in its efforts, New York searched for a carrot-and-stick formula that would allow it to govern Vermont effectively. At first, Governor William Tryon held up the carrot by offering to issue confirmatory patents for half the standard fees, successfully courting many in the Connecticut River valley. He proved equally willing to use the stick, as evidenced by a March 1772 midnight expedition by Yorker Justice of the Peace John

Munro to Arlington to arrest Remember Baker. However, neither approach provided resolution. The Crown refused to honor confirmatory titles, and although Munro initially captured Baker after a bloody struggle in which the latter lost his thumb, Arlington and Sunderland neighbors rescued him a few hours later on the road to Albany. And later that spring, Robert Cochran and a party of Green Mountain Boys seized Hugh Munro, an ex-soldier surveying lands he claimed in Rupert under a military patent, and administered severe whippings to him and his companions.

Anxious to stem the tide of violence, Tryon turned to the olive branch, writing a conciliatory letter to Rev. Jedediah Dewey of Bennington, asking that settlers send spokesmen to New York to negotiate. Stephen and Jonas Fay did travel to meet with Tryon and his council, and they agreed to accept New York jurisdiction if authorities could secure confirmation of the validity of their New Hampshire titles. They struck a compromise in which the council promised to suspend all civil suits contesting New Hampshire titles until the Crown rendered its decision, provided all settlers were left undisturbed and New York law upheld. Bennington residents enthusiastically approved the plan to secure "Universal peace & Pelenty Liberty & Property."[19]

Yet the speculative value of the lands continued to undermine the peace on the Grants. When New York surveyor William Cockburn was discovered by Seth Warner and Remember Baker surveying along the Winooski River in the heart of the Onion River Land Company holdings, a contingent of Green Mountain Boys "arrested" him and destroyed his instruments. According to Cockburn's letter to James Duane, they "intended to murder us if we did not go from thence."[20] The same contingent that harassed Cockburn also forcibly evicted some Yorker settlers occupying land in Panton that Ethan Allen claimed under a Wentworth title. And, in late September 1772, Baker and Ira Allen seized Benjamin Stevens, another New York surveyor, near Burlington, and sent him packing. This last in a series of incidents pushed New York authorities beyond their limit, and they issued warrants for the arrest of Baker and Allen, with the offer of huge rewards.

As the stakes rose, Ethan Allen and his cohorts moved from a reactive to a more anticipatory stance. In November 1773, in an enormous show of force, Allen and Baker led an armed band of one hundred thirty men into Clarendon, where many who were sympathetic to New York had obtained a confirmatory patent for the town of Durham. In the dead of night, Allen and his men rousted from his bed Benjamin Spencer, the outspoken

Yorker partisan who performed duties as a New York justice of the peace, and forced him to watch as flames enveloped two of his compatriots' homes. Declaring that if the Green Mountain Boys ever returned, they would "reduce every house to ashes and leave every inhabitant a corpse," Allen and fellow "judges" Baker, Seth Warner, and Robert Cochran conducted a kangaroo court in which they found Spencer guilty of showing "respect and obedience" for New York, and ignited the roof of his home.[21] Although Spencer gave no more trouble, Rev. Benjamin Hough, a neighbor and Baptist minister of the town, journeyed to New York City to give an eyewitness account of what the "Bennington mob" had done in Clarendon. Upon his return, two of Allen's men seized him and delivered him to Allen and Warner in Sunderland for "trial," at which he received a sentence of two hundred lashes as "full punishment for his crimes."[22] Upon release, Hough was subsequently banished from the Grants.

The extraordinary bravado exercised by Allen and his cohorts provoked an unprecedented reaction from New York. In March 1774, New York's General Assembly issued a strong antiriot law aimed at "preventing tumultuous and riotous Assemblies" and facilitating "the more speedy and effectual punishing of the rioters." It declared that individuals who engaged in any assemblage of three or more persons for "unlawful intent" would be liable for one year's imprisonment, as would anyone caught "harbouring, abetting, or succouring" Allen and his seven closest colleagues. More draconian yet, the law gave officials enforcing this provision free reign to injure or even to kill, while anybody who interfered with and obstructed an officer attempting to disperse a mob, or who refused to obey an order to disperse, became subject to a death penalty.[23]

This "Bloody Act," as Allen labeled it in his published response, underscored the frustration of New York officials at being unable to put down the frontier rebellion and their hope that, by imitating Allen's tactics of intimidation, they might bring the rebellious Yankees into submission. Instead, the action produced the opposite reaction. Allen and six of the others named in the law (James Breakenridge did not sign) issued a reply condemning it as unconstitutional because "it is not a law for the Province of New York in general, but . . . for part of the counties of *Charlotte* and *Albany*, viz. such parts thereof as are covered with the *New-Hampshire* charters; and it is well known those grants compose but a minor part of the inhabitants of the said Province; and we have no representatives in that assembly." Defending their defiance of New York magistrates on the grounds that "we are necessitated to oppose their executive of law, where it points directly at our property or give up the same," Allen and his colleagues matched the death threat of the New York law itself with the promise that "if the executioners approach us, they will be as likely to fall victims to death as we."[24] Compromise became impossible, as the spirit of defiance gained vigor and strengthened Allen's hand. A convention held in Manchester passed a resolution forbidding any inhabitant of the grants to "hold any office of honor or profit under the colony of N. York."[25] To further demonstrate their power and their anger, a party of Green Mountain Boys seized Dr. Samuel Adams, a New York sympathizer from Arlington, marched him to Bennington, and hoisted him in an armchair to the top of the signpost outside the Catamount Tavern, where he swung for several hours, as a reminder that no westsider could feel safe expressing sympathy for the New York side of the dispute.

Dr. Samuel Adams of Arlington hoisted into the air at the Catamount Tavern, while below, Green Mountain Boys administer what they called the justice of the "beech seal." From Zadock Thompson, *Civil History of Vermont* (1842).

View of Bennington, painting by Ralph Earl. The view includes Isaac Tichenor's house (center foreground), the Parson Dewey house (far right), and the Elijah Dewey house (gambrel-roof structure right foreground). *Courtesy of the Bennington Museum.*

Despite this string of successful actions, the Green Mountain Boys and their supporters in western Vermont remained in a state of waiting, still lacking a solid plan for guaranteeing permanent control of their land claims. This continued to be the situation when they began receiving the benefits of events not of their own making. Specifically, they began drawing strength from the series of challenges to the legitimacy of British authority that was gaining momentum across the colonies. In fact, the consequences of the 1773 Boston Tea Party and, most importantly, the harsh British countermeasures, which included shutting down the Port of Boston completely and dispossessing Massachusetts residents of their political rights, reverberated with great intensity in these northern frontier lands. Vermonters found themselves fighting for their cause within a much larger revolution.

By 1774, the population of the Grants numbered between twelve and thirteen thousand. The majority remained in the southeast, with Guilford the most populated town, while Bennington and a few other southwestern communities followed close behind in size. Frame homes and occasional brick or stone dwellings enhanced a resemblance to New England villages to the south. Small saw and grist mills dotted the waterways, typically built with incentives from proprietors or early residents to promote settlement and increase property values. Taverns and rudimentary general stores also began to appear. Yet a fundamental instability undercut the facade of social order. With few exceptions, the inhabitants were farmers and most had incurred debts in their quest to purchase land, livestock, implements, and seed. Thus, during this period most families experienced larger expenditures of money than receipt of income. Ordinarily, debtor-creditor problems could be resolved with considerable leeway; but with the growing economic dislocation in revolutionary Boston, coastal merchants and others began calling in debts.

Confronting the economic deterioration in the spring of 1775, even the law-abiding southeasterners found themselves embracing the spirit of insurgency. On March 10, "about forty good, true men" from Rockingham met with Thomas Chandler, the chief judge of New York's Cumberland County court, to discuss the court session scheduled to begin four days later in Westminster. They pointed out that as a consequence of extraordinary economic circumstances an unprecedented number of debt cases crowded the docket. Could the judge, recognizing the revolutionary fervor abroad, consent to a postponement of the session, lest violence occur? According to the account written by Reuben Jones, clerk of the Cumberland County court, the judge concurred that "it would be for the good of the county not to have any court, as things were," but noted that a murder case needed to be heard, "and if it was not agreeable to the people, they would not have any other case." Beyond that, he insisted upon consulting his associate judges before rendering the final decision.[26]

On March 13, a mob of one hundred men, distrustful of Judge Chandler's promise not to have the court deal with foreclosures, occupied the Cumberland County courthouse at Westminster. The "rioters" reasoned that if the court could not convene, creditors could not take action. Sheriff William Patterson of Hinsdale (Vernon) assembled a posse, marched to Westminster, and ordered the "damned rascals" to disperse. They steadfastly refused. At this point, Patterson and his posse retreated to Norton's Tavern, ostensibly to discuss their next move. Accounts of what happened next are colored by whose side of the story one consults. Patterson insisted that, in the clearest of minds, he and his posse returned about midnight, figuring that the vast majority of the insurgents had grown bored and returned home. Those who remained, however, refused to heed the sheriff's demand to vacate the building. Partisans within the courthouse insisted that the sheriff, being inebriated, climbed to the top of the courthouse step, lost his balance, and subsequently fell. Patterson insisted he had been pushed back and clubbed by guards defending the entryway. Reuben Jones mentions no such mishap, only that the sheriff and his company "marched up fast, within about ten rods of the door, and then the word was given, take care, and then, fire." In the brief period it took the posse to rush the building "with guns, swords, and clubs" and subdue the unarmed "rioters," two inside the courthouse were killed and eight others wounded, while two of the sheriff's posse received slight flesh wounds. The posse took seven as prisoners in the melee and crowded them along with the wounded into two narrow and unheated "dungeon-like" rooms for the remainder of the night.[27]

News of the situation spread so quickly that by noon the next day an outraged assemblage of several hundred men had convened. They proceeded to recapture the courthouse and to jail the sheriff's posse and the judges. On the following day, the arrival of Robert Cochran and a band of forty Green Mountain Boys, dispatched by Ethan Allen from the west, gave to this local event an increased significance. For the first time, moderate easterners listened intently as Cochran declared the "Westminster Massacre" an uprising against New York tyranny and offered the services of the Green Mountain Boys to assist their new eastside allies in avenging the blood spilled.

Acting Governor Cadwallader Colden of New York did not miss the significance of the event. Colden reported to London superiors that he had "no doubt" that the eastsiders would "be joined by the Bennington Rioters, who will endeavor to make one common cause of it, though they have no connection but in their violence to Government."[28] The Westminster affair signaled the end of New York's continued operation of courts or any other institution in the Grants. Henceforth, as advocates for violence gained the upper hand throughout the colonies in their determination to throw off the continued injustices of British rule, their calls to remember the "Massacre" significantly bolstered the cause of independence.

Joining the Fight for Independence

With the firing of the "shot heard 'round the world" at Lexington and Concord on April 19, 1775, the pace of change accelerated. Opposition in the Grants no longer focused exclusively upon New York landjobbers, but now included the "tyrant" King George III. Also, the people's right "to alter or to abolish" unjust government, once confined to Vermont's frontier, now enveloped the American mainstream.

The transformation of Ethan Allen and the Green Mountain Boys from "outlaws" to patriot "rebels" occurred naturally, according to Allen, and as a result of "a sincere passion for liberty."[29] Allen's linking of the American cause with that of the Grants settlers' own struggle against "arbitrary power" rapidly led him to involvement in the war. When Samuel Parsons, a member of the Hartford Committee of Correspondence, promised to fund an attack on Fort Ticonderoga to acquire critically needed artillery to resist the siege of Boston, Allen eagerly agreed to lead the effort. Espionage information added urgency to the project, revealing the fort to be exceedingly vulnerable and the British unfamiliar with events unfolding to the south.

The idea for capturing Ticonderoga actually had been planted in Parsons's mind through a chance meeting with Benedict Arnold, who then lost out to Ethan Allen in a competition for leadership of the attack. The meeting occurred as Arnold traveled to Cambridge to persuade the Massachusetts Committee of Safety to fund this bold venture with himself as a commissioned colonel at its head. After the Committee granted his request and he began soliciting troops in western Massachusetts, Arnold learned of Allen's plan. Hurrying northward, he met with members of Allen's force in Castleton, and followed them to Shoreham, at Hand's Cove, where Allen and his men made preparations to cross Lake Champlain. Arnold, dressed in his blue uniform of the Connecticut footguard, insisted

"Col. Allen demanding the surrender of Ticonderoga." Wood engraving from Charles A. Goodrich, *A History of the United States of America*, (c. 1834). *Courtesy of the Fort Ticonderoga Museum.*

that he alone possessed authority to lead the attack. Ethan left the decision up to his men, who steadfastly refused to pledge allegiance to anyone other than their own commander. Arnold had no option but to comply.

Allen recorded his recollection of the Ticonderoga attack in his *Narrative*, published only after his career had been tarnished by his unauthorized mission to capture Montreal that ended ingloriously in his own captivity. He asserted in the *Narrative* that the Ticonderoga attack "was carried into execution" without a hitch. In actuality, the incursion survived several hitches. Allen's failure to procure the boats needed to ferry his men across the lake set off a frenzied search in the early morning hours of May 10, 1775. Able to obtain only two vessels, he could transport over the lake before daybreak just 83 men of the 230 assembled. Allen's recollection obliquely mentions that a lone sentry he encountered had been able to fire point-blank at him, although the piece failed to discharge. As a further embarrassment (also not acknowledged by Allen's recollection), he mistakenly identified Lieutenant Jocelyn Feltham, the fort's second in command, as Captain William Delaplace, its principal officer, delivering to him the famed surrender demand, "In the name of the great Jehovah, and the Continental Congress," or, as his men later recalled, a more direct "Come out of there, you Damned British rat!"[30]

Still, nothing could detract from the significance of Allen's achievement. The surprise capture of the fort, the first offensive victory scored for the patriotic cause, and its role in providing artillery used to defend Boston, constituted a feat of extraordinary proportions, and the name of Ethan Allen quickly circulated as America's first Revolutionary hero.

That heroic image proved to be short-lived, however. Allen celebrated his victory by commandeering the ninety gallons of rum from Captain Delaplace's private cellar "for the refreshment of the fatigued soldiery." During the extended festivities, Benedict Arnold, his status bolstered by the arrival of a hundred of his Massachusetts troops, sailed a captured sloop north to St. John, where he seized its small garrison and the heavily armed British sloop *Enterprise*, thus giving the patriots total control over the lake. Allen, not to be outdone, organized a hundred-man force to row four bateaux up the lake to St. John to capture the city itself. Meeting Arnold halfway, Allen refused to be dissuaded from a plan that Arnold described as "a wild, impractical scheme."[31] Allen's force forged on until finally collapsing, exhausted and hungry, along an exposed riverfront on the outskirts of St. John. Early the next morning, they were unceremoniously roused by cannon fire unleashed by a British unit recently dispatched from Montreal. The attack caused Allen to retreat quickly, leaving three of his men behind and one captured.

That blundering episode apparently had a dramatic effect on his men who, while reveling with him in the seemingly risk-free enjoyment of bullying Yorker sympathizers, now reconsidered Allen's military prowess in the face of war-ready British troops. On July 26, after a convention of westside representatives learned that the Continental Congress had authorized a Green Mountain Regiment to be incorporated as a regular unit into the Continental army, they selected Seth Warner as its leader over Allen, by a lopsided 41 to 5 vote.

Ethan Allen, dejected by the actions of those he disparagingly labeled "old men," impulsively withdrew from the organization he had formed five years earlier and offered his services as a civilian scout to General Philip Schuyler at Ticonderoga. However, he quickly grew restless with Schuyler's ambivalence about launching an offensive against Canada at a time when, he insisted, it was ill-prepared for war. That impatience precipitated Allen's ill-fated and wholly unsanctioned attempt to capture Montreal on his own, with a force of one hundred men, in September. The effort culminated in defeat and capture. For the next two and a half years Allen remained out of combat as a prisoner of war, transported to England, Ireland, and back to America, where he languished in a New York prison until being exchanged for a British colonel in May 1778.

Across Québec, news of Allen's capture "put the French people into great consternation," according to his compatriot Seth Warner. That view was echoed in a British partisan's gleeful observation that "the Canadians before were nine-tenths for the Bostonians. They are now returned to their duty."[32] The broader patriotic cause at home, George Washington reported, had similarly felt the "unfavorable effects" of the hero of Ticonderoga's capture, adding that "his misfortune will, I hope, teach a lesson of prudence and subordination to others who may be ambitious to outshine their general officers."[33] Two months after Allen's capture, the American army, led by General Richard Montgomery, seized Montreal. That victory, however, was undercut by a failed assault on Québec in late December that left Montgomery dead and the frontier again vulnerable.

In an ironic twist, Benedict Arnold returned to Vermont the following summer to take command as chief protector of the Revolutionary cause. Having demonstrated considerable bravery in the failed offensive upon

"God Bless Our Armes," and "New England Vessels at Valcure Bay." Watercolor by C. Randle. *Courtesy of the Fort Ticonderoga Museum.*

Québec in which he had been severely wounded, Arnold, now as a brigadier general, held responsibility for maintaining the patriots' advantage on Lake Champlain against an expected British counteroffensive designed to reclaim the lake and a substantially reconstructed Fort Ticonderoga. Convinced that American naval superiority on the lake would preclude any advance by the large British army in Canada, Arnold employed more than two hundred carpenters working day and night at Skenesborough with green wood to construct an eight-gun schooner, eight gondolas (crude, flat-bottomed vessels resembling large bateaux), and four galleys. The new construction completed his flotilla of fifteen vessels carrying 86 guns, 152 swivels, and 500 men.

Arnold lacked any knowledge of the size of the British fleet. He discovered just what his forces faced only as the British made final preparations. The three-masted *Inflexible* alone had eighteen cannon delivering twelve-pounders capable of pulverizing the American fleet. Two schooners of fourteen and twelve guns accompanied the *Inflexible*, as did the raft-like *Thunderer*, equipped with fourteen heavy guns. Twenty gunboats of one gun each rounded out the force. Arnold quickly scrapped his plan for a first-strike strategy in the open lake and anchored his vessels in a hidden sanctuary behind Valcour Island. Anticipating that the large British warships would sail past his crescent-shaped battle line of ships, Arnold hoped to use the element of surprise to bombard the British vessels with heavy shells, and then exploit their lack of maneuverability as they attempted to tack back against the wind into the shallow channel where Arnold's fleet was anchored. His trap worked. Although the fierce battle on October 11, 1776, destroyed all but four American warships and left the British in control of the lake, the damage inflicted on Sir Guy Carleton's navy proved sufficient for him to reconsider his attack on a well-armed Ticonderoga. On November 1, with cold weather setting in, and uncertain of what remained of Arnold's forces, Carlton turned his fleet around and sailed back to Canada for the winter. Thanks to Arnold, Americans now had another year to prepare for the British offensive. Over the winter of 1776–1777, the Americans worked busily to reinforce Fort Ticonderoga and construct a pontoon bridge across the narrows to Mount Independence where an American garrison perched high over the water was meant to defend the barrier to British ships, expected to resume their campaign south the following season.

Vermonters used this interim to complete their own revolution within a revolution. In January 1776, delegates from eighteen southwestern townships meeting in Dorset had voted to send Heman Allen, one of Ethan's younger brothers, with a petition to the Continental Congress requesting that the Grants be recognized as independent from New York military authority. However, those with whom Allen spoke in Philadelphia—even those favorably inclined—advised him that the proposal contained a fatal flaw: It lacked support from the residents in the southeastern Grants.

In fact, despite the Westminster Massacre, many moderate southeasterners, inspired by the revolutionary fervor that followed Lexington and Concord, had promised "with the utmost cheerfulness and alacrity, to unsheath the sword in defence of the lives and properties of the good people" of the "ancient and truly respectable patriotick colony of New York."[34] Militias had been formed for both Cumberland and Gloucester counties. Eastern moderates such as Jacob Bayley had laid aside their misgivings and pledged allegiance to fight, under New York rule, against the larger threat of George III. As some delegates of the Continental Congress advised, until the inhabitants of the Grants could "consult suitable measures to Associate and unite the whole of the inhabitants of said Grants together," the bid for independence would go nowhere.[35]

In the summer of 1776, southwestern delegates met with the Committees of Safety of Cumberland and Gloucester counties to solicit support for the Grants' independence. A third Dorset Convention held in September 1776 included eight self-appointed delegates from Cumberland County, among them two former leaders of anticourt riots. Still, their ability to advance the cause of unifying the Grants owed far more to the actions of New Yorkers than to their convention's rhetoric. Jacob Bayley, commissioned by the newly formed revolutionary Provincial Congress of the State of New York in 1776 as brigadier general of Gloucester and Cumberland counties, had remained aloof from discussions about the Grants' independence. In April 1777, however, New York's issuance of its new revolutionary constitution compelled Bayley to reconsider his position. The new constitution, far from espousing revolutionary change, stood as a highly conservative document that underscored the determination of New York's ruling elite to oppose most internal political changes, with the exception of ridding themselves of the British imperial administration.

New York's authorities—these "reluctant revolutionaries"—offered a governing system that gave little encouragement to Grants settlers.[36] It provided the Grants with only token representation in New York's assembly and senate; insisted that high property requirements for suffrage be sustained; granted the governor extraordinary powers to control and even dismiss the legislature; and most dramatically, conferred on New York judges life tenure with good behavior. This government structure was profoundly in conflict with political ideas widespread in the Grants. In a June 1777 letter addressed to the New York assembly, Bayley reported that "the people before they saw the constitution, were not willing to trouble themselves" with separation, "but now almost to a man they are violent for it."[37] Union with the west now seemed the least onerous of available options.

Fighting a Revolution Within a Revolution

With Ethan Allen still in captivity, the challenge of verbally capitalizing on New York's actions fell to his youngest brother, Ira, a contrast with Ethan both physically (nicknamed "Stub" by his brothers in reference to his diminutive stature) and in his preference for quietly managing the brothers' Onion River properties. In a pamphlet entitled "Some Miscellaneous Remarks," distributed throughout the region, Ira chose to extol the unassailable logic of independence with little of his brother's familiar bombastic style. "The great distance of road betwixt this district and New York," he observed, "is alone a convincing argument that the God of Nature never designed said district should be under the jurisdiction of said State." Furthermore, in contrast to New York's constitution, Allen promised that Vermont's assemblies and courts "will have quite short sessions," judges elected for short terms, and officers' fees set "at a reasonable rate." Thus Allen appealed to "the impartial reader" to reflect upon which "would be best, wisest and cheapest."[38]

Before Grants residents could cement their unity, however, they faced more immediate tasks, related to the revolutionary struggle against Britain. As had occurred many previous times, the strategic Champlain Valley became transformed into a highway for war. Lake Champlain had already served as a staging point for an American attack on Montreal. Now, in early 1777, a British force of seventy-five hundred men began assembling under the command of General John Burgoyne in Canada to be marched down to Albany. Burgoyne planned to meet Barry St. Leger's troops, then join with Lord Howe's army on the Hudson, to isolate the rebellious New Englanders from the remainder of the colonies.

In mid-June, news that Burgoyne's force had begun moving sent shock waves throughout the Champlain Valley and forced widespread evacuation of the sparsely settled northern frontiers. As British troops freely trampled corn fields in northwestern Vermont, a large assemblage of delegates, with a majority from the east, convened in Windsor on July 2, 1777, for the purpose of uniting the Grants into a single, independent state. On May 15, 1776 the Continental Congress had issued a resolution "to the respective Assemblies and Conventions of the United Colonies, where no government sufficient to the exigencies of their affairs has been hitherto established, to adopt such government as shall in the opinion of the Representatives of the people best conduce to the happiness and safety of their constituents in particular and America in general." Although strictly speaking the document did not apply to them, the Vermonters took advantage of it, along with the collapse of royal authority, the confusion of wartime administration, and the revolutionary fervor sweeping the land, to declare themselves an independent state and draft a constitution.[39]

To assist the inexperienced delegates in their deliberations, Ethan Allen's boyhood friend, Thomas Young, had sent a letter in April 1777 advising them that "you have nothing to do but send attested copies of the

[May 1776] Recommendation to take up government to every township in your district, and invite all your freeholders and inhabitants to meet in their respective townships and chuse members for a General Convention, to meet at an early day to chuse Delegates for the General Congress, a Committee of Safety, and to form a Constitution for your State."[40] Along with his letter, Young sent a copy of Pennsylvania's 1776 constitution—

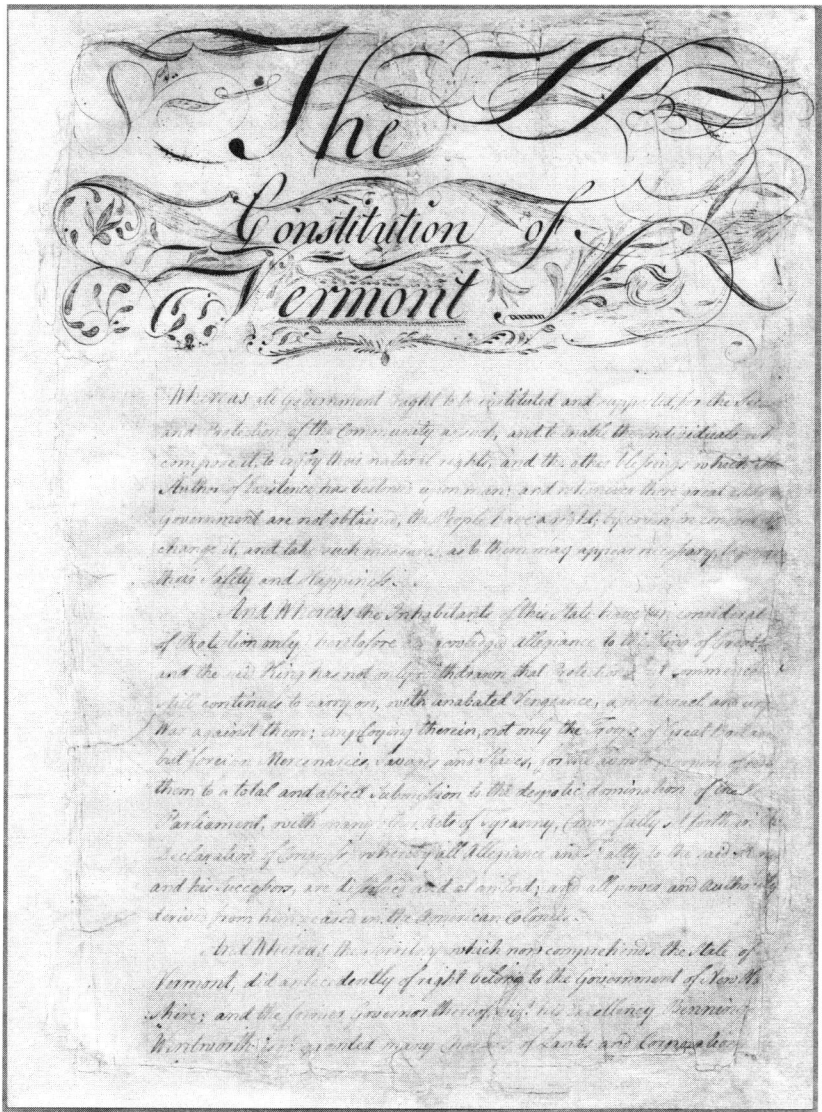

First page of the manuscript copy of the Constitution of the State of Vermont, 1777.
Courtesy of Vermont State Archives.

one of seven written by the breakaway states in 1776 and 1777, and generally considered the most radical—which, he advised, "with a very little alteration, will, in my opinion, come as near perfection as any thing yet concerted by mankind."[41]

Vermont historians have traditionally held that convention delegates, in response to the intense pressure of Burgoyne's invasion, acted in haste to embrace Young's document of 1776 as their own, made only a few nonsubstantive modifications, commissioned Ira Allen to have it printed, and then quickly adjourned to meet the emergency of the advancing British army. Ira Allen's own singular account describes the serendipitous intervention of a severe thunderstorm that prevented delegates from disbanding before completing the work of drafting the constitution. The way the document took shape, therefore, and the genesis of some of its contents, remain cloaked in doubt; but many of its elements, even the document's preamble, which Ira Allen later claimed to have authored and added in December, captured the distinctive mood of Vermont's "revolution within a revolution."

The first two paragraphs of the preamble followed closely both the ideology and language of the Declaration of Independence, proclaimed just a year earlier. The breakaway Vermonters thereby associated themselves with the high principles of liberty rather than mere self-interest, with the revolution in progress rather than mere rioting, and with the nation struggling to form itself rather than petty intracolonial squabbling. They, like their fellow Americans, called upon a theory of natural law and social contract to proclaim their independence from King George III, who had carried on "with unabated vengeance, a most cruel and unjust war" with the intent of reducing the population "to a total and abject submission."[42]

The remaining sixteen paragraphs of the preamble, however, recited in elaborate and colorful detail a litany of abuses suffered not at the hands of Great Britain but rather New York. Grievances included the regranting of land "to certain favorite land jobbers in the government of New York," the dispatch "of savages on our frontiers," and the issuance of rewards for capture of "those very persons who have dared boldly, and publicly, to appear in defence of their just rights."

A comparison of Vermont's 1777 constitution with the other state constitutions of the revolutionary and postrevolutionary period illuminates the radical character of the Windsor document. Like many of the documents drafted in the states between 1776 and the 1780s, Vermont's constitution places a "Declaration of the Rights of the Inhabitants" ahead of the "Frame of Government." The Vermont Declaration, which once again paraphrases the 1776 Declaration of Independence, affirms the origins of government in the people and the existence of inalienable individual rights and liberties as the foundation of any form of government. This line of reasoning, which had developed in North America from the 1680s, and had become solidified in the assertions of the Declaration of Independence of "certain inalienable rights," had been key to the evolution of a distinctly American approach to constitutionalism. The mere act of writing a constitution, as opposed to the British system of an unwritten constitution encompassing the entirety of British statutes, represented, as historian Bernard Bailyn has commented, "efforts to abstract from the deep entanglements of English law and custom certain essentials—obligations, rights, and prohibitions—by which liberty, as it was understood, might be preserved."[43]

Foremost among the nineteen articles delineating individual rights in the Vermont Constitution was article one, which declared "that all men are born equally free and independent, and have certain natural, inherent, and unalienable rights, amongst which are the enjoying and defending life and liberty, acquiring, possessing and protecting property, and pursuing and obtaining happiness and safety," language borrowed from the Pennsylvania Constitution. The Vermonters went a step further, however, and in fact went beyond any other state, by prohibiting slavery of males over the age of twenty-one and females over age eighteen "unless they are bound by their own consent, after they arrive to such age, or bound by law, for the payment of debts, damages, fines, costs, or the like." This statement anticipated by about a generation the emancipation of servants, slaves, and apprentices by state constitutional or statutory means elsewhere in the North and reflected what historian Gordon Wood has called "the contagion of liberty" in the era of the Revolution.[44] It represented as well the unique situation Vermonters placed themselves in by using the absence of any effective colonial authority to strike out on their own and put into practice what the ideology of the age preached in theory.

Article 2 likewise broke new constitutional ground by declaring "that private property ought to be subservient to public uses when necessity requires it, nevertheless, whenever any person's property is taken for the use of the public, the owner ought to receive an equivalent in money." This concern for balancing individual rights with the public or communal good permeates the remaining articles of the Declaration of Rights. Article 9 declared that "every member of society hath a right to be protected in the enjoyment of life, liberty and property," then insisted on the obligation "to contribute his proportion toward the expense of that protection." Article 6, perhaps the most radical of the items in this section of the constitution, declared the "government is, or ought to be, instituted for the common benefit, protection, and security of the people, nation, or community" and guaranteed Vermonters "an indubitable, unalienable and indefeasible right to reform, alter, or abolish government in such matter as shall be, by that community, judged most conducive to the public weal."

The "frame of government" likewise embodied much of the enlightened spirit of revolutionary change. The Vermonters adopted many elements from the Pennsylvania Constitution warmly recommended by Young, in many cases copying the model word for word, but they also added some elements from the Connecticut charter—for example, the Freeman's Oath, which came to Connecticut from Massachusetts—with which many of Vermont's earliest political leaders were familiar.[45] The Vermont document followed Pennsylvania by creating a unicameral legislature, thereby proclaiming republican distrust and rejection of any institution that threatened to impose an aristocratic principle, and symbolically striking at both the New York state constitution, which had created an upper house, and England's House of Lords. The same distrust of power exercised beyond the reach of citizens led the Vermonters to adopt the Pennsylvania model of an executive council rather than a single executive, and to establish a supreme court and other courts as a separate branch of government (although the conditions and terms of appointment were not specified in the document). As a further check on the government, the constitution included in Chapter II Section 44— the final section of the document—a provision for the election every seven years of a thirteen-member "council of censors." These men, elected at large, with the restriction that none could currently be serving in either the General Assembly or the Governor's Council, had the responsibility "to enquire whether the constitution has been preserved inviolate in every part; and whether the legislative and executive branches of government have performed their duty as guardians of the people." Given broad powers to examine "persons, papers, and records," the council also had authority for one year to censure public officials, order impeachments, repeal any laws "as appear to them to have been enacted contrary to the principles of the constitution," and call for a constitutional convention "if there appears to them an absolute necessity of amending any articles of this constitution which may be defective."[46]

Whether from pragmatism or conservatism, the Vermonters departed from the Pennsylvania document in some significant details. Recent historians, closely comparing the language of the two constitutions, have made much more of these variations than their nineteenth-century predecessors. In the spirit of democracy, Pennsylvania elected no officials on a statewide level and barred all members of the executive branch (councilors, lieutenant governor, and governor) from seeking reelection. Vermonters adopted neither of these provisions, electing their entire executive—the governor, lieutenant governor, state treasurer, and twelve members of the governor's council—on a statewide basis but requiring a majority of the votes cast to secure election of the executive officers and giving the legislature and council joint responsibility to determine the election in cases where no candidate won the majority. The apparent contradiction of permitting reelection of the executive was offset by the requirement for annual election and by denying the executive office any veto power. Nonetheless, by permitting reelection, the Vermonters created the conditions that would allow for a small coterie of men to govern Vermont year after year, which became the case when Thomas Chittenden, who served as governor for all but one of the next twenty years, became the leader of an increasingly powerful faction known as the Arlington Junto. In addition, by not specifically precluding the possibility of individuals serving in multiple offices within state government, Vermont created a situation in which, during the earliest years, judges often served as members of the executive or legislative branches while, in the absence of stipulations giving the assembly full control over passing public bills, "the governor and council participated in and dominated the legislative process." Thus, a relatively few men in Vermont exercised an extraordinary degree of control in writing, enacting, and ultimately adjudicating the law.[47]

The spirit of conservatism appeared elsewhere as well, fueled by continued broad adherence to the traditions embodied in the "New England way." Although this stance was modified as early as the 1786 revision of the document, Vermont's first constitution stipulated that only Protestants were protected against being "justly deprived or abridged of any civil right as a citizen."[48]

Giving the towns priority over individuals in the political system, the Vermont constitution departed from the Pennsylvania model by providing for equality of representation based on a one-town-one-vote model (except for towns with populations over eighty, which received two votes) rather than apportionment by population. Towns were privileged in other respects, both in the constitution and in early legislation, which gave the town meeting the right to determine who would be counted as a freeman, based on whether the person was of "a quiet and peaceable behavior."

Vermont's English settlers brought the institution of the town meeting with them when they migrated from Massachusetts and Connecticut. Accustomed to governing their church affairs through congregational meetings, early New England settlers rapidly adapted that mechanism for self-governance to town affairs and by the mid-1630s town meetings had become a feature of the political life of settlements around Boston, where freemen were obliged to attend a meeting to discuss town affairs as frequently as once a week. Absenteeism soon led to adopting the expediency of appointing or electing a selectboard to conduct town affairs, and town meeting became an annual event.[49] By the mid-eighteenth century the annual town meeting had become a fixed institution in New England, and New Hampshire charters establishing communities in Vermont included stipulations for a town meeting to be held on a Tuesday in March (regularized in 1880 as the first Tuesday in March).[50] Once the institution of town meeting had been regularized and legalized, according to political scientist Andrew Nuquist, it "became the formal legislative body for the community. All powers of control were lodged in the Meeting, and it was empowered to choose such officers as the needs of the time demanded" and to formulate and execute "its own policies, within the limits prescribed by the state legislature."[51]

By contrast with its conservative elements, the Vermont Constitution contained some forward-looking provisions. Section 40 of chapter II, for example, specified the legislature's right to establish a school or schools in each town "for the convenient instruction of youth . . . one grammar school in each county, and one university in this State." Much like Thomas Jefferson's "Bill for the Diffusion of Knowledge" which Virginia's legislators rejected, Vermont's 1777 document called for state-mandated education to facilitate a citizenry distinguished by talent, intellect, and virtue. The Vermont document also eliminated property requirements for suffrage, replacing them with a poll tax. In so doing, it placed the Vermont "experiment" at the vanguard of radical revolution.

All told, the declaration and establishment of an independent Vermont signaled the convergence of people inspired by Enlightenment thought and radical ideas of individual liberties with social and religious moderates guided by a more traditional desire to uphold the principles of the "New England Way."

One significant departure from this radical republicanism was the failure of the Windsor convention to place the constitution before the towns or the people of Vermont for ratification. In this respect, however, the Vermonters followed the practice adopted by the other states that rewrote their constitutions at this time, although it is perhaps worth noting that here, too, Vermont did not follow the example of Pennsylvania, which was the only state to submit the text to public scrutiny and discussion before its legal adoption.[52] Nothing in the document itself required such approval and the tumultuous events taking place at the time became either the cause or the excuse for setting up a government without it. Following adoption of the Constitution of 1777, therefore, the delegates at Windsor agreed upon a compromise candidate, Thomas Chittenden, to lead the twelve-man Council of Safety charged with governing the state until elections could be held. Within a short period, Chittenden, a middle-aged, recently settled resident of Williston, with political experience as a Connecticut representative, formed allegiances with the Allens and their clique that would begin to fracture on both geographic and philosophical lines the fragile coalition that came together in the summer of 1777 to create an independent state.

For the moment, though, focus during the first week of July 1777 was directed at General John Burgoyne as he guided his well-disciplined army of seventy-five hundred men southward through the Champlain Valley and into position for an attack on Fort Ticonderoga. A detachment of Burgoyne's forces hastily constructed a road up the seven-hundred-fifty-foot Sugar Loaf Hill (later renamed Mt. Defiance), situated to the south of the fort, and left undefended by American forces, who believed it to be too steep to be fortified. The British used oxen, however, to deliver eight pieces of artillery to its summit and thereby threatened the Colonial garrison on Mt. Independence.

With Ticonderoga now subject to a punishing barrage of cannon fire, General Arthur St. Clair and his American force of more than three thousand men concluded that their only option lay in retreat. In the dead of night early on July 6, St. Clair's army traversed a floating bridge built across the lake earlier to deliver supplies from Vermont, and moved along the only road still open leading southeast to Hubbardton and Castleton. The American hold on Lake Champlain, gained two years earlier, had been lost.

British troops commanded by General Simon Fraser pursued the retreating forces, finally making contact in Hubbardton early on July 7. St. Clair had positioned his most experienced unit, the Green Mountain Regiment commanded by Seth Warner, in the rear guard, hoping to deter the British pursuit. For more than half an hour Warner's men, and elements of the 11th Massachusetts regiment, held off Fraser's attackers. The arrival of Von Riedesel's German reinforcements, however, and a subsequent deadly bayonet charge against Warner's right flank, turned the tide of battle. His troop lines broken, Warner shouted at his men, as they scattered through the woods, to reassemble with him at Manchester. St. Clair's forces, confronted by the fleeing forward line, turned about and also resumed retreat. Altogether, the battle at Hubbardton cost the Americans 354 men killed, wounded, or captured; the British suffered 183 casualties. Despite their losses, Warner's regiment had managed to stop Fraser's pursuit and bought the time needed for American forces to regroup further south.

News of St. Clair's retreat from Ticonderoga and Mount Independence deflated American morale, George Washington judging "the affair" to be "so mysterious that it baffles even conjecture."[53] The triumphant Burgoyne, however, immediately confronted problems with his supply lines. Hoping to ease the shortages, he dispatched Lieutenant Colonel Frederick Baum and a force of German mercenaries to Bennington to capture a supply of oxen, corn, cattle, and horses that Seth Warner and his men had collected there. General John Stark and a band of fellow New Hampshiremen had moved into the vicinity, and, learning of Baum's planned attack, bolstered their troops with militia from Massachusetts and from towns around Bennington, and a company of Stockbridge Indians. On August 16, his corps of eighteen hundred men attacked Baum's contingent, numbering nearly fifteen hundred, stationed on a steep hill above the Walloomsac River, six miles northwest of Bennington (in present-day New York state). Stark's small army routed the British forces in fighting that continued until after sunset. The American victory at the "Battle of Bennington" cost Burgoyne two hundred dead and seven hundred prisoners, approximately one-tenth of his army. He wrote to Lord George Germain that Vermont, which had been thought of as an essentially unpopulated wilderness, now "abounds in the most active and most rebellious race of the continent and hangs like a gathering storm on my left."[54]

The Bennington success also restored American morale. Subsequent continental military offenses broke Burgoyne's lines of communication, forcing his troops into a defense at Ticonderoga and Mount Independence.

Within a month, Captain Ebenezer Allen regained Sugar Loaf Hill, while other efforts reclaimed all the British shipping at Lake George and Champlain landings. Two thousand Vermont militiamen joined in the second Battle of Freeman's Farm on the heights above Fort Edward. And when John Stark blocked the retreat of the weakened British forces at Saratoga on October 16, 1777, Burgoyne surrendered his remaining army of almost six thousand men.

While the victory at Saratoga bolstered American spirits and proved crucial for winning French support for the war, Vermonters received little credit and no gratitude from a Continental Congress that remained unwilling to acknowledge the state's claim of independence. Moreover, Vermonters' most immediate challenge was the task of funding their participation in the war. In the face of Burgoyne's advance from Canada, the Windsor convention had authorized the newly formed Vermont Council of Safety to raise the funds needed to maintain Vermont's militia. Ira Allen, following through on his threats in "Miscellaneous Remarks," recommended that a commission of confiscation be formed to seize loyalist properties. Sequestration courts operating in other states served as models for punishing loyalists by selling their "movable" property and renting out their land until they pledged allegiance to the patriotic cause. Allen proposed that commissioners, serving as judges on one of two courts located on either side of the mountains, seize "goods and chattel of all persons who had or might join the common enemy."[55]

The two courts were duly established but differed markedly in their definition of who was subject to the law. The western court engaged in brisk activity, bolstered by Ethan Allen's return from captivity and appointment as a judge in 1778. A noteworthy case involved "seventeen wicked Tories" delivered by Allen to the Albany jail. Petitioning New York's governor for release, the seventeen insisted their only crime had been in "acknowledging themselves to be subjects of the State of New York, and not recognizing the validity and existence of the State of Vermont."[56] Between March 1778 and February 1779, seventy parcels of confiscated land were sold in the west, compared with only one in the east. Clearly, the banishment of "enemies" yielded many advantages for the Bennington interests.

For Jacob Bayley, now a member of the Governor's Council, and for other eastern moderates, the steady operation of the confiscation courts underscored yet again the unscrupulous propensity of the "Arlington Junto"—led by the Allens, Moses Robinson, and Governor Chittenden—

to champion their own self-aggrandizement. To his dismay, Bayley found no recourse in the Vermont Assembly against their actions. Having agreed to the constitution's scheme of representation providing towns of fewer than eighty inhabitants with one representative and larger towns with two, Bayley assumed the more populous east would maintain a numerical advantage in the body. However, at the first meeting of the Assembly, Bayley realized he had been outfoxed when he discovered a large number of representatives from "settled" Champlain Valley towns within the purview of the Allens' Onion River Land Company.

In a conscious effort to wrest power from the Junto, Bayley agreed to sponsor an effort by sixteen New Hampshire towns situated along the Connecticut River to gain entry into Vermont. The so-called "Eastern Union" attracted frontier towns disaffected with New Hampshire's newly created scheme of proportional representation, which deprived smaller towns of representation and left them unprotected against the "iniquitous intrigues and secret designations" of vested coastal interests "in imitation of their late *British* oppressor."[57] With backwater discontent heightened by the perception that Vermont had a far more equitable system of representation, delegates from the disaffected New Hampshire towns joined with Bayley in convincing the Vermont Assembly on June 11, 1778, to accept admission of the Eastern Union towns into the independent state of Vermont.

Answering this challenge to the Arlington Junto, Governor Chittenden dispatched Ethan Allen to the Continental Congress, where he learned that congressmen had been shocked by the Vermont Assembly's action. Allen offered his apologies to New Hampshire's delegates for "the Imbecility of Vermont, in the matter of the Union," then returned from Philadelphia to advise the Vermont legislature. "From what I have heard and seen of the disapprobation, at congress, of the union with sundry towns, east of Connecticut River," Allen warned, "I am sufficiently authorised to offer it as my opinion that, except this state recede from such union, immediately, the whole power of the confederacy of the United States of America will join to annihilate the state of Vermont."[58] Amid escalating fears, the Vermont Assembly voted on October 21 to retract its support for the Eastern Union and effectively declare it "totally void, null and extinct."[59] Jacob Bayley and twenty-four of his supporters in the Assembly walked out of the session in protest.

Ethan Allen achieved a similar victory over a contingent of vocal

Yorkers in southeastern Vermont who persisted in denying Vermont's legitimacy and soliciting New York support. Encouraged by New York Governor George Clinton, who continued to grant appointments to military positions and civil offices, these partisans openly rebelled in the spring of 1779. Refusing to be conscripted into Vermont's militia after Governor Chittenden announced a draft to reinforce frontier garrisons, Yorkers further insisted they were not subject to a "fine" demanded as a substitute. With the fine roughly equivalent to the value of a cow, Yorker rebellion took the form of "cow wars," masterminded by a New York-commissioned colonel, Eleazer Patterson, who boldly led his partisans in a quest to "liberate" cows before they were auctioned off.

Fearful that the insurgency would fester, Governor Chittenden responded by calling upon Ethan Allen to ride to Putney and restore order. News of Allen's pending arrival provoked a note to the governor of New York requesting assistance, "otherwise our Persons and Property must be at the disposal of Ethan Allin which is more to be dreaded than Death with all its Terrors."[60] The New York governor, however, did not answer their pleas and Allen, armed with a writ charging forty-four men with "enimical conduct," rounded up and arrested thirty of the ringleaders and delivered them to Westminster for trial. Early in the trial the judge cited the famed English jurist Blackstone's *Commentaries* to reduce the charges against the first defendants to breaking the peace of the Republic, and then to rule favorably on a motion by counsel for the defense to drop all charges against several other prisoners. An outraged Allen interrupted with the retort that, "with my logic and reasoning from the eternal fitness of things, I can upset your Blackstones, your whitestones, your gravestones, and your brimstones." A lengthy tirade followed, with Allen demanding that the "enemies of our noble State" receive the harsh sentence of banishment. On this occasion, Allen was overruled. The conspirators in the "cow wars" controversy received only minor fines and "a friendly admonition," as though to belittle their actions, and Chittenden himself issued a blanket pardon to all who had revolted. Internal challenges to Vermont's legitimacy had clearly been addressed.[61]

By late 1779, Vermonters in general and the Arlington Junto in particular had overcome a multitude of problems. Their largest remaining issue, however—gaining recognition of Vermont as a new state from the Continental Congress—remained unresolved. In the Congress few delegates spoke openly on Vermont's behalf, fearful of incurring New York's wrath or, in several cases, of bolstering similar secessionist movements in their own states. Congress, in fact, traditionally had been too fractured and too preoccupied to consider the Grants issue at any length. However, with congressional opposition to an independent Vermont growing in the aftermath of the Eastern Union dispute, and with New Hampshire now adding its voice to those of Massachusetts and New York in laying claim to sections of Vermont, the Continental Congress turned its attention to resolving the crisis.

In June 1779, Congress sent two delegates to interview Governor Chittenden to determine how to defuse the Grants situation. They posed the question: Would Vermont consider giving up its independence if New York agreed to recognize the legitimacy of the New Hampshire grants? Chittenden responded that too much had transpired, Vermont could not turn back: "We are in the fullest sense as unwilling to be under the Jurisdiction of New-York as we can conceive America would to revert back under the Power of Great Britain . . . and we should consider our Liberties and Privileges (both civil and religious) equally exposed in future Invasions."[62]

Notwithstanding the Continental Congress's insistence that it would quickly resolve an issue that some in Philadelphia feared might soon endanger the country's future unity and peace, Chittenden and his cohorts refused even to accept Congress's right to determine Vermont's fate. Having been ordered not to issue any further land grants pending a decision from Congress, Vermont's Assembly responded defiantly in October 1779, voting to bestow upon its two Revolutionary native sons, Ethan Allen and Samuel Herrick, two islands in the northern part of Lake Champlain, henceforth to be known as the Heroes, North and South.

In September 1780, Chittenden dispatched Ira Allen and Stephen Rowe Bradley to Philadelphia with a new and explosive warning. Given Congress's reticence to accept Vermont's admission into the Union, the State of Vermont remained "at liberty to offer, or accept, terms of cessation of hostilities with Great-Britain, without the approbation of any other man or body of men."[63] Very simply, Vermont considered itself free to negotiate with Canada for readmission into the British Empire.

The Allens, in fact, had conversed at length with the British in the so-called Haldimand Negotiations. "The return of the people of Vermont to their allegiance," Lord George Germain wrote in February 1781, was "an event of the utmost importance to the King's affairs."[64] Through such a "return," the British hoped to prevent any further military offensives launched against them from the Champlain Valley and to drive a wedge deep into the New England–New York region. Conversations had begun in the fall of 1780 when Ethan Allen met in Castleton with a former Green Mountain Boy, Justus Sherwood, representing the commander-in-chief of the British army in Canada, General Frederick Haldimand. Advising Allen "that Congress was only duping them and waited for a favourable opportunity to Crush them," Sherwood posed a question: Would Allen consider Vermont becoming a British province with the assurance that Vermont's land titles would be validated? Allen remained noncommittal, but accepted Sherwood's offer to call a temporary truce as a sign of good faith while insisting the conversations be kept secret.[65]

When news of the surprising British offer reached the Vermont legislature, rumors began to circulate among opponents of the Arlington Junto of involvement by Ethan Allen in secret negotiations with the British. Denouncing "such false and ignominious aspersions" leveled against him, Allen publicly resigned his position as a brigadier general.[66] To Seth Warner, he acknowledged receipt of letters inviting him to deliver Vermont to the British, yet insisted he had not responded. Still, he declared defiantly that the Continental Congress's failure to provide recognition meant that Vermont had "an indubitable right to agree on Terms of Cessation of Hostilities with Great Britain." Vermont interests, he concluded, would be upheld at all costs: "Rather than fail, [I] will retire with hardy Green Mountain Boys into the desolate Caverns of the Mountains, and wage war with Human nature at large."[67]

With Ethan Allen under public scrutiny, the responsibility of conducting subsequent negotiations now fell to brother Ira. From late fall 1780 until May 1781, Ira Allen debated the specific terms for readmission, frustrating both Sherwood and Haldimand by insisting on separate occasions that the two men lacked the necessary authority to authorize such terms. The frustrated Haldimand had earlier described Allen and his followers as "a collection of the most abandoned wretches that ever lived" and by August 1781, had concluded that the negotiations were nothing but a ruse.[68] Should the British win the war, "Vermont will gladly become loyal," Haldimand observed; "if the contrary, she will declare for Congress, being actuated as well by interest as Heartfelt Attachment to their cause— In six months she will be a Respectable Ally to either side."[69]

At the height of the Haldimand conversations, the Eastern Union revived. With Connecticut River towns vulnerable to British attack seeking refuge under Vermont's truce, the Vermont General Assembly voted to annex thirty-four river towns. This time, the Allens not only supported the Union but worked with a group of fifteen Hudson Valley towns that, for reasons similar to the Connecticut River towns, proposed to secede from New York and join Vermont. The admission of both the "Eastern" and "Western" unions doubled Vermont's size, greatly enlarged its population, and extended its jurisdiction west to the Hudson and north through the Champlain Valley to Canada.

The issue of "Greater Vermont" quickly became folded into the Haldimand negotiations. At a September 1781 meeting the British issued Ira Allen an ultimatum either to negotiate forthrightly or face renewed warfare; Ira ended the deadlock and agreed to terms. Vermont would reenter the British Empire, provided it gained validation of all New Hampshire titles, assurance of free trade with Canada, and inclusion of the Eastern and Western Unions as part of Vermont. Ira devised a strategy for implementing the plan. A large British force, led by General Barry St. Leger, would be dispatched from Montreal to Ticonderoga. Upon receiving word from Ira, General St. Leger would issue a proclamation incorporating the already agreed-upon terms. At this point, the Allens, whether admitting their complicity or not, would convince the newly elected assembly to accept the terms.

Were the Allens serious? Historians Henry Steele Wardner and Chilton Williamson maintain that the Allens' actions were governed by their recognition that the future of their Onion River Land Company rested in cheap trade with Canada. Wardner insists a "round robin" letter, signed by the Allens, Governor Chittenden, and several other members of the Arlington Junto and forwarded to Haldimand in September 1781, is conclusive proof of intent.[70] Other scholars, however, insist that the Allens' failure to provide General St. Leger with a signal as promised demonstrates that the negotiations were simply an ingenious ploy designed to draw Congress's attention to reconsidering statehood for Vermont. Whatever the case, news of Lord Cornwallis's defeat caused General St. Leger's expedition to return to Canada, and the British shelved the plan. Nevertheless, six months later, in June 1782, the British Secret Service operating in the Champlain Valley dispatched agents to kidnap Jacob Bayley, whom the British viewed as their chief obstacle to reviving plans to return Vermont to the Crown. However, Bayley discovered their intentions and escaped to

Haverhill, New Hampshire. After the declaration of peace between the United States and Great Britain in 1783, the British finally terminated their Vermont efforts.

Meanwhile, Congress, ever conscious of the "Canada option," had remained unwilling to employ violence to resolve the "Vermont problem." Shortly after the creation of "Greater Vermont" in August 1781, congressmen hinted they would consider admitting Vermont as a state if the two Unions were dissolved. George Washington tendered this offer himself five months later. "It appears," he wrote to Chittenden in January 1782, "that the dispute of boundary is the only one which exists, and that, this being removed, all further difficulties would be removed also." Vermonters thus complied, only to discover that Washington could not deliver. New York held firm in its opposition, and retained the support of Virginia, the Carolinas, and Georgia. James Madison attributed these states' resistance to solving the Vermont problem to their concern for "the influence of the example on a premature dismemberment of the other states" and, as well, to "the inexpediency of admitting so unimportant a state, to an equal vote, in deciding on peace." Almost another decade would pass before the final obstacles to Vermont statehood finally yielded.[71]

The Rise of Rival Leadership

By 1783, long-settled Vermont communities such as Bennington, Windsor, and Springfield exhibited a degree of sophistication befitting mature New England towns. In many areas social structures already had begun to stratify. An analysis of probate estates left by Bennington County residents who died between 1778 and 1783 reveals enormous differences in the accumulation of wealth. At the bottom of the economic scale stood propertyless servants, laborers, tenant farmers, transients, and—remarkably—slaves, still allowed under the terms of Article I of the state's constitution. A case in point is a "Negro boy" valued at £60 and listed among the probated "property" of farmer John Armstrong. Modest landowners comprised a second, and far larger class of residents. Typically, these individuals had been able to acquire their land with a three- or four-year mortgage and no down payment. They accounted for more than three-quarters of the estates probated in Bennington. A small elite of large property holders sat atop the social pyramid. This group included men such as James Breakenridge, Samuel Robinson, and Rev. Jedidiah Dewey, who "financed and led the town's settlement and, thus, controlled its land supply." These men had accumulated the largest proportion of their wealth from land sales, supplemented in some instances by their ownership of saw and grist mills and inns. Unsurprisingly, the sons of these fathers would also wield enormous financial and political influence in their communities for years to come.[72]

Evidence of similar stratification appeared even in the newer settlements to the north, where early migrants selected the choicest lands, acquired large holdings, and sold land at considerable profit. In Addison County towns, for example, land prices rose tenfold between 1777 and 1783. However, as new settlements opened in the northern reaches, many who arrived with little or nothing were obliged to operate on marginal lands. Elias Smith, recalling his family's August 1782 journey to their new home in Woodstock, remembered that the land had been represented to them as "Canaan; a land of hills and valleys, flowing with milk and honey." "The first part," he noted, "I found true." Yet the reality of subsisting on a diet of "a little milk thickened with flour" in the weeks prior to harvest led Smith to fantasize the "rich living" within their reach "if we could have been supplied with a sufficiency of potatoes."[73]

Seth Hubbell recorded a more graphic tale of "sufferings" in his account of the Hubbell family's experience as the first settlers in Wolcott following their migration from Norwalk, Connecticut, in February 1789. Hubbell trekked through snow depths of four feet, lost one of his oxen to starvation, and arrived having "not a mouthful of meat or kernel of grain for my family, nor . . . a cent of money left to buy with." He traded a sable skin "carried fifty miles" for half a bushel of wheat, and acquired moose meat from "an Indian." Denied fifty acres that had been promised him, he sold his remaining ox and horse to buy his land, leaving him only a single cow, which he lost in June in an accident. Possessing only "one axe and an old hoe," he cleared two acres along the river during his first year, pausing "when too faint to labour" to catch fish which his family broiled and ate "without bread or salt." His "misfortunes" continued, as an early frost destroyed his corn crop, obliging him to travel twenty miles to exchange two and a half yards of whitened linen (doubtless spun and woven by his wife, part of her contribution to the household economy, although Hubbell is silent on the matter) for eight quarts of seed corn, a transaction he characterized as "extortion." In early fall, he traveled forty miles to Grand Isle to exchange his labor in harvesting a wheat crop for a bushel and a half of the

A HOME IN THE WILDERNESS

Above, "A Home in the Wilderness," from *A Vermont Settler's Own Story*, reprinted from the *Original Narrative of Seth Hubbell, First Settler of Wolcott, 1789*, privately printed for Marvin E. Hatch, Solitarian Press, Hartland, Vermont, Christmas, 1941. Right, detail from "A Correct map of the state of Vermont from actual survey; exhibiting the county and town lines, rivers, lakes, ponds, mountains, meeting houses, mills public roads, &c." (1796), by James Whitelaw; engraved by Amos Doolittle. In contrast with the wilderness homestead with its tree stumps still littering the cleared field surrounded by forest, Whitelaw's map shows a settled, orderly, and prosperous farmstead. *Both from the Vermont Historical Society.*

grain, which he brought back to his family "and was welcomed home with tears." Similar arrangements in harvesting potatoes, and in hunting and bartering with neighbors, provided Hubbell short-term "sustenance" until his farm could sustain his family. Forty years later, in recording his "narrative of sufferings," the pioneer farmer could only express "wonder and astonishment" at his ability to bear up, in the face of "slow progress" emanating from his "raw and inexperienced" efforts to clear his lands and meet the family's food needs amid such recurring and unexpected hardships.[74]

Few pioneers in Vermont during the 1780s left such extensive narratives to corroborate or challenge the typicality of Seth Hubbell's "sufferings." Visitors, however, who traversed large sections of the state, provide extensive evidence that the Vermont frontier of that period was multidimensional and diverse. Jonathan Carpenter, a soldier in the Revolution

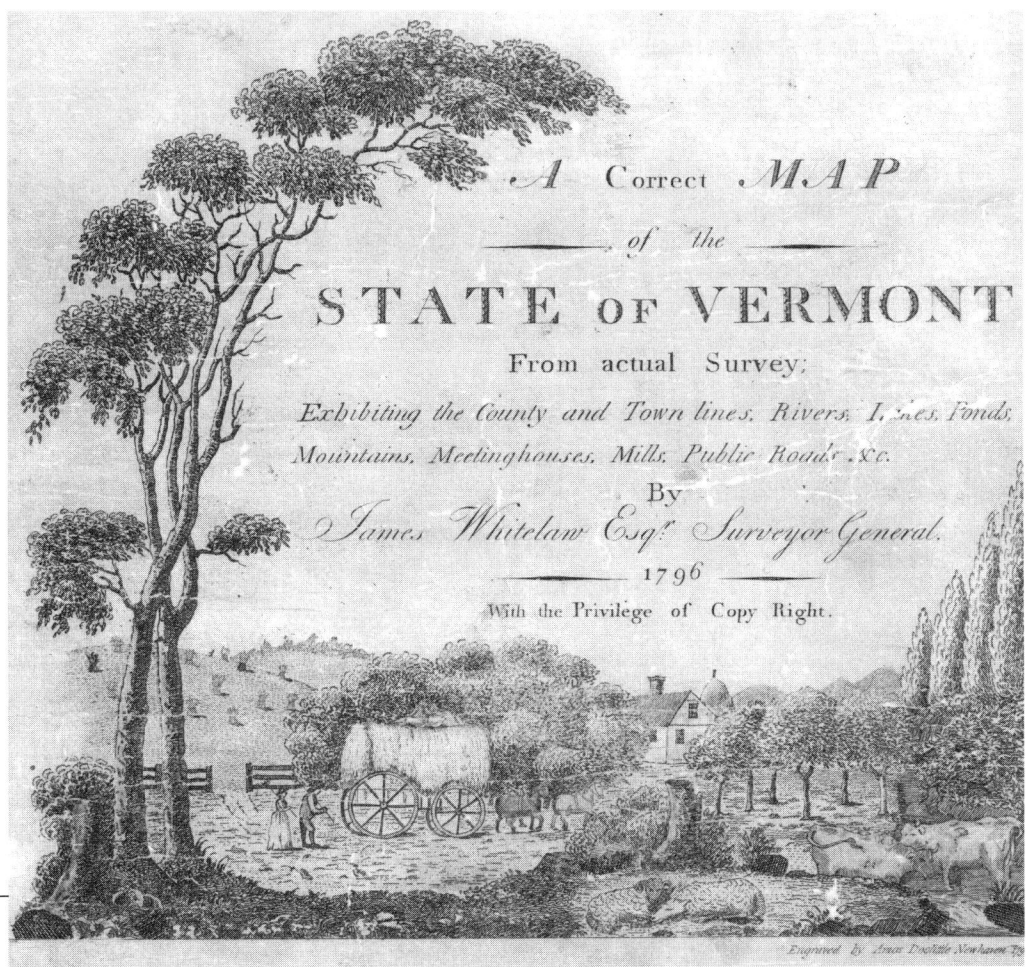

from Rehoboth, Massachusetts, kept a diary from 1774 to 1789 that provides his accounts of both the war and his later years as an early settler in Randolph, Vermont. His experience was far less traumatic and dramatic than Hubbell's and he reported a regular round of seasonal activities of planting, sowing, reaping, and tapping maple trees for sugar. Occasional natural disasters struck, such as an invasion of worms in July 1781, or the annoyance of wolves attacking livestock each August. But his experience of frontier Vermont was generally far more benign than Hubbell's and he recorded, for example on May 2, 1782, from Pomfret, where he worked as hired help, "nothing remarkable all generally Healthy in these parts. ye snow ben gone 2 weeks."[75]

The Reverend Nathan Perkins, a Congregational minister who undertook a missionary tour of the "new settlements" during the late spring of 1789, captured this diversity of conditions and lifestyles in early Vermont in his "narrative." Entering Vermont at Pownal, he found "poor land" occupied by a "miserable set of inhabitants—no religion, Rhode Island haters of religion—baptists, quakers & some presbyterians." Yet his next stop, Bennington, was a "good town of land," with "people proud" who had created an impressive community with "some elegant buildings," including a "tolerable Court-house & jail" and a "good grammar school." As he traveled northward into the newest settlements, conditions grew increasingly primitive in the eyes of the cleric: "Far absent—in ye wilderness—among all strangers—all alone—among log-huts—people nasty—poor—low-lived—indelicate—and miserable cooks." On the other hand, Perkins acknowledged the impressiveness of Governor Thomas Chittenden's farm in Williston: "1000 acres,—hundred acres of wheat on ye onion river—200 acres of extraordinary interval land." So, too, he described General Samuel Strong's home in Addison as "a pleasant place on ye Lake." Although in good Calvinist style Perkins expressed gratitude for having endured "ye perils of journeying," his narrative underscored a vast range of frontier landscapes and experiences.[76]

Throughout the 1780s, the combination of new settlers and changing economic circumstances associated with the end of the war contributed to a new political landscape in which the authority of the Arlington Junto faced a challenge from a growing rival leadership. Allegiances that had formed amid the political intrigues of the 1770s no longer commanded the spirit of urgency or the loyalties of newcomers, whose suspicions were raised by "irregularities" within the prevailing political process.

The most prominent public figure to fall from grace during the 1780s was Ira Allen. A mainstay of Vermont politics from his arrival, Ira had persuaded his older brother Ethan to invest in and later to defend the Onion River lands against "Yorker" encroachments, and had spearheaded the drive for Vermont independence in 1777. In succeeding years, Ira Allen wielded tremendous power in his often-overlapping tenures as state treasurer, surveyor-general, member of the Governor's Council, propagandist, and unofficial ambassador-at-large. Yet, as his critical role in the Haldimand negotiations demonstrated, he maintained his power on a shaky foundation of clandestine deals, dubious policies, and irregular financial practices. With the end of war, Ira's vulnerability rendered him a prime target for a new breed of politicians.

Isaac Tichenor played the central role in Allen's downfall. A Princeton graduate, Tichenor had come to Bennington in 1777 as an army supply officer and remained to develop a highly successful political career. Nicknamed "the Jersey Slick" for his origins and his own political finagling, Tichenor initiated attacks on Allen in 1782 for his unaudited records as state treasurer. In 1785, Tichenor sponsored an act that annulled all of Ira's town surveys on the grounds that his slovenly practices had produced innumerable boundary disputes. The act also prohibited Ira from ever again practicing his occupation as a surveyor in the state of Vermont. Over the next five years, Tichenor forced Allen to resign or lose all his statewide offices and most of his political power.

Tichenor was only one of the new breed of politicians who joined the so-called rival leadership. Nathaniel Chipman enlisted, as well. After serving under George Washington's command at Valley Forge, the youthful and ambitious Yale graduate migrated from Litchfield County, Connecticut (where Ethan Allen spent his early years), to seek his fortune on the Vermont frontier. In stark contrast to Allen, however, Chipman set up a law practice in Tinmouth. Only the third lawyer to settle in Vermont, Chipman aspired, as he wrote a Yale classmate, "to become the oracle of law to the state."[77] With considerable legal trade arising from the instabilities generated by war and land disputes, Chipman succeeded in acquiring a statewide reputation, which he parlayed into a position as Rutland County state's attorney in 1781 and, in 1784, as Tinmouth's representative to the Vermont Assembly.

Chipman's arrival in the legislature corresponded with a growing controversy surrounding the Betterment Act. Following the 1780 passage of a Redemption Act restoring property and civil rights to Loyalists, Governor Chittenden and his Arlington Junto colleague, Matthew Lyon, had convinced the Assembly that settlers who occupied the properties during the Revolution should be reimbursed for all improvements, or "betterments," made during their tenure. Chipman steadfastly insisted upon a strict adherence to law, asserting that because the settlers were "trespassers" who had illegally occupied land they did not own, they deserved no compensation.[78] The General Assembly, divided along factional lines and deadlocked on this issue, submitted the question to an advisory referendum in 1783. However, even after voters approved an act for full compensation, Chipman, Tichenor, and their supporters joined together and refused to pass the bill that Lyon and Chittenden favored, demanding instead a compromise restricting the amount dispossessed settlers could collect. The 1785 Betterment Act, finally accepted by the legislature, contained the Chipman faction's limiting amendments.

Although Matthew Lyon portrayed the contest as one pitting "democrats" against "aristocrats," Chipman's political conservatism continued to gain support in the face of growing economic difficulties. By late 1785, Vermont followed the rest of America into a deep depression resulting from the closing of lucrative British markets in the West Indies and the loss of British specie. Alternative currencies existed in the form of state notes issued during the war; yet the proliferation of these notes without solid backing in gold and silver rendered exchange of diverse state currencies problematic. Merchants, obligated to purchase British goods with British specie, insisted that they, too, be paid in specie.

In rural areas such as Vermont, where exchanges had traditionally been paid in produce or paper notes, the deteriorating economy created a growing number of debt cases that once again clogged the courts. As before, popular discontent found a voice in public rallies, mobs, and court riots. On October 31, 1786, a mob of thirty men armed with "guns, bayonets, swords, clubs, drums, fifes, and other warlike instruments"[79] under the command of Robert Morrison, a Hartland blacksmith, and Benjamin Stebbins, a Barnard farmer, threatened to close the Windsor courthouse. The mob dispersed, however, before the sheriff arrived. Three weeks later, a group of men calling themselves "regulators" similarly assembled at the start of the Rutland County court session to decry the high costs and numerous debts contracted by citizens to satisfy court and attorney's fees. Threats to bring a halt to court sessions, banish lawyers, and resist the sheriffs resounded throughout Vermont's countryside.

In an effort to diffuse public tensions, Governor Chittenden submitted proposals to the February 1787 assembly session in Bennington. One proposal called for a General Tender Act that would permit farmers devoid of specie to repay debts with farm produce, including "neat cattle, beef, pork, sheep, wheat, rye and Indian corn,"[80] which were assigned an inflated value. In addition, Chittenden proposed creating a state bank that would allow farmers to obtain mortgages on property and possessions, and that would be authorized to issue scrip as legal tender. Chipman quickly mobilized his colleagues in opposition to the bills. While acknowledging that the short-term issuance of scrip would benefit large landholders including the Governor who "is [$]3000 in arrears to the treasury [to] discharge the same

Above: From 1781 to 1791 the State of Vermont issued fiscal paper, or bills of credit, to cover costs incurred by government. The first bills were printed in eight specific denominations. Later the state issued these "check-like" bills, printed with blanks for recording the certificate number, date, amount, and signature of the state treasurer (Ira Allen, 1778 until 1787; Samuel Mattocks, 1786 until 1800). Forbidden under the U.S. Constitution to continue issuing its own currency, the state ceased to produce these bills after 1791.

Left: From 1785 to 1788 the state also issued copper coins under its own authority, to serve as small change for local transactions. The reverse of this "landscape" design featured an "all seeing eye" with fourteen rays and the inscription, "Stella Quarta Decima"—the fourteenth star, a reference to Vermont's expectation of being admitted to the Union as the fourteenth state. *Both from the Vermont Historical Society.*

[with] paper money," Chipman warned that spiraling inflation over time would depreciate the notes at a rate of "a thousand to one," bankrupt "every merchant and trader in the state," and place farmers who held mortgaged lands in severe jeopardy of forfeiting their properties. The populist cures proposed by Chittenden, Chipman concluded, would "greatly increase and prolong the sufferings of the people."[81]

This time, Chipman succeeded in capturing public opinion. By a referendum margin of more than four to one, Vermonters rejected Chittenden's state bank and General Tender Act, allowing Chipman to substitute a Specific Tender Act requiring that only "such articles of personal property as the debtor had contracted to pay" be accepted by the creditor.

Vermonters' growing support for Chipman and his rival leadership's advocacy of fiscal restraint and political conservatism underscored a growing shift taking hold in Vermont politics.

While Chittenden and the Arlington Junto now hesitated to join the Union based on their concerns about the validity of their old New Hampshire land titles and the future of Vermont's trade relations with Canada, events unfolding outside Vermont's borders further strengthened Chipman's advocacy for Vermont statehood. Deteriorating economic conditions in Massachusetts spurred debt-ridden farmers, led by revolutionary Captain Daniel Shays, to rise in armed insurrection against the state government in the summer of 1786. Shays's efforts were eventually defeated, and many of the rebels sought refuge in Vermont, including Shays himself. Notwithstanding Governor Chittenden's proclamation warning Vermonters not to "harbor, entertain, or conceal" the insurgents, authorities made no effort to round up leaders and return them to Massachusetts for trial. These events propelled the movement to revise the Articles of Confederation, which resulted in the drafting of a new Constitution in 1787. They also raised new concerns among the northern states about Vermont continuing to remain outside the Union.

Even before America's constitutional delegates assembled in Philadelphia in May 1787, to discuss "the exigencies of the Union," the problem of creating new states from the existing ones had emerged as a political issue threatening the new and fragile union. As historian Peter Onuf has demonstrated, "the Vermont problem" was but one of several similar conundrums facing the Constitutional Convention. Although the specter of Vermont was prominent in the minds of delegates for its seeming advocacy of a dangerous brand of democratic demagoguery, they were mindful that the residents of Kentucky had petitioned Congress to make a state from that western portion of Virginia. The interests of sectional balance, therefore, began to play a role in moving Congress toward seeking resolution of these territorial disputes. The convention solved the problem of state-making with Article IV, section 3, which provided for making new states "formed or erected within the Jurisdiction of any other State [or] formed by the Junction of two or more States, or Parts of States" with "the Consent of the Legislatures of the States concerned as well as of the Congress."[82]

What remained, after solving the constitutional problem, was, on the one hand, to secure the consent of New York to relinquish its claim to Vermont and, on the other hand, to secure the consent of Vermont to the terms of separation and the terms of admission to the Union as a state. Seizing the moment provided by anxieties about Shays's Rebellion, Nathaniel Chipman wrote to Alexander Hamilton on July 15, 1788. Chipman advised Hamilton, now serving in the New York State legislature, of Vermonters' excitement about the promise of the new federal Constitution and their willingness to enter the Union if given assurances that federal courts would not invalidate New Hampshire titles and that some form of "compensation" arrangement could be reached with New York. Hamilton agreed that Kentucky's bid for independence from Virginia rendered this a "favorable moment" for effecting Vermont's entry into the Union, and promised to use his influence to arrange an agreement with New York.[83] In February 1789 the lower house of the New York legislature passed a bill granting consent for Congress to acknowledge Vermont as a state. Although it suffered defeat in the state senate, the bill signaled a change of opinion and opened the way for serious negotiations. Governor Chittenden, however, still worried that Congress might reject the deal with New York, thereby leaving landowners with New Hampshire titles vulnerable to enormous debts or losses, refused to promote the drive toward statehood and insisted that Ira Allen be appointed one of three negotiators dispatched to Congress. Only the outbreak of the "Woodbridge scandal," involving the assembly's discovery that Chittenden had granted Ira Allen a town charter without consent of the Council, finally enabled Chipman to conclude his campaign to guide Vermont's entry into the Union. The scandal led to Chittenden's defeat in the October 1789 election.

With Chittenden temporarily removed from power, discussion resumed toward reaching an agreement with New York that would clear the way to statehood. By March 1790, the New York and Vermont legislatures appointed new commissioners to negotiate the terms for separation and New York's consent to Congress to acknowledge the state, to determine boundaries, and to agree upon compensation to New York for the loss—as it insisted on terming it—of lands on its eastern border. On October 7, the commission finally issued its report, which included the settlement of the western boundary of Vermont and compensation to New York of $30,000 to be paid by June 1, 1794. The Vermont General Assembly passed the bill confirming the agreement on October 28, 1790.

Anticipating the final resolution of this long struggle and the consequence of recognition and admission to the Union by an act of Congress, the General Assembly also passed a bill calling for a state convention to meet in January 1791 to consider ratification of the United States Constitution—the last hurdle barring the way to statehood. A new generation of leaders took their places to enact this last scene of Vermont's march toward statehood and the first act of its union with the new nation. Of the 109 delegates who convened at the 1791 statehood convention at Bennington, only twelve had been present at the 1777 Windsor convention that declared Vermont's independence. Gone were the cohort of Green Mountain Boys, including Ethan Allen (who died in 1789), Seth Warner (1784), and Remember Baker (1775), and while the governor, Thomas Chittenden (reelected in 1790) and Ira Allen attended, neither played important roles. With two-thirds of Vermont's residents newly arrived since 1783, lawyers, large landholders, and merchants now led the cause of union. Nathaniel Chipman proclaimed in his keynote address to the convention that statehood offered Vermont the opportunity to break out of her "narrow limits," to resolve economic instabilities, and to share in "the reflected greatness of the empire with which we unite."[84] On January 10, 1791, by a vote of 105 to 4, the delegates ratified the United States Constitution and on March 4, Vermont finally gained admittance "as a new and entire member of the United States of America."[85]

With Vermont finally ensconced in the Union, the state's politics became subsumed within a larger political dynamic. Rivalries erupting at the national level between strong Federalists led by Alexander Hamilton and Democratic Republican followers of Thomas Jefferson spilled over into Vermont. Nathaniel Chipman quickly gave his allegiance to the Federalist party, serving as the first federal judge for the District of Vermont, and then, in 1797, as United States senator. Despite these contributions to early Vermont, Chipman's later undying devotion to Federalist politics led to the collapse of his political career and slide into relative obscurity. Today, as historians Samuel Hand and Jeffrey Potash noted, "Vermont hearts seldom quicken at the mention of [his] name. Neither can he be said to occupy a conspicuous place in the state's collective memory."[86]

A more colorful political career was that of Ethan Allen's protegé and Governor Chittenden's son-in-law, Matthew Lyon. An Irish immigrant who had fought with the Green Mountain Boys, Lyon developed the town of Fair Haven into a thriving community complete with store, hotel, mills, forges, an iron furnace, and a newspaper. Gradually he emerged as the chief spokesman for Jefferson's Democratic Republican views in Vermont. Lyon

February 21st. — Coll. Humphreys appointed this day Minister resident to the Queen of Portugal.

Congress of the United States:

AT THE THIRD SESSION,

Begun and held at the City of Philadelphia, on Monday the sixth of December, one thousand seven hundred and ninety.

An ACT *for the* ADMISSION *of the* STATE *of* VERMONT *into this* UNION.

THE State of Vermont having petitioned the Congress to be admitted a member of the United States, *Be it enacted by the* SENATE *and* HOUSE *of* REPRESENTATIVES *of the United States of America in Congress assembled, and it is hereby enacted and declared,* That on the fourth day of March, one thousand seven hundred and ninety-one, the said State, by the name and title of "the State of Vermont," shall be received and admitted into this Union, as a new and entire member of the United States of America.

FREDERICK AUGUSTUS MUHLENBERG,
Speaker of the House of Representatives.

JOHN ADAMS, *Vice-President of the United States, and President of the Senate.*

APPROVED, February the eighteenth, 1791.

GEORGE WASHINGTON, *President of the United States.*

DEPOSITED among the ROLLS in the OFFICE of the SECRETARY of STATE.

Th: Jefferson, Secretary of State.

Presented to the Historical Society of Vermont by Frank M. Etting of Philadelphia.

Act of Congress admitting Vermont to the Union as one of the United States. Approved, February 18, 1791. *Vermont Historical Society.*

"Congressional Pugilists," a contemporary cartoon depicting the fight between Representatives Roger Griswold of Connecticut (right, brandishing a walking stick), and Matthew Lyon of Vermont (wielding the fire tongs) on the floor of Congress, Philadelphia, February 15, 1798. *Vermont Historical Society.*

spearheaded the state drive in the early 1790s to organize "Democratic Societies" to counter the pro-British leanings of the Federalists and allow "the great body of people themselves [to] undertake to watch over the government." In 1796 Lyon gained election to Congress from the western district of Vermont. Possessing an acerbic tongue and a hot temper, he acquired national notoriety when a heated exchange with Connecticut Federalist Roger Griswold culminated with Lyon spitting in Griswold's face in response to an accusation of cowardice during the Revolution. The Vermonter escaped congressional expulsion at the hands of Federalists who nevertheless labeled him a "kennel of filth." He had less luck with Griswold himself, who chose to retaliate by attacking Lyon at his desk in the House chamber, striking "more than twenty blows on his head" with his cane before Lyon managed to retrieve a pair of tongs to defend himself.[87]

Undeterred by these events, Lyon next became entangled in the national controversy brought on by President John Adams's legislative efforts to muzzle attacks against his administration's pro-British stance. Known as the Sedition Act of 1798, the legislation sought to punish "any false, scandalous and malicious writing" that brought "disrepute on the President or Congress." Lyon quickly thrust himself to the forefront of the Jeffersonian opposition. He charged that Adams had shown an "unbounded thirst for ridiculous pomp, foolish adulation, or selfish avarice,"[88] and his writings in his newspaper *The Scourge of Aristocracy* earned him the distinction of being one of only eighteen Americans indicted under the Sedition Act. Found guilty in federal circuit court in Rutland, Lyon received a fine of one thousand dollars and a sentence of four months in a Vergennes jail cell. The Federalist *Hartford [Connecticut] Courant* newspaper trumpeted that "the beast was now caged and on exhibit in Vergennes,"[89] but Lyon's conviction elevated his status to Republican martyr and he gained reelection to Congress while confined to his cell.

Despite Lyon's colorful career, the title of Vermont's most flamboyant politician during the 1790s justly belongs to Ira Allen. During the 1780s Ira experienced waning political influence. In addition, Ira's involvement with his brother Levi in the timber trade with Canada brought a disastrous decline in their economic circumstances as a result of plummeting prices and other complications. While Montreal merchants acknowledged the importance of Vermont lumber, the rate of exchange had so far deteriorated, Levi wrote Ira in 1787, that he "would sooner take my pistols and commence a highwayman" than seek to negotiate with his Montreal creditors.[90] Unwilling to ascribe his difficulties to his own financial miscalculations, Ira grew increasingly obsessed with building a canal around the Richelieu rapids, to prevent the significant losses that occurred when his lumber, traveling the rapids, became splintered and commercially worthless. More than that, Ira wanted direct access to the ocean and a method for bypassing the merchant middlemen who, he believed, denied him his rightful profits.

In the late 1780s he failed in an effort to gain Haldimand's help in funding a canal, and he relinquished increasing amounts of his Onion River lands to pay his bills. His continued obsession with a Richelieu canal, however, led him, in December 1795, to plead his case directly to Britain. To finance his mission, he put up forty-five thousand acres of his choicest lands as collateral. In London, Ira contacted William H. C. Bentinck, the home secretary in William Pitt's government, proposing a project that involved the construction of a sixteen-mile ship canal extending from St. John to the St. Lawrence River. The negotiations with British officials consumed four months but yielded no formal decision.

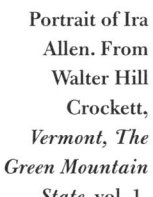
Portrait of Ira Allen. From Walter Hill Crockett, *Vermont, The Green Mountain State*, vol. 1.

Frustrated at the unresponsiveness of the London bureaucracy, and increasingly worried about his family's economic survival, Ira set out on a quite different scheme. He traveled from London to Paris in late May 1796, where he arranged to acquire twenty thousand guns from the revolutionary French government, the Directory. In this transaction, Ira ostensibly acted on a commission given him by Governor Chittenden to purchase European arms for the state militia. Historians long believed, however, that Ira's true intent in the arms acquisition was simply profiteering. Documentary evidence recently discovered in the French National Archives reveals that neither explanation was correct. The archival records show that Ira actually had made an agreement with the French government to assist in fomenting a revolution in Canada to overthrow British rule. The Directory promised to dispatch French fleets to subdue the Maritimes and move toward Québec in the late summer of 1797, while Ira would oversee the arming of American adventurers and French Canadians at Missisquoi in a land attack from the south. Victory in this undertaking, and the subsequent creation of a new republic, United Columbia, would not only wrestle Canada away from the British and lead to the latter's financial collapse but, of equal importance for the French revolutionaries, also liberate Québec from the stranglehold exercised by the Catholic Church and permit the redistribution of Church properties among the poor. Ira's commission from Chittenden to buy European arms would merely serve to divert suspicion when he returned to the United States with the twenty thousand French muskets.

Prior to embarking on the plan, Ira went back to London to learn of any forthcoming progress on his canal proposal. Advised that the British did not view him as "a Man of Sufficient Property or any way Equal to Undertake So Great Business,"[91] Allen now had no reluctance to forge ahead with the French scheme. He returned to the French coastal port of Ostend, loaded his muskets and cannon aboard a chartered American ship, the *Olive Branch*, and departed for home.

Unfortunately for Ira, however, after eight days out, a British warship stopped and seized the *Olive Branch* on grounds that it had engaged in illegal trade. Ira retreated to France in May 1798, to obtain documentation from the Directory that would convince the British to release his cargo of arms. Instead, French authorities immediately imprisoned him; his trip back to London so soon after negotiating the arms deal had raised doubts in the Directory about his loyalties.

After languishing in a French prison for more than a year, and in ill health, Ira finally obtained his release. Upon returning to Vermont in May 1801, he found his financial affairs in disarray and numerous persons, including the heirs of his brothers, suing him for failing to provide them with their fair shares from the Onion River Land Company. Granted one year's special immunity from arrest at the hands of his creditors by the Vermont Assembly, Ira was forced in 1803 to deed his remaining property to a son of his brother Heman and flee Vermont to escape imprisonment for debt. He traveled first to Kentucky for a stay with his friend Matthew Lyon and then took up residence in Philadelphia, where he spent his final eleven years suing and being sued. Ira Allen died on January 15, 1814, at the age of sixty-two, and his body was buried in an unmarked pauper's grave in Philadelphia's Free Quaker burial ground.

Vermont Frontiers

In the nineteen years after achieving statehood, Vermont grew at an annual rate of eight percent, nearly tripling its population from 85,000 to almost 218,000. Much of that growth resulted from migration by settlers from other states, lured by the wide expanses of available land and the optimistic promise of a fresh start. It was, largely, a migration of youth, as reflected in the federal censuses of 1791 and 1800 which showed a majority of all Vermont residents to be sixteen years of age or younger.

Where did these newcomers choose to settle? After 1791, few desired to locate in the mature towns of the state's southern sections. In that year, Vermont's two largest communities, both situated on the state's southernmost border, were Guilford with 2,422 residents, and Bennington with 2,358, the only localities in the state with more than two thousand residents. Nine years later, in 1800, Guilford and Bennington remained Vermont's two most populous towns, yet each had actually experienced declines (of two hundred and one hundred, respectively). Indeed, both were shortly to be eclipsed by three new communities located further north: Rutland in the west, Windsor in the east, and Woodstock, conveniently located in the valley as a link between the other two. Between 1800 and 1810, the proportion of Vermont's total population that resided in the four southernmost counties fell from four-fifths to less than one-half.

The primarily northward thrust of migration between 1791 and 1810 followed the routes of least resistance, in the direction of Vermont's most fertile lands. The rush to settle on prime agricultural lands meant that few newcomers placed a premium on transplanting New England village life or even, for that matter, residing in close proximity to neighbors. An examination of settlement patterns in the rich farmlands of Addison County's Champlain Valley supports this conclusion, revealing a process determined essentially by the quality of available soil. Modern-day soil survey maps indicate roughly one-third of Addison County soils to be of the "Vergennes-Covington association" type, a clayish soil deemed most suitable for farming.[92] Transposing settlement patterns in 1791 onto modern-day soil maps reveals that, with few exceptions, settlers flocked to these soils, consciously ignoring even marginally less productive lands.

Focused on staking their claims to the soils that promised the highest agricultural yields, newcomers exhibited little interest in amenities that, in more recent times, rendered certain sites far more attractive than others. Lakefront property is one illustration. In the period of settlement, narrow twenty-six-acre second-division lots abutting Lake Champlain in Shoreham were consolidated and sold at prices equivalent to or actually lower than those of other Shoreham properties. Similarly, sites with fast-running waters suitable for mills rarely, if ever, were selected early in the initial settlement process and, indeed, incentives often had to be offered to entice someone to build sawmills and gristmills.

The logic for these choices was simple. The vast majority of migrants, estimated at eighty to ninety percent, planned to take up farming. Contrasted with the exhausted soils of southern New England from which most had come, Vermont's best soils promised astounding productivity. Whereas the nutrients in southern New England soils had depleted to the point that farmers had been forced to substitute corn for wheat as their primary grain staple, newly cleared Vermont lands commonly produced twenty to thirty bushels of wheat per acre. High demand to the south, Samuel Williams reported, meant that "the first crop of wheat will fully pay him [the farmer] for all the expense he has been at, in clearing up, sowing, and fencing his land."[93] Thus, wheat became a key "cash crop," alongside potash. In 1792, western Vermont farmers exported thirty thousand bushels of surplus wheat. New settlers anticipated that two or three years of hard labor clearing lands and growing wheat could be parlayed into economic independence.

Problems of transportation, however, limited what Vermonters could produce. Champlain Valley farmers desiring to ship their produce northward faced a quandary similar to the challenge Ira Allen had confronted leading to his obsession with building a canal around the Richelieu rapids. So, too, Connecticut Valley residents, desiring to ship southward, encountered a series of rapids on the river that required that goods be unloaded, transported overland, and then reloaded, adding significantly to their transportation costs. Yet for a growing number of communities located at considerable distance from navigable waters, the most important problem in the 1790s was the absence of a full-fledged network of roads. The military roads remained the best routes for overland transport. Farmers, initially preoccupied with clearing, cultivating, and improving their properties, rarely had the time to travel and had little inclination to be taxed to build roads. Where efforts at road construction had been undertaken, the results appeared as "hardly more than broad paths through the forest," typically widened only enough to accommodate ox-drawn carts leading from hamlet to hamlet and perhaps to a neighboring village. Where they crossed water, these "roads" presented a line of ruts with frequent mud holes and, where dry, they produced heavy dust. Road builders typically removed only the largest stones and stumps absolutely necessary to permit passage.

Visitors in the 1790s became acutely aware of such shortcomings.

Timothy Dwight, perhaps New England's most well-traveled tourist, described the road between Rutland and Middlebury in 1798 as "little wrought and of course indifferent, and the last part of the distance for about eight miles was to us dangerous. . . . [W]herever a rill crosses the path, it becomes speedily soft, and ultimately a quagmire."[94] Under such conditions, the cost of overland travel severely restricted the movement of goods both into and out of the state. Few items could withstand the expense of transportation beyond a ten- or fifteen-mile radius and still accrue a profit for the producer. Wheat was one of them. Other precious items, commanding high prices relative to their bulk, included salted meats, salted butter, and pot and pearl ashes.

Vermont's farms were, by modern standards, small yet remarkably diverse. While farm properties averaged one hundred acres or more during this era, farm families rarely cultivated more than twenty acres. In part, that reflected the prevailing tendency to rotate lands, allowing fallow land time to regenerate vital nutrients before reusing it. On the cleared acreage itself, farmers labored to produce wheat, rye, and barley for the family's consumption, along with an array of vegetables including peas, turnips, and pumpkins. They raised corn and hay primarily for the livestock, which usually included cattle, pigs, sheep, and horses. Hemp and flax were planted to provide the raw materials for the family's clothing. Orchards were also common, with apple cider deemed more healthy than water and, as it fermented during the cold winters, more satisfying.

Uriah Brigham's description of his Bakersfield farm between 1800 and 1802 illuminates the workings of an early Vermont agricultural operation. Brigham wrote to Massachusetts relatives, "we have got a very good House and Barn and about 20 acres of land under improvement which yields Us a plentiful supply of provisions and fodder." His animal stock included "a good yoak of oxen two Cows and a yearling Heifer a likely Breeding Sow 10 hens and 2 Hunting Cats." He had slaughtered one hog in the winter, "that weighed 243 lb.," and planned to kill two more in the spring "that I expect to weigh 200 lb each." Brigham also reported raising "a Great deal of Poultry and take the good of eating of it." Having sold his mare, "I live very much retir'd I sildom goe further from home than to Mill about half a Mile." Still, he had raised forty bushels of wheat, sixty-five of corn, two hundred of potatoes, and fifty pounds of flax. "I am not in extreme Poverty nor great Affluence," he concluded; "we have vituuls enough to Eat and some to sell, we are Comfortable for Cloaths ant none to spair."

The large size of the Brigham family, numbering seven children, was not unusual given the labor needed to sustain the farm. "Idleness we are strangers to," Uriah reported.[95] When Ira Allen observed in 1798 that "the labours of the family are divided and proportioned according to their strength, ingenuity, and sex,"[96] he meant that the males of the family had responsibility for tilling, planting, and harvesting the crops at varying intervals between spring and fall; repairing equipment; cutting firewood; and keeping animals fed, clean, and warm during the winter. The combined labor of wives and daughters was directed toward the chores of food preservation and preparation; caring for the vegetable, herb, and medicinal gardens; and, often, for feeding the animals. Daughters in the Brigham household were taught to "spin knit and sowe very well,"[97] tasks essential not only to clothe the family but, as general-store account books indicate, to exchange excess cloth for essential items such as salt and coffee, which could not be generated on the family farm.

Vermont folklore suggests that the vital farm partnership of husband and wife occasionally encountered problems, as in the case of the farmer "John Grumlie." Grumlie exchanged plowing responsibilities for his wife's domestic chores to prove the more demanding character of men's work, but his exasperating experience with milking cows, feeding animals, and spooling yarn obliged him to acknowledge,

> When the old woman came home from work,
> He said he could plainly see
> That she could do more work in one day
> Than he could do in three.[98]

Scholars likely have exaggerated the self-sufficiency and independence of Vermont farmers of this era. These were extraordinarily enterprising individuals, anxious to improve the quality of their lives through all available means. Consequently, despite severe limits on what they could export, Vermonters invested much energy in developing networks of internal exchange. Studies of agricultural records for the early settlement period demonstrate this scenario. The account book of Titus Hill, a Cornwall farmer whose vast land holdings placed him among the town's wealthiest residents, reveals that he generated substantially more income renting his oxen to neighbors for "plowing" and "dragging," and his horse for pulling a sleigh or making deliveries to and from the local mill, than he earned from agricultural produce. A study of Addison County probate inventories reveals that many households were deficient in such vital goods as vegetable crops, wool, animals, grain, or grasses while maintaining substantial excesses in other goods. It is not surprising, then, that local shopkeepers accepted as payment for debts corn, hay, potatoes, and other bulky produce unmarketable outside the immediate area.[99]

Residents displayed ingenuity in seizing on other opportunities that arose during the 1790s. As increasing populations boosted the volume of agricultural surpluses that could be grown yet not transported, breweries and distilleries emerged to convert the grain portion of that surplus into a "cash crop" for local as well as more distant markets of thirsty consumers. Weathersfield residents conducted a lottery in October 1789, to raise money to build a malthouse and brewery, for the purpose of "makeing of malt and also both Strong and Small Beir." In appealing for popular support, its boosters mixed economic, moral, and health motives, arguing "it will Greatly encourage the Raising of Barley and the Drinking of that most Salutiferous Liquor beer [and] prevent in a Great measure the Consumption of distilled Liquor So destructive to the health the morals and the fortunes of the Good people of this State and prevent Great Sums of Ready Cash Going out of the State."[100] Two years later, Canadian investors selected Middlebury as the location for a new five-thousand-dollar distillery because its distant location from any markets assured a low price for grain. Perhaps most interesting of these ventures was the 1792 construction of a ten-thousand-dollar distillery in Rutland, funded from the proceeds of a lottery chartered by the Vermont legislature. Advertisements for the lottery claimed the project reflected the General Assembly's patriotic wish to promote the manufacture of brandies and strong beer. By 1800, the patriotic fervor had burgeoned to the point that two hundred distilleries and breweries were scattered across the state.

Although bountiful, these enterprises did not constitute the most attractive Vermont industry. As populations grew, so did the construction of mills wherever running "water rights" could be obtained. Gristmills were by far the most plentiful type, as residents willingly paid the "toll," mandated by a 1779 Vermont law, of two quarts per bushel of Indian corn or wheat to a local miller to relieve them of the tedious task of making flour with a mortar and pestle. Sawmills, often one-man businesses, also grew in abundance as residents sought boards and planks to build frame houses and staves to produce barrels. Other critical services congregating around water came from fulling mills (cleaning and shrinking homespun cloth), oil mills (pressing linseed oil for use as a base for paints), cider mills, and paper mills. Tanneries, although not strictly mills, required copious supplies of water for tanning pits.

The abundance of water sites, the relatively small expense of constructing mills, and the unwillingness of residents to travel long distances combined to create multiple village or hamlet sites within Vermont's towns. Given the large numbers of mill owners, tanners, and blacksmiths who serviced small rural populations, many split their energies between their business and a farm. That was true, too, of shopkeepers, who typically maintained a small stock of "essentials" brought from the outside—nails, salt, imported cloth, rum—that they offered to exchange for "most kinds of country produce," running the gamut from grain to grasses, animals to vegetables. All told, these small hamlets and villages that delivered rudimentary yet essential services to the area's farming community comprised a vital element of Vermont's "self-sufficient" landscape.

Often, the multiplicity of hamlets within a township generated major disagreements over the site of the actual hub of the township. Locating a town meetinghouse typically occurred after the town had grown large enough to warrant one rather than at the inception of settlement. And it often provoked fierce disagreements among residents who understood the far-reaching ramifications of the decision. In the case of Cornwall, heated debates raged for more than a decade, with weekly religious meetings split between sites in the east and west, before settlers in 1796 finally compromised and agreed to build a meetinghouse at the precise geographic center of the town.

Disputes within townships, however, paled in comparison with the more intense competition between Vermont communities to lay claim to what historical geographers refer to as regional "central place" status. The rivalry often originated in a battle to become a county's "shiretown" and its center for court and administrative activity. Forward-thinking residents recognized that such a designation provided opportunities to further centralize regional commercial, communication, and cultural activities to efficiently service the needs of broad hinterlands.

Debates over "central place" location usually originated in claims of geographic advantage. Communities competing for the location of shiretowns frequently petitioned the Vermont legislature to consider their "natural advantages" while soliciting representatives from surrounding towns to describe such natural obstacles as "an impregnable Swamp," "impassable hills," or "unhealthy marshes" within competing towns. Such impediments obviously rendered their competitors' selection "unjust and grevously Burthensom to the greatest Part of the People Inhabiting Sd County."[101]

The overall magnitude and reliability of sources of waterpower proved to be another important factor in town growth. Towns usually developed at locations where the largest possibilities existed for industrial expansion, as, for instance, along the Otter Creek at Rutland, Middlebury, and Vergennes. And towns also emerged where roads converged or water transport facilitated the movement of goods, as along the upper Connecticut River at Norwich and Newbury. So, too, the launching of a ferry service between Shelburne and Willsboro, New York, by "Admiral of the Lake" Gideon King, and his shipping of goods between Burlington and St. John, Québec, proved instrumental in Burlington's growth.

While resources played a critical role, successful growth in these early years also appears to have depended upon the quality of local boosters. Middlebury's rapid ascent provides an example. The town contained a fine source of power with falls at the Otter Creek, yet in 1791, with a mere 395 residents, it ranked as only the ninth largest community in Addison County. Gamaliel Painter, Middlebury's ingenious "town father," proceeded systematically to bolster the town's fortunes. First, he successfully petitioned to relocate the county courthouse from Addison to Middlebury on the grounds that his town's geographic centrality would permit residents to "more easily attend to transact their necessary business."[102] At the same time, having acquired title to the lands abutting the falls, he proceeded to dispose of small lots, at little or no cost, to persons whom he judged could solidify Middlebury's "central place" status. By 1799, his valuable riverfront properties had become home to merchants, tanners, carpenters, blacksmiths, a cabinetmaker, a gunsmith, and a tavern owner. Next, he invited the Vermont legislature to hold session in Middlebury, and working in concert with Middlebury attorney Seth Storrs and other Congregationalists eager to provide higher education in a religious context, strong-armed lawmakers into granting, in 1800, a charter for Vermont's second college.[103] A scant ten years later, Painter had succeeded in boosting Middlebury's stature above that of its regional neighbors, Vergennes and Fair Haven, and had laid the groundwork for Middlebury's growth in the following decade.

Painter and his fellow Middlebury boosters also became active participants in what historians describe as a "turnpike mania" that enveloped Vermont after 1796, as the state sought to overcome its transportation constraints. Recognizing that residents of rural Vermont communities would continue to resist paying taxes to construct better-quality roads, enterprising individuals formed companies to obtain private charters from the Vermont Assembly providing monopoly rights of way. Altogether, the Assembly chartered ninety-one "toll roads" in Vermont within the span of a decade.

The Centre Turnpike Company, spearheaded by Middlebury "town fathers," offers a good illustration of an early toll road venture. The company sold a total of 279 shares of stock at $10 apiece for a turnpike to expand Middlebury's trade networks to the east, with links to Woodstock and the Connecticut River. Construction of a corduroy road, in which logs were laid across and then covered by soil to produce a relatively comfortable ride, was projected to cost $1,000 per mile. These projections proved fanciful, however, when actual costs mounted as the road began its climb into the Green Mountain foothills. Skeptical stockholders, assessed upwards of $170 per share to continue the project, finally balked in 1810. Stock values plummeted to $4, at which point officials formally dissolved the company, and the vision for a road through the mountains abruptly ended.

Many private road-making projects shared the Centre Turnpike Company's experience. Less than one-third of the toll-road and plank-road companies chartered between 1796 and 1810 became fully operational. And as visitors to the state readily testified, the improvements in travel proved to be not always as good as promised. In 1807, the English visitor John Lambert reported that the Burlington-to-Vergennes toll road "for the most part . . . lay through woods, where it required all the skill and dexterity of the driver to avoid deep ruts, huge stones, logs of wood, felled timber, and stumps of trees. . . . [T]hese obstructions continually obliged us to run in a serpentine direction."[104]

Still, the completion of some roads, combined with the construction of three small canals along the Connecticut River, which after 1802 permitted navigation of the river southward from Bellows Falls, signaled Vermont's commitment to developing stronger networks to draw closer to the world beyond the state. By 1809, stagecoaches connected Middlebury with Boston in two days and Middlebury with Troy in thirty-six hours. Other

Signboard, Peru Toll-Gate, 1814. *Vermont Historical Society.*

RATES OF TOLL

	CENTS
A FOUR WHEELED PLEASURE CARRIAGE DRAWN BY TWO BEASTS	50
EACH ADDITIONAL BEAST	4
A TWO WHEELED PLEASURE CARRIAGE DRAWN BY ONE BEAST	25
EACH ADDITIONAL BEAST	4
A WAGON DRAWN BY TWO BEASTS	25
EACH ADDITIONAL BEAST	4
A HORSE WAGON DRAWN BY ONE BEAST	20
EACH ADDITIONAL BEAST	4
A CART DRAWN BY TWO OXEN	20
EACH ADDITIONAL BEAST	3
A PLEASURE SLEIGH DRAWN BY TWO HORSES	20
A PLEASURE SLEIGH DRAWN BY ONE HORSE	12½
A SLED OR LUMBER SLEIGH DRAWN BY TWO BEASTS	12½
A SLED OR LUMBER SLEIGH DRAWN BY ONE HORSE	8
EACH HORSE AND RIDER	6
ALL HORSES MULES OR NEAT CATTLE	2 CENTS EACH
ALL SHEEP OR SWINE AT THE RATE OF	6 CENTS A DOZEN

noteworthy developments permitted the exchange of vital communication: By 1798, mail deliveries occurred once a week each way between Windsor and Burlington via Woodstock, and, during the course of that year, the Woodstock post office reported receiving a total of 180 letters and mailing out 120.

The rapid proliferation of newspapers within the state presented an even more dramatic example of increased information exchange. By 1801, nine of Vermont's leading towns (Bennington, Brattleboro, Burlington, Middlebury, Peacham, Randolph, Rutland, Vergennes, and Windsor) boasted newspapers, communicating a range of vital information to residents. "Foreign Affairs" and "American Affairs" usually occupied the front page, with news of the former typically dated three months earlier and news of the latter extracted from other selected newspapers, a month or more old. Poetry, editorials, and self-help articles typically rounded out information drawn from afar. Local "news" took more varied forms, including announcements by shopkeepers of the arrival of various goods for sale at "cheap," "cheaper," or "cheaper than cheap" prices, and solicitations by artisans both for new business clients and for the immediate payment of overdue bills, lest they "may expect to be called on in a more serious way without further notice." The papers also displayed advertisements for land sales, announcements of lotteries, stock offers, "lost and found" reports, and announcements by spurned spouses advising readers that, as a consequence of "elopement" or abandonment, "I hereby forbid all persons harboring or trusting [him/her] on my account as I will pay no debts . . . after this date." The proliferation of newspapers in this period both reflected and contributed to what William J. Gilmore describes as widespread literacy in Vermont, making it, he claims, the most literate society in early American history.[105]

The increasing integration of Vermonters' lives into the larger world became apparent at the close of the eighteenth century when orthodox Calvinist missionaries from Connecticut and Massachusetts entered the state to ignite fires of revivalism that had already revitalized church membership in southern New England. Vermont's notoriety as the residence of "ye Awful Infidel" Ethan Allen gained further enhancement from missionaries' reports that the rough-and-ready lifestyle of the Vermont frontier reinforced "deists and proper heathens," while leading others "gradually to lose their religious impressions and the habits of seriousness" they had adhered to in their former homes. Appalled by what he saw and experienced on his journey to Vermont in the spring of 1789, the Congregational missionary Nathan Perkins confided to his journal:

> About one quarter of the inhabitants and almost all of the men of learning deists in the state. People pay little regard to the Sabbath; hunt and fish on that day frequently. Not more than 1/6 of the families attend family prayer in the whole state. About 1/2 would be glad to support public worship & the gospel ministry. The rest would choose to have no Sabbath—no ministers—no religion—no heaven—no hell—no morality.[106]

While the image of a godless Vermont served to inspire the orthodox faithful of southern New England to contribute generously to secure "the welfare of the regions beyond," upwards of one hundred churches were already planted throughout the state and fully nine-tenths of these were Calvinist (Congregational and Baptist). A more accurate albeit less seductive truth was the fact that, in a state where orthodox churchgoers resided alongside equal if not larger numbers of nonchurchgoers or members of competing sects, the orthodox church was at the same time likely to define social class and economic and political affiliation but unlikely to function as the center for the community's larger social life. Where neighbors interacted in town and congregational meetings, in barn and house raisings, bees, sporting events, and militia trainings, the more common gathering place, with its accommodating hours, its welcoming inclusivity, and its atmosphere of comfortable camaraderie, was the tavern. And even the former bastions of orthodoxy such as the lower Connecticut River towns and Old Bennington that had planted churches concurrent with settlement by 1800 sported more taverns than houses of worship. "The prevalence of folly, and the introduction of frivolous amusements, gambling and Intemperance," warned Bennington publisher Anthony Haswell, particularly exhibited by Bennington youth, threatened to render its sons "worse husbands and worse men" and its daughters "more lonesome and unhappy women."[107]

The contest to reverse the tide of infidelity translated into a thirty-five-year-long effort, known as "The Second Great Awakening," to bring the church to the un-churched. It also fostered competition among Congregationalists, Methodists, Baptists, and other sects for the right to the largest share of Vermonters' souls. By the early years of the nineteenth century, Vermont towns that formerly had one church or none at all suddenly found themselves the host of several. As a result, a corps of dedicated itinerant preachers traveled the countryside, invited into communities by splinter groups, dissenters, and small circles of ardent Christians seeking personal reformation, as well as by orthodox congregations wary or even fearful of the proliferation of such sects. In response, Middlebury College, already claiming a strong foundation in religious orthodoxy from the founding days, redirected its energies to producing orthodox ministers to bolster the cause of religious revival and personal reform with the framework of Congregationalism.

The frontier stage of Vermont's development drew to a close in the first decade of the nineteenth century. By that time, little remained of the vast expanses of open lands that had magnetically attracted floods of newcomers, and by 1810 larger numbers chose to exit rather than enter the state. For more than four decades, Vermont had functioned as New England's dynamic frontier. It attracted a vast assortment of people possessing diverse political views, religious allegiances, and economic desires. At no time did the collective experience of frontier Vermonters reflect unity either of purpose or action. The primary force uniting them was the lure of the land. Not all who came to frontier Vermont chose to stay. For those who did—persisting through the fighting of a "revolution within a revolution"; enduring the long struggle for entry into the United States; and surviving the uncertainties of the first years of statehood—the land nurtured a spirit of enterprise and hope. "Would that all mankind were as happy this minute as the Vermontese," Ira Allen had written in 1798.[108] In years to come, however, the primary challenge facing Vermont would be answering the question of whether the land could sustain its people.

4
Years of Optimism and Anxiety
1807–1850

The Price of Statehood: Jefferson's Embargo

In spring of 1791, Secretary of State Thomas Jefferson and his friend, Virginia Congressman James Madison, made an excursion into New England, collecting botanical specimens and fishing, but also sounding out anti-Federalist political sentiment. The two men visited Bennington during their tour, and soon afterward, with the aid of Matthew Lyon and others, Democratic Societies espousing Jeffersonian principles began forming in the state.

Jefferson's rising influence affected not only Vermont's political dynamics, but also the state's religious life. Just as Federalism and Calvinist Congregationalism existed in close alliance across New England, many of Jefferson's political followers belonged to the diverse collection of non-Calvinist sects that had been spreading rapidly since the 1780s, and would continue to do so during the evangelical "awakening" of the next decades.[1] Of these groups, Methodists, Universalists, and Free-Will Baptists were most prominent. Among the tenets separating them from Congregationalists was the latter's Calvinist doctrine of election, which held that, by grace alone, God selected for salvation a few individuals—"Saints"—through whom He accomplished His will on earth, and that all others, as embodiments of humanity's disobedience, were doomed to eternal damnation.

In 1783, Vermont legislators had codified these Congregational politico-ecclesiastical pretensions in a Green Mountain version of the old Connecticut Standing Order. This legislation, despite wording intended to take account of the presence of diverse religious views, permitted communities to tax residents "to enable Towns and Parishes to erect proper Houses for public Worship, and support Ministers of the Gospel."[2] The upstart sects, as well as orthodox "separatists," New Lights, and Quakers, wanted to repeal this law formally connecting church and state, convinced

The Vermont State Prison in Windsor, in an 1832 etching. *Courtesy of Special Collections, Bailey/Howe Library, University of Vermont.*

that doing so would promote not only the rights of conscience on matters of religion but also democratic principles of limited government.

In 1807, they got their political chance. In that year, Israel Smith captured the governorship as the candidate of Jefferson's Democratic-Republican Party, defeating ten-term incumbent Federalist, Isaac Tichenor; and the Jeffersonians gained control of the General Assembly. Legislators promptly abolished the Standing Order authority, "the better to promote harmony, and good order in civil society," making Vermont the first New England government to cut the tie of church and state.[3]

On this and other public matters in 1807, many Vermonters, with rising optimism about their land and future, believed themselves on the cutting edge of history. Over the next forty years, however, events gradually tempered their sanguineness and expectations. The state's economy flourished initially, then absorbed wartime setbacks, and slowly overcame them, while developing an increasingly precarious agricultural dependence on a single crop, wool. The state's population continued to grow, but the shrinkage of available land, as the state moved beyond the frontier stage, brought gradually dwindling opportunities for young people and newcomers and contributed to a widening gap in material well-being among Vermonters. At the same time, reservoirs of religious optimism and secular idealism nourished three decades of robust revival and moral and cultural reform in the state. These efforts climaxed in the 1830s in quarrels among revival leaders, popular disillusionment with religious excesses, and widespread disagreement and disappointment over results. Grassroots involvement declined and reform leaders altered their methods for achieving social change, turning away from the revival-inspired technique of moral suasion and toward more practical strategies of political coercion. These developments, in turn, contributed to the fragmenting, reconstruction, and fragmenting again, of Vermont's nascent political party structures. By the late 1830s, the state had entered a more anxious time, and by 1850 a more wary realism had replaced Vermonters' turn-of-the-century exuberant democratic and frontier optimism.

When Governor Israel Smith took office in 1807, he epitomized the optimistic, expectant spirit of the times. Smith presented himself as a reformer with a vision. He wanted "to teach each individual of the community the necessity of self-government."[4] With the dismantling of the Standing Order completed, he focused on Vermont's treatment of law violators. The governor exhorted legislators to enact new penal reform measures that emphasized rehabilitation rather than the sort of retribution called for in the state's rigid Calvinist blue laws, drawn from the criminal code of Connecticut. For individual misconduct, the state's laws continued to stipulate the harsh corporal punishments codified in the 1770s, such as cropping of the ears, whipping, branding, or being put in stocks. Legislators had generally assumed that by applying severe and publicly visible physical punishment, the sorry plight of the law violator would be a cautionary example and serve as a deterrent.

Smith endorsed rehabilitation through incarceration as an enlightened alternative to such coercive punishments and "particularly suited to an advanced state of society." Asserting that "confinement and hard labor" could be combined for the purpose of teaching the "culprit" habits of constructive employment and that it would produce a more positive effort than would the noose and whipping post, Smith asked lawmakers to authorize construction of a state prison similar to those recently opened in Philadelphia and Massachusetts.[5]

The General Assembly responded positively to Smith's call, enacting his proposal and appropriating thirty thousand dollars for the prison's construction.[6] A legislative commission selected Windsor as its location. Completed three years later, the massive three-story stone structure became the largest and most expensive building in the state. Replete with individual cells to house one hundred seventy men and a workshop to assist with reform and rehabilitation, the Vermont state prison stood as a dramatic testament to a vision of a brighter future.

Signs of "progress" appeared everywhere. In 1801, the University of Vermont had put an end to years of delay by admitting its first class. Although the Vermont Constitution of 1777 had declared a "university in this State, ought to be established by direction of the General Assembly,"[7] the 1786 Constitution dropped reference to a state university. Lawmakers did not finally establish the Corporation of the University of Vermont until November 1791,[8] and Ira Allen's donation of land helped secure the school's location in Burlington. The charter directed that the university's "rules, regulations, & by-laws shall not tend to give preference to any religious sect or denomination whatsoever," making it the nation's first public institution of higher education with such a mandate.[9]

Economic developments strongly contributed to the spirit of optimism and progress. Canadian trade on Lake Champlain increased yearly, and new technology promised an acceleration of that trend. Soon after Robert Fulton launched his steamboat, the *Clermont*, on the Hudson River in

The "College Edifice" (1801–1807) was the University of Vermont's first building. From Zadock Thompson, *A History of Vermont, Natural, Civil and Statistical* (Burlington, Vt.: Chauncey Goodrich, 1842). *Courtesy of Special Collections, Bailey/Howe Library, University of Vermont.*

1807, Burlington investors induced the Winans brothers, John and James, to bring the new invention of steamboating to Lake Champlain. The Winans, Quaker shipbuilders in Poughkeepsie, New York, had built the hull of Fulton's *North River*. When launched from the Burlington waterfront in June 1809, the Winans-constructed 120-foot *Vermont* became only the second steamship in the world to operate on a regular schedule.

Equipped with a sidewheel powered by a single-cylinder, twenty-horsepower engine, and containing only one Spartan room below deck for eating and sleeping, the *Vermont* proved that steamboats could operate in open waters and against adverse winds and large waves. At a time when Vermont's transportation remained in an early stage of development, water transport by way of steamship met a growing commercial passenger demand. Moreover, the flow of the lake northward made Canada a natural partner for the Champlain Valley and western Vermont, vastly increasing the region's access to markets and trade. The Winans' steamship could make the 150-mile trip between Whitehall, New York, at the lake's southern tip, and St. John at the falls on the Richelieu River in Canada, situated at the northern end of lake navigation, in twenty-four hours.[10]

Broadside for the steamboat *Gen. Greene*, one of several Vermont-based ferries providing service on Lake Champlain in the 1820s. *Vermont Historical Society.*

Developments on the east side of the state exhibited the spirit of economic and transportation progress too, as resourceful engineers found ways to circumvent the drop in the course of the Connecticut River at Bellows Falls of more than fifty feet in a distance of one mile. The solution, a system of locks constructed between 1792 and 1802—much of it with English capital—made possible one of the first canals built in the United States for navigation purposes and opened the way for shipping goods from eastern Vermont as far north as McIndoes Falls, and southward to markets in Boston and Long Island Sound in New York.

The General Assembly contributed to this optimistic mood in 1805 by selecting Montpelier as the permanent seat of state government. In the period since 1777, the legislature had convened two or three times a year, for sessions of a few days in length, in more than a dozen different locations, almost evenly divided between the east and west sides of the Green Mountains. Among the towns participating in this rotation were Woodstock, Westminster, Newbury, Rutland, Middlebury, Vergennes, Burlington, Windsor, and Danville. The arrangement caused numerous troubles, including elaborate travel inconveniences, difficulties in maintaining and preserving the official records of government activities, and, perhaps of greatest political significance, persistent rivalry among towns desiring the prestige of hosting a legislative session.

In 1805 the General Assembly decided to select a "permanent seat of the legislature for holding all their sessions." On November 8, motivated largely by a desire to allay the east-west and town rivalries, legislators voted—"as a measure of peace"—to locate the capitol at Montpelier, a politically innocuous village of twelve hundred residents nestled approximately in the center of the state, "among the mountains, but on neither side of them." A condition of the decision was the agreement of Montpelier citizens to construct a capitol building and convey its title to the state. In 1808 legislators met at Montpelier for the first time in their new three-

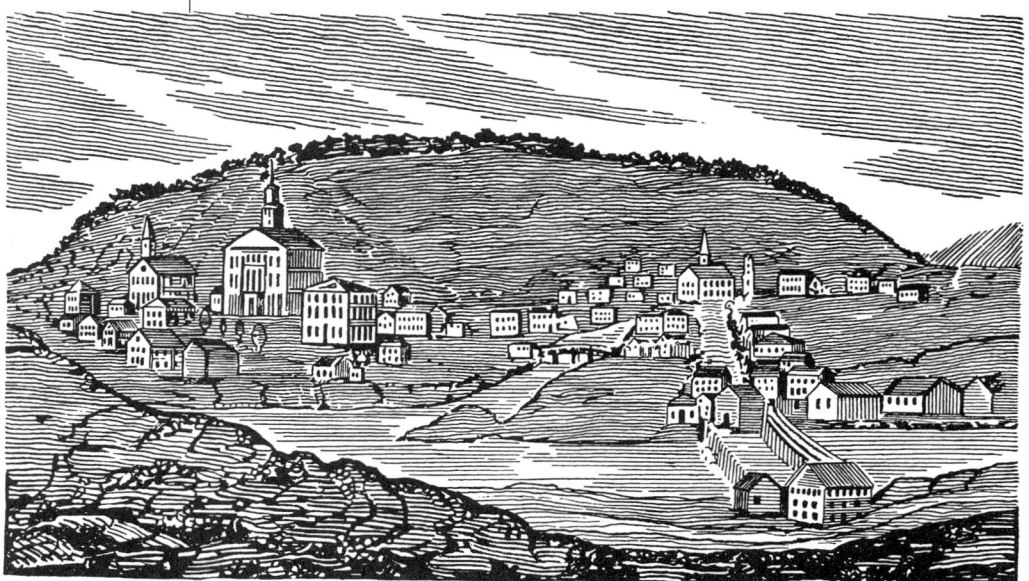

The earliest known picture of the village of Montpelier (1821). *Vermont Historical Society.*

story, rectangular-shaped, plainly finished wooden State House (including .... Hall). Although this structure was .... al Greek Revival granite building, the .... ernor had finally found in Montpelier

.... ate savored this period of "prosperity .... ing in distant places that would bring .... une, undercut its optimism, and force .... ices. Vermonters soon found them- .... lving Europe's greatest powers that .... state's striving for economic growth .... nwavering quest for independence. .... ame world events, vigorously pushed .... tional markets and free trade while .... liances, and found themselves in the

.... fore was the resumption of war by .... parte against Britain in 1803. Within .... nated and the adversaries turned to .... ockading the other's high-seas trade. .... g, and insisting on its trading rights .... nited States briefly emerged as the

.... s position, however, ... the British and .... y claims and .... nited States trade. American ships, regardless of their location on the seas or the content of their cargoes, became subject to seizure by one or the other of the belligerents. Concurrently, the British Navy, hoping to relieve problems brought on by a severe shortage of sailors, stepped up its boarding of American vessels that harbored British deserters. The "impressments" issue, as it came to be known, reached a climax in late June 1807 when the captain of the USS *Chesapeake*, plying international waters off the coast of Virginia, refused to surrender four

A thirteen-inch terrestrial globe, c. 1810–1815, made by James Wilson (1763–1855), a Bradford farmer and self-trained engraver and cartographer. Wilson manufactured the first terrestrial and celestial globes on a commercial basis in America. *Vermont Historical Society.*

deserters to the British frigate *Leopard*. The *Leopard* opened fire, killing three American sailors and crippling the American vessel. Its sailors boarded the *Chesapeake* and forcibly removed the deserters. Outraged Americans demanded a robust military response.

President Thomas Jefferson, however, sought to avoid being drawn into Europe's war while nevertheless bringing the belligerent powers to terms. He decided to use economic pressure. In December 1807, at Jefferson's urging, Congress passed an Embargo Act that forbade virtually all exports from the United States to any country. Jefferson hoped that by withholding all produce and dry-docking America's merchant marine, he could starve Britain into recognizing America's neutral trading rights and also protect American ships from encounters involving either of the European adversaries' warships.

Vermont's Democratic-Republican congressmen generally supported the embargo, on the presumption that it would not apply to overland trade with Canada. On March 12, 1808, however, Jefferson added a land embargo as well. The decision threatened economic disaster for the many Vermonters in the Champlain Valley who had participated in an increasingly lucrative trade with their northern neighbors in recent years. Pork, beef, and other farm produce; potash; and lumber regularly flowed up the lake and across the border, to be exchanged for finished goods, foodstuffs, and liquor. Participants feared that without "commercial intercourse with Canada," the hard-earned yield from their soil would become "useless trash."[13]

Vermont's Collector of Customs, Jabez Penniman, warned President Jefferson that because of the law's potentially negative economic consequences for the state, many Vermonters might ignore it. Jefferson responded by directing the United States marshal to raise a posse to assist Penniman in enforcing the embargo. He also activated units of Vermont's militia as federal enforcement agents, and ordered that two gunboats be built at Whitehall. Finally, in a proclamation to all Vermonters issued on April 19, Jefferson warned about "sundry persons" believed to be "confederating on Lake Champlain and the country thereto adjacent, for the purpose of forming insurrections against the authority of the laws of the United States." He called on public officials to enforce the embargo "by all the means in their power, by force of arms or otherwise."[14]

As Penniman and the state's congressmen feared, the land embargo triggered widespread denunciation. Citizens felt its effects all over the state. Federalists, several of whom possessed large land holdings and sizable investments in Canada trade, led many of the protests. Martin Chittenden, a Federalist legislator, charged that Jefferson, in fact, intended the embargo to break and humble the party and its members.

Opposition to the land embargo and to Jefferson's warning came from Democratic-Republicans as well as Federalists. "TRUE AND FAITHFUL CITIZENS" of St. Albans who "furnished NO cause for such Proclamation" joined with residents of Burlington, Shelburne, Milton, and other Champlain Valley towns to denounce the president's actions. Maintaining that Jefferson had been guided by erroneous information from persons of ill repute, erstwhile supporters of the president insisted that "as FREE and INDEPENDENT REPUBLICANS" they retained the right "to examine the measures of government." A group of citizens in St. Albans asserted that responsibilities of good citizenship required that "individuals, finding themselves and their families on the verge of ruin and wretchedness . . . evade the embargo restrictions."[15]

The embargo took effect, by chance, in late spring, at the traditional commencement of Lake Champlain's rafting season. Burlington merchants reported that their local market contained more than four hundred thousand dollars worth of timber and potash ready for sale in Canada. Needing the sales to repay debts and discharge large advances of money and finished goods, some of the merchants decided to move their cargoes quickly before enforcement of the embargo could be fully implemented. Accounts from Québec described the arrival on rafts of "immense quantities of Produce [that] come in by every fair wind from Lake Champlain."[16]

Customs Collector Penniman, operating with limited resources, sought to inspire obedience to the embargo by pursuing only the most flagrant violators. Foremost among those proved to be the crew of the *Black Snake*, a forty-foot-long, open-decked, single-masted cutter whose tarred hull enabled it to elude visibility as it transported contraband barrels of potash from the Burlington area to Canadian markets. Penniman targeted the *Black Snake* for seizure at any cost. His chance came when a lakeshore resident in the islands advised the captain of the revenue cutter *Fly* that the vessel was on its way up the Winooski River to Joy's Landing to receive a load of contraband potash bound for Canada. A small force of twelve officers surprised ten of the smugglers on August 4, 1808, as their boat lay beached and with its crew ashore. In the ensuing confrontation, two of the officers and a local resident who had stumbled accidentally onto the scene were killed. The remaining forces overpowered the smugglers and, with the exception of two who escaped and were arrested later, delivered them to the Burlington jail for trial.

Many Vermonters—including large numbers of Federalists—sympathized with the smuggling, but not with murder. Nevertheless, some of the state's leading Jeffersonian supporters professed to see dark Federalist motives in the incident. In August, they directed a broadside "To the People of Vermont" warning that blatant acts of "treason, rebellion, and murder" threatened the very "existence of your government."[17] Such pronouncements helped intensify the excitement and partisan emotions that accompanied the convening of the state Supreme Court in Burlington on August 23. Placed on trial were the captain of the *Black Snake*, Truman Mudgett, of Highgate, and seven of his men (from Alburg, Highgate, Swanton, and Milton). The court eventually handed down verdicts of murder against three of them. Only one, Cyrus Dean, received a sentence of death. On November 11, 1809, approximately ten thousand people—roughly six times the population of Burlington at the time—gathered in front of the courthouse to observe the unrepentant Dean on the scaffold. According to an unsympathetic commentator, prior to the condemned man's hanging he exhibited "a hardihood and careless unconcern perhaps never equaled in this part of the country."[18]

The *Black Snake* affair marked a victory for the government but deepened the division between Vermont's Democratic-Republicans and Federalists. In state elections during September 1808, Federalist Isaac Tichenor swept in again as governor, and Federalist candidates won three of the state's four congressional seats. Nevertheless, in the presidential balloting Vermont delivered its six electoral votes to Democratic-Republican candidate James Madison, and repeated the feat again in 1812, the only state in all of New England to do so.

With so much trade at stake for Vermonters, the *Black Snake* controversy and subsequent events did little to staunch the flow of goods into Canada. Smugglers knew too many routes and ingenious approaches. Missisquoi Bay, the northern part of which lies in Québec, provided the most inviting opportunities. Smugglers sailed to the vicinity of the boundary line, abandoned ship, then watched as "friendly" Canadian hands boarded and delivered the goods to their destination. Similarly, runners drove cattle overland to the boundary line and they ambled across, "of their own volition." Places such as "Smugglers' Notch" and countless other roadways carved out across Vermont's wide border with Canada provided virtually endless possibilities for disregarding the embargo. Jefferson might decry the "traitorous and diabolical traffic" of the Champlain Valley, but his proclamation did little to stifle efforts of Vermonters of all political persuasions to find ways of thwarting the law as they transported ashes, lumber, grain, pork, and cheese to the lucrative Canadian market. A Highgate resident of the time described his neighbors engaged in smuggling as "not so much enemies to their country as friends of gain."[19]

Historian H. Nicholas Muller's study of the Canadian customs records for goods entering the port of St. John details the magnitude of this illegal trade. Records reveal that trade passing north through St. John in 1808, after the embargo took effect, actually increased by 31 percent over the embargo-free previous year. In 1809, that figure doubled the 1808 totals, and in 1810 trade grew by another 41 percent. Much of this increase came from Champlain Valley agricultural products that, prior to the embargo, had been shipped for sale in the Hudson Valley or other parts of New England. Those markets, however, had become awash in locally grown commodities that previously had gone abroad, prompting the affected Champlain Valley producers to divert their goods to the Canadian trade. Unsurprisingly, a resident of Québec writing to a Vermont acquaintance highlighted these "beneficial" effects and declared "God grant that your Embargo Law may continue forever."[20]

The smugglers' early successes signaled an opportunity for others to follow. An examination of Champlain Valley newspapers underscores the brisk trade with the north among local shopkeepers. Far from evidencing persistent shortages or diminished stock, advertisements such as those of David Page appearing in the *Middlebury Mercury* reported an abundance of Canadian shad and salt, while his competitor William Hooker assured customers that he possessed adequate supplies of rum and cognac, undoubtedly also acquired from Canadian sources. Indeed, an examination of merchant George Cleveland's account books reveals that sales in the first year of the embargo averaged 25 percent higher than before it had been imposed.[21] If Middlebury's shopkeepers typified others across the Champlain Valley, a number of Vermont merchants appear to have profited handsomely from the embargo.

As the embargo wore on, other opportunities to capitalize emerged as well. The prohibition on British goods provided tremendous incentive for domestic manufacturing in Vermont and throughout New England. Across the state a sizable number of small factories, and a few large ones, got their start. In Northfield, Elijah Paine built a five-story woolen factory along the Dog River, costing forty thousand dollars and providing employment in the vicinity, directly or indirectly, to several hundred workers. In Middlebury, a new cotton factory and a six-story stone gristmill appeared in 1811, and a fledgling Middlebury marble factory owned by Eben Judd enjoyed considerable prosperity as a consequence of the declining availability of white Italian marble.

If the embargo was extensively evaded in Vermont (and in other states, as well), it also failed to bring either England or France to terms. In February 1809, Congress repealed the embargo, replacing it with a Non-Intercourse Act barring British and French vessels from entering American ports. A thicket of additional diplomatic moves resolved little, and by 1812, relations with England had so deteriorated that President Madison concluded he could not avoid a military confrontation. On June 1 he sent Congress a war message and on June 19 he proclaimed a state of war with Great Britain.

The War of 1812 in the Champlain Valley

The United States' move from embargo to war had immediate effects in Vermont. Townships along the Canadian frontier, including Troy, Westfield, Derby, Lowell, and Brownington, hastily took defensive steps, erecting a small fort, barracks, and a guardhouse, and stocking ammunition for the local militia, including muskets, bayonets, powder, and lead.[22] Meanwhile, much of the populations of these settlements retreated southward. On Lake Champlain, ten days prior to the formal declaration, Isaac Clark of Castleton, newly appointed colonel of the Eleventh U.S. Infantry, arrived under orders to Burlington and purchased two five-acre lots overlooking the lake for a military headquarters. During the next month, he fortified the bluff with approximately two thousand men, created earthen embankments, and mounted six large guns.

In addition to defensive measures, the war declaration also rekindled old offensive hopes among some Vermonters for an invasion of Canada that would drive the British from North America. Burlington's Democratic-Republican representative to the General Assembly (and later governor), Cornelius P. Van Ness, called for "a war of offense . . . [and] a war of conquest." On this issue most Vermonters, however, likely agreed with the state's Federalists who expressed skepticism. Martin Chittenden, the only Vermont congressman who voted against Madison's war request, warned that United States efforts to "visit the peaceable, and, as to us innocent, colonies of G. Britain with the horrors of war" would only result in more war.[23] Antiwar sentiments, fueled by Federalists, heightened across the state. In Montpelier, Federalist opponents of war interrupted a prowar demonstration in front of the State House. The town of Rockingham refused to enlist soldiers, and Poultney would not pay them. In Bennington, antiwar protesters disrupted a militia muster.

While Federalists and Democratic-Republicans debated through the press and in public forums, Burlington turned to meeting the needs of the two thousand newly arrived soldiers, roughly equal to the town's own population. Each soldier received a standard daily ration of one pound of beef or pork, one pound of bread, and four ounces of rum, whiskey, or brandy. Supplying these rations provided area farmers, merchants, millers, and tavern owners with abundant opportunities. The *Vermont Centinel* (later, *Sentinel*) advertised jobs for shoemakers, printers, blacksmiths, druggists, weavers, and hatters, while Burlington's only cooper employed ten additional workers to assist him "at trimming [the] government provisions in this place."[24]

The onset of war stimulated other economic activity. Iron works in Vergennes and elsewhere produced shot for the army. A dozen cotton factories employed hundreds of workers. Investors established potteries in St. Johnsbury and Monkton. A glass works commenced in Salisbury. Farmers increased production of wool and flax. Across the state, where grain crop surpluses proved unable to sell, distilleries burgeoned. At the height of the war, Peacham claimed thirty operating distilleries.

If commerce flourished, support for the war effort did not. Enlistments in Burlington fell short of desired numbers, in part reflecting the gap between the five-dollar monthly pay of a private and more than eleven dollars earned by laborers in the area. Chief army hospital surgeon James Mann found many of the soldiers who arrived in Burlington to be "habitually intemperate," in poor health, or men "who, in consequence of bad habits, and infirm constitutions, could find no other employment."[25] The troops' lack of preparation bolstered the natural caution of General Henry Dearborn, commanding the troops at Burlington, with the result that the army remained fixed at its Burlington base as winter set in at the close of 1812.

During the winter of 1812–1813, the Burlington camp suffered an outbreak of pneumonia in epidemic force that further complicated military preparations. Within a month, the epidemic had spread throughout the city, eventually causing approximately one hundred civilian deaths, and extending to every part of the state. The failure of standard "bloodletting" practices to stem the tide led Burlington physician John Pomeroy to prescribe expectorants to relieve congestion, supplemented by warm teas and sweat baths. The results proved encouraging and, by late winter, physicians had brought the epidemic under control. With an estimated statewide death toll of more than 6,400, including 750 soldiers, Dr. Joseph Gallup, one of the state's most prominent physicians, described it as "the most severe epidemic disease that has ever afflicted the inhabitants of Vermont."[26]

In April, news that American troops had captured York (modern-day Toronto) along the Niagara frontier bolstered hopes in Vermont for an attack on Canada originating from the Champlain Valley. In June, however, British forces foiled this possibility by gaining control of the lake in a punishing battle during which the United States lost two vessels and 112 men. Then, in July, the British landed a fleet (including the two captured vessels) at Plattsburgh, bombing and burning several buildings. From there, the ships proceeded toward Burlington, where American forces had assembled three thousand troops and eight hundred militiamen in anticipation of the British offensive. According to one eyewitness account, the attackers "shot a number of 24 lb. balls into the village. . . . One struck the roof of a house & lodged in the lower room, which was about all the damage that was done."[27] Still, the British had made the point of their military dominance.

Meanwhile, the war intensified the political conflict between Vermont's Federalists and Democratic-Republicans. A Jericho resident wrote to his brother, "the war is very troublesom in this part of the country . . . the party spirit runs high the people are devided about half in favour of the war and the rest oppose it. . . . Here is more politicks than religion."[28] Political leaders viewed their parties' future as riding on the war issue, and consequently took unusual measures to influence voter turn-out. On election day 1813, hoping to deter antiwar Federalist gains, Major John McNeil marched two hundred soldiers from Burlington to the polls in Colchester, ostensibly to avoid the large lines of voters in Burlington. Observers reported that, under the dual influences of alcohol and their commanding officers, the soldiers received instructions to vote for the Democratic-Republican incumbent for governor, Jonas Galusha.

Galusha won a plurality of votes in the election, but the resultant uproar and nullification of the Colchester vote (won by the Democratic-

Republicans, 258 to 38) coupled with unhappiness over the economic effects of the war, deprived him of a majority, and threw the election into Vermont's General Assembly. There, amidst claims of the outright purchase of votes, Galusha's former brother-in-law, Federalist Martin Chittenden, won election by the margin of a single vote in a legislative body controlled by Federalists. Candidates from Chittenden's party also won all of the state's six congressional seats.

Unaffected by the excitement accompanying his victory, Chittenden boldly used his inaugural address to question the existence of "adequate cause for a protracted, expensive and destructive war."[29] To punctuate his point, Chittenden insisted that Vermont's militia should provide defense and not participate in the invasion of foreign nations. On November 10, 1813, he distributed a proclamation countermanding the orders received by Vermont's Third Militia Division to participate in General Wade Hampton's expedition against Canada. He commanded the troops to return to their homes "forthwith."[30]

Chittenden's proclamation brought quick negative reaction. From their camp at Plattsburgh the Vermont officers, eighteen in all, responded to the governor, "we shall not obey your Excellency's order for returning; but shall continue in the service of our country until we are legally and honorably discharged." (The militia, nevertheless, did return prior to its scheduled release, and without further incident.)[31] In Washington, Chittenden's action provoked a motion in Congress calling for his prosecution as a traitor for enticing soldiers in the service of the United States to desert. Chittenden's actions, while daring, likely reflected the views of a small majority of Vermonters who stood opposed to the war by 1813.[32]

Trade with the enemy, meanwhile, quietly continued throughout the fighting. Although a Democratic-Republican–controlled State Assembly, in November 1812, had passed "an act to prevent intercourse with the enemies of the United States on the northern frontiers," it had had little effect.[33] Officials on both sides of the border confronted the smuggling by simply following the logic of profit. Canadians issued special British passes to the New York merchant John Jacob Astor so he could transport furs from Montreal through Lake Champlain to New York. (Astor employed Burlington's Gideon King, "the Admiral of Lake Champlain," in these undertakings). Burlington Customs Collector Cornelius P. Van Ness acknowledged his own permissive wartime customs policy in a sworn deposition rendered after the war. A merchant wanting to import goods from

Lower Canada would "give notice to the Collector of his intention, previous to the importation," then retake possession of his seized property through a remission from the government after the sale, minus a surcharge and a "few dollars worth of fees."[34]

Thus, American goods maintained a steady flow northward. Rafts carried naval supplies for the enemy shipyards at Ile aux Noix and St. John, and numerous Champlain Valley war profiteers smuggled food provisions to the British army. With the price of beef rising more than 25 percent during the war, entrepreneurs drove hundreds of cattle across the border daily. British commander Sir George Prevost wrote to Lord Bathurst, secretary of state for war and the colonies, that his army lived on "Beef provided by American Contractors drawn principally from the States of Vermont and New York." This active trade with the Canadian foe infuriated Colonel Zebulon Montgomery Pike, commander of the 15th Infantry at Burlington, who declared Vermont citizens "void of all sense of honor or love of country."[35]

In late 1813, as the war entered its second winter, the army at the Burlington battery suffered another outbreak of disease. Medical officials this time removed those affected to a quarantine camp set up south of Burlington, away from populated areas. The move may have contributed to the military post's experiencing one-quarter fewer deaths than in the previous year's epidemic. In March, with expectations that additional troops would join the three-thousand-man force already stationed at the Burlington camp, the army sought the use of facilities at the University of Vermont. The university, beset at the time by mounting debts, negotiated a rental fee of five thousand dollars, and accommodated the arrangement with a hasty late-March commencement and early dismissal of students and faculty.[36]

Masthead of the Burlington newspaper, the *Northern Sentinel*, during the War of 1812. *Vermont Historical Society.*

In 1813 and 1814, the Champlain Valley became a center of activity for United States forces preparing a move on Québec. When eleven thousand British regulars under the command of Sir George Prevost began forming in Montreal for a strike at New York, however, American plans shifted from offensive to defensive. Captain Thomas Macdonough, the thirty-year-old United States naval commander on the lake, put his forces to work in the late winter and spring of 1813–1814 preparing for the expected land and water invasion. Macdonough summoned artisans at Vergennes, at the falls of the Otter Creek, and acquired supplies from Troy and Boston to construct a flotilla by late May consisting of a twenty-six-gun schooner, two smaller schooners with multiple guns, and six gun-boats each with two guns. Two months later he added another ship and four additional gunboats.

In September, Prevost's land and water forces launched their southward campaign. Prevost moved his army across the Canadian border and down Lake Champlain's western shore, before settling near Plattsburgh, along the Saranac River, to await the arrival of his naval support. This formidable army boasted eleven thousand British regulars, most of them hardened veterans of the Napoleonic Wars. A French-Canadian militia and a small body of Odanak Abenakis (seeking to regain lands on the Missisquoi River that had been lost to post-Revolutionary War settlers) also joined Prevost. It stood as the strongest, best disciplined, and most completely equipped army the British had ever sent to North America. As events transpired, it became, also, the last great military force to campaign on the ancient Champlain route. With his naval flotilla's assistance, Prevost planned to capture Plattsburgh, clearing the way for further southward advance.

Against these approaching forces, General Alexander Macomb positioned his American defenders along the bank of the Saranac River, on the south end of Plattsburgh Bay. His stopgap army relied on a combination of regular troops, militia, and volunteers from New York and Vermont, many of the latter being formerly feuding Federalists and Democratic-Republicans who had set aside their animosity to confront the advancing British threat. A witness from the town of Highgate later recalled that "nearly every family had sent some of its members with such weapons as could be procured, either guns or pitchforks, to the scene of action. Life or death hung in the balance."[37] Macomb's total force of 3,300 amounted to less than half that of the British. With Prevost's enormous land advantage, the United States would need control of the lake in order to turn back the British advance.

A depiction of the Battle of Plattsburgh, September 11, 1814. From Paris M. Davis, *An Authentic History of the Late War Between the United States and Great Britain* (New York: Ebenezer F. Baker, 1836).

Historians have ranked the subsequent Battle of Plattsburgh, on September 11, 1814, with Samuel de Champlain's 1609 encounter with the Iroquois and Benedict Arnold's 1776 Battle of Valcour as among the most fateful in Lake Champlain's history. On that day, Prevost planned to move his army forward across the Saranac in two places as his naval forces engaged in Plattsburgh Bay. The confident and poised British navy possessed superior size, manpower, and, most critically, firepower, boasting ninety-two guns and sixteen vessels to Macdonough's eighty-six guns on fourteen vessels. Macdonough prepared for the anticipated battle by anchoring his fleet in a northeasterly line across the narrow channel between Crab Island and Cumberland Head in Plattsburgh Bay. The American naval captain calculated that with the wind blowing from the north, the British fleet would first have to face the wind that had brought its ships around Cumberland Head before it could gain position to fight. The situation could provide opportunities for Macdonough's forces to bring the British under withering fire from close range.

At approximately 9 a.m., the British vessels moved into view along the lake from the north, as expected. When the British *Confiance* came into range at 350 yards, and began to maneuver, Macdonough fired the largest guns of his biggest warship, *Saratoga*. Multiple battles quickly erupted, engaging all the ships. The cannonading could be "distinctly heard" as far away as Swanton and Highgate at the Canadian border.[38] In one deadly barrage from the *Saratoga*, following a maneuver in which Macdonough used his anchors to haul the ship around in order to gain the use of its port battery, *Confiance* suffered crippling damage and its captain, British Commander George Downey, received fatal wounds. Meanwhile, Prevost's shore batteries failed to provide support for his struggling ships. Two hours and twenty minutes after the battle had begun, the British ships' guns fell silent and the entire fleet, except for its gunboats, surrendered. The frustrated Prevost, no longer in control of the lake and fearing that the naval defeat posed a threat to his supply line, withdrew his army to Canada.

Prevost left behind weapons, tons of biscuits, and hundreds of gallons of rum for a boisterous American victory celebration. In Burlington, Macdonough received toasts as "the Hero of Champlain," and in Washington, D.C., Congress commissioned a gold medal to commemorate his triumph. By an act of the General Assembly on November 11, the State of Vermont made a gift to him of one hundred acres overlooking the scene of the battle.

The Plattsburgh Bay victory strengthened the American bargaining position in the peace negotiations, underway since August. The discussions climaxed on Christmas Eve 1814, with the signing of the Treaty of Ghent, which reaffirmed the prewar status quo between the two countries and formally ended the war. Two weeks after the signing, but before news of the event had traveled across the Atlantic, Andrew Jackson and a rag-tag military crew at New Orleans decisively defeated a troop of veteran British regulars. American victory at the Battle of New Orleans created an occasion for Democratic-Republican claims of national vindication in the war and triggered an outpouring of national pride and patriotic sentiment.

For Vermont's Federalists, many of whom had opposed the war, it was an awkward time. A secret meeting of New England Federalists at Hartford, Connecticut, in mid-December compounded their embarrassment. Rumors spread that the Hartford Convention entertained a secessionist agenda driven by individuals with maritime interests who had absorbed deep financial losses as a consequence of the embargo and war. Although Green Mountain Federalist leaders had chosen not to attend, two Vermont delegates did participate, one officially representing Windham County, the other, Secretary of State Josiah Dunham of Windsor, as an observer. Though the set of resolutions adopted by the convention included no secessionist actions, news of the signing of the Treaty of Ghent and the victory at New Orleans stimulated a deluge of ridicule of the Hartford gathering and denunciations of the Federalist Party as petulant and a source of national discord. Vermont's General Assembly, controlled by Democratic-Republicans, deemed the meeting sufficiently significant to formally condemn it. Federalists, who prior to the war were viewed by many as merely elitists and foes of democracy, now additionally appeared discredited as plotters and disunionists.

In 1815, Vermont's Democratic-Republicans took advantage of Federalist weakness to recapture the governorship for Jonas Galusha. In the next year's elections, Democratic-Republicans expanded their political hold on the state, maintaining the governorship, winning all six congressional seats, and claiming a solid majority of the Vermont legislature. A Federalist candidate never again gained the Vermont governor's office and the party itself rapidly disappeared as a political entity. For a decade after 1817, Democratic-Republican candidates for governor won their annual races without challenge from any organized party opponents.

In fact, party identities, on both state and national levels, now appeared in decline. Galusha extended a political hand to Federalists in his 1815 inaugural address, rejoicing "that we have been so far united"; and in 1817, new president James Monroe, fresh from easy victory over Federalist Rufus King of New York (his waning party's last presidential nominee), described the American people as "one great family with a common interest."[39] Vermonters appeared ready to forego party identities in the way that the heroic Green Mountain volunteers had done when they set partisanship aside and fought together against Prevost at the Battle of Plattsburgh.

In the summer of 1817, President Monroe took a tour of New England, the former Federalist heartland, in a further gesture at consensus building. Entering Vermont in July, he met, in an apparently genuine display of unity, with the Hartford Convention participant, Josiah Dunham. During the next few years, the surface unity continued, party identities faded, and popular interest in elections fell off. After voter turnouts that ranged between 70 and 80 percent in the ten-year period after 1806, elections in the 1818 to 1828 period struggled to draw 30 percent of the vote. The significant divisions in the Vermont legislature appeared now to be not the old party variety but between Canada-oriented and United States-oriented commercial interests.

Calamity, the New Commercialism, and the Selective Nature of Growth

The end of war ushered in a period of "good feelings," but it also put in motion circumstances that undermined much of Vermont's fledgling economy. In 1815, Great Britain declared war on American industry, unleashing stockpiles of manufactured goods on the nation's shores. Britain determined "to stifle in the cradle those rising manufactures in the United States, which the war has forced into existence, contrary to the natural course of things," a parliament member boasted.[40]

The strategy achieved devastating effect in Vermont. In 1816, confronted by the "crowded state of the market for iron," the Monkton Iron Works stopped production and dumped its "scrap" iron at two dollars per ton. In Middlebury, woven cloth that had sold for fifty cents a yard during the war fell to six cents a yard by 1816, forcing the town's mills to discontinue production. Eben Judd's marble works recorded a 75 percent drop from wartime sales. Shopkeepers struggled, many of them shutting down in the year after the war's end. The Lake Dunmore Glass Works, which at the height of war had employed forty men, also closed its doors permanently. Its owner, Epaphras Jones, penned his personal "epitaph" as a last entry in the company journal:

> Here lies Epaphras Jones beneath this sod
> Who was thought a shield but proved a rod
> And when he left this mortal soil
> He ran his race and ceased his toil
> To farthest west he sped his way
> And left his friends his debts to pay.

Jones's decision to abandon Vermont for the "farthest west" foreshadowed the state's emerging problem of out-migration that persisted through the rest of the century.[41]

Natural calamity brought additional misery. In the afternoon of June 5, 1816, a cold front swept into northern Vermont and pushed to the southeast, causing temperatures to plummet from the 80s F into the 40s in less than twenty-four hours. A freak blizzard accompanied the front. On June 7, Bennington farmer Benjamin Harwood recorded in his log that in "ploughfields and other parts the surface of the ground was stiff with frost—the leaves of the trees were blackened." A blanket of snow covered the northeast plateau, with twelve inches on the ground at Craftsbury, and similar drifts in the hills overlooking the statehouse in Montpelier. The next day, "the awful scene" persisted. Harwood noted "sweeping blasts from North . . . with light snow squalls. . . . So cold in the morning that we were absolutely compelled to send for our mittens and wear them till near noon-day." For the next three nights his farm experienced frost, with his corn "badly killed."[42]

In late June, temperatures returned to nearly normal, but in July northwest winds again brought chilling Canadian air, light frosts, and record low temperatures. Throughout the period, virtually no rain fell, and the consequent drought, along with statewide frosts on August 21 and 28, led farmers to abandon hope of a corn harvest and to mow entire fields for fodder. The dry conditions resulted in several severe forest fires in late summer and early autumn. According to Burlington's *Northern Sentinel,* smoke from the fires, ranging from Plattsburgh down to Ticonderoga, impeded navigation on the lake and reduced visibility to twelve feet along the roads of western Vermont. Finally, a series of deep killing frosts swept down the Champlain and Connecticut valleys during the last week of September, marking the end of what Governor Galusha described in his October inaugural address as the "foreboded evil of this unparalleled season."[43]

Perhaps the most notable testimony from among the survivors of 1816—that "year without a summer"—came from an anonymous rhymer, probably Theophilus Wilson Fitch of Hyde Park, whose rough doggerel captured the religious anxiety as well as the discouragement evoked by an extraordinary winter-in-summer season:

> If God withholds those milder rays
> And sends us frosts & chilling days
> E'en snow as late as eighth of June
> That nips the fruit in early bloom
> Shall we be frightened by such things?
> No, rather frightened at our sins[44]

In fact, Vermonters shared the "evil" season with much of the world's population; meteorologists have since traced the freakish 1816 weather to a massive volcanic explosion on Mt. Tambora, near the Bali Sea in Indonesia. The event sent tons of dust and ashes into the atmosphere, producing, among other things, an especially capricious weather pattern.

Despite the postwar hard times, Vermont's economy began a steady growth by the early 1820s that did not halt until the national Panic of 1837. The increase in activity, however, showed a mixed pattern, with abundant warning signs of economic fragility, one of which came by way of the United States census. Vermont's population grew by only 8 percent (from 217,895 to 235,966) between 1810 and 1820, an expansion that compared unfavorably with the state's growth rates of 80 percent and 40 percent for 1791–1800 and 1800–1810, respectively. In addition, the economies of many localities were in the midst of a shift from relative self-sufficiency to commercial agriculture and small manufacturing, a transition that while bringing expansion and prosperity for many, led to struggle and decline for others.

In the decade after 1820, although the population increased by almost 19 percent, to 280,652, a large number of towns actually lost population. These included eight of sixteen communities in Bennington County, longer-settled farm towns with populations of roughly fifteen hundred residents or more. Other "losers" included almost all of the prosperous farm communities dotting Lake Champlain, including Orwell and Shoreham in Addison County, Charlotte in Chittenden County, and Highgate in Franklin County. Residents participating in the exodus included landless immigrants and disheartened farmers with small holdings, but also native sons confronted by the natural limits on land acquisition in a maturing population.

Other places grew, however. Many of these were interior hill towns that had earlier been only sparsely settled as a consequence of moderate or fairly extreme undulating landscape. The most dramatic growth came in the relatively underpopulated Washington County towns that, by 1820, fueled a countywide expansion of 45 percent. This same pattern appeared in eastern Vermont, within towns along the foothills of the Green Mountains, including such places as Townshend, Jamaica, and Londonderry in Windham County, and Bethel, Ludlow, and Plymouth further north.

As a harbinger of developments to come, Vermont's commercial "central places" enjoyed significant growth in these years. Along the west side of the state, Middlebury (population 2,535) and Burlington (population 2,111) enjoyed the greatest increases, with both towns consolidating their holds on the surrounding hinterlands through expansion of their artisan and commercial corps. By 1820 nonfarmers made up the majority of taxpayers in those two communities. Significant growth in Montpelier (population 2,308), and in Vermont's two largest towns, Windsor (population 2,956) and Springfield (population 2,702), signaled the magnetic draw of commercial centers that continued over the next decades.

Growth required better transportation. By 1820, the "mania" for private turnpikes had largely dissipated and canals became the new rage. The Connecticut River canal projects caused a drop in transport costs by approximately half, on some shipments, and an increase in trade on the river. On the western side of the state, help came, ironically, from former cross-border nemesis, New York. In the years following the War of 1812, New York's Governor DeWitt Clinton backed the projected Erie Canal that promised to reroute trade from the rapidly growing Great Lakes trade region and Montreal to the Hudson River and New York City. Clinton also joined with New York merchants and industrialists to promote a second canal running from Whitehall, New York, at the south end of Lake Champlain, to the Hudson River. This canal, forty-six and a half miles long, funded and operated by the State of New York, offered the prospect of diverting the products of Lake Champlain trade from lower Canada, and sending it south instead. Raw materials, including timber (which suffered from the bruising journey through the Richelieu rapids), iron from northern New York, Vermont marble, and various foodstuffs could help build a busy trade on the new canal, and with a reduction in transport costs of as much as 90 percent. In addition, Vermont consumers might now gain access to imported goods at a significant reduction in price.

The *Gleaner* of St. Albans, loaded with wheat and potash, became the first ship to pass through the Champlain Canal when it opened on October 8, 1823. "It went forward to New York, welcomed by booming cannon, brass bands and dinners to the owners."[45] Prior to the canal's opening, an estimated forty ships regularly plied Lake Champlain's waters; within five years, that number rose to more than two hundred. Toll revenues grew from $26,000 in 1823, to $46,000 in 1824, to $72,000 in 1825, to $107,000 in 1828.[46] Within only a year after the completion of the canal, trade between Canada and the Champlain Valley all but dried up.

Western Vermont quickly felt the canal's impact. Benefits for industrialists came through the expanding activity that centered on the lumber trade at Burlington's waterfront, and in the nearly 50 percent growth in sales of Eben Judd's Middlebury marble factory. Commercial storehouses burgeoned along the lake, assembling agricultural produce and exchanging it for imported goods. Across the Champlain Valley, farmers expanded cattle herds and utilized advanced breeding practices to the extent, according to Shoreham farmer (and future governor) Silas Jenison, that "butchers could distinguish by the appearance and feel the fat cattle from this part of Vermont from those in the market from other places."[47] The economic emphasis within agriculture began shifting from broad-based self-sufficiency to larger-scale commercial ventures, favoring already well-established and wealthier farmers who possessed both the capital and the larger land holdings needed to expand their herds.

This growing prosperity in western Vermont, and the rising concern about diversions of trade away from Boston markets to New York, led merchants in Bellows Falls, Brattleboro, Montpelier, and other towns to hold conventions at Windsor and Montpelier to explore the potential for building canals connecting the Champlain Valley with the Connecticut River valley and to improve and extend the Connecticut River canal artery with Boston. Even more challenging, army engineers in May 1825 investigated the terrain between Lake Memphremagog and Barnet to ascertain a route for connecting the Connecticut River, via the St. Francis, to the St. Lawrence. Eager to encourage such projects, Vermont's legislature joined with Governor Cornelius P. Van Ness to support a small appropriation for funding additional surveys. In the end, however, Vermont's hilly terrain precluded the construction of any such canals, forcing the Connecticut Valley to wait for the "railroad revolution" before it could attempt to reclaim trade west of the Green Mountains.

Managing the state's emerging new canal-stimulated economy proved difficult. During construction of the Champlain Canal, a state legislative committee speculated that farmers' response would be to produce "an immense surplus of grain" for export at "the nearest seaport." And in the canal's first full year of operation Champlain Valley farms did so, delivering more than forty-one thousand bushels of grain to New York City. But in the next few years Vermont farmers moved rapidly away from wheat raising, and in 1826 *Niles Weekly Register* estimated that the state imported yearly approximately fifteen thousand barrels of flour. This figure quadrupled to sixty thousand barrels in a scant eight years.

What explains this unexpected development? Many Vermont farmers had quickly adjusted to the new commercial possibilities. The tradition of self-sufficient farming based on diversified agriculture and barter had begun yielding to new circumstances ruled by monetary exchange. The case of Hiram Harwood, in Bennington, provides an example. In 1826, Harwood ceased planting wheat and the following year purchased his flour in nearby Troy. He then planted his newly freed fields in additional corn and hay to use as feed for his expanding dairy herd. Harwood's actions proved common for farmers who had struggled with wheat's viability for more than a decade. As Vermont's original cash crop, "wheat, wheat and more wheat was the goal" of early farmers, especially in the Champlain Valley. But it was a labor-intensive produce and sensitive to weather conditions. In addition, it had generated progressively diminishing yields, the result of chronic problems, including spring killing, blight, rust, and generalized soil exhaustion. This situation and the cheap availability of a superior western wheat by way of the new canal sped the transition to other agricultural products.[48]

Vermonters' efforts in the mid-1820s to enlarge their herds of cattle and sheep necessitated greater energies in corn production. And cultivating corn called for heavy time commitments. In spring, fields needed to be spread with barnyard dung, and plowed. Then came planting and hoeing, in early summer. During September and October the crop was harvested. The cycle ended in the winter months, with husking and grinding. However, because these labors did not interfere with later summer harvesting of hay and grain, many small farmers could maintain independent stock and harvest corn while hiring themselves out as labor for the critical hay season.

National politics, too, influenced Vermonters' shift toward the cultivation of grazing animals for commerce. In 1824, Kentucky Senator Henry Clay proposed a set of legislative initiatives termed the "American System" that included numerous tariff features protecting American manufactures and a national system of internal improvements encouraging economic development through improved transportation. One of Clay's proposals called for a small protective tariff favored by wool-growing and woolen textile interests, intended to stem the tide of English wool. The bill, promising to expand the domestic market for northeastern states' wool and textile products, met opposition from farmers in southern states who viewed it as having the effect of an unequal tax, awarding privileges to selected segments of the economy and driving up prices. Congress nevertheless enacted the tariff, and it triggered a new wave of enthusiasm for sheep raising on Vermont hillsides. William Jarvis's efforts in Weathersfield had introduced the Spanish merinos in 1811, but farmers now turned to the

The celebrated Vermont sheep importer, William Jarvis (1770–1859), of Weathersfield, is shown energetically engaging a presumed client, while a larger-than-life merino sheep looms in the background. *Vermont Historical Society.*

Saxony merinos, which possessed finer, silkier wool that produced "a fabric of striking beauty."[49] By the middle of the decade, Vermont's sheep population rose beyond one-half million.

The sheep growers' optimism, however, soon dissipated. The Tariff of 1824 did not halt British traders from "invoicing their goods far below their cost." An 1826 memorial submitted to Congress by Woodstock growers suggested that the tariff constituted "a perfect nullity."[50] The lure of larger commercial profits remained strong, however, leading sheep farmers to demand still higher tariffs.

In 1828, Congress again delivered, enacting the so-called "Tariff of Abominations" that included an effective doubling of the duty on wool. Prices for wool that had fluctuated between thirty-seven and forty-two cents per pound for the previous five years began an immediate climb, increasing by nearly 50 percent over the next five years.

The dramatic increase in the wool price came on the heels of a natural catastrophe for wheat growers earlier in the spring. The sudden appearance of a seemingly invincible enemy, the wheat midge, triggered the setback. According to one farmer, the midge "blasted the expectations of the wheat grower and rendered all his efforts to procure a crop abortive."[51] The collapse of the wheat crop, in conjunction with the new tariff, altered the face of Vermont agriculture forever. The "sheep craze" had begun, and with it came a quickening of Vermont agriculture's integration into the wider markets beyond the state and increased exposure to the vicissitudes of government regulation.[52]

Nathan Hoskins, in his 1831 *History of the State of Vermont,* wrote that "the soil is such, and the seasons are so uncertain, for the perfection of crops of grain, that grazing is the most sure and profitable branch of agriculture which the farmer of Vermont can attend to with success." And it was "from this source," he observed, that "the principal exportations are derived."[53] Indeed, Vermont farmers eagerly sought to supply the raw material for rapidly proliferating textile mills in southern New England and, on a smaller scale, in the Green Mountains (the state claimed 156 such mills, and 2,300 textile workers, by 1850). Farmers acquired staggering numbers of sheep, allocated increasing amounts of land to graze them, and during most of the 1830s enjoyed enormous profits. Harriet Martineau, in her travels along the Atlantic seaboard, noted that Vermont no longer provided Boston with fowl, butter, and eggs in quantities of previous years, "partly owing to an increased attention to the growth of wool there for the manufactures."[54] The shift to sheep diminished also the number of horses, mules, neat cattle, and swine, as well as poultry and hogs on Vermont farms.

Sheep-induced prosperity brought with it other costs to Vermont's traditional identity. The growing demand for grazing acreage substantially boosted land prices. The boost, in turn, changed the requirements for farming success and provoked increased disparities of wealth within Vermont's agricultural communities. In the past, many people had been able to parley the savings from a few years of labor into a small farm, but Nathan Hoskins in 1831 reported that the bidding up of land prices meant "it now takes much severe labor and hazardous enterprize to gain a competence, and much more to rise to easy and independent circumstances."[55]

Farm consolidation increased rapidly in some sections of the state. Over time, according to one Vermont farmer, as "men counted their flocks by thousands, and as they grew more and more rich in money and sheep, they bought farm after farm adjoining their own and turned them into pasturage."[56] As Addison County's sheep population rose to more than one hundred thousand in 1832 (still only 40 percent of what it would ultimately total), the impact could be seen on several levels. Whereas a majority of resident artisans in 1829 owned small farms, by 1835 the figure had dropped to one-third. In Shoreham the farm size for the wealthiest residents had grown by an average of 15 percent and the average flock by 125 percent, while middling and poorer residents showed little or no gain in their financial circumstances.

Many farms across the state, however, remained small in size, and life and labor on them changed little in the first half of the nineteenth century. Peacham's grand list in 1813–1814 showed that among the 136 resident farmers owning more than ten acres, the extent of the average farm was 124 acres, with about half of it improved, or about what one farmer and his immediate family could manage. By 1850, not much had altered in this regard. The average farm size in Vermont was 139 acres, with 63 percent of that land improved.[57] Few could afford to pay wages for the help of more than an occasional farm laborer. And in that year, new labor-saving machinery still had not ousted hand processes on most farms. The curved snath (or handle) and cradle scythe had generally replaced the more awkward scythe and sickle after the 1820s, and iron plows were superseding wooden ones. But until the 1850s, threshing machines did not come into general use, replacing the trodding of oxen or horses on the threshing floor; and mowing machines did not generally begin to replace the scythe for cutting hay. Corn planting and cultivating continued to be done by hand. Moreover, farmers continued to rely on their own skills, or that of a neighbor, in meeting such day-to-day demands of the farmyard as making an ox yoke, constructing a barrow or a wagon body, laying a stone wall, or providing veterinary care for animals.

The 800-acre farm of Judge Elijah Paine, in Williamstown, one of the largest in the state, provides a view of workaday farm tasks in the years prior to the large-scale introduction of mechanical innovations that came in the period after 1850. According to a memoir by Charles Paine, a grandson of Judge Paine and a nephew of Governor Charles Paine, a viable farm worker of this period continued to need to become competent in many tasks. The grandson relates that his education on the Williamstown farm included learning "to plough, to plant and to harvest, to chop and to saw wood, to make sugar, soap and candles. . . . I learned . . . to ride, to drive, to care for the horses, to milk the cows, to stable and feed the oxen, to bring the cattle or the horses or the hogs from pasture, to salt the sheep and to drive them to and from pasture along the highway, to help in the washing and shearing, catching the animals and taking them to the men, to spread and rake hay, to bind grain, to shock, to husk and to shell corn, to thrash and winnow the grain, to mow, to cradle, to reap."

According to Paine's memoir, "the only machinery was a winnowing mill, lately introduced. The neighbors used a two-handed fan for winnowing. Oats were cradled but other grains were reaped with a sickle and threshed with a flail, precisely as in Scriptural days. . . . The oats were threshed on the barn floor, between the bays, by riding over the bundles on a horse, while a man stirred the bundles with a fork to keep the heads of the grain towards the outside."[58]

In the next decades, technological innovation, the wide-ranging impact of the Civil War, and fundamental shifts in perspectives led to agriculture's embrace of machinery and opened the way to a basic restructuring of Vermont farm life. Accompanying the stepped-up pace of change in the succeeding generation was the surprising emergence of almost plaintive expressions of nostalgia for the life of the farmer of the 1820s, 1830s, and 1840s on the part of some Vermonters. In 1877, a resident of Middletown (renamed Middletown Springs in 1884), moved by a sense of loss that he perceived had accompanied the alterations of the intervening years, deplored the "great change, going on" that he asserted had "severed our connection with the good old times" of those earlier years. Gone, now, "and left . . . behind us," were "the times when the ox-yokes, the ox-bows, the whip-stocks and other necessary implements, were made in the long evenings before a blazing fireplace—the times when he was considered the best manager who did 'everything within himself'—the times when, as the men worked, the hum of the little linen-wheel, or the large wheel for spinning wool, or the rattle of the shuttle and treads in the loom mingled with the crackle of the fire and the sounds of the axe and the drawing knife."

The Middletown citizen continued: "As some one has written: 'The women then picked their own wool, carded their own rolls, spun their own yarn, drove their own looms, made their own cloth, cut, made and mended their own garments, dipped their own candles, made their own soap, bottomed their own chairs, braided their own baskets, wove their own carpets, quilts and coverlids, picked their own geese, milked their own cows, fed their own calves, and went visiting or to meeting on their own feet, and all this with much less fuss and ado than our modern ladies make when they are simply obliged to oversee the work of an ordinary household in these days.'"[59]

The rising market economy and increasing land prices, combined with a static number of farms, permanently altered the broad pattern that had existed at the turn of the century, of independent yeomen farmers providing for themselves most of the necessities of life. Concurrently, the prospects for agricultural hired hands also receded. Lacking the opportunity, or the capital, to purchase a farm of their own, these men in large numbers abandoned hopes for land ownership, drifted to employment as small tradesmen, mechanics, or factory workers in larger Vermont communities and southern New England industrial towns, or abandoned the Green Mountains for the West.

Revivalism and Reform

From the 1790s to the 1840s, Vermonters engaged in a succession of fervent religious revivals that expanded church membership rolls, enlivened social consciences, influenced three decades of benevolent and humanitarian reform initiatives, and kept the state's social and political landscape in a condition of almost perpetual embroilment. The religious enthusiasm was part of the Second Great Awakening, an evangelical movement that held believers in thrall from New England across much of New York and the Old Northwest to Kentucky and the Appalachian west.

In Vermont, Congregational and other Calvinist missionaries from Connecticut led early forays, beginning in the mid-1790s, motivated by the assumed spiritual neglect of the frontier and by fears, as well, of the purported antireligious influences of the rising Jeffersonians and their Democratic Societies. Their evangelical mission aimed at stirring spirits, arousing the backwoods communities' unacknowledged Elect, and gaining commitments from all society's members to "live the Christian life."[60]

One Federalist minister who delivered New England Calvinist orthodoxy to the frontier was Lemuel Haynes. Described as a "magnetic revivalist," he started life as the illegitimate son of a slave and a white woman in West Hartford, Connecticut. As a young man, Haynes served with American forces in several Revolutionary War engagements, including the Battle of Fort Ticonderoga. In 1780, after a period of study, he became a licensed Congregational minister and in this role in 1785 undertook a missionary preaching tour through Vermont. Reputed to have become, in Connecticut, the first black pastor of a white congregation in the United States, he returned to Vermont in the late 1780s to serve a church in West Rutland, where he remained approximately thirty years. He occupied other pulpits in Vermont, and elsewhere in New England, preaching a Calvinist gospel in which God provided salvation for a regenerate few while denying the unregerate a capacity to influence their own regeneration. He died at age eighty in 1833, a staunch upholder of Congregational and Federalist orthodoxy to the end.[61]

Rev. Lemuel Haynes, prominent Congregational minister and outspoken Federalist. *Vermont Historical Society.*

Non-Calvinist sects, including Methodists and Free Will Baptists, also moved into Vermont, conducting their own revivals. Their message, however, was "popular evangelicalism," offering the availability of redemption not just for an Elect, but for all who faithfully sought it. Methodist circuit riders became the effective leaders in espousing this doctrine of "free will," and the emotional energy that often drove its attraction is evident in early documents of the Methodist Church in Vermont.

A reminiscence provided by a rural Methodist minister told of an incident that occurred about 1801 in Huntington, involving "an old fashioned Calvinist" pastor and the grieving parents of a four- or five-year-old daughter who had recently died. While preaching the funeral sermon in the family's home, the minister, faithful to Calvin's doctrine of predestination, declared to the parents, "there were nine chances for their child to be lost, for one for it to be saved." At that, the father interrupted with "a heavy stamp with his foot," and said, "Hold your tongue; I will have no such talk in my house. I don't believe my child has gone to hell. I believe it has gone to heaven; and I just mean to go there too." He then beckoned to a friend: "Neighbor Norton, won't you bring a Methodist preacher to see me?"[62]

Historian David Ludlum has suggested that this era's revivalism drew strength from desires to extend the benefits of "Christian living" but also to expand the ways of democracy and the "natural rights liberalism" familiar to the Jeffersonians' Democratic-Republicanism. From this perspective, Vermont's early-nineteenth-century revivals represented a profoundly democratic development. They offered a message of greater opportunity to attain salvation, delivered in language familiar to ordinary people—often by clergy with little more training or education than audience members—and brought forward with an evangelical fervor that generated a multitude of moral and cultural reforms and "good works." As the Methodists believed, "if the man's soul was saved fundamental social change would inevitably follow."[63]

Religious enthusiasm declined during the 1812 War years, but a new revivalistic surge commenced in 1816. The combination of natural catastrophe and financial disarray that followed immediately after the war, and the state's ambiguous performance in the war itself, likely disposed many Vermonters to respond positively to renewed religious appeals. However, other influences, including a felt need for a new spirit of self-discipline, also were probably at work: An observer reported it was a time in which "profanity, Sabbath breaking, intemperance, and a general dissoluteness of life and manners, were becoming fearfully prevalent."

The evangelical efforts in 1816 and 1817 brought gratifying results. Churches in Middlebury and Cornwall reported their largest-ever "harvest of souls," and Asa Burton of Thetford observed that, because of the revivals, "the state of morals has been greatly improved, vice has been put to the blush, and in many remarkable instances, infidelity has received a fatal shock."[64] They even earned some credit for the decline in partisan politics across the state following the postwar Federalist Party collapse. In a lay testimonial of the revival's power, Peacham resident William Chamberlain reported in a letter to a friend in 1817 that the intense political fractionalization formerly subsuming the community had subsided "almost entirely."[65]

In the late 1820s and early 1830s the revivalist surge took on new energy. This fresh round of religious excitement signaled the arrival in the Green Mountains of the so-called evangelical "new measures"—or spontaneous revivalistic methods—that had been developed in camp meetings in western and central New York by famed itinerant Congregational evangelicalist Charles Grandison Finney. The "new measures" represented for Congregationalism an attempt to align the traditionally elitist tenets of orthodox Calvinism with the strongly egalitarian social trends of the postrevolutionary period. Finney, utilizing a fiery and dramatic style of oratory, proposed to his orthodox congregations a spiritual possibility that non-Calvinist sects had already embraced: salvation by the power of individual free choice through acts of faith and good works, for all who believed.[66]

Congregationalists heretofore had viewed the revival as "a surprising work of God," an outpouring that came in God's own good time. The "new measures," however, rendered it possible for ministers and congregations to create, rather than await, revivals. The "new measures" evangelists thus launched protracted meetings of three and four days duration, often running continuously day and night (later they would extend to thirty days). Assuming salvation to be in reach of every churchgoer, they made the gaining of converts a central goal.

To that end, revivalists introduced the use of "anxious benches" and extended prayer sessions in which participants prayed for family members, friends, and other "receptive" individuals by name. As explained by Rev. Joshua Bates, president of Middlebury College, the congregation needed to "be told plainly, authoritatively, yet affectionately, if we do not enjoy a revival it will be because of the inequities of the church—because professors of religion desire the perishable objects of this world more than they desire the conversion of sinners."[67]

Armed with the "new measures," revivalists achieved extraordinary numbers of converts. Half the Congregational churches (99 of 197) in Vermont reported revivals during 1831, with the addition of more than fifty-five hundred new believers. Baptists reported more than two thousand five hundred new converts. The sheer magnitude convinced church members of every denomination that an extraordinary "work of grace" was underway. Hazen Merrill of Peacham, writing to his brother in Indianapolis, reported two hundred fifty new converts in his town during the 1831 revival, and described how long-held "divisions among us . . . [over] a few months have vanished in thin air."[68]

The magnitude of the revivalist outburst led some churchgoers to fundamentally alter their theological thinking. For them, a "new era" in "the ushering in of millennial glory" appeared to be foreshadowed.[69] Envisioning that Christ's Second Coming would occur not during the apocalypse but rather through the ultimate conversion of all hearts to Christianity, they believed the time had arrived for Vermont's "Christian army" to redouble its efforts to purify their communities of society's various ills, and advance the cause of righteousness. The spirit of "ultraism"—the embrace of extreme measures in the singular pursuit of the salvation of humankind—had taken hold in the Green Mountains.

In 1835, ultraistic evangelicals brought their efforts to Burlington. From earliest settlement, the Queen City held a reputation as a freethinking community. One of its residents had been Ethan Allen, the man Congregational missionary Nathan Perkins called "an awful infidel, one of ye wickedest men yt ever walked this guilty globe." The town also served as the location of the University of Vermont, which boasted a charter instructing the institution to eschew denominational allegiances.[70] This stance had provoked Middlebury's Calvinist town fathers to such an extent that they founded Middlebury College in 1800 as their own citadel of orthodoxy. Whereas the University of Vermont emphasized rationalism and encouraged its graduates to pursue careers in law and public service, Middlebury College distinguished itself through its emphasis on religious instruction and the training of Calvinist ministers. During the 1820s and 1830s Middlebury graduated three times as many students as the University of Vermont.

The Rev. Jedediah Burchard, a renowned itinerant revivalist from western New York's "Burned-Over District," came to Burlington in December of 1835 at the invitation of clergy in that city, for a revival that proved to be pivotal for the state's evangelistic future. Recently, the power of his "new measures" tactics had been on display at a great meeting in Middlebury that netted approximately two hundred converts. Middlebury College's president Joshua Bates, Thomas Merrill, long-time minister of the sizable Middlebury Congregational Church, and several Middlebury College students joined Burchard in his Burlington crusade.

The University of Vermont's campus community and Burlington residents proved invulnerable to the "new measures," however. Word of Burchard's flamboyant style preceded his arrival and bolstered the resolve at the university to oppose him. In addition, Russell Streeter, a widely known Universalist, published an unsympathetic description of Burchard's revival in Woodstock entitled *A Mirror of Calvinistic Fanaticism*, including the minister's insistence that "anxious benchers" convert in five minutes or less or suffer the eternal wrath of God. In these instances, Burchard counted down the time on a clock. University faculty members joined Streeter in characterizing Burchard's measures as "fanaticism" and expressed disdain for the numerous Vermont congregations' infatuation with him. Episcopal Bishop John Henry Hopkins added his voice to the opposition denouncing the revivalist's "lack of humility," and former University of Vermont president James Marsh dismissed conversions rendered in the excitement of mass emotional outpourings as altogether spurious.

Yet Burchard himself ultimately did the greatest damage to his cause. Learning that two University of Vermont undergraduates had been hired by bookseller Chauncey Goodrich to transcribe the revivalist's Burlington sermons, Burchard sought to buy the confidence of one of the students by "offering him a large sum." Although the student accepted his invitation, he refused to hand over transcripts or absent himself from subsequent meetings. Burchard became enraged at his failure to have the two students removed, and refused to continue. As one unsympathetic observer noted, the lengthy silence stirred irritation among his followers, who became "mad because they came to see the elephant and the elephant won't play for fear his tricks shall be noted down."[71]

News of Burchard's behavior emboldened critics from across the state, including former supporters in the Rutland Association of Congregational Ministers who concluded that "the system of measure" that he used had greatly diminished "the ordinary ministrations of the Gospel." They pronounced Burchard's revivals as being "not merely distasteful, but indecently low & personal & harsh."[72] Middlebury College paid a heavy price for its support, its enrollments plummeting from 168 in 1836 to 46 in 1840 and graduation diminishing by three-fifths. The University of Vermont's enrollments tripled during the same period. The power of ultraism, and revivalism as well, had begun to wane.

The combination of religious and social tensions that produced the revivals also led to campaigns for reform. Influenced by the "new measures" setting, earnestly committed to new codes of behavior, and believing "what ought to be done can be done," many Vermonters dedicated themselves to drives for social change. The temperance, antislavery, and antimasonic movements claimed the largest numbers of dedicated supporters, with the promotion of temperance emerging earliest. In 1817, the formerly competing religious sects cooperated to persuade the Democratic-Republican-controlled legislature to organize a committee to investigate "the too free use of ardent spirits."[73] The committee, chaired by Governor Galusha, estimated that Vermonters spent more than one million dollars each year for strong drink, a figure that exceeded the total expenditure for schools and other town services.[74] Outraged that taverns in Vermont outnumbered churches and attracted more people, the religious constituencies led the committee to blame "intemperance for every evil from crime to political excesses and 'taxes to support the poor.'"[75] Resistance to reform, however, held strong. The 1810 census showed 125 distilleries thriving in the state, some of them producing fifty gallons a day; the home consumption of cider was enormous; and alcoholic excess punctuated almost every public gathering. At this early stage in the campaign, the rhetoric against intemperance exceeded the legislature's willingness to act formally.

Not until the mid-1820s did an organized effort to promote sobriety take hold. In February 1826, Rev. Joshua Bates, Woodstock lawyer Charles Marsh, and other prominent Vermonters attended a meeting in Boston that formed the American Society for the Promotion of Temperance. Two years later, the two men spearheaded the organization of the Vermont Temperance Society. Modeling their efforts after the religious revivals, the group pledged to form local societies and encourage members to dedicate themselves to eliminating "that loathsome vice which completes the degradation of degraded man."[76] Many ministers preached temperance as a necessary requirement for legitimate conversion. Temperance tracts, similar to the religious ones, blanketed the state, continuing an earlier theme that blamed alcohol for most of society's failings. Its negative consequences purportedly even included poor citizenship because traditional Election Day toasting caused voters to render their decisions not "in faith to the Constitution, but under the bias of whiskey."[77]

The conduct of members of the Vermont militia in company June Training days stood as another alcohol-provoked civic blight, in the eyes of reformers. A state law required every company in the state militia to be inspected, drilled, and trained on the first Tuesday in June of each year. In fact, this annual day became an occasion of great community fun, highlighted by the long-standing practice of "treating" militia members (by law, all able-bodied male white citizens, 16 to 45 years of age) with alcohol, as a reward for their service. "The staple refreshment was whiskey," a St. Albans resident recalled, "and under its influence, a continued popping of fire-arms was kept up, until some time after sunrise."[78] An irate temperance letter-writer in the Danville *North Star* called for "less draining of bottles and more training of the musket." In Montpelier legislators adopted a resolution declaring the practice of "treating" militia members "burthensome to officers, corrupt to the morals of soldiers, tends to introduce disorder, confusion & disobedience, and ought to be discountenanced by all classes of community." Despite such appeals, changes were not forthcoming.[79]

Commencement of the "new measures" revivals in the late 1820s, however, clearly advanced the Vermont Temperance Society's efforts. By 1832, approximately two hundred local societies existed across the state, with a total membership of thirty thousand. An average of one in every four adults volunteered to take the temperance pledge. These local societies formed Temperance Houses so that principled travelers could avoid the temptations of the tavern. Reporting that "the success of the temperance reformation [is] of vital importance to the interests of true religion," the General Convention of Congregational Churches encouraged "all the friends of God and the human race to make vigorous efforts to sustain and carry on this blessed work, and not to remit their efforts till the way for the Second Coming of Man is every where fully prepared."[80]

As the revivalistic fervor intensified, newer converts to the temperance cause began to exercise a degree of zealotry that exceeded their forbears' more moderate views. A meeting of the Rutland County Temperance Society illustrated the division. A spirited debate arose between the moderate founders of the society who advocated abstinence only from "strong liquor," most notably rum, and "ultraistic" radicals who demanded abstinence from all intoxicating beverages, including hard cider. Especially fanatical were two Rutland physicians, a Dr. Hale who advocated that cordials and essences be banned ("and this is the reason, sir, why your scented lady is almost always in such fine spirits!"), and a Dr. Bowen who insisted that long-term consumption of alcohol raised the possibility of spontaneous combustion of the human body.[81]

Such warnings doubtless proved less threatening to the rural farmer, however, than the proposals of some advanced temperance advocates that apple orchards be destroyed. The consumption of hard cider, especially on farms, remained enormous, helped along, perhaps, by the fact that it was a product easily made "by exposing the cider to freezing weather, then removing the surface ice as it formed, leaving the remainder of higher alcoholic content."[82] Charles Paine, the nephew of Governor Charles Paine, recalled the central role of cider on his grandfather Elijah Paine's large farm in Williamstown. The farm boasted three sizable orchards providing mainly apples that were turned into cider, stored for a year in Paine's cellar, and then served in the fields to his farm workers "instead of water." The nephew recalled that "the jug came up to be filled with every load of hay or grain that was sent to the barns." In addition, his grandfather "always drank cider at every meal in small quantity, and there was *always* a pitcher of cider on the sideboard."[83]

Unsurprisingly, thousands of farmers opposed any intrusion in their cellar stocks of hard cider, and by 1836 had withdrawn from the temperance movement, striking it a substantial blow. When antiliquor leaders revived the call several years later, they jettisoned the use of moral suasion and the soliciting of converts to take the pledge in favor of a strategy of government-imposed prohibition.

Rousing greater moral and political ardor among Vermonters than temperance or any other reform was the issue of Antimasonry. The fraternal order of Freemasonry had come to America from England early in the eighteenth century and had grown rapidly during the period of the break with the British, attracting to its membership many of the leading figures of the revolutionary cause. A group of civic leaders in Springfield established the first lodge in Vermont in 1781, and other units followed, claiming many of the prominent and ambitious men in the growing towns.

Masonry also attracted opponents, however, who, as early as the 1790s, denounced the order as dangerously antidemocratic and elitist, citing its secret rites, elaborate regalia, and mysterious titles. The disappearance in September 1826 of William Morgan, a resident of Batavia in western New York's revival-prone "Burned-Over District," brought antimason emotions to a peak. Morgan had authored a pamphlet ostensibly revealing the secrets of Masonic rituals, and his sudden absence provoked suspicions. Accounts circulated in the press that he had been kidnapped and killed in an act of retaliation, and Masonry opponents grew quickly in number across New England and the old Northwest.

Vermonters of diverse backgrounds—"a coalition of the religiously zealous and socially discontent"—were drawn to the movement. Many were hard-pressed farmers and artisans uneasy about the emerging commercial market system and upset at the perceived privileges of those more successful in navigating the economic transition. To these groups in many towns, the more nimble economic gainers appeared as a new homegrown aristocracy that included lawyers, merchants, physicians, small manufacturers, and tavern owners (all "nonlaborers"), sharing disproportionately in the local wealth and power and participating disproportionately in the Masonic order. For them, this emerging "new, secular standing order" represented a failure of economic equity, a retreat from the ideals of the fading Revolutionary generation, and a development tantamount to "treason against republicanism."[84]

The Masons, however, drew complaints from other groups, as well. Christian women, troubled by what they perceived as immoral behavior, denounced the drinking and smoking that occurred behind closed doors of men's clubs. Free Will Baptist and Methodist leaders, fueled by ultraism and opposition to "hyper-Calvinism," paired their denunciations of Masonry as anti-Christian with affirmations of religion-based democratic ways, claiming that true doctrines of faith recognized an equality of spiritual footing among believers and thus stood in opposition to hierarchies of either church or state. Other evangelicals denounced Masons' perceived indifference to revivalism and characterized the group's fraternal attachments as representing direct competition with churchly institutions.

Vermont's newspapers carried dozens of stories over a period of months in 1826 and 1827, discussing William Morgan's possible fate and the case's potential implications. Numerous public meetings fanned already combative feelings. At a gathering in Randolph in May 1827, participants repeated the common antimason themes, denouncing the order for establishing "an unnatural and unwarranted distinction, a species of favoritism and aristocracy, derogatory to the equality of a free and independent people."[85]

As Antimasonry gained strength, it also drew critics who unleashed aggressive attacks of their own. The editor of the *Bennington Gazette* denounced the "antimasonic excitement" as "deplorable" and equated it with the "persecution and hanging of persons imagined wizards and witches" in Massachusetts a century and a half earlier. The *Burlington Sentinel* charged that the movement fed upon the prejudices of the lower classes, and dismissed the movement's leaders as "a mass of stupidity—a collection of individuals hardly qualified for *hog-reeves*."[86] Other defenders claimed the existence of a counter-conspiracy among antimasons that included anti-Calvinist, Universalist, and Baptist ministers. The Vermont Grand Master of Masons also tried, however ineffectively, to defend his order. In a public statement, he grandiloquently defined Masonry's purpose as the "great work of reforming and happifying the world" through "enlightening the understanding, cultivating the mental faculties and improving the moral virtues of men, and teaching them their duties and relations to each other, in connection with their religious obligations."[87]

Undeterred, the antimasonic movement swiftly shifted from a loose alliance to an organized political party, spreading across the eastern United States and to western Pennsylvania and Ohio. In Vermont, weakened political loyalties presented opportunities. From the close of the War of 1812, descendents of the old Democratic-Republicans controlled the governorship and legislature. In the winter of 1824–1825, however, after the disputed presidential election victory of John Quincy Adams over Andrew Jackson, national and state Democratic-Republican coalitions finally came apart. By the spring of 1825, Adams's supporters, including offspring of the old Federalists, began calling themselves "National Republicans," and Jackson's followers in several states, including Vermont, formed a new "Jacksonian" version of the Democratic-Republicans. In the 1828 presidential election, Adams and his new party gained three-fourths of Vermont's ballots, although the ticket lost to Jackson nationally in a landslide.

These shifting Vermont alignments provided the context in which the Antimason political party took form. Social activists in 1828 and 1829 who otherwise might have joined the National Republicans, moved toward the start-up Antimasons. Others who joined the new third party identified with Jackson's championing of the Common Man—his espousal of equality of opportunity and calls for the benefits of society to be fairly shared—but drew back from his energetic defense of slavery and his opposition to the protective tariff and internal improvements. Following a series of town gatherings in 1828, Antimasonic delegates met at Montpelier in August 1829 in what became the first political convention ever held in Vermont.[88] Chaired by Nathaniel Colver, a Baptist evangelist from Addison County, later described by John Quincy Adams as the most effective extemporaneous speaker he had ever heard, the Montpelier convention launched the Antimasons on their first political campaign. In that initial

As this 1830 publication indicates, even the cover pages of almanacs became fodder for the antimasonic campaign. *Vermont Historical Society.*

1829 outing, the new party elected William Cahoon, a farmer and veteran of the War of 1812 from Lyndonville, to Congress, and thirty-three Antimasons to the General Assembly. In the gubernatorial contest, the party drew 7,376 votes, only half that of the winning National Republicans but almost twice the totals of the Jacksonian candidate, an extraordinary beginning for a start-up party.

The new Antimason party rapidly became the state's strongest political force. Among northeastern states, only in Pennsylvania did Antimasons accrue the political strength exercised by the Vermont movement. In 1830, the new party's nominee for governor lost again, but attracted enough votes to send the contest to the legislature for a decision. In 1831, Antimason candidate William Palmer of Danville captured the governorship, the first of his four consecutive victories in that office. And in 1832, Vermont gave its electoral votes to the Antimason candidate for president, William Wirt of Maryland, the only state to do so, and sent Antimason William Slade to Congress.

The party's decline, however, proved to be as meteoric as its rise. By 1834, the movement's original target, Vermont Masonry, was in disarray, with most of its lodges either having suspended operations or surrendered their charters. This success, in turn, left the movement, whose state assembly members had seldom voted as a bloc and whose statewide office holders tended to follow a policy line similar to National Republicans, without its *raison d'être*. In addition, its national party offered no hope for success in the upcoming 1836 presidential race.[89]

Hastening the Antimasons' political demise was the new Whig Party that had emerged in time for the 1836 elections. The Whigs existed as a loose umbrella coalition of various anti-Jackson forces that included National Republicans, descendents of the old Federalists, and activists for anti-Catholicism, anti-immigration, antiliquor, antislavery, and other single-issue causes. The party's general strategy aimed at branding the Jacksonian Democratic Party as opposing not only the tariff, sound currency, and internal improvements, but abolitionism, temperance, and other reforms backed by churchgoing Vermonters. It specifically hoped to co-opt Antimasonic voters by depicting the Democrats as a "tyranny" more significant now than the Freemasons. They succeeded. The Antimasonic Party, with its members' energies increasingly redirected to other campaigns, notably temperance and antislavery, endorsed a slate of state and national candidates in 1836 identical with that of the Whig Party, and disappeared from view.[90] The Whigs carried the election, and for the next sixteen years the Vermont legislature and governorship resided, however tenuously, in Whig hands.

The revivalist-reformist temper of the 1820s and 1830s also stirred Vermont's organized antislavery movement. From the drafting of its 1777 constitution, Vermonters—whose landscape of harsh seasonal weather and small family farms discouraged economic interest in slavery—had maintained a consistent opposition to the institution, articulated on moral and religious grounds.[91] A small number of blacks did reside in Vermont in these early years, scattered from Hyde Park to Vergennes to Windsor, and elsewhere. Historian Randolph Roth estimates that approximately 250 blacks lived in the Connecticut Valley in the late eighteenth century, primarily in towns, where they catered to the needs of the wealthy, were not always treated respectfully, and "were not recognized as equals by other Vermonters."[92] Although blacks in Vermont did not confront legal barriers to voting as was common in other antebellum northern states, the question of racial equality in the Green Mountains, as elsewhere, was generally separated from the issue of slavery. Consequently, the handful of "slave" ownership cases on record resulted in court findings consistent with the slavery prohibition plank in the state Constitution. And the "higher law" legal argument that prosecutors utilized in these cases became a central feature in the claims of the later abolitionist movement.

Antislavery moved directly into the state's political consciousness in 1819 and 1820. The Vermont General Assembly joined the debate then under way in Congress over Missouri Territory's application for admission into the Union as a slave state. Legislators adopted resolutions declaring slavery "a moral and political evil"; that "the right to introduce and establish slavery, in a free government, does not exist"; and that Congress possessed the authority to "inhibit any further introduction, or extension of slavery, as one of the conditions upon which any new State shall be admitted into the Union."[93]

Beyond opposing its spread, however, Vermonters disagreed over just what should be done about slavery. The question attracted fresh attention after William Lloyd Garrison, a young Massachusetts journalist, arrived in Bennington in 1828. At the invitation of local citizens, he had accepted the editorship of the *Journal of the Times*, a campaign newspaper supporting the reelection of President John Quincy Adams. At the time, antislavery activism mainly involved fundraising efforts of the state chapter of the American Colonization Society (formed in 1819). The Society proposed using the funds to purchase slaves and return them to Africa, a goal that, when accomplished, according to Rev. John Kendrick Converse of Burlington, would "free this country from the unnumbered evils of a colored population."[94]

Garrison, whose views on slavery were in an early stage of development, embraced the colonization approach of gradual emancipation, and he supported removal but only for those liberated slaves "desirous of emigrating." He also urged a more activist program, advocating the formation of local antislavery societies as the basis of a proposed national antislavery movement. In January 1829 he forwarded a petition with 2,352 Green Mountain signatures to Vermont Congressman Jonathan Hunt urging the gradual abolition of slavery in the District of Columbia.

Garrison's efforts won him little support from prominent state politicians or clergy, however, and his verbal adroitness alienated others, earning him the title of "'My Lloyd' know-it-all" and a reputation as a man apparently on a mission "to civilise the Green Mountain Boys."[95] Many distinguished Vermonters, including former Governors Cornelius P. Van Ness and Ezra Butler, aligned themselves instead with a new Colonization Society drive to collect thirty-one thousand dollars for use in sending six hundred free blacks to Liberia, ostensibly as agents to Christianize the African continent. Disgruntled by his experience in the Green Mountains, Garrison offered "a word about Varmaount" to a friend in March 1829, as he described his imminent return to Boston: "I came to this state, you know, with extreme reluctance. . . . I leave it with *precipitate* delight, caring not whether I again see an inch of its territory, and, I had almost said, any of its inhabitants."[96]

Back in Boston, Garrison soon became founding editor of the *Liberator* newspaper and by 1831 had emerged as the national voice of the militant abolitionist movement, advocating a new policy of immediate emancipation. In 1832 Garrison organized the New England Antislavery Society, and that summer assigned Orson Murray, a recent convert to the energetic Christian life, to be its Vermont agent for three months. The Society espoused the view that because of its "sinfulness" slavery should be abolished immediately. Garrison, as well, began evolving his denunciation of the U.S. Constitution for its compromises with slavery, using the pages of the *Liberator* to brand the union of states a criminal compact, and eventually declaring the Constitution "a covenant with death and an agreement with Hell." This radical position, which appeared to eschew any role for political action, or compromise, provoked intense emotions across Vermont and New England, including fears for the future of the Union.

Audiences for the Vermont lectures of Murray and his fellow agent Oliver Johnson were invariably loud and unruly. In October, college students interrupted an address in Middlebury by "scraping of feet, frequent showering of corn over the room, and other disturbances designed to break up the meeting." When Murray arrived for a speaking engagement at the Congregational church in Bennington, he found an assembly already convened, with speaker after speaker portraying "in glowing clouds, the effects and consequences which must unavoidably accrue in case Garrison and his fanatical co-agitators could carry their mad project into effect."[97] Murray and his colleagues managed to form twenty local societies across the state, barely one-tenth the number established by the temperance crusade.

Such opposition reflected the reticence of numerous Vermonters at the time, including many church congregations, to embrace Garrison's "too enthusiastic" approach, and their greater comfort with the more moderate goals and methods of the Colonization Society.[98] That more conservative course, and the strong conviction with which many embraced it, was manifest in the stance of Elijah Paine of Williamstown, a United States district judge and former judge of the state Supreme Court. According to the memoir by his grandson, Paine, who was born in 1757 and served for several years as president of the Vermont Colonization Society, "belonged to the generation which solemnly agreed to the compromise with slavery contained in our Constitution, and he proposed to live up to it, cost what it would." To the judge and his family, consequently, abolitionists were "vile" attackers of the Constitution, "false to all obligations, deliberate repudiators of contracts, who renounced the vows made for them by their fathers." Raised in this atmosphere, the grandson added, "I really supposed . . . that there were no baser mortals than they."[99]

Abolitionists, however, continued to gain strength. In Middlebury, on May 1, 1834, antislavery activists founded the Vermont Antislavery Society as an auxiliary to the American Antislavery Society, formed five months earlier in Philadelphia. Among those attending the Middlebury meeting were former Governor Samuel Crafts and Ferrisburgh Quaker Rowland T. Robinson, who with his wife Rachel Gilpin Robinson had such dedication to the cause that they offered their home, Rokeby, as a stop along Vermont's informal network of the Underground Railroad and boycotted goods such as cotton and sugar associated with slavery.[100]

The eighty-six Middlebury convention delegates voted to expand the use of paid agents and continue to spread the gospel of "immediatism," agreeing with the American Antislavery Society founders that "no scheme for the abolition of slavery in the United States, which offers any prospect of success, has ever been proposed but that of Immediate Emancipation."[101] By its third anniversary, the Vermont Antislavery Society had grown to ninety chapters, with an estimated eight thousand members.

The various antislavery efforts, and the drift of national events, emboldened some of Vermont's political leaders to take more advanced positions of their own. Vermont's Congressman William Slade and Senator Benjamin Swift attracted national attention with ringing speeches on the floor of Congress denouncing "gag rules" aimed at halting the presentation before the two legislative bodies of antislavery petitions. In Montpelier, the Vermont legislature began peppering Congress with appeals against slavery's spread to the West. Resolutions in 1837 called on the state's Washington delegation to oppose admission to the Union of any new slave states, including Texas, and asserted the constitutional authority of Congress to abolish slavery in the District of Columbia and to legislate an end to the interstate slave trade. Presenting these petitions in the upper chamber, Swift told senators they came not from "fanatics" but from "the legislature of Vermont"; they were "the result of no party effort," but "the united voice of the whole state of Vermont." At the same time, Slade condemned the "gag rules" on the House floor as an attack not only on those who opposed slavery but on the right of free inquiry itself. "I cannot stand here as a freeman and the Representative of freemen," he told House members in one of the most bitter condemnations of slavery yet delivered in that chamber, "without declaring in the face of this House and of the world, that the right to hold men as goods and chattel . . . should cease and be discontinued instantly and forever."[102]

Many Vermonters nevertheless feared the possible effects of the various antislavery strategies. As Slade championed "free inquiry" in Congress, abolitionist supporters and agents found themselves silenced in many Vermont communities. During the fall of 1835, an Antislavery Society lecturer, calling for immediatism, faced down unruly mobs in several communities, with commercial and trade towns providing much of the resistance. At Montpelier, a prominent local banker interrupted a lecture and demanded an end to the speaker's "ungospel and anti-union harangue."[103] The major religious denominations in the towns of Randolph Center, Woodstock, and Windsor, reluctant to embrace immediatism, closed their meetinghouses to abolitionist speakers.

In some villages, opponents pelted the lecturer with eggs and booted him off the stage. At Newbury, where a mob had gathered to silence the speaker, violence broke out, resulting in arrest and conviction of several people for disturbing the peace. Even the great black abolitionist Frederick Douglass found the Green Mountains a difficult challenge. After attending an antislavery convention in Middlebury, he wrote of the "disrespect" he received during his state travels, and the failure of his efforts there: "Few people attended our meeting, and apparently little was accomplished by it."[104] The momentum of antislavery would soon strengthen, however, as national events turned the movement in more directly political directions during the decade of turmoil that lay immediately ahead.

The international dimension of Vermont's reform impulse during this era was on exhibit in Green Mountain reactions to the "*patriote*" uprising in Lower Canada in 1837 and 1838. At the center of this controversial political and military venture clustered a group of largely French-speaking Lower Canada reformers, or "*patriotes*," who demanded a greater voice in the popularly elected provincial assembly. Faced with English-speaking Canadian and official British intransigence, they launched a small-scale rebellion on November 23, 1837, at the village of St. Denis on the east bank of the Richelieu River. Officials dispatched British troops who quashed the insurrection and captured and imprisoned approximately five hundred *patriotes*.

Equal numbers of the rebels, however, fled across the United States border into New York and Vermont. In Alburg, Highgate, Swanton, St. Albans, and Burlington, the surviving insurgents plotted their return. The United States officially claimed neutrality in the dispute, and Governor Silas Jenison issued a proclamation reiterating that position. However, between December and January almost a dozen Vermont communities held public meetings to aid the refugees' cause and a reported 107 clandestine "hunters' lodges" formed to back military incursions into Lower Canada. The arrest in Windsor of two *patriotes*, Doctor Robert Nelson and C. H. O. Cote, for breach of American neutrality after a raid from Alburg in February 1838, provoked large public displays of support.

Following a jury's acquittal, a public banquet in Montpelier honored the pair. The attending celebrants offered twenty toasts, among them "Liberty," "Exiled Canadians," and "Green Mountain Juries," reflecting the connection felt by many Vermonters to the *patriote* cause, and their continued interest in a Canada free from British rule.[105]

In the end, however, support proved more rhetorical than revolutionary. Forays across the border, originating in Troy and Derby, did not succeed; and Canadian forces put down the movement in November 1838. The uprising's legacy for Vermont lay in the *patriotes'* exposure to bustling Burlington. As evidenced in the brief publication of a newspaper, the *Patriote Canadien*, in the Queen City in 1839–1840 by exiled *patriote* Ludger Duvernay, Burlington appeared as a prosperous industrial community "which presents to the traveler one of the picturesque and remarkable sights of Switzerland."[106] The refugees' exposure led to a significant increase in the French-Canadian population of the city.

For most Americans, however, 1837 was not remembered as the year of the "patriote uprising" but of the "great panic" and the onset of a nation-wide depression. Prosperity had reigned, generally, in the state and nation for a dozen years, but in the spring of 1837 the bubble burst. From March, and continuing into the fall, businesses failed from New Orleans to New England. Inflated real estate values collapsed, stock and commodity prices fell, and an acute banking crisis ensued. In southern New England, the Panic shut down mills, halted manufacturing, bankrupted large commercial concerns, and threw thousands out of work.

Although speculation in land values played a lesser role in Vermont than in Western states, the Green Mountains could not avoid being pulled into the national depression. In an uneven pattern, activities across the state, at many levels, felt the impact. The price of wool slumped by 25 percent. Some Vermont banks went under and others stopped specie payment. In Swanton, "most of the business men became embarrassed," and marble operations there and in Middlebury collapsed. While Rutland's prosperity was only "somewhat checked," the economic reversals forced several business enterprises in Bennington into liquidation and Bennington Seminary and Bennington Academy to close their doors. At Middletown, the shaken "credit system" proved "disastrous to many industrious and honest farmers." Danby farmers, as well, "suffered severely" and business experienced "a great decline" that lasted "for several years," prompting the community's citizens to begin plans for constructing a town poor house to cope with the crisis. The University of Vermont weathered the depression, but not before its president, John Wheeler, reported the school had been "sued for a large debt; the . . . Library was attached, and advertised at a Sheriff's Sale." On the positive side, the pace of emigration from the state actually slowed for a number of years as the West and other distant attractions temporarily lost their allure.[107]

The Panic of 1837, which did not generally abate until 1843, marked a fundamental divide in Vermont between the optimism of the postrevolutionary era—undergirded by economic growth and revival and reform idealism—and the more anxious outlook of the following decades. The economic setbacks, ultraism's excesses, and the increasingly divisive relationships among church and political groups as temperance and antislavery efforts moved away from moral suasion to controversial strategies of legislative coercion, signaled that the "Second Great Awakening" in Vermont, unequivocally, had reached an end.

Anxiety Replaces Optimism

As the decade of the 1830s closed, Vermonters struggled with the effects of the Panic and depression. For farmers, sheep still appeared to be the economic key. Significant problems with the corn harvest throughout the 1830s, associated with changing climatic conditions, rendered it all the more important to concentrate energies on grazing and haying. Even when wool prices dropped, farmers continued to expand their herds, anticipating an eventual return to higher prices. In 1836, the state's sheep population stood at slightly more than a million. Four years later, the U.S. census reported a total of 1,681,000 sheep, or six for every person in the state. Addison County, which led the way, with an average of 373 per square mile, "raised a greater number of sheep and produced more wool, in proportion either to territory or population, than any other county in the United States."[108] Approximately two hundred sheep per square mile or more could also be found in Chittenden, Windsor, Rutland, and Grand Isle counties.

The sheep mania continued to encourage farm consolidation. This tendency, along with the absence of available new farm acreage, in turn contributed to a persistent exodus from the land, begun in the 1810s and 1820s, of small farmers and landless sons. The 1840 census revealed the magnitude of this leave-taking from the state's farming communities.

Although Vermont's population increased by 4 percent during the decade, to slightly less than 292,000, five counties (Addison, Bennington, Rutland, Windham, and Windsor) each recorded net losses. The biggest shrinkage came in moderately large (populations of 1,500–2,000) commercial farming communities.

Growth persisted within selected urban centers. Montpelier's population increased from 2,985 to 3,725 residents, and Burlington's catapulted from 3,526 to 4,271, enabling it to lay claim as Vermont's largest city. Montpelier's rise derived from growth of the state government, but also from the continued expansion of trade and transport within Washington County. Burlington's prosperity rested on a number of factors: improvements to the town's inferior harbor by lengthening the breakwater; expansion of industrial frontage on the lake; and investments of capital to modernize small-scale glass, pottery, machinery, textile, iron-working, boat-building, and wood-fabrication industries. By 1840 Burlington's harbor area boasted a lighthouse, three thriving commercial wharves, and an annual wholesale trade estimated at over one million dollars. Burlington attracted wholesale, banking, and insurance enterprises, and a growing professional class including doctors, lawyers, teachers, and architects. In 1840 the city business directory listed seventy-three lines of business, including professions such as architect, auctioneer, brewer, carpet weaver, organ maker, and stucco worker.

Yet just as rural dwellers understood the mixed consequences in the relationship between increasing commercialization and the exodus of many native sons, urban dwellers also saw a double-edged sword in continued growth. The docks, building trades, factories—and, later in the

Brattleboro, shown here in the 1840s, joined Montpelier and Burlington among urban centers experiencing steady growth as the state approached mid-century. *Vermont Historical Society.*

decade, railroads—attracted new immigrant laborers who did not readily assimilate with the native population. Irish and French-Canadian arrivals brought distinctive ways and habits and, perhaps most disturbingly, their Roman Catholic faith. Although the 1840 census showed only small numbers of Irish and French-Canadian immigrants in the state, many Vermonters shared the nativist sentiments of Nathaniel Hawthorne, who observed of Burlington's Irish newcomers during a visit in the summer of 1835, "they swarm in huts and mean dwellings near the lake, lounge about the wharves, and elbow the native citizens entirely out of competition in their own line. . . . [I]t is difficult to conceive how a third part of them should earn even a daily glass of whiskey, which is doubtless their first necessary of life—daily bread being only the second."[109] By 1850, stimulated by the railroad's arrival, the Irish accounted for one-third of Burlington's population and performed approximately four-fifths of its manual labor.

The immigrant presence triggered considerable fear and anxiety in railroad communities across Vermont. In Barnet, a town father called for guarantees from the Connecticut & Passumpsic Railroad that the Irish would depart the area when their work on the rails was completed. The Newbury editor of the *Northern Protestant and American Advocate* insisted in 1847 that all Catholics, including increasing numbers of French Canadians, be deported from the state.[110] Many Vermonters reacted with consternation, consequently, when news spread in the late 1840s and 1850s that at St. Albans, Fairfield, Milton, and Burlington, prominent citizens, including the editor of the *Burlington Free Press* and his wife, had abandoned their Protestant denominations to become Catholic converts and fellow worshippers with the Irish and French Canadians.[111]

Other democratizing forces also fed Vermont's anxieties. The 1830s, a decade dominated by three-party political races, was a period of rising interest in public affairs and increasing voter participation in the state's elections. Turnouts grew from 25 percent of eligible voters for the governor's race of 1827, to 82 percent in 1840. This expanded electorate, with its fragmented party loyalties, created new complications. The state constitution required that successful candidates for executive offices must receive a majority of the total votes cast. Consequently, in this period of three-party politics, races for governor frequently had to be decided in the General Assembly because no candidate garnered a majority of votes. Moreover, dissatisfaction with the effectiveness of the single legislative body, the House, in this role contributed to the decision in 1836 to amend the state constitution by eliminating the Governor's Council and creating a thirty-member Senate, apportioned among the counties, to serve as a coordinate branch of the legislature with the House of Representatives.

Political party leaders, anxious about democracy's unpredictability, also sought to better manage the growing pool of voters. To this end, they brought into being an elaborate system of local, county, congressional district, and state conventions and rallies, guided by networks of party committees, coordinated at the town and state level. They hoped that such efforts would keep enthusiasm constantly stirred and result in high voter turnouts for their candidates. These activities tracked a new campaign style taking hold across the country that emphasized "dramatic spectacles . . . the mass rally, the procession, and the employment of banners, emblems, songs, and theatrical devices," and that fostered "club-like associations, colorful personalities, and emotionally charged appeals to party loyalty."[112]

In these efforts at voter management, party-affiliated newspapers gained importance in spreading the candidates' message. Thus, the *Burlington Free Press*, in addition to printing the local and village gossip, declaimed the slogans and epithets of the state's Whigs, making no distinction between news and editorial copy; the *Burlington Sentinel* did the same for the Democrats; and readers entered their subscriptions accordingly. Partisanship won readership: Of twenty-six long-lived Vermont weekly newspapers published in the 1840s, twelve carried the Whig banner, five identified with the Democrats, and two with the Liberty and Free Soil parties. The rest circulated as denominational or reform presses.[113] Historian Randolph Roth estimates that by 1835 four-fifths of households in the Connecticut Valley received such party-affiliated newspapers each week.[114]

Dewitt Clinton Clarke provides an example of a civic-minded citizen recruited to political involvement in the emerging new setting.[115] Clarke, who held numerous positions of state prominence during the 1840s, 1850s, and 1860s, received his start in politics as a young "doer and joiner" in Brandon. After moving to that village in 1837 at age twenty-six, where he worked for the Conant Iron Works, Clarke became a tireless community activist, helping to organize the village fire company and its library society, joining its reading society, serving as president of the Brandon Literary Association, as a justice of the peace, and on committees to improve local schools.

In 1839, Clarke joined the new Whig political party. Brandon party members selected him in June of that year as a delegate to the Whig state convention in Woodstock where he gained appointment as one of the convention's secretaries. At a county convention, delegates again chose him as secretary and appointed him to the Whig three-member county committee. Soon after, he delivered his first speech of a political sort at a Whig convention in Salisbury. Although he failed in a bid for his party's nomination to the state legislature, he did gain a patronage appointment in February 1840, as editor of the presidential campaign organ, the *Rutland and Addison County Whig,* and earned a place in the Vermont delegation to the National Convention of Whig Young Men, held in Baltimore, Maryland.

Clarke described himself, during this busy period, as in "a state of constant political animation."[116] In fact, he and fellow political operatives did function in a perpetual campaign atmosphere made necessary by state laws requiring annual election, on the first Tuesday in September, of representatives for the General Assembly, senators, and statewide officials, including a governor, lieutenant governor, and treasurer. Historian T. D. Seymour Bassett writes that Vermonters of the antebellum era "probably devoted more time to politics than to any other organized activity."[117]

The 1840 presidential election displayed the new party system at work. The campaign matched Whig candidate, military hero General William Henry Harrison, against incumbent Democrat Martin Van Buren. Vermont's Whigs copied the national party's leadership in running a "log cabin and hard cider" campaign touted as a people's crusade against the "aristocratic" Van Buren presidency.

The Whigs convened their state convention on June 25, in Burlington, under a banner announcing "the dawn of a brighter day." A parade of Whig supporters of "Tippecanoe and Tyler too" marched behind twelve "superb grays" hauling a twenty-foot by ten-foot cabin, the symbol of their candidate, a purported sturdy son of the frontier and simple man of the people. Gubernatorial aspirant Charles Paine of Northfield had constructed the cabin, mounted it on wheels, and driven it to Burlington, serving hard cider "from the door to all who cheered for the Whig candidates."[118]

Starting at the Burlington courthouse and marching eight abreast with flags and brass bands on that June parade day, the first of an estimated twelve thousand participants had already returned from the two-mile march around the town's borders before the last had even begun. The *New York Star* declared it the largest gathering of freemen New England had ever seen. Attendance estimates ranged from fifteen thousand to twenty-five thousand participants.[119]

The campaign's most memorable event, however, occurred two weeks later, on July 8, at the Bennington and Windham County Convention, on Stratton Mountain, where an estimated ten thousand Vermont Whigs assembled to hear the oratory of the United States Senator from Massachusetts, Daniel Webster. Although no text exists for Webster's speech, his correspondence reflects some of the themes he addressed. While the election of 1840 rested ostensibly on the overthrow of Democrats faulted for the depression, Webster framed the campaign in a way that captured the locally originating anxieties of many Vermonters: "We are either on the high ground to the accomplishment of the greatest civil revolution ever yet achieved in this country, or else we are in an enchanted ground, surrounded by farriers, fancies, phantoms, and dreams."[120]

During the election drive, the singing of campaign songs, often originating extemporaneously, and usually containing many verses, became common political fare. The flamboyant Dewitt Clinton Clarke again epitomized the young Whig Party's exuberant, aggressive spirit. A witness recalled that Clarke entertained his Brandon neighbors "by singing Whig songs from the platform around the pump in front of one of the taverns."[121] The importance placed by state leaders on this form of campaign expression is evident in a letter from a Democratic activist to party power broker and editor Charles G. Eastman, known also as a leading Green Mountain purveyor of light verse. Eastman's correspondent urged him to "write more [songs] . . . and send them on for the people must sing and if we suffer them to sing Whig doggerel when you can give them good poetry we ought to be crucified."[122]

Eastman and the Democrats, however—defensive over the economic depression and divided on moral issues of temperance and slavery—never had a chance in 1840: Vermont gave Harrison—a candidate with few known views—his largest majority, in proportion of votes cast (60 percent), of any state in the Union. And the military hero at Tippecanoe carried nineteen of the twenty-six states, with almost four-fifths of the nation's eligible voters casting ballots. In 1840, both of Vermont's U.S. senators and all five of its congressmen were also among those carrying the Whig banner.

No group celebrated Harrison's victory more optimistically than Vermont's sheep farmers. They hoped to be rewarded for their votes with tariff relief. None, however, was forthcoming. Reduced tariffs on wool, mandated by the compromise Tariff Act of 1833, took effect in 1840 and 1841, causing a further slump in wool prices. In New York, the price of wool experienced an additional drop of almost one-third, to roughly forty-four cents, and by the summer of 1842 some Vermont herdsmen claimed that costs exceeded income by more than one million dollars.

A Burlington poet active in state Democratic politics, John Godfrey Saxe, could not resist commenting on the Whigs' wool disappointments. He called his rhyming effort "The Whig's Lament."

> Oh dear! Oh dear! The times, the times—
> When will the story end.
> In spite of Tip and Tyler Too
> The times refuse to mend.
> We ask for change of government—
> Alas! The cry was rash—
> For though we've got a change in men—
> We've got no *change* in cash.
>
> In old Vermont-mont-mont
> We're in a dreadful state.
> Instead of fifty cents for wool
> We can't get thirty-eight.
> They promised if we'ed vote for Tip
> That wool would surely rise;
> But all they've done with wool has been
> To pull it o'er our eyes. [123]

Most devastating to Vermont sheep farmers, however, was the continued growth of supplies of cheaper western wool, transported to eastern markets via the Erie Canal. Additional trouble came in 1846 when the national Democrats, controlling both houses of Congress, finally succeeded in their quest to completely eliminate the tariff on wool. Prices slid to thirty cents a pound. With each animal averaging three pounds of fleece and the annual costs averaging $1.20 per animal, in contrast to $1.00 or less per head in the West, most Vermont farmers found themselves unable to continue. Observers reported that whole flocks were delivered to the Brighton market for slaughter. "What are we coming to?" asked one Middlebury farmer, as Vermont's sheep population fell by more than six hundred thousand in the four years following the tariff decision.

In one answer to that question, wool producers began forming market cooperatives, or associations, similar to the union organizations of wage-workers then being attempted in the larger cities of southern New England and, more pertinently, to the dairy unions that Vermont farmers would eventually organize in the 1930s and 1940s. Assuming that strength resided in numbers, they hoped, by acting together, to achieve more satisfactory relations with the purchasing agents of the large textile mills of southern New England. The cooperatives established depots for wool clip at Addison in 1847 and at White River Junction in 1849.

John Orvis, writing in *The Harbinger,* described how the cooperatives functioned: "Each farmer took his wool to the depot, where it is assorted into several qualities, each distinct quality being weighed and washed and marked, for which the owner receives, if he wishes, an advance of two-thirds the current price of wool of that quality. He will thus be enabled to wait until the wool can be disposed of at its full value. There will be one or two agents connected with a depot, who will attend to the assorting, weighing and selling, and whose expenses are to be defrayed by those interested. The effect of this arrangement will be to equalize the profits of wool growing, and to protect small farmers against speculators, whilst it will guarantee that reward to the growers of superior qualities of wool, to which their enterprise entitles them, and establish a unity of system in the wool trade throughout the country."[124]

These cooperatives, however, faced too large a challenge from the competition of Western growers to be able to save Vermont's wool industry. The state's flock size had reached a peak in the mid-1830s with an estimated 2.1 million sheep. By 1850 the number had dropped to 1,014,122 sheep and the decline continued steadily, if less precipitously, thereafter.

The slavery issue provided another destabilizing influence for the Whigs, and for the state's fragile political order. The congressional "gag rule" controversy (1836–1844), the United States acquisition of Texas (1845), and the Mexican War (1846–1848)—for which Vermont produced only one company of volunteers—brought slavery to the fore as the leading issue in state and national politics, galvanizing antislavery feelings, and increasing the difficulty of political compromise. Vermont abolitionists formed affiliates of the single-issue Liberty Party and Free Soil Party, with the latter making rapid gains and imposing new pressures on Vermont Whigs and Democrats, whose national party constituencies included a significant representation of proslavery Southerners. Whig Governor Carlos Coolidge illustrated the growing dilemma when he unceremoniously declared "hostility to Slavery is, in [Vermonters], an instinct,"[125] at the same time that his national party was cautiously seeking ways to make less obvious the division of its northern and southern branches.

In the 1848 presidential election, dissatisfied Whig leaders in Vermont and other New England states made an attempt to "abolitionize" their national party. The effort failed, however, when the Whigs selected as their nominee for president Zachary Taylor, a slave owner who agreed to adopt the party line of merely opposing slavery's extension. Whig strength in Vermont thereafter commenced a fatal decline.

The state's other parties, however, also struggled unsuccessfully with the slavery issue. Active for less than a decade, the Liberty Party in 1848 merged with the Free Soilers, who, in turn, a year later, in May 1849, entered a brief, abortive coalition with Vermont's Democrats hoping to take advantage of the weakened position of the Whigs. This alliance with the Democrats, whose party at the national level continued to be dominated by Southern and proslavery interests, only confused matters for those most committed to abolitionism. Free Soilers subsequently joined the Whigs in the downward slide.

The Democrats fared no better in their brief and fruitless coalition with Free Soilers. Throughout the 1830s and 1840s they had remained a minority party, unable to win the governorship or majorities in the legislature. Their struggle to accommodate to antislavery sentiments led them to create their own splinter groups under labels such as Independent, Locofoco, and Barnburner. These efforts not only failed to win more votes, but further discredited the party with its 1849 Free Soil alliance, giving it the appearance of a purely opportunistic organization, committed to no principles and interested only in gaining political power. In Vermont, as in a number of other states, the political picture that emerged by midcentury was one of fragmenting parties unable to come to terms with the volatile politics of antislavery.

Although Vermont's religious excitements had largely dissipated by the early 1840s, the state's landscape during this period nevertheless nurtured two remarkable religious innovators, John Humphrey Noyes and William Miller. (One of their contemporaries in religious innovation, Joseph Smith, 1805–1844, founder of the Mormon Church, was born in Sharon, Vermont, but departed with his parents for New York as a boy.) Both

Noyes and Miller sought to correct the "errors" of the earlier Awakening by fashioning their own religions. And the efforts of each climaxed in rounds of both confidence and anxiety for Vermonters with whom they came in contact.

John Humphrey Noyes started life in 1807, the son of a prosperous Putney merchant and Vermont congressman. Educated as an orthodox Congregationalist at the respected institutions of Andover, Dartmouth, and Yale, he used his learning to arrive at unorthodox conclusions. Noyes was attracted to the revivalist excitement of the 1820s and 1830s, and when the revivals' collapse came he viewed it as a failure not of intent but of execution. As he saw it, a religious conversion experience transported the individual into a state of temporary "perfection" that was difficult to sustain as one returned to the fallen world. Yet perfection, Noyes insisted, remained humanly possible: Humans could become free of sin, conduct themselves as God's coworkers, and establish the Kingdom of Heaven.

He believed the evils of humankind derived from society's breach with God, epitomized in a marital system that enslaved women, a labor system that oppressed men, and the human fear of death. Noyes thought that he had identified a form of community living and "chain of redemption" that would reconcile men and women with their God, restore "the true relations between sexes," reform the industrial system, and culminate with "victory over death." These views, according to historian Vernon Louis Parrington, made Noyes "probably the most radical American of the times."[126]

Noyes returned to his hometown of Putney in 1838 for the purpose of implementing his theory of Bible communism, as he referred to it. By 1843, he and his followers ran two farms and a local store. During these years Noyes extended his principle of communal sharing to sexuality, insisting that males could control, "by the moral faculty," what he called "amative" as opposed to "propagative" relations. While "complex marriage" liberated Noyes and his followers from the unnatural rule of the "one love theory," news of the goings-on in his experimental community led his Putney neighbors to drive Noyes and his followers from the town and the state in 1848. Their migration to the western frontier village of Oneida proved eventually to be New York's gain and Vermont's loss as the community gradually abandoned its more distinctive features and became wealthy through the manufacture of traps, hardware, embroidery silks, and silverware.[127]

The Baptist preacher, William Miller, enjoyed a significantly larger following than Noyes. Miller was born in Pittsfield in 1782 but moved with his parents to Poultney at age four. A convert to Baptist tenets during the revivalistic upsurge following the War of 1812 and a self-educated biblical scholar, he scrutinized apocalyptic references in the Bible to ascertain the exact moment the world would end. Miller concluded the date would be sometime "around 1843."[128] During the ultraistic revivals of 1832 he disseminated his findings to interested church members in Poultney and Pawlet. When the revivals ended, Miller shared his insights with a Baptist minister in Boston named Joshua V. Himes, and thereafter his message spread across the country in newspapers (including Boston's *Sign of the Times* and New York's *Midnight Cry*), pamphlets, and periodicals, drawing attention especially among communities of Methodists and Free Will Baptists.

Miller's Vermont followers believed that the recent revivals marked the last gathering of saints before the launching of Christ's thousand-year reign on earth. Determining the right time, exactly, thus became of central importance. Although Miller offered no precise date, followers selected March 21, 1843. Armed with this wisdom, they sang a camp meeting ditty: "Oh! The world will be burnt up in 1843; and then we'll have a great Jubilee!"[129] As the day grew near, many gave away their possessions and prepared to meet their maker. However, on March 21 nothing happened. Responding to the pleas of his followers, Miller asserted that his initial error was predicated upon his failure to use a Jewish calendar.

He offered other explanations, as well. Not long after the 21st had passed, the memoirist Charles Paine attended a Millerite meeting held at a starch factory in Waterbury. Miller impressed Paine as "an earnest, plain speaker of the Methodist style, without any effort at eloquence." The minister approached his subject at Waterbury by beginning "at the beginning, first demonstrating the reliable character of the Bible by pointing out how many of its prophecies had been fulfilled; second, the equal value of those relating to the 'Coming of our Lord'; third, the calculation of the fixed date which he still maintained had been correctly determined, since . . . the Lord had 'thrown in' repentance time and several other periods for which an arbitrary measure seemed to be assumed. . . . He still seemed to believe he could name the day, approximately."[130]

Miller did indeed ascertain a new date: March 21, 1844. And as the appointed time again drew near, frenzied followers sought to settle their accounts to enter the Kingdom. On the fateful day, many ascended to high places, climbing hills, trees, or buildings where they could "go up" with ease. According to one report, a Rutland resident constructed wings, climbed to the top of his barn and, at the appointed moment, leaped into a flight that became a free fall resulting in a broken leg. Again, the date proved wrong. When a third date, October 22, 1844, also proved disappointing, Miller's followers largely abandoned him. A number of small Adventist churches, nevertheless, persisted under his influence, and one Millerite offshoot formed the Seventh Day Adventist Church in 1863.[131]

The experiences of the Millerites stood as decidedly unusual, yet their behavior punctuated a changing mood among Vermonters who exhibited a lessened faith in the power of moral suasion to usher in a new millennium. Attitudes toward social reform underwent a similar review. As the optimistic belief that religious conviction could guide people to renounce sinful behavior receded, the reform activity that flourished in the 1840s relied increasingly on legislative action and the courts, rather than persuasion, to achieve desired ends.

Temperance provided a prime example. For three years following the Panic of 1837, the movement had languished in Vermont as it had in other northeastern states. In the summer of 1841, however, agents of a Baltimore-based group of self-described reform drunkards called the Washingtonians conducted "experience meetings" across Vermont, preaching the gospel of recovery. The emotional intensity of their meetings revitalized the call for action.

This time, however, activists pushed not for temperance but prohibition. Erastus Fairbanks, the St. Johnsbury manufacturer who later became governor, exemplified this new spirit. Under Fairbanks's leadership, the heretofore conservative Temperance Society joined a growing call for rigorous regulations. A memorial to the legislature from the Society provided the new direction's rationale: "It is a principle of law well established, and everywhere recognized, that no man is at liberty to use even his own property in such a manner as to essentially injure others, or to become a public nuisance."[132]

During the 1840s, the temperance crusade took up various strategies for achieving a viable prohibition law. A system of licensing of the sale of liquor by towns and counties became the central interdictive procedure. In 1844 the General Assembly enacted a bill with a local option approach, barring towns from licensing the sale of alcoholic beverages that had not provided formal authorization to a board of county commissioners as grantors of licenses. A law in 1847 prohibited all licensing of liquor sales unless a majority of Vermont towns approved licensing.

Speaking for many opponents of these attempts at prohibition, however, Vermont's Episcopal Bishop John Henry Hopkins warned against the infringement of public liberties and, over the decade of the 1840s this criticism largely stymied the prohibitionists' efforts. For example, the legislature did not reenact the 1847 bill the following year. Proponents of temperance nevertheless continued to see in prohibition the means to achieve what persuasion had fallen short of accomplishing. Finally in 1852, the General Assembly enacted a version of the famous Maine law, outlawing all sale and manufacture of alcoholic beverages, without qualification.

The campaign for school reform also gained strength during this period. As with the evolving antiliquor efforts, the school drive envisioned an increased role for state government in fostering education while also continuing to rely on innovative individual initiatives. Vermont demonstrated early that it offered fertile ground for educational innovation. In 1814, Emma Hart Willard established a visionary school for young women in her home at Middlebury before marrying and relocating to Troy, New York, where she founded the Troy Female Seminary, the first woman's high school in the United States. In Concord, Vermont, in 1823, Samuel Read Hall, a licensed Congregational minister, established the Concord Academy, the first normal school—or teacher-training institute—in the United States, using his own text, *Lectures on School-Keeping,* the first American book on teacher training (1829). Alexander Twilight, the first black graduate of an American college (Middlebury College, Class of 1823) and a licensed Presbyterian minister, brought unusual talent for teaching and enormous energy to Brownington, where he erected a four-story, fifty-room stone academy building in 1835 that he proudly named "Athenian Hall" and created a curriculum that included chemistry, botany, history, Latin, English, and music.[133]

Initiatives for common school improvement came, with mixed results, during the governorship of Cornelius Van Ness in the 1820s. The governor chastised his legislature for "so long [having] delayed to lend its direct and efficient aid to the general purposes of education,"[134] and persuaded it to create, in 1827, a Board of School Commissioners of Common Schools, the first such body in New England. Van Ness charged the board with the task of improving education by standardizing textbooks that parents purchased for their children. The proposal triggered a negative public reaction that led to the disbanding of the commissioners. According to a commission report, "the attempt, however well-intentioned, to dictate the books to be used in our common schools is regarded by many as invasion of the right of private judgment, and consequently incompatible with the genius of our free institutions."[135]

School reformers nevertheless persevered. By the 1840s activists drew inspiration from Horace Mann of Massachusetts, that state's first commissioner of education. One of Mann's initiatives called for the imposition of statewide standards for teacher preparation as well as textbooks. Mann influenced Vermont Governor William Slade and his successor Governor Horace Eaton, who simultaneously served as Vermont's first state superintendent of education, to implement a similar system. They achieved it in an "Act Relating to Common Schools" in November 1845.[136]

Seeking to correct what had earlier been characterized as a "checkerboard" in quality among local schools, the act created a hierarchical system of supervision, involving local overseers, county superintendents, and finally a state superintendent of common schools. The county superintendent possessed the central responsibilities of examining and certifying qualified teachers, calling annual conventions of educators, and compiling reports on school conditions. The new county superintendent's role, however, did not last long. Negative public reactions again surfaced, and the legislature, yielding to cost concerns and the powerful hold of localism, eliminated the office in 1849, and a few years later balked at funding the state superintendent's position, as well.

The language used by the first state superintendent, in his initial annual report, nevertheless underscored the importance that he and other prominent Vermonters placed in public education. Concerned by indications of social stratification that had been apparent from at least the 1770s, Eaton noted that "as society advances in age, there is ever growing up a tendency to widen disparities of rank and condition." He asserted that public education needed to function as an instrument through which "an equalizing power" would ensure against the emergence of class animosities. Viewed in light of an earlier attack by the *Rutland Herald* on Vermont's public schools as a "farce" and its criticism of the growing movement of wealthy Vermonters to withdraw their children and place them in private academies,[137] the act of 1845 constituted an important effort to reassert control over Vermont's future.

At the same time, Vermonters also sought to gain control of their past. In 1846, Norwich University professor James Davie Butler presented an address to the fledgling Vermont Historical Society, entitled "Deficiencies in Our History."[138] The Historical Society had been formed in 1838 by a select group of Vermonters who had figured prominently in the reform efforts of the previous decade. The founders included woolen manufacturer, temperance leader, and antiquarian Henry Stevens, its president, political figure and novelist Daniel Pierce Thompson, abolitionist-lawyer George Mansur, and lawyer-financier Oramel H. Smith, all of Montpelier.[139] These men sought to recapture what they saw as Vermont's lost identity—to gain control of their state's past. For them, that identity derived from the formative years between 1770 and 1791. As depicted in Thompson's *Green Mountain Boys* (1839), the era epitomized industriousness, decency, courage, independence, and enlightened compassion.

Stevens, Thompson, and Mansur (Smith played no active part in the organization after its founding) were part of a small but widening group, primarily in the older states of the northeast in the 1830s and 1840s, concerned about the absence of reverence shown by citizens for their collective past and the loss of imagined pioneer virtues. (The American Historical Society had been formed in Washington, D.C., two years earlier.) To these three, however, Vermont's situation appeared especially dire. Governor Chittenden's correspondence had been sold to a peddler as rags. Maps captured at the Battle of Bennington had been "used as curtains until all, save one, perished." Trophy arms and a drum captured at the same battle and presented to Vermont's governor and council had been "vilely thrown away." Observing that "young nations live in hope rather than in memory," Butler in his 1846 address depicted the resurrection of Vermont's past as nothing short of a moral imperative. As midcentury approached, however, some Vermonters found only meager evidence that the state's citizens shared any common set of values or experiences connecting them to this mythic past.

The emerging commercial economy's impact appeared to illustrate the point. In the 1840s it had begun to yield larger benefits for industrialists, merchants, some commercial farmers in the Champlain Valley, and, in scattered towns across the state that had hit upon a successful specialty product of some kind, for manufacturers. By 1850, the U.S. Census of Manufacturing listed among industries in Vermont twelve plants categorized as metalworking, machinery, tool, and instrument shops; twenty-four woolen mills; six enterprises classified as quarries, stone mills, and mines; and nine plants related to the cotton industry. The times, however, also bolstered the growth of an increasingly diverse laboring class. As large, expen-

Edward Norton, in top hat, sits with employees of the U.S. Pottery Company, founded at Bennington in 1800. Norton joined his family's prosperous firm as a partner in 1850. *Courtesy of Bennington Museum.*

sive Greek Revival homes appeared, reflecting the wealth of the 1840s, so did town poor farms come into view, in growing numbers, as communities turned to institutional means for coping with the indigents in their midst, their "physical unfortunates," and victims of the recent financial panic. For many Vermonters, the prosperity could be measured in an array of material improvements—in the proliferation of fine soaps, imported whale oil, new furniture, musical instruments—and in the number of formal holidays. Yet, at the same time, the prospects for property acquisition among growing numbers of propertyless rural and urban wage earners continued to fall.

The optimistic vision displayed by many Vermonters, so apparent a half-century earlier for two of the young state's key institutions, the prison and the university, now also flickered less brightly. The state prison at Windsor had been constructed at the direction of the 1807 legislature in the idealistic hope that an enlightened, new approach to punishment—replacing whipping, branding, and physical mutilation with confinement in a house of detention—could lead to reform of inmates' character. After its opening, however, the new facility struggled with inadequate sanitation, heating, and lighting, the consequence of underfunding and poor supervision by a neglectful and parsimonious legislature. It rapidly became overcrowded and its superintendent instituted a regime of harsh physical punishments to enforce discipline that, observers concluded, broke rather than mended the spirits of inmates. The superintendent, in addition, began the practice of contracting out prisoners as workers in the local machine-tool industry. Supporters of the prison only narrowly defeated a legislative bill in 1847 that would have closed the prison and moved it to the site of a marble quarry on Isle La Motte.

The University of Vermont also yielded disappointing returns. Opened in 1801 with hope and a flourish, it suffered through temporary wartime closure, religious controversy, insufficient financial support, a disastrous fire, and low enrollments. Further, it found itself mired in a struggle for preeminence with state rivals Middlebury College and Norwich University, a military college founded at Norwich in 1819. Finally, in 1836, the University of Vermont's medical department, begun in 1822 for the purpose of training physicians, had been forced to terminate its program because of insufficient student interest.[140] By the late 1840s, UVM—that "frail college"—feared for its very survival; and for the second time in thirty years, the school considered, but turned back, a proposed merger with Middlebury College.

Yet, for anxious Vermonters, perhaps the most telling development at midcentury was contained in a report by the United States census that during the decade of the 1840s, the state's population grew by less than 4 percent. In fact, the inability to keep up with the national pace in population growth had caused a reduction of Vermont representation in the House of Representatives from six in 1812 to five in 1822, and to four in 1842. The 1850 census provided a further disturbing population revelation: That the exodus of residents from the state, initially noted in 1810, continued and expanded. Forty-two percent of all native-born Vermonters now resided outside the state. It appeared likely that if children of natives born outside Vermont were included, the population totals would show more Vermonters living outside than within the state.

Vermont residents in 1850 faced the future with ambivalence. The spirit of enterprise and hope evident in 1807 had helped shape Vermont's peculiar—and ultimately triumphant—participation in the United States's second war with Great Britain; and it drew many of its citizens to an idealistic dalliance with democratic rebels in neighboring Canada. It had also energized the transitions of practical Vermont farmers from subsistence agriculture to the market system, business enterprisers from home industry to the beginnings of expansive commercial and manufacturing activity—including the railroad revolution of the second half of the nineteenth century—and its overwhelmingly rural population to increased contact with the larger world. But many reasons to be anxious remained: the nagging fact of the state's falling population growth rate, its basically flat economy, the dissipation of revivalist passions, a rising uneasiness concerning "foreign immigrants," and an enlarging sense that an era of social and political ferment had passed.

5
Links to the Nation
1850–1870

The Iron Horse in the Green Mountains

"If anyone wishes to visit Vermont I advise them to wait until the RailRoad is made, which will probably be next Summer." Addison Bancroft of Philadelphia had just returned home from a grueling trip from Boston to Cabot in August 1847. In his journey, Bancroft used every form of transportation available in his day: horse and wagon, horseback, foot, stage, steamboat, canal boat, and, outside Vermont, the railroad. The roads in Vermont were bad, he reported, and the stage coach crowded and bone shaking.[1]

Bancroft was overly optimistic. More than two years later, on December 31, 1849, a locomotive of the Vermont Central Railroad finally steamed into Burlington, completing a 117-mile trip across the state from Windsor on the Connecticut River to Lake Champlain. Although ignored by the press, the trip nonetheless ushered in both a new decade and a new era in the history of Vermont. The twenty-year period that followed the arrival of

Construction site on the St. Johnsbury and Lake Champlain Railroad (c. 1895). Although not among the first railroads built in Vermont, the St. J & L.C. encountered many of the same difficulties of overcoming topography and geology, as demonstrated in this photograph of a crew laying rails along a steep escarpment. *Vermont Historical Society.*

the railroad in Vermont encompassed important changes in the landscape and the political, economic, and social life of the state. Now, more physically connected to other eastern states, more economically connected to the larger markets for its agricultural and industrial products, and more politically engaged in the ferment of mid-nineteenth-century America, Vermonters became increasingly integrated into the outlook and institutions that so significantly shaped the nation during this watershed era.

The completion of the rail connection between the east and west boundaries of Vermont was a bittersweet triumph for the Vermont Central's president and former Vermont governor, Charles Paine. The climax of almost twenty years of planning and scheming, Paine's locomotive was the second railroad to cross the mountains. Barely two weeks earlier, on December 18, trains starting from Bellows Falls and Burlington met on the tracks of the Rutland and Burlington Railroad at Mount Holly, where workers excavating for the rail bed in 1848 had uncovered the skeleton, tusks, and teeth of a prehistoric mammoth. Where the two trains met, a celebration took place that included mixing kegs of water from Boston harbor and Lake Champlain. Because the rail connection to Boston was not yet completed, the ceremony only symbolically linked the former inland sea with the Atlantic Ocean. Yet all present acknowledged that this event lowered the barriers that separated the east and west sides of the Green Mountain State and tied Vermont more securely to the economic centers of the east coast.

Railroads came late to Vermont, a reflection on the state's geography, its small and slowly growing population, and its comparative poverty at mid-century. Plans began to be laid for building railroads as early as 1830, when rival entrepreneurs Charles Paine of Northfield and Timothy Follett of Burlington met with others at the Pavilion Hotel in Montpelier to discuss their interest in bringing the new transportation technology to the Green Mountain State. A year later Rutland caught the railroad fever that was sweeping the state and a series of mass meetings whipped up enthusiasm but no capital for the expensive and formidable task. By 1835, Paine had a charter from the state to build a railroad across the Green Mountains, but he, too, was unable to accumulate the necessary capital and the Panic of 1837 forced further delay.

Although the expectation of enormous profits drove the railroad promoters and entrepreneurs, it was clear from the beginning that Vermont traffic alone could not support the enormous costs of building and maintaining a railroad. Paine, Follett, and their financial backers therefore intended to make Vermont the connecting link between Canadian markets in the north; Boston to the east; Long Island Sound, New York City, Philadelphia, Baltimore, and Washington, D.C. to the south; and the Great Lakes to the west. The 1843 session of the Vermont General Assembly passed bills authorizing the construction of four railroad lines that reflected these goals: the Vermont Central, connecting the Connecticut River with Lake Champlain; the Champlain & Connecticut River (later called the Rutland & Burlington and eventually the Rutland Railroad), going south from Burlington through Addison, Rutland, and Windham or Windsor counties to "some point on the west bank of Connecticut river, as such Company shall designate"; the Connecticut & Passumpsic, going north along the Connecticut River valley to reach Canada; and the Vermont & Massachusetts, going south from Brattleboro to Fitchburg, Massachusetts.[2] A railroad convention in Montpelier in January 1844 expressed renewed enthusiasm for the project and by November of that year a survey of the land was underway to determine feasible routes.

Encouraged by the revived interest, Paine began selling stock in the Vermont Central in 1845, and in June that year the first stockholders' meeting elected him president of the company. By that time he had accumulated $2 million in capital investments, $1.5 million of which came from Boston. A year later Paine hired Seward F. Belknap to build the Vermont Central Railroad from Windsor to Burlington.

Belknap divided the project into three sections: Windsor to White River Junction (15 miles); White River Junction to Northfield (53.51 miles); and Northfield to Burlington (48.21 miles). The route itself was controversial, determined as much by politics and personal gain for Paine as by the dictates of the difficult terrain. This was to be one of the problems that would plague Vermont's railroads throughout their history. Paine insisted on taking the tracks through Northfield, his home town. This meant that the road would cross the height of land at Roxbury and enter the Winooski River valley west of Montpelier, thereby missing the state capital and Barre, which were to be connected by a spur. The alternative route, north from Bethel and crossing the height of land at Williamstown Gap, would have been five miles shorter and taken the train through Barre and Montpelier, but Paine insisted that his route would cost less and take less time because the elevation at the highest point was lower through Roxbury. Unstated, but nonetheless important, was the fact that Paine himself was heavily invested in properties in Northfield and used his position as president of the company not only to determine the route, but to make that town the railroad's operating center.

Ground breaking for the Windsor-to-White River Junction stretch took place on December 15, 1845. Crews of predominantly Irish laborers—Vermont's first major non-Yankee immigrant population—constructed all three legs of the route simultaneously. The unforgiving topography slowed the pace of work and money was a constant problem, sometimes halting work entirely and on one occasion resulting in Vermont's first labor strike, the "Bolton War."

On July 3, 1846, laborers near Richmond in the Bolton flats walked off the job, disgusted at not having received any pay since they began work in April. Frustrated still further when money sent to the subcontractor was used to pay for food and supplies, the laborers blocked the road between Burlington and Montpelier, took the subcontractor hostage, and sent his assistant back to Montpelier to get the payroll. The local sheriff called for help and on July 4 the Burlington Light Infantry marched into Bolton Valley, joined by the local fire company, deputized and armed. A Catholic priest convinced the laborers to release their hostage and disperse, only to see a dozen of the leaders jailed and many denied their wages.

Commenting on both the cause and effect of this collective labor action, DeWitt Clinton Clarke, who had only recently acquired the *Burlington Free Press*, wrote in its July 10, 1846 issue a remarkably balanced opinion. The workers "ought to have been promptly paid," he asserted. Unsympathetic though he was to the walkout and the workers' collective action, Clarke also castigated the owners of the railroad for their part in provoking the crisis. "Holding all resistance to the LAWS, and all illegal combination for the purposes of redressing even *real* wrongs, in utter abhorrence, and believing that they should be suppressed, promptly and if necessary by armed force, we yet unhesitatingly affirm that these laborers, indefensible as their conduct became, were NOT *the first wrongdoers.* That sin must lie at the door of those who, knowing their necessities, continued to receive the benefit of their unrewarded labor."[3]

Passenger service in Vermont began on June 26, 1848, when the Vermont Central opened twenty-seven miles of track between White River Junction and Bethel. The *Vermont Watchman*, July 6, 1848, published an enthusiastic report of the event, and predicted a bright new future for the state's economy.

> Three beautifully finished cars were filled with passengers, among whom was the honorable Abbott Lawrence of Boston. . . . The cars were about an hour going to Bethel, where upon our arrival, we found an extensive table bountifully spread with all the substantial comforts that could be desired. The Hon. gentleman seemed highly pleased with . . . that portion of the Central Road over which he had just passed—so thoroughly and faithfully constructed, and forming an important link in the great chain of railway communication that is to develop our resources and bring us into close contact with the Atlantic Border and the Great Lakes of the Northwest; so that Vermont can be called an inland state but a short time longer, so far as the term relates to the development of our dormant resources and the immeasurably increased facilities of approaching the great markets . . . . [A]ll present, seemed inspired with the importance of the opening to Vermont of the great future. . . . [W]e congratulate all our friends. . . on the prospect before them—on the prospect of having through the very heart of Vermont one of the most thoroughly and substantially built railroads in the country.[4]

On October 10 service reached as far as Northfield; on February 13, 1849, freight and passenger service was in operation between Windsor and White River; and three days later full service began between Windsor and Northfield. On July 4, 1849, a revenue train entered Montpelier on the promised spur from the junction of the Dog and Winooski rivers west of the city. The tracks reached Middlesex by August, Waterbury in September, and Burlington at the end of the year. By that time, however, Paine and his railroad were in dire financial straits. The 116 miles of track cost over $4.1 million to build. The wood-fueled steam locomotives, climbing steep grades, had to stop every thirty miles to refuel—a boon to the lumber and wood-cutting industry, but a factor that drove the cost of operations ever higher. Moreover, as predicted, Burlington's small population of 7,585 proved inadequate for generating sufficient passenger or freight revenue to maintain the railroad. In order to compete with steamboats on Lake Champlain that carried goods and people south to Whitehall with its rail connections to Albany and points south, the Vermont Central had to negotiate low rates that brought business but failed to cover costs. In his memoirs, Jonas Wilder, acting as agent for the Vermont Central, described shipping barrels of lime from Burlington free to generate business: "The scheme worked and orders came in and the result was that [Judge Underwood] had to build six more kilns and gave the R.R. line nearly a $1,000 freight per month." Another time, Wilder conducted impromptu negotiations for a rate of $4.00 per thousand board feet of prime Canadian pine to stimulate the market. Neither the shipper nor the railroad agent knew if this was a good price, but it soon became the standard for the Burlington railhead.[5]

Worse still, the rail service that ran between Ogdensburg, New York, and Lake Champlain, connecting the Great Lakes and west with the Northeast, terminated at Rouses Point. To secure freight contracts, the Vermont Central had to lease steamboats to carry goods across the lake to its Burlington terminal, further driving up costs.

The Vermont Central was saved from early ruin when Paine negotiated an agreement linking his line with John Gregory Smith's Vermont & Canada Railroad. Chartered in 1845 and headquartered in St. Albans, the Vermont & Canada provided the crucial rail connections to Rouses Point, Montreal, and Ogdensburg, gateway to the productive western states. Paine and Smith agreed to connect their lines east of Burlington at Essex Junction and in 1851 a rail connection from Highgate to Rouses Point completed the first through route from Boston to the St. Lawrence River. The accomplishment was celebrated in Boston with three days of festivities attended by U.S. President Millard Fillmore, the governor general of Canada, the governors of Massachusetts, New Hampshire, and Vermont, and railroad officials.

The alliance between Paine and Smith eventually cost Paine the directorship of his railroad. His financial collapse and the reorganization of his company were harbingers of things to come. More important, the merger undermined any hope for the financial success of the Burlington & Washington Railroad, now called the Rutland & Burlington.

"The history of the Rutland," writes geographer Harold Meeks, "tells of a railroad going from nowhere to nowhere, trying to get somewhere."[6] Although Timothy Follett's railroad provided through service between Boston and Burlington by December 24, 1849, without a connection to Canada or the road west, the future was limited at best and bleak for the Rutland road. Follett tried to secure rights of way for a rail line to St. Albans, where he hoped to connect with the Vermont & Canada, but Smith and Paine—both with excellent political connections—blocked him at every turn and by 1851 Follett admitted defeat. When a scheme to combine rail and water transport proved unprofitable, Follett negotiated a series of leases that eventually gave the Rutland & Burlington control of tracks built by the Rensselaer & Saratoga, Bennington & Rutland, and Troy & Boston railroads. This combination opened routes to Albany and New York City but did not solve the problem of obtaining a northern connection. Financial irregularities put the railroad in peril and in 1867 John Page, president of Howe Scale Company in Rutland, took it into receivership and reorganized the business as the Rutland Railroad.

Page saw opportunities for coercing the Vermont Central into cooperation. Between 1867 and 1870 he succeeded in leasing several more lines, which gave him connections south to Massachusetts and Long Island Sound. He began operating the steamer *Oakes Ames* between Plattsburgh and Burlington. Faster and more reliable than its predecessors, the boat service cut deeply into the rival Vermont Central's growing lumber business. Page's final triumph came in 1870, when he assembled a combination of leases that gave the Rutland its long-sought connection north. The Vermont Central was finally forced to negotiate with the Rutland. On December 31, 1870, the twenty-year rivalry came to end when a newly reorganized and renamed Central Vermont signed a lease giving it control of the Rutland Railroad tracks, including a lease on the *Oakes Ames*, a boat that it did not need, in return for payments totaling $7.14 million over twenty years.

While initial railroad planning focused on southern connections to Boston and New York, an alternative route took shape in the mid-1840s, when John Alfred Poor of Maine began an intricate set of negotiations to lay tracks between Portland, Maine, and Montreal. He quickly found Canadian backers interested in connecting Montreal with the Eastern Townships. In August 1846 work began on 165 miles of railroad going west from Portland and in October Canadian crews began laying rail beds going east from Montreal 132 miles to the U.S. border at Norton, Vermont. The centerpiece of this complicated international arrangement was the agreement to make Island Pond, Vermont, located almost exactly midway between Portland and Montreal, the terminal for two independent railroads. Service between Portland and Island Pond opened in May 1853 and the Island Pond-to-Montreal stretch began operating in July.

By this time, the rail connections between Brattleboro and Boston had opened in 1849 and the Vermont Valley Railroad, connecting Bellows Falls with Brattleboro, began service in 1851. However, the fourth railroad envisioned by the Vermont General Assembly in 1843 took longer to complete. The Connecticut & Passumpsic provided service between White River Junction and St. Johnsbury by 1850. But no further construction took place for over a decade. In 1863 track reached Newport and the Canadian border, but again came to a dead end for four years. Meanwhile, another Vermont industrial magnate, Horace Fairbanks, president of E. & T. Fairbanks Scale Company, began his own efforts to establish an east-west connection across the top of the state. In 1864 Fairbanks assembled nine colleagues and secured a charter for the Essex County Railroad to build twenty-two miles of track connecting St. Johnsbury with Lunenburg on the Connecticut River, with the intention of linking up to Portland. Two years later, Fairbanks joined with twelve other financiers to charter the Montpelier & St. Johnsbury Railroad. As president of both companies, Fairbanks planned to make St. Johnsbury a northern hub providing through service in all four directions. However, the Central Vermont refused to provide the switching agreement that Fairbanks counted on, thus cutting off the link to the west, and Montpelier's merchants and residents disappointed Fairbanks by refusing to approve bond money to build the northern connection. Faced with this double failure, Fairbanks plotted a new route 100 miles across the state from St. Johnsbury to Swanton. Portland businessmen, lured by a shorter through route to the west, now joined Fairbanks to charter the Portland & Ogdensburg in 1868. Work began in December 1869, but the route presented many obstacles and service did not open until 1877.

By then the first stage of railroad building was over. The four routes chartered by the legislature in 1843 were established, providing the state with over five hundred miles of track. Moreover, through acquisition, financial collapse, restructuring, and leases, the congeries of corporations that built Vermont's first railroads merged into a few large corporations operating the railways that connected Vermont to larger markets north, south, east, and west. Infilling with short lines, spurs, and connections over difficult terrain to serve communities and businesses in the interior, took place in the three decades from 1870 to 1900.[7]

The railroad had a profound and far-reaching effect on Vermont politics, its economy, social, and cultural life, and on the land. Railroad building and operation in the 1850s and 1860s required more capital than anticipated, involved higher-stakes political and financial dealing than the state had ever seen, and called upon extraordinary ingenuity, initiative, experimentation, and boldness. Vermont, and America as a nation, had never before seen such capital accumulation nor such a constellation of business challenges associated with one type of enterprise. Not even the textile mills and canals of the previous generation—the two other major financial and management enterprises of the early nineteenth century—compared with railroads in the size or complexity of initial costs, operating expenses, payrolls, or technically difficult decisions.[8]

The railroads created fortunes for some, catapulted a few into political power, and altered the lives and vocations of many. Four railroad builders in the 1840s to 1860s became governors: Charles Paine (1841–1843), J. Gregory Smith (1863–1865), John B. Page (1867–1869), and Horace Fairbanks (1876–1878). Others associated with the railroad would follow them into the governorship later in the century and into the first quarter of the twentieth century before railroading went into steep decline. Many Vermonters saw their lives completely altered by the railroad. Thomas H. Canfield of Arlington started life on a farm, studied engineering, then became a successful and prosperous merchant and wholesale shipper in Burlington in the 1840s. Associated with Timothy Follett's shipping company after 1848, Canfield soon supervised an elaborate network of wharves, warehouses, and steamships that moved manufactured and agricultural goods across as well as up and down Lake Champlain. He helped organize and finance one of the first telegraph lines in the Champlain Valley from Troy to Burlington. Through Follett's involvement in the Rutland & Burlington, Canfield was drawn into railroading, first as a manager and then as superintendent and president of the Rutland & Washington, then as private lease holder of the railroad. In 1852 he organized the first direct run between New York City and Montreal. He then moved west, where he became active in building the Chicago & Northwestern Railroad. Called to Washington, D.C., during the Civil War, Canfield served as assistant secretary of war in charge of railroads around the District of Columbia. Immediately following the war he went west again where, as an associate of John Gregory Smith of St. Albans and Frederick Billings of Woodstock, Vermont, he became a director, general agent, member of the board, and finally manager of the Northern Pacific Railway, one of the largest corporate enterprises in nineteenth-century America.

Thomas H. Canfield. *Vermont Historical Society.*

Canfield's career, so intimately linked with railroading, nonetheless shows the transition from one mode of transportation to another. He never completely abandoned an interest in water transport, holding the position of general superintendent of a steamer on Lake Champlain during the Civil War and, after he moved west a second time, negotiating the sale of the Oregon Navigation Company to the Northern Pacific.[9]

Jonas Wilder was another Vermonter whose life became intertwined with the young railroad industry. His biography shows how the industry itself grew, improvised, and invented new patterns of operation and organization. Born in Wendell, Massachusetts, in 1813, Wilder left farming to become a cobbler, then at age sixteen a peddler, achieving sufficient success within five years to pay off family debts. He migrated to Vermont and took a job on a construction crew of the Vermont Central. Within a few years he was in charge of the commissary and supply departments on the Vermont Central, then added to his responsibilities supervision of a division of track construction. He next moved into the operations division where he managed the freight, tickets, and organization of the stations of the western division (Waterbury to Burlington), and brought the Vermont Central some of its first big freight contracts. He improvised shipments of freight across Lake Champlain by sled and steamboat, negotiated contracts with Great Lakes steamboat companies, suggested the idea and supervised construction in 1852 of the first refrigerator freight cars for shipping butter, invented the coupon ticket to simplify passenger booking for through services over different railroad lines, and worked with quarry owners in Vermont to provide rail service for marble and slate. After ten years with the Vermont Central and the Rutland & Washington, Wilder resigned in 1858. He bought a wood lot near the railroad, sold wood for fuel and ties, and opened a general store that he turned into a small department store that did business of $50,000 a year until 1861, when he returned to railroading. In 1893, at the age of 80, Wilder retired—a prosperous man with an impressive record of service and innovation.[10]

Most of the stories of life on the railroad were not so happy. Those who built the roads, mostly recent Irish immigrants, endured dangerous working conditions when embankments or bridges collapsed, explosions went off prematurely, or equipment cars derailed. They and their families lived migratory lives, received low wages and sometimes no pay for long periods of time, and had few prospects for upward social mobility. Constantly on the move, most Irish workers rarely stayed in a community

The locomotive "T. M. Deal," built in 1865 as the "St. John," rebuilt in 1881 and used until 1899. *Vermont Historical Society.*

long enough to be counted in two successive decennial censuses. They held a disproportionately high number of unskilled jobs. In 1850, Irish men comprised just under 10 percent of the male work force in Northfield but 22 percent of its unskilled labor force. Irish women fared no better. Most unmarried or divorced women found work as domestic servants; married women took in washing.[11]

Laborers on the construction gangs occupied the lowest of many rungs on the ladder of railway employment. Incomplete records and unreliable census data make it difficult to say with certainty how many people the railroads employed in their first two decades of operation in Vermont. In the 1860s, however, Vermont Central Railroad payrolls stood at approximately twelve hundred workers. In addition to construction crews, the railroads employed more-specialized laborers such as locomotive engineers, firemen, brakemen, conductors, station agents, carpenters, machinists, and painters. Many of these men were recruited from other transportation concerns—the steamboat and stagecoach companies being driven out of business by the railroads—or from apprentices in machine and blacksmith shops. A significant number of young men came off the farm to work for a few years on the railroad before going on to other trades or occupations. Wages, benefits, and prestige varied greatly, as did mobility within the industry; but in contrast with the Irish gang laborers, the highly skilled engineers and conductors enjoyed some of the highest-paying and most respected jobs in mid-nineteenth-century Vermont.[12]

The railroads touched the lives and work of many people in addition to those they employed directly. Large industrial concerns such as Fairbanks Scales in St. Johnsbury, Howe Scales in Rutland, Estey Organ Company in Brattleboro, the Rutland-area marble and slate quarries, and lumber and wood-products companies, suddenly found new, faster, and less expensive ways to serve national or international markets. Lumber especially benefitted from the rail connections to Boston and coastal markets. Steamboat traffic struggling to maintain passenger excursions after the railroad made the connections to Boston, New York, and Montreal, surged briefly as millions of board feet of Canadian timber moved on barges up the Richelieu River, through the Chambly Canal, to the Burlington wharves where they were sawed, planed, loaded on railroads, and shipped east or south. By 1860 Burlington was handling 40 million board feet of Canadian and Adirondack pine, spruce, and fir. In 1868, according to historian Ralph Nading Hill, some four hundred American and Canadian vessels serviced the Burlington lumber wharves. At the height of the lumber boom, around 1873, Burlington ranked among the largest lumber ports in the nation, served by 1,021 registered steamers, ships, and canal boats that brought 170 million board feet to its wharves. Lumberyards covered thirty acres around the wharves and held the dressed wood for shipment by rail to meet the construction needs of cities throughout the east. Related industries, such as furniture, bowls, and wooden implements, also thrived and used the railroad to ship goods to distant markets. Within two decades, however, western lumber had made deep inroads into the business of the Canadian and northern Adirondack suppliers and the lumber business collapsed, taking with it much of the lake freight traffic.[13]

With more money in circulation and a dramatic increase in the volume of goods passing through Vermont by rail, banking and insurance companies became more ubiquitous, sometimes more profitable, and more risky. In a period when the railroads were at the center of change in the kinds and operations of business, banks found themselves handling enormous sums of money, saddled with bad loans, or issuing too much in bank notes in proportion to their cash reserves. As inventories grew, entrepreneurs built or expanded mills and factories, hired large numbers of new employees, and created a demand for fire and life insurance to protect themselves and their companies against losses.

Rutland & Burlington Railroad. Advertisement for Independence Day excursion, July 4, 1853. *Broadside, Vermont Historical Society.*

The railroad also took a leading role in the burgeoning tourist industry, promoting day excursions for holidays and special events as well as interstate travel for summer residencies. In addition to timetables, railroads published tour books describing scenery, points of interest, accommodations, and nearby facilities. Vermont's mineral springs, an attraction for health-seeking tourists since the early nineteenth century, now became a mecca for the fashionable, who traveled great distances to take the waters at Vermont's hotels. With only a few exceptions, the most successful mineral spring hotels were within five miles of a railway depot, with convenient, if not always comfortable, stage connections. Vermont's Southern clientele, numerous in the middle decades of the century, dropped off abruptly when the Civil War began; but the popularity of mineral springs as resorts continued to soar throughout the second half of the nineteenth century.[14]

Where the railroad passed, towns and villages frequently reoriented themselves to take advantage of new opportunities. Hill towns, such as Rutland, Bellows Falls, and Randolph, moved down to the valley; other towns, such as Danby, Essex, St. Albans, Newport, Barton, Newbury, and Hartford, shifted their centers to meet the tracks. The railroad created some new communities, such as the villages of Island Pond and Essex Junction. Wherever the tracks ran, the landscape changed, property values soared, and homesteads improved. Forests disappeared to feed the iron horse, giving farmers a new source of income until coal from Pennsylvania began to replace wood in the early 1860s. And although most stockholders lost money, the railroad made great fortunes for a few men and transformed the rural economy of Vermont by reducing the amount of barter and expanding the volume of cash purchases of a wider variety of goods brought from a wider range of production centers. With the railroad came the telegraph, faster postal service, and quicker, more reliable communication with a wider world. Newspapers, which only a generation earlier had reprinted accounts that editors read from colleagues down country, now scrambled to keep up with news of national and world events arriving by train and telegraph. A few weeklies became dailies; other printers kept their presses running by turning out the business forms, advertising broadsides, and train schedules required in the increasingly sophisticated and complex business environment.

The railroad even altered the compositions of artists, who now began to abandon the sublime style of the Hudson River School, with its rugged

VIEW OF THE EAST DORSET.
Italian Marble Mountain & Mills.
PUBLISHED BY D. L. KENT & CO, EAST DORSET VERMONT

"View of East Dorset Marble Mill," by Frank Childs. Childs painted this scene c. 1875. It was later published as a color lithograph by D. L. Kent and Company. *Vermont Historical Society.*

and barely inhabited forests and streams, and to include trains in their landscapes as symbols of progress in the midst of Vermont's still rural and pastoral environment. Frank Childs's painting of a view of East Dorset (c. 1875), subsequently published as a color lithograph, typifies the transformation of images of Vermont landscapes to feature industrial buildings, the railroad depots, and "the machine in the garden." (See color plate I.)

Not everyone was pleased with the railroads, however. One of their most tenacious and powerful critics was George Perkins Marsh, scholar, linguist, U.S. representative from Vermont's 3rd District from 1842 to 1849, diplomat, and beginning in 1857, Vermont's first legislatively appointed commissioner of railroads. In his annual reports to the legislature, Marsh minced no words castigating the railroad owners for their greed, inefficiency, and failure to think of their businesses, so handsomely supported with public monies, as a public service. "It is notorious," he wrote in the commissioner's *Third Annual Report* (1858), "that, not to speak of the monstrous venality which has attended the granting of many railroad charters, the railroad companies, in some of the United States, are so numerous, and so strong in pecuniary resources and in the personal influence of their managers and shareholders, that they both exert great weight in modifying the legislation of the State in matters affecting their corporate interests, and even control the political action of the government and the people." Vermont escaped some of the worst abuses, according to Marsh, because the capital required to build and maintain the roads greatly exceeded the financial resources available within the state. Investors, therefore, were mainly outside the state. "It is for such reasons that we, as a State, and as individuals, have escaped the enormous moral, political, and financial evils to which the almost universal corruption of great private corporations has elsewhere given birth." But he warned that vigilance and a strong hand were required to keep the railroads in check and make them serve their passenger and freight customers.[15]

In his best-known work, *Man and Nature,* published in 1864, Marsh continued his attack on the railroads. A work of broad scope and vision, encompassing history, geology, geography, natural history, and philosophy, *Man and Nature* contained Marsh's analysis of the human impact on the natural world from ancient times to the present. Drawing on his observations from his own travels and his extensive reading in several languages, Marsh argued that human society has altered and abused the natural world, placing itself not in nature, but above it, thereby causing continual and in some cases irreparable damage to the forests, waters, sandy areas, and wildlife that inhabit them. "Man is everywhere a disturbing agent," he asserted. "Wherever he plants his foot, the harmonies of nature are turned to discords. The proportions and accommodations which insured the stability of existing arrangements are overthrown." Every step that humankind takes to improve its own condition breaks down another fragile ecosystem. Every promise of technological progress for people carries with it a new threat to the balance in nature.

The railroad featured prominently among Marsh's examples of human progress run amok in the wilderness. While he conceded that the surveys that preceded railroad construction furnished an enormous amount of information about geology, topography, hydrography, flora, and fauna, Marsh described in a long footnote the sordid history of railroad building, its damage to nature, and its corrupting influence on society. "Joint-stock companies have no souls; their managers, in general, no consciences.... More than one American State is literally governed by unprincipled corpo-

George Perkins Marsh. Appointed railroad commissioner in 1857, Marsh rode every mile of Vermont railroads before issuing his thorough but scathing criticism in his 1858 report. Photograph from *The Vermonter* (October 1903).

rations, which not only defy the legislative power, but have, too often, corrupted even the administration of justice."[16] He did not discuss here the extent to which his experience in Vermont brought him to this dismal conclusion, but it is clear that he spoke from first-hand knowledge.

One of Marsh's persistent complaints as railroad commissioner was the inconvenient scheduling and placement of the connections between the Rutland and Central Vermont railroads at Essex Junction. The corporate shenanigans that resulted in placing the state's most crucial railroad junction six miles east of the state's largest population and business center, and scheduling its departures in such as way as to cause the greatest inconvenience for passengers and freight customers, infuriated Marsh. He called upon the state to make the Central Vermont accountable to the traveling public and to rectify this "flagrant and wanton abuse." A generation later Middlebury native Edward J. Phelps, professor at Yale Law School, president of the American Bar Association, and U.S. ambassador to Great Britain, repeated Marsh's complaint in his famous satirical poem, "The Lay of the Lost Traveler."

> Here Boston waits for Ogdensburg
> And Ogdensburg for Montreal,
> And late New York tarrieth
> And Saratoga hindereth all!
> From far Atlantic's wave swept bays
> To Mississippi's turbin tide
> All accidents, mishaps, delays,
> Are gathered here and multiplied!
> Oh! fellow man, avoid this spot
> As you would Peter Funk shun!
> And I hope in hell his soul may dwell
> Who first invented Essex Junction![17]

The railroad thus touched almost every aspect of and every place in Vermont life. While Vermont's infant industries and financial institutions appeared to be the main beneficiaries of the coming of the iron horse, the state's traditional economic basis, agriculture, was also profoundly affected by the changes brought by the railroad.

Agriculture: From "Competency" to Market Farming

A report in the 1845 issue of *The Cultivator* gives us a concise sketch of agricultural conditions and practices in Vermont on the eve of the railroad era:

> The plow is not extensively used in this part of the country—the object of farmers being generally to raise only about the quantity of grain and vegetables required for home consumption. It is, however,

stated by those best qualified to know, that Addison county produced last year a considerable surplus of bread-stuffs, beyond supplying the inhabitants. Wheat has been less cultivated since 1830 than formerly, owing to the attack of the wheat midge (*Cecidomyia tritica*). . . . Indian corn is cultivated with success on some of the lighter and warmer soils. On the best lands, and with good cultivation, it frequently yields sixty, and sometimes eighty bushels per acre. . . .

Potatoes flourish remarkably well, and are of superior quality. They are in some instances raised for the purpose of fattening stock, and for feeding sheep and store cattle through the winter. . . . Other vegetables [notably sugar beets] are in some instances cultivated for feeding stock.

We observed that it is a very uniform practice in this district to manure the ground intended for corn and potatoes very heavily. . . .

Buildings, Barn-Yards, Fences, & C. — The buildings through this district are generally in good repair. Many of the houses are of a superior style—are convenient and well furnished, and are sometimes tastefully ornamented with trees and shrubbery. Less care and judgment is generally shown about the barns and outbuildings. . . .

The fences generally preferred are cedar rails and stakes. It is laid in the form of what is called "worm fence" in some sections . . . Stone walls are sometimes made, and are, when well built, an excellent fence for all stock but sheep. But as sheep are the chief stock, and they are apt to run over the walls, rail fence is most common. . . .

Grass Lands.—The section of country is particularly favorable to the growing of grass. Judging from appearances, it is our opinion that we have never seen any other land which is capable of sustaining as much stock to the acre. . . . The hay made from these lands is of the most nutritive quality. . . . In fact, so excellent is the hay which is made here, and so fine is the pasturage, that some of the best 'grass beef' that is brought for the Brighton [Mass.] market is found here. . . .

Orchards, Fruits, & C.—Though the winters of Vermont are long and cold, the hardier fruits, as the apple, pear, and plum, thrive well. We have never seen finer apples than we tasted at several places.[18]

A long section of this report, written for one of the many new magazines devoted to scientific management of farms, describes the still abundant merino sheep flocks and Morgan horses. The writer was dismayed that

Vermont farmers paid so little attention to raising cattle for milk or beef.

This portrait of Vermont agriculture changed remarkably quickly once the railroads began operating in 1850.[19] The most dramatic alteration was the decline of the number of sheep on Vermont farms. Flock size, which reached its peak by the mid-1830s, declined steadily thereafter. The last time there were more sheep than people in Vermont was 1890, when the population was 332,422 and flock size was 333,947.

The declining number of sheep was offset by the increasing yield of fleece, the result of careful breeding. Among William Jarvis's original merinos in 1812 the fleece accounted for 6 percent of total body weight. By 1865 merino fleece was 21 percent of total body weight. The 1850 agricultural census reported that Vermont sheep provided 3.4 million pounds of wool, almost half the total New England yield, and an estimated twelve to twenty pounds of wool per animal.

Although sheep raising declined precipitously in Vermont in the 1840s, those who had registered breeding stock held on for a generation, making a handsome living from the breeding capacity of their flocks. A reporter for *The Cultivator* in 1849 mentioned several breeders with flocks of three hundred to five hundred animals in Bennington, Rutland, and Addison counties.[20] This brief revival lasted through the Civil War, when cotton supplies were cut off from the South and wool became the standard material for Union soldiers' uniforms and blankets. Even this development, however, did not save Vermont's sheep-raising enterprise and by 1880 there were fewer than half a million sheep in the state.

If the railroad was a factor in killing off Vermont's sheep boom, it also contributed to the next stage of Vermont agricultural history. Most important among the new directions for Vermont farmers was dairying. Before Jonas Wilder designed the first refrigerator cars, Vermont milk was consumed locally, churned into butter that was heavily salted for export in winter and early spring, or processed as cheese. Before 1850, cheese was made mostly for local consumption, produced in the home by women. Along with butter, eggs, and a few other commodities produced or watched over by the women of the farm family, cheese was part of a small agricultural economy that was meant to supply the needs of the family or, as part of a network of neighboring farms, the needs of the nearby community. Farmers expected little from their work beyond a comfortable self-sufficiency, what the age called a "competency," which included the ability to obtain by barter or purchase (when necessary) objects and goods not produced on the farm or the small luxuries that raised life above the level of mere subsistence.[21]

By 1850, however, dairy farmers had new opportunities to broaden the distribution of their products. In response they expanded their herds, introduced and monitored the purity of breeds that provided more milk or higher butterfat for butter and cheese production, and participated in greater number in a complex regional market for dairy products. The agricultural census for 1850 counted 146,000 milch cows, almost 3 percent fewer than in 1840; but in 1860 the number increased to 175,000, and in 1870 reached 180,000. The number of farms increased over this twenty-year period from 29,763 in 1850 to 33,827 in 1870, with slight gains in the productivity of the land. In 1870, 67.3 percent of the farmland in Vermont was listed as "improved," suggesting that after they cut down their forests for lumber, farmers put any usable land under cultivation or into pasturage.

The shift from sheep to dairy production was the most dramatic but not the only change in Vermont agriculture. As with wool, the western lands and railroad played important roles in defining competitive crops and markets for Vermont farmers. Wheat and corn continued to decline in importance and were kept in cultivation almost exclusively for local use, as feed crops. Writing to *The Cultivator* in April 1849, J. S. Pettibone of Manchester, Vermont, asserted, "In this section, grain is out of the question. There is no more raised than is necessary for our own consumption, and of wheat not sufficient for that." Similarly, Z. E. Jameson, writing on agriculture in Orleans County for Abby Hemenway's *Vermont Historical Gazetteer*, commented that "the wheat raised is not nearly enough to supply the home demand."[22] By contrast the "small grains"—barley, oats, rye, and buckwheat—served a specialized market and played an increasingly significant role in the Vermont farm economy.

Similarly, potatoes had a variety of markets and uses—in the kitchen, as stock feed, for starch and whiskey. The first agricultural census in 1840 reported that Vermont produced almost 3.9 million bushels of potatoes. Production increased to 5.2 million bushels in 1860 and reached a peak of 5.8 million in 1877, when 44,000 acres were devoted to potato growing. Almost every farm cultivated two or three acres to potatoes and in towns with starch factories, as many as twenty acres, with yields as high as 400 bushels per acre. Until the outbreak of the Civil War, Vermont potatoes found a ready market in the South and as much as 40 percent of the crop was exported annually. Blight, pests, and early freezes periodically devastated the crop, however, and the susceptibility of potatoes to such ravages encouraged experiments in hybrids. In 1860 Albert Breese of Hubbardton introduced the "Early Rose," which quickly became the most commonly grown potato variety in late-nineteenth-century America.[23]

Apples, too, provided a significant income for Vermont farmers in the mid-nineteenth century. Although the temperance movement curtailed the production of apples for cider, the fruits found ready markets in the South and in England. During the Civil War, barrels of Vermont apples followed Union troops as a staple in their diet. Small fruits, such as strawberries, also supplemented farm income. On Bradford's Upper and Lower Plain, nearly every farmer raised strawberries in the 1870s. The railroad allowed growers to get these extremely perishable foods to the Boston market in satisfactory condition.[24]

A few other marginal crops and agricultural products made brief appearances in Vermont. An experiment in hops growing produced a brief boom starting in the 1850s. That year, Vermont hop yards in Windham, Windsor, and Orleans counties produced 292,000 pounds, with a market value of about $1.00 per pound. In 1860 the volume reached its high point of 638,677 pounds, but declined to 527,929 pounds in 1870, the last year of major hops production in the state. That year Orleans County growers brought in more than half the state's yield, but it accounted for only 2.1 percent of the national total. By 1880 the boom was over. Again, the western territories proved more productive, especially for a crop highly sensitive to climate and temperature, requiring a high level of capitalization, labor, and fertilization. "In many ways," writes historian Thomas Rumney, "hop cultivation typified nineteenth-century farming in the state, as Vermonters sought above all a commercial crop that could enable them to survive in an increasingly competitive, interregional agricultural market. Interestingly, since few Vermont farmers grew hops exclusively, they were better able to survive the post-1870 decline in hop production."[25]

Undeterred by failed experiments, Vermont farmers continued to supply distant markets—especially Boston—with livestock including swine, beef, and poultry. Turkey and goose drives were a feature of rural life into the 1880s as drovers walked flocks to the nearest railhead. In her reminiscences of nineteenth-century Vermont, Daisy Dopp of Glover recalled the stock and poultry drives: "In those days [after 1848] our farm was a well-known stopping place for large herds of cattle that were driven to

Boston by men on foot. The drovers brought news and gossip gathered along the trail. Big flocks of turkeys and geese were also taken through the state. [It is said that in 1870] two brothers Cromwell and Amos Bean . . . drove 1,000 turkeys on the highway from their farm in Glover to Washington, Vermont, a distance of 50 miles."[26]

Other livestock declined in number. Oxen, commonly used for field work as well as beef in the late eighteenth century, began to be replaced by draft horses and beef cattle.

By 1860 Vermont agriculture was in the midst of a crisis and realignment. The staple crops of an earlier era—wheat, corn, sheep—were steadily disappearing to be replaced by dairy cows, hay, some small grain, and other specialty market crops. While the number of farms held steady or increased slightly in the period 1850–1870, the average size of farms declined by a few acres.

A brief report on farming in Vermont in the March 1859 issue of *The Cultivator* painted a rosy picture, but one of greater diversity in agriculture than a decade earlier.

> We are inclined to think that there is no State in the Union where the labors of the farmer are better paid than in Vermont. Though emphatically a mountain State, her valleys are traversed by railroads, by which a ready market is provided with but little cartage, in almost, if not quite, every county of the State. In horses and sheep, she does a large business with the Southern and Western States, while her grain crops, her dairy products for which she is celebrated, and her fine beef, pork, and mutton, are unsurpassed in the Boston market. In the Co. Gent. [probably *Country Gentleman*] of Jan. 13, we gave a statement of the shipments of butter and cheese during the year 1858, from which it appeared that over $600,000 worth were sent to market from a single depot in Franklin county. In the *Middlebury Register* of Jan 26, we find the proceedings of the annual meeting of the Addison Co. Ag. Society, from which it appears that cash prizes were awarded for the following crops:
>
> *Winter Wheat*—34½ and 31¼ bu. per acre.
> *Spring Wheat*—35½ bu. per acre.
> *Indian Corn*—123¾ and 121¼ bu. per acre.
> *Oats*—71 and 65½ bu. per acre.

Peas—35 bu. per acre.
White Beans—41¾ bu. per acre.
Potatoes—225 and 182½ bu. per acre.
Sugar Beets—340 and 250 bu. per half acre.[27]

In some ways, the life of the farmer changed very little before 1870. The daily and yearly round of chores continued much as they had since "all-around" farming began in Vermont in the early nineteenth century. Some improvements in farm implements appeared, such as scythe snaths and cradles, and plows designed by John Deere and Frederick Holbrook of Brattleboro that were better suited for deep tilling and working the rocky, clay-filled soil of Vermont. Early experiments with mechanical reapers and rakes also made the work of sowing and reaping more efficient, but only slightly easier or less time consuming, as the sources of power remained largely a combination of animals and humans. Farmers continued to need a variety of skills as carpenters, builders, and tinkerers, as well as managers, agronomists, and animal husbanders. The increasingly competitive market and the growing interest in scientific farming pushed agricultural occupations to new levels of expertise in handling and developing a wide variety of crops and livestock.

Four young men with forkfuls of hay, Waitsfield, c. 1890. The application of technology to haying had not changed much from the mid-nineteenth century to the time when this photograph was taken. *Vermont Album Collection. Vermont Historical Society (ATX 269).*

To help them keep abreast of changes and developing trends, farmers had several formal and informal institutions. Almanacs, printed continuously in Vermont from early in the nineteenth century, provided traditional guidance for planting, tending, and harvesting, as well as advertisements for new agricultural products. As spring militia training faded in the 1840s, it was replaced as a community event by fall agricultural fairs, where farmers and farm wives displayed their prize crops and livestock, and learned about new developments, products, markets, and tools. Vermont held its first state fair September 10-11, 1850, in Middlebury. *The Cultivator* reported in its November 1851 issue that twelve thousand people attended and saw exhibits that included 400 horses, 300 meat cattle, 1,100 sheep, 50 lots of poultry, and 1,200 "inanimate objects." The growing number of voluntary agricultural societies and their publications, and the new agricultural college, created as part of the Land Grant College Act of 1862, drafted and shepherded through Congress by Vermont's U.S. Representative, Justin Smith Morrill, also helped disseminate new information on horticulture and animal husbandry.[28]

State government maintained a low profile in promoting or regulating agriculture until the 1870s. But farmers and agriculturists themselves formed associations and organizations to disseminate information and represent agricultural interests to business and industry. Beginning as informal local clubs and a few scattered county agricultural societies, these organizations slowly coalesced and in 1850, at the conclusion of the state fair, a small group met to create the Vermont State Agricultural Society. The new society elected as its president Frederick Holbrook of Brattleboro (governor of Vermont, 1861-1863), and as vice presidents, William Nash, Joseph Coburn, Henry Bradley, and Erastus Fairbanks of St. Johnsbury (governor of Vermont, 1852-1853 and 1860-1861). This group met again on September 25, 1850, to draw up a petition to the legislature for incorporation, which was finally accomplished in 1857. Although the Vermont State Agricultural Society held annual exhibits and fairs and its leaders helped establish the New England Agricultural Society in 1864, it was not a strong organization. Berated in the press for its lack of results or products to help farmers, the organization languished in the years after the Civil War, when Vermont as a whole struggled to revive its agriculture under the twin handicap of a shortage of men to work the farms and more attractive opportunities for agriculture in the American West.

A decade later, in 1869, another group of fifty men met, this time in a committee room of the Vermont Senate, and formed the Vermont Dairyman's Association. The founders included twenty-three members of the legislature who were involved in dairying. Avowedly political and interested in reform, the association provided dairy farmers with information about production techniques, livestock maintenance, and market analyses in addition to being an advocate for improved technology and higher prices for butter. By 1870 membership had grown to 120, with 65 percent of the members from Chittenden County, 10 percent from Rutland and Addison counties, 10 percent from Washington County, and slightly less than 15 percent from the eastern side of the state.[29]

Concern about Vermont's competitiveness in an expanding and increasingly complex market for agricultural goods reached a climax in the 1870 session of the legislature. For many years the legislature had received and acted on petitions to underwrite expenditures by voluntary agricultural organizations for prizes, premiums, and equipment at local fairs and exhibitions. Increasingly, the legislature also received petitions to have Vermont follow its neighbor states to establish a state board of agriculture. In 1860 Governor Erastus Fairbanks urged the legislature to consider the question, but lawmakers delayed taking action and in 1861 the pressing concerns of outfitting Civil War units and the temporary profitability of supplying Union troops with agricultural goods diverted their attention. At the conclusion of the war, however, Vermont farmers once again faced the increasing unprofitability of raising grain, wool, and meat in competition with the West; the shortage of manpower due to devastation of the war and emigration; and the abandonment of farms and marginal uplands. In October 1870 Charles Heath of Plainfield introduced a resolution in the Vermont Senate calling on the Committee on Agriculture to establish a "commission for the promotion of agriculture, manufactures, quarrying, and mining." The committee responded with a rapidly drafted bill to establish a State Board of Agriculture, Mining, and Statistics—the last of the eastern states to do so. The bill quickly passed in both houses and by the end of the 1870 legislative session Vermont had a state Board of Agriculture consisting of the governor, the president of the University of Vermont and State Agricultural College, six members appointed by the governor and, *ex officio*, a secretary of agriculture. In 1870, with a federal land grant college system emerging to support agricultural education and boards of agriculture established in all the New England, Middle Atlantic, and several other states, government was now solidly in the picture of American and Vermont agriculture.

Urban and Industrial Growth

Vermont farmers' struggle to make their work profitable reflected a deeper shift in the state's economy and society: the beginning of a reorientation toward urban life. In the years following 1820, not only did Vermont's population grow slowly, it began to grow around urban nodes, while rural areas showed an overall trend of population decline. Burlington became Vermont's most populous town in 1840, with 4,271 residents. A decade later the population reached 6,110. In 1851 a group of citizens began agitating with the legislature for incorporation as a city—the first since Vergennes had won a charter in 1788 (for diplomatic reasons). The Burlington petitioners argued that the growing population made the direct democracy of town government impractical; but they also saw incorporation as a way to attract new businesses. In 1865 the push for a city charter finally succeeded. By then Burlington had over 7,700 residents, including seventy-three manufacturers employing 948 laborers, who produced goods valued over $1.2 million. A few years later, in 1870, the number of manufacturers had increased slightly to seventy-nine, but the number of workers rose to 2,713 and the value of goods produced leaped to almost $5.2 million.[30]

Burlington, from the lake. From a bird's-eye view of Burlington, 1858, published by H. P. Moore, Concord, N.H. *Vermont Historical Society (VHS 145).*

The growth of an urban core and manufacturing in Burlington is the most dramatic example of trends throughout the state. With the exception of some growth in the rural towns of Lamoille and Orleans counties, rural population in Vermont reached its peak in 1850 and declined steadily thereafter. By contrast, those towns with developing industrial and manufacturing activity (Burlington, Colchester, St. Johnsbury, Rutland, Springfield, Bennington), or those that became railroad centers (Hartford, Northfield, Brighton), showed the greatest population gains in the decades after 1850.[31] The growth of manufacturing centers in turn affected the overall economy of rural households. Cottage industries, such as small-scale weaving and other cloth manufacture, shoe making, braiding palm-leaf hats, and furniture making, could no longer compete with the large manufacturing concerns that produced the same articles. Young girls with fewer opportunities to earn a living at home and discouraged by the mores of the time from striking out on their own to go west, sought new economic opportunities by abandoning their home spinning wheels and looms to work in the cloth mills that sprang up throughout Vermont and elsewhere in New England. By 1845, 75 percent of the young women working in Lowell textile factories came from northern New England; twelve hundred of those workers came from Vermont. One of these, fifteen-year-old Mary Paul, wrote to her father in Barnard, explaining her decision to go to Lowell: "I want you to consent to let me go to Lowell if you can. I think it would be much better for me than to stay about here. I could earn more to begin with than I can anywhere about here [Woodstock, Vt.]. I am in need of clothes which I cannot get if I stay about here and for that reason I want to go to Lowell or some other place." A few months after she arrived in Lowell, Mary wrote her father again, full of enthusiasm for her life of independence and income. "I think the factory is the best place for me and if any girl wants employment I advise them to come to Lowell."[32] Among the forty-six woolen mills operating in Vermont in the period 1850–1860, females outnumbered male laborers overall, sometimes by as much as two to one.[33]

Several other large industrial enterprises shaped the communities in which they were located. E. & T. Fairbanks & Company employed 250 workers at its scale factory in 1860 and dominated the landscape, economy, and cultural life of St. Johnsbury. The marble quarrying boom in Rutland and half a dozen foundries and iron products shops in Brandon helped make Rutland County the fastest-growing area in the state in the

1850s; a smaller boom in the slate industry placed Fair Haven among the four dozen towns whose population increased by one hundred or more between 1850 and 1860.[34]

The Civil War, with its drain on manpower and demand for goods to feed, clothe, equip, and move the Union army, accelerated the change in Vermont from a predominantly agricultural economy to one with a substantial manufacturing sector, and from rural to village society. At the same time, the five-year boom caused by wartime demand for goods masked some of the most troublesome issues related to the very changes it helped stimulate. Large-scale emigration from Vermont continued with little immigration to the state to replace those who left. Consequently, Vermont's population remained almost level for the remainder of the century. Consolidation of farm lands and the difficult competitive situation of marginal upland farms distant from transportation routes forced many farmers off the land. The changing nature of rural work, in the process of being transformed from small enterprises serving local markets to factory-oriented businesses serving regional and national markets, brought about changes in the distribution of population in the state. Limited capital made it difficult for Vermont business owners and industrialists to compete successfully in big markets. Similar expansions of agricultural markets affected the size and number of farms.

By 1850, Vermont was the only New England state where a majority of men remained employed in agriculture—but it was barely a majority. That, too, changed within two decades. "The period 1830–1870 in the rural life of New England hills," wrote historian Harold F. Wilson, "saw the transition from self-sufficient to commercial agriculture, from a household to a factory industry; it witnessed an increasing differentiation of occupations and of customs between the rural and the urban people."[35]

Politics: Disintegration and Realignment

While Vermonters in the 1850s wrestled with the problems of an uncertain agricultural economy and adjustments to an urban, industrial society, no political issue was more divisive or influenced the shape of Vermont politics more than antislavery. Two national political crises hastened the process of political realignment in Vermont. The first was the Compromise of 1850. Forged by Daniel Webster, Henry Clay, and John C. Calhoun, the omnibus bill allowed congressional Whigs and

Democrats to reach temporary accord over the admission of California as a free state. Other provisions fixed the border of Texas but left the matter of the extension of slavery into New Mexico open to future determination. In the District of Columbia, slavery was left untouched but the slave trade was abolished. As a final concession to the South, the compromise strengthened the fugitive slave laws.

Vermonters rejoiced in the creation of a free California. Continuation of slavery in the District of Columbia, however, where federal authority and not state sovereignty was the controlling power, aroused immediate and vigorous resistance. Since the 1820s, the Vermont legislature had passed numerous resolutions denouncing slavery and calling upon Vermont congressmen and senators to work to end the slave trade and oppose the spread of slavery by every constitutional means. With passage into law of this provision of the Compromise of 1850, the flood of protest was renewed.

The main focus of anger and resistance to the Compromise of 1850, however, was the Fugitive Slave Act. Under this law, federal commissioners had authority to issue warrants, assemble posses, and force citizens to participate in the capture of runaway slaves. A resolution of the legislature passed in October 1850 put Vermont on record again in opposition to compliance with a law that it characterized as both offensive to civil liberties and a violation of state sovereignty. The legislature went a step further by passing the Habeas Corpus bill to impede the execution of the new federal law. The new state law required judicial and executive officers in Vermont counties to intervene in suspected or anticipated captures of fugitive slaves, notify the state's attorney, and impede through court order and physical protection the capture and return of fugitive slaves.[36]

The next great crisis, and the one that finally broke apart Vermont political coalitions, was the Kansas-Nebraska Act of 1854. Introduced by Vermont-born Stephen A. Douglas, U.S. senator from Illinois, the bill initially proposed no more than to allow states formed from the Nebraska Territory to determine the issue of slavery by a vote of the citizens—"popular sovereignty" as Douglas insisted on calling it. Convinced by Southern senators that they had the power in Congress to block him, possibly spurred by his presidential ambitions, and probably motivated too by his enthusiasm for railroad building and western development, Douglas at the last minute acceded to demands of Southern senators to include in his bill an amendment repealing the Missouri Compromise of 1820, which for thirty years had defined the northern boundary for the spread of slavery and had helped establish a balance of slave and free states. Securing in advance the written assurance of New Hampshire-born, Democratic President Franklin Pierce that he would not veto the bill and that he considered the Missouri Compromise inoperative, Douglas proceeded to submit his amended bill.

The Kansas-Nebraska Act shook Vermont politics to its roots. Douglas made an appearance in Vermont in February 1854, which only hastened the disintegration of Vermont's Democratic Party. The Whigs, unable to stop passage of the act, were equally discredited and in disarray. The Free Soil Party abandoned its coalition with the Democrats but had done itself irreparable damage through its association with proslavery policies. Mass meetings in March and April denounced the Kansas-Nebraska Act and those who had conspired to pass it. At a meeting in Montpelier on March 2, a new coalition of disaffected Democrats, Whigs, and Free Soilers adopted a resolution protesting the act as "treason to the cause of human freedom; as a clear violation of the faith of the Government, which was pledged to the people 'forever' by the very terms of the act of 1820; and as intended to extend the unrighteous and abominable system of American slavery into a vast territory, which has been sacredly dedicated to Freedom."[37]

The political avalanche continued through the spring and early summer of 1854. Town meetings throughout the state adopted resolutions condemning the Kansas-Nebraska Act and repeal of the Missouri Compromise. Voters in Charlotte censured Senator Douglas. In Springfield, voters resolved that "We will vote for such men, and such men only, as will use their vote and influence to protect this territory from the encroachments of slavery." In Rutland, a mass meeting called for repeal of the "repealing clause," adding that "if disunion be the result, let the guilty authors of the unnecessary measure be responsible for the consequences." Meetings in Burlington, Vergennes, and St. Albans also protested repeal of the Missouri Compromise.

Condemnation of the Kansas-Nebraska Act was not universal in Vermont, however. The Democratic Party's nominating convention in June 1854 declared its loyalty to President Franklin Pierce and adopted a platform plank endorsing Douglas's policy of "squatter sovereignty." However, in a sign of disintegrating party unity and discipline, the convention also resolved that "we don't propose to make difference of opinion among Democrats in relation to the policy of the provisions of the bill establishing a territorial government for Nebraska and Kansas a test of party faith."[38] Democratic Governor John Robinson, elected by the legislature in 1853 by a coalition of Democrats and Free Soilers, declined his party's nomination for a second term. This further splintered the coalition with the result that each party now put up its own candidates for governor and lieutenant governor.

The Whigs fared no better. Their convention in early June began with receipt of a letter from Erastus Fairbanks of St. Johnsbury declining to be a candidate for governor. Fairbanks had been the Whig candidate in 1852, when he won the governorship, and again in 1853, when, lacking the required majority, he was defeated in the legislature by the Democratic-Free Soil coalition. Fairbanks's withdrawal from the race was an ominous sign for the Whigs. The Whig convention, carefully managed by Eliakim P. Walton of Montpelier, the ardently antislavery editor of the *Vermont Watchman and State Journal*, adopted a plank that vigorously denounced repeal of the Missouri Compromise and a recommendation on party procedure that hinted at schism. It then nominated Stephen Royce of Berkshire for governor and Oscar L. Shafter of Wilmington for lieutenant governor.

But the political maneuvering for 1854 was not yet complete. Walton and Lawrence Brainerd, chairman of the state committee of the Free Soil party, called for a mass convention "without distinction of party" to meet in Montpelier. On July 11 over six hundred Free Soilers, breakaway Whigs, and disaffected Democrats convened at the State House under the label of "unionists." Adopting an uncompromising position against slavery—repeal of the Fugitive Slave laws, termination of all slave trade, abolition of slavery in the District of Columbia, prohibition of slavery in all territories of the United States, and no more admission of slave states—the unionists declared themselves the Republican Party and nominated for governor Ezekiel Walton, Eliakim's father, and Ryland Fletcher of Cavendish for lieutenant governor. As this Unionist/Republican convention broke up, the dissident Democrats, calling themselves Free Democrats, convened a meeting of their own and adopted the Republican platform. In hurriedly assembled county meetings, Democrats, Whigs, and Free Soilers realigned. When the elder Walton withdrew from the race, the Republicans offered the nomination for governor to Stephen Royce, a temperance man, abolitionist, and for twenty-five years a judge of the Vermont Supreme Court, who possessed the doubtful qualifications that he had "never mingled in the slightest degree with party politics." Then Oscar Shafter withdrew and the Republicans completed their coalition building by offering the lieutenant governor candidacy to Fletcher.[39]

The general election itself proved an anticlimax to the nominating process. Royce, running for governor as a Republican/Whig, received 62 percent of the popular vote; and Fletcher, running for lieutenant governor as a Republican, received 65.5 percent. The Free Soil Party, redundant now that the Republicans emerged unequivocally as the antislavery party, disappeared in the debacle; the Democrats feebly struggled to hold on; the Whigs, though moribund as a party, retained enough local strength to elect all three of their candidates to the U.S. House of Representatives, two of whom endorsed the Republican platform. Almost with its dying breath, the Whig Party launched the extraordinary political career of its third successful candidate for Congress that year, Justin Smith Morrill.

A native of Strafford, Vermont, the son of a blacksmith, Morrill was a self-made man. Born in 1810, he went off to Maine in 1828 to clerk at a general store. Returning to Vermont in 1830, he set up his own business and kept a general store until 1850, learning from that profession to observe the shifting tide of politics and the economy in Vermont. His formal schooling ended at age fifteen with no more than two terms at grammar school. Nonetheless, he had a high regard for learning, founded a subscription library in 1827, helped start a lyceum in 1831, and began to acquire his own library in the 1830s. In 1841 he traveled west, keeping a careful record of his observations. He eagerly studied and absorbed the learning and style of Victorian America and in 1850 designed a house and grounds in Strafford in the popular Gothic Revival style that announced to the world that he was a man of substance and culture. Quietly forming personal alliances with important men in Vermont politics, Morrill made his first bid for public office in the tumultuous year 1854, running for Congress in Vermont's Second District. By adhering tenaciously to the Whig label, but hinting at his acquiescence to the Republican platform while keeping some distance from legislative and party fights over railroads, liquor, and abolitionism, Morrill barely managed to win the difficult election by capturing just over 50 percent of the vote in his district. Responding to the contemporary political transition, however, he cast his first vote as a Congressman for the Republican contestant for Speaker of the House, and in 1856 ran for reelection under the banner of the Republican Party.

Justin Smith Morrill, portrait by Thomas Waterman Wood, 1892. This portrait of Morrill, painted near the end of his career, was presented to the Vermont Historical Society by the artist, who, well known for his work as a genre painter (see chapter 6), was also famous for his portraits. *Vermont Historical Society.*

Morrill's first years in Congress were active if undistinguished. He satisfied his sheep-raising constituents by opposing a low tariff bill in 1857 and guiding a high tariff bill through the House in 1860. He spoke for a free Kansas and thus established his antislavery position in Congress. He introduced a resolution for a national agricultural school early in his congressional career and saw it come to fruition with passage of the Land Grant College Act in 1862, by which time he had accumulated seniority and prestige in the House. Although he neither wrote nor even conceived of the bill, a fact he freely acknowledged, he championed it and used his skills as a floor manager and parliamentarian to maneuver around the states' rights opposition, who objected to the federal government interfering with the sale of public land (except, perhaps for railroad building). When the Southern states left Congress in December 1861, Morrill took advantage of the weakened opposition to bring the bill forward for a vote.

Morrill remained in the House for twelve years, after 1856 as a Republican, typically taking 75 percent of the popular vote in each of his reelection bids. In 1866 he waged a careful, tactful, effective behind-the-scenes campaign to win appointment to the Senate seat left open by the death of Jacob Collamer. In the Senate, he served on the Committee on Buildings and Grounds, where his interest in architecture found an outlet in his proposal to establish Statuary Hall in the Capitol Building and in his efforts championing the designs for the Library of Congress and the Washington Monument. Throughout his congressional career he was closely involved in finance, first as chairman of the House Ways and Means Committee, then as chairman of the Senate Finance Committee, where he sponsored a number of bills designed to boost tariffs, raise revenues, and reform tax and monetary policies. Morrill died in office in 1898, with thirty-one years of service in Congress, one of the longest congressional careers in American history.[40]

Back in Vermont, the coalition of Whigs and Republicans hastily assembled in 1854 solidified and in 1855 Governor Stephen Royce ran again, now as a Republican. He easily beat back challenges from Democratic, Temperance, and American or "Know-Nothing" party candidates, to garner 59 percent of the popular vote. Nationally, the Republican Party presented John C. Frémont as its first candidate for president in 1856. That year, Vermonters voted more than three to one for Frémont over the successful candidate, Democrat James Buchanan. Vermont thereby established a tradition of support for Republican presidential candidates that remained unbroken until

1964. By 1860, the Republican Party was so firmly established in Vermont that all its candidates for statewide office and congress garnered majorities of about 70 percent of the popular vote. In the presidential election that year, Vermonters gave 42,419 votes to Republican Abraham Lincoln, 6,849 to Democrat Stephen Douglas, and about two thousand votes combined to Southern moderate John Bell, of the Constitutional Union Party, and Southern Democrat John C. Breckenridge.[41]

Attracting increasing attention during this period of political reshuffling was the rising popularity of a new political faction in Vermont: the American Party, also known as the Know-Nothings because their members were sworn to secrecy. Established in 1849 in New York, the American Party represented a nativist reaction to immigrant groups, especially Irish, and expressed virulently anti-Catholic sentiments. It allied with antislavery groups but opposed slavery on racial and economic rather than moral grounds, seeing the spread of the slavery as a threat to the economic well-being of white society. In Vermont, the new Republican Party during its coalition-building stage included several Know-Nothing leaders, and when the Know-Nothings finally emerged as a party after 1854, offering its own candidates, it posed a threat to the Republicans, still trying to cement their own coalition. The American Party was mistrusted more for its practices than its policies and its strong showing in 1855 demonstrated that it had the sympathy of many voters. In a letter to Erastus Fairbanks, dated April 19, 1855, George Perkins Marsh summarized both the concerns and attractions that the Know-Nothings held for many.

> No man can be better convinced than I of the impropriety and danger of all secret combinations and organizations whatever for political purposes, and indeed for any other object, and if I could be persuaded that the Know-Nothings were likely to retain that objectionable feature as a part of their policy, I should be ready to take any lawful measure almost to resist them. I believe, however, that they must and will abandon their whole foolish machinery of lodges & wigwams, sachems, oaths, secrets, and all the like silliness, which...will otherwise infallibly destroy the party.
>
> For the present, therefore, I do not believe in the necessity of any special effort to resist the movements of the party, and, committed as I have publicly been for more than twenty years to their avowed principles—which I understand to be repeal or at least restriction of the

right of naturalization, and resistance to catholic commandments—I cannot participate in any steps which would expose me to the suspicion of having abandoned these *principles*, barely because I disapprove of the *means* which are resorted to advance them.[42]

Nationally, the Know-Nothings were primarily an urban political party, playing on the fears and prejudices of eastern business and labor groups. In Vermont their strength resided mainly in the largest towns, but they found some support from anti-Catholic farmers who feared the growth of French and Irish Catholic populations. Nonetheless, the Know-Nothings had a short-lived and ambiguous success. In 1855 they ran James L. Slade as their own candidate for governor, who garnered only 8 percent of the vote, but endorsed Ryland Fletcher for lieutenant governor and Henry Bates for treasurer, both of whom, although they ran officially as Republicans, were also prominent Know-Nothings. In 1856 and 1857 Fletcher won substantial majorities as the Republican candidate for governor and Slade reappeared, now as the Republican candidate for lieutenant governor, and also won handily. Know-Nothing candidates also gained extraordinarily strong representation in the 1855 Council of Censors. Thus, without gaining ascendancy as a party, the Know-Nothings exercised considerable power within the solidifying Republican coalition, but then faded from the political picture as the Republican Party rose to dominance on the platform of union, antislavery, and anti-Catholicism. By 1860 the Republicans had assembled a strong statewide organization that allowed the party to hold power for a century in Vermont and, in the time of crisis that lay ahead, to muster the energy and resources of Vermont's independent-minded communities.

The Civil War in Vermont

On the night of April 14, 1861, as Confederate shells fell on Fort Sumter in Charleston harbor, South Carolina, Governor Erastus Fairbanks received a brief telegraph from President Abraham Lincoln: "Washington in grave danger. What may we expect of Vermont?" The governor is said to have replied, "Vermont will do its full duty."[43] The next day Lincoln issued a nationwide call for troops to put down the rebellion that had been simmering for so many years. In response to the president's request for a regiment from Vermont, Governor Fairbanks immediately issued a proclamation to raise the troops and then called a special session of the General Assembly to meet on April 23. In his address to the joint session, Fairbanks reviewed the events of the previous two weeks and called upon the legislators to support the Union and the Constitution "at whatever cost of men and treasure."[44]

The legislature rose to the occasion. In a series of war-related acts passed during a frenzied four-day session, the General Assembly not only endorsed Fairbanks's actions but authorized up to six additional regiments, two to be raised immediately and four as needed. To the federal pay of $13 a month, the legislature added a state bonus of $7 a month from the time of enlistment through active duty, and stipulated that the state supplement would be set aside as assistance to the families of Vermont soldiers or, upon termination of service, paid out in a lump sum. In all, the General Assembly approved $1 million—twice the amount initially requested—to purchase equipment, weapons, and supplies for Vermont regiments; $4 million in pay supplements; and a war tax of ten cents on the dollar of the grand list.

By May 2, companies from Brandon, Woodstock, Cavendish, Middlebury, Swanton, Burlington, St. Albans, Rutland, Northfield, and Bradford began to assemble at Rutland as the First Vermont Regiment. Under the command of Mexican War veteran Colonel John Wolcott Phelps, and Woodstock lawyer Peter T. Washburn, the First Vermont mustered in for three-months duty on May 8. The regiment's 728 officers and soldiers headed off by train to Washington, D.C., then marched to Fort Monroe in Virginia, where a portion of the regiment saw action in the first skirmish of the war at Big Bethel. Three months later, on August 2, their enlistment term ended and the regiment disbanded. Six hundred of its members reenlisted, now for three-year tours of duty. By that time the Second Vermont, 868 men, had assembled at Burlington on June 6, gone south at the end of the month, and fought at First Bull Run. The Vermont Third, 882 men, assembled in St. Johnsbury about the same time, but too late to fight with their neighbors at that first turning point in the war.

How to account for this generous, even extravagant response by Vermont to the opening months of the war? A population of barely 315,000, still mostly rural—less than 9 percent of the population lived in the five most populous towns—and still largely dependent on agriculture for its income, pledged a huge proportion of its male population and its fortune to the war. There can be no doubt that the response to the first call came from deep within the moral and political fabric of the citizens of the state. For at least forty years, Vermonters had listened to and participated in the increasingly noisy and angry debate over slavery, first as a moral and religious question, then as a political one.

Some in Vermont condoned slavery. Episcopal Bishop John Henry Hopkins defended the "peculiar institution" using the Bible as his authoritative text as late as 1861. And some who entered the war continued to express doubts about imposing abolition on the South where the Constitution had clearly provided for the continuation of slavery. Copperheads (a northern splinter group more formally known as "Peace Democrats"), who opposed the war, continued to capture as much as 25 percent of the vote in Vermont for statewide offices and Congress. Anger against them flared and their civil rights to express their opposition came dangerously close to being extinguished. Lieutenant Governor Paul Dillingham told a gathering in Montpelier that it was important "to stop, as far as possible, free speech," by which he meant finding fault with the progress of the war. A U.S. Marshal, C. C. P. Baldwin, arrested three individuals "for expressing secessionist sentiments," but to its credit the Vermont grand jury refused to bring an indictment and instead fined Baldwin for unlawfully suspending habeas corpus. Even the songs "Tenting Tonight" and "When This Cruel War is Over" were considered subversive by some people.[45]

Assessing their commitment to the war required Vermonters to think about the meaning of the war in the context of their own history. Where the heated political debates of the 1850s had focused on checking the spread of slavery or abolishing it, according to all official propaganda the war in 1861 was being fought to save the Union—an issue of broader appeal and less open to controversy. Vermonters, too, had flirted with abandoning the United States in the Haldimand negotiations, resisted federal policy during the embargo of 1806, and had some experience with nullification during the War of 1812 and the personal liberty law of 1851, which defied the Fugitive Slave Act. But these acts of resistance and dissent had all been conducted cautiously and with reference to the state's role within the Union. Nothing in their past resembled the South's violent attempt to break away from the Union. Their own history thus propelled Vermonters into the Civil War with enthusiasm.

The stunning defeat of Union troops at Bull Run on July 21, 1861, sent the grim message that, contrary to initial expectations, this war was to be long, exhausting, and costly. With two regiments in the field and a third about to depart for the front, Governor Fairbanks ordered a fourth to assemble on July 30 and called for two additional regiments of three-year enlistees. By the time Fairbanks left office in October 1861, Vermont had raised six regiments and a company of sharpshooters. The next two governors, Frederick Holbrook of Brattleboro and John Gregory Smith of St. Albans, called for still more Vermont units. By the war's end, Vermont had fielded seventeen regiments of infantry, a regiment of cavalry and a company of cavalry to patrol the border with Canada, three artillery batteries, and three companies of sharpshooters, in addition to 619 men who served in the navy and marines.

At Bull Run the Second Vermont had its first encounter with massed Confederate forces. After a "double quick" march of six miles, the Vermonters fought for about thirty minutes. "It was awful," wrote Edson Emery of Tunbridge in his diary. "The bullets come like hail. Then we retreated in confusion. Loss is heavy." On April 16, 1862, William Farrar "Baldy" Smith led the Vermont Brigade—the Vermont Second, Third, Fourth, Fifth, and Sixth Regiments—in an attack on Confederate troops at Lee's Mill dam on the Virginia Peninsula. Soldiers slogged through unexpectedly deep water, across logs and debris, to face entrenched fire pits. The battle was a disaster of tactics and communication, resulting in 65 dead and 148 wounded.

The Vermont Brigade fought again at Antietam, near Sharpsburg, Maryland, on September 16, 1862, where the Second Vermont Sharpshooters had already participated in the bloodiest fighting of the day. Two months later the Vermont Brigade saw action again at the first Battle of Fredericksburg, another military disaster for the Union, then settled into winter camp near the battlefield.

Artist James Hope, who until war broke out enjoyed a fine reputation as a landscape painter in the Rutland and Castleton region, served as a captain and topographical engineer in the Union army, making sketches as he moved from battle to grisly battle. Late in the war he painted several battle scenes. On commission from Charles B. Stoughton, commander of the Fourth Vermont Regiment, Hope used his sketches for a large painting of the Vermont Brigade encamped at Fredericksburg. Under a glowing winter sky, with a beautiful landscape in the background, Hope showed the ravages of war—woods cleared for rows of tents and camp fires and in the foreground graves of Vermont soldiers who succumbed to injuries and sickness.

When military action resumed in 1863, fresh troops from home joined

Vermont's Old Brigade, as it was now called. The Second Vermont Brigade, comprising the Twelfth, Thirteenth, Fourteenth, Fifteenth, and Sixteenth regiments, started into the field with five thousand men in October 1862. The Eighth Vermont was far away in Louisiana; the Ninth was near Richmond, Virginia; the Tenth protected Washington, D.C.; and the Eleventh had been transformed from infantry into an artillery unit. The First Vermont Cavalry also received reinforcements during the winter of 1862 with new men and five hundred fresh mounts, mostly Morgan horses.[46]

Early in May fighting resumed near Fredericksburg and the First Brigade took heavy losses. With barely time to gather their knapsacks, the Old Brigade moved on to Chancellorsville and another devastating Union defeat, then took to the road leading to Gettysburg.

The Union Sixth Corps, including the First Vermont Brigade under the command of Lewis A. Grant of Brattleboro, was thirty miles from Gettysburg on July 1, 1863, when General John Sedgwick issued the famous order, "Put the Vermonters in the lead and keep the column well closed up." The Old Brigade was by now known for its speed and endurance on the march and Sedgwick had the Vermont regiments set the pace for the troops moving toward battle. The Second Vermont Brigade, under General George Stannard, was already at Gettysburg, occupying a central position on the battlefront at Cemetery Ridge, and the First Vermont Cavalry was deployed.

The third day of the battle, July 3, became the Second Brigade's finest moment. As Confederate infantry ran across a mile of open field toward the Union line in what became known as Pickett's Charge, Vermont regiments stood to meet them. In a crucial maneuver that sealed the fate of the attack and the battle, two Vermont regiments under Stannard wheeled like a hinge and fired on the flank and rear of the attackers. The timely movement broke the charge and earned for Vermont regiments additional praise as disciplined and persistent soldiers.

Gettysburg was the "high-water mark" of the Confederacy, the climax of Lee's plan to invade the north. After July 4, 1863, the Union took the offensive and pursued Confederate troops back into the South. Even on the defensive, however, Southern troops fought back ferociously and many more campaigns lay ahead. During the bloodiest weeks of the war, beginning on May 5, 1864, Vermont soldiers participated in a running battle from the Wilderness to Spotsylvania Courthouse, where at the infamous

"Bloody Angle" fighting reached a peak of frenzy with hand-to-hand combat. The two armies, locked in a grim dance of death, then moved on to Cold Harbor, and finally settled into an exhausting siege at Petersburg. The campaign saw some of the fiercest and most costly fighting of the war, with losses on the Union side averaging fifteen hundred men each day of combat. In what became known as "the Forty Days," the Vermont Brigade lost almost two-thirds of its men: 249 killed, 1,231 wounded, 170 missing, and 400 emotionally broken under the strain of the carnage and discharged or sent to Northern hospitals.[47]

The War at Home

The war back home in Vermont had its own dynamics, as legislators, farmers, manufacturers, and private citizens responded to the escalating needs for men, money, and materials. Having already committed $1 million to support troops, including a new regiment of cavalry, the legislature, when it convened for its regular session in October 1861, now acceded to the U.S. Congress levy of $20,000,000 from direct income and property taxes by imposing a tax on grand list valuation, with the intent of paying up to 50 percent of the levy from current revenues year by year. In 1861 the surtax was fifty cents on the dollar of assessed value; in 1862 it rose to eighty cents; it went up again in 1863 to one dollar and remained at that level through 1891, when Vermont paid off its portion of the national levy.[48]

Private philanthropy supplemented government funds to care for wounded soldiers and provide small items to comfort the men at the front. Women in Vermont collected money and goods for the nationwide Christian and Sanitary commissions: $900 in 1862, $700 in 1863 to help furnish the military hospital at Brattleboro, and in 1864, after the terrible fighting in May, $5,000 plus $1,000 from benefit lectures and entertainments.

Lydia E. White of Topsham wrote an account of her effort to raise money for the Christian and Sanitary commissions. Published in October 1864 as a supplement in New York weeklies, the report later circulated as a pamphlet and as a feature story printed by newspapers throughout the North. "The Record of a Day" described White's visits to all the houses in her neighborhood to collect cash contributions and articles to send to the field hospitals. White described each of her stops, sometimes coaxing reluctant givers, sometimes grieving with recent widows, parents, or siblings of young men killed in battle.

White's account, stylized and perhaps fictionalized though it may be, provides an extraordinary glimpse into the conditions of and attitudes toward the war. We see the household economy of a small community, with stores of cloth and linen, small reserves of cash, but widely varied resources—reminders of the old agrarian ideal of farming for a "competency." Many families on Lydia White's route already had sent all their sons to war; at one stop she talks with the mother of five young men who went to war—two dead at Antietam, two at Fredericksburg, and the fifth lying wounded in a field hospital in Alexandria, Virginia. At another stop, White shares a midday meal with a widow whose only son died from wounds at Gettysburg; at the drygoods store she learns that the proprietor's brother has died from wounds received at Fredericksburg. We learn about the work of the Christian and Sanitary commissions, forerunners of the American Red Cross, that kept track of wounded soldiers and supplemented the materials and supplies provided by the government for the military hospitals. We also hear the voices of a community and their response to war, from the devout and patriotic to the dubious. White describes the hypocritical fervor of the town recruiting officer, "an excitable, bustling, portly man of almost forty-five; and on account of the *conscription law*, he was overanxious that the wheels of time should roll round as swiftly as possible, that he might attain that desirable age."

White's route brings her to the home of Herman Green, who opposed the war. She writes of him, "At the outset of the war, he took a bold stand for the South; but certain of his neighbors informed him that it would not be safe for him to avow such principles so, to 'save his bacon,' as the boys said, he kept comparatively quiet, although the most casual observer could not but see that he deprecated every Union victory and rejoiced at every defeat." Rebuffing White's request for a contribution, Green gives voice to what must have been an unusual, or at least rarely heard, attitude toward the war in Vermont. "'I can give nothing to help this unjust war along. The Southerners have been abused and I admire their grit. I hope they'll hold out to the end. The Abolitionists caused this war and I wish to mercy they had to bear all the burden.'"[49] Such resistance is the exception, however, and White's one-day effort yielded about $50 and a substantial box of items: shirts; blankets; quilts; cotton, linen, and flannel cloth, which a local sewing club cut and sewed into bandages in a six-hour marathon; sheets, towels, and other linens; slippers and shoes; dried and fresh fruit; preserves; maple sugar; books and pamphlets.

Vermont women also used their skills in the domestic sphere to contribute to the war effort, rolling bandages, sewing socks, and knitting garments. Abby Estey Fuller, in her recollections of Brattleboro during the war, wrote that "it was considered a disgrace to attend a concert or lecture without taking a soldier's sock for knitting." The results were always appreciated but not always useful. Mrs. Fuller recalled one soldier's complaint about a garment he received that "he was sure was made for a four-legged animal—it could not be put on a human being." She also remembered some gentler admonitions from the reformer Dorothea Dix to "try to remember that the soldiers were human beings like our fathers and brothers and not monstrosities."[50] Alice Watts Choate of Peacham tried to knit two hours a day and joined a circle of women who met once a week to sew for soldiers. In one of her letters to family members she reported that young people in the community produced "an old folks concert and tableaux at the [Peacham] Academy on Christmas night that earned forty-six dollars for the sewing project."[51]

Raising troops was the next challenge. In the first flush of patriotism, regional pride, and sectional antagonism, young Vermonters rushed to volunteer for the regiments being formed at Rutland and Brattleboro. The First Regiment formed in a matter of weeks; the First Brigade was on the field in three months. This was all the more impressive because the town militia system, which should have served as the recruiting and training base for a volunteer army, had fallen into disuse since the late 1840s. The traditional June muster days—more noted for the quantity of spirits consumed than the quality of military training—had earned the opprobrium of temperance crusaders and other town critics. By midcentury agricultural fairs and field days had replaced the musters. Probably no less sober occasions for some, the field days nonetheless reflected the growing interest in scientific agriculture, domestic economy, and rural skills and became community events that allowed the participation of women and families, and deemphasized what had remained of the military aspects of summertime frolics.

When the war broke out, therefore, only a few Vermont communities had the organization or experience to recruit or train volunteers. Moreover, as the fighting dragged on enthusiasm for the war flagged, communities began to feel more acutely the stress created by shortages in the labor force, and recruitment became increasingly difficult. In 1862 the legislature adopted a draft law for men between the ages of 18 and 45, and passed another bill authorizing towns to pay bounties to volunteers. The smaller towns, already having difficulty meeting their quotas, had to resort to the bounty system to recruit men to fill the ranks. A year later the legislature made another effort to make military service attractive by giving volunteers the option of accepting a $125 bounty at the time of enlistment or taking the $7 monthly supplement to their military pay. At the same time, the 1863 legislature authorized towns to offer bounties to draftees in addition to the state bonus and family support.

The offers were often very attractive. On December 9, 1863, Huldah Morse wrote from Woodbury to her son Franklin, stationed in Louisiana with the Eighth Vermont, that "your uncle Truman Lawson has enlisted[.] there has a good many gone from woodbury[.] they get six hundred (600) dollars bounty[.] they go for Calais[.] the town of Calais pays three hundred and the government three hundred . . . Quite a temtation for anyone." A week later she wrote to Franklin that his younger brother, Orlando, was about to enlist for Marshfield. The town will pay $225 and the government $302. This at a time when the average wage for a farm laborer was about $300 a year.[52]

Despite these financial enticements, recruitment remained sluggish. On October 28, 1863, Governor John Gregory Smith issued a proclamation announcing that Vermont had to provide 3,300 more men to meet its quota for the 300,000 additional troops called for by President Lincoln. In addition, the state had to fill 1,923 positions in existing units, left vacant through casualties or termination of duty, for a total of 5,223 men. The carrot-and-stick rhetoric in Smith's proclamation hints at the difficulty the state, and the Union in general, faced in meeting these goals. "[F]or the purpose of avoiding if possible a resort to another draft, the President proclaims the offer of large and generous bounties to all such as may now enlist voluntarily. . . . I would therefore most earnestly invite the people of the State to respond promptly to this call . . . as the only means of averting another draft, which, if it must finally be resorted to, will of necessity be enforced with more rigor, and in such manner as to secure beyond possibility of failure the complement of men, so much needed by the Government."[53]

The promise of generous pay worked for some, but not all Vermonters, and the state again resorted to the much resented draft. Some avoided conscription by purchasing their way out of service and paying a "substitute." Even that tactic was not always successful. On August 27, 1862, Harriet

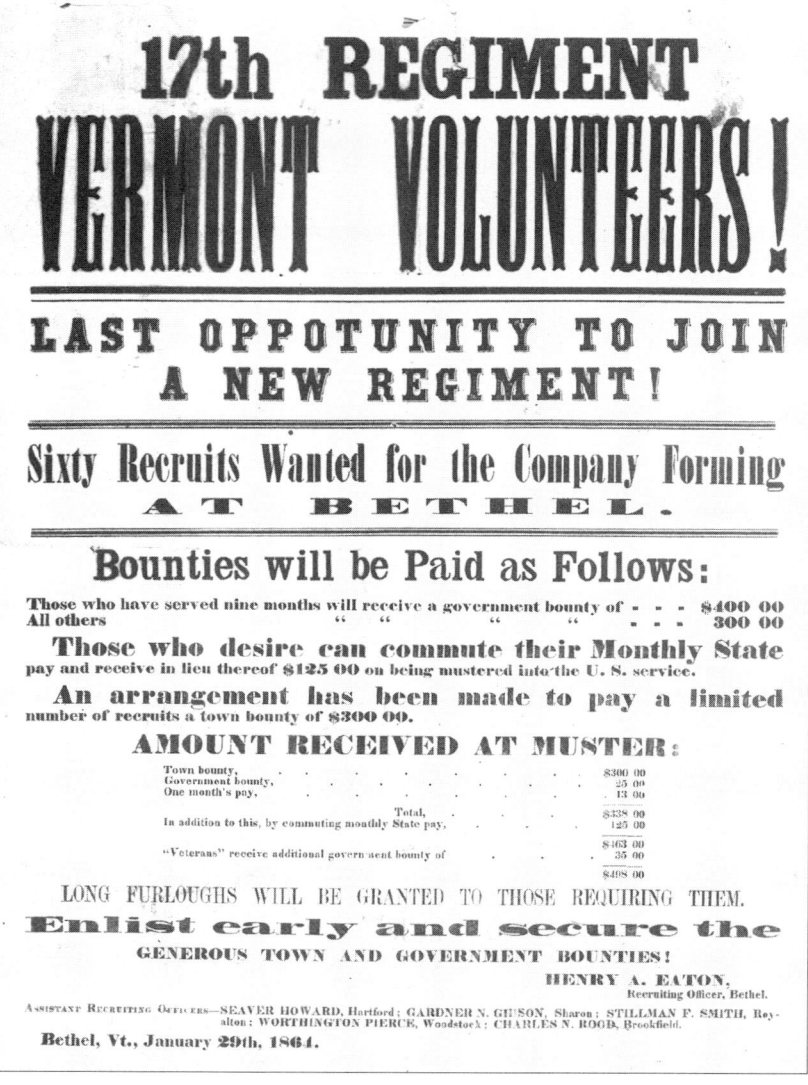

Recruiting broadside for the 17th Regiment, Vermont Volunteers, Bethel, January 29, 1864. *Vermont Historical Society.*

Lawson wrote Franklin Morse, "the drafting scar[e]s the boys[.] some of them have gone and got Certificates and paid two dolars for them and they ain't going to do them eny good[.] they will have to go just the same." A year later George Morse wrote to Franklin, "they have been drafting up this way lately and I sent you some daily [newspapers?] that had a list of the drafted in [T]hose that was drafted in Woodbury payd 300 all but one or two and that cleard them." But George also expressed frustration with the war: "You know the drafting law is the meanest law that ever was made[.] if they wanted men why did not they draft men and not money[.] money wont put down this Rebeldom but they don't want to stop this war[.] the officers are getting to[o] big pay."[54]

In Rutland, resistance to the draft took a more violent turn. On June 16, 1863, Irish laborers in the marble quarries obstructed the work of the Enrollment Board. The following day five hundred resisters, armed with clubs, stones, guns, and ammunition they had been collecting for about three months, and "openly avow[ing] their intention to resist with arms any attempted enforcement of the enrollment or draft," attacked the provost-marshal of the district, the enrolling office, the deputy sheriff of the county, and the surgeon of the Board of Enrollment.[55]

Recruitment rolls and rosters for Civil War units give us a glimpse at one sector of Vermont's population that has been little studied: African Americans. Prevented from serving in Vermont units, or indeed from any other units early in the war, African Americans from Vermont found an opportunity in the famous Massachusetts 54th. The *Revised Roster of Vermont Volunteers, 1861–1865* lists sixty-eight Vermonters in that regiment. All but a handful enlisted between November 1863 and early January 1864, and about a dozen of the remainder enlisted in July and August 1863—before Lincoln's call for three hundred thousand more men. More recent research reveals that 150 African Americans from Vermont fought in the war, serving also in the 10th Regiment Infantry U.S. Colored Troops, the 31st, 41st, 43rd, and 45th infantry regiments, and the somewhat less famous Massachusetts 55th Regiment.[56] These recruits came from many areas of Vermont—Bennington and Pownal in the south to St. Albans in the north. The largest concentration of residences, however, were around Rutland (20), Woodstock and its environs (13), and Ferrisburgh and its neighboring communities (11). A roster of "Miscellaneous Recruits," most of whom enlisted about a year later, gives us an even more scattered list of towns where African Americans resided, from Guilford to Peacham, Shaftsbury to Grand Isle.

Our knowledge about these families is limited, but their residences at the time of enlistment suggest that some may have been descendants of runaway slaves of an earlier generation who, as they passed north with the help of free blacks and sympathetic antislavery whites, settled into farming communities and villages rather than continuing on to Canada. Vermonters had been active in antislavery activity since the 1830s and by

1850 the state was clearly and by statute defying the Fugitive Slave Law, which made settlement for runaway slaves relatively safe. But some of the African Americans who volunteered from Vermont came from families that had been living in the state for several generations. Among the twenty volunteers for the Massachusetts 54th from the Rutland area, most had been born in Vermont. Only one, George Hart, was known to have been a former slave, born in Louisiana. Further evidence that these men were not themselves runaway slaves but must have had a fairly long residence in Vermont before enlisting comes from U.S. Senator Jacob Collamer, who reviewed the troops and noted that "every man among them wrote his name to his articles of enlistment; not one made his mark." Southern laws prohibited teaching slaves how to read or write. Some of the Rutland recruits were farmers; others were laborers, servants, cooks, and domestics.[57] Census data reveals that African-American volunteers from the Hinesburg-Huntington area had roots in Vermont going back to at least 1800 and possibly earlier.[58]

Materials and supplies constituted the third corner of the triangle of support Vermonters gave to the war effort. The war brought both high prices and prosperity to Vermont. Lydia White's article confirms reports that sugar had become very costly and that many Vermonters resorted to using maple sugar—although some had boycotted sugar for years because it was associated with slave labor. Other documents and letters tell us similar stories of high prices and shortages. Alice Watts Choate wrote on May 6, 1862, "All sorts of goods are pretty high here . . . Tea all the way from .75 to 1.25 per pound"; Abby Fuller remembered that "yard wide cotton cloth was thirty-five, forty, and even forty-five cents a yard. If you thought it dear, you knew it would be dearer tomorrow."[59] The cost of all commodities and services jumped 13 percent in the first year of the war, and leaped 67 percent between 1861 and 1865.[60]

For those selling supplies to the military the boom was immediate and sustained. In the first year of the war the state spent half a million dollars on provisions for its troops. Vermont suppliers, unprepared for the sudden demand, lost out to out-of-state merchants in the first months, but quickly caught on to possibilities. T. D. Seymour Bassett calculated that "rations for the first five regiments in Vermont camps came to $27,000 . . . mostly to hotel keepers and wholesale grocers. . . . Brattleboro business boomed in 1862, when eight regiments encamped at Camp Holbrook. . . . Twelve dealers in lumber, stoves, iron, tinware, and dry goods grossed $4,600 from the state in 1862; some grocers and bakers received twice as much, and others including Governor Holbrook, Levi K. Fuller, Estey & Green, and the Brattleboro House, supplied wood, straw, and incidentals. . . . Rutland kept the Seventh in the winter of 1862 with corresponding profits."[61]

In addition to supplying local needs, some Vermont merchants and manufacturers did well competing for contracts with the federal government, especially in ordnance and wool cloth. Lamson, Goodnow, and Yale in Springfield, pioneers in the production of rifles a generation earlier, enjoyed a new boom in 1861 with a contract for 110,000 Sharps carbines worth $2,800,000, followed by more contracts for the duration of the war. The Bennington Powder Company produced gunpowder at great risk but significant profit. Woolen mills in Winooski and North Pownal won contracts worth hundreds of thousands of dollars, and Vermont sheep raisers enjoyed a brief burst of prosperity with the new demand for their fleeces.

Conversion to produce war-related materials helped other manufacturers. Fairbanks Scales produced harness irons. Railroad shops in St. Albans, Rutland, and Brandon produced locomotives and transport cars to move men and supplies to the front. The demand for wood to build barracks, hospitals, and other military buildings and to build, repair, or replace railway trestles and ties put lumbermen and lumber mills back to work. The wartime demand for copperas for ink, dyes, fertilizer, and disinfectant helped revive the copper mines in Orange County. A handful of Vermont foundries and ironworks also benefited from the demand for war-related products.[62]

Even the agricultural sector enjoyed a share of the boom. Wool for uniforms, blankets, and other cloth; Morgan horses for officers, artillery teams, and cavalry; hay to feed them; cattle, swine, grains, potatoes, and apples to feed the men, all contributed to the rising demand and rising prices for Vermont agricultural products.

Supplying the demand was often a challenge. With so many men away at war, farm labor was at a premium. Women took a larger role in harvesting and farm production and the recently introduced mechanical mowers increased productivity at haying season. But the capital investment for these new machines was high and many farming families simply resorted to cooperation and pooled labor to get the work done.

Getting farm products to the front, like getting troops to the front, was the role of the railroads, and here the iron horse proved its value. With its extensive network of railways, the Union was far more efficient and effective than the Confederacy in moving troops and supplies to the places where they were critically needed. Railroad companies in Vermont thrived during the war, as did water transportation on Lake Champlain and Lake Memphremagog. The railroad also helped bring the troops home—both those who returned for burial and those who returned for recovery and recuperation.

As the war ground on, the facilities for treating sick and wounded soldiers near the battlefields were taxed beyond their limits. By the end of 1862 the government reluctantly acknowledged the need for more hospitals and began building or using facilities throughout the Union to care for soldiers whose illnesses or injuries permitted them to be transported back to their home states.

In 1894 Frederick Holbrook described his complicated negotiations with federal officials to establish the Vermont hospitals. Following a visit to the field hospitals in and around Washington, D.C. in December 1862, Holbrook claimed that he convinced President Lincoln and Secretary of War Edwin Stanton to overcome their doubts that the experiment would be "inexpedient and impracticable of execution. It was thought that many of the disabled men would die under the fatigue and exposure of such long transportation back to their state; and it was suggested that possibly some might be lost by desertion. It was also said that the plan would be an unmilitary innovation." Holbrook claimed that he overcame these and budgetary concerns by offering to use the existing campgrounds and barracks buildings in Brattleboro, already owned by the federal government, and to have the State of Vermont "remove them to a sheltered situation at one end of the grounds, placing them in a hollow square, and to fit them up with plastered walls, nice floors, chimneys, provisions for ventilation, an abundance of pure spring water, and all needed appliances and facilities for hospital purposes." Holbrook's bargain with the government included assurances that the hospital would be operated as a military facility, that the secretary of war would authorize transfer of patients from field hospitals, and that the experiment, as Stanton continued to call it, could be revoked in six month's time if it proved unworkable.

By the summer of 1863 the hospital in Brattleboro was treating fifteen hundred to two thousand patients. The barracks buildings were full and tents accommodated the overflow. According to Holbrook, the facility easily passed its first inspection by government officials and "was soon credited by the United States medical inspector, with perfecting a larger percentage of cures than any United States military hospital record elsewhere could show.... The experiment of establishing this hospital proved so successful that similar hospitals were provided in other northern states."[63]

The Brattleboro hospital was one of three military medical facilities in Vermont. It handled more patients than either of the other two—4,402 between June 1, 1863, and October 5, 1865; but it was not the first to open.

The Marine Hospital in Burlington was already receiving sick and wounded from the war in May 1862. Originally built between 1856 and 1858 with a congressional appropriation of $39,000—a political patronage reward for Judge David Smalley, head of the Vermont Democratic Party—the hospital sat two miles south of the village on Shelburne Road on ten acres of land commanding "a fine view of the lake and village.... It is 2 stories high, with a basement; built very thoroughly, with ample and convenient rooms for the use intended." In 1862 the hospital stood unused and was turned over to the government.[64] The first patients arrived in May. Renamed the General Hospital in April 1863, then Baxter General Hospital in September 1864, to honor Vermont's U.S. Representative Portus Baxter, the facility treated a total of 2,406 patients before it closed its doors in July 1865 and transferred its remaining inmates to a temporary post hospital elsewhere in Burlington or to Sloan General Hospital in Montpelier.

Vermont's third military hospital opened in Montpelier in June 1864. Named in honor of W. J. Sloan, U.S. medical inspector for the Department of the East, the hospital occupied a site known as the fair grounds, a plateau at the top of a hill one mile east of the State House. Dr. S. W. Thayer, surgeon general of Vermont, selected the location for its altitude, available fresh water, and access to the railroad. The State of Vermont built twenty-four hospital and service buildings in a roughly circular plan, connected by a covered walkway, and enclosed to create a secure quadrangle. The facility, one of the first to use the improved "pavilion plan" developed by the Army following guidelines developed by Florence Nightingale, was designed to accommodate five hundred patients, hospital staff, and one company of Vermont reservists who served as hospital guards. On April 25, 1864, Governor Smith turned over the buildings to the U.S. War Department and in mid-June the first three hundred patients arrived.[65]

264 FREEDOM AND UNITY

Views of the three Vermont Civil War Hospitals: Top: U.S. General Hospital (later called Smith General Hospital), Brattleboro *(Vermont Historical Society)*; Bottom: Baxter General Hospital, Burlington *(Vermont Historical Society)*; Opposite: Sloan General Hospital, Montpelier *(from Henry Janes scrapbook, Special Collections, Bailey/Howe Library, University of Vermont)*.

By October the hospital was under the direction of Waterbury physician Henry Janes, who had three years of intensive experience with wartime medical practice. Janes brought his experience with battlefield medicine and a commitment to rehabilitation of wounded soldiers to Sloan General Hospital. He followed the progress of many of the gunshot patients and, like some other surgeons, used the new technology of photography to record wounds and progress. Janes commanded the Montpelier hospital from October 15, 1863 until it was decommissioned on December 12, 1865, by which time the facility had treated 1,670 patients. It was the last of the Vermont military hospitals to close its doors.

Holbrook had argued that soldiers sick with malaria, swamp fever, and a variety of illnesses bred by close and unsanitary conditions in the camps and field hospitals would recover better and sooner if removed to a healthier climate. The majority of patients sent north for treatment were diagnosed upon admission with "chronic diarrhea," high fever, or one of several diseases associated with overcrowding and poor sanitation, and hospital records for Brattleboro and Burlington show far more deaths from these causes than from battle injuries. However, of the 8,574 patients admitted to the Vermont hospitals (including Burlington's post hospital) from May 1862 to December 1865, only 175 died while under treatment. Most of the rest returned to duty or were discharged from military service when the war ended in April 1865. The results vindicated Holbrook's optimism in the face of Lincoln and Stanton's skepticism, served as testimony to Vermont's mountain air and relatively clean water, and demonstrated the effectiveness of the improved hospital design employed in the building of the Vermont facilities.

Within a year of the end of the war all three military hospitals shut down. The government sold the Burlington hospital to the Home for Destitute Children for $7,000. Eventually the buildings were razed to make room for a shopping mall on Shelburne Road. The Montpelier Seminary, relocating from Newbury, Vermont, bought the buildings of Sloan General Hospital for $15,500 in 1866. Some of the hospital structures were reused for dormitories, and a few were moved to new locations and survive on and around present-day College Street. The Brattleboro hospital barracks were eventually razed and the site is now occupied by the Brattleboro high school.

The war raged on through the early fall of 1864. On October 19 soldiers from the Eighth, recently brought north from Louisiana, and Tenth Vermont regiments and the regiments of the Old Brigade fought at Cedar Creek in the Shenandoah Valley. The Eighth got chewed up in the early hours of the surprise attack by Confederate troops, while the Tenth, brought up as reinforcements, was able to hold its ground. The Old Brigade came into the fight at midday. When General Philip Sheridan rallied his battered and retreating troops with his famous twelve-mile ride to the battlefield at full gallop, it was the Vermont Eighth that first broke the Confederate lines.

On the same day that Vermont troops fought in the Battle of Cedar Creek, the war came home to Vermont in a new and totally unexpected way. Far from the front lines, most Vermonters never expected to become directly engaged in the war. On October 19, however, St. Albans became part of the war zone for a few dramatic hours. In the middle of the afternoon, about twenty Confederate soldiers led by Bennett Young of Kentucky simultaneously robbed the three banks in St. Albans.[66] In half an hour they seized more than $200,000 in greenbacks, bills, and other U.S. currency. Making their escape on stolen horses, the raiders fired their pistols and attempted to set the town ablaze with grenades of Greek Fire, but the incendiary devices failed to ignite. The Confederates made a dash for the Canadian border, where they had assembled a week earlier to plan the raid. An impromptu posse, led by Captain George Conger, a veteran of the First Vermont Cavalry, pursued the raiders across the border and captured several of them, including Bennett Young. Canadian authorities, notified by telegraph that the raiders were headed their way, also rounded up the fugitives, but insisted on taking all of them into custody. Conger reluctantly surrendered his prisoners to the Canadians, who led fourteen of them back to Montreal. In a tense exchange of diplomatic correspondence, the United States government demanded extradition of the raiders and the Canadians resisted. Finally, a Canadian magistrate ruled against extradition, but Canada returned $88,000 of the stolen money to the St. Albans banks. The pursuers picked up other cash dropped by the raiders along the escape route.

The St. Albans raid was more startling than damaging. The raiders shot three men, one of whom subsequently died. One raider was seriously wounded; one bridge on the escape route was charred by a successful application of Greek Fire; one dumbfounded farmer barely escaped being shot by the pursuers, who mistook him for a Confederate.

Despite its tactical failure, the raid had larger consequences. Relations with Canada grew tense and border towns became nervous. A broadside issued at Barton on October 20 urged "Orleans County, Awake! Rebels in Vermont!" Rumors of more raids resulted in the dispatch of Norwich University cadets to Newport, where they barely avoided opening fire on several confused civilians disembarking from a ferry. In November the General Assembly passed two bills expanding the death penalty to individuals who conspired to levy war against the state or participated in raids that brought harm to persons or property. Governor Smith, whose wife had been in St. Albans at the time of the raid, called out a corps of veterans to guard the town. Eventually a cavalry unit was assigned to patrol the border under the command of George Stannard, recently returned from Petersburg, Virginia, where his right arm had been shattered, then amputated. The northernmost skirmish of the Civil War, the St. Albans Raid has become one of the mythic tales of Vermont and Civil War history.

By spring 1865 the military advantage had finally and irrevocably shifted in favor of the Union. Vermont troops continued on active duty at the siege of Petersburg through the winter of 1864, the last major battle for Vermont's First Brigade. On April 3, the Ninth Vermont Regiment led the Union Army into Richmond, the capital of the Confederacy, abandoned to its fate by a retreating, hard-pressed army. With complete victory now obviously close at hand, Vermonters began to celebrate. In Montpelier the *Watchman*

"Orleans County, Awake! Rebels in Vermont!" Broadside printed October 20, 1864, immediately following the St. Albans Raid. *Vermont Historical Society.*

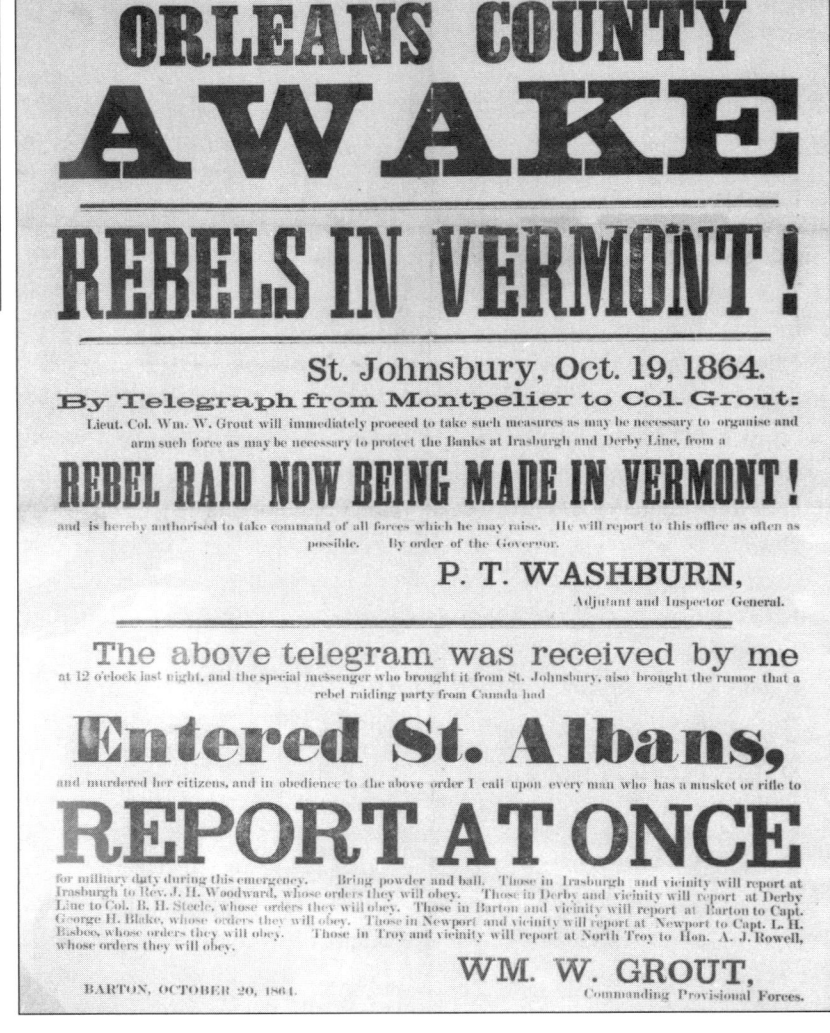

reported on April 8 reaction to news of the capture of Richmond: "The people of Montpelier are in an ecstasy of joy—business suspended, stores, shops, and corner groceries closed, bells ringing, bunting flying, and cannon roaring. Everybody screams at everybody; everybody laughs with everybody; everybody cheers with everybody."[67]

Farther south, the Seventh Vermont Regiment joined other Union troops preparing to take Mobile, Alabama. Vermont infantry regiments moved through the Shenandoah Valley, fighting skirmishes with a now ragged, dispirited Confederate army. On April 9, the First Vermont

Cavalry had just taken its place for an attack on Confederate troops near Appomattox when word arrived of General Lee's surrender.

On his way to dinner on April 13, 1865, President Lincoln received an urgent request from Alfred Burbank Darling, a native of Burke, Vermont, and at the time the owner of several hotels, including the Battle House in Mobile, Alabama. With the war over, Darling was eager to inspect his property. He therefore appealed to Lincoln, probably through an intermediary, for a pass. Apparently not yet having the news that the city fell the day before, Lincoln picked up a scrap of paper and scribbled on it a few words: "Allow the bearer, A. B. Darling, to pass to, and visit Mobile, if and when that City shall be in our possession. A. Lincoln. April 13, 1865."[68] The next night John Wilkes Booth shot Lincoln at Ford's Theater.

Lincoln had enjoyed enormous popularity in Vermont. In the November 1864 elections, with the war draining the state of most of its able-bodied men and people weary of the defeats and disasters, Vermonters had given Lincoln a second resounding vote of confidence with a better than three-to-one victory over his former general, George McClellan, who ran on a Democratic Party peace platform. Once again public and private business stopped throughout the state as celebration of the end of the war turned to mourning for the slain president.

Troops began returning to Vermont in mid-June. Throughout the summer men arrived back home to pick up the pieces of their lives or recover from the grueling experiences of war. Last to return was the Seventh Vermont Regiment. Following a long, unhappy service in Louisiana and Mississippi, then a final action in the siege of Mobile, the Seventh was sent west to patrol the Rio Grande valley in late April 1865. Finally mustered out in Brownsville, Texas, in March 1866, the men of the Seventh at last returned home in April 1866, a full year after the war ended.

Vermont sent 34,238 men into the war: one in every ten of the population, more than half of the total number of men eligible for military duty. Of those who served, 5,224 died in action or from wounds, diseases, and other causes. With a total value of $85 million in property in 1861, the state spent $9.9 million for the war; $5.2 million of that amount was spent by the towns without expectation of repayment. The numbers of men sent to war and the casualties taken by Vermont were among the highest of the Union states.[69]

The war made the reputations and reshaped the future of many. Four military commanders—Peter T. Washburn, Roswell Farnham, Samuel E.

Pingree, and Urban A. Woodbury—later served as governors of Vermont. Redfield Proctor, who as commander of the Fifteenth Vermont helped put down the New York City draft riots in July 1863, also later served as governor of Vermont, U.S. senator, and secretary of war in the cabinet of William Henry Harrison. Charles H. Joyce, who early in the war won dubious notoriety for charging his superior officer, Henry Whiting, with cowardice, went on to serve eight years as a representative in Congress. Cavalry officer William Wells represented Waterbury in the Vermont House, Chittenden County in the Senate, and was appointed collector of customs. Wheelock Veazey, commander of the Sixteenth Vermont at Gettysburg, became a justice of the Vermont Supreme Court. General George Stannard was appointed customs collector in Burlington and later doorkeeper of the U.S. House of Representatives. In 1866, veterans of the war formed the Grand Army of the Republic (GAR)— an organization that both kept alive and before the public the memory of the war and became a vehicle for catapulting many former soldiers and officers into prominence, prosperity, and public office.

For many returning soldiers, however, the transition back to civilian life was quick and less dramatic. Franklin Morse of Wooodbury left the army in June 1864. His diary for 1863–1864 laconically records his departure from the war.

> Mon. 20 June. Clear and plessant arived to Brattleboro 3.15
> Tues. 21 June. Plessant Musterd out of the United States Service
> Wed. 22 June. Paid State Pay. Verry hot
> Thurs. 23 June. Paid and Left for Home on the Night Train
> Friday 24 June. Arived Home at Noon
> Saturday 25 June. Hoed Corn . . .
> Monday 27 June. Began to Fraim the Barn . . .
> Friday 1 July. Raised the Barn

For others, of course, the return was even less joyful or promising. With over five thousand dead and over four thousand wounded from the war, there was much to mourn. Many returned only briefly, then emigrated to cities or to the western states, where their pensions and pay allowed them to find new opportunities for prosperity.[70]

The War Enshrined

An abundance of visual images kept the Civil War in people's memory. In the early years of the war, Vermonters, like others throughout the North, received news and pictures of the war through daily papers and other periodicals. *Harper's Weekly,* among others, featured wood engravings of battle scenes made from sketches drawn by artists acting as war correspondents or by photographers using a variety of technologies to capture details of war and camp life. Two Brattleboro natives, Larkin G. Mead and George H. Houghton, helped shape the image of war for those back home in Vermont and elsewhere in the North.

Mead was already a famous sculptor when war broke out in 1861. His allegorical figure, "Agriculture," adorned the top of the new State House dome, and in October 1861 he was completing a larger-than-life-size statue of Ethan Allen for the State House portico as regiments gathered at the army camp in Brattleboro. In February 1862, Mead headed south to join the troops, hired as a technical field artist by General William Farrar Smith to provide the Vermont Brigade with drawings and topographical surveys of Confederate installations. He soon began sending drawings to *Harper's Weekly,* which rendered them as wood engravings. Mead left the war in late June or early July 1862 but continued providing sketches to *Harper's.* His last battlefield image appeared on August 2, 1862. In October 1862, Mead settled in Florence, Italy, where he opened a studio. After the war, he won the commission to produce the sculptures for the monument to Lincoln in Springfield, Illinois. A study for the bust of Lincoln, donated by his widow in 1910, sits in the Vermont State House.[71]

George H. Houghton was one of many photographers who followed the war. Still a relatively new technology when the war began, photography was already evolving from the one-of-a-kind daguerreotypes, introduced about 1840, toward wet and dry plate processing, which allowed the photographer to record a subject in a shorter time and make multiple prints from a negative. Taking his cue from Matthew Brady's commercial success, Houghton left Brattleboro in late 1861 in the first of two visits to record the peninsula campaign. He met up with Larkin Mead and photographed some of Mead's sketches. He took about a hundred photographs of men, scenes, and engagements of Vermont regiments and appears to have made a handsome living from the sale of prints. In 1864 Houghton collected his wartime photographs into an album, which he presented to the Vermont Historical

Above, "The Vermont Soldiers Inspecting the Lincoln Gun at Fortress Monroe, March 24th, 1862." Drawing by Larkin Mead. Below, "When Will This Cruel War Be Over." Photograph by George H. Houghton. *Vermont Historical Society (Houghton Album, 1413)*.

Society. The Vermont *Phoenix* called it "one of the most valuable and reliable historic collections made since the commencement of the rebellion."[72]

Photography democratized the face of war. The common soldier could easily and inexpensively get his portrait taken as a daguerreotype, tintype, or ambrotype, or as a reproducible photograph, often placed on a *carte de visite* sent home or left behind as a memento for his loved ones. Whereas for previous wars we have only the portraits of officers and prominent political figures, for the Civil War we have thousands of bust and full-length photographic portraits of the common soldier and his equipment.

Visual images of the war appeared everywhere during and after the conflict. Panorama painters turned out large-format canvasses trucked from village to village by lecturers who used the sequential scenes as the backdrops for narratives of major conflicts. Lantern slides served the same purpose. Both kept audiences on the home front apprised of the progress of the war—forerunners of the newsreels of the next century. Even after the war ended, the panorama and lantern slide shows continued. A 125-foot-long, 7-foot-high panorama painting by Vermont artist Charles Hardin Andrus, created in the last years of the nineteenth century, contains twelve scenes from the Civil War, from the firing on Fort Sumter to Grant and Lee at Appomattox. Apparently commissioned by the GAR in Vermont, the panorama painting helped veterans remember their experiences, taught the history of the war to the next generation in life-size images, and may have been used to generate enthusiasm for the Spanish-American War.

After the war another new technology, chromolithography, helped perpetuate memories of service. Printed unit rosters with decorated borders depicting scenes from the war circulated widely. Some included portraits of corps commanders and other high-ranking military figures, allowing the printer to do large runs of the basic format, which could be overprinted with lists of the names of the unit's soldiers and officers. In many cases, an area was left blank for the purchaser or his family to place his own portrait on the roster. As the GAR grew in significance, convened its state and national reunions, and established its own hierarchy, medals, badges, buttons, and similar items made their way into the materials of everyday life or into family scrapbooks.

The fine arts thrived as well, with commissions for portraits, battlefield scenes, commemorative sculpture, monuments, and *bas reliefs* that kept artists busy into the next century. In 1868 St. Johnsbury, Swanton, and Derby erected statues to their Civil War veterans. The following year Williamstown set up a statue to commemorate the war.[73] In 1870 the Vermont legislature

Soldiers Record, Company C, 9th Vermont Volunteers, Addison County. *Vermont Historical Society.*

authorized Governor John W. Stewart to contract with Julian Scott, a native of Johnson, Vermont, for a historical painting illustrating the Vermont troops in action. Scott accepted the commission for $5,000 and offered to paint a scene from Antietam, where he had seen action as a fifteen-year-old boy. However, a reunion of veteran officers in 1871 passed a resolution requesting that he portray the Battle at Cedar Creek, where more Vermonters came under fire than at any other engagement. Scott visited the battlefield in June 1871 and agreed to the subject. Four years later he produced a monumental work ten feet high by twenty feet wide, for which the legislature voted an additional $4,000. The painting now occupies an entire wall in the Reception Room (sometimes called "the Cedar Creek Room") of the State House.

The State House in fact became something of a shrine to Vermont's participation in the Civil War. In 1865, veterans of the war presented sixty-five regimental flags to the state. A few years later the banners went into display cases outside the House chamber. Portraits, commemorative plaques, and battle scenes continued to arrive at the State House in the century following the war. In 1993 the State House purchased a portrait of General William Farrar Smith by Julian Scott, and in 1995 it added to its collection a painting of Vermont at Gettysburg.[74]

Julian Scott, "The Battle of Cedar Creek" (1875). The enormous canvas, measuring twenty feet wide by ten feet high, hangs in a reception room at the Vermont State House, Montpelier. Photo by Marie Charbonneau. *Courtesy of Friends of the Vermont State House.*

The Civil War thus brought together, often in gruesome perfection, many technological advances, social and political changes, and economic shifts that had been taking place for the past decade or more in Vermont, no less than in the nation as a whole. For Vermont, perhaps more than for most other states in the North, the Civil War represented a triumph of commitment and dedication. With the adoption of the Thirteenth Amendment to the U.S. Constitution, the state's long-standing constitutional, religious, and political opposition to slavery became the law of the land. With a proud record of human and financial sacrifice to the principles of personal freedom and union, Vermont more fully emerged from being a remote and largely self-contained frontier into national politics, economics, and culture. Moreover, with the infrastructure created during the war, Vermonters saw their local and state governments transformed into larger and more powerful institutions that exercised much greater influence over their lives and fortunes.

Politics and Society: The "Little Republics" and Reform, 1850–1870

Although slavery and the war preoccupied Vermonters from the mid-1850s until the end of the 1860s, other items of unfinished business remained on the political agenda. Temperance activism had played a role in shaping political and social alliances since before the war and culminated in passage of the state's version of the Maine Law in 1852. It was a victory for the big towns. Spurred on by the Know-Nothing Party, urban voters and big business leaders focused their concerns about public disorder on Roman Catholic Irish and French Canadians and used their control of large voting blocs among laborers at factories, quarries, and lumber mills to push prohibition. While voters in a majority of small towns cast ballots against statewide prohibition—in short to maintain local option and assert the sovereignty of the town—the state's population had shifted sufficiently to give the prohibitionists in the large towns the popular vote they needed to have their way.

The Know-Nothings exercised political power one more time during the brief period of party fluidity after 1852 by dominating the 1855 meeting of the Council of Censors. Lacking a strong town-based organization themselves, the Know-Nothings at this septenary gathering successfully promoted proposals to amend the state constitution's provision for electing state representatives and senators. In its report to the people of the state in February 1856, the council asserted that "the present constitutional provision giving each organized town one representative [in the Vermont House of Representatives] without regard to population, is wrong in principle, unjust in its operation, and unnecessarily expensive. This Council adhere to the more reasonable doctrine that population and representation should be equal, and can see no good reason why equal numbers should be unequally represented. . . . [U]nder the present system," the council report continued, "one quarter of the inhabitants of the State have nearly the same number of representatives as the other three quarters, thereby giving the controlling power of legislation to a minority."

In its discussion of the biennial legislature, the council report complained that "It appears to us, that annual sessions of the Legislature, especially with the present number of representatives, have a direct tendency to render the system of legislation unstable. The laws of one session of the legislature are not unfrequently altered, amended or repealed by subsequent enactments, before their import is understood, and before their practical operation could be tested by the people. This has become so great an evil as to be almost universally felt and complained of by business men." Even

Second Vermont State House, designed by Ammi Young and built in 1833. Fire destroyed much of it on January 6, 1857. Daguerreotype, c. 1850. *Vermont Historical Society.*

lawyers, the council added, had a hard time knowing what the law was.

To remedy this inequity, the Council of Censors called for a constitutional convention to amend Vermont's charter by reducing the number of representatives, providing representation by population rather than by town in the House, and holding biennial rather than annual sessions of the General Assembly. A majority vote of the delegates to the constitutional convention was required to amend the constitution, with each town sending one delegate to the convention. Shrewdly assessing the small likelihood of achieving these constitutional reforms under the existing procedures, the council continued its attack on the political power of the small towns by proposing new ones. Noting again the growing disproportion between the number of towns and the distribution of the population, in a startling maneuver, the council called a convention to be composed of only ninety delegates chosen on a proportionally representative basis.[75]

The 1856 legislature, not at all pleased with the report of the Council of Censors, called into question its authority either to propose such amendments to the constitution or to alter the composition of the constitutional convention. Thus, when the convention did meet on January 7, 1857, it faced several challenges, including the question of its jurisdiction.

Before the convention could get to work, however, it had to find a place to meet. On the night of January 6, 1857, the janitorial staff of the State House stoked the fire boxes to warm the building for the next day's meeting. By midnight fire had broken out and in the morning the superb structure designed by Vermonter Ammi Young in 1833 had been reduced to a burned-out shell.

When the convention finally settled down to work, it took a dim view of the amendments proposed by the Council of Censors. Population-based representation clearly posed a threat to the traditional power of the towns—"the little republics"—and they came prepared to fight back. In a strongly worded resolution the convention quickly rejected the amendments.

Reorganizing the legislature on the basis of population did not reappear as an agenda item in 1862, but emerged again at the meeting of the Council of Censors in 1869. By then, however, the Republican Party had assembled an effective town-based political organization and had little to gain from pressing for this reform. The Know-Nothings, who as an urban party had the most to gain from population-based representation, had disappeared from the political scene; and the Democrats, discredited by their association with slavery and the Confederate cause (Democrats in

Congress after the war continued to resist abolition and provided all the votes against the Thirteenth Amendment to the Constitution eliminating slavery), wielded negligible power or allegiance beyond the ethnic Irish and French population in Vermont's larger towns. Those ethnic, Catholic groups faced a suspicious Protestant majority, secure in their political hegemony, which they exercised through the power of the towns in the legislature. It would be almost a century before the issue of population-based representation and reform of the legislature emerged again, this time under a Democratic governor and under the threat of a federal lawsuit following a U.S. Supreme Court decision imposing on state legislatures the principle of "one person, one vote."

The challenge by the big towns did not end with the defeat of the amendments proposed by the 1855–1856 Council of Censors. The ashes of the old State House were barely cold before a fight broke out over relocating the state capital. Burlington, Middlebury, Northfield, and Rutland, among others, vied to become home to state government and sweetened their offers with promises of cash contributions toward constructing a new state house. Montpelier did the same and played upon the antagonism of the rural towns toward the big-town bullying that had soured the 1857 constitutional convention. At a special session of the legislature called on February 18, 1857, the debating and canvassing became intense, with much of the discussion revolving around which town was most lax about enforcing the statewide ban on alcohol. On February 27 the Senate voted 13 for Montpelier, 11 for Burlington, 4 for Rutland, and 1 for Middlebury. The House voted 138 for Montpelier, 80 for Rutland. A few days later Montpelier citizen George W. Cree wrote to his brother, T. Jefferson Cree of Wheelock, Vermont, describing the struggle: "Never did two contending armys work with more desperation and determination than Montpelier and Burlington." "In the end," writes historian T. D. Seymour Bassett, "mileage and rural antagonism to the largest village and its methods triumphed, for the incumbent. Burlington was not enough larger than her rival to steamroller or cajole the votes, and the backfires raised by others in favor of removal to their towns canceled out much of Burlington's strength."[76]

When the Council of Censors met again in 1869, it placed before the citizens of Vermont six proposals, including biennial elections to replace annual terms and biennial legislative sessions to replace annual meetings; a procedure for popular ratification of constitutional amendments to replace the council and constitutional convention; and the issue of suffrage for women. In support of its proposal for two-year terms and biennial sessions, the Council of Censors' report emphasized the facts that nothing was likely to change, as officers and legislators traditionally served two years; that frequent elections tended to promote small-faction fighting and petty ambitions; and that short annual terms deprived officeholders of the opportunity to gain expertise in their office, resulting in poor law making and improvised administration.

The proposal to abolish the Council of Censors was more complicated and controversial. The council had the authority to propose amendments with a simple majority of its vote. Because its members were elected at large, the council increasingly reflected the interests of the larger communities against the small towns, even though a two-thirds majority vote was required for the council to call a convention to amend the constitution. The convention in turn was composed of delegates elected by town caucuses, and a simple majority vote in the convention could pass the proposals to amend the constitution. Since 1777, when this system was devised, most of the council's proposals for amendment had been rejected. The council itself had been severely discredited by its 1855 proposals, and its recommendation now to abolish the procedure carried the echo of that earlier opprobrium. In its place the council recommended a procedure whereby every ten years the Senate could propose amendments by passing articles of amendment by two-thirds majority votes, with concurrence of majority votes in the House and majority votes in each house in the next session, and then submitting the articles to the people as a referendum. This complicated system (modified in 1974 to reduce the time lock to four years), finally approved by the convention of 1870, abolished the Council of Censors, preserved the power of the towns, and kept the Vermont constitution one of the briefest, because most difficult to amend, of the state constitutions.[77]

The council's proposal to extend suffrage to women did not enjoy such success in the 1870 constitutional convention. In the years before the Civil War women had played prominent roles in antislavery and temperance activism. One wing of the antislavery campaign had already raised the question of enfranchising women, although this radical idea had been beaten back by the mid-1850s. Among those speaking on behalf of antislavery and for women's suffrage was Clarina Howard Nichols, a native of West Townshend, who had married a Baptist minister and moved to

Clarina Howard Nichols. *Vermont Historical Society.*

upstate New York in the 1830s, where she ran an academy and raised three children. In 1840 she left her husband and returned to Vermont, where three years later she married George W. Nichols, the editor and publisher of the *Windham County Democrat*. When he fell ill, she took over the paper and served as its editor for ten years, writing editorials opposing slavery—an unusual position for a Democratic newspaper—and in favor of reforms including legal and property rights for married women. In 1852, already a practiced speaker on behalf of women's rights, Nichols addressed a joint session of the legislature—the first woman to do so—urging support of a bill to allow women to vote in school district meetings.

All but a few legislators stomped and jeered at Nichols and then voted down the bill. The following year she and her family moved west to participate in the antislavery struggle in Kansas.[78]

In the shuffle of political party realignment between 1852 and 1856, voting rights for women disappeared from the reform agenda. It reemerged as a national issue as the postwar amendments to the U.S. Constitution moved toward ratification. The Civil War gave women new and unprecedented opportunities to participate in civic activities and work outside of the home. Women throughout Vermont, as elsewhere in New England and the North, raised money for the Sanitary and Christian commissions, took on a wider variety of jobs on farms and in factories, and with an acute shortage of young men, stepped into the role of schoolteacher in greater numbers—commanding far less pay, as school districts gleefully observed. Their involvement in such activities continued after the war through participation in the freedmen's bureaus and schools and other social welfare activities. Now more acutely sensitive to both their contributions to society and their legal and political subordination to men, a new generation of women leaders renewed efforts to win the right to vote.

When the Council of Censors met in 1869, some among them also believed the time had come to expand suffrage to include women. In their report to their colleagues on the council, the Special Committee on Woman Suffrage—Jasper Rand of St. Albans, Charles Read of Montpelier, and H. Henry Powers of Morristown—argued that

> even-handed justice, a fair application of the principles of the Declaration of Independence and of our State Constitution . . . give woman the ballot, and do not shut out from it one-half of the intelligence and more than one-half of the moral power of the people. Custom and prejudice alone stand in the way. . . . We know no good reason why the most ignorant *man* should vote, and the intelligent *woman* be refused. . . . Now woman sits by the side of man, is his companion and associate in his amusement, and in all his labors, studies, pursuits, and interests, save the one of governing the country. And it is time that she should be his associate in this.[79]

Convinced by this argument, the council eventually voted 9 to 4 to include among its six proposals for amendments to the Vermont Constitution one mandating full suffrage for women.

Supporters of the amendment had seven months to convince the delegates to the constitutional convention to approve it. In January 1870, Rand, Read, and Powers established the Vermont Woman Suffrage Association (VTWSA), an entirely male organization including newspaper editors, clergy, lawyers, businessmen, and politicians, to coordinate the campaign. Early in February the VTWSA invited several prominent women from the moderate American Woman Suffrage Association to attend a convention in Montpelier. Among those who spoke at this meeting were Julia Ward Howe, Mary Livermore, and Lucy Stone, already among the leading national figures in the women's suffrage movement. Late that month a second convention met in Rutland, followed by March meetings in Brattleboro, St. Johnsbury, St. Albans, and Burlington. William Lloyd Garrison shared the platform with Julia Ward Howe in Rutland; Lucy Stone spoke in Brattleboro.

The "invasion of strong-minded women," as one newspaper editor called it, ended in April when the most well-known speakers for women's suffrage ceased to appear on Vermont platforms. Local organizers and supporters continued the effort to convince voters to elect pro-suffrage delegates to the constitutional convention, but similar efforts elsewhere in the nation brought only discouraging news. Although Wyoming and Utah passed legislation giving women the vote, similar proposals went down to defeat in Colorado, Kansas, and on a veto by the governor in Minnesota. In a last-ditch effort to win support for the amendment in Vermont, women throughout the state signed petitions that they presented to the constitutional convention when it convened in June.

Perhaps only the lopsided vote count surprised observers when the women's suffrage amendment went down to defeat. Only one delegate among the 232 men elected to the convention voted in favor of the proposal. The lone supporter, Harvey Howe of Fair Haven, later published a pamphlet, "The Last Resort," defending his position, claiming that "many of the best and most progressive minds of both men and women in Vermont are decidedly in favor of woman suffrage," and predicting that the day was not far off when women would receive the vote. Howe may have overstated support for the amendment and was certainly too optimistic in his prediction, for not until 1880 did Vermont women get the right to vote in local school district meetings, and full suffrage had to wait until passage of the Nineteenth Amendment to the U.S. Constitution in 1920.[80]

The 1870 census recorded a population in Vermont of 330,551, an increase of just over 5 percent from 1850. By contrast, the entire population of the United States increased by over 70 percent in the same twenty-year period. The small rise in numbers in Vermont tells many stories. In those twenty years, Vermont lost many young men to the West and the Civil War, and many young women to the mills, factories, and industrial centers of New England. The railroad brought the state into closer and sustained contact with the rest of the East Coast and with the newer communities and states developing beyond the old Western Reserve. Within the state, population shifts tell similar stories. In 1850 Windsor County had the largest population in the state, Burlington—the largest town—had 6,110 inhabitants, and just 7 percent of the population lived in the five largest towns. Twenty years later, Rutland County, spurred by marble, railroads, and manufacturing, had the largest concentration of Vermonters, Burlington now had 13,596 people (roughly 4.1 percent of the entire state population), and almost 12.5 percent of the people lived in the five largest towns. What T. D. Seymour Bassett called in the 1930s the "urban penetration of rural Vermont" began in 1850 with the coming of the railroad. By 1870, what Bassett called in the 1990s "the growing edge" had clearly shifted away from rural communities to those that provided opportunities in manufacturing, transportation, and finance in the same location. Some Vermonters saw the changes coming and leaped at the opportunities. Some saw the entire fabric of society changing. Two of those people determined to capture the memory of the past and record the changes taking place around them.

Pliny Holton White (1822–1869) crammed a lot of activity into his short life. Lawyer, newspaper editor, Congregational minister, businessman, public servant, educator, and civic leader, White was a prolific writer, passionately concerned with the history of his native state and the towns where he lived and worked. In 1858 he settled in Coventry, in Orleans County. That year he published *The Life and Services of Matthew Lyon*; two years later he brought out a collection of *Early Poets of Vermont*. At the end of his life he compiled the first bibliography of Vermont, which he published in periodical form in 1869. In an article for a St. Johnsbury newspaper, White called upon his fellow citizens to take an interest in local history and he set an example by writing a history of Congregationalist churches in Orleans County, planning to expand the work to include the entire state.[81]

White's devotion to local history and especially his suggestion that each

Two Vermont historians: Pliny Holden White (right), whose article advocating local history inspired Abby Maria Hemenway (left) to undertake her monumental *Vermont Historical Gazetteer*. *Vermont Historical Society.*

town write its own history, struck a responsive chord in the imagination of Abby Maria Hemenway (1828–1890). A native of Ludlow, Vermont, with a classical education from the Black River Academy, Hemenway had just published her first book, *The Poets and Poetry of Vermont*, in 1859 and, as she put it, was "looking about for something of a Vermont character to do," when she read White's article on local history. His plan for a book-length history of each town struck Hemenway as infeasible, but she determined to collect in a series of volumes historical sketches of each town written by local correspondents.

Initially greeted with skepticism, Hemenway persisted and assembled a corps of writers, including Pliny White, whose work she edited, annotated, supplemented, and saw into print at her own expense between 1868 and 1891. She planned to publish three volumes, but her persistence and the material, although not financial support, that she gathered forced her to expand the project to five published volumes and a sixth completed but unpublished at the time of her death.

For Hemenway, as for White, the project had urgency. "Our historical material," she wrote in her preface to volume one of the *Vermont Historical Gazetteer*, "is becoming—and will continue to become—daily more and more indistinct and irrecoverable; . . . Our past has been too rich and in many points, or some, too unique and romantic to lose."[82] The richness she claimed for Vermont's past she demonstrated in the eclectic nature of the material she published: narrative histories; biographical and genealogical sketches; church and institutional histories; statistics on population, agricultural production, prices, and weather; lists of town officers and participants in the Civil War; short works of oratory, prose, and poetry. With entries varying in length from one paragraph to many pages, Hemenway's *Vermont Historical Gazetteer* provided contemporary readers with an enormous body of facts, recollections, and impressions of Vermont's communities. The Vermont Historical Society, founded a generation earlier, rewarded her efforts by making her the first female member admitted to the Society.

Still a unique and invaluable resource for comprehending the first century of Vermont history, the *Gazetteer* is a monumental work and a reflection of the expanding world of Vermont in the middle and late nineteenth century. Vermont writers in the next generation, like some of those of the previous generation, lamented the lost world of frontier and rural society and recreated it in fiction and other works of the imagination. Many of Hemenway's writers, by contrast, still in the thrall of a rising industrial society, recorded the facts and figures of Vermont's towns and managed to capture the living memories of the passing generation of founders and builders.

It is testimony to the continuing dominance of the towns in the lives, landscapes, and imaginations of Vermonters that Hemenway conceived the idea of assembling a history of the state and executed it as the assembled histories of its towns. However much state government had grown in its scope, authority, and presence for Vermonters in the course of the two decades from 1850 to 1870, and however much state pride had shown itself a force in the national cataclysm of the Civil War, the town remained in 1870 the locus of memory, political participation, and identification for most Vermonters. Hemenway's most recent biographer, Deborah Clifford, concluded that "Abby Hemenway saw her history as uniting Vermonters, not dividing them. Each town in its individuality was part of a larger whole. In this way she nourished a communal pride. Towns, not the state, came first, and even the smallest, poorest community had something to contribute to the whole. The *Gazetteer* gave Vermonters a newfound pride in their local places and their local people."[83]

6

The Reconfiguration of Vermont

1870–1900

Vermonters on the Move

In his inaugural address to the General Assembly on October 6, 1870, Governor John W. Stewart confidently asserted that "there are encouraging signs of advancement in our State. Our population and resources have materially increased within the last decade."[1] A decade later, a worried John L. Barstow offered the legislature a different view of Vermont's future. Concluding his farewell speech, Governor Barstow had this to say about the general condition of the state:

"The census of 1880 again shows that our rural population and wealth are decreasing, while our villages and cities gain only a little more than enough to compensate for the loss in the country towns. The reduction of our representation in Congress [Vermont fell from three to two House districts in 1882] also forcibly reminds us that our beloved State is not keeping pace with others in material prosperity and development."[2]

Barstow identified several possible causes for this decline in prosperity and shift in population. He cited poor and discriminatory management of the railroads, which put Vermont farmers at an economic disadvantage as shippers of goods to the Boston and New York markets and discouraged capital investment in the state. He mentioned a lack of legislation to encourage manufacturing, mining, and quarrying; a critical shortage of labor; and failure to attract a new labor force from the immigrants entering the United States. Postwar prosperity had gone bust. Vermont, like much of the nation, had suffered under the burden of a depression in the early 1870s; but unlike many other areas of the country, Vermont was not making a good recovery. The lack of population growth especially disturbed Barstow.

When Governor William P. Dillingham gave his valedictory in 1890, he also reported an alarming number of abandoned farms and shortage of labor. Referring to his own efforts to recruit "the best class of Swedish emigrants to come to Vermont and settle upon what are known as unoccupied or abandoned farms,"[3] which for many years had been declining in value, he challenged the legislature to continue his experiment as one way to revitalize Vermont's economy and boost its population.

Something odd was happening in the last third of the nineteenth century. While the nation's population increased steadily at rates of over 25 percent every ten years, Vermont's population showed barely any increase at all. Moreover, continuing a disturbing trend that began in the 1820s, large numbers of native-born Vermonters were leaving the state, often for manufacturing and industrial jobs in nearby Massachusetts, New Hampshire, and New York, and sometimes to travel farther afield to the upper Midwest and far West. "In a new and growing country like our own," Dillingham said, "there have been opportunities for young men who were strong, temperate, intelligent, industrious, enterprising, and ambitious to seek and make fortunes in the commercial and manufacturing centres, and in those portions of the west where speculative values have afforded opportunity for the exercise of sagacity and sound judgment."[4] Vermont had raised its share of such men and women; but they had gone elsewhere to exercise those qualities. (One Vermonter who left, Chester Alan Arthur, became president of the United States in 1881.) The 1880 census counted 430,041 native-born Vermonters, only 251,780 of whom—about 58 percent—lived in Vermont. The entire population of the state that year was 332,286. The 1890 census identified 424,286 Vermont-born nationwide; only 250,320 of them still living in the state (a decline in the native-born population); and a negligible increase in the state population to 332,407.

Some of the large number of "Vermonters abroad," as the magazine *The Vermonter* called them, retained their affection for their native state and by 1895 Vermont associations met annually in Boston, Worcester, Springfield, Lowell, and South Framingham, Massachusetts; Manchester, New Hampshire; Providence, Rhode Island; Hartford, Connecticut; Washington, D.C.; Brooklyn and Buffalo, New York; and in the western cities of Detroit, Chicago, Minneapolis, Des Moines, Omaha, Denver, and San Francisco. The constitutions and bylaws of these associations spoke of promoting acquaintances, cultivating friendship and mutual benefits among Vermonters, and, as in the case of the Pacific Coast Association Native Sons of Vermont, "the collection and preservation of important information relative to the early and subsequent history of the Green Mountain State."[5] Many of these organizations were for native sons and served as networks for business and political advancement among their members. A few admitted women, and in Boston the women organized themselves in 1894 to create the Daughters of Vermont, whose membership included "any woman born in or having been a resident of Vermont for three years and of good moral character."[6] Membership in these Vermont associations typically exceeded two hundred individuals, many of them prominent in business, politics, and education. The clubs sent rosters and reports back home to *The Vermonter*, founded in 1895, which published them with bittersweet pride in the accomplishments of lost native sons and daughters.

The long period of migration from Vermont and no growth in its total population has long mystified and concerned Vermont historians. In fact, the total population of Vermont remained at the same level for almost a century beginning in the years after the Civil War, and Vermont thus earned a reputation as a good place to come from but not a good place to

"Birds Eye view of Burlington and Winooski, Vermont" (1877). Drawn by E. Meilbek, published by J. J. Stoner, Madison, Wisconsin. *Vermont Historical Society.*

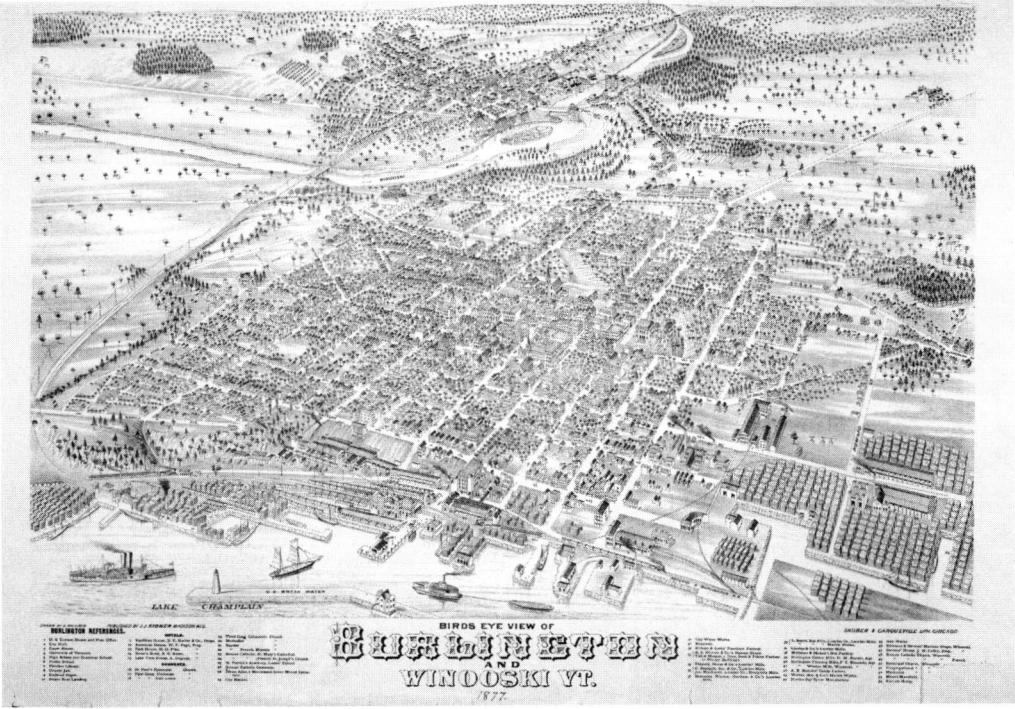

live. However, this formulation masks some important changes that took place in the composition and distribution of Vermont's population and consequently the reconfiguration of economic, political, social, and cultural life in the late nineteenth century.

Urban Growth

The raw demographic data noted by successive governors underscored just one part of the population change affecting Vermont. For while many people moved out, many also moved within Vermont. This internal migration depleted many rural communities while it stimulated some villages to accept the responsibilities and structures of urban life. In the period 1850 to 1910, according to historian Barry Salussolia, "an average of 151 towns lost population every decade . . . while the twelve largest towns grew more rapidly than the state at large."[7]

Until 1865, Vermont had only one community incorporated as a city: Vergennes, then as now one of the smallest cities in the nation. By contrast, Burlington, in 1865, the most densely populated community in the state, remained a village. When Burlington businessmen promoted a plan that year to reorganize their village as a city, they looked forward to additional growth and to attracting new investment in manufacturing and trade by offering better services: sewers, water, police and fire protection, greater control over finances and administration, and more adequate representation in the legislature. Opponents—primarily Burlington's Irish and French Catholics, who together comprised almost 54 percent of the local population—feared that losing the direct democracy of town meeting would disenfranchise them and open the door to corrupt government by a city council and mayor drawn from the elite. Another argument centered on the general distaste for what many Vermonters perceived as the moral evils of urban life. It took a decade of negotiating and failed referenda before citizens finally voted to divide Burlington into a city of roughly 8½ square miles and a new town of South Burlington of roughly 14 square miles of mostly agricultural land.

The expectations of the business leaders and promoters of city autonomy were largely fulfilled over the next three decades. By 1870 Burlington had almost fourteen thousand inhabitants, almost twice its population in 1860. Burlington's lumber industry revived in the late 1860s in part because nearby Canadian lumber could enter the U.S. duty-free, in part because

Burlington's rail access to Boston provided an inexpensive outlet to national and world markets. A host of allied industries grew up around the lumberyards: sash, Venetian blind, door, box, and carriage makers; iron works; furniture and picture-frame makers. This economic activity attracted yet a wider circle of manufacturers and merchants. By 1892 Burlington supported 129 manufacturers and more than six hundred merchants and small businesses, including at least one hundred women listed as dress makers, embroiderers, milliners, and private nurses. The city boasted five banks, four large hotels and twenty-six boarding houses (eighteen run by women), electric street lighting, an advanced water and sewer system, and a Board of Trade that promoted new business and continual growth.

The wealth created by this activity in turn generated additional urban amenities and services. In 1873 Mary L. Fletcher, widow of one of the wealthiest men in Vermont, and her daughter, Mary Martha Fletcher, gave the city $10,000 for books and $10,000 for construction of a free library. Three years later Mary Martha Fletcher, now the sole heir to an estate of over $400,000, arranged for a gift of $25,000 to purchase land and buildings for a hospital, $75,000 to build it, and $110,000 to endow the institution, which opened on January 27, 1879. Another Burlington business entrepreneur, John Purple Howard, included an ornate and spacious opera house in the commercial block he constructed in 1879.[8]

To meet the challenges of urban life, so much feared and anticipated in the debate over incorporation in the 1850s and 1860s, groups of Protestant women, the wives, sisters, and daughters of middle-class and wealthy merchants and business leaders, organized and supported several charitable institutions. These included the Home for Destitute Children formed in 1865; the Ladies Aid Society, organized after the Civil War and renamed in 1882; the Howard Relief Society, named for its major contributor, Louisa Howard, older sister of John Purple Howard; the Ladies of Nazareth; Adams Mission Home; and Burlington Cancer Relief Society. Similarly, the wives and daughters of Burlington's Jewish merchants organized Hebrew Charities. These organizations in some ways mirrored larger trends in philanthropy and charitable works across the nation, but according to historian Marshall True, they were distinctive in two respects. First, Burlington's organized charities began at about the time the city gained its charter and therefore grew with the city and helped shape social policy. Second, possibly reflecting and building on the moral authority women's organizations earned in the previous generation, when they took an active role in antislavery and temperance reform, these Burlington women exercised an unusual degree of control and autonomy in the leadership of their charitable organizations from the beginning, and "used this position to alter public policy toward the poor and establish a fragile bridge over some of the issues of class and ethnicity that divided women."[9]

Concentration of population and economic activity occurred in several other locations around Vermont. Rutland's population briefly surpassed Burlington in 1880, and although it did not maintain that lead in the next census count, it remained Vermont's second-largest community, with a population of 11,499 in 1900. Rutland followed a typical pattern of growth in the early nineteenth century, becoming by 1830 a market and small manufacturing center for woolens, whiskey, and cider brandy. Rich deposits of iron ore in the area around Rutland also made it the leading center in Vermont for the production of cast and forged iron in the second quarter of the nineteenth century. An 1840 census of ironworks credited Rutland County with eleven blast furnaces which produced 3,365 tons of cast or pig iron, employed 363 workers, and represented capital investments valued at $275,050, about half the total investment and output of Vermont's iron industry.[10] Rutland Town benefited from this small but active industry by becoming a center for production of agricultural implements, stoves, and iron ware. By 1850, however, the iron industry in Vermont entered a period of instability and decline because of the opening of local markets for agricultural tools in Western states, the rise of steel to make rails for the ever-expanding rail system, and the easier access to coal of Western factories. Consequently, Rutland faced the danger of economic stagnation. In the words of labor historian Leon Fink, "a combination of rail and rock reversed Rutland's slide into historical obscurity."[11] By the 1870s six railroads converged at Rutland, making it a transportation center connecting Vermont with Boston, New York City, Albany, Troy, Connecticut and Long Island Sound, Montreal, and routes to the west. Although Vermont's railroad industry ultimately proved unprofitable for its investors, it provided jobs and social mobility for unskilled, semi-skilled, and skilled workers, made personal fortunes for a few families, and provided the launching point for the political prominence of several Vermont governors—including two from Rutland: John Page (1865–1867) and Percival Clement (1919–1921).

Generous deposits of marble provided the other pillar of Rutland's prosperity. The marble deposit extends the entire length of Vermont's western boundary, from the Massachusetts border to Canada, and the stone has been quarried in Danby, Middlebury (where the first quarry opened in 1804), Monkton, Isle LaMotte, and Swanton, as well as Rutland. By the 1830s, however, the deposits in the Rutland area took the lead, and as the marble industry grew in the years following the Civil War, Rutland County became the marble center of Vermont and the nation. The marble industry sustained Rutland's economy and pushed it toward urbanization in the 1880s and 1890s. By 1881 Rutland's ten marble companies, led by the Sheldon and Slason quarries and the Vermont Marble Company, employed fifteen hundred workers. The quarries and finishing companies in turn provided a market for foundries, stonecutters, and machine makers. When Howe Scale Company moved from Brandon to Rutland in 1877, the town's population ballooned and briefly passed Burlington. In addition to these large enterprises, Rutland had more than seventy manufacturing firms, at least one hundred stores, five banks, three large hotels, and nine churches. The Ripley Opera House, named for General E. H. Ripley, was destroyed by fire in 1874, then rebuilt on a grand scale: three stories high with a seating capacity of eight hundred. A great fire in 1863 became the stimulus for Rutland to reconsider its water supply and by 1878 the town invested eighty-five thousand dollars in the construction of a water supply and distribution system "fully adequate to all demands."[12]

Redfield Proctor provided the leadership for much of this phenomenal growth. In 1870 Proctor took over operations of the Sutherland Falls Marble Company, which had fallen into receivership of the firm where he practiced law. Within ten years he had revived the company, bought out the New York-owned Rutland Marble Company, and secured control of 55 percent of the marble trade nationwide. In 1883 he created a cooperative called the Producers Marble Company, with four of the other major marble firms in the state. The five companies produced 98 percent of Vermont's marble and for four years were able to control prices and drive out smaller competitors. By 1891 Proctor had bought out all major competitors. In 1894 his Vermont Marble Company employed eighteen hundred workers.

The success of his marble company propelled Redfield Proctor into local, statewide, and eventually national prominence. He served as a selectman in Rutland in 1866, and represented Rutland in the General Assembly in 1867 and 1868. He became state senator in 1874, lieutenant

Redfield Proctor, photographed while he was a U.S. senator. *Otto T. Johnson Collection, Vermont Historical Society.*

governor in 1876, and governor in 1878. Appointed secretary of war by President Benjamin Harrison in 1889, he retained that post until 1891, when he gained appointment to the U.S. Senate to succeed George F. Edmunds. Proctor won election to the Senate in 1892 and retained his seat until his death in 1908.

Proctor's growing prominence had an effect on the development of Rutland. Considered in his day a benevolent employer, Proctor nevertheless opposed the organization and political aspirations of labor, as did industrialists, entrepreneurs, and merchants elsewhere in New England. In July 1883, for example, when copper miners went on strike against the Vermont Copper Mining Company and took up arms demanding payment of wages owed them, Proctor volunteered to join the Rutland unit of the Vermont Militia called out by Governor Barstow. While he utilized an open-handed approach in his philanthropy—building a library for his village and later a hospital for his workers—he balked at sharing political power with wageworkers and ethnic groups in Rutland. This reluctance shaped the resistance by Proctor and his colleagues to efforts beginning in 1886 to transform Rutland's town government into a city charter structure.

As their counterparts had done for Burlington, businessmen initiated Rutland's drive to incorporate as a city in 1880, hoping to consolidate the multiple and competing layers of authority among village, town, and county jurisdictions. Proctor's opposition, however, along with that of the outlying agricultural population, and the rural sympathies of the state legislature, doomed the effort.

A turning point in Rutland's history came in 1886, when the town's laboring classes formed a political bloc under the leadership of the Knights of Labor. Founded in Philadelphia in 1871, the Knights opened their ranks to skilled and unskilled laborers, including immigrants, African Americans, and women, and advocated an eight-hour workday, a graduated income tax, consumer and producer cooperatives, prohibition of imported contract labor, and an end to the monopoly power of railroads and banks. In Rutland, the Knights organized Local Assembly 5160 in January 1886, drawing members from the upper levels of workers and skilled laborers, and eventually from the area's Irish, Swedish, and French-Canadian workers. By March 1886 West Rutland's fifteen hundred to two thousand marble workers, encouraged by reform-minded Catholic clergy, began joining Local Assembly 5160. Under the banner of a United Labor party, the Knights organized a political convention in 1886 and drafted a slate of candidates for village offices, all of whom won election in September 1886.

United Labor called for civic improvements including better roads, electric lights, a public library, and school reform. They also wanted the abolition of the town trustee process, election of town overseers of the poor, and the adoption of four labor-related reforms: weekly cash payment of wages, employer's liability laws, free evening school for six months of the year, and a law requiring a ten-hour work day. The Democratic Party in Rutland joined United Labor in pressing again for incorporation of Rutland as a city, in order to replace the town meeting, dominated by the merchant and industrial elite, with representative government in a city council.

Proctor and other industrialists, including the owners of Howe Scale Works, the largest employer in Rutland village, moved quickly to protect their interests by persuading the legislature to divide the town into three government units: Rutland, West Rutland, and Proctor. While one faction of United Labor hoped to bring all of Rutland under a city charter, the coalition began to break up over the issue of division.

In November 1886 the legislature approved a bill to create the towns of Rutland, West Rutland (taking 14 square miles from Rutland), and Proctor (created out of 6.25 square miles from Rutland and Pittsford). In the same bill, however, the rural-dominated legislature struck back at labor by depriving Rutland Town of its right to elect municipal judges, making them appointed officials instead, requiring local trustees to post bonds of $1,000 to $5,000 before taking office (thereby effectively excluding lower-income candidates), voiding the terms of Rutland's fifteen recently elected Justices of the Peace, and giving the governor authorization to make interim appointments until the next regularly scheduled election.

The following spring, at its first town meeting, the citizens of Proctor elected Redfield Proctor moderator and adopted his slate of candidates for town offices. Thereafter the town of Proctor enjoyed several institutional advancements, including a company cooperative store, an employees' savings bank, the nation's first industrial nurse (1895), a hospital and free medical services for Vermont Marble Company personnel, and a branch of the Young Men's Christian Association.

West Rutland, dominated by Irish laborers, continued to advance ethnic and labor interests for several years following its separation from Rutland Town. A moderate, nonpartisan coalition swept the 1887 West Rutland elections and installed Irish marble workers and two French Canadians among the town officers. A year later, however, working-class leadership lost the support of its main constituency when it failed to secure wage and working condition improvements from manufacturers. By the mid-1890s the Knights of Labor leadership was gone and labor could only restrain but no longer direct the actions of the town's trustees.

Rutland Town after division in 1886 became smaller by about one-third of its land and population. United Labor swept the elections of 1887, with 75 percent of eligible voters participating. By the end of the year, half of Rutland's officeholders were under the age of thirty and largely second-generation Irish-American skilled laborers. Business interests remained implacably antilabor, however, and created their own Citizens Union Party of Order. The Citizens Party recaptured town government in 1888 and returned to the legislature with a request to charter Rutland City in 1892. The legislature again divided the area roughly in half, creating the current units of Rutland City and Rutland Town.

In Bennington, Vermont's fourth-largest population center in 1870 and 1880, the cloth industry continued to thrive and bring the town a significant measure of prosperity. Child's *Gazetteer and Business Directory of Bennington County for 1880–1881* reported that the H. E. Bradford Hosiery Mill, manufacturer of men's shirts and drawers, employed one hundred workers; Green Mountain Mills, established in 1857 to produce knit goods, employed eighty; the Hosiery Mill of George Rockwood and Company, manufacturing shirts and drawers, also employed eighty operators; Bennington Woolen Mills, established in 1865 as a manufacturer of cloth for heavy overcoats, had four hundred employees. In neighboring North Bennington allied industries such as Globe Button World, and Christopher Cooper and Tiffany and Cooper, two makers of sewing machines, further swelled the number of laborers. The Vermont Mills employed ninety workers in the production of cotton print cloth and J. S. Lyman Mill, manufacturer of print cloth, employed seventy workers.[13]

Across the mountains, Brattleboro in the late nineteenth century had developed a specialty market in the reed organ business. As early as the 1840s the village served as home for several instrument makers. Its access to power from the Whetstone Brook, abundant supplies of lumber, and, after 1850, railroad links to major urban markets allowed Brattleboro to flourish as a center for instrument making.

Among the thirty-four manufacturing companies listed at Brattleboro in Child's 1884 *Gazetteer* for Windham County, the Estey Organ Company took the lead. Its sixteen buildings on more than sixty acres of land on Birge Street included eight nearly identical manufacturing halls, 100 feet long, 30 to 38 feet wide, and three stories high—each equipped with an Otis elevator—and an impressive wood-drying house, 140 feet long by 50 feet wide. The founder, Jacob Estey, built the company from a modest lead pipe and pump business to one of the nation's largest manufacturers of reed organs and served as its president from 1854 to his death in 1890. Known locally and even nationally as a benevolent industrialist, Estey set aside part of the area as housing for factory workers who developed it cooperatively with Estey, many of them building their own homes. The *Vermont Phoenix* reported that by 1894 the area known as Esteyville had seventy-eight houses for 106 families (a total of 424 people), a primary school with a basement meeting room used by several town organizations for public gatherings,

Estey Organ Company trade card, c. 1885. The image shows the complex of buildings on Birge Street in Brattleboro on the far left. Above the reed organ is a portrait of founder Jacob Estey. The reverse of the card lists the addresses of Estey Organ Company salesrooms in New York City, Chicago, St. Louis, Philadelphia, Boston, Atlanta, and London, England. *Vermont Historical Society.*

and its own fire department that frequently assisted the town's firefighters. Estey's five hundred employees formed the single largest bloc of workers in Brattleboro, and constituted 10 percent of the entire population of the village. The workforce appears to have been treated well by Estey, and, according to recent research, the few surviving personal records of Estey employees "suggest a progressive factory atmosphere and a healthy community environment in comparison to situations in many American manufacturing centers."[14] Estey employed mostly skilled workers. The workforce included a significant number of women in the crucial reed-filing operation, and a large number of German and Swedish craftsmen. Some of the Swedes settled with other countrymen in a section of the village that became known as Swedeville. The neighborhood church counted 170 Swedish members. Irish and French Canadians constituted another large segment of Brattleboro's non-Yankee population.

Two other reed organ manufacturing plants—E. P. Carpenter & Sons and J. D. Whitney & Sons—settled in Brattleboro, making the village a major center for the manufacture and nationwide sale of instruments that became a marker of American middle-class wealth and culture. Brattleboro also was the site of an early spa—the Wesselhoeft Water Cure—that drew tourists and "patients" from throughout the Eastern states in the 1840s and 1850s, and the state's first mental hospital, the Brattleboro Asylum for the Insane, which, since its founding in 1832, had accepted both private patients and those supported by state funds.

Child's *Gazetteer* for 1884 praised Brattleboro for its "many beautiful private residences ... two hotels, four banks, the extensive buildings of the Vermont Asylum for the Insane, two enterprising weekly papers—the *Vermont Phoenix* and the *Reformer*—two literary journals, [and] six churches. ... The village is well supplied with illuminating gas and with water of an excellent quality."[15] The *Gazetteer* also made note of the Brattleboro Telephone Exchange, established in 1881, with 180 subscribers and 160 miles of pole lines connecting subscribers in Brattleboro, other villages in Windham County, and in Cheshire County, New Hampshire.

Domination by a single industry became the pattern for several Vermont towns. St. Johnsbury and the E. & T. Fairbanks & Company were "almost synonymous" according to Child's *Gazetteer of Caledonia and Essex Counties* (1887), "for it is this large firm that has made the village what it is—a thriving, prosperous center."[16] Founded in 1831 and incorpo-

E. AND T. FAIRBANKS AND COMPANY.
SCALE MANUFACTURY.
ST JOHNSBURY, VERMONT, U.S.A.

The E. & T. Fairbanks & Company complex in St. Johnsbury. By J. S. [?] Landis, Newark, Vt. (no date). *Vermont Historical Society.*

rated in 1842, the company made world-famous platform scales. By 1887 the firm employed over six hundred skilled artisans and mechanics who produced eighty thousand units—eight hundred varieties of scales—each year. Fairbanks shipped scales from St. Johnsbury throughout the United States. Among its largest contracts were three thousand postal scales for the U.S. Post Office in 1875 and scales for the U.S. Navy Yard in Washington, D.C. It also shipped scales abroad to Russia, Austria, Germany, Brazil, Chile, and Australia. To make this worldwide concern operate smoothly, the Fairbanks family invested in banks and railroads, built a factory complex of twenty buildings—mostly brick— on twelve acres of land near the center of town, and invested heavily in civic improvement in order to attract and keep skilled workers.

Erastus Fairbanks, one of the two brothers who founded the business, became first president of the Passumpsic River Railroad and twice served as governor of Vermont (1852 and 1860). Thaddeus, the mechanical genius who developed the patent for the platform scale, kept a somewhat lower public profile, but served as a benefactor of the St. Johnsbury Academy. Horace, one of the sons of Erastus, followed his father's bent to business and public life, as president of the scale company, president of the First National Bank of St. Johnsbury, and governor of Vermont (1876–1878). In 1870 he presented to the town of St. Johnsbury the Athenaeum, a library of ten thousand volumes and an art gallery complete with works of European and American art. He served as a trustee of the University of Vermont and of Andover Academy. Franklin, second son of Erastus, became manager of manufacturing at the scale works. In 1889 he presented the town with a museum and natural history collection of fifty thousand specimens. Other members of the family held prominent positions in business, academic, and professional life.

Around this phenomenally successful industrial complex and dynasty grew the town of St. Johnsbury. By the late 1880s it hosted more than twenty manufacturing concerns, four banks, twelve churches (two of them founded and heavily supported with Fairbanks money), and three newspapers. The late-nineteenth-century reformer Charles Edward Russell, sent as a youth from the Midwest to study at St. Johnsbury Academy, bitterly characterized the town as a medieval "barony, and so far as autocratic rule was concerned, reproduced neatly the status of a Rhine village in the Middle Ages. The baronial family lived in the castle on the heights; the townspeople kow-towed below. . . . [M]embers of the Fairbanks family were the barons; in effect their word was law. Without assuming any ostensible place or reachable responsibility in the government, they ruled it absolutely."[17] Russell resented the Fairbanks's puritanical piety, missionary zeal in the matter of temperance, and loathing of tobacco, claiming that they imposed their own beliefs in these matters on their workers and on the town as a whole, and kept their skilled workers dependent on them by paying them poorly while threatening them with dismissal if they strayed from the family's religious and moral code. And in the absence of any state law before 1892 requiring the town to issue ballots for local and statewide elections, the Fairbanks Company printed ballots that allowed company officials to see how workers voted.

Historian Allen Yale, in his close examination of the Fairbanks Company, concluded that the Fairbanks family probably did insist on regular church attendance, although not necessarily at the Congregational church. It is uncertain whether the Fairbankses required a temperance pledge of their workers, although they clearly forbade any consumption of alcohol in the workplace, did select workers on the basis of their temperance practices, and did dismiss workers who were arrested for public drunkenness.

Yet Yale's work with Fairbanks Company papers and diaries of workers modifies Russell's picture of a benevolent despotism of capitalism. The average daily wage for skilled mechanics was $2.25 for a ten-hour day, amounting to $13.50 for a six-day week. The average wage for all workers was $1.68 per day, amounting to annual earnings of $525. This compared favorably with $18.65 a month for farm laborers in 1884—the highest wages paid in the period 1870–1900—and with wages ranging from $315 to $395 per year for industrial workers elsewhere in New England. Room and board at one of the St. Johnsbury Academy boarding houses was a relatively modest $3.00 to $3.50 per week. Moreover, in times of economic downturn the Fairbankses attempted to keep workers engaged by reducing hours, spreading work, or sometimes temporarily reducing wages for those not on shortened hours before resorting to layoffs. Although the company did not have a workers' compensation or retirement program, the Fairbanks family, like the Estey Company in Brattleboro after 1894, helped workers establish a mutual relief association that supported injured workers through their recovery and provided a fund of money for funeral expenses and family survivors when a worker died. Yale concludes that "in general, compared with the standards of the day, the scale workers at E. & T. Fairbanks & Company fared well," earning higher wages than most industrial workers in New England, enjoying a community rich with resources for leisure and recreation, relatively safe working conditions, and stable employment.[18] Fairbanks Scale Company grew steadily throughout the last half of the nineteenth century, drawing almost two-thirds of its workers from Vermont, with French Canadians and Irish laborers comprising the largest ethnic groups among nonnatives. The prosperity of the scale company helped to swell the population of St. Johnsbury, which grew from 2,758 in 1850 to 7,010 in 1900.

Vermont's third largest city in 1900 was Barre, chartered in 1895 following a fifteen-year period of unparalleled growth. In 1880 the population stood at 2,060; by 1900 it had leaped to 8,448. Like Brattleboro and St. Johnsbury, a single industry dominated and spurred growth, in this case the quarrying and finishing of granite for construction, monuments, and cemetery markers. Unlike the other industrial towns, however, no one family or company dominated Barre industry or the community. Barre, more than most late-nineteenth-century communities, brought together diverse ethnic and immigrant groups—Scotch, Italian, Spanish, and French Canadian—and blended traditional European guild and clan organizations with more modern forms of capital accumulation and industrial processes. Following the European workshop tradition, workers frequently became owners, and small shops managed to operate alongside much larger companies.

Granite quarrying for cobblestones and smaller building elements had begun early in the nineteenth century, but the steam engine and railroad, which arrived in Barre in 1875, introduced new possibilities for moving the heavy stone in larger units and greater volume. When late-Victorian sentiment turned cemeteries into monumental gardens, granite as a material for sculptural applications went into high production. More durable than marble or slate, but equally susceptible to artistic sculpting and able to take a high polish, granite became popular in the 1870s and 1880s. By 1889, when Hamilton Child published his *Historical Gazetteer of Washington County, Vermont*, thirty-four companies in Barre engaged in one or more aspects of granite fabrication, from quarrying to specialized carving. Two years later, when George E. Norris published his second bird's-eye view of Barre, he listed sixty-five granite companies.[19] Some shops employed as few as four men in design and sculpture. By contrast, Jones Brothers, established in 1886, employed seventy-five stone cutters and twenty-five to thirty quarrymen, in addition to teamsters, clerks, and

Main Street, Barre, c. 1894. This block of granite, part of the Leland Stanford mausoleum, was being hauled to the railroad depot in Barre. *Courtesy of the Aldrich Public Library, Barre.*

Central Vermont Railroad station, St. Albans. *Vermont Historical Society postcard collection.*

other office workers; and the Vermont Granite Company, established in 1887, owned 110 acres of quarries and shops (known as "sheds") for turning out finished stone, and employed over 100 workers.

The prosperity of the granite industry propelled civic improvements in Barre and by the end of the century the city had electric lighting, a modern water system, an opera house, two banks, six churches, common schools, a graded school, and the Goddard Seminary, sponsored by the Universalist society, which graduated 228 students in 1889.

The town of St. Albans became preeminently a railroad community after former Governor J. Gregory Smith moved the Central Vermont Railroad's shops and administrative headquarters from former owner Charles Paine's hometown of Northfield to his own home location in Franklin County. In 1883, when Hamilton Child published his *Gazetteer and Business Directory of Franklin and Grand Isle Counties, Vt.*, St. Albans's population stood at 7,195, larger than St. Johnsbury, Brattleboro, or Bennington. The railroad and its shops employed many hundreds of workers, making it one of the largest railroad centers in the state; and Child trumpeted the Central Vermont depot as the largest in New England.[20]

The fortunes of the railway company influenced those of many of its citizens and entrepreneurs. Although the town served as home for only a few manufacturing companies, the largest of them were related to or served the railroad industry. The St. Albans Foundry, established in 1840, flourished under the influence of the railroad. In 1883, according to Child, it employed seventy-five workers and ranked "among the best establishments of its kind in the country," doing machine and foundry work, repairs, jobbing, and producing railroad car wheels and castings for the Central Vermont. In addition, the foundry produced a wide range of agricultural implements, circular and drag saws, stoves, and—its specialty item—Old's patent horse-power and threshing machines, which, in this transitional period from the use of animal to machine power, gave the foundry a national market. The St. Albans Iron and Steel Works, established in 1873, generated cast iron products until 1878, when it began to manufacture products using steel imported from England and Scotland and produced about 25 percent of its own steel in open-hearth furnaces. It employed 175 men and manufactured twenty thousand tons of rails a year. As the Vermont railway industry began to fade in the 1880s, the company shifted to serve a national market and by 1883 was sending nearly half its products to the West.

The National Car Company owned about 4,000 railroad cars, which it rented to various railway companies. Chartered in 1868, the company enjoyed steady growth, and in 1883 began planning to invest $50,000 to build its own repair shops. By 1891, however, the company had moved its shops to Detroit, Michigan, and Elsdon, Illinois; and according to Lewis Cass Aldrich, had "no more than a nominal existence" in St. Albans.[21] The Vermont Construction Company, which built bridges for railway companies, cities, and towns, established itself in St. Albans in 1890.

The presence of several railroad workers' associations in St. Albans similarly demonstrated the influence of the railway industry on the economy and social life of the town. The Order of Railway Conductors had a fifty-member branch, founded in 1870; while its rival Independent Order of Railway Conductors, whose members stood "unalterably and absolutely opposed to strikes among employees of any road or system of roads," organized in 1890 and three years later had thirty-two members.[22] Other railroad workers' associations with headquarters in St. Albans included the Green Mountain Division, No. 330, of the Brotherhood of Locomotive Engineers, with fifty members; the Champlain Division No. 352 of the National Brotherhood of Locomotive Firemen, also with fifty members; and the Green Mountain Division, Brotherhood of Railway Brakemen.

The importance of the railroad for Vermont's dairy industry was reflected in the St. Albans butter market, which in 1883 "show[ed] the heaviest transactions of any in the country." The St. Albans Point Creamery, located in St. Albans Bay, two miles from the village center, manufactured butter and cheese from the milk of eight hundred cows from the surrounding area.[23]

The railway also served the local tourism industry. St. Albans, with its location near Lake Champlain, accommodated its many seasonal visitors in three large brick hotels, the largest of which, The Weldon House, stood five stories high, with two hundred rooms and suites, a grand dining room, and three levels of verandahs. Child pronounced it "one of the largest and best appointed hotels in New England."[24]

After calamitous fires in 1869 and 1871 destroyed town records and twenty-five commercial buildings, the village reorganized its fire department into a company of fifty salaried men and invested in a reservoir, aqueduct, and hydrants. By 1880, the village acquired gas lighting, and the next year a telephone exchange installed over forty miles of lines, connecting the village with Swanton and outlying areas. In 1881 the women of St. Albans formed an association to receive and administer a $25,000 dollar gift from Chauncey Warner of Cambridge, in Lamoille County, which they used to purchase land and establish the Warner Home for Little Wanderers—a home for destitute children.

With a more diverse economy than many of its larger neighbors, Montpelier shared many of the characteristics and changes taking place in Vermont's urban communities. As the state's capital, Montpelier served as both the symbolic and administrative center of government. However, with no official residence for the governor, short legislative sessions through most of the late nineteenth and early twentieth centuries, and a still relatively small government bureaucracy that had no permanent offices (many officials worked out of their homes, where they kept their official records), the presence of state government had less impact on the town than did its role as a manufacturing and financial center. Split off from East Montpelier in 1848, which retained the bulk of the land of the original grant, the capital city ranked as one of the smallest units in the state, and its incorporation as a city in 1894 made it one of the smallest state capital cities in the nation. In 1870, Montpelier had a population of only 3,024, most of whom lived and worked in the narrow valley formed by the confluence of the

Winooski River and its Worcester or "North" branch. Montpelier grew rapidly in the thirty years following the Civil War. At a time when the number of citizens in the state remained almost unchanged, the population in Montpelier rose by almost 1,000 in just twenty years, and doubled to reach 6,216 by 1900.

The falls of the North Branch of the Winooski provided power for a succession of saw and gristmills, including E. W. Bailey and Company, the last and largest of them, with an enormous elevator at the confluence of the Winooski and North Branch that continued to operate into the 1960s. The other mills gradually closed, replaced in the 1860s by foundries and machine shops. The Lane Manufacturing Company, established in 1863, and the largest of the three machine shops in the village, built a complex of eleven buildings along the North Branch in 1890—many of them brick—and employed 100 workers, with a weekly payroll of about $1,000, making parts for sawmills, turbines, planers, and other woodworking machinery. Thirty granite sheds, one of which also dealt in marble, and the Sabin Slate Company, with a quarry working a 200-foot-deep vein of black slate, exploited the mineral resources of the area. The C. H. Cross & Son bakery produced the "Montpelier cracker" that became a staple item in Vermont

Laying electric railway tracks in Montpelier, 1898. *Vermont Historical Society.*

pantries for over a century. Its complex of buildings occupied a central location in Montpelier's compact downtown area. Two firms, the Colby Wringer Company, manufacturer and repairer of clothes wringers, washing machines, mangles, polishers, fluters, and carpet sweepers, and the United States Clothespin Company, provide a glimpse of how industrialization had begun to change domestic chores for women. The clothespin factory, founded in 1897, employed thirty workers by the end of the century who operated new machinery made especially for the company. A tannery, nickel-plating factory, and carriage company occupied some of the buildings that lined the south bank of the Winooski. Across the river the Central Vermont Railroad operated a depot and spur connecting the village center to the main line at Montpelier Junction one mile west of town, and the Montpelier & Wells River Railroad maintained tracks, a depot, and shops that provided crucial transportation links to towns north and east as far as St. Johnsbury, and to the larger railroad systems that connected Vermont with major markets and population centers. This second stage of growth in railroad connections helped overcome the initial disadvantages Montpelier suffered when the Central Vermont laid out its original route in 1849 to bypass the state capital.

Three major insurance companies anchored Montpelier as a financial center. National Life Insurance Company, in business since 1848, had almost seventeen thousand policies in force, confining itself to Vermont and other Northern states "as people living in this section are generally longer lived and freer from epidemics and scourges."[25] Vermont Mutual Fire Insurance Company, chartered in 1827, and the Union Mutual Fire Insurance Company, incorporated in 1874, confined their business to Vermont and to insuring buildings against loss. Between them in 1889 they insured almost fifty-six thousand properties in the state against loss from fire. As symbols of their success, the insurance companies constructed major buildings on Montpelier's State Street. The Vermont Mutual building, built in 1870 in an elegant mid-Victorian style, occupied a lot near the Central Vermont depot, the State House, and the Pavilion Hotel, the city's most elegant accommodation. Next door, National Life constructed in 1891 a palatial four-and-a-half-story brownstone and brick building.

Fire played an important role in shaping Montpelier's look and future. The fire that destroyed the second State House in 1857 resulted in the construction of the imposing third State House, a structure that dominated the town. Two fires in 1875 destroyed thirty-eight buildings in the commercial center. "Never was more energy displayed than in the rebuilding of the burned districts," Abby Maria Hemenway wrote in her *Historical Gazetteer*; "the smoke having barely cleared away when several large and splendid brick blocks were underway in the course of erection, some of them occupied within four months." The town passed an ordinance prohibiting construction of wooden structures in the village center that transformed the downtown. Four new adjacent brick buildings on Main Street set a standard for downtown and encouraged additional commercial and residential block construction in the 1880s and 1890s. The enormous Blanchard Block, built in 1883–1884, included the Blanchard Opera House that accommodated an audience of one thousand and provided a full-size stage. For twenty-five years, the opera house served as a busy performance space that drew talent traveling the "golden triangle" between New York, Boston, and Montreal. Sometimes offering as many as three performances a week, the Opera House attracted audiences from throughout central Vermont, many of whom came to town using special passes and excursion rates offered by the railroads. The arrival of moving pictures at the turn of the century created competition with live performances and the opera house closed in 1910.

The fires of 1875 also stimulated Montpelier to improve its water system. By 1888 the town had completed laying water pipes from Berlin Pond, installed almost seventy hydrants in the central area of the village, and begun negotiations with the Town of Berlin to purchase the pond to ensure an adequate and secure water supply. A telephone exchange began operation in 1881, and in 1885, the Standard Light and Power Manufacturing Company took over lighting the city's streets from the local gas light company. With an expanding infrastructure and population, the town petitioned the legislature for a charter change and became a city in 1895.[26]

Although still a rural state in 1900, Vermont ended the nineteenth century by undergoing a transformation of its traditional economy to adapt to the needs of the increasingly centralized organization of American manufacturing and industry. These changes also transformed the look of many Vermont communities and affected both the composition and distribution of its population. At the same time that urban centers within Vermont drew laborers, craftsmen, and merchants from rural communities, many Vermonters left the state to pursue farming opportunities in the Western states or higher-paying jobs in the large industrial and commercial centers springing up throughout the nation. As well, a working-class population drawn from French-Canadian, Irish, Italian, and other European immigrants entered the state to fill jobs created by some of the new or expanding manufacturing firms. Industrial growth also began to draw workers off farms and away from the agricultural sector, who in previous generations might have split their time, perhaps on a seasonal basis, between farming and small-scale, local workshops. This, too changed the population and character of many rural communities.

Rural Stability

The picture in rural Vermont appeared very different from the tableau of changes taking place in the burgeoning urban centers. Observers in the late nineteenth century, and during several decades into the twentieth, focused on the lack of growth in rural areas, or their emptying out, and proclaimed what Harold Fisher Wilson called the onset of "a severe winter season."[27] Wilson and others took their cues from the comments of public officials in the period 1870–1900 who decried the abandonment of hill farms, the stagnating or declining population of rural towns and villages, the failure of Vermont's farmers to adapt to the changes wrought by the opening of western lands after the Civil War, and most important, the creation of area and national markets as the railroad continued to create a web of regional and transcontinental transportation. This critique of rural Vermont society, coupled with concern among the Yankee elite about the immigration of ethnic groups, especially Irish and French-Canadian Catholics, led observers in the late nineteenth century to deplore Vermont's lost vigor and Puritan pioneer spirit.

When the editors of *The Vermonter* published the names of former Vermonters who gained prominence in Midwestern and Western states, along with lists of members of Vermont Associations far and wide, they joined the chorus of voices lamenting the loss of the Green Mountain State's best and brightest to migration outside its borders. "Our young men," wrote Albert Dwinell of Calais, "*our men of ability and enterprise, have been and are constantly leaving us.* . . . We who are left, are left to suffer loss, and feel the paralyzing effects of a virtue, a strength, a motive power, gone out from us."[28]

It is undeniably true that population in rural towns and counties experienced decline after 1870. Census data show that population in Addison and Orange counties, two of Vermont's most rural areas, decreased steadily through the second half of the nineteenth century and into the first decades of the twentieth. Addison County's population reached a peak of 26,549 in 1850, then dropped by over a thousand every decade until bottoming out at 17,944 in 1940, lower than its population in the 1810 census. Orange County had 27,873 residents in 1840 and then moved steadily lower until it reached 16,694 in 1930, almost two thousand fewer people than the count in 1800. Lamoille County hovered between 12,311 in 1860 and 12,289 in 1900 before dropping to 10,947 in the 1930 census. And while the population of Vermont's ten largest towns grew from 15 percent of the whole state in 1860 to 25 percent in 1900, the total population of the 124 smallest towns declined from 30 percent of the whole state to just over 20 percent in the same period.

Agricultural reformers and political commentators saw in these figures an alarming trend of stagnation, or worse, the disintegration of Vermont's rural and agricultural traditions. Zuar E. Jameson of Irasburg, in an 1872 speech that he titled "Vermont as a Home," delivered before the State Board of Agriculture, mourned the decay of rural communities and tried to make the case for opportunities on Vermont farms.[29] At the same time that Redfield Proctor and Jacob Estey were seeking to recruit Swedish workers for their industries, Governor William Dillingham's Commissioner of Agriculture and Manufacturing Interests, Alonzo B. Valentine, recruited fifty-five Swedish families to work abandoned uphill farms in Weston and Wilmington. Even this government-sponsored effort failed, however, because the new immigrants saw greater opportunities in industrial centers, and the official publications of the period continued to reflect frustration and pessimism about Vermont's agrarian future.

A closer look at small-town life and economy in Vermont during the late nineteenth century, however, tells a somewhat different story. Historians in the first half of the twentieth century generally accepted the contemporary pessimistic interpretations as accurate descriptions of the decline of old rural Vermont, but more recent historical studies of rural communities suggest new ways of understanding late-nineteenth-century developments. These studies indicate that it may be more appropriate to characterize the last three decades of the nineteenth century as a period of stability rather than stagnation.

By 1880 the number of farms in Vermont had actually increased to an

View of Chelsea, c. 1860. From the Vermont Album Collection, #137. *Vermont Historical Society (ATX 725).*

all-time high of 35,522 with 4.8 million acres in farmland—82 percent of the state's total acreage. Moreover, the average size of farms in Vermont had grown since the Civil War. In a close study of one rural community, Chelsea, historian Hal Barron demonstrates that neither the number of farms, nor their size, location, or output changed significantly until the late 1890s. Chelsea farmers relied on a combination of wool, butter, cheese, and maple sugar to secure a competency until the price of wool, which rose temporarily during and immediately following the Civil War, fell dramatically again in 1894. In short, Chelsea's agricultural history showed remarkable stability through the late nineteenth century. Barron concludes that "the constant number of farms and level of farm production suggest that agricultural development in Chelsea had reached the limits of its growth and had leveled off."[30] If farmers earned less, it was because wool growing was now less profitable than dairying; however, a shortage of farm hands caused by the out-migration of Chelsea's nonfarm and nonprofessional workers prevented farmers from increasing the labor-intensive dairying operations that offered greater profitability and they had to make the rational choice of continuing to raise a mix of sheep and cows. Moreover, Barron demonstrates that the critical change in population occurred among the nonfarm laborers—skilled and semiskilled workers—who migrated to urban and industrial centers because the transportation revolution brought about by the railroads now made rural crafts and industries unprofitable. In short, Chelseans with long residence and well-established agricultural occupations stayed, while more recent immigrants moved on.

Barron's findings are corroborated in studies of eleven Vermont towns reported by H. Nicholas Muller III. Muller's examination of Jericho—like Chelsea, a rural and largely agricultural community—revealed a decline in population of around 25 percent between 1880 and 1890. Some of this decline is attributable to deaths of town residents, some to migration to the urban centers of Burlington and Winooski. Other migrants moved only short distances to be closer to railroads. And as with Chelsea, the data for Jericho suggest "that the town did experience selective migration. . . . Those with the greatest stake in the town in terms of property and position, the farmers and the professionals, remained, while farm laborers and tradesmen, many of whom were foreign born, moved on."[31]

With the loss of their semiskilled and skilled workers, artisans, and small-business owners, Vermont's rural towns went through a significant social and cultural reconfiguration. In contrast with urban centers, where social and economic cleavage became more pronounced at the end of the century, Vermonters in small towns remained more similar to each other in their social and economic status. And where urban ethnic and economic groups created new institutions to help establish their place in these new environments, "those who stayed behind" also found ways to create social cohesion and community consensus. These came mainly through a rich array of voluntary associations, such as temperance leagues, literary and debating societies, sewing circles, baseball and other athletic clubs, town bands, and local chapters of state and national veterans' organizations and agricultural reform groups, which in turn produced an active social and cultural life within the towns. Late-nineteenth-century broadsides from the village of Cavendish, for example, reveal a constant round of community entertainment events, presented by both homegrown and imported talent, including itinerant theater troupes, dance bands, and traveling circuses.[32]

To outsiders, and especially to residents of the burgeoning cities of Vermont and other New England states, however, the strength of the emerging social and cultural consensus that held towns together, combined with ever-tightening webs of kinship ties created by the stability of Vermont's rural town populations, seemed oppressive and stultifying. To reformers of the late nineteenth and early twentieth centuries, the rural Vermont communities seemed stagnant and ingrown. These impressions fueled their concern for finding the "right kind" of new Vermonters, and efforts to reconfigure and reform institutions such as education. They made efforts to revive the rural economy by promoting agricultural reform to make Vermont's farmlands more productive, and encouraged tourism to bring the abandoned hill farms back into habitation and stimulate local economies. These efforts, not unique to Vermont, but significant for the image of Vermont that they presented to the wider world, would eventually come together early in the twentieth century to produce the "country life" movement, government-sponsored tourism promotion, and proposals to dispose of what became known as "submarginal" farm lands for more profitable second-home sites for "down country visitors."

Government and Reform

Vermonters emerged from the Civil War period with new experiences of state government and new expectations of its role. Over two decades, from 1850 to 1870, state government had played an increasingly prominent role in monitoring, promoting, and managing the resources and prosperity of the state, from taking a larger hand in regulating railroads to commandeering men, goods, and tax revenues to support the war effort. As the 1860s closed, Vermont state government continued to expand its regulatory and promotional activities. Some areas of involvement, such as providing prisons, care of the mentally retarded, and especially education, had deep roots in Vermont history, but several were entirely new.

The state began regulating railroads as early as 1855, when the legislature created the first railroad commissioner to inspect facilities, equipment, finances, debt structure, rates, safety of operations, services, and railroad crossings. By the 1880s a railroad commission had been established that included three members appointed by the governor to two-year terms. Vermont farmers and small-industry owners complained bitterly of the long-haul discount rates that favored Western states and drove up costs for getting local products to markets throughout the state and in New England. Until the federal government took control of rates through the

1887 Interstate Commerce Act, Vermont's railroad commissioners filled their reports with angry comments about this abuse.

Another early regulatory function was oversight of fish and game. In 1866 the General Assembly authorized the governor to appoint two fish commissioners for five-year terms and created the local position of town fish warden. In 1892 the legislature gave the fish commission oversight of game and added a third member. The state issued its first license for harvesting wildlife in 1894, when it granted limited authorization for netting fish in Lake Champlain.

The state's role in social welfare was apparent in its involvement in corrections, beginning with construction of the first state prison at Windsor in 1807. In 1865 the state built a reform school in Waterbury, later relocated to Vergennes when the school's first building burned in 1874. In 1876 the legislature authorized construction in Rutland of a workhouse for convicted felons between the ages of sixteen and twenty and for elderly convicts. Although care of the poor remained the responsibility of towns until the 1960s, the state took over supervision of mentally ill, retarded, and severely disabled persons. In 1872 the state provided a total of $2,000 for training "feeble minded and idiotic children." The amount went up to $11,000 in 1898 and included special education for those without hearing, speech, or sight. In 1904 the legislature increased funds to $20,000 a year, which went up to $30,000 in 1913, the year the state built the Brandon Training School, a residential facility for the mentally retarded. Until 1890 the state paid for institutionalization of mentally ill people at the private Brattleboro Asylum. After many years of debate and urging by Vermont's governors, the legislature in 1890 authorized construction of a state mental hospital in Waterbury, although some state patients continued to be treated at Brattleboro.

The state became involved in public health in 1886 when the General Assembly created one of the nation's first state boards of health. The three members of the board, appointed by the governor, served six-year terms and appointed an executive secretary who was required by statute to be a "reputable, practicing physician of this State."[33]

Road building in Vermont until the late nineteenth century remained a job shared between private concessions and towns. The turnpikes of the first half of the century were built and operated under monopoly arrangements with the state legislature while inventive neighbors traced "shunpikes" through nearby wilderness in order to avoid the tolls charged by the proprietors. In a transportation act of 1892, the state began assuming responsibility for coordination, construction, and maintenance of a state network of roads. The act authorized the governor to appoint a commission to examine and report on the extent and condition of roads in the state. The commission submitted an interim report in 1894 and a final report two years later. The 1892 act also provided for the election of a road commissioner in each town and levied a tax of twenty cents on the grand list to support town roads and an additional five cents to support state roads. Simultaneously with passage of the transportation act of 1892, a group of Vermont citizens organized the Vermont League for Good Roads, part of a nationwide movement to improve transportation networks. Open to all citizens, the league stated its goals to be "to awaken general interest in the improvement of public roads, determine the best methods of building and maintaining them, secure the legislation (State and National) that may be necessary for their establishment and support, and to conduct or foster such publications as may serve this purpose."[34] The legislature renewed its effort to inventory and coordinate road building in 1898, when it created the state highway commission. Two years later the commission issued its first report, noting that it had spent $87,257.17 and counted a total of 14,825 miles of roads in the state. That total remained almost unchanged for the next half-century.

While the governors of Vermont in the late nineteenth century loudly and frequently proclaimed the decline of agriculture, the legislature with its one town-one vote system of representation found ways to promote and assist the agricultural interests that continued to dominate economic and social life in the majority of towns. In the area of agricultural reform, public institutions and voluntary associations worked parallel paths, with the voluntary organizations frequently prodding the legislature to take action. The Vermont Dairyman's Association (VDA), established in 1869 to inform dairy farmers of scientific progress and economical methods for production and marketing, won a measure of public support when the General Assembly granted $500 for the publication of the association's annual report. Legislators renewed the grant in 1874 and regularly thereafter, giving $1,000 a year from 1887 until 1923 to support the annual meeting and prizes. Annual meetings became favorite places for political figures and those aspiring to political power to make an appearance. But the Dairyman's Association did not represent the interests of most rural farmers and its membership never rose beyond 550.

In 1870, a year after formation of VDA, the legislature created the Board of Agriculture, Manufactures and Mining. Although the board attempted to assist farmers by sending out speakers and sponsoring meetings, it too failed to address more basic needs of farmers, who viewed it with suspicion and dismissed it as yet another example of "book farmers" trying to instruct those who struggled with the practicalities of changing markets, small or no capital reserves, and a disappearing labor force. The board's earliest regulatory activities included monitoring dairy herds for tuberculosis and other diseases, setting standards for butter and cheese flavor, and restricting the sale of oleomargarine. But its failed effort under Alonzo B. Valentine to recruit Swedes and other immigrant groups to take over abandoned hill farms stood as just one example of what many rural Vermonters considered inefficiency, lack of organization, and condescension toward working farmers. These criticisms brought about a temporary suspension of the board when in 1878 the legislature replaced it with a superintendent of agriculture, only to reverse itself in 1880 by reviving the board, finally appointing a salaried commissioner of agriculture in 1908.

In contrast with government leadership in agriculture, which failed to win the confidence of the majority of farmers, several new voluntary associations served the political, educational, and social needs of specialized agriculture and "all around farming." In addition to organizations for Morgan horse and merino sheep raisers, the Vermont Maple Sugar Makers Association organized in Morrisville in 1893 and the Vermont Horticultural Society in 1895. Both received subsidies from the General Assembly and eventually came under the wing of the Board of Agriculture.

By far the most popular and for a while the most influential farmers' organization was the Patrons of Husbandry, commonly known as the Grange. Part of a nationwide movement begun in 1867, the Vermont State Grange formed in 1870 at St. Johnsbury and grew rapidly during its first few years, achieving by 1875 a membership of 11,110 in more than 160 local chapters. These were its most politically active years in Vermont and across the country, especially in the Midwestern states of Illinois, Kansas, Iowa, Wisconsin, and Minnesota, where the state granges created slates of candidates that won key elections. The political strategy of granges in those areas was to work between the two major political parties to win votes. But the two-party system ultimately proved too strong and by 1875 activists within the Grange movement found it more effective to work within the Republican or Democratic parties.

Vermont's Grangers never had the opportunities enjoyed by their Midwestern brethren, because by 1870 the state's Republican Party had already achieved near-monopoly status. After 1875 membership in the Vermont Grange dropped off, reflecting a national trend but also disagreement with the national organization's efforts to promote high prices for grain, and by 1885 only about a thousand members remained in the state. Membership surged again after 1890 when the Grange led the fight for reform of agricultural education at the University of Vermont and for tighter control of railroad rates and discriminatory practices. By 1911 the Vermont Grange boasted a membership exceeding twenty thousand, making it one of the largest organizations of any kind in the state. The Grange provided a way for farmers to purchase affordable insurance, and operated as an umbrella organization for buying cooperatives, a voice for farmers in politics, and as a social organization for men and women in agriculture. It served as well as an unofficial watchdog over the UVM Agricultural College and the State Department of Agriculture and as an advocate for education reform in rural communities. Urged on by a standing committee on education of the National Grange, established in 1876, Grange organizations throughout the nation advocated the teaching of "practical agriculture, domestic science, and all the arts which adorn the home," and an annual review of the content and pedagogy offered in schools serving rural and agricultural communities.[35]

No area of public life in this era saw greater change, or greater growth of state government involvement, than public education. As was the case throughout the nation, public education became a consistent target of reformers beginning in the decades following the Civil War. The disputes over what needed to be changed in public education, and how and where those changes would be initiated, raised important questions—which Vermonters continue to debate in our own day—about the relationship between towns and state government in Vermont.

The 1777 state constitution had mandated that schools be maintained in each town. Vermonters fulfilled this obligation with the formation in every town of a number of independent school districts. By 1846, when Horace Eaton served simultaneously as Vermont's governor and first state superintendent of education, the situation had become chaotic, with more than two thousand independent school districts scattered across the state enrolling an average of thirty-seven pupils each. Eaton had sought consolidation of public schools and an infusion of state money to improve the condition of schoolhouses, the materials available for instruction, and the salaries paid to teachers, another detail that the state constitution had left to the towns. Eaton's proposal, resisted by the towns and districts alike, became the opening salvo in a contest between local control and state authority over public education.

Thirty years later, little change had occurred in the local autonomy of school districts. Thetford, with a population of 1,610, had fifteen school districts. The 1869 state report on education noted with exasperation, "Here are over 2,000 little educational republics, practically independent of each other and of all the world, remote from intellectual centres and wedded to practices which were necessitated by conditions in earlier times.... They have been able to say, Keep off! We manage our schools in our own way; and if it is a poor way, it is a cheap one and we intend to perpetuate it." Hoping for a minimum of consolidation, the report dared to suggest that "If all the schools are put under control of the towns, it will bring the schools out of little intrenched [sic] hiding-places called districts, into the light of larger public opinion."[36]

The results of this fragmented, antiquated, and parsimonious educational system were dismal. Critics estimated that as late as 1886 only about 60 percent of Vermonters between the ages of five and twenty had attended school at all; school terms were as short as eighty-eight days a year; student-teacher ratios varied widely from one teacher for fewer than fifteen pupils to one teacher for one hundred scholars. In most schools a single teacher supervised pupils in every grade from the newly instituted kindergarten, if the school offered that option, until they entered high school. Teachers were themselves frequently not much older than their charges, some being as young as sixteen years of age. Most teachers possessed uncertain training; many worked with short-term contracts and generally earned lower wages than dairy maids, shoe-shop girls, stenographers, teamsters, house servants, or woodchoppers. Except for compulsory temperance training, required by the legislature in 1882, no uniformity existed in curriculum or in text book usage within the schoolhouse, least of all from district to district. In most cases, students had to provide their own books, placing an additional financial burden on them or their families and thereby erecting yet another barrier to attendance and progress in their studies. The schoolhouses varied widely in their condition and equipment, leading a writer for the *Rutland Herald* to describe them in 1854 as "black, rickety, ugly boy-killing affairs where comfort never comes, and where coughs, consumptions, fevers, and crooked backs are manufactured wholesale."[37] A frustrated school superintendent in Thetford complained of the lack of blackboards, maps, or even globes (which could be purchased for as little as $2.50).

In 1870 the legislature took a tentative step in the direction of the school consolidation proposed in the 1869 state report by passing an act permitting schools to reorganize under town authority rather than in independent districts. In the period 1870 to 1892 forty towns participated in this voluntary experiment, but fifteen gave up and reverted to districts. Over the next three decades, the legislature, prodded by a succession of energetic state superintendents of education—Edward Conant (1874–1880), Justus Dartt (1880–1888), Edward Palmer (1888–1892), and Mason S. Stone (1892–1901, 1905–1916)—made several more forays into education policy. In almost every session between 1872 and 1896, the legislature passed acts mandating education reforms: more equitable taxation for schools and distribution of the proceeds, more effective training and licensing of teachers, free textbooks, compulsory attendance, longer school terms, and the establishment of high schools in towns with a population of 2,500 or more. The district school boards, ever vigilant to protect their traditional and, as they saw it, constitutionally sanctioned autonomy, resisted each step of what they saw as state encroachment on their privileges. The key victory for education reform, however, came in 1892, when support for small autonomous districts had weakened sufficiently to allow the legislature to abolish them. The new law, called by its critics "the vicious act of 1892," gave towns sole authority for defining and enforcing educational policy within their boundaries. By 1901, when Mason S. Stone left his post as state superintendent of education for what turned out to be a four-year leave of absence in the Philippines, the state had won what John C. Huden called "a slow battle of attrition against the district schools."[38] These changes set the stage for more extensive involvement by the state in educational policy, practices, and organization, in which Stone acted as a leading participant when he returned to Vermont for a second period as state superintendent from 1905 to 1916.

The turbulence surrounding reforms in public education at the grammar school level had some parallels in higher education. Citizens increasingly called upon the General Assembly to investigate, mediate, and subsidize the training of Vermont's teachers and farmers. Although defining the qualifications for teachers remained a constant concern among education reformers, the state government stayed out of this quagmire through most of the nineteenth century. It left licensing teachers to district, town, or county boards and superintendents. The legislature also left teacher training to private initiatives and institutions such as Jacob Eddy's classes for young men in Danby (1785 and following), Emma Willard's School for young women in Middlebury (1814–1818; thereafter in Troy, New York), and Samuel Read Hall's courses on school teaching in Concord (1823 and following). In 1866, however, the legislature succumbed briefly to the clamor for more involvement in teacher training by authorizing the creation of three state normal schools, one for each of what were then Vermont's three congressional districts. The availability of former county grammar school buildings at Johnson in Lamoille County, Randolph in Orange County, and Castleton in Rutland County aided advocates for state involvement in the normal school movement. Exercising its usual caution and parsimony, however, the General Assembly merely authorized the establishment of the teacher-training institutions, carefully stipulating that they "shall be established and maintained without any expense to the State, excepting the payment of the Board of Education for their services."[39] The institutions enjoyed limited and inconsistent success, limping along for a century with minimal state support, dependent on the whims of legislators and the energy or inventiveness of their principals.

Vermont state government's major commitment to higher education has been the University of Vermont, chartered by the General Assembly in 1791, but until 1865 operated almost entirely without state funds. The Morrill Land Grant Act of 1862, shaped and shepherded through Congress by Vermont's U.S. Congressman Justin Smith Morrill, opened new possibilities for the state, but the legislature responded only slowly to the offer of income from the sale of federal government lands in the West to support higher education. Although the original intent of the Morrill bill had been to encourage and facilitate higher education in sciences and the useful arts—among which was agriculture—*alongside* the liberal arts, it finally emerged from Congress and received President Abraham Lincoln's signature as an act supporting agricultural schools.

This gap between intention and outcome precipitated a fight in Vermont over the use of the proceeds of the sale of public lands. An initial plan to merge Middlebury College, Norwich University, and the University of Vermont and use land grant revenues to support a Vermont State

University and Associated Colleges stalled when Middlebury College trustees balked and vocal agricultural interests protested, demanding a separate agricultural college. The legislature acquiesced in 1864 by passing a bill to create the Vermont Agricultural College, with Congressman Morrill as one of its incorporators, pledging the use of Vermont's land grant money to support the new institution, provided it would raise an additional $100,000 from private donations. Efforts to meet the challenge failed and in 1865 the new institution had a charter but no prospective home. The legislature once again reluctantly took action by amending the University of Vermont charter to create the University of Vermont and State Agricultural College, the former operating largely as a private institution dedicated to classical liberal arts and the latter as a public institution devoted to military tactics, agriculture, and mechanical arts. Both institutions were to be governed by a single board of trustees.

The uneasy alliance of the two schools proved to be initially also an unequal one. The university trustees and administration sought to fulfill their obligations to provide agricultural education by adding a few courses to the liberal arts curriculum addressing plant and animal anatomy and physiology, soil chemistry, and mineralogy, offered by the Agricultural and Scientific Department. The school also organized a series of lectures on agricultural topics, offered in February and March. University trustees argued that creating a separate College of Agriculture would be expensive and inimical to the university's mission of educating "the whole man" by integrating classical with scientific knowledge. Farmers, by contrast, complained that the offerings failed to meet their fundamental needs and that the few students enrolled in the agricultural course had been recruited from the classical studies program.

In the 1870s the tension erupted into a challenge by the agricultural community to the university's administration of land grant funds. The General Assembly appointed a joint committee in 1874 to examine the issue but when it exonerated the trustees of charges of misuse of funds, the farmers took a more aggressive tack. Members of county agricultural societies, the Vermont State Grange, Vermont Dairyman's Association, Farmers' League, and newspapers maintained pressure on the legislature to make the university create a separate college of agriculture and to acquire an agricultural experiment station. In 1883, A. B. Franklin, master of the state Grange and a member of the Vermont House of Representatives, proposed the purchase of an experiment station with an annual appropriation of $3,000. Although the bill failed, the Grange kept up the pressure to force the university to take a more practical approach to agricultural education by operating a farm. The university finally yielded and in 1886 the legislature, anticipating additional funds from the national government, appropriated $3,500 for the purchase of a farm near the university campus in Burlington.

Encouraged by this action, the farmers' coalition led by the Grange persisted in its demand for a "complete divorce" of the Agricultural College of Vermont from the "literary institutions" of the university to which, in the view of the Grange, it had been yoked. In 1890 the legislature formed another study committee and urged the university to offer more concessions, including the purchase of another farm, more agricultural courses, new equipment, and scholarships to farmers.

Debate on the separation bill in 1890 was intense and bitter. The university brought in fifteen agricultural students and Morrill himself, since 1867 a U.S. senator, to argue that separation would be uneconomical—always a strong argument with the legislature. The university offered to institute some compromises in governance, but the House of Representatives passed the bill for separation with a wide majority, strongly encouraged by the agricultural towns where sentiment against the university ran high. Confident of victory, the Grange pressured members of the Senate, presenting a petition signed by five thousand farmers supporting separation. In a surprise reversal, however, the Senate narrowly defeated the bill. It was not a real victory for the university, however, which for the next twenty years failed to win the trust of the General Assembly—dominated by legislators from rural and agricultural communities—and consequently failed to receive any appropriations from it, the only one of the forty-five land grant colleges in the nation that had no support from its state government.

Politics: Little Republics and the Mountain Rule

Even where it provided no monetary support, Vermont state government found itself involved in an ever-widening circle of economic and social issues as the end of the century approached. Public officials in Vermont, like those in most other states, became caught up in the conviction that through scientific management government could be the means for providing solutions to a wide range of social and economic problems.

Consequently, a proliferation of boards, commissions, secretariats, and other government agencies sprang up in the 1880s and 1890s. And as state government grew the political structure that undergirded it also took on a higher degree of organization and articulation.

By 1860 the Republican Party enjoyed hegemony in Vermont state politics. For the rest of the century and well into the next one Republicans uninterruptedly held Vermont's three U.S. House of Representatives seats (two beginning in 1882, after Vermont lost one following the 1880 census; then one seat beginning in 1932), both U.S. Senate seats, all elected statewide offices, all but a handful of seats in the Vermont House of Representatives and, with the exception of five legislative sessions, every seat in the Vermont Senate.

The Democratic Party picked up an occasional seat where a disaffected Republican bolted the party or some other challenger made a successful foray into local politics. Moreover, since it was predominantly associated with Irish laborers concentrated in the larger towns and cities, and with small interest groups scattered throughout the state, the Democratic Party could count on winning majorities in few legislative districts. The other major ethnic voting bloc in the state, Franco-Americans, rarely participated in politics in these years, except in a few communities, such as Winooski, and were reluctant to associate with the Irish or other ethnic groups. Unlike its successful rival, therefore, the Democratic Party had little in the way of statewide organization, and could offer only the few federal patronage positions that came as perquisites of loyalty during Democratic presidential administrations. Whatever disaffection existed within the Republican ranks showed itself in elections for statewide officers, where non-Republican candidates of any stripe occasionally garnered as much as one-third of the popular vote.

The Republicans sustained their hegemony by the exercise of a formidable if informal system of party discipline and rewards. The most visible feature of party discipline was the so-called "Mountain Rule," operating to distribute statewide political offices since the earliest years of statehood and firmly in place by 1854, when the Republicans gained their ascendancy. Under this widely acknowledged yet unwritten arrangement, the key statewide elected offices of governor and lieutenant governor rotated alternately between the east and west sides of the Green Mountains. John W. Stewart, Republican from Middlebury, achieved the governorship in 1870, followed by Julius Converse from Woodstock in 1872, succeeded by

Asahel Peck from Jericho in 1874, who was followed by Horace Fairbanks of St. Johnsbury in 1876, and so on. The pattern repeated itself in a mirror image at the level of lieutenant governor, with an east-side lieutenant governor elected to serve with a west-side governor, succeeded by a west-side lieutenant governor to serve with an east-side governor. Not once until the 1940s did this pattern of east side-west side alternation falter.[40] This informal system had applied to Vermont's two U.S. Senate seats as early as the state's admission to the Union, with one seat reserved for an east-side candidate and the other for a west-sider. The arrangement proved easily enforceable because the General Assembly elected U.S. senators until 1913, when the Seventeenth Amendment to the U.S. Constitution mandated popular election.

An important companion tradition to the Mountain Rule was the practice, established by the Whig Party beginning in the mid-1840s, of having governors and lieutenant governors serve no more than two years in office—that is, two one-year terms—and then retire. That practice, combined with the ladder of succession, ensured that no ambitious candidate had to wait more than four years to make his bid for governor. According to historian Samuel B. Hand, the Republican Party's success in cementing the Mountain Rule to the principle of rotation in office "kept the party open at the top and inhibited long-term organized factional alliances within the Republican Party."[41]

The Republican Party nominating convention of 1872 demonstrates how the Mountain Rule damped down discord, maintained party unity, and reinforced party strength. That event almost became the exception that proved the rule. The 1870 amendment to the state constitution that created two-year terms for all elected positions raised the question of whether the principle of rotation was now to be interpreted as serving two *years* in office—that is, a single two-year term—or two *terms*, now extended to two years each. When the 405 Republican Party delegates assembled at Montpelier, many anticipated continuing the two-year tradition, assumed that Governor John W. Stewart of Middlebury—the first governor to serve a two-year term—would step aside, and came prepared to nominate a candidate for governor from the east side of the state to succeed him. The two people touted as likely candidates to succeed Stewart were Frederick Billings and Julius Converse, both of Woodstock.

Billings, a native of Royalton, had gone to California to make his fortune in real estate and then in railroad building with the Northern Pacific. He returned home in the early 1860s to assist with munitions purchases for the Union armies. By then a rich and famous man, he purchased the Woodstock estate of Charles Marsh, where George Perkins Marsh grew up. There, in addition to his duties with the Northern Pacific, Billings concentrated on reviving and leading agricultural reform efforts and implementing conservationist ideas he had first encountered in Marsh's book, *Man and Nature*. By 1872 Billings had become deeply involved in developing his estate as a model for progressive agriculture and had made some tentative forays into local government and politics.

Converse, a long-time resident of Woodstock, a lawyer, and an experienced political figure, had represented Bethel and Woodstock in the General Assembly, and Windsor County in the senate for three terms. From 1850 to 1852 he served as lieutenant governor. Although Converse had made a bid for nomination as governor in 1869, the party had passed him over in favor of Peter Washburn, also of Woodstock and a Civil War hero. In 1872, at age seventy-four, Converse had been out of public office for twenty years. He may still have aspired to the governorship as the capstone of his career in public office, but he apparently had no great hopes of attaining it because he was out of state at the time of the Republican nominating convention.

Governor Stewart threw the convention into turmoil when he announced his intention to run for a second two-year term. "The governor question" thus drew the attention of the delegates and the convention became deadlocked on the first ballot. Stewart agreed to withdraw in favor of Converse, who narrowly defeated Billings on the second ballot. Billings then dutifully addressed the convention, calling for party unity and harmony, especially important in a year when the Democratic candidate was also running as the nominee of a splinter group that labeled itself Liberal Republican. Billings perhaps anticipated he would have another opportunity for gaining the governorship in 1876 and recognized the necessity of reuniting the Republican Party if he were to have any chance of being its candidate in the future—an event that failed to materialize. Converse learned of his nomination the following day in the newspaper.

Interpretations of these events differ. Robin Winks, Billings's most recent biographer, believes the convention was orchestrated to deprive Billings of the governorship. His many years away, relatively recent return, and association with land speculation in California, Winks argues, made him suspect in the eyes of many Vermonters. Although a native of

Vermont, he undoubtedly seemed to the experienced politicians a newcomer to state and even to national Republican politics, whereas Converse appealed to voters as a veteran with long experience and diverse state service. Winks argues further that in addition to spoiling the nomination bid for Billings, Stewart maneuvered to get for himself the Republican nomination for U.S. Representative from Vermont's First District (the eastside district).[42] He did eventually gain the House seat in 1882.

Samuel B. Hand argues that "the governor question" concerned more particularly redefining the tradition of rotation in office under the new term limits. The question facing Stewart and the convention became whether rotation would now take place every two years or every two terms. Many had argued and would continue to argue that the rapid turnover in government promoted party unity at the expense of efficient and effective government; and that two years provided insufficient time for either legislators or governors to grasp the complexity of issues or the diverse institutions in rapidly expanding government, and strategies for dealing with them. Stewart's short-lived bid for a second two-year term may have been meant to address these problems; his retreat—or defeat—at the convention settled the issue in favor of one-term rotation and party unity for the next fifty years, until John Weeks served two two-year terms, 1927–1931.[43]

Even at the local level Republicans maintained party discipline and rewards with a version of the Mountain Rule and rotation that operated to elect state representatives and senators. Few members of either house of the General Assembly served consecutive terms, thereby assuring that representation within the town or senate district was handed around. In 1884 only twenty-one of 239 members of the House succeeded themselves; and in 1888 only twelve members of the House had been there the previous session. In the Senate, typically, one or two members returned for a second consecutive term. On the other hand, members of both houses frequently served subsequent nonconsecutive terms. In 1884, forty-six representatives had previously served in the House and six had been members of both the House and Senate. That same year, nineteen senators had previous experience in the House. In 1888, twenty-two of the thirty state senators had previously served in the House and only five members possessed no previous legislative experience. Thus, while composition of the legislature changed year to year, the legislative and executive branches clearly maintained a core of experienced leaders.

Not that these men's duties overburdened them. The legislature abandoned annual sessions in 1870, convening only every second year for an average of fifty-five days. Despite the expanding responsibilities of state government, legislators and governors alike remained loyal to the ideology stated by Governor Urban Woodbury that "it is better to do too little than too much."[44] And although the legislature, by delegating authority to commissions and boards, gave state government an increasingly visible and powerful role in a growing range of activities, it continued to confine its deliberations to a narrow period of time, as if to reinforce Woodbury's formula that less is more.

Two issues clouded the political landscape and disturbed Republican Party unity in this period: female suffrage and temperance. Both had long histories in the political life of Vermont; their overlapping constituencies tied them to each other; and neither achieved resolution until amendments to the U.S. Constitution compelled the state government to take action.

Although woman suffrage did not directly disrupt Republican Party discipline, it continued to challenge at least some assumptions and practices in the operation of politics. At various times in the late nineteenth century the party officially endorsed limited female suffrage, but members of the legislature simultaneously continued to vote it down. Following the defeat of a full suffrage amendment in the 1870 constitutional convention, legislative supporters introduced two bills in the 1872 session of the General Assembly—one to give tax-paying women the right to vote in school district meetings; the other once again proposing full suffrage. Both went down to defeat. Although the more limited proposal for franchise in school issues passed in the House, the Senate defeated it by only one vote.

As women continued to be active and take leadership roles in the temperance and prohibition campaigns, they acquired increasing experience, skill, and visibility in speaking out and organizing for political action. Not all women active in temperance, however, wished to press forward on winning the right to vote, and this caused a split within the temperance movement itself. For almost a decade, women interested in securing the vote therefore had to follow another path, often without their former colleagues in the Women's Christian Temperance Union (WCTU).

By 1880, however, the two issues again began to converge. In 1879 the annual meeting of the Vermont chapter of WCTU, which had earlier renounced any broader political aspirations, unanimously resolved that as a way to secure their goal of suppressing intemperance they would petition the next session of the General Assembly "to allow us to vote for school

Women's Christian Temperance Union (WCTU), Weston, Vt. The chapter was founded December 10, 1884. *From Vermont Album collection, Vermont Historical Society (ATX 175).*

committees, hoping thereby that we may be able to place temperance textbooks in our public schools."[45] In 1880 the legislature passed an act giving tax-paying women the right to vote and hold office in school districts. This limited franchise, affecting the relatively few women who held property and paid taxes in their own names, encouraged organization for wider suffrage. In a series of meetings around the state speakers from the Boston-based American Woman Suffrage Association attempted to build support for measures that would allow women to vote in municipal elections. The campaign culminated in a two-day convention at St. Johnsbury in November 1883 featuring prominent suffragist leaders Lucy Stone, Julia Ward Howe, and Henry Blackwell, who encouraged and helped the assembled women organize a state association.

Beginning in 1884 the Vermont Woman Suffrage Association (VWSA) petitioned every successive session of the legislature to pass a bill giving women the right to vote in town and city elections. On a few occasions, their efforts succeeded in one chamber, only to suffer defeat in the other. In 1886 the Vermont Republican Party convention proclaimed itself in favor of woman suffrage but in such equivocal language that in 1888 the legislature had no difficulty defeating the bill that would have granted it. As the century closed, woman suffrage appeared to be making no progress at either the state or national levels, and while the VWSA won a small but ultimately significant victory in 1900 with passage of a law that allowed women to serve as town treasurers, town librarians, and notaries public, the prize so eagerly sought since 1870 continued to elude them.

The movement for temperance and prohibition had an equally turbulent history but produced more widespread disruption of the political landscape. Vermont law had prohibited the sale and manufacture of alcoholic beverages (except for medicinal purposes) since 1852, when legislators narrowly approved a version of the 1851 Maine Law. However, the war against intemperance suffered some setbacks following the return of soldiers from the Civil War. The easy availability of liquor in camps and its liberal use as an anesthetic and sedative in Civil War medicine had the inevitable effect of undermining antebellum temperance reform back home. Moreover, among Vermont's postwar immigrants were such ethnic groups as the Irish, French Canadians, and Italians, for whom alcoholic beverages were important parts of cultural and social life. Many immigrants were like Mrs. Bianchi, the Italian woman whom Robert L. Duffus recalled in his memoir of Williamstown in 1898. Arrested for selling wine in her home and locked in what served as a jail in the basement of the Williamstown Town Hall, Mrs. Bianchi complained bitterly over the abuse of power of the Yankee town fathers. From the point of view of these immigrant newcomers to Vermont, "It was Constable Nichols . . . who had done wrong, not the Italian woman. She had been doing what she would have done in Italy, and no criticism from anybody. . . . The Italians in general agreed with her. They felt that when she was arrested, in her own house, while attending to her own affairs, it was not she alone who was being persecuted, it was Italy and the whole Italian race that were being put upon."[46]

For liquor's foes, however, the "war against rum" became part of a larger effort to restore and retain what they believed to be the orderliness and safety of agrarian, preurban, Christian (by which they meant Protestant) society. They marched against the sale of alcoholic beverages in places such as Burlington, Rutland, and the railroad towns of Northfield and St. Albans. In these outings, however, the crusaders, especially the women who formed the most visible groups such as the Women's Christian Temperance Union and its offshoots in towns throughout the state, also struggled against the rowdiness of saloons and brothels, the violence and disorder that they perceived as the concomitant evils of alcohol and the disruptive changes that accompanied the growth of urban and industrial society.

The WCTU and its offshoot organizations grew dramatically through the end of the nineteenth century in Vermont. By 1888 the WCTU claimed 2,375 members, mostly native-born Americans of Anglo-Saxon Protestant stock. They did not confine their efforts to cities, however, and brought their message also to rural and farming communities. Although officially the state barred liquor consumption, local enforcement—in the hands of men—seemed to the reformers lax in both rural and urban areas. And while the legislature enthusiastically passed a law in 1882 requiring schools to teach children about the harmful physical and moral effects of alcohol—even going so far as to violate its hands-off policy in education by requiring uniform textbooks when it came to this matter—shutting down saloons in villages and cities proved hard to accomplish because it continued to be an entirely local matter. By the end of the century large-town support for prohibition, which had been responsible for passing Vermont's version of the Maine Law in 1852 despite opposition from the small towns, had now shifted, and the small towns advocated prohibition laws while the cities pressed for local option. In effect, according to Samuel B. Hand, the push for repeal of the 1852 law and replacement by local option represented "a variation of the little republic concept, in which each town would decide whether to permit the sale of alcoholic beverages within its boundaries."[47]

The little republics and the mountain rule together served as ways to acknowledge local differences while allowing for majority rule, and handle cracks and fissures in the political landscape while creating unity through party discipline. On the whole, these political arrangements and informal institutions, even as they dampened some opposition voices within the party by shutting them out of the political arena, helped Vermonters regroup and recreate community and regional identity in the aftermath of the social and economic disruptions of the post-Civil War era. These layers of local, regional, and national identity showed up not only in political disputes and political arrangements, but also in the cultural and social life of Vermont at the end of the nineteenth century.

Looking Forward; Looking Back

The dramatic shifts in demographics and economic circumstances that characterized late-nineteenth-century Vermont presented many challenges and opportunities as Vermonters struggled to redefine the contours of their social, cultural, political, and economic lives. Small rural towns and larger industrial and commercial communities alike coped with the changes. A close look at how Vermonters spent their leisure time in the last third of the century reveals the heightened sense of community identity that emerged in Vermont's towns.

In his study of Chelsea, Vermont, Hal Barron noted that "after the Civil War, a plethora of voluntary associations developed in Chelsea as in other rural communities and small towns and established additional common grounds among the local inhabitants."[48] Religious or religion-based organizations, such as the International Order of Good Templars; reformist societies like the Sons of Temperance and WCTU; and fraternal and quasi-political organizations such as the Masons, GAR, and the Grange led the list of associations that helped define and strengthen community ties. Many Vermont communities could also boast of one or more baseball teams, drama clubs, reading societies, and brass bands. The events sponsored by these voluntary associations, usually open to all, helped create or solidify community identity and cohesion.

Fads in sports invaded the Green Mountain State as elsewhere in the nation. Bicycle enthusiasts formed the Vermont Wheel Club of Brattleboro in 1885 with a membership of 250 and a long waiting list. Golf courses in Manchester (1894), Burlington (1897), and St. Johnsbury (1899) catered to wealthier sportsmen, but dozens of Vermont towns had baseball teams, in part a result of the popularity of that sport in Civil War military camps. Winter sports included snowshoeing, ice hockey, and tobogganing and coasting. In 1886 the Burlington Coasting Club sponsored a five-day "Carnival of Winter Sports" that attracted thousands of visitors from surrounding towns as well as Boston, Albany, and Montreal. Coasting and tobogganing slides provided winter entertainment in Rutland, Hinesburg, Montpelier, St. Johnsbury, and other towns until the fad declined at the end of the 1880s.[49]

Other forms of recreation also reflected community pride and identification. Brass bands, long a feature of community life in New England, proliferated following the Civil War. The American band movement of the late nineteenth century helped encourage the composition and performance of music for various combinations of instruments, primarily brasses. Meanwhile, improved techniques in the manufacture of valve instruments, which eventually replaced the more-difficult-to-play keyed brasses, encouraged wider participation. By 1907, Walton's *Vermont Register* listed

Above: Barnet Band at Harvey's Lake, West Barnet, in the 1890s. *From the Vermont Album collection, Vermont Historical Society (ATX 347).*

Right: "Programme of entertainment, Cavendish, February 12, 1880." *Broadside, Vermont Historical Society.*

Left: "Cole's Circus Museum and Trained Animal Exposition, Ludlow, June 24, 1895. *Broadside, Vermont Historical Society.*

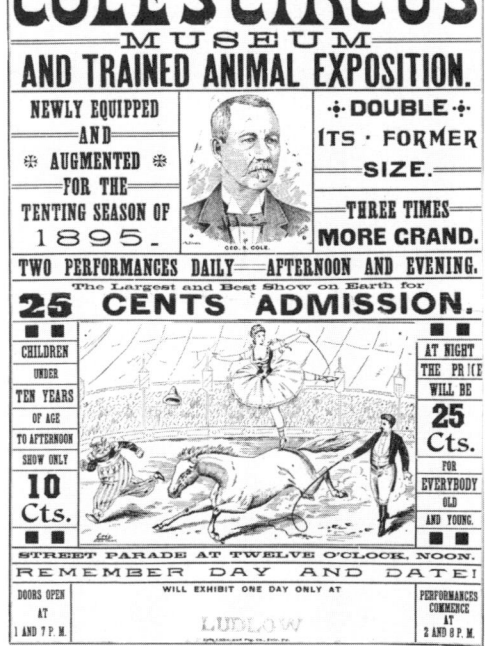

sixty-four brass bands in Vermont. An additional twelve are known from contemporary documents and photographs. The groups ranged in size from the eight-piece North Hero Cornet Band to the thirty-member Sherman Military Band in Burlington. Lyndonville and Montpelier boasted military bands, and St. Albans had two groups: the Ransom Guards Band and Ye Ancient Horribles, who, in contrast with the ensembles arrayed in military-style uniforms, presented themselves in work clothes or ragged costumes. Town bands played at dances, community events, and patriotic holidays, especially Memorial Day and the Fourth of July. In many cases the town bought and owned the instruments; in a few cases, funds were raised by subscription. Several towns built elaborate bandstands for the summer outdoor concerts.

Choral groups played a similar role in the life of the community. Continuing the tradition of the eighteenth- and early-nineteenth-century singing schools, itinerant "singing masters" instructed groups and conducted concerts, usually comprised of selections from their own printed collections, which they sold as part of the course of lessons. Occasionally, professional traveling soloists performed with community choruses, making these presentations major events in the annual cycle of community concerts, recitals, and cultural soirees. For many adults and children, however, these community "musical conventions" were as much social as cultural gatherings.

Large numbers of itinerant entertainers supplemented the local talent. Musicians, circus performers, and drama troupes made regular tours throughout the state. Traveling lecturers utilized extravagant props such as historical and travelogue panorama and diorama paintings and magic lantern shows. Most towns were now easily accessible because of the network of railroads connecting Vermont communities to each other and to "the golden triangle" of Boston, New York, and Montreal.

To accommodate this much-expanded cultural life, many enterprising businessmen and community benefactors constructed theaters and opera houses. By the end of the century, elaborate and well-equipped opera houses existed in Barre, Bellows Falls, Bennington, Brattleboro, Burlington, Derby Line, Enosburg, Manchester, Montpelier, Newport, Rutland, St. Albans, White River Junction, and St. Johnsbury.[50] To decorate and enhance the use of these buildings, owners, operators, and sometimes the town itself, commissioned painted theater curtains from a local or itinerant artist or purchased them from a distant production studio.

Drop curtain for the Hardwick Town House. Painted by Charles Henry, (1902). *Photograph by M. J. Davis.*

Some curtains depicted local scenes, such as the curtain for North Hyde Park, with its scene of Lake Eden, painted by Charles Hardin Andrus of Enosburg Falls, or a curtain with a painting of Lake Morey produced by an unknown artist for Fairlee. Others featured representations of historical events, such as a Civil War battle scene painted for the GAR in Chittenden by Andrus, and a depiction of the Coliseum in Rome, with a chariot race in progress, painted by Vermont artist Charles A. Henry. Many featured distant, exotic, or imaginary landscapes, like the Venetian display produced by "Mr. Huiest of the Theatrical Co of Troy New York" for the Barre Opera House in 1899, a similar scene painted in 1904 by Erwin LaMoss of Boston for the Haskell Opera House in Derby Line, a painting of Cape Wrath in Scotland produced for Shaftsbury by L. L. Graham of Brooklyn, New York, or the many imaginary rustic scenes created by Henry as he toured the state with his family of singers, instrumentalists, and actors.[51] The opera houses, band stands, community halls, and their decorations—even a few art museums such as the St. Johnsbury Athenaeum (1870) and the T. W. Wood Collection in Montpelier (1895)—were physical manifestations of civic pride and community identification as well as symbols of Vermont's lively interior life and its connections with a wider world of arts and entertainment.

Another expression of this heightened sense of community identity was the production, in increasingly large numbers, of maps and prints of bird's-eye views, or panoramas, of many of Vermont's smaller villages as well as its large industrial and commercial centers. As historian J. Kevin Graffagnino has demonstrated, these artistic and cartographic specimens, depicting major commercial landmarks along with private homes, public monuments, and prominent geographical features, almost always portrayed an idyllic landscape, along with symbols of progress and prosperity, such as railroads, factories, or quarries.[52]

While many Vermont communities worked at creating cohesion or redefining themselves to conform to the changing conditions of late-nineteenth-century society and economy, state government and entrepreneurial institutions such as railroad companies busily sought to open new economic opportunities by promoting tourism. Although lacking the historical and patriotic sites associated with the Revolution, or the rugged mountains that evoked the "sublime" landscape that attracted tourists elsewhere, Vermont's geology, with its abundance of mineral springs and its many "picturesque" and accessible mountain tops, helped launch a tourism industry early in the nineteenth century. Geographer Harold Meeks counted 131 mineral spring locations in use in Vermont in the late 1880s, noting that at one time or another thirty-two of them supported hotels. "Some, such as Clarendon, Sheldon, Guilford, Highgate, and Middletown, were large and diverse recreation spas with bowling [greens], croquet lawns, bottling works, and livery stables. Others, such as Wheelock,

Trade card for The Montebello Sulphur & Iron Spring resort, Newbury, Vt. 1880s. *Vermont Historical Society.*

Plainfield, Waterville, Barre, and Hartland, were much smaller." The more elegant hotels created a summertime high society in Vermont. Mountain roads and hotels or "mountain houses" perched near or at the summits of Killington Mountain, Mount Mansfield, Camel's Hump, Mount Ascutney, Breadloaf Mountain, Mount Equinox, Mount Anthony, and Grandview Mountain (now Snake Mountain) provided stagecoach access for day trips and accommodations for overnight visitors from afar as well as some local tourists. Where railroad tracks were nearby, these resort areas thrived, and the railroads took a hand in both promoting and profiting from this variety of tourism, sometimes by building and operating hotels, often by advertising their own and other facilities in printed schedules and illustrated tour books that they produced themselves.[53]

In the decades following the Civil War, tourist interest in the mountain houses and mineral springs tapered off, as the more spectacular and rugged scenery of New Hampshire's White Mountains and New York's Adirondacks, and the more elegant spas and resorts at Saratoga, gained in popularity. Some of the grand hotels and mountain houses burned and were never rebuilt; others lost out to facilities closer to railroad stations. The decline of visitors from the southern United States, some impoverished by the war, others resentful of the North, also affected Vermont's first era of tourism.

Other factors, however, began to bolster the state's nascent tourism industry. The shift in Vermont's population from rural to urban communities, the stagnation in overall population growth, and the supposed decline of its rural towns alarmed state government officials—perhaps more than it did those who continued to reside in those towns. State government responded to this perceived rural crisis by promoting a new form of extended vacation and tourism based on an appeal to Americans' enduring if somewhat abstract and nostalgic affection for their agrarian past, and on the supposed healthful benefits of time spent away from the cities in a wholesome country environment.

The celebration of Old Home Week was first promoted in 1899 by New Hampshire's Governor Frank Rollins. According to historian Dona Brown, Vermonters quickly and successfully adopted it, with August 16—Bennington Battle Day—conveniently providing an occasion to combine patriotic sentiment with summertime recreation. Calling on those who had left the state to return for this brief visit and also targeting those who had no roots in Vermont itself, but who might wish to associate themselves with the mythic virtues of New England individualism and rural simplicity, Old Home Week celebrations adapted the symbolism of agrarian tradition and rootedness—the old oaken bucket, the steepled church, the red schoolhouse—to appeal to a broader society of Americans increasingly mobile and heterogeneous.[54]

Vermont actually began its own publicity campaigns to attract visitors a decade before Old Home Week crystallized the theme of New England tourism. In 1891 the Vermont Board of Agriculture tried to find new uses and new owners for abandoned uphill farms by publishing a series of pamphlets including "Resources and Attractions of Vermont," "Vermont... A Glimpse of Its Fertile Farms and Summer Homes," and "A List of Vermont Farms at Low Prices." The shift of emphasis away from attempting to find new farmers to the goal of encouraging seasonal residents demonstrated the growing awareness of Vermont's potential as a destination for summer travelers. At the same time, the Board of Agriculture helped promote an expanding business in summer boarders at farms, where weary city folk could restore themselves with clean country air and "plain country fare."

These preliminary efforts bore fruit in a steady increase in vacationers. By the middle of the 1890s the Board of Agriculture's annual report recorded between fifty and sixty thousand summer visitors who found accommodations in no fewer than 650 hotels, resorts, boarding houses, and farms. Accommodating vacationers rapidly became Vermont's second most profitable economic activity, behind dairy farming. Like so many other aspects of Vermont life in these years, promoting the state as a destination for visitors and vacationers presented a double image: one that looked back to a supposed healthier and more virtuous life of rural simplicity and yeoman strength of character, and one that looked forward to commercial enterprise, economic growth, and progress.

The tension, if not incompatibility, involved in the rush toward the economic and social busyness of urban industrial life, and the nostalgia for a disappearing rural culture that lay beneath the surface of efforts such as tourism development, rose to the surface in much of the writing, art, and pageantry of late-nineteenth-century Vermont.

The writings of Rowland Evans Robinson, including short stories, sketches of rural life, and history, exemplify the effort to recapture and reify a fading ideal of bucolic innocence and rugged independence from an earlier age of Vermont's past. The oldest son of prominent Quakers and antislavery activists Rowland Thomas and Rachel Gilpin Robinson, Rowland

Evans was born in 1833 at Rokeby, the family farm in Ferrisburgh. Less committed to the Quaker ways and ideals than his parents, he went off to New York City in his teen years with the intention of becoming an artist and illustrator. After two extended stays in New York, neither of which resulted in fame or fortune, he returned to the family farm in 1873, disillusioned with big-city life. At Rokeby he continued to paint and sketch, but devoted most of his efforts to raising sheep and other livestock. In the mid-1870s his life took another turn when he sold his first story about rural life to *Scribner's Magazine*. There followed a steady stream of essays, sketches, and stories that won for Robinson both the commercial success he failed to achieve as a draftsman and a reputation as a limner in words of Vermont's receding rural landscape and culture. He also contributed an article on Ferrisburgh to Abby Hemenway's *Vermont Historical Gazetteer* and wrote his own history of Vermont, which he characteristically subtitled "A Study of Independence." It was his many stories of the fictional community of Danvis and the cast of characters he created to inhabit it, however, that made Robinson famous and an enduring literary figure in Vermont history.

The Danvis tales were eventually collected and published in six volumes, two of which appeared after his death in 1900. Through his characters—the elderly cobbler Uncle Lisha Pegg and his wife Aunt Jerusha, the strapping outdoorsman Sam Lovel, the officious Solon Briggs, and the much-abused French Canadian Antoine—Robinson constructed a vision of a Vermont that few in his own day might have recognized, yet one that resonated to the image that many Vermonters had of their own past. Of his fiction, Robinson commented: "It was written with less purpose of telling any story than of recording the manners, customs, and speech in vogue fifty or sixty years ago in certain parts of New England. Manners have changed, many customs have become obsolete, and though the dialect is yet spoken by some in almost its original quaintness, abounding in odd similes and figures of speech, it is passing away."[55]

Those imagined times of Robinson's tales were not entirely idyllic, and the characters were not without faults, rivalries, provincialism, and occasional disagreeableness. Yet Robinson noted, with obvious disapproval of his own times, that "it is all changed now: Danvis has daily mails, the telegraph almost touches its border, and its mountains echo the shrieks of locomotives and the roar of railroad trains. The people, generally, wear as fine and modern clothes as any country folk, and it is doubtful whether there is one adult who has not seen something of the bustle and life of at least one of Vermont's two cities, if not those of even greater marts. An aristocracy has sprung up, and people are losing the neighborly kindness of the old times when none were rich and none were poor, and all were in greater measure dependent on each other."[56] For Robinson, clearly, the "Gilded Age" in which he lived was one of lost innocence and decline from its imagined Yankee purity. In his history of Vermont, Robinson combines episodes from the state's past, folklore, and some bitter, ugly commentary on non-Yankee ethnic groups—especially Franco-Americans—to reiterate his nostalgia for a lost society and a lost time.

As with Robinson, the artist Thomas Waterman Wood portrayed in his genre paintings the sights, customs, and attitudes of rural society, which he contrasted with the more morally complicated mores of urban life. Born in Montpelier in 1823, Wood began to learn his art from an itinerant artist and by drawing the people and surroundings of his native town. He then went to Boston to study painting, and as a young portrait artist made a good living and gained a wide reputation from commissions in Washington, D.C., Baltimore, Nashville, Louisville, and several Canadian cities. He also traveled to Europe, where he broadened and deepened his training by viewing and copying old master paintings. Some of these copies he included in his gift of art works to the town of Montpelier in 1895.

Following the Civil War, Wood turned to genre painting, and again enjoyed success. As a member, vice president, and then president of the National Academy of Design, he became one of the most prominent practitioners of and spokesmen for a style of painting that replaced the sublime with the picturesque. The sublime had been the central element in the rugged, untamed landscapes of the Hudson River School, in which human figures were lonely intruders in a forbiddingly awe-inspiring wilderness. Wood and his contemporaries Charles L. Heyde and James Franklin Gilman, in contrast, depicted scenes contrived to imitate everyday life, and landscapes that everywhere showed the effects of human intervention and "improvement."

In his genre paintings, sketches, watercolors, and etchings from his middle years as an artist, approximately 1865 to 1890, Wood turned for subjects to his neighbors in Montpelier, where he continued to spend his summers. He drew upon the capital city residents' activities to create a vision of the simple virtues of rural America: a little girl's trusting leap from a hay loft into the arms of her uncle; men sharing "a pinch of snuff"; the

Vermont centennial and dedication of Bennington Battle Monument, August 1891. The Grand Ceremonial Arch, canvas covered and painted to look like granite, spanned Main Street, Bennington. *Vermont Historical Society.*

intimate community that gathered in a country store; the patriotism evoked by veterans of the Civil War. It was a vision that seemed to be disappearing under the burden of technological change and the more complex human interactions of urban life, depicted in his paintings—which sometimes border on being caricatures—of Irish, Yankees, African Americans, and other diverse American men lined up to vote at the polling place, or in his monumental painting of the drama between a drunkard's wife and child and the corpulent innkeeper who, by his shrug, refuses to take responsibility for the tippler lying at his feet. Late in his career, from 1890 until his death in 1903, Wood returned to portraiture, rendering in near photographic detail the faces and characteristics of individuals of both local and national prominence. His portrait of Justin Smith Morrill, now hanging at the Vermont Historical Society, was exhibited at the Vermont pavilion of the World's Columbian Exposition of 1893 in Chicago.[57]

Public rituals, too, played their part in defining and reinforcing community, state, and national identity. The anniversary of the Battle of Bennington, August 16, had been a day of celebration for Bennington residents as early as 1778—a mere two years after the event. For the next fifty years the annual celebrations became more elaborate and attracted increasingly large audiences of spectators and participants. As a result, in 1853 a small group of prominent Vermonters began planning a monument to commemorate the battle as a symbol of Vermont's identification with the great cause of American independence. The Bennington Battle Monument Association (BBMA) failed to gather sufficient funds or enthusiasm for its project and in 1874 a new group reorganized the BBMA with the intention of raising the monument in time for the centennial of the battle. Another shortfall in funds again thwarted realization of the association's plans and a dispute over the design, which had originally featured a statue of General John Stark, caused further delays. Hiland Hall, a Bennington resident and former governor, led efforts to redesign the monument, which resulted in the adoption of a plan submitted by Boston architect J. Phillip Rinn. After further modifications of the design, work began on the 300-foot-high tapered shaft. Supporters laid the cornerstone on August 16, 1887, and fifteen months later the two-ton capstone was set in place. The dedication ceremony, which took place on August 19, 1891, combined a commemoration of Vermont's participation in the war for independence with the centennial celebration of Vermont's entry into the Union as the fourteenth state.

The elaborate pageant of patriotism at Bennington attracted more than thirty thousand people. Participants in the grand parade to the monument included President Benjamin Harrison, accompanied by his secretary of war, Redfield Proctor; Vermont's two U.S. Senators, George Edmunds and Justin Smith Morrill; Governor Carroll S. Page and ex-governors of Vermont, Massachusetts, and New Hampshire; and dignitaries from New England and New York. In his dedication oration, Edward J. Phelps, Vermont's most prominent Democrat but also a nationally known lawyer, U.S. minister to Great Britain, and a renowned public speaker, expounded on the two themes of military valor and national unity that converged in the day's ceremony. In the peroration, Phelps looked for a larger significance in the monument: "Gazing forward, in the light of the after-glow of the dying century, we discern with the eye of faith and of hope, what this sentinel pile shall look out upon, in the days that are before it. It will look out upon Vermont: on whose valleys and hillsides the seed time and the harvest shall never fail; a land to which its people shall cling with an affection not felt for the surface of the physical earth, by any but those who are born among the hills, hallowed to them as to us by its noble traditions."[58]

Following the celebrations at Bennington, President Harrison made a two-week tour of the state.[59] In Fair Haven, heart of the booming slate district, he praised its workers and entrepreneurs who, "When you found the stones too thick to make agriculture profitable, you compelled the rocks to yield subsistence." At Brandon he spoke of "a type of the diversity and yet the oneness of our people." In Middlebury he praised its college by observing that "a free land rests upon the intelligence of its people, and has no other safety than in well-grounded education and thorough moral training." In Vergennes he recalled the valor of the Vermont Brigade in the Civil War; in Burlington he praised Edmunds, who had served as the senior U.S. senator from Vermont since 1866, and regretted his decision to retire from public life. From Burlington the president's party sailed up Lake Champlain to Swanton, then proceeded to St. Albans where he stayed with former governor and railroad baron J. Gregory Smith and visited the St. Albans Creamery. After brief stops at Richmond and Waterbury, the president addressed the legislature in Montpelier. Boarding the Wells River Railroad, Harrison and his party stopped at Plainfield, Wells River, McIndoe Falls, and Barnet on the way to St. Johnsbury, where he stayed at the home of Franklin Fairbanks. "You have here," he proclaimed in his speech at the Athenaeum, "manufacturing establishments whose fame and products have spread throughout the world. You have here public-spirited citizens who have established institutions that will be ministering to the good of generations to come. You have here an intelligent and educated class of skilled workmen."

The tour continued to Bradford, White River Junction, and Windsor. It concluded on August 29 at Rutland, where Harrison praised the city as "one of the best in American life," and openly endorsed the appointment of Redfield Proctor to succeed Edmunds in the U.S. Senate (Proctor received that appointment from the state senate the following November).

For two heady weeks Vermont stood in the glow of presidential politics, its accomplishments, history, and society inspected, rehearsed, and praised by the nation's leader in a characteristically American ritual of local, regional, and national celebration.

Only a few years later, Vermonters once again found themselves celebrating military heroism and national unity. On May 1, 1898, Montpelier native George Dewey, commodore of the Asiatic squadron of the United States Navy, steamed into Manila Bay in the Philippines and in a few hours crippled or destroyed the ships of the Spanish fleet, thereby helping to launch the United States' entry into world politics and global imperialism. The Spanish-American War, unpopular in our day, was controversial in its own time. Justin Smith Morrill, in one of his last acts as Vermont's senior U.S. senator, opposed the war and the acquisition of offshore territories, even though his junior colleague, Redfield Proctor, had helped start it by giving a stem-winding speech in the Senate denouncing Spain's cruel treatment of its Cuban colonial population. The war encountered opposition on other fronts, but when the Vermont General Assembly met in a special session on May 5, 1898, it unanimously approved a resolution supporting President McKinley's declaration of war, and agreed to send a regiment of enlisted men into service. This unswerving support of the war effort was almost immediately rewarded when news arrived later that day of Dewey's spectacular naval feat at Manila.

A few months later Vermonters could boast again, this time of Bradford native Charles E. Clark's participation in the naval battle in Santiago harbor on July 3, following a hurried voyage of 14,900 nautical miles from San Francisco around Cape Horn to Cuba in sixty-six days. Clark's voyage around South America fueled national enthusiasm for a ship canal across the isthmus of Central America. The legislature honored him by commissioning his portrait by Thomas Waterman Wood to hang in the Vermont State House.

The one disappointing episode in this string of local triumphs was the fate of the Vermont regiment. Sent off in May with great ceremony and fond memories of Civil War triumphs, the soldiers languished at Chickamauga Park, Georgia, where hundreds fell ill and twenty-seven succumbed to typhoid fever and other camp diseases. The regiment returned to Vermont in late August without having seen action.

Dewey's exploit, however, electrified the nation. Around the country musicians wrote songs about him; biographical sketches appeared in bookshops almost overnight; children contributed dimes for a silver trophy; cities renamed streets and schools after him; parents named their newborn sons in his honor. His portrait became more widely viewed than any other American's; the Navy promoted him from commodore to rear admiral and soon thereafter admiral. A few days after the victory at Manila, on May 9, 1898, ten thousand people gathered at Montpelier, Dewey's hometown, to celebrate his accomplishment. Such excited responses, however, were merely a prelude to what followed.

Dewey returned to the United States in 1899. He took an unprecedented triumphal tour of the nation and by the time he finally arrived in his home state in October, celebrations reached a fever pitch. Following receptions in Washington, D.C., and New York City, his first Vermont stop came in Bennington. Accompanied by Governor Edwin C. Smith and Col. W.

Dewey Day in Montpelier, October 1899. *Vermont Historical Society.*

Seward Webb of Shelburne, he boarded a special train that took him to Rutland, Middlebury, Vergennes, Shelburne, and Burlington, then on to the climax of the tour, Dewey Day in Montpelier, on October 12, 1899. An estimated forty thousand people, the largest crowd in the state's history, jammed the streets of the narrow valley city to greet the hero of Manila Bay. Railroad firms constructed thirteen special tracks to accommodate the assembling crowd. Celebrants draped patriotic bunting and strung electric lights on the State House and every other public and commercial building in the small downtown. Bonfires, fireworks, speeches, and parades climaxed the triumphal homecoming of America's most famous man.

The event, of course, was symbolically bigger than Dewey and his military feat. It celebrated the emergence of America as a forward-looking worldwide power. At the same time, it celebrated the myth of opportunity and fame open to every small-town American boy. The books written about him, and Dewey's own autobiography, chuckled and winked at his youthful high jinks—sledding down Montpelier's steepest hills, pummeling his teachers and schoolmates with snowballs, running blindfolded and backwards down the steps leading to the State House. This confirmation of small-town life, Yankee high-spiritedness, and independence fit well with the image of Vermont and the nation. A century after their state had cast its lot with the American Union, Vermonters on the eve of the twentieth century embraced identification with their nation's vigorous military exploits and its vision of progress, prosperity, technological innovation, and economic advance. At the same time, Vermonters celebrated the nation's reliance on the culture and values that had produced men like Dewey, molded by and in many ways personifying the traditions of Yankee individualism, ingenuity, spunk, and independent thinking, now bursting on the scene of world politics as uniquely American traditions and characteristics. In a state struggling to resolve the tensions between its traditions of rural life, agriculture, and small-town independence of mind and action on the one hand, and the emerging culture of urbanism, industrialism, and national identity on the other hand, Dewey Day was an eloquent expression of what Vermonters valued, sought to retain, and saw themselves more or less willing to sacrifice as they tried to define a valued place for themselves in a changing, expanding nation.

7
"Behind the Times"
1900–1927

Glimmers of Modernity

On October 4, 1905, Joseph A. DeBoer gazed out at a large Montpelier audience gathered to celebrate the one-hundredth anniversary of the establishment of the state capital in that city. DeBoer was chief executive of the National Life Insurance Company, a prominent Republican leader, and reputedly the Green Mountains' best orator. A colleague described him as "probably the ablest man of Vermont."[1] On this day, with Montpelier's buildings festooned in flags, bunting, and thousands of electric lights, and before an audience containing many of the state's dignitaries, DeBoer expressed a concern about Vermont's future that, although delivered in less anxious phrasing, was similar to those voiced by Governor Barstow in 1870 and Governor Dillingham in 1890. During the recent Dewey celebrations, Vermonters had readily identified with the nation's vision of progress, prosperity, and economic advance. Yet the state—as a whole, not merely its rural towns—appeared to lag behind the nation. DeBoer conceded his worries about the state's trends in farming, industry, and population during a portion of his speech in which he defended Vermont against claims of its shortcomings.

"True it is," DeBoer acknowledged to his distinguished audience, "that our people have been charged with being behind the times, as somewhat set in their ideas, slow going, hide bound and unprogressive." He acknowledged that Vermont "may not have figured so largely as some of its neighbors on a money basis or as numbers go in politics." And he conceded that many of the state's villages and towns had suffered a diminishing of their populations "from natural causes"; and that its people might presently have "a tendency to live more closely up to earning capacity than formerly." Nevertheless, he insisted, "Vermont is better to-day than ever, better traveled, better heated, better lighted, better fed, better transported, better educated, better served with news, and has a better market in which to trade and to which to sell." Vermont was in fact a progressive state—although one with a special character. Vermont had indeed made advances, DeBoer asserted, and a main reason had been "a firm adherence to the usage and practice of the past" and to the principle of making "haste slowly." "At points there are reverses . . . but, as a whole, our people are today enjoying as large and pleasant a prosperity as in the past."[2]

To some observers at the beginning of the new century, however, Vermont adhered, too much, to the past. From a national, or even regional perspective, the state appeared to stand outside the mainstream. Evidence of its divergence emerged in many measurements of development. Vermont remained a relatively remote and—at 343,641 residents—a scarcely growing state. Its geographical distance from major markets discouraged the kind of industrial development that drove expanding economies in states in southern New England, the middle Atlantic, and the upper Midwest. Vermont persisted, consequently, with a largely rural work force, relatively low incomes, few urban centers, transportation problems, and a population that had hardly increased in fifty years. In 1900, Vermont could claim no town with a population as large as twenty thousand, and only two towns, Burlington and Rutland, with as many as ten thousand. And, although DeBoer's 1905 audience could not know it, many of the most worrisome trends would increase. Between 1910 and 1920, the state would actually lose population for the first decade in its history. Even more ominous, the percentage of the working-age population (15 to 40 years old) would decline while that of older citizens increased.

Even compared to its two neighboring northern New England states, Maine and New Hampshire, Vermont appeared at variance: It possessed the largest population living on farms or in rural communities (78 percent); the smallest percentage of foreign-born in its population (13 percent); and lagged far behind in annual gross value of its manufacturing product. In an era of urbanizing, industrializing, and expanding growth, Vermont appeared out of step.

Still, subscribers to this anxious view, and those who shared DeBoer's more balanced depiction of Vermont, could both find some confirmation. Over the turbulent three decades that followed, encompassing the "Progressive Era," World War I, and the difficult 1920s, Vermonters struggled to apply their "usage and practice of the past" to the era's dynamically

Plate I. *View of East Dorset Marble Mill* (c. 1875). By Frank Childs. *Vermont Historical Society.*

Plate II. This 1939 publication by the Publicity Service of the State of Vermont's Department of Conservation and Development was part of an expanded effort to boost Vermont tourism. *Vermont Historical Society.*

Plate III. Arlington artist Norman Rockwell published *Freedom of Speech* in 1943 in the *Saturday Evening Post* as part of his famous wartime depiction of America's *Four Freedoms*. *Printed by permission of the Norman Rockwell Family Agency, Copyright 1943, the Norman Rockwell Family Entities. Collection of The Norman Rockwell Museum at Stockbridge, Norman Rockwell Art Collection Trust.*

Plate IV. *Champlain Valley* (1984). By Sabra Field. Woodcut, 11½ x 19½ inches. *Courtesy of Sabra Field.*

Plate V. *Dawn Loading* (2003). By Kathleen Kolb. Oil, 27 x 40 inches. *Courtesy of Kathleen Kolb.*

Plate VI. *High Summer* (1972). By Wolf Kahn. Oil on canvas, 50 x 50¾ inches. © Wolf Kahn/Licensed by VAGA, New York, N.Y. *Courtesy of the Smithsonian American Art Museum.*

Plate VII. Illustration for *Snowflake Bentley* by Jacqueline Briggs Martin (1998). By Mary Azarian. Woodcut, 17 x 8¾ inches. *Courtesy of Mary Azarian.* Wilson A. Bentley (1865–1931) of Jericho began photographing snowflakes at the age of fifteen. He began publishing his photomicrographs in 1898 and achieved wide national recognition for his work, which eventually included 2,500 images.

Plate VIII. *Black Bonnyvale Ridge* (2003). By Eric Aho. Oil on canvas, 62 x 80 inches. *Courtesy of Eric Aho.*

changing forces. Issues that commanded attention early in the period—election reform, railroad and utility regulation, child labor and workman's compensation legislation, school reform, and protection of the state's forests and woodlands—suggested a state in the throes of modernization. The experiences with reform, and with the war period of 1917-1918, in turn, generated new interest in problem-solving through techniques of centralized planning. Modern technology, meanwhile, in the form of telephones, electric appliances, and automobiles, penetrated the hill farms and began a gradual transformation of the state's rural life. A new age did not emerge, however. As the new technology crept slowly out from towns to hillside farms, and as some prewar currents of change found extended life in the 1920s, other initiatives were turned back or stalled. And intimations of social fragmentation that had surfaced over past years gained new energy in the postwar decade to accompany, and feed on, the economic malaise that dogged the entire era.

On that crisp fall Montpelier day in 1905, DeBoer insisted, correctly, to his assembled throng that Vermont did not stand moribund. In towns such as Burlington, Rutland, Brattleboro, St. Johnsbury, and Barre the characteristic features of modern society—industrial enterprise and urbanization—had in fact begun to take hold in the previous century. Manufacturing plants, quarries, and lumber mills, although small in number, already produced more wealth than the state's agriculture, and governors of the era sought ways to accelerate this manufacturing growth. Fletcher Proctor (1906-1908) expressed their shared view in his 1906 inaugural address, calling on the farmer-dominated legislature "to foster and not to discourage industry, to promote and not to retard prosperity."[3]

By the early twentieth century, consequently, Vermont's principle industrial towns, while comprising only a small segment of the state's population, already exhibited the more complex, stratified, and cosmopolitan features associated with industrializing centers elsewhere in the Northeast. Diverse populations were one of their common denominators. Although the Irish had been the first non-English immigrant group to enter Vermont in significant numbers, congregating primarily in railroad towns in the 1830s-1860s, French Canadians outnumbered them in the state by 1900. Small groups of Québec farmers had begun moving into Vermont's northern tier of counties early in the nineteenth century. Later, as crop failures and general economic decline expanded the cross-border flow, Québecers turned to jobs in Green Mountain mills and quarries. Their presence in towns from Highgate to Bennington expanded, as mill owners put entire families, including children, on the payroll.

The influx transformed Winooski and the Lakeside area of Burlington into vibrant Franco-American communities, with neighborhoods of close-knit families, benevolent societies, and networks of French-speaking tradesmen, carpenters, ship owners, and lawyers. They supported their own doctors, a hospital (Fanny Allen, founded in 1894), and French-speaking Catholic priests. While the state as a whole lost population between 1910 and 1920, the Queen City, spurred by the French Canadians, but also by new arrivals from Italy, Lebanon, Syria, Greece, and Germany, achieved a population gain of 11.3 percent

Vermont's French Canadians and Irish helped make Roman Catholicism the state's largest religious denomination by the 1890s, outnumbering the four largest Protestant churches, the Congregationalists, Methodists, Baptists, and Episcopalians. Discord, however, emerged early in the relationship of the two Catholic groups. When French-speaking worshipers requested a larger role in church administration and greater use of their language in rituals of worship and parochial classroom instruction, Irish church leaders resisted. Attempts to alleviate the conflict led in 1850 to the establishment in Burlington of St. Joseph's, the first French-speaking Catholic parish in New England. By 1904, St. Joseph's church had established St. Michaels College in Colchester and a growing parochial school system in Burlington and Winooski that included bilingual instruction (French in the morning and English in the afternoon) in three schools enrolling more than seventeen hundred students. This bilingual approach became the model for French-dominated parochial schools across the state.

Immigrants from southern and eastern Europe, part of a massive late-nineteenth- and early-twentieth-century influx to America's shores, also found their way to Vermont. In Winooski, Poles, Armenians, Syrians, and Lebanese joined the Canadian French and the Irish. Immigrants from Russia, Italy, Greece, and Poland entered the work rolls of machine-tool plants in Springfield and Windsor. Arrivals from the same groups, augmented by Czechs, Hungarians, and Austrians, came to the state's slate-district towns of Poultney, Fair Haven, Castleton, and West Pawlet, where they joined a large community of Welsh slate craftsmen who had settled in the area a half-century earlier. The Welsh workmen, unlike many of the new European arrivals, had managed to bring wives and families and to

Granite workers in Barre's Boutwell, Milne, and Varnum Quarry, c. 1910-1915. *Courtesy of Aldrich Public Library, Barre, Vermont.*

reproduce the institutions of their homeland in their new surroundings. By the turn of the century, consequently, Poultney supported Welsh-speaking Presbyterian, Methodist, and Baptist church congregations. And the community boasted Welsh musical societies, brass bands, and charitable, social, and literary organizations. The Welsh settlers' avid cultural interests, Protestant religious convictions, and inclination to vote Republican on election day served partially to undercut their Yankee neighbors' skepticism and distrust of the numerous foreign newcomers in their midst.[4]

The diverse new arrivals to the state in fact provided fresh cause for anxiety for many Vermonters, including Joseph DeBoer. Noting "the great shift in the character of city population now going on in different parts of Vermont," DeBoer—a Dutch-born immigrant who had worked his way through Dartmouth College—lamented to his 1905 Montpelier Centennial audience that the "lack of perfect assimilation" in certain communities was apparent in "changes in recent political conditions."[5]

The "changes" DeBoer had in mind probably involved nearby Barre, whose turn-of-the-century population transformation stood as the most dramatic among the state's larger cities. After the late 1870s, when Barre gained its spur line to the Central Vermont Railroad, the area's granite industry greatly expanded from a workforce of one hundred in 1880 to three thousand in 1910. Barre's population also grew rapidly; by 1910 the city claimed 10,734 residents, with European immigrants accounting for most of the increase. A one-time Barre mayor described the city as "Vermont's outlander" because of the many nationalities drawn there by the granite industry.[6]

A sizable number came from northern Italy (by 1910, more than one-fifth of the population), and they predominated in Ward 5, located in the city's north end, where they made up almost 60 percent of the residents. Barre's Italians formed their own mutual aid societies, social clubs, and cooperative stores, and published their own newspapers. The schedule at the Barre Opera House, which opened in 1899, regularly included programs of opera favorites performed by Vecchia Filodramatica. Other, "smaller-sized ethnic colonies were spread throughout Barre. Syrians, Scandinavians, and Scots all had their own geographical communities, with Irish, Canadian, German, Greek, and Austrian people between them."[7]

These Barre newcomers—quarrymen, stoneworkers, and sculptors—brought with them economic and political views shaped by their Old-World experience. They quickly established Barre as a staunch union labor town. By 1900 the area boasted fifteen unions, with 90 percent of the workforce as members. The local branch of the Granite Cutters National Union (GCNU) formed in 1886. The GCNU demonstrated its effectiveness during the 1890s by negotiating a series of victories over the granite companies that gained for Barre stoneworkers a closed shop, limits on the rents of company housing, rejection of a proposed company store system, and establishment of standard rates and regulations for worker tasks. The Quarry Workers International Union (QWIU) organized in the town in 1903, and Barre soon was designated as its national headquarters. Even the city's bartenders, laundry workers, musicians, retail clerks, and teamsters organized into unions.

In the new century's first two decades, consequently, Barre became the indispensable center for efforts to organize workers in the Green Mountains. Although the drive remained small and fragmented, it succeeded in establishing a structure and leadership from which emerged a significant statewide union movement during the 1930s and 1940s. Barre's leadership role flowed naturally from its heavily unionized workforce, but also from the wide range of radical political perspectives that thrived there during the early twentieth century, most visibly through ethnic political clubs. Several of the city's Italians considered themselves anarchists and syndicalists. Anarchist outposts took hold also in Italian communities of the surrounding granite-industry towns of Montpelier, Northfield, and Hardwick. Convinced, in general, that all forms of government were oppressive and should be abolished, Central Vermont's anarchists, like colleagues in Europe, nevertheless divided into factions over specific ends and means, including whether or not to support the union movement that embraced the relatively modest goal of expanding labor's rewards within the existing system of capitalism. Although most Italian workers became loyal union members, their full participation in union affairs came more slowly than for the Barre granite district's other ethnic groupings.

Through Luigi Galleani, Barre earned a brief international reputation as a center for anarchist activity. Galleani, a leading European anarchist writer, publisher, and political organizer, fled to the United States in 1901. After being indicted for inciting to riot in Paterson, New Jersey, in 1902, he escaped to Canada, and later took up residence in Barre at 29 Pleasant Street for a number of years. Using an assumed name, he spent his time writing and producing the *Cronaca Sovversiva*, or *Subversive Chronicle*, an incendiary weekly newspaper with a subscriber list of more than five thousand readers in the United States and abroad. Galleani moved his base of operations from Barre to Lynn, Massachusetts, in 1910, and nine years later, at the height of the post-World War I "red scare," federal authorities deported him to Europe. After Galleani's departure, the local anarchist presence faded in significance, dying, according to Barre author Mari Tomasi, "to grey ashes."[8]

The anarchist presence in Barre nevertheless earned the city a wide reputation for dangerous radicalism, for a while. Barre's Socialist Hall, on Granite Street, represented the "outer reaches of libertarian political thought," for one homegrown townsman.[9] In Boston, in 1906, an unfounded rumor circulated with broad acceptance, that Italians from Barre had gathered huge quantities of dynamite for the purpose of blowing up the Hoosac Tunnel docks.[10]

A large contingent of the town's stoneworkers, including many in the

Scottish immigrant community, deemed themselves socialists, an identification that remained strong in the city well into the 1930s. The Scots, who made up 17 percent of the city's population by 1910—second in size, after the Italians, among the immigrant groups—began arriving in significant numbers in the late 1880s, bringing with them strong traditions of trade unionism and independent labor politics. They quickly assumed leadership of the Barre granite district's trade union movement.

The mix of Barre radicalism's ethnic backgrounds and cultural roots led to occasional local confrontations. An incident of violence in 1903 symbolized the tensions that existed between anarchist and socialist political factions. On October 1 of that year, a feud apparently rooted in a dispute over upkeep of Socialist Hall erupted at an open meeting of workingmen at the Hall. Socialists had scheduled as speaker a New York newspaper editor who possessed an antianarchist reputation. When the speaker's arrival became delayed, a fight broke out, and someone fired gunshots, accidentally killing Elia Corti, one of the city's most respected sculptors.

Another event nine years later, however, exhibited the solidarity of spirit that existed across ethnic and political lines during much of this period. When textile workers at the American Woolen Company in Lawrence, Massachusetts, went on strike in 1912 in protest against wage cuts, Barre workers supported the strikers (many of whom were Italian) and closely followed the labor action's almost ten-week course. A Lawrence strike committee formed in the city and anarchists and socialists joined with local merchants and outlying Yankee farmers to take in several dozen of the Lawrence textile workers' children, to assure their safety for the duration of the Massachusetts strike.

The city's various strands of radicalism appear to have had little dramatic impact on local Barre politics. Although one granite district labor leader, Ben F. Healy, called for "the class conscious use of suffrage," voting patterns indicate this generally did not occur.[11] From the late 1880s through the first decade of the twentieth century, candidates of the local Socialist Party and various fusion "independent labor" parties regularly lost in annual city mayoral elections to homegrown members of the Barre business community. Why these outcomes? Many workers likely looked to their trade union as the effective agent for advancing their most important interests and viewed city government's elected officials as of marginal importance to their lives. Also, many newcomer stoneworkers, including members of the large Italian community, who had had little or no experience in electoral politics in the "old country," were slow to become voters in the "new." Italians in 1910 comprised 70 percent of the residents in Ward 5, one of the city's largest (of six) wards; nevertheless, it regularly recorded the lowest turnouts in city elections, a pattern that did not change on those occasions when labor and socialist mayoral candidates appeared on the ballot.[12]

When a labor candidate finally won a mayoral election in 1910, backed by a coalition of independent and socialist party factions and trade unionists, the campaign benefited from the first serious economic difficulties to emerge in the local granite industry in two decades. A slumping granite market, labor strikes in 1908 and 1909–1910, and concern over increases in stoneworkers' black lung disease brought on by introduction in the sheds of new dust-creating pneumatic tools, energized blue-collar voters. Boosted by the biggest turnout for a mayoral race in Barre history, John Mutch, a politically moderate member of the Tool Sharpeners' branch of the Granite Cutters' Union, won the election.

Mutch claimed no allegiance to socialism; nevertheless, his success attracted the attention of Eugene V. Debs, national leader of the Socialist Party of America, who came to town to help celebrate the victory. Debs was but one of several national leaders—including American Federation of Labor president Samuel Gompers, labor firebrands Mother Jones and "Big Bill" Haywood, and anarchist leader Emma Goldman—who made their way to the Granite City for speaking engagements during this period. In 1916, the coalition of Socialists and trade unionists re-formed to support the mayoral candidacy of Robert Gordon, who won a one hundred-vote victory over the editor of the *Barre Daily Times* to become the city's first Socialist mayor.

A handful of other labor and Socialist Party political victories occurred in Barre City and Barre Town in the years 1910–1916, but these electoral successes lacked clear mandates. Only Mutch, of the period's successful citywide workingmen's candidates, managed to serve a second term. And the issues and records of these labor politicians indicate they largely differed only in emphasis from their merchant and proprietor opponents. Successful as practical coalition builders, they "fused" with storekeepers and independent factions on such issues as lower taxes, more sidewalks, and upgraded road surfaces; and they cooperated with local municipal reform interests to achieve city ownership of the waterworks, municipal regulation of the gas works, and oversight of trolley rates and services, all of which were characteristic "progressive" municipal reform issues of the pre–World War I period. The limited strength of radical politics in Granite City balloting appeared never more evident than in the 1912 elections for state and national offices, in which Barre's Fred Suitor ran on the Socialist Party ticket for governor of Vermont but could finish no better than fourth among Barre voters; and Eugene V. Debs, running as the Socialist Party's presidential candidate, managed a fifth-place finish in a field of six, polling only 184 votes out of 1,532 cast.

In these years of few or no class-based political accomplishments, Barre's pragmatic workingmen nevertheless created a vibrant trade union movement and laid the groundwork for the larger role that organized labor would later play in the economic and political events of twentieth-century Vermont. The city's union leadership formed the Vermont Federation of Labor (VFL) in Barre in 1903, and soon thereafter launched legislative lobbying efforts in Montpelier and union organizing projects beyond the granite district, initially targeting lumber workers in Burlington, employees at the Fairbanks Scales Works in St. Johnsbury, and textile mill hands in Winooski. In these activities, Ben F. Healy, James Lawson, Fred Suitor, and others accumulated leadership skills as spokesmen and strategists for a growing, previously voiceless, segment of the Vermont workforce.

As with Barre, the cities of Rutland and Burlington possessed sizable blue-collar populations and wide ethnic diversity, but they failed to develop the Granite City's dominating union presence. At Rutland in 1904, the American Federation of Labor (AFL) sought to organize marble industry workers. The drive, including an attempted strike, failed largely because of the efforts of the Proctor family, owners of the Vermont Marble Company. The Proctors mollified worker discontent and undercut union appeals by the astute use of philanthropy and benevolent paternalism. The marble company constructed a clubhouse for employees and their families, reorganized the company store as a cooperative, and made available generous medical and other social services. The strategy succeeded. In 1911, Rutland's city directory listed seventeen labor organizations but none in the marble industry. The marble-district workforce remained reliably docile until the depression years of the 1930s.

Rutland's marble workers fared little better at finding a political voice than in their efforts at economic organization. After the brief triumph of the Knights of Labor in the city's municipal elections in the 1880s, blue-collar citizens and "friends of the workingman" had local political success only in 1904 when Labor Party candidate Jack S. Carder, a violin-playing marble worker from Cornwall, England, won election as mayor. Carder sandwiched his mayoral term between those of two of the city's marble dealers. Like Barre's labor mayors of this period, he appears to have owed his election largely to coalition building. When he failed to win reelection, the local press faulted his campaign for lacking pivotal issues.

A year prior to Carder's victory in Rutland, Burlington voters also chose a workingman mayor, rejecting standard Yankee leadership for the first time. The Queen City's new mayor, James E. Burke, a blacksmith by trade and the son of Catholic Irish immigrants, had run on both the Democratic and Local Option tickets and won by eleven votes. A strong union presence did not exist in the city, which possessed organized locals only in the small Typographical Union, Team Drivers' Union, and the Brotherhood of Painters, Paperhangers, and Decorators. Nevertheless, Burke had built a reputation as a champion of "the people's" interests, and a reporter described him as having "struck a popular chord in the hearts of the proletariat among whom his strength has been greatest."[13]

Burke's 1903 campaign emphasized reform themes familiar at the time in many urban centers across the country, including Barre and Rutland: "clean government" and public ownership of services. Burke called for public ownership of electric power and the waterfront, and a publicly controlled street commission. He also advocated increased representation in the legislature for Burlington and the state's other sizable towns. The polls reflected his popularity. In 1904 he won reelection by the largest margin ever given a Burlington mayor (the turnout was 84 percent of the voting list); and he won again in 1905, carrying every ward except one.

A canny political pragmatist, the Democrat Burke often described himself as a "[Theodore] Roosevelt Democrat." In 1909, in an act that defined his political distance from counterparts in Barre, Burke barred Emma Goldman, the famous anarchist leader, from fulfilling a scheduled speaking engagement in his city. His accomplishments during his several terms in the mayor's office (eight years between 1903 and 1914 and one term in the 1930s) included a water filtration plant, a municipally owned light plant, a public dock, the construction of Union Station at the base of College Street, and establishment of a municipal employee retirement fund. Burke's political career peaked in 1908 when he gained the Democratic nomination for governor, but his most important accomplishment may have been his extensive tenure in the mayor's office, strengthening his Democrat constituency's influence in the state's most populous community.

The 1902 Gubernatorial Campaign

Despite the population shifts and power realignments occurring within Vermont's larger towns in the last years of the nineteenth century and the early years of the twentieth century, the locus of political power statewide remained rural, agrarian, and Republican. Nevertheless, as the century opened, even the seemingly immutable Republican organization sat at the edge of change, prodded by those same shifts and realignments, by the concurrent slippage of the small rural towns, and by the force of external events.

Republicans had dominated Vermont politics from the party's formation in 1854. After marble magnate Redfield Proctor's 1878 gubernatorial victory, however, the party had appeared to acquire a more centralized direction, and political observers began attributing the party's leadership to an informal, not clearly delineated, "Proctor Machine." Unquestionably, by the 1880s the Proctor family had become the party's vital center. Built initially on the support of returned Civil War veterans, the Proctor influence derived its staying power, in part, from the family's control over one of the state's most important industries, marble, but also from the substantial leadership skills of Redfield Proctor and his eldest son, Fletcher. Their extended circle originated with like-minded friends and allies, and had expanded, by 1900, to encompass most of the state's largest business and industrial interests.

The Proctor circle exercised its power largely by influencing the process by which the party chose nominees for public office, primarily the governorship. They operated with few formal constraints because Vermont, like most other states, provided no statutory regulation over nominating candidates or getting out the vote, and did not require any form of party registration. Consequently, a well-organized faction could decisively influence the election of state officers by closely supervising the nominating process. Over the years, according to political scientist Andrew Nuquist, a system gradually emerged, so closed in its operations, that "the rank and file of the citizens played no role save that of sheep herded to the polls to cast ballots for pre-selected candidates."[14]

Constraints on the control of the Proctor faction did exist, however, in the form of long-standing Vermont political customs. These included the informal "Mountain Rule" system of candidate recruitment, the practice by which governors served a single two-year term, and the somewhat loosely enforced apprenticeship tradition for attainment of the state's highest offices, in which aspirants worked their way up, in orderly process, from General Assembly service to legislative leadership to governor.

Such constraints presented the Proctors with a system that they could strongly influence but not fully control. For Vermont voters, the combination of political custom and factional influence resulted in an electoral process not as predictable as Nuquist suggested but that nevertheless offered few surprises. In Republican primaries, with limited eligibility pools, candidacies tended to be driven by personalities more than by issues. On occasions when several Republicans vied for a nomination, the Proctor circle worked to settle rivalries early—and desirably prior to the start of the convention season—by exercising pressure and influence in the town caucuses, where the selection of delegates for the state nominating convention occurred.

Proctor hegemony went uncontested until the governor's race of 1902. The unlikely challenger to the "machine's" smooth running that year was Percival Clement, son of a wealthy Rutland marble dealer. Clement owned a thoroughly mainstream political resume, but he possessed several assets advantageous for an independent race. He owned the Rutland Railroad, the *Rutland Herald* newspaper, a bank, hotels, and a brokerage firm in New York City. He was also a proven vote getter as the former mayor of Rutland and a former legislator in both houses of the General Assembly. In addition, the public knew him as a "bitter political foe of the Proctor family,"[15] his antagonism stemming from conflict over local option but also from a long-standing rivalry of the two "industrial baron" families, the Clements and the Proctors, for economic and political primacy in the Rutland area. Clement, by 1902, served as a magnet for anti-Proctor sentiment in both political parties.

Clement openly campaigned for the nomination. Although he lacked any political organization, and despite indifferent oratorical skills and an undiplomatic personal style, the Rutland millionaire spent a vigorous six weeks prior to the Republican state convention touring the countryside, making a direct appeal to Vermont voters—as he claimed—"over the heads of the bosses" and their "paid army." In this campaign, "unconventional" by Vermont standards,[16] he visited the state's major towns by rail, using his personal railroad car, the "Grand Isle." A horse and carriage delivered him to smaller communities. A brass band and a singing group, described by the state's newspapers variously as Clement's "colored minstrels" or his "coon quartet," accompanied the candidate on most of his stops; and a Southern revivalist minister, the Reverend Sam Small, frequently shared the speaker's platform with him, at which times the candidate occasionally donned a Mexican sombrero.

This "melodramatic stumping tour" attracted crowds of people for the entertainment. Many in his audience, however, also supported Clement's central campaign issue: his call for a local option proviso to the state's half-century-old statewide prohibition of alcoholic beverages. He condemned the act as an infringement on the rights of the people. Local option, in contrast, he argued, would allow each town to decide on the legality of liquor sales within its borders. And he used the issue to attack the Proctors directly, branding their steadfast prohibitionist stance as but one more example of their seeking to rule people's lives.[17] Republican leaders responded by denouncing the Clement campaign as, among other things, a menace to party regularity, and they were furious that he had interjected the historically volatile liquor issue into the gubernatorial debate.

At the state convention in June, Party regulars managed to turn back Clement's bid. John G. McCullough, of Bennington, captured the nomination on the third ballot. Dissatisfied Clement delegates then bolted from the convention, branding the proceedings corrupt, and (ironically) accusing the wealthy McCullough of spending money lavishly in his own interest. In July they held a third-party convention under the banner of the Local Option League and named their man as candidate for governor, setting the stage for "the most bitterly fought contest in the history of Vermont politics."[18]

Clement's campaign used a three-pronged attack. First, he repeated his call for the repeal of the prohibitory law. Second, he demanded caucus reform, renewing his claim that bribery had occurred in the election of delegates to the Republican state convention and that the principal guilt lay with Proctor's "machine." "A few men have controlled official positions and legislation and have traded out the various offices from governor down, year after year, saying, 'You support me this time and I will support you next,' and upon that platform they have gone through the state with their strikers, hat in hand, begging votes." "The time has come," Clement told his audiences, "when we have got to purify the Republican Party from the damnable machine which has been on top of it."[19]

Clement's third line of attack was to denounce Proctor-era waste and inefficiency, and to call for a new "business administration of state affairs." He claimed that Vermont's total expenses had increased extraordinarily during the thirty-year period preceding June 30, 1901, while the state's population had expanded by less than 4 percent during the same period. Republican leaders responded by acknowledging the large increases in state expenses, but claimed accurately that the cause had less to do with corruption and mismanagement than with the long-standing bipartisan policy by which the state had taken on many of the financial burdens of the small rural towns.

Despite his energetic campaign, Clement's independent bid fell short in the September general election. His vote total (28,201), however, combined with that of the Democratic Party candidates (7,364), deprived McCullough (31,864) of a majority. In such circumstances, the Vermont Constitution mandates that the choice be made in the General Assembly. With Republican stalwarts solidly in control at Montpelier, they easily handed the governorship to their candidate.

Although the Clement movement failed to win the governor's race, it could claim significant accomplishments. It delivered a jolt to the "Proctor machine." Never before had Vermont Republicans failed to win a popular majority for one of their statewide nominees. In addition, Clement won his fight against prohibition. The 1902 legislature enacted a local option law. However, lawmakers attached to it a clause calling for a state referendum in which voters chose between two enactment dates, the first Tuesday in March 1903 or the first Monday in December 1906. Opponents of the new law supported the 1906 date, which if adopted, provided the next legislature time for repealing the act. Although the 1906 date carried in almost 70 percent of towns below median population, eight of the ten largest towns voted heavily for March 1903 and that date won in the voting, signaling the threats presented to small-town interests if, in the future, popular majorities displaced "Little Republic" governance in the state.

Finally, Clement's charges of widespread fraudulent practices and the buying of votes in town caucuses pressured party leaders to devise a popular referendum on the caucus reform issue. The 1902 legislature had enacted a Corrupt Practices Act addressing the role of money in election campaigns, but several influential newspapers, endorsing Clement's campaign claims, pushed for a caucus reform bill. The *Burlington Free Press* made the case: "The number of instances of the securing of fraudulent nominations by packing caucuses with men and boys who have no right to vote in them, has become so great and the consequences so serious, that to permit the practice to prevail any longer would be to outrage the moral sense of the honest persons who constitute the great majority of our people." In 1904 the General Assembly enacted caucus reform legislation which, although weakened in final passage, did assert state oversight of the caucus process by mandating the use of party check lists (subsequently repealed), publicly called meetings, and publicly supplied ballots.[20]

Progressive Politics

The Republican Party's flexibility on the issues of local option and caucus reform—apparent in its response to Clement's 1902 electoral challenge—signaled that the party understood that the price of its continued control would be a willingness, occasionally, to mollify insurgents' demands for change. This lesson in political accommodation came in a timely way for the party. Reform efforts and legislative innovations in many areas of Vermont public life followed in the fifteen years following 1902, the period of popular restiveness known nationally as the "Progressive Era." As R. L. Duffus recalled in Waterbury, "We were getting into the day when muckrakers were taking a long look at American business and finding much of it unethical . . . there was a kind of unrest that may have upset a good many men in Vermont who always voted Republican, but were not quite sure . . . that this was the best of all possible worlds."[21]

Progressivism emerged across the country on a wave of compassionate concern to ameliorate injustices wrought by the Industrial Revolution. Its leaders addressed mainly urban concerns of economic fairness, workplace protection for women and children, widespread poverty, and the challenge presented by large corporations to strongly held traditional notions of equity. Increasingly, reform groups looked to government, guided by freshly reinvigorated democratic processes, to arbitrate economic conflicts, check ensconced private and local power, and take on larger responsibilities to further social justice. The great social and economic upheavals reverberating nationally had been felt in Vermont mostly in the industrial towns, and not at all, in any direct sense, in many of the state's villages. Nevertheless, over much of the first two decades of the new century, Green

Mountain residents, prompted partly by the influence of national-scale events, but impelled primarily by the growing need to address problems arising from a constellation of the state's own economic, demographic, and political changes, built their own solid record of reform accomplishment.

By the start of the century, Vermont already had more than four decades of experience in using government as a reform instrument. Beginning in the 1870s, the state had created numerous commissions, boards, and agencies to monitor and regulate Vermont's prosperity and resources. And when small towns, driven by rural poverty, had turned to the state for financial aid in bearing local responsibilities such as keeping up roads and schools, and providing for the welfare of disadvantaged community members, the legislature, motivated primarily to preserve "little republic" vitality, had acted positively. As well, the state acquired a role in election processes when the legislature in 1890 permitted use of the Australian ballot at town meetings and gave the state responsibility for printing ballots. Such innovations in public planning, in the centralizing of management responsibilities, and in the "equalizing" of expense and effort stood as available models for Vermont's Progressive Era reformers. When in 1914 the Vermont Republican platform declared that "new complex social and economic conditions" necessitated imposing "novel duties and obligations" upon "the agencies of government," not all of the conditions, in fact, had been new or novel.[22]

Fletcher Proctor, elected governor in 1906, showed a particularly deft hand in responding to the era's rising spirit of change. "One of the most progressive governors Vermont has had," declared a contemporary observer.[23] Proctor understood that compromises and enticements might ameliorate reform sentiment while also protecting entrenched leadership; that reform could serve not only as an instrument for social improvement but that, in circumstances of economic and social uncertainty, it could be a method for maintaining control.

Proctor presided over a term of unusual accomplishment. In a quest for more efficient government, he modernized the state's bookkeeping practices and instituted a wide-ranging judicial reform plan that resulted in a four-judge supreme court and a new six-judge superior court. With his business experience concerning the dangers of worker discontent, he managed passage of a bill that had failed in 1902 and 1904 directing corporations to pay employees' wages on a weekly basis.[24]

Proctor also addressed one of the era's biggest issues. A major theme of progressivism nationally was dissatisfaction with the irresponsible exercise of power and influence by large corporations. In Vermont, such dissatisfaction took form as a call for public regulation of privately owned "natural monopolies" such as railroads, utilities, and express and telegraph companies. Discontent with the conduct of Vermont railroads had simmered for decades, dating back to George Perkins Marsh's harsh and eloquent criticisms in the 1850s. The Railroad Commission established by the legislature in the 1880s had been given the power to do little more than make recommendations, however. Despite the Commission, issues of safety, financing, and passenger displeasure remained inadequately addressed.

By 1906, legislators in the neighboring states of Massachusetts and Connecticut, facing similar dissatisfaction, instituted comprehensive new state railroad safety regulations. Aided by a 1906 report to the Vermont General Assembly scathingly critical of the railroads' operations in the state that singled out Percival Clement's Rutland Road for special criticism, Governor Proctor urged the Vermont legislature to take action also. Recent tragic railroad accidents at Vergennes and Bennington had swung popular support for a strong bill, and senate leader Ernest W. Gibson, of Brattleboro, provided effective leadership. Despite stiff railroad opposition, the General Assembly gave Proctor the bill he wanted creating a new Board of Railroad Commissioners, with expanded duties and authority. In a set of related enactments, the legislature also tightened regulations on rail transportation charges and increased railroad tax assessments.[25]

Proctor's successor, George H. Prouty (1908–1910), continued the regulatory push. In his gubernatorial primary campaign, Prouty promised to expand the state's supervision of utilities and, despite strong opposition from those companies, he managed to win the Republican nomination and to defeat the Burlington Democrat, James E. Burke, by a wide margin in the general election. Influenced by enactment of public service regulatory laws in New York State, the General Assembly—after heated debate—gave Prouty a bill expanding Vermont's regulatory powers to cover gas plants, electric light plants, telephone and telegraph services, and express companies—as well as railroads—under a newly created Public Service Commission, with the authority to issue orders and decrees. Prouty signed the bill into law in January 1909. Opponents of the legislation took solace, however, in the knowledge that they could successfully appeal commission decisions to state courts friendly to the utilities.[26]

Events in the election year 1912 increased the reformist momentum in

Progressive Party presidential candidate Theodore Roosevelt, speaking before a large Barre audience, August 31, 1912. In the background is the Barre Opera House. *Vermont Historical Society.*

Montpelier. In the presidential race, incumbent William Howard Taft faced former president Theodore Roosevelt and Democrat Woodrow Wilson. Roosevelt had seized the banner of progressive leadership as his only route back to the White House, but the other two men also embraced "progressive" campaign agendas. Taft, whose father was born in West Townsend, Vermont, and whose grandfather and great-grandfather were early settlers in Windham County, enjoyed wide backing in the state. But Roosevelt claimed numerous supporters as well.

Early in 1912, Roosevelt's boosters formed the Vermont Progressive Republican League with an eye toward winning control of the state party and forwarding a program of legislative reforms. However, at the Republican state convention in Montpelier, on April 10, they lost a bitter struggle to the Taft regulars. In June, they followed Roosevelt's national lead by breaking away to create a state version of their leader's national Progressive Party. Composed largely of individuals inexperienced in elective politics, the new party met in Burlington on July 23, where they chose Roosevelt electors to attend a national Progressive Party convention and named Frazier Metzger, a Randolph clergyman, as the party's candidate for governor.

Republicans, confronted by this inexperienced but "thoroughly organized" new party, as historian Walter Crockett described it, launched a "battle royal" to hold the state for their ticket.[27] Trips into Vermont by Roosevelt in August, and Taft in October, highlighted the campaign. Metzger led the state Progressives with an issue-focused attack. He declared that "Democracy is on trial" in the election, and his party's platform denounced "the constant efforts of crooked business in unholy alliance with crooked bosses to usurp the powers of government through control of party machinery," and called for a direct primary as the remedy. On issues of "social and industrial justice," Metzger advocated suffrage for women, effective employer liability and child labor laws, and a statute limiting the hours of labor for women.[28]

The results of the election on November 5 demonstrated Republican weaknesses and the strongly progressive temper of the times. The nation chose Wilson as president, with Roosevelt a close second, followed distantly by Taft. Vermont went for Taft—but by a mere 1,200 votes—joining only Utah in the Republican column. In the competition for governor, Progressive novice Metzger captured 25 percent of the votes, and the Democratic candidate Harland B. Howe claimed 32 percent, thus depriving the Republicans of a majority and forcing the decision into the General Assembly for the second time in a decade. Embarrassed by having won only slightly more than one-third of the gubernatorial votes, the Republicans nevertheless handily controlled the new legislature, thus guaranteeing the governorship for their candidate, Allen Fletcher of Cavendish, a relative of the Proctors.

After confirming Fletcher, the legislature proceeded to act on a laundry list of progressive bills. The new governor had in fact campaigned on an aggressively reformist platform drafted at the state convention with significant input from the party's progressive faction, prior to its third-party bolt. Regular Republicans had permitted the platform concession to progressives as part of a futile attempt to head off the party split. After the election, Republicans again tried to lure the Progressive wanderers back into the fold by acting promptly on many of their main issues. The postelection atmosphere was thus conducive to legislative action; the General Assembly sat for an unusual five-month term and enacted a number of significant bills.

The 1912 session and subsequent ones prior to World War I were notable for the roles played by civic interest groups that had formed only recently, or previously had only marginal participation in Vermont politics.

Ten-year-old Addie Laird, a spinner at the Vermont Cotton Mill in North Pownal. Lewis Hine, of the National Child Labor Committee, took this photograph in August 1910. *Courtesy of Library of Congress.*

The Vermont branch of the National Child Labor Committee (established in Burlington in 1910), the Episcopal Diocese of Vermont, and the Vermont Federation of Women's Clubs (formed in 1896) all contributed investigative reports on the "many evil conditions prevalent in the state."[29] Testifying before legislative committees, and in other public forums, these groups, whose members resided primarily in the larger towns, provided information on a number of social and economic justice issues.

The Vermont Federation of Women's Clubs had become active politically in the state after Florence Kelly, of the National Consumers League, visited Burlington in 1903, advocating laws protecting children in the workplace. The Vermont Federation responded by forming its own Consumers League committee with an agenda focusing on children. Other committees of the Vermont Federation investigated the state's penal institutions; participated in drives against tuberculosis and venereal diseases; and promoted bills for compulsory medical inspection in schools, pensions for widowed mothers, and the establishment of children's traveling libraries under the guidance of the State Library Commission.

By 1912, the poor conditions for workers, especially children, in many of the state's mills and factories attracted the concern of several civic-minded groups, in addition to the Consumers League and the Vermont Federation of Labor. The issue of protection for children in the workforce, however, had also come up in previous legislative sessions. Prompted partly by disclosures from the state branch of the National Child Labor Committee, the Vermont General Assembly passed two statutes in January 1911 intended to protect the health and educational rights of child workers. Assisting in the drive for passage of that legislation had been Lewis W. Hine, a young New York City photographer employed by the National Child Labor Committee. Hine, who later gained recognition as one of the great photojournalists of his era, photographed children as young as seven or eight years of age working at mills and quarries in Winooski, Burlington, Proctor, Rutland, Barre, and Bennington. The enactments of the 1910–1911 legislative session, however, had proved unsatisfactory, as had earlier regulatory efforts in 1904 and 1906, because of the absence of an effective enforcement mechanism. Not one prosecution had occurred under any of the acts.[30]

In September 1912, the Episcopal Diocese of Vermont again drew public attention to working conditions of female and child employees. The report of a three-person diocese commission detailed circumstances in factories in Bennington, Rutland, Burlington, Winooski, Hardwick, Barre, Bethel, and Bellows Falls. It exposed the low wages and long workdays at textile mills, in particular, and cited cases in which 11-to-14-year-old boys and girls worked 60 to 72 hours per week, or more, with earnings as small as $4 per week. Reports on textile mills in Winooski and Burlington, owned by the American Woolen Company, included an instance of a pregnant woman required to work within ten days of delivery, and of the employment of at least thirteen children less than six years of age.

The findings attracted wide attention. A legislative committee's tour of Burlington-area textile mills turned up its own evidence verifying the commission's findings and undermining factory owners' opposition to new regulations. After further intense lobbying by the Episcopal Diocese, the Burlington-based Workmen's Political League, and the *Burlington Free Press*, and also the strong urging of Governor Fletcher, the legislature enacted a factory inspection bill establishing machinery for investigating and inspecting the state's industrial workplaces. In addition, it provided a system of enforcement noticeably absent from the earlier labor welfare laws. Governor Fletcher signed the bill on February 18, 1913, six weeks after signing other new legislation establishing a maximum 58-hour work week for women and children. (Farm labor was exempted from these provisions.) The worker-protection momentum continued two years later, with enactment on April 1, 1915, of a workmen's compensation bill that made employers legally responsible for injuries sustained by employees in the course of work. The new law, which had been strongly backed by the Vermont Federation of Women's Clubs, provided for weekly employer payments to widows and children of men killed in industrial accidents, and payment of medical and hospital costs to employees injured on the job. The number of accidents in Vermont quarries dropped significantly in the years following the law's enactment.[31]

One of the period's most far-reaching government initiatives proved to be the launching, under Fletcher's leadership, of a fundamental reassessment of Vermont's educational system that climaxed in sweeping changes that centralized the administration of the schools. The groundwork for this initiative had been prepared by state Superintendent of Education Mason S. Stone, recently returned from a stint as a school administrator in the Philippine Islands (1901–1905). In 1892, during an earlier tour as state superintendent (1892–1901), he had backed the law that attempted to replace Vermont's district school structure with a town-based system providing one school district for each town.[32] The new plan's supporters hoped once again to encourage a voluntary reduction of the one-room schools. The consolidation of schools, they anticipated, could enable the adoption of a graded system based on age and skill levels that was not possible in the one-room schools, and gain a wider tax base making possible the hiring of better-trained teachers and providing a more centralized professional administration of the schools. Although Vermont's cities and larger towns employed trained educators as superintendents, rural schools in almost all cases possessed superintendents without qualifications or training for their positions. Teachers in rural schools were often inadequate, as well. According to a rural Methodist minister who served, without qualifications, as superintendent in two towns, "almost anything could get by in the open country. I had plenty of tragicomic examples of rural instruction."[33]

These Vermont efforts reflected widely diffused national trends at the turn of the century. The National Education Association endorsed the goal of rural school administrative consolidation in 1895; and a few years later President Theodore Roosevelt's Commission on Country Life identified the poor quality of rural schools in the United States as a significant problem for which school consolidation was a recommended solution. The more broadly focused Country Life Movement of this period, composed largely of social scientists, religious leaders, and philanthropists, concerned itself with a diverse agenda of perceived rural social ills that prominently included rural education. The Country Life Movement's goal, of reconstructing the local institutions of rural America in the service of "better farming, better living, and better business,"[34] found its models in the social and management efficiencies of urban life and its supporters—including those in Vermont—primarily among individuals with an urban perspective. The Country Life Movement never gained much footing in rural communities, however, neither in Vermont nor across the country, and it came to an end with the onset of World War I.

Early in the new century, prior to Fletcher's initiative, Vermont had taken additional steps in the centralization of school administration. A 1906 law allowed the voluntary joining together of towns in "unions" to form larger supervisory districts and to employ a full-time professional superintendent. As incentives, the new act provided that half of the superintendent's salary would come from the state and allocated $20,000 for state reimbursement to towns for elementary-school transportation. In 1912, following recommendations from a conference of school superintendents and principals, a law was enacted transferring the responsibility for choosing the state's chief education administrator from the legislature to a new five-member State Board of Education, appointed by the governor. The new board was also charged with establishing qualifications for union superintendents and teachers.[35]

By 1913, Governor Fletcher had made education reform a part of his, and the Republican Party's, plans for improved governmental administrative efficiency. At Fletcher's urging, the legislature created a nine-member Vermont Educational Commission to study "the educational condition of the state."[36] Chaired by state Supreme Court Chief Justice John H. Watson, this group

Peacham Corner School in 1902. *Vermont Historical Society.*

engaged the Carnegie Foundation to make a study of the rural schools. Two years later the commission filed a report, based on the Carnegie survey, extremely unfavorable in its conclusions. The report found the typical rural Vermont schoolteacher ill prepared; elementary school curricula inadequate; and the physical state of schoolhouses typically "dilapidated." According to the report, the central problem lay with the schools' decentralized administrative organization and the lack of skilled supervision in local hands. Until the state created an effective comprehensive administrative system, with a clear statewide educational policy, no real progress could be made in addressing the schools' problems. With its almost seventeen hundred schoolhouses, of which approximately fourteen hundred were one-room structures, many of them inefficient and uneconomical, Vermont's system remained too rigidly tied to local control. Ultimately, the report concluded, the state's schools reflected a "failure to adapt . . . to modern conditions."[37] The report specifically recommended that union supervision for groups of towns, optional since 1906, be extended and made mandatory as a step toward centralizing the state system.

The 1915 legislature embraced much of the commission's report. Governor Charles Gates signed a number of bills—the so-called "Carnegie legislation"—into law. The package lengthened the school year to thirty-four weeks; established uniform courses of study; authorized state sponsorship of teacher-training courses; established a minimum weekly salary for rural teachers, with the additional salary payment provided by the state; and created a program of vocational education. It encouraged school consolidation by providing transportation for pupils living one and one-half miles or more from school, with all expenses paid by the state in towns with grand lists under $5,000; towns above that amount shared with the state the cost of transportation, the amount determined by a formula based on the size of each town's grand list.

Of most importance, the legislation reorganized and further centralized school administrative structures, increasing the Board of Education's powers, and mandating the board to form the state into a system of sixty-six rural supervisory unions composed of groups of towns, with professionally trained administrators for each union. Under this plan administrators would be appointed by the state board and have their salaries paid by the state. To fund these additional school expenditures, the state property tax, originally imposed in 1890 for the support of schools, was increased.[38]

The chairman of the House Committee on Education, Arthur W. Hewitt, a clergyman from Plainfield, described the atmosphere in which he and fellow legislators had worked: "For a generation there had been wrangling and confusion and charges of [educational] incompetence.... This was the crisis of a generation.... If we did not save the wreck now, education in Vermont had little hope." For Hewitt, the bills' provisions were "revolutionary."[39]

A rigorous statewide debate preceded enactment of the "Carnegie legislation." Many Vermonters liked the initiatives for their promise of improved student performance, greater administrative efficiency, and economy. Many others, however, opposed large parts of the package. Critics in both poor and wealthy districts had long feared that consolidation initiatives would bring loss of local control over school districts and, consequently, of the school budget, as well. Specifically, the smaller districts anticipated that consolidation would likely be accompanied by new state-mandated standards at added cost; and more prosperous districts worried that their entering into consolidation with more needy districts would result in unwanted increases in their own taxes.[40]

Not all complaints were related to money. Some people feared that closing schools in a quest for consolidation would strike a disastrous blow to unity, social life, and local pride in the affected communities. Others put forward safety concerns about transporting young children longer distances, over unpaved roads, to a large and unfamiliar centralized school, especially during winter months and the state's two lengthy "mud seasons." Still others claimed that the social environment of centralized schools created "rude pupils." Some people simply did not agree that a crisis existed in their schools and did not like the idea of "outsiders," such as the Carnegie Foundation, criticizing their state. The report faced inevitable doom, according to one commentator, "because Vermont does not care as a rule to follow in the train of other states; because Vermonters do not take kindly to the advice of outsiders; because as has been aptly said, 'Vermonters would rather go to hell in their own way than to heaven in your way.'"[41]

The most vocal opposition, nevertheless, came from those anxious about the widening influence of state authority in local education matters, and the accompanying loss of control for districts and villages. In their view, local control had been replaced by unelected, centralized administrators. State Superintendent of Education Mason S. Stone led the resistance. In his two decades as superintendent he had pushed hard for increased standardization and modernization, with emphasis on professional supervision of local schools. But for him, the recent legislation had ceded too much local educational control to the state. When the newly created Board of Education invited him to become the first Commissioner of Education, he agreed to accept only on an interim basis, and resigned in 1916.

Stone and other advocates of a more dispersed and voluntary system of administration persisted in their dissent. After serving as lieutenant governor in 1918, Stone gained election to the House of Representatives in 1919 and 1923, where he helped roll back several of the 1915 enactments. By then, the spirit in Montpelier had shifted regarding the centralizing movement of previous years. The General Assembly took away the Board of Education's authority to appoint union superintendents and gave it back to local officials. It reduced the board's size from five members to three, and reduced the size of its staff, as well.[42] More importantly, it backed away from the entire supervisory concept, eliminating its compulsory aspect and replacing it with a plan of school supervision by which towns could choose to operate either with a town superintendent or a supervising principal, or to join with other towns in a union, administered by a union superintendent. In fact, the years after 1915 had yielded little consolidation; by 1919, over twelve hundred one-room schools still existed, and the state possessed only forty consolidated rural school districts.

A few years later, writing in *History of Education: State of Vermont*, Stone elaborated on his opposition to the 1915 centralization effort, which he depicted as part of larger, more disturbing Green Mountain trends. Stone attributed the 1915 legislature's actions to "a state of mind" that had emerged, to a large extent, because of changes in the state's composition. He lamented, among other things, the influence of "foreign" populations and expanding factory towns. As "large manufacturing centers developed . . . in agrarian states like Vermont, a strong centripetal tendency set in and a rapidly growing urbanization. . . . With centralization of people came centralization of government and with centralization of government came more officials, more autocratic power, and more expense."[43] Stone's views resonated not only with a wide circle of discontented Vermonters but also with a broad spectrum of Americans who, by the 1920s, had begun to draw back from prewar optimism about centralized management of public affairs. Educational consolidation would have to come at a slower, more incremental pace than 1915 reformers had anticipated.

A crowning political accomplishment of Vermont's progressive era came in 1915 with the enactment of a direct primary bill. In state capitals across the nation, the call for greater participation in the political process topped legislatures' reform agendas. For Vermont, that call took shape as a movement for a more open nominating process, made necessary, according to its supporters, by the failure of the 1904 caucus reforms to bring an end to manipulation of candidate selection. By 1914, broad-based support existed for a plan to replace the caucus-convention process with a direct primary. It came from individuals in all three political parties; from all of the larger towns; and from the editorial pages of several of the state's most prominent newspapers, including a new (1914) weekly, the *Vermont Advance*, an opinion vehicle of the state Progressive Party, which embraced the motto, "It's time to set the Public Welfare in the first place." The direct primary became an issue Montpelier lawmakers could not avoid.

Reluctant to buck the proposal's numerous advocates, but wary of its small-town-based opponents who rightly believed its passage would lead to a shift of power to the larger towns, legislators skirted decisive action. Instead, they fell back on the familiar device of the popular referendum, ostensibly to determine the electorate's precise wishes on the issue. Two referenda were held. One in March 1914 presented a convoluted ballot in which voters could choose a binding or preferential primary, or neither. More people favored the direct over the preferential primary but no option received a majority. The second referendum, an up-or-down vote on the direct primary in 1915, verified its popular support, and resulted in enactment of direct primary legislation.[44]

Governor Charles Gates touted the new law as a Vermont advance in popular government. For small towns, however, it had the effect their leaders had feared by undermining political power they had long enjoyed. Under the old town caucus system the state's smaller communities had exercised influence vastly disproportionate to their population or voting participation. Replacing the town-based system with the new law's mandate that all voters be counted equally with no attention to town residence and allowance of nomination by plurality made inevitable a reduction of rural communities' influence. After 1915, in the statewide candidate selection process and in the election of county representatives to the state senate, town interests lessened and cities' gained; the long decline in influence of agricultural interests in the legislature that extended throughout the twentieth century had entered a period of acceleration.

In 1917 the legislature moved on a number of fronts relating to the care of needy and unfortunate Vermonters. Reacting to pressure from the private Vermont Conference of Charities and Corrections, newly formed in Burlington in 1916, lawmakers gave governor Horace F. Graham (1917–1919) bills that he signed into law stopping the practice of keeping children on poor farms; creating the Board of Charities and Probation to oversee cases of persons in need or under supervision of the courts; providing funding for the Brandon State School for the Feebleminded; and setting up a state program for aid to dependent children. The legislation had the effect of placing the state rather than private relief societies, as in the past, at the forefront in providing for Vermonters' social welfare needs.

Vermont's forests, too, came under the expanding administrative power of the state in these years. Groups influential in other reforms—opponents of the public abuse of private economic power, and supporters of administrative efficiency—provided much of the impetus in this early movement for environmental conservation. President Theodore Roosevelt emerged as a symbol of the movement nationally in 1901, when he proclaimed the protection of forest and water resources to be a critically important national problem. By that year, however, the need for forest conservation programs and for greater participation by the state in promoting preservation had become accepted wisdom among some Vermonters. Of this group, none made a greater contribution than Joseph Battell (1839–1915) of Middlebury. A man of wide interests, outsized idiosyncrasies, and inherited wealth, Battell was also the largest landholder in the state.

Battell's real estate possessions included a tract of land in Ripton containing Bread Loaf Mountain that he purchased in 1865 after being awed by the area's scenic beauty. At the mountain's base, he built and personally managed an inn, where he entertained his guests with voluble discourses on his many enthusiasms, ranging from physics, photography, mathematics, and cartography, to European travel.

Battell, however, was not content with talk. In his eight terms in the state legislature, representing Ripton and Middlebury, and in the pages of the *Middlebury Register* newspaper, which he owned, he functioned as a rigorous policy advocate on such topics as the need for protection of the Morgan horse, the menace of automobiles, and the virtues of William Jennings Bryan's bimetalism. In the 1896 presidential election year in which the Democrat/Populist Bryan embraced "free silver," Battell even accepted the nomination of the Vermont People's (Populist) Party for governor. Battell managed to attract only 831 votes, of almost 70,000 cast in the election, and soon afterward he drifted back into the progressive wing of the Republican Party and became a strong supporter of Theodore Roosevelt.

Battell reserved his most passionate concern for the uncertain future of the state's forests. Vermont had reached its maximum in timber depletion following the Civil War, when approximately 80 percent of the state's land area stood cleared of trees, including almost all land below two thousand feet in elevation. Floods and forest fires had been factors in this decline. But contributing most destructively to deforestation had been wasteful methods of lumbering, such as clear-cutting, which had spread by the extension of post-Civil War railroad lines from the Champlain and Connecticut River valleys to upland timber areas. Loggers of this era, while improving their access to timber sources and their processing technology, had largely ignored timber renewal programs that might have assured a continual lumber supply, a healthy wood industry, and intact forests.

Because the timber industry provided Vermont with one of its greatest sources of income, the shrinking forest cover appeared to imperil the state's economy. In addition, it compromised the capacity of hills and mountains to hold their soil against stream runoff, a result that caused cleared land to become steadily less productive and wildlife and fish less abundant. In Battell's view the dangers George Perkins Marsh had warned of fifty years earlier had become a reality, and the great writer's conclusion on the interrelatedness of humanity and nature never seemed truer. A further concern was that the declining forests robbed Vermonters of the beauty of their natural environment and jeopardized efforts begun in the 1890s to use the state's scenery as a lucrative tourist attraction.

During the last years of the nineteenth century, voices calling for conscious management of forestland grew more numerous. Beginning in the 1880s, several owners of large landholdings, including Battell, Frederick Billings of Woodstock, William Seward Webb of Shelburne, Marshall Hapgood of Peru, and Silas Griffith of Danby independently began experimenting with scientific conservation management on their own vast estates.

The first formal step toward creation of a state policy on forest preservation came in the 1882 Vermont legislative session when Battell, then a House member from Middlebury, won adoption of a resolution calling for creation of a commission to study and evaluate the problems confronting Vermont forests. The Vermont Forestry Commission included three of the state's most powerful and influential public figures, Redfield Proctor, Edward J. Phelps, and Frederick Billings. The commission's subsequent report, submitted in October 1884, documented the crisis facing Vermont's forests but nevertheless foresaw a limited role for Montpelier in seeking solutions, because of the absence of publicly owned forest land and because of the committee members' own reluctance to recommend state intervention in private land-use practices. Of the commission's various recommendations, consequently, education in the schools, among farmers, and for landowners generally became the primary tool for change.[45]

Dissatisfied by the commission's limited accomplishments, Battell agitated for a larger state role in forest conservation, an issue he saw as a matter of right and wrong. He viewed Vermont's lumbermen and paper companies as primary culprits against which the public needed protection. In a plea to the legislature in 1890, the blunt-spoken Battell denounced the timber industry's method of clear-cutting large areas, and described its practitioners as "timber butchers" and "soulless corporations." Particularly in northeastern Vermont, they had "left broad areas that were covered by handsome forests, naked, barren and desolate." Battell wanted legislation "authorizing the State to purchase its best lumber lands yet untouched, that can be purchased low, and to place the same under a proper management." Drawing on his own experience at Bread Loaf Inn, he also made a pitch for conserving the state's forests as a tourist attraction, suggesting that "one summer hotel with the capacity of 200 boarders" should bring into the state revenue at least the equivalent of five million feet of spruce per year.[46]

Governor Urban M. Woodbury, in 1894, pushed the conservation issue along, warning the legislature that "Owners of timberlands in our state are pursuing a ruinous policy in the methods used in harvesting timber," and asking for enactment of "some measure . . . to lessen the wanton destruction of our forest resources."[47] Meanwhile, Battell used his own resources to begin buying up as much forest land as he could, including Camel's Hump, Lincoln Mountain, the entire central ridge of the Green Mountains, and subsidiary peaks for the specific purpose of protecting their scenic beauty from the woodchopper's axe. Battell once explained his purchases this way: "[People] go to Europe and pay $10,000 for a painting and hang it up in their home where none but their friends can see it; I buy a mountain for that money and it is hung up where everybody can see and enjoy it."[48]

In 1904, Vermont's "forestry movement" finally emerged. A number of influences helped it into existence, including the efforts of Battell and fellow activists, and the lobbying of professor L. R. Jones, a botanist at the University of Vermont. Another was the 1902 annual report of the Vermont Fish and Game Commission which contained a warning of the destruction occurring to the state's trout streams—and thus their lucrative recreational potential—through river silting brought on by the depletion of the state's forests. Two other disparate developments also provided catalysts for action. In 1903, a series of forest fires raged across northeastern Vermont and the Adirondacks of New York, provoking a new sense of urgency; and, in January 1904, Gifford Pinchot, whom Theodore Roosevelt had appointed head of the United States Division of Forestry, and an outspoken advocate of the scientific management of forests, made a brief visit to the state. In a speech at Burlington, Pinchot discussed the need for managing forest resources for economic purposes and the forests' multiple role as provider of watershed, wildlife, and recreation. The chief forester's visit left a strong impact. Soon thereafter, a small group of conservation-minded patricians formed the Forestry Association of Vermont, an organization that sought, among other things, to reconcile the interests of forest conservationists and commercial woodsmen, and to push the idea that scientific management of forests could serve the interests of both groups.

The belief that part of the conservation solution must lie in the public ownership and management of land also gained support. Battell and a few others, less optimistic than many of their "forestry movement" colleagues that private and corporate owners could lead the conservation movement, began making grants of land to the state. In 1911, Battell made a public gift of one thousand acres, including the summit of Camel's Hump Mountain (he inserted a stipulation for the Camel's Hump tract that it be used as a public park forever and that "no growing trees" could be cut in it except for the purpose of building roads).[49] At his death in 1915 he left to Middlebury College approximately thirty thousand forested acres along the Green Mountains in Fayston, Warren, Granville, Ripton, and Hancock—land that in the 1930s became foundation blocks in Vermont's present-day state forest and Green Mountain National Forest. (In an earlier gift of a similar nature, Mount Mansfield's two largest landowners gave to the University of Vermont in the 1850s all of that mountain's area above timberline, accompanied by restrictions on commercial development).

Battell's gifts, although the largest, did not represent the first of the state's acquisitions. In 1909 the Board of Agriculture and Forestry approved the purchase of a 450-acre tract in Plainfield known as Old Goshen Gore. Subsequently, Charles Downer of Sharon made the first gift of land for a state forest—340 acres in Sharon. In 1910 Peru lumber mill owner and preservation-oriented philanthropist Marshall Hapgood, who, like Battell, had concluded that only government action could hold back forest devastation, gave the summit of Bromley Mountain and the adjacent mountain range to the state. Hapgood, who admired Theodore Roosevelt and liked to think of himself as "Vermont's rugged reformer,"[50] stipulated in his gift that no tree should ever be cut on the mountain's one-hundred-acre summit. Hapgood's and Battell's grants led Vermont officials to begin exploring the prospects for establishment of a state forest system.

The state's first formal step toward accepting a management role over Vermont's forests came in 1904 with the enactment of legislation, drafted by the Forestry Association, authorizing the governor to appoint a member from the Board of Agriculture to serve as Commissioner of Forestry, and to set up a fire protection program in cooperation with local selectmen. Additional legislation in 1906, backed by Professor Jones, created a state nursery for research and production of forest seedlings with an annual appropriation of $500. Two years later, following the urgings of Governors Fletcher Proctor and George H. Prouty, both friends of the forestry movement, the legislature replaced the Board of Agriculture with a Board of Agriculture and Forestry. Prouty, whose family in Newport owned one of New England's largest lumber firms—though operating primarily in Canada—had only recently set aside his skepticism of the conservation movement.

The 1908 law also created the position of state forester, filled the next year by Austin F. Hawes, a graduate of Yale University's Forestry School. Hawes focused his work primarily in three areas: expansion of the state's holdings, providing advice on forest management to loggers, and developing a reforestation program for public land. In 1910, he oversaw planting of a total of sixty-nine thousand trees. Budget constraints, however, limited his effectiveness, and timber industry attitudes remained a problem. Hawes reported that the International Paper Company, with its vast forest holdings in Vermont, "did not even care to make a bluff at practicing Forestry," and that the company's superintendent of forests consistently "worked against me."[51]

In 1912, Governor Fletcher warned the legislature that "our forests by reason of mismanagement are ... rapidly ... disappearing. ... If we continue our present method or lack of method" in dealing with Vermont's forests, "we shall, in another fifty years, have few forests on which to place value."[52] At Fletcher's urgings, the legislature for the first time established an appropriation, amounting to $7,500, "to purchase lands in the name of the state, to be held, protected and administered as state forests," thus providing a name for the disparate land parcels the state had acquired. The bill also charged the new forest service with setting up a "reforesting" program on the state lands.[53] In that year, Vermont's State Forest included seven areas totaling less than three thousand acres; by 1920, the amount had climbed to thirteen areas totaling 20,950 acres. Finally in 1923, Vermont set up a separate Forest Service. Over the next decade, forest conservation gradually matured from a "movement" and became "an accepted institution, often regarded by woodsmen as an inconvenience, sometimes disregarded entirely, but the message of woodland preservation had been put across."[54]

Kathleen Norris, Catherine Robbins, and Hilda M. Kurth became the first women to hike the entire length of the Long Trail, September 1927. *Vermont Historical Society.*

Before its demise, around 1916, the Forestry Association along with many of the state's most prominent men joined in the efforts of James P. Taylor, then associate principal of Vermont Academy at Saxtons River, to organize the Green Mountain Club. Taylor, committed to making "the Vermont mountains play a larger part in the life of the people," worried that of all the state's mountains, only eight possessed trails to the summit. "Should the Green Mountain Range continue to be sacrosanct to the spirits of the first 'Green Mountain Boys,' and to hedgehogs, and untouchable to everybody else?" he asked. In fact, Taylor's claim that Vermont's mountains lacked hiking trails was an exaggeration. Laura and Guy Waterman, in their research on the history of hiking in the northeast United States, identify almost forty Vermont mountains possessing trails at that time.[55]

Taylor formed his new organization in 1910 and set it the task of constructing the Long Trail, a well-marked path that would open the Green Mountains to hikers and travelers. Battell, who had built a buckboard road up Mount Abraham in 1899 and a trail along the ridge of Lincoln Mountain, boosted the Long Trail project by allowing the Green Mountain Club to locate its new footpath over Lincoln Mountain and through his vast wilderness holdings north to Camel's Hump. By 1931, the Long Trail traversed the entire state, 270 miles, from the Massachusetts line to the

Canadian border, making Vermont the only state with such a footpath.[56]

Despite the activity embodied in Vermont's progressive era, Joseph A. DeBoer in 1905 accurately depicted the experience of large numbers of Green Mountain citizens when he claimed that the state, as it moved forward, made "haste slowly." In fact, the first years of the new century brought only modest shifts and changes for many Vermonters, altering their lives in small ways, if at all. The role of state government in these shifts—and the impact on cherished traditions of independence, self-reliance, and "local control"—drew considerable discussion, nevertheless. Farmers, who in the opinion of many remained the most authentic expression of the state's mind, were sensibly ambivalent in this dialogue, if a modest little volume entitled *The Gentleman from Hayville* was to be trusted to represent "the farmer's voice." Published in 1909 by the *Rutland Herald*, the book was the work of *Herald* editor, H. L. Hindley. During the 1908–1909 legislative session Hindley kept a whimsical, humorous diary in which he wrote sketches purportedly authored by a bemused farmer-lawmaker, communicating the Vermont farmer's perspective on the pressing public issues of the day. It sold widely.[57]

In his "diary," the apocryphal "new member" of the legislature from "Hayville" held forth on issues that supposedly most riled the small farmer. For example, the Hayville lawmaker opposed a bill before the legislature creating the position of State Forester, declaring that he "Hain't a going to have no expert poking round my wood lots and telling me what I can't do." The legislator applauded the death of a bill that would have prescribed "just how big we shall pack our apples, top or bottom the barrel." He added that "Down our way we consider that a mans own personal business." As for the proposed enactment of a licensing fee for deer hunters, he opposed it too, observing it was a "funny thing if we got to keep them deer around the place for a year and then pay to go out and shoot 'em."[58] (The first legal restrictions on the hunting of deer had been established in Vermont as early as 1779, and on fishing in 1819.)

The Hayville "gentleman's" jottings exposed the wide gap of distrust that existed between the state's agricultural communities and its industrial workers. Explaining why he joined with other "farmers" to defeat a proposed employers' liability bill, he wrote, "it was [caused by] them labor union men and if they's one class of critters I despise, its them strikers that slugg honest workmen and burns bridges and knocks streetcars off the track. It's about time us members let them labor men understand they . . . don't cut no figure up here to the legislature."[59]

Although this rural "legislator" opposed state regulation in many arenas, he along with many Vermont farmers welcomed its beneficent reach in others, revealing the prevailing ambivalence among farmers about the expanded uses of state power. For example, he eagerly supported bills to regulate the service provided by telephone companies: "Every sence the New England refused to connect us with Boston, New York and Hancock, I ben in favor of a law to make them do it." As for automobiles, he also favored regulation: "I'm in favor of separate highways for them machines any way. . . . Make 'em keep off the trunk lines and then post the branch roads and gess we'd have them autos where we want 'em." And he enthusiastically supported a bill establishing a bounty for the killing of bobcats: "Them pesky critters does more harm than a bear. They kill young deer, lambs, poltry and hain't got no objection to carrying off a bob veal calf. So long as we got to have a [state budget] deficit any way, us farmers reckoned we might as well vote for a little protection." For all his posture of independence and self-sufficiency, the Hayville gentleman seemingly epitomized the beleaguered turn-of-the-century Vermont farmer, whose eyes focused pragmatically on economic viability.[60]

Certainly the continuing trends in Vermont of expanded state government and reduced local control had been partly driven by the rural communities' increasing need for help in providing basic local services such as schools and roads, and the consequent need for more efficient administrative processes. However, legislators in the century's first two decades were also responding to the principal progressive pressures of that national era of reform, in increased state promotion of citizens' health, morality, and welfare, and in protecting the public interest from some of the most destructive effects of large irresponsible private interests. In doing so, Vermont state government gradually took on expanded roles as supervisor of election processes; owner, custodian, and model conservator of forest land; nurturer of the state's fish and deer; regulator of roadway travel; administrator of public school education; protector of women and children in the workplace; and guarantor of compensation for workplace injuries for the state's industrial employees. It was a period of unusual accomplishment that, according to historian Lorenzo D'Agostino, writing thirty years later, included enactment of "the most important public welfare legislation in the

State's history."[61] And despite their protests, the Hayville farmer and his hillside neighbors found much to embrace in the era's record.

Infrastructure of Modernity

Additional alterations crept into the lives of many Vermonters in these years through piecemeal application of modern technology. The automobile occupied the vanguard of these changes, but it was an innovation that required time getting used to. In fact, some Vermont residents who had fought to protect the state's forested hills from "greedy loggers" viewed the automobile as an equally greedy menace to the state's horses, the preservation of which was now deemed threatened.

Joseph Battell was one of the auto skeptics. Battell loved horses as much as he loved trees and this affection led him to become a leading breeder of the famous Vermont Morgan horse, a strain that at the turn of the century stood at the brink of extinction. He spent several years and a considerable amount of money locating as many Morgan horse pedigrees as possible, which he compiled and published as the *Morgan Horse Register*, a three-volume work, the first of which appeared in 1894. In 1907, he made a gift of his four-hundred-acre Bread Loaf Morgan horse stock farm in Weybridge township to the United States, in exchange for a government commitment to continue his work on the perpetuation and improvement of the breed.

Battell's protective concern for horses put him in the forefront of the short-lived but intense struggle over public policy concerning automobiles that, for a few years after the turn of the century, became one of the state's most heated controversies. At issue was whether, or how, to accommodate the automobile, because when occupying the open road the new vehicles left little room for horse-and-rider, or horses hitched to wagons or sleighs. The nation's first automobile manufacturing company had opened its doors in 1895; by 1899 the "horseless carriage" arrived in Rutland and, the next year, in Woodstock. In 1903 an eccentric Burlington physician, Horatio Nelson Jackson, contributed to the invention's growing popularity by becoming the first person to cross the United States in an automobile, driving from San Francisco to New York City in two months and nine days.

As the number of noisy, fast-moving new machines increased in the state, so did roadway confrontations. Concern for horse-and-rider safety, especially on Vermont's narrow mountain passes and rural back roads, led to passage in 1902 of the state's first legislation specifically restricting the operation of a motor vehicle. This horse-friendly enactment warned automobile drivers to exercise "every reasonable precaution" necessary "to prevent the frightening of . . . horse or horses, and to insure the safety and protection of any person riding or driving the same." The bill went on to set speed limits for autos at fifteen miles per hour outside town limits and six miles per hour in towns and villages.[62] In 1904 the legislature enacted the first law requiring registration of motor vehicles and a license for their use.

Battell and other implacable antiautomobilists deemed such gestures at regulation drastically inadequate. Even when governor Charles T. Bell and several legislators suggested restricting automobiles to a few trunk-line roads, Battell voiced skepticism that the "death wagons," as he called them, could legitimately use *any* existing public roadway. "Let the owners of the highway dragons build their own roads," he argued in 1906; "It is impossible that highways can be used with safety and comfort by the two methods of travel." The automobilists, he asserted, "should be compelled to use roads constructed exclusively for their machines. They could be run parallel to the public highways but certainly not nearer than four rods."[63] As evidence of the auto's menace, Battell launched a project to collect stories from across the northeastern United States of automobile-related violence, which he reprinted in his Middlebury newspaper. Perhaps as further confirmation of Battell's assertions of their dangerous unpredictability, the first fatal auto accident in Vermont actually occurred not on a road at all, but in a pasture, when, in 1910, Albert J. Kinneson, of Brookfield, lost control of his vehicle while driving through a farmer's field and crashed into a barn.

Although Battell's was the dominant Vermont voice in a short-lived chorus of similar voices nationally, he was no more content merely to talk on this issue than on forest conservation. In 1910, while serving in the legislature, he introduced a bill that would have prohibited automobiles from using the busy Hancock-Ripton road that led past his Bread Loaf Inn. He also briefly took the law into his own hands by placing barriers on the road and, later, by scattering materials on this road's surface that made the thoroughfare hazardous to a car's passage. Reacting to such provocation, the legislature made it a violation of state law to "cause to be placed upon any highway tacks, nails, wire, scrap metal, glass, crockery, or other substance injurious to the tires of vehicles."[64]

Battell's death in 1915, at age seventy-six, ended his long antiauto war in behalf of the farmer and the farmer's horse. (Ironically, a motor-driven hearse delivered his coffin to the cemetery.) By then he had already lost the fight. In 1906, only 373 motor vehicles were registered in the state. But in 1913, after Henry Ford had begun producing his relatively inexpensive Model T, Burlington, Rutland, St. Johnsbury, and Brattleboro each had more than two hundred citizens with registered automobiles. In 1920, one of every four Vermont farmers had become an automobile owner. By 1930, with secondhand farm trucks available for the modest price of $35, the ratio had increased to two out of three. (Numerous farms, nevertheless, continued to rely on oxen for field work; in 1930, a total of 657 of these animals were reported in the state.) Certainly, at an early point most farmers in Vermont, as elsewhere, realized that the motorcar might not only offer certain advantages in getting goods to market, but also by breaking down isolation and bringing urban amenities within their reach, could contribute significantly to making farm life more attractive.

The automobile's emergence, meanwhile, placed renewed emphasis on the importance of good roads. In 1916, with the number of autos on the nation's roadways multiplying, Congress passed the Federal Aid Road Act. Vermont quickly embraced the requisite federal guidelines by organizing a state highway system, which qualified for one of the first federal grants—to be matched by a state grant—under the program. The state's roads nevertheless remained inadequate, with mostly dirt or gravel surfaces, often deeply rutted, that became quagmires when snow melted, and nearly impassable from March to June each year. These circumstances, combined with the inexperience of drivers and scarcity of traffic laws, ensured that motor vehicle travel would continue to be a precarious enterprise. As bleak evidence, *The Vermonter* reported that in the year 1921, cars in the state collided with 51 cows, 269 teams of horses, 139 dogs, 15 hogs, 1 sheep, 27 trains, 27 trolley cars, and 184 pedestrians.[65]

The automobile brought not only new attention to the state's inadequate roadways but also changes in the physical appearance of towns. As horse-and-buggy transportation gradually disappeared from the landscape, so did the services of the town blacksmith shop begin to slacken. Gas stations, overnight lodging facilities, and billboards emerged to compete for space alongside roadways. Communities cleaned up streets and buildings' facades in hopes of attracting the increased flow of auto tourists. The commercial centers of towns gradually shifted away from the vicinity of the railroad to the main auto thoroughfares. In 1911, state government hastened the pace of these developments by creating a Bureau of Publicity to promote tourism. The new vehicles also made easier the process of school consolidation and interdenominational cooperation of churches in villages with declining populations. As with railroads before them, automobiles gradually began reconfiguring the face of the state.

Other transforming developments paralleled the auto's rise. The first two decades of the century brought the age of the trolley to Vermont's larger towns. This electrically powered form of local mass transportation became available for a number of years to citizens in Burlington, Rutland, Bennington, Barre, Montpelier, Bellows Falls, Springfield, Waterbury, Stowe, and Brattleboro. Burlington established the state's first electrified street trolley in 1887. The Rutland Street Railway Company made its debut in 1894, replacing a horse-drawn railway in operation since 1867. In 1906, the company extended service beyond the town to Castleton, Lake Bomoseen, Fair Haven, and Poultney, thus becoming the "real colossus of Vermont's electric railways." At its peak in 1913, the Rutland trolleys carried over three million passengers on their thirty-five miles of track.[66]

The trolleys, like the autos, had their opponents, who claimed that while enhancing travel efficiency, they added congestion, noise, or worse. The English author Rudyard Kipling, who for a number of years resided

The horse-and-buggy met the trolley at a busy downtown Barre intersection in the early years of the twentieth century. *Courtesy of Aldrich Public Library, Barre, Vermont.*

Erecting telephone poles in the White River Valley, c. 1905. From *The Vermonter* (December 1906).

in Dummerston, protested the trolley construction in nearby Brattleboro with all the fervor of the antiautomobilists. The trolley line, he charged, "permanently disfigures streets already proven to be inadequate to any extra strain of traffic; . . . wholly destroys the beauty for which Brattleboro is so greatly famous; . . . enormously increases the risk of fires, at the same time adding to the perils of extinguishing them; and . . . in every city of the Union has invariably been followed by the violent death or mutilation of human beings."[67] When the trolleys began their decline in the early 1920s, the cause was not the persuasiveness of critics such as Kipling but competition from the ubiquitous automobile.

Unlike trolleys and autos, some changes of the era appeared more unambiguously constructive to Vermonters. In the 1890s, the United States Post Office Department inaugurated the free delivery of rural mail in horse-drawn postal wagons, and by 1903 the service had reached the Green Mountains. Also, early in the new century telephone lines appeared along village roads after having first established a foothold in several larger towns in the 1870s and 1880s. St. Johnsbury acquired the state's first telephones when on July 20, 1877, a line was strung from a drugstore operated by C. C. Bingham to his house. Montpelier opened a telephone exchange in the winter of 1880–1881; Brattleboro in 1881; Dorset and Manchester in 1883. The Weathersfield Telephone Company organized in 1905. By 1930, most of the houses in tiny Peacham had been wired for telephone service, as had 60 percent of the state's farms.

During the 1880s, electric light companies, relying on hydroelectric power, had begun delivering public lighting to Vermont's largest towns. Montpelier hung its first lights in 1886, about the same time that a power company in Burlington organized to distribute lighting power to a two-mile circuit from a hydro-generation plant at Winooski Falls. By 1890, thirteen Vermont communities possessed electrical hookups, powering streetlights and home conveniences; by 1900 the number had climbed to forty-five and increased rapidly thereafter.

In the first decade of the twentieth century electricity gradually began reaching beyond the towns into the countryside, making possible fundamental alterations in the lives of rural Vermonters. The farmer and his wife might now replace the less luminous, more dangerous kerosene lamp with the incandescent light bulb in house and barn. Electricity might now begin to ease their basic chores of hauling water, feeding the animals, and transporting milk and other crops. A dairyman and his wife owning twenty cows and spending two hours milking them by hand might now anticipate acquiring one of the newly invented electric milking machines. And electric refrigeration could gradually begin replacing ice as a means of keeping the farmer's milk from spoiling, a shift that signaled the beginning of the end of the time-consuming and laborious annual cycle of tasks that included cutting the ice at the nearby pond, packing it in sawdust, and hauling it to storage, with its requirement of more-or-less continuous "tending" until needed.

The arrival of electrical power promised changes in the farm family's household chores, as well. An electrical hookup might eventually make possible the acquisition of such drudgery-relieving amenities as washing machines (relieving hours of hot and backbreaking, monotonous hand labor); electric irons (replacing the hefty flatiron that required continual reheating); and cook stoves (eliminating the tasks of hauling wood or coal, tending an uneven fire, and perpetual ash clean-up). Although electric service made work easier, an ironic long-term impact of such "labor-saving" devices as washing machines and vacuum cleaners for some women was a "raising of the bar" in household maintenance, resulting in new forms of domestic drudgery and scant gains in free time. In addition, some chores heretofore done by helpers or those outside the home now fell exclusively to the farm wife.[68]

By 1930, too, a majority of Vermont farms, some of them through the application of electricity, had acquired running water, and almost one fourth of farmhouses enjoyed water piped to bathrooms. Indoor plumbing brought an end to the daily ordeal of hauling large amounts of water from a stream or well for cooking uses, baths, laundry, dishwashing, and chamber pots, and then hauling the wastewater back outdoors when these activities were completed. The spread of electricity to the countryside, however, was slow; by 1920 only one in ten Vermont farmers had acquired electricity, many initially for lights only. By 1930, 30 percent of farms possessed hookups, a rate well above the national average of 13 percent but last among New England states.

An unintended casualty of the era's technological advances was a widely popular annual event on the social schedule of many Vermont communities known as Chautauqua Week. Staged usually in July or August in many parts of the United States in the early twentieth century by troupes of traveling or "circuit" performers, the Chautauqua visits offered a mix of entertainment and "improvement" presentations produced under a circus tent in an open field or on the local school grounds.

For most audience members, the programs provided a level of intellectual stimulation and social excitement unavailable at local church fairs, drama clubs, and town hall dances. A young Chautauqua enthusiast, Dorothy C. Walter, of Lyndonville, described the "Week" in her town during August 1915, in a letter to a friend. She excitedly characterized herself as "just like all the rest of the people in Lyndonville, Orleans, Hardwick, and other towns that have been having the meetings; I can't talk of anything else!" The line-up at Lyndonville included a singer performing selections from *The Barber of Seville;* instrumentalists playing the banjo, xylophone, cornet, and piano; an Italian band; and a professor from the University of Pennsylvania who delivered a lecture on "ethics" ("really it was on selfishness").

Other events involved a debate on the merits of woman suffrage; an antiwar lecture (from a woman whose announced topic had been about birds); and a lecture "on the Mormon kingdom of today" that held the "large audience breathless through several hours." The presentation of *Much Ado About Nothing* before "a large and enthusiastic crowd" provided another highlight for Walter. She wrote, "they do not make any attempt at scenery but play the plays as Shakespeare meant them to be played, with no breaks at all. They have money to put into costumes on account of not lavishing it on scenery. The best of it is that they are all good. They don't try to have stars as so many companies do."

With her sister, Walter attended "every afternoon and evening for six days and once Sunday morning." She noticed in the audience "folks whom you wouldn't expect to be interested in the best music and lectures." "That pleases me," noted Walter, daughter of Lyndonville's newspaper editor, "for it means that the Chautauqua idea is working out as it is advertised to do and as it ought to do to be truly democratic. It ought to please those artists to know that one's hired hand and one's French neighbors recognize a good thing when they hear it."[69]

By the 1920s, the Chautauqua circuit faced increasing competition for its village and rural audiences from other forms of entertainment. Several towns acquired motion picture theaters in the 1910s, and by the 1920s residents in larger communities had the choice of three or more movie theaters, with an admission cost of no more than ten or fifteen cents. In 1930, the Flynn Theater opened in Burlington as the first theater in New England built specifically for the presentation of movies with sound. A study of Orleans and Rutland counties in 1931 reported "ten theatres conducting movie shows daily or at least four times a week." Chautauqua courses, in contrast, had been offered in only three communities in those two counties during the previous year.[70] The proliferation of radio receivers and automobile ownership likely further diverted one-time Chautauqua enthusiasts, so that by the early 1930s the era of the circuit Chautauqua had closed.

Despite such losses, the arrival of automobiles, electrical power, trolleys, telephone service, Rural Free Delivery, labor-saving devices, and increasing access to home radio sets and motion picture theaters contributed to making the lives of many Vermonters less hard and more interesting. By lifting some of the workload and isolation of the family farm, lessening transportation difficulties, easing the means of communication between rural households, and opening village life to further outside influences, the first years of the new century became, for many Vermonters, a time of broadening possibilities and rising expectations.

Vermont and World War I

When war came to Europe in August 1914, most Vermonters either took scant notice or rejoiced that the United States remained uninvolved. By spring 1917, however, American participation loomed as a near certainty, and many in the state favored intervention, influenced, as were most Americans, by two and a half years of pro-British newspaper coverage and German submarine attacks on American ships. On March 27, Governor

Horace F. Graham, anticipating President Wilson's April 2 request to Congress for a declaration of war, delivered his own "war message" before a joint session of the legislature and a packed gallery. Embracing the coming war, Graham urged each Vermonter to "light upon the alter of his heart the divine fire of patriotism and keep it ever burning; and then repeat these words: 'Our country, may she always be in the right; but our country, right or wrong.'" The speech brought flag-waving legislators to their feet, and the gallery audience broke into a spontaneous singing of the "Star Spangled Banner," followed by "America the Beautiful." Four days later, on March 31, Graham signed a "war-purposes" bill in which the legislature appropriated one million dollars to equip and supply the Vermont National Guard and authorized borrowing three million dollars more in support of military forces the state might have to provide. This bullish action drew brief national notoriety to the Green Mountain State for its having declared war on the Central Powers before the United States.[71]

As they did in 1861 and 1898, Vermonters quickly embraced the war, many of them viewing it along with most Americans more as a great moral crusade than a matter of national self-defense. Reflecting public opinion in Vermont, a Methodist minister in Windsor declared that the American soldier would be fighting for a "holy and righteous" cause, and that consequently "God will give him victory."[72] Voluntary enlistments in the state proved so numerous that few slots required filling in the initial round of draft calls. They did not fight as discrete Vermont units, as in previous wars, and most of the enlistees ended up in the 26th Yankee Division and the 101st Ammunition Train. Eventually, approximately fifteen thousand Vermont men served in the military during the eighteen months of United States participation (one for every seven men between the ages of nineteen and fifty); more than half saw duty abroad, and 612 lost their lives from battle wounds or disease.

In April 1917, Fort Ethan Allen, the state's only United States military post, rapidly became transformed into a training camp for recruits. Congress had authorized the creation of the base in 1892, at the urging of Redfield Proctor, whom President Benjamin Harrison had rewarded with appointment as secretary of war, and the fort opened two years later on six hundred acres of land in the towns of Essex and Colchester. During the Spanish-American War and the 1916 border skirmish with Mexico, Vermont's regiments had used the fort and the nearby Vermont National Guard campground as mobilization points for departing the state. Other notable troops garrisoned there in its brief history included an African-American unit, known as the "Buffalo Soldiers," from 1909 to 1913.[73] In 1917, Fort Ethan Allen received its most important assignment, and during the eighteen months of United States involvement in World War I, approximately six thousand men received training there.

Elsewhere on Vermont's home front, citizens threw themselves into the struggle. Eager contributors oversubscribed three federal Liberty Loan drives to help pay for war expenditures; schoolboys and schoolgirls, estimated at approximately thirty thousand, enrolled in a Green Mountain Guard to increase food production and conservation; and women, numbering in the thousands, engaged in food production programs and Red Cross knitting and sewing projects. The Vermont Committee of Public Safety, a group of public-spirited businessmen appointed by the governor, conducted campaigns in every township in the state aimed at whipping up patriotic fervor against the "Prussian" foe. Governor Graham, who had earlier drawn attention by advocating warrantless arrests of any individual suspected of aiding the enemy, stoked patriotic emotions further by publicly disagreeing with President Wilson's request to the nation that, during prosecution of the war, Americans should view as the enemy the German leadership, not the German people.

Legislators embraced the war spirit by enacting some of the most severe anti-treason measures in the nation. The legislation authorized Graham's warrantless arrests and once again imposed the death penalty for persons convicted of attempts to kill or injure individuals or destroy property in wartime.[74] Town governments also acted on security concerns. In February 1917, after President Wilson broke off diplomatic relations with Germany, residents of the White River Junction area began posting armed guards at the town's two railroad bridges and halted pedestrian traffic, apparently seeking to foil possible attempts at sabotage by German agents.

Vermonters who disagreed with Wilson's intervention decision risked becoming targets of persecution. Among the state's war dissenters, Clarence Waldron, a Baptist minister in Windsor, attracted the most notoriety. On December 21, 1917, a federal prosecutor accused Waldron (who possessed both pacifist convictions and a German-born mother-in-law) of violating the 1917 Espionage Act when the minister circulated views to his parishioners that purportedly intended to "prevent young men from performing their duty" under the recently enacted U.S. Selective Service law. In various statements, Waldron had made clear to his congregation, including its military-age young men, that he stood "opposed to the war and to all other wars"; but he had also denounced the Kaiser and told the young men of his church to "do their duty as they saw it."

A Brattleboro jury failed to reach a verdict in the case in January 1918. In a second trial held in Burlington in March, however, the jury found the Baptist minister guilty, and he received a fifteen-year sentence in a federal prison in Atlanta, Georgia. United States Attorney General Thomas W. Gregory attracted national attention to the Burlington verdict, calling it "an effective deterrent against a very dangerous type of antiwar propaganda." It was the nation's first important case involving religious opposition to the war, and Waldron's punishment was the most severe handed down since the Espionage Act's enactment. (After the war, President Wilson commuted Waldron's sentence, enabling him to be released from federal prison in April 1919.)[75]

The patriotic and anti-German spirit also altered other Vermonters' lives during the war. Two days after Waldron's conviction, a creamery worker in Holland named Harold Mackley, a "native born person of German descent," also received fifteen years in a federal prison for making "seditious statements." A professor of German at the University of Vermont, Anton Hermann Appelmann, resigned his faculty post under pressure; and in Wilmington, a public school student who refused to salute the American flag was driven from the community, along with his parents. A handful of Protestant ministers who shared Waldron's pacifist beliefs left their pastorates.

In the heated wartime atmosphere, even the appearance of a German connection caused trouble. To clarify its own patriotic sentiments, the village of West Berlin changed its name and post office, in 1918, to Riverton. A Vermont-initiated rumor reached as far as Washington, D.C., resulting in the labeling of Frazier Metzger (the Progressive Party candidate for governor in 1912) as a "German spy" by the United States Justice Department based on no evidence other than his name. Governor Graham interceded to squelch the rumor.

Wartime emotions carried over to the postwar years. Less than six months after the armistice, against the backdrop of social unrest in Europe, a slumping state and national economy, and numerous domestic labor strikes, U.S. Attorney General A. Mitchell Palmer warned of a "Red Threat" across America. Prominent Vermonters shared Palmer's concern. John T. Cushing, of St. Albans, editor of an official history of Vermont's part in the war, cited Palmer's report of "increasingly dangerous radical activities." Cushing concluded that radicals threatened the "utter destruction of the whole social fabric upon which rests the safety of the advancement of humanity." Governor Graham made clear who he believed sought "revolutionary overturning of order" by specifically calling on the "laboring men of Vermont" to enlist in the antirevolutionary cause. Not wanting to take any chances, Montpelier lawmakers in 1919 swung into action against the possible postwar menace, enacting a vaguely worded bill promising three years imprisonment for individuals involved in "the promotion of anarchy," and another bill mandating six months in jail for individuals displaying a red or black flag for political purposes, or any flag that contained an inscription "opposed to organized government, or sacrilegious in its nature, or opposed to public morals."[76]

Although legislators' fears of alien and labor subversion in the Green Mountains lacked credibility, many Vermont residents in the last months of the war and its immediate aftermath did confront a genuine mortal crisis. The great "Spanish Flu" epidemic—the terrible plague that swept the world in 1918—ravaged the state from September to November, and its effects lingered for many months afterward. Medical historians believe the virus struck first in a handful of cases at a military post in Kansas in March 1918. From there it spread to European fighting fronts and to ports around the world, assisted by the wartime conditions of crowding and high troop movement. By fall the malady reappeared in the United States with the returning soldiers, and it moved rapidly through New England and across the nation. More than half a million people died in the United States during the epidemic.

In Vermont, the "grippe," as residents sometimes called the sickness, hit the central part of the state hardest. One-fourth of all deaths occurred in Washington County, with Montpelier and Barre particularly hard hit. "Every stone shed, in fact every industrial and office plant in the city [Montpelier] has been hit by the epidemic," reported the *Montpelier Evening Argus* on September 27. By October 4, an estimated fourteen hundred cases had been diagnosed there. During the first week of October, Barre had two thousand reported cases. All available spaces in the town, including living rooms, back porches, garages, and icehouses, became storage spaces for corpses. The area's granite quarries, already slowed by a war-induced labor shortage, lacked enough healthy workers to stay open. The Republican Party canceled its state convention, and relatively unaffected towns banned visits from residents of communities hard hit by the disease. On October 4, the State Board of Health ordered the closing of public meeting places statewide and prohibited all public assemblies.[77]

By November, the epidemic's force had largely dissipated and the statewide ban on public meetings was rescinded. In Chittenden County, relieved residents greeted the ban's lifting with "an outbreak of drunkenness as people vigorously drank to their continued health."[78] On Armistice Day, November 11, Montpelier's citizens had recovered sufficiently to celebrate the war's end with a street parade. Three months later, the flu had almost disappeared from the state, leaving behind about fifty thousand cases of illness and more than seventeen hundred deaths, a total that far exceeded Green Mountain casualties in the European war. It would stand as the most severe death-causing natural disaster to hit Vermont in the twentieth century.

The flu outbreak exposed deficiencies in the state's health services that precipitated a number of changes. In 1919, the Vermont Conference of Social Work (formerly the Vermont Conference of Charities and Corrections) presided over the creation of the Vermont Children's Aid Society, a new statewide social welfare organization to serve the large number of needy children orphaned by the devastation. That same year, the legislature acted to strengthen the state's public health role by committing $10,000 for rural sanitation projects. Of most importance, the legislature abolished the town health officer, a position often not filled by a physician, and put in place a more centralized state system directed by the State Board of Health. The new structure organized Vermont into ten state-funded sanitary districts, each headed by a physician and supported by adequate staff competent to deal with public health threats. The legislation established Vermont as the first state to provide such rural health services.

These innovations also represented, however, a loss of power and independence by the towns, and by local physicians, with regard to public health. Guardians of town sovereignty fought back, as they did in the controversy over management centralization in public education. The 1923 legislature, as part of the so-called "back to the towns" effort of that year, repealed the appropriation for the 1919 act and reestablished the town health officer. The new legislation empowered town selectboards to nominate candidates for that office and to set and pay the officeholder's salary, but reserved approval of nominees to the discretion of the State Board of Health. In 1931, a citizens' research group acknowledged the influence of

An innovation of the Progressive Era, this traveling library wagon, accommodating three hundred books, was given to the state in 1922 by the Vermont Federation of Women's Clubs. *Vermont Historical Society.*

decentralizing pressures on the lawmakers' decision and concluded the 1919 "experiment" had been "too much ahead of public opinion."[79]

Politics in the Twenties

World War I and its aftermath narrowed and redirected Vermont's engagement with the progressive spirit. By 1918 most of the Bull Moose insurgents of 1912 and 1916 had returned to the Republican Party, which again enjoyed unchallenged statewide political dominion. In the 1920s, leadership gradually drifted back into familiar "old guard" hands, and the preceding two decades' concerns for political and economic reform receded from public discourse. What followed was a period of relative lethargy in public affairs that, despite the presence of such volatile issues as prohibition, woman's suffrage, and a surging Vermont version of the Ku Klux Klan, did not give way until the crisis of the 1927 flood and the Great Depression of the 1930s.

Republican political campaigns of the period seldom wavered beyond a skeletal agenda that headlined more efficient management, followed by calls for reduction of state spending. Ritual recognition was provided for some other issues: improvement of rural schools, expansion of hard-surfaced roads, eradication of bovine tuberculosis from the state's dairy herds, and promotion of agricultural products and tourism. The ongoing need for more government income made taxes a continuing issue, as well, but prior to the 1927 flood crisis the only impositions passed during the decade were a tax on the sale of gasoline in 1923 (the revenue to be used for highway construction) and a 1925 tax on intangibles that yielded disappointing revenue results.

One failed effort at increasing taxes brought attention to an important power shift underway within the legislature in these years. Rural towns continued to control the House of Representatives and to exercise political influence far out of proportion to their population through the generosity of the House's one-town, one-vote system. The composition of the state Senate, however, was undergoing change. After the 1915 direct primary law weakened the rural towns' power in the Senate, that body gradually drifted into alignment with urban business and commercial interests. The fate of an income tax bill in 1923, which the House of Representatives passed, demonstrated the shifting influence. Rural communities had hoped that enactment of the bill, the first attempt at adopting a state income tax, would ease the increasing pressure on local property tax assessments by creating a tax plan—similar to the late-nineteenth-century school and road programs—not based on town or county of residence. In 1923, however, the Senate, reflecting its emerging new constituency, rejected this attempt at equalizing the tax burden at the expense of the urban business centers, and the bill died.

Management efficiency was an issue the Old Guard and progressives alike could support. Governor Horace Graham (1917–1919) used his term to establish a Director of State Institutions and a Board of Control that he hoped would bring business-minded order to the various state agencies. In this spirit, in 1923, a progressive coalition of social reformers drawn from private charity work, child welfare, academe, and state government persuaded the legislature to create an encompassing new agency, the Vermont Department of Public Welfare. The new body took on the duties of the Board of Charities and Probation, the Director of State Institutions, the Vermont Sanitarium, and the Board of Supervisors of the Insane and of the Tuberculosis Hospitals. It also acquired supervision of all other indigent and dependent Vermonters in state care.[80]

The policy solidarity within the party—especially the focus on government reorganization—held, even for two governors, Percival Clement (1919–1921) and James Hartness (1921–1923), who won election as party mavericks, opposed by the state Republican establishment. Their back-to-back victories had other similarities. In gaining the Republican nomination (tantamount to election), both men demonstrated the opportunities for nonregular candidates that the new direct primary law made possible. The 1915 law that replaced the caucus-convention process allowed a mere plurality to determine the nomination. This proved ideal for men such as Hartness and Clement, both of whom possessed great wealth and a willingness to use it in the search for votes. Clement, whose 1918 gubernatorial victory came after losing bids for the governorship in 1902, 1906, and 1914, used a generous purse, statewide contacts, and years of political visibility to finally overcome Proctor organizational strength. He won nomination with a bare plurality, attracting 12,060 primary votes of a total 32,592 cast.

Hartness, a self-educated Springfield engineer, inventor, and machine-tool businessman, had never participated in politics even at the grassroots level, prior to his 1920 bid. Spending money to gain voter familiarity, sell his candidacy, and overcome his substantial shortcomings as a public speaker, became crucial for his success. His campaign introduced to Vermont the joining of traditional electoral politics with the sophisticated techniques of modern advertising. Hartness showered voters with pamphlets, buttons, and cards, and his supporters plastered roadside trees and fence posts across the state with posters bearing his likeness. In the last weeks of the campaign he broke additional new ground by releasing a movie, "The New Era," depicting his industrial accomplishments. He made special efforts to reach out to women voting for the first time since ratification of the nineteenth amendment to the U.S. Constitution, and to organized labor. Hartness won the Republican primary, attracting 23,733 votes after spending an unprecedented $38,560 on his campaign, compared to a combined vote of 37,105 (and spending total of $4,377) by his three opponents.

Outsiders as candidates, these two idiosyncratic and strong-minded men in office were able to accomplish little, and each left the governorship frustrated and disappointed by the experience. Hartness was especially disconsolate. He did accomplish a reorganization of the highway department as part of his effort at greater government efficiency, and he gained an increased budget for the state development office. However, legislators and Vermonters in general gave scant backing to his other exertions in behalf of industrial development. More than other Republican gubernatorial candidates of the era, he had emphasized the importance of robust industrial growth and new industrial job creation, yet in office those themes—and most of his other ideas—made little headway. One of his critics described him as naive and ill prepared for his job, "wholly unaccustomed to the requirements of politics and legislation."[81] Some, more bluntly, likened him to a company chief executive officer who expected the legislature to follow his orders. A sympathetic Hartness biographer, however, attributed his difficulties to "a strong political machine that would try to block any changes he tried to introduce," despite the common political ground he shared with the party on most issues.[82]

After the maverick interludes of Clement and Hartness, the Republican regulars reclaimed the governorship in the successive terms of Redfield Proctor (1923–1925) and Franklin S. Billings (1925–1927). Proctor, whose father (Redfield) and brother (Fletcher) had preceded him in the governorship, managed to push forward Hartness's management goals, eliminating Graham's Board of Control and establishing a series of departments with specific functions—Agriculture, Finance, Education, Public Health, and Highways—in a system administered directly by the governor. Again charges surfaced from dissatisfied Republicans that the party had come under "machine" control. One frustrated loyalist candidly lamented that the Party enjoyed "not too much active participation" at the grassroots, yet completely "dominated the state political scene."[83] Meanwhile, Vermont Democrats, widely viewed as the political home for immigrants, Roman Catholics, urban poor, and antiprohibitionists, continued to fare badly against the Republicans in general election match-ups.

Republicans' firm grip on Green Mountain politics did not loosen even after one of the state's worst political scandals. Shortly after Horace Graham vacated the governorship in 1919, he was indicted and convicted for acts of malfeasance that occurred during his lengthy tenure as state auditor of accounts (1902–1915). The ex-governor received a sentence of five-to-eight years in state prison for his misdeeds but managed to avoid jail when his successor, Percival Clement, pardoned him unconditionally shortly after sentencing. (In 1923, the town of Craftsbury sent him back to Montpelier as its elected state representative.) For many people the Graham scandal served as a reminder of the rarity of incidents of political corruption in Vermont's history. William Allen White, the confidante of Theodore Roosevelt and peripatetic progressive editor of the Emporia,

Kansas, *Gazette*, proposed an explanation for this northern New England phenomenon. "The point is," White offered, "that there are so few pennies in the state treasury that every Vermonter knows where every one of them is, all the time."[84]

The Republican Party's control in Vermont never seemed more triumphant than in the mid-1920s, when one of its own, Calvin Coolidge, occupied the presidency of the United States. Coolidge had left the state at age nineteen for Massachusetts, where he attended college and where his legal career and political fortunes later blossomed. At the time Coolidge became president he had never traveled outside the United States and seldom outside New England, but he had gone a considerable distance from his rural Vermont childhood. The British ambassador once commented about him, "I never saw a man . . . who looked less like the son of a farmer."[85] Nevertheless, during his six-year stay in the White House, Coolidge's upright, austere bearing and thrifty ways endeared him to many Americans as the idealized embodiment of his home state's character—an example of the value and strength of Vermont ways. In fact, the scene of Justice of the Peace John Coolidge swearing in his son as the nation's thirtieth president by the light of a lantern in Plymouth following Warren Harding's unexpected death in August 1923 became one of the iconic moments of Vermont history. Few state Republican regulars in those proud, exhilarating days wished to recall that only three years before, as Massachusetts governor, Coolidge had been the center of a short-lived presidential boomlet, and Vermont's Republican delegates had opted to support the candidacy not of their native son but of war hero General Leonard Wood.

The legislature's response to two controversial political issues shoved forward by the war demonstrated the political lethargy of Vermont in the 1920s. Both resulted in United States constitutional amendments—establishing national prohibition and woman suffrage—and ambivalent Vermont legislators failed, in both instances, to make a timely ratification. The prohibition question arrived on legislators' desks first. Liquor consumption, a potent issue in Vermont politics for many years, had surfaced most recently in Percival Clement's 1902 gubernatorial campaign and in the "local option" drive of 1903 that brought an end to fifty years of state prohibition. Ironically, Clement sat as governor in 1919 when the Eighteenth Amendment, mandating a nationwide end to the production, sale, importation, and consumption of intoxicating beverages, came before the Vermont legislature for ratification. He adamantly opposed confirming the amendment, describing it in his inaugural address as an issue of states' rights. The proposed amendment, he asserted, "abrogates certain powers of self-government, which the state has always retained, and deprives our citizens of time-honored rights."[86]

Vermonters held mixed views on the issue. Three years earlier, a state prohibition referendum had failed in every county except Orleans, suggesting popular contentment with local option; yet, only thirteen towns and cities actually voted to license liquor sales by 1918. When the legislature finally approved the vote on the Eighteenth Amendment, on January 29, 1919, national ratification had been completed thirteen days earlier.

Enforcement of Prohibition in the Green Mountains, as elsewhere in the nation, proved to be almost impossible. Congress enacted the strict Volstead Act (1919) to implement the Amendment and successive Vermont governors pledged to "faithfully execute" the law. However, violators remained active throughout the Prohibition Era. Large-scale smuggling activities along the Vermont-Canada border kept a steady flow of alcohol arriving from the north. Enterprising bootleggers simply overwhelmed United States Customs Service border patrols, utilizing boats and barges on Lake Champlain and Lake Memphremagog, speedy automobiles, railroad freight cars, and river vessels to bring contraband beer and hard liquor to Vermont cities and towns, and through Vermont into southern New England.

The smugglers—and home manufacturers—embraced daredevil strategies in their efforts. Between 1924 and 1930 a well-known East Montpelier rumrunner made regular nighttime trips to Montreal for loads of liquor, driving without lights on back roads, in an old Cadillac automobile buttressed with reinforced springs. For safety in emergencies on his two-hundred-mile round trip, he established hiding places every twenty-five miles or so, and even occasionally drove into roadside haystacks to elude pursuers. A group of bootleggers in Barre, using Packards and Cadillacs, also enjoyed considerable success "running" the thinly patrolled border. "We ran mostly ale," Frank Cardini later recalled; "we got it in Canada for five bucks a case and sold it here [Barre] for fifteen or twenty. You could load a lot of ale into those big crates we had. We kept five or six cars on the road at the time." His customers cut across local society: "We sold everybody in Barre and Montpelier from the poolroom crowd to the town big shots."[87] To elude a vigilant sheriff in the White River Junction vicinity, "runners" used a Cadillac touring sedan rigged with an elaborate device known as a "smoker." A driver could pull a cable located under the car's dashboard that released a thin stream of raw oil onto the vehicle's overheated manifold. The cloud of dark smoke thus created provided sufficient cover for the driver to escape from the pursuing authorities.[88]

As enforcement problems mounted through the decade, and support for Prohibition waned in Vermont and across the country, many citizens concluded that liquor's ills would not likely be solved by such methods. When repeal of the Eighteenth Amendment came in 1933, few Vermonters opposed the decision.[89]

Indecisive on Prohibition, the Vermont legislature acted no more forthrightly regarding the proposed Nineteenth Amendment granting suffrage to women. When suffrage surfaced as a national issue at war's end, it followed a twenty-year period in Vermont during which a friendlier attitude toward votes for women had gradually emerged. In that time, dedicated suffragists, despite lacking broad support from the state's women, and despite continued claims from Vermont men that "Nature" rendered females "unfit" for the "strenuous and nerve-racking burdens of political activity,"[90] had nevertheless persisted in petitioning for a voting rights bill in every legislative session. Small victories had come in legislation in 1880 and 1900, granting limited voting access in school district elections and the right to hold certain town offices. Another law, in 1917, allowed taxpaying women to vote in municipal elections. Although the 1917 initiative made Vermont the first New England state to take such a step, fourteen Western states had already granted women full, unrestricted voting rights.

Legislators nevertheless continued to turn back efforts at full suffrage until 1919, when a bill permitting women to vote in presidential elections finally passed both legislative houses. When it arrived on his desk, Governor Clement vetoed it, and the House of Representatives sustained his veto. Nationally the issue remained alive, energized by war-driven momentum, and on June 4, 1919, Congress passed the Nineteenth Amendment and sent it to the states for ratification.

Vermont women immediately requested the legislature to take up a state ratification bill. To do so required calling a special session and in April 1920 Clement received strong pressure to convene one. Prompt action would enable Vermont to provide the final state ratification needed to put the Amendment over the top. Governor Clement refused to act, however,

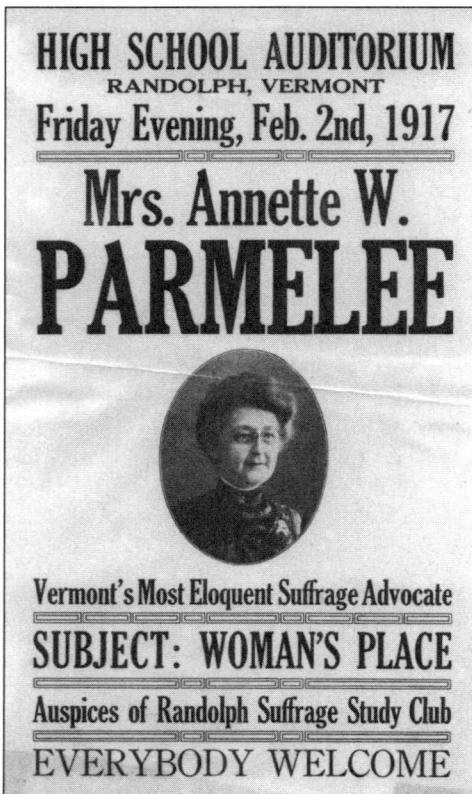

Broadside publicizing a 1917 woman's suffrage rally in Randolph. *Vermont Historical Society.*

convinced that women had strongly opposed his long crusade for local option liquor sales. When the General Assembly finally did give its formal endorsement to votes for women, on February 8, 1921, it came six months after Tennessee became the decisive thirty-sixth ratifying state and three months after Vermont women had cast their first presidential ballots.

The enfranchisement of women brought no dramatic changes to Vermont's political landscape, but the influence of the new voters quickly became visible. In the 1920 gubernatorial election, Clement's candidate lost in the Republican primary to James Hartness, a leading male voice in the state for ratification. Contemporary estimates gave Hartness about 75 percent of the ten thousand or more votes cast by women in the election, and in his 1921 inaugural address, he thanked them. "Women's coming into full equality in suffrage," Hartness declared, "bodes well for humanity."[91] In Northfield, female voters' presence led to alterations in the appearance of the community's town hall voting location. Local officials in 1920 removed the sawdust that customarily covered the floor to absorb tobacco juice, disallowed smoking in the building, and placed chairs along the walls to enable women voters to sit. According to the *Northfield News*, "female voters of the town cast their votes as if they had done the same for years."[92] The most substantive early change came the next year, when Edna L. Beard of Orange won a seat as the first female representative in the history of the Vermont legislature. In 1923, Beard set another precedent by becoming the first woman elected to the state senate.

A greater challenge to Vermont's postwar status quo than woman suffrage came from the brief foothold gained in the state by the Ku Klux Klan. The secret hate organization had initially formed in the South after the Civil War, and enjoyed a brief existence forwarding policies of white supremacy in relations with ex-slaves. In 1915, William J. Simon, an Alabama Baptist minister and organizer of fraternal organizations, revived the defunct group at a gathering at Stone Mountain, Georgia. By the early 1920s the Klan no longer restricted its animus to blacks, extending it now to all who lacked credentials as "one hundred percent Americans." Uneasy white Protestants across the country took notice, especially those harboring economic complaints, or fears and resentments of Catholics, immigrants, Jews, or "Reds." The organization thus found acceptance for a number of years in many sections of the country, including several communities in Vermont that contained sizeable Catholic populations.[93]

Estimates of Vermont members of the Klan ranged from ten thousand to fourteen thousand, but historian Kenneth Jackson doubts the total exceeded two thousand.[94] Klan organizers appeared in the state for the first time in spring 1922. A serious membership drive did not begin until 1924, however, organized out of the northern New England Klan headquarters located at Rochester, New Hampshire. The organizers came from other states, many from Indiana. They worked quietly at first, distributing literature, advertising in newspapers, and initiating members at secret meetings, with those in attendance sworn to secrecy. Admittance to these meetings often required the inspection of invitation cards. By the summer of 1924, after several Vermont towns had been canvassed and members enrolled, organizers began holding open meetings in fields and meadows where large groups could assemble under a huge burning cross, to hear speeches and initiate the new recruits. At these Vermont events Klan members wore white robes and hoods.

White-sheeted public gatherings, including occasional cross burnings, became familiar Vermont sights during the decade, primarily in railroad towns, whose populations generally contained larger-than-usual numbers of Catholics and immigrants. Washington County's first large outdoor Klan gathering occurred in 1924. A rally near Montpelier a year later drew almost ten thousand people, and a public "konklave" at the Lamoille County fairgrounds in Morrisville attracted five thousand men and women.

The Klan's presence kindled strong opposition. Several newspapers, including the *Rutland Herald*, editorially denounced the organization's gatherings and its leaders. The *Burlington Free Press* told readers their community needed the Klan as much as they needed a consuming plague and predicted that the hooded group would find the Green Mountains about as poor picking as "Mormon missionaries or Communist agitators."[95] A number of towns passed "anti-mask" ordinances. In 1923, however, the Vermont Senate killed a bill that would have prohibited the public wearing

of "masks and disguises," and in 1925 it failed to act on proposed legislation requiring secret associations to file their lists of officers and members with the secretary of state. Although reports of Klan-related physical violence were few, some rough incidents did occur. On Christmas Day 1927 in Northfield, for example, local Klansmen burned a fiery cross on a hill above the town and triggered a brawl with a crowd of Klan opponents.

Klan activities deeply divided many communities, sometimes with a stridency that influenced legal proceedings and cast doubt on the state's justice system. In Montpelier, officials charged two local men with burning a cross on the front steps of St. Augustine's Catholic Church on November 25, 1925. Their trial, which attracted a pack of unruly spectators to the courtroom, eventually ended without a decision. Deane C. Davis, of Barre, lawyer for one of the men and a future Vermont governor, explained the jury's inability to reach a verdict. According to Davis, within the Montpelier community the case had created "an awful lot of angry division"; "it took days to get a jury, because if you found anybody who said they had no opinions one way or the other about the Ku Klux Klan, he had to be a liar or living under a haystack. We finally ended up with six Catholics and six Protestants on the jury, and when the case was over we had a hung jury."[96]

A court case in Burlington attracted statewide attention. Three Klansmen stood trial for the theft of religious items from St. Mary's Catholic Church of the Immaculate Conception on August 9, 1924. As the three fled the

A Ku Klux Klan rally and picnic near Montpelier, July 4, 1927. *Vermont Historical Society.*

building, one of the men fired shots from a revolver. At the end of their trial, to the great relief of Burlington's agitated Catholic community, a jury convicted the men of grand larceny. Although the presiding judge sentenced the ringleader to a two-to-three-year prison term and the others to four-to-six months each, Governor Redfield Proctor pardoned the two followers after they had served less than sixty days, and Governor Franklin Billings later pardoned the ringleader after he had served less than a year.

By the last years of the decade, the Klan had gone into decline locally and nationally. Corruption charges against Klan officials in several Vermont communities undermined the movement in the Green Mountains, and scandal and corruption dogged national officers as well. Ultimately, however, its demise likely followed from its members' gradual realization that the hate group had no capability of delivering on its promise of a "pure" and "protestant" bastion, in Vermont or anywhere else.

Economic Malaise

The years 1900–1930 were a hard period for the Vermont economy. As the new century opened, farming remained the primary way of making a living, claiming 36.6 percent of the workforce. Agriculture nevertheless continued to be fraught with difficulties. The total number of farms in the state dropped steadily, falling from 33,000 in 1900 to 29,000 in 1920, and to 25,000 in 1930. The amount of acreage under till declined, as well, even though the size of farms increased as more prosperous farmers bought out less successful neighbors. By 1930, the isolated backwoods and hilltop farms, where poverty ran deepest, and where the economic base remained a combination of subsistence, barter, and scarce cash, had almost vanished from the landscape. In addition, by the end of this period Vermonters employed in agriculture had dropped to 27 percent of the workforce, second now to manufacturing with 28 percent.

Farmers who survived did so through dogged perseverance and a practical willingness to make adjustments to the market. Since the late nineteenth century, the more successful had turned to highly specialized agriculture, mainly the staples of butter and cheese, whose prices remained stable and which were easily distributed to distant markets by rail. Hill country hay fields and well-watered pasturelands were ideally suited to this kind of agriculture. Farmers with land not well adapted for dairying shifted to other specialties, particularly tree crops such as apples and maple products, high-grade seed potatoes, and poultry. Most numerous, however, were dairymen. In the last three decades of the nineteenth century the number of dairy cows in the state doubled and the 1900 census reported that half of farmers claimed dairying as their principal income source. In that year, Vermont led the nation in butter production.[97]

Despite such production, Vermont dairymen still found it difficult to compete profitably against the butter and cheese of Western farmers. In the years before World War I they began switching to highly perishable milk and cream, dairy products in growing demand in the rapidly expanding metropolitan markets of Boston and New York. These commodities, expensive to ship and easily spoiled, had the advantage of not being threatened by competition from the West. By 1905, railroads had established shipping stations for fluid milk at seven points in Vermont, and in the next fifteen years the Boston milk shed—the system of milk-gathering and shipping stations that serviced the Boston-area market—had enlarged to include all of Vermont.[98]

The war years 1914–1918 brought a brief boost in Vermont's farm income. Overseas food shipments caused new demand for wheat and increased prices for corn, oats, barley, and potatoes. Dairymen, with the aid of a war-emergency pricing system, managed to sustain favorable price levels throughout the war. By 1919, the total value of the state's agricultural crop, including its expanding dairy products sector, had risen significantly. In the war's aftermath, however, the demand for wheat and other products slackened and prices sagged faster than did those for industrial goods, putting many farmers in Vermont and across the country in a disadvantageous price squeeze, and contributing to the nation's slide, during 1920–1921, into the worst economic slump of the new century. The national agricultural downturn continued through the decade.

The shift to fluid milk by Vermont farmers persisted in the 1920s despite the agricultural difficulties. By 1928, two-thirds of the milk received in the Boston market came from Vermont dairy farms. The move to milk appeared so complete that one local observer concluded Vermont's farmers were now doing little "except buying a few cows and shipping their milk to Boston."[99] In 1930 Vermont had more cows per farm than any other state in the Union; almost 58 percent of its farms were classified as dairy farms; and dairy products accounted for about 65 percent of the total state farm income. The transition to dairying brought changes to the land. Alterations occurred in the physical appearance of farms as dairymen constructed larger, sturdier stables and barns to accommodate cattle and hay through the winter months, and added milk houses and silos for corn fodder. Vermont boasted 9,445 silos by 1921, one for every thirty cows.

Dairymen found that by entering the highly specialized fluid milk market, they moved into even greater dependence on outside forces. The costs associated with getting milk transported from the farm to the consumer represented a major continuing problem. The transportation dilemma had two parts. One challenge, especially in warm weather, centered on the daily expense and hazard of hauling the fluid milk by wagon to the distant railroad shipping station and its refrigerator milk trains without it souring along the way. (Not until the wider availability of autos and trucks and improved roadways in the late 1920s was this "initial haul" problem alleviated.)

The other problem grew out of issues relating to costs of rail transportation to the Boston and New York markets, pricing, and production planning. The expanding operations of city milk dealers had greatly stimulated production, especially after 1915. The power of the larger dealers, however, enabled them to dictate the price to consumers and the amount of return to producers. Boston milk prices consequently stayed low. These circumstances produced a brief unsuccessful "Boston Milk War" in 1910, initiated by New England farmer-members of the Boston Cooperative Milk Producers Company. In a further attempt to improve their bargaining position on prices and transportation rates with the dealers, dairymen in

Vermont, Massachusetts, and New Hampshire organized the New England Milk Producers' Association. By the beginning of the 1920s, this "collective bargaining" group boasted twenty thousand members (with 5,810 from Vermont), and controlled four-fifths of New England's milk production.[100]

Farmers and public officials who had consistently denounced labor unions and the collective action of Vermont's industrial workers now found themselves turning increasingly to collective methods in the service of their own practical needs. Dairyman-owned cooperative plants, such as the Cabot Farmers' Cooperative Creamery, which formed in 1919, offered the producers themselves the possibility of processing the milk and preparing it for market, an advantage they could use to gain price concessions and better working arrangements from Boston milk dealers. In 1920, desiring more local control than the New England Milk Producers' Association made available, a number of state cooperative creameries formed a federation, the Vermont Cooperative Creameries, Incorporated, which bought supplies for the creameries and sold the products manufactured by member creameries in Boston, explicitly identifying them as *Vermont* products.

Vermont Commissioner of Agriculture Elbert Brigham (1913–1924) encouraged the move toward cooperatives among Vermont's farmers. "In the days when each farmer marketed his surplus produce in his local village, cooperation was not necessary," he declared, "but now when a great part of the farmers' produce must pass through several handlers, all well-organized, he himself must organize for his own protection."[101]

In addition to boosts from the cooperatives, Vermont's farmers also received increasing amounts of assistance from public sources. Initially reluctant and skeptical about learning methods of better farming from agricultural journals and state agricultural reports, many had lessened their resistance by the early twentieth century. The process had been helped along by efforts of the Vermont agricultural experiment station, established in Burlington in 1886, and soon after the turn of the century by the Vermont State Agricultural College's program of sending out extension agents to work with farmers and raise their awareness of new techniques in farming.

The state expanded its commitment to farming education in 1908 with creation of the position of Commissioner of Agriculture. An early initiative of that office was the Better Farming Special, set up in 1910 as a traveling exhibit mounted on railway cars of the Rutland Road that provided horticulture and forestry demonstrations and displays of modern farm machinery, fertilizers, and feeds. A more comprehensive approach to agricultural education became possible in 1914, when Congress passed the Smith-Lever Act. This legislation provided $10,000 in federal funds annually for extension work, with additional money available if matched by state and local funds. In 1915, the Vermont legislature responded to Smith-Lever by establishing an annual appropriation of $8,000 (financed by taxes on the towns in each county) and requiring that expenditures by county agricultural associations be supervised by a director of the Vermont State Agricultural Extension Service, then operating under the aegis of the University of Vermont.

With these federal/state incentives, Vermont began developing a county demonstration program that by the 1920s had distributed extension agents across the state. In addition, home demonstration agents provided advice to farm wives on diet, nutrition, and household problems; and county club agents worked with boys and girls in 4-H club activities. By 1930, a total of 450 active 4-H clubs existed in the state.

Around 1910, farmers in each county who were interested in working with the extension agents began forming themselves into county farm bureaus. In 1918, most of the county demonstration programs had gradually been reformed as Farm Bureau associations, and in that year a state federation of county Farm Bureau associations came into existence. In 1919, Vermont became one of twelve states to participate in forming the American Farm Bureau Federation, and soon afterward, the state's aggressive young chapter, headed by Arthur Packard, began challenging the more cautious Grange for political leadership of the state's farmers.

While Vermont farmers appreciated "aid," they remained skeptical of regulation, whether from state or federal sources. This skepticism became evident again in the 1920s, just as it had been for H. L. Hindley's "Hayville gentleman" in 1909. Beginning in the 1890s, the Department of Agriculture and Forestry worked hard to eliminate the hazard presented to Vermont's dairy herds and to the quality of their milk by the disease bovine tuberculosis. However, after a voluntary testing program, begun in 1894, led to the slaughter of several thousand cattle, many farmers became reluctant to cooperate, fearful of further losses and unwilling to support compulsory testing. In 1925 the General Assembly enacted a bill providing for the disease's elimination but the new plan still contained voluntary features and the farmer-dominated House of Representatives underfunded

Agriculture Commissioner Elbert Brigham's efforts in the 1920s to apply it. Another decade passed before lawmakers, anxious to hold onto Vermont dairymen's prominence in the Boston milk market, finally provided adequate legislation and funding for a successful program.

That same concern to maintain Vermont's milk market prominence provided the force behind enactment of another significant regulatory bill. In 1912, the General Assembly passed a Creamery Inspection Act that imposed sanitation and health standards for all plants handling dairy products and a schedule of periodic inspections, to be carried out by examiners employed by the state.

In the 1920s, Vermont's farmers struggled to survive, but they remained generally better off than their contemporaries in Western and Southern states. Historian Arthur F. Stone, writing in 1929, made this point while nevertheless expressing justifiable concern for the state's agricultural future. "The farm situation today, in Vermont as elsewhere, is not particularly pleasant," he noted; at the same time, Green Mountain farmers were "not in such a slough of despond as some would have us believe." Conditions appeared better in Vermont than for farmers in states outside New England largely because of the region's shift in agricultural emphasis to its specialty crop, dairy products, supplied to reliable nearby niche markets. Many of the region's farmers thus were able to keep their prices high during the economic downturn, in contrast to the collapse of prices on basic commodities experienced by Western and Southern farmers who mostly competed in glutted and unregulated international markets.[102] Although the number of Vermont farms and farm acreage did continue to decline in the decade, the value of farmland, buildings, implements, and livestock increased. In addition, while lagging behind some other New England states, farmers in Vermont possessed auto ownership, electrical connections, and telephone hookups in proportions exceeding those of farmers nationally. Dorman B. E. Kent, the long-time librarian of the Vermont Historical Society, concluded in 1930 that "the voice of discontent uttered by our [farm] people here, compared with the kick put up by the millions of farmers in the West . . . is about as the tweet, tweet of the sparrow to the roar of fifty ferocious lions."[103]

Vermonters thus also eluded the harshest aspects of the brief national depression of 1920–1921. Indeed, the depression's ironic effect in Vermont was to create a momentary upturn in the state's rural population. Many who had earlier migrated to industrial centers in search of jobs returned to the relative security of Green Mountain farms owned by family and friends who had chosen not to leave. In 1922, the writer Dorothy Canfield Fisher, of Arlington, elaborated on this point: "Now, when times are hard and manufacturers are flat and the mills in the industrial states around us are shut down, and newspapers are talking about bankruptcies and bread-lines, the Vermont family, exactly as rich and exactly as poor as it ever was, remarks with a kindness tinged with pride, 'Well, we'd better ask Lem's folks up to stay for a spell, till times get better. I guess it's pretty hard sledding for them.'"[104]

Fisher understood the candidly temporary character of such retreats to the farm and the high likelihood of Vermont's continued long-term rural population losses. Hopes for halting the losses nonetheless provided the impetus for state efforts in the era to encourage farm cooperatives, develop healthier herds, expand programs in agricultural education, and increase efforts to repopulate abandoned—and apparently no longer agriculturally viable—hillside farms with tourists rather than farmers. Such efforts, if they bore fruit, would be a key to revitalizing local economies and erasing negative trends in Vermont's struggling villages. Meanwhile, by 1930, at the end of one hard era—and the beginning of another—the farmers themselves left a mixed set of impressions on the landscape that included, according to agricultural historian Howard S. Russell, not only "backwoods and hilltop farm buildings . . . burning, decaying, slumping into cellars," but also "good dairy, fruit, and garden farms . . . [with] dwellings, thousands of them, well-clapboarded and painted white or buff with lead and oil, border[ing] county roads."[105]

In manufacturing, too, the early twentieth century presented a picture of little growth and limited gains. In the new century's first decade and through World War I, a handful of industries expanded production but others slipped backward, and the 1920s brought an almost across-the-board decline. Machine tool production enjoyed the most consistent prosperity. The Windsor-Springfield area, known since the mid-nineteenth century for firearms and rifle manufacturing, had lately become a home to the machine-tool industry, supplying high-quality turret lathes, drills, and milling machines to an international metalworking market. The industry's development experienced an important turning point in 1889 when James Hartness, at age twenty-nine, arrived in Springfield to become superintendent of the Jones & Lamson Machine Company. The enterprise had located in Springfield only a year earlier, after transporting its possessions over Skitchewaug Mountain by oxcart from Windsor. Hartness, the future governor, focused the company's manufacturing on a product of his own design, the flat turret lathe, capable of making longer and heavier metal cuts at faster speeds than competitor lathes.

The strategy succeeded and under his leadership the company enjoyed its most prosperous years. As the business thrived, two of Hartness's colleagues, Edward R. Fellows and W. J. Bryant, departed Jones & Lamson to start their own companies in Springfield: Fellows's plant (1896) manufactured gear shapers, and Bryant founded the Bryant Chucking Grinder Company (1909). These three firms along with the Windsor Tool Company, in Windsor, formed Precision Valley's central core. The two communities grew rapidly between 1900 and 1920, with Springfield tripling in size and becoming the state's most important industrial city. Ralph Flanders, a Jones & Lamson engineer and future United States senator, characterized the vibrant town of Springfield in its sublimely rural setting as "an island of heavy industry entirely surrounded by cows."[106]

The economic stimulus of the World War brought temporary advances in some segments of Vermont's manufacturing economy, and setbacks in others. The machine tool industry, already stimulated by expanding automobile manufacturing, boomed as war-driven orders doubled and then doubled again. War contracts also brought prosperity to Swanton, where the Remington Arms factory manufactured four million cartridges a week to fill orders from the American and French governments. The war also boosted production at the state's woolen and lumber mills and garment manufacturing plants. The E. & T. Fairbanks & Company's scale factory also made gains.

Industries not essential to the war effort, however, experienced difficult times. Stone companies and quarries were hard hit by declining demand but also by a shortage of labor brought on by the military draft and the emigration of workers to higher-paying jobs in the booming war-industry plants of southern New England. A year into the war, the state's labor supply dropped by 35 percent, but by almost 60 percent in the granite and marble industries. Springfield's machine shops responded to the state worker shortage by taking the unprecedented step of hiring women—almost two hundred strong. Precision Valley shop owners arranged separate shop entrances for their new female employees, and hired "matrons" to look after their welfare while on the job.

After the armistice, war-related manufacturing orders dried up across the country and industrial output dropped, triggering the brief but severe national economic downturn of 1920–1921. Vermont's industrial sector thereafter stabilized but did not prosper. In the course of the decade that followed, seven out of the ten major industries showed a decline in the value of their products. The stone and machine tool industries made marginal gains, but struggled with declining demand caused by shifting markets. The transfer of textile mills outside the state continued a long-standing New England trend, and lumber and timber products declined from a 1907 peak, tracking a drain in high-grade, profitable timber that was a consequence, in part, of inadequate cutting policies of lumbermen. Paper and printing also remained flat through most of the decade.

In 1921, Governor Hartness had called for a "general plan of increasing the industrial activity in Vermont," but it attracted little support, and none of the three governors who followed during the decade took up the issue.[107] The continued shift of people from farm to towns stimulated urban construction activity but otherwise the state's manufacturing struggled at the periphery of a decade-long national prosperity heavily reliant on the expanding automobile industry and its satellites, steel, petroleum, and rubber. The total number of manufacturing concerns in Vermont dropped from 1,790 to 927 in the 1920s, and the number of workers dropped also, so that despite a late surge of growth, by 1930 industrial labor's proportion of Vermont's workforce stood at only 28.4 percent, down from a high of 30.2 percent in 1920.[108]

The slumping Vermont economy provided the setting for two of the most bitter labor strikes in the state's history, at Bellows Falls against the International Paper Company's plant, and at Barre against a phalanx of large and small quarry owners. Both strikes attracted the support of their workers' local communities but drew strong condemnation in other parts of the state. In fact, efforts at establishing labor organizations in Vermont, from their earliest attempts, had met with vigorous resistance from the state's predominately rural population and skepticism from its rural-based legislature and statewide elected officials in Montpelier. Some labor opponents viewed unions as offenses against hardy independent-mindedness or threats to good industrial order. Others considered them straight-out "alien" organizations. Among the supporters of the union cause were many of the state's immigrant newcomers, thus making it a target of ethnic and religious prejudice as well as antiunion sentiment. A business-financed survey of Vermont industry in the late 1920s boasted that the "majority of the population is native-born . . . and not disposed toward industrial disturbances."[109] The *Poultney Journal*'s response to a union organizing effort in the ethnically diverse slate-producing region of Castleton, Poultney, and Fair Haven illustrated the general distrust of unions. The newspaper asserted its preference for having twenty thousand men sit idle for five years "if that will effect . . . an end to these miserable labor organizations."[110]

The strike at Bellows Falls began in 1921. The town had been a center for the production of pulp paper for almost three decades when in 1898 the large International Paper Company came to town. Over the next two decades the company acquired a payroll of more than five hundred employees and a reputation for difficult labor relations. The 1921 stoppage climaxed several years of labor conflict that included five other strikes since 1898. After a strike in 1912, workers had managed to gain a union contract that assured them an eight-hour day and wage payments at a rate of time-and-a-half for overtime work. In 1919, however, International Paper demanded that employees accept an open-shop labor policy, an increase in the workday to nine hours, a 30 percent cut in the hourly wage rate, and an end to special rates for overtime pay.

Union members voted to walk out rather than accept the terms. Negotiations quickly stalemated, and the Bellows Falls community launched mass meetings in the summer of 1921 in support of the strike. On July 15, two men were wounded by gunfire, and ten days later rioting occurred in Bellows Falls. Governor James Hartness called out the Vermont National Guard to keep order. Physical threats and confrontations continued to occur, nevertheless, between strikers and "scabs," through the summer and fall. The union insisted on a mediated settlement, a solution the paper company steadfastly rejected. On January 8, 1926, four and a half years after the strike began, and with none of the disputed issues resolved, International Paper shut down completely and moved its operations to Three Rivers, Québec, leaving Bellows Falls's economy badly crippled and its workers destitute.[111]

The trouble in Barre began after owners announced a decision to cut wages and abandon the closed-shop union contract that had governed the granite industry for several years. At the end of 1921, workers responded with a strike; the manufacturers, in turn, announced a lockout. The standoff gripped the granite district through 1922. Several owners, attempting to maintain production, began replacing the union men with unskilled strikebreakers from Canada and Massachusetts and "anyone who was willing to learn the work."[112] French-Canadian farmers arrived in large numbers to take the jobs. According to one account, "Anybody was employing the Frenchmen as soon as they came across the border."[113] Historian Ann Banks writes that quarry owners arranged to have newly arrived scabs "paraded up [Barre's] Main Street to the music of bands and fed free Sunday dinners of chicken and ice cream."[114] The enmity that formed along ethnic lines between strikers and French-Canadian replacement workers caused several instances of violence and left a legacy of animosity that lingered in central Vermont for decades. Although a few smaller companies broke management ranks and signed union contracts, the strikebreaking strategy won out for the majority of Barre firms, and by 1923 the owners had generally instituted the open shop and the 1921 wage reduction. Barre's closed-shop era had ended—at least for a while.

As the economy lagged through the 1920s, many leading Vermonters continued to share the view, widely held at least since the 1890s, that their picturesque natural landscape offered a potentially rich resource for boosting the state's prosperity—a lure to entice the "cash crop" of summer tourists, sightseers, and nostalgia seekers. By the end of the decade, among those who had been attracted by Vermont's natural environment were a growing number of out-of-state novelists, poets, and painters who envisioned it as an ideal setting, not for tourism, but for the creation of their art. Vermont's remoteness, pastoral surroundings, and its citizens' willingness to leave visitors alone, offered artists the promise of seclusion and tranquility they viewed as necessary conditions for their work. They came both as periodic visitors and as full- or part-time residents.

The state's southwestern corner was a popular destination, and in the 1920s an active community of musicians, artists, and writers formed there. Novelist and essayist Dorothy Canfield Fisher settled in tiny Arlington as a permanent resident in 1915. The town also drew composer and painter Carl Ruggles. Poet Robert Frost kept a home in South Shaftsbury beginning in 1920. Nearby lived other artist residents: poets Sarah Cleghorn and Walter Hard (a Vermont native) in Manchester; writer Zephine Humphrey in Dorset; and artist Rockwell Kent in Sunderland.

Artist enclaves formed elsewhere as well. In 1926 Middlebury College established the Bread Loaf Writers Conference at the inn in Ripton formerly run by Joseph Battell.[115] Each summer it attracted a group of the nation's outstanding writers of poetry and fiction. In 1928, two years prior to his winning the Nobel Prize for literature, Sinclair Lewis, with his wife, Dorothy Thompson, bought a home in Barnard. For Lewis, who famously ridiculed small-town life in his satirical novel *Main Street* (1920), the decision to take up residence in small-town Vermont ended an extended search for a "a place to spend the rest of my life," although his divorce from Dorothy Thompson led him eventually to leave.[116] Lewis's feelings for his adoptive state, however, were never in doubt. He boasted to his publisher, Alfred Harcourt, that he felt "about one million per cent better up here than in New York." "For me," he wrote, Vermont embodied "peace and work and home."[117]

Neshobe Island in Lake Bomoseen, near Castleton, provided the location of perhaps the most colorful of the artistic gatherings in the 1920s. A group of New York City writers and actors renowned for their wit and style, known collectively as the "Algonquin Round Table," made annual summer visits to the seven-acre island beginning in 1925. Led by theater critic Alexander Woollcott, the group included playwrights George S. Kaufman and Moss Hart, songwriters Howard Dietz and Irving Berlin, and writers Heywood Broun and Edna Ferber. Other frequent visitors included writer and actor Robert Benchley, *New Yorker* founder Harold Ross, playwright Robert Sherwood, writer Ring Lardner, comedian Harpo Marx, and poet and short story writer Dorothy Parker. Lured by the beauty of the area's surroundings, Woollcott initially rented the island and its residence, and later he and his friends bought it. "The thing we cherished . . . along with its natural beauty," Harpo Marx explained, "was its isolation." They vacationed there, used it as a long-term residence, and as "a working refuge" through the 1940s.[118]

Closer to the cultural roots of Green Mountain residents in the decade of the twenties was the literary and publishing work of Walter John Coates and J. Howard Flower. The two men, lifelong friends and colleagues, had common backgrounds as theology students and also shared a love of poetry, a desire to do what they could to foster a distinctive and vital Vermont literature, and a commitment to the community life of rural Vermont. Coates, after completing student pastoral assignments in Marshfield and Calais, took up the life of a storekeeper and printer in North Montpelier in 1922. Flower chose a vagabond existence in the Hartland vicinity as an itinerant printer, schoolteacher, and odd-job man after giving up his Unitarian pastorate in Glover. A vegetarian, pacifist, and proponent of women's rights, Flower dressed unconventionally and wore his hair flowing long past his shoulders.

Flower acquired a small press in 1907 and printed town reports until he had earned enough money, by 1917, to begin publication of *Free Soul*, a literary monthly he described as "a journal of personal liberation and eternal youth." He also founded Solitarian Press, through which, for forty years, he published poems, essays, and pamphlets by local and regional writers, often selling them himself, door-to-door.

Coates formed a publishing entity of his own, the Driftwind Press, in 1926, in the back of his North Montpelier store, utilizing a seventy-five-year-old foot-powered press that he had purchased from a business in Enosburg Falls that printed labels for horse liniment bottles. In that year Coates began publishing his own literary magazine, *Driftwind*, subtitled "a tramp magazine issued for the love of literature." Coates hand-sewed the first *Driftwind* issue himself, with birch bark covers, and he bound many of Driftwind Press's later imprints in wallpaper. Like *Free Soul*, it served as an outlet for his and Flower's poetic and literary efforts while also providing encouragement and a publishing opportunity for other Vermont poets.

That the works he and Flower published were often of negligible quality did not deter Coates; he wanted to encourage the development of a distinctly Vermont literary voice. With his energy centered on that goal, he turned his North Montpelier home into a salon for local talent and his store was mostly an excuse for more social intercourse. He also set to work on the compilation of a bibliography of Vermont literature, and edited and collaborated on several collections of Vermont verse. With Arthur Peach of Norwich University, he founded the League of Vermont Writers for the purpose of raising literary consciousness in the state, and served for a decade as its president.

Most of the poetry and essays that appeared in Coates's and Flower's publications were of minor status, and the consensus view of scholars concerning Coates is that his most lasting contribution was his work on the bibliography of Vermont literature. To his contemporaries, however, his influence was measurably larger. Vermonter Vrest Orton, who worked in New York City as an editor and publisher during the 1920s, described Coates as a good example of the old-time, independent and courageous "early-American fighting editor."[119] Sinclair Lewis also held him in high regard, as is clear from an article written by the Nobel Prize winner advising students at Yale University on ways to build a literary career: "I really know a poet, a good poet, who keeps alive by conducting a grocery store, with a gasoline pump in front of it, in Northern Vermont. He had time not only to write, but to edit and, himself, by hand, to print a small magazine. I know of no chromium-plated, streamlined writer of magazine serials who has half his leisure or a tenth of his dignity."[120]

These years marked the flourishing of small literary magazines in Vermont that included, in addition to *Free Soul* and *Driftwind*, the publications *Hill Trails* (1936) and *Ghost* (1944). These journals, and the small presses that produced them, operated hand-to-mouth, but also with their editors' hope that they were contributing, in the words of Coates, to a "new renaissance movement, looking toward literary self-discovery here in our state."[121]

By 1928, however, Vermont, appeared distant from a "renaissance movement" of any kind. Despite many changes in the first quarter of the twentieth century, Vermonters had not put behind them the worries of 1900. It remained a poor state, desperate for growth, its population shrinking, its farms dropping in number, its industry stagnant. At the same time, the small-scale, local economy of the nineteenth century that had nurtured cherished attitudes of self-reliance, independence, and caring for one's community continued to recede, although the attitudes themselves still strongly colored Vermonters' thinking. Few would have guessed that Vermont stood on the threshold of a period of "advance"—one that would profoundly challenge its people's "firm adherence," as Joseph A. DeBoer expressed in 1905, "to the usage and practice of the past."

8
Floods, Depression, and War
1927–1945

The Great Flood and Vermont's Future

Rain came down almost daily in the month of October 1927, nearly 50 percent above normal amounts for the state. The prolonged drenching so saturated the hills and valley floors that by the end of October, much of the precipitation simply ran off as surface water. Then, on Tuesday, November 1, a tropical storm pushing up the Atlantic coast from the Gulf of Mexico, which had been expected to move out to sea, made contact with a high-pressure barrier off New England, which diverted it inland. The warm moisture-laden storm churned its way up the Connecticut River valley where it collided with a cold rainstorm moving northeast out of New York State. Meteorologists had been anticipating fair and colder New England weather for that day; instead, a furious downpour struck all across the region, but most heavily in Vermont.

In the next three days—November 2nd, 3rd, and 4th—seven to nine inches of rain fell on Vermont. With the land already sodden, the new accumulations rushed almost directly into river systems, and in amounts far larger than the watercourses could handle. Streams across the state became torrents, overflowing embankments and filling the narrow and low valleys so rapidly that farm families in their paths could not save movable property or animals—or even flee. For a while, on the night of the 3rd, water levels climbed at a rate of four feet per hour. The rushing currents broke through dams and reservoirs, adding to the avalanche of water, washing out roadways and bridges, thrusting railroad tracks into the air, and carrying along on their crests entire houses with families in them, telegraph and telephone poles, dead farm animals, and fallen trees. The Winooski, Missisquoi, Ottauquechee, Jail Branch, Dog, and Lamoille rivers, and Otter Creek, all reached exceptional flood stage.

Devastation was greatest along the Winooski River. In Montpelier, situ-

During the 1927 flood, the rising waters of a Winooski River tributary overwhelmed residences along Webster Avenue in Barre. *Vermont Historical Society.*

ated at the convergence of three rivers including the Winooski, water crested in the early morning of the 4th, at twelve feet above street level. At Barre, four miles east of the capital, seven citizens drowned, including Vermont's lieutenant governor, Hollister Jackson, who failed to escape from a swollen brook in which his car had stalled. In the vicinity of Waterbury, twelve miles downstream from Montpelier, twenty people drowned and water reached a high point of eighteen feet on Main Street. At Bolton, across the river from the base of Camel's Hump Mountain, at least fifteen people in a boarding house swept to their deaths over Bolton Falls. Along some sections of the Winooski, northwest of Waterbury, the swollen river channel extended to a mile in width, and further down the valley, at Essex Junction, the flood crested at fifty-one feet above normal street level.

Years later, many survivors of the tragic flood of 1927 viewed it as the first in an era of crises. Before the worst of the flood-related troubles had been resolved, Green Mountain residents confronted another great collective challenge with the onset of unprecedented national economic depression. The scale of these two ordeals overwhelmed the best applications of Vermonters' preferred ways of problem solving and governance. The responses they did devise, in turn, helped prepare them to face the period's third great ordeal, the reentry by the state and nation into another devastating world war. For many, the experiences of 1927–1945 signaled the completion of Vermont's move from "independence" to full participation—and integration—in region and nation, and provoked renewed awareness that fidelity to the state's traditional values would necessitate new approaches and new ways of thinking.

When the rain finally ceased falling on November 5, 1927, the northern part of the state stood almost completely isolated, its bridges destroyed and public services broken off. For thirty hours, until a transmitter could be rigged, Montpelier lacked communication to the outside world, fueling a rumor that two hundred lives in the town had been lost by the collapse of a reservoir (in fact, only one capital resident died in the flood).

Rescue forays commenced before the rain had stopped. On the 5th an airplane began making landings on Towne Hill, at the edge of Montpelier, delivering supplies and mail. National Guardsmen and federal troops from Fort Ethan Allen assisted in policing the city's streets, barring movement without a pass, and instituting a community curfew and a plan for rationing food and fuel. A United States Army detachment traveled through Smugglers' Notch to reach Waterbury with wagon trains of medicine and food. The *Burlington Free Press* reported that airplanes stationed at Fort Ethan Allen dropped "messages" over twenty-five to thirty flooded towns, "each containing a letter asking the people if there was anything they particularly needed," and giving "instructions as to how to indicate by a panel system on the ground what they might need."[1] On Lake Champlain, the old side-wheeler, *Chateaugay*, became a mercy ship, staying in motion for sixteen days, plowing "through minefields of debris on the swollen lake," delivering food, mail, and construction materials from Port Kent, New York, to Burlington, and ferrying refugees to the western shore.[2]

By the 7th, the water began to recede, revealing the scope of the devastation: eighty-four lives lost—fifty-five in the Winooski River basin alone; scores of towns inundated, partly or wholly; almost ten thousand people driven from their homes; $30,000,000 worth of property destroyed, including a cost to twenty-three manufacturing plants of $2,812,500; many miles of railroad track washed away, never to be replaced. In Montpelier, where only two stores carried flood insurance, the staggering losses averaged $400 for every man, woman, and child in town. Barre absorbed $1,250,000 worth of damage, and its granite operations remained closed for almost four months. According to the 1928 farm report of Agriculture

Commissioner Edward H. Jones, 187 houses, 200 barns, and 257 other outbuildings had been swept away; and 1,704 head of cattle, 202 sheep, 469 swine, and 7,215 chickens drowned. The State of Vermont calculated that the storm had destroyed or severely damaged 1,258 bridges and that the cost of damages to highways and bridges amounted to $7,755,000. Estimated total damage resulting from the flood reached $35,000,000. The state had experienced other destructive floods—in 1785, 1811, 1830, 1850, and 1869—but Governor John E. Weeks pronounced this one "the greatest catastrophe in Vermont's history."[3]

Initially, however, the 74-year-old Weeks had misjudged the scale of the devastation. Early in the crisis, a U.S. Army captain, Charles S. Ferrin, stationed at Fort Ethan Allen, managed to reach Montpelier, traveling by horseback and on foot through Smugglers' Notch and over Hunger Mountain to inform Weeks that Major General Preston Browne, commander of the First Corps Area in Boston, had put the Army at the governor's disposal. According to Ferrin, Weeks defensively responded, "Captain, Vermont can take care of its own." Shortly afterward, however, Vermont Adjutant General Herbert T. Johnson took Ferrin aside and said, "Charles, send the troops"—and the troops came.[4]

On Sunday, November 6, Weeks began an anxious search for even more outside assistance. That night he made a telephone call to President Calvin Coolidge, in Washington, D.C. Weeks later recounted his exchange with the president, who apparently had been in a humorous mood: "I said to him, 'President Coolidge, I want [Herbert] Hoover [secretary of commerce] up here to look this thing over.' The President laughed out loud, so loud that Mr. [Fred A.] Howland who was near me, heard him, and he replied, 'You want Hoover? Who put you up to that?' I said, 'Yes, we are in a sad situation here and I think you should send Hoover to us.' 'I will see about it and let you know' was his answer. Early the next morning he wired me, 'Your man Hoover is on his way.'"[5]

Hoover faced a task in Vermont similar in many respects to one he had carried out for Coolidge seven months earlier in the Mississippi Valley. In March and April of 1927, the Mississippi River had gone on the worst rampage in its recorded history. Coolidge had dispatched Hoover to coordinate efforts of the Red Cross and establish temporary bank credit corporations to meet the crisis as it affected the states of Illinois, Missouri, Tennessee, Kentucky, Arkansas, Mississippi, and Louisiana. The assignment had occupied several weeks of Hoover's attention.

On November 17th, Hoover personally surveyed the Winooski Valley flood area, accompanied by U.S. Attorney General John G. Sargent, a native of Ludlow. As Hoover completed his tour, the *Burlington Free Press* called for quick action on federal aid for the state: "It can not be that a Congress which finds it easy to vote millions for the aid of Russia and other devastated countries in the old world can refuse similar appeals from our own Americans." Vermont's U.S. Senator Porter H. Dale had already approached the congressional flood committee, "urging prompt and adequate action for the relief of New England flood sufferers."[6]

Hoover's visit resulted in a series of recommendations to the president. "The cost of rehabilitation," he reported, extended "beyond the means" of the stricken districts, and outside assistance would be needed. He proposed that federal government funds be made available for the purpose of reconstructing Vermont's federal-aid roads; that financial aid to industrial plants, commercial establishments, and farmers should come through private low-interest loans to be extended by the New England Bankers Association or the New England Council, a Boston-based banking and industrial group; and that the many Vermonters made homeless by the flood should look for assistance to the Red Cross and other private charity organizations capable of sending out calls for public contributions. Hoover's proposals became the blueprint for subsequent actions.[7]

Assured by Hoover that the state would not be forced to rely solely on its own resources, Weeks convened a special one-day session of the legislature on November 30, and proposed a plan of action for reconstructing the state's roads and bridges. With towns unable to afford the high cost of repairs, Weeks saw no alternative to a vastly expanded state role, even if it came at the expense of local control and autonomy. Lawmakers embraced Weeks's proposal that the state take over the towns' responsibility for repairing highways and bridges, and that the work be carried out under complete control of the State Highway Department. In order to gain immediate funding for the needed repairs they also agreed to bypass the legislature's long-standing pay-as-you-go policy, and authorized a bond issue of $8,500,000, and a flood tax to retire the bond.[8]

In addition to this self-help, aid flowed in from private sources beyond the state. Acting on Hoover's recommendation, the New England Council formed the Vermont Flood Credit Corporation, capitalized at $1,000,000, to make loans available for flood-damaged businesses. Of the many private gifts and contributions, the largest came from the Red Cross, which brought $600,000 into the state for use by flood victims, $170,000 in Montpelier alone.

In March 1928, assistance arrived from Washington. Congress used a rider to an agriculture bill to appropriate $2,654,000 for repairing damages to the state's federal aid road system. The appropriation vote followed House debates in which Vermont Representative Elbert Brigham unambiguously presented the state's case for "outside" help: "This is the first time that representatives of Vermont in the 136 years of its membership in the Union have appeared before a committee of Congress, asking for relief. Such calamities as we have had heretofore have been within the capacity of our self-reliant people to meet. I assure you that we appear here now only because a disaster has befallen our State so overwhelming that it is without parallel in her history."[9]

Washington also provided help in another form. In February, U.S. Representative Ernest W. Gibson, Sr., had given the chairman of the House Committee on Flood Control petitions, signed, according to the congressman, "by hundreds of Vermont citizens asking the Federal Government to take some [flood control] action for their protection." The chairman assured Gibson that a pending appropriation bill allocated funds that would meet his request for the Army Corps of Engineers to conduct surveys to determine practicable ways "of controlling floods or lessening the damages therefrom."[10]

State officials fitted the federally funded repair work into a schedule of general highway improvements launched in 1927, prior to the flood. The federal aid made possible, among other things, the complete replacement not only of washed-out bridges but also decrepit and surviving spans long in need of repairs but unaffordable by cash-strapped towns. From 1927 to 1933, in addition to the emergency program expenditures, and despite the onset of the Great Depression, the state spent more than $4,500,000 annually on highways, amounting to more than one-third of each year's approximately $12,000,000 state budget. By contrast, allocations for health and education amounted to only $1,000,000 annually. As a result, by 1933 Vermont possessed 1,100 miles of paved highways. State financing for the program came almost entirely through funds collected from automobile license and registration fees and the revenue from the state gasoline tax.

Despite the federal aid dollars and other outside assistance, flood cleanup remained a local task. Individual communities assumed the massive chore of removing mud, silt, and downed trees from their streets and roads; reestablishing telephone, water, and sewage lines; and burying drowned cattle and other animals. In Montpelier, according to the capital city's commissioner of public works, "between 300 and 400 names were on the weekly [cleanup] pay rolls. Some 50 or 60 trucks and teams were worked at one time, and in a couple of months probably over 50,000 loads of material were moved." Piles of trash and refuse awaiting removal were so massive "that if we could have collected enough trucks to have had loaded all this material at one time, the fleet . . . would have reached from Montpelier to Washington, D.C."[11]

Vermont's response to the Great Flood of 1927 had enduring effects, both accelerating well-established trends and pushing the state in new directions. Hence the huge amount of flood-related state expenses, along with the onset of the national depression, forced the legislature to embrace new methods of government funding. In 1931, acting on initiatives from the Vermont Farm Bureau that already had earned broad support prior to the flood, lawmakers ended their reliance on a statewide property tax as the source for most of the state's money and implemented an income tax (thus also easing the tax burden on income-poor Green Mountain farmers), a step only one other New England state had taken.

The flood had other important effects. The legislature's decision to centralize management of road repairs represented a significant strengthening of state authority and weakening of town government and local autonomy. The decision to borrow money for the roadwork marked a fundamental departure from a pay-as-you-go fiscal policy as old as the state itself. The expansion of Montpelier's responsibility for roads and the emphasis on hard-surfaced roads speeded the creation of a modern state highway system. The concentration on road reconstruction while accepting the permanent loss of many miles of rail track hastened a decline in the state's economic reliance on railroads and a shift to highways. The natural calamity in its sheer magnitude forced Vermonters, as they turned to Washington and elsewhere for assistance, to confront the practical limits of self-help. Finally, the Great Flood instigated the dissolution of the state's political tradition of only two years of service for its governors, and with it, a time-honored bar to enhanced executive authority: Weeks sought a second two-year term in 1928, insisting on the need for continuity in completing the recovery effort, and gained easy reelection.

In the flood's aftermath, two surprising themes emerged in Vermonters' thinking about the ordeal, revealing confusions characteristic of transition times. Within two years, influential individuals began publicly characterizing the disaster as a fortuitous turning point for the state. An opinion column in the mainline *Vermonter* magazine in September 1929 declared unequivocally, "The flood was a blessing." Written by its editor, Charles R. Cummings, the piece—a meditation on the virtues of bridge and road construction—asserted that the flood had "yanked Vermont out of the doldrums. Our advance since that visitation of 1927 has been revolutionary."[12]

The other strain of thought embodied a conviction in many people's minds that Vermont had overcome the flood tragedy without help from others. The crisis rather quickly came to be seen as another chapter in the state's remarkable commitment to self-help, local autonomy, and independent ways. In 1937, Governor George D. Aiken spoke what had, by then, become the standard view within the state. Recalling predictions that Vermonters could never recover from the flood's terrible destruction, Aiken declared, "the people who made these predictions did not know the true temper of Vermonters. We did not solicit charity nor appeal to the federal government to sustain the loss that had been inflicted upon us. We stood upon our own feet, repairing our own damage, maintaining our own self-respect and won the admiration of the nation by so doing."[13] Four years later, in another remembrance of the flood, William H. Rice asserted flatly in *The Vermonter*, "the state refused offers of outside help."[14] So durable was this myth that the *Burlington Free Press*, in a 1952 retrospective on the flood, concluded, "Vermont paid its own way out of the mess."[15] Consuelo Northrop Bailey's autobiography, in 1976, recalled Governor Weeks's statement that "Vermont wants nothing. She will take care of herself" as evidence of an unwaveringly self-reliant Vermont and as an inspiring moral guidepost.[16]

In 1928, with Vermont ostensibly "out of the doldrums," and with the flood's worst effects in the past, two hundred prominent citizens launched an ambitious civic enterprise known as the Vermont Commission on Country Life (VCCL). This private group, chaired by Governor Weeks, trained its attention on perceived continuing problems of rural Vermont. Declining population and economic stagnation in rural areas had been sources of worry for many years. By 1928, the concern had produced a constituency of public-spirited volunteers from the state's leadership ranks, sharing many guiding assumptions of the old Country Life Movement and receptive to a call for devising "a constructive plan" in the "interest of a sanely progressive future for our beloved state." The commission's executive director, Henry C. Taylor, a rural sociologist from

Northwestern University, described its members as infused with the same spirit that characterized the state's reaction to the previous year's flood. Vermonters' "magnificent response" to the flood disaster, Taylor wrote, had given them "a fuller sense of their power and gave them a new impulse" with which the VCCL could "synchronize" its own work.[17]

In their desire to improve the state's rural life, commission members directed considerable interest toward the social and spiritual condition of rural citizens. This emphasis largely reflected the commission's origin as an offshoot of the research interests of a University of Vermont professor of zoology, Henry F. Perkins. Three years earlier, Perkins had begun a project called the Eugenics Survey of Vermont (ESV), premised on a belief fashionable at the time in some scientific, social, and political circles in the United States and Europe, that "the science of human breeding" could be the basis for building a healthier society. Perkins's search for funding for his research activities brought the VCCL into existence. Funds from the Social Science Research Council and philanthropic grants for "a comprehensive survey of rural Vermont" provided the VCCL's necessary financing; they enabled Perkins to hire the highly respected Taylor, and made possible the continued financing of his own Eugenics Survey efforts. Under the commission's organizational structure, the Eugenics Survey became the Committee on the Human Factor.[18]

The commission, with Perkins serving as its secretary, divided its work into seventeen committees and more than thirty subcommittees, and over a three-year period examined a wide range of topics affecting rural Vermonters. In addition to the economics of agriculture, they investigated aspects of farming as a way of life, the natural environment, medical services, education, recreation, processes of governing, religious practices, and other elements of rural living. The VCCL published a final report in 1931 called *Rural Vermont: A Program for the Future, by Two Hundred Vermonters*, and sent it to every library in the state. The report, which included findings and recommendations of each of the major committees, emphasized the need for improved education, supported cooperative efforts by farmers, called for a state utilization commission to address submarginal land issues, singled out tourism and summer residents as offering promise to become the state's new economic foundation, stressed the protection of the state's natural beauty and historical heritage, and urged the reinvigoration of local leadership. A surprisingly small number of its recommendations offered direct economic benefit to Vermont farmers.

The commission subsequently also published several volumes celebrating the state's cultural and artistic heritage—its "traditions and ideals." The most significant of these cultural efforts resulted in the rich collection of folk ballads and songs assembled by Helen Hartness Flanders, who searched through the state's rural areas and small towns armed with an old Dictaphone to record words and music. The premature exhaustion of her commission stipend did not halt her work, which continued for more than a decade.

One of the points of emphasis in the VCCL's *Rural Vermont* report involved Henry Perkins's eugenics assessments. Although in the 1920s Vermont possessed the lowest rate of illiteracy in the New England states, Perkins had become disturbed by United States military data from the World War that indicated, in his words, an unusually high number of "physical and mental defectives" among Vermont boys drawn to military service. His Eugenics Survey, examining the apparent problem of "degeneracy" in the state, led Perkins to report that "'blood has told,' and there is every reason to believe that it will *keep right* on 'telling' in future generations."[19]

In the next years, Perkins's research assistants had gathered information on a number of Vermont families that he identified as "low-grade," including more than four thousand six hundred individuals in whom he claimed to detect a pattern of elements that "seems to encourage defectiveness, crime and pauperism." The scientific standards that Perkins employed were not rigorous; nevertheless, he believed he had detected a hereditary degeneracy in large numbers of Vermont's rural French-Canadian and Abenaki populations.[20]

In several of *Rural Vermont*'s committee final reports, influences of Perkins's work appeared indirectly, and in many others, they were not evident at all. However, in a long section entitled "The People of Vermont," written by the Committee on the Human Factor (for which Perkins served as executive secretary), the committee asserted that a need existed not only to protect the state's natural beauty and historical heritage but also its "Old Vermont Stock." The "hardy pioneer stock" that had been out-migrating for the past one hundred years needed to be replenished. Thus, also, Vermont needed to reduce the population's percentage of individuals of foreign birth. "If the valuable characteristics of our old Vermont stock are to be conserved and passed on to future generations for the good of the state and the nation, conditions must be brought about which will favor the maintenance of that stock as far as possible." The Committee on the

Human Factor urged "that the doctrine be spread that it is the patriotic duty of every normal couple to have children in sufficient number to keep up to par the 'good old Vermont stock.'"[21]

Needed, as well, according to the report, although the word "sterilization" did not appear, was a method of not only managing but preventing the misery of the poor—and a method of preventing the feeble-minded segment's proliferation in the state's rural population. In a section of *Rural Vermont* titled "The Eugenics Aspect," Perkins wrote that through the guidance of eugenics, "our children's children will be less hampered by the social and economic drag of avoidable low grade Vermonters."[22]

In 1931, a few days prior to the publication of *Rural Vermont*, the legislature enacted a sterilization law that Perkins had a hand in drafting.[23] In various forms, for twenty years, sterilization bills had appeared before the legislature, including one vetoed by Governor Allen Fletcher in 1912, and one that passed in the house but failed in the senate in 1927. The 1931 law, by which Vermont became the thirty-first state to legalize sterilization of the handicapped or "feeble-minded," received the endorsement of an influential roster that included the president of the Vermont Children's Aid Society, the education commissioner, the state public welfare commissioner, and the president of the University of Vermont, all of them also members of Perkins's Eugenics Survey advisory committee. Over the following five decades, the state carried out more than two hundred sterilizations under this law before the legislature finally repealed it in 1981.

The Vermont Commission on Country Life completed its work and disbanded in 1931, leaving a legacy ambivalent in retrospect. One historian has called the commission's final report "a sweeping program for social development through political action" that became "the footing for the state's efforts to create a healthy and prosperous twentieth century society."[24] However, historian Nancy Gallagher, in her book, *Breeding Better Vermonters: The Eugenics Project in the Green Mountain State*, concludes that the report's "tragic flaw" lay in "its assertion of Yankee Protestant tradition and heritage as the model for future community development."[25] Their backward look for models provided barriers to the commission members' efforts to significantly influence the decline of farm populations or make rural life more appealing. However, in their support of expanded planning efforts and the greater mobilization of state resources, they helped prepare Vermonters for a constructive engagement with Franklin D. Roosevelt's New Deal, which lay directly in the state's future.

Though cramped and narrow in aspects of its social vision, and indefensible in some of its conclusions, *Rural Vermont* did represent an ambitious first formal effort to assess the state's needs in a wide range of areas and chart a plan for future growth. Highly esteemed by many in the state's leadership circles, its recommendations became a reference point for an era in the state's history, and influenced several other attempts that followed, in the New Deal years and beyond, at making long-range plans for the state.

The Depression and New Deal in the Green Mountains

The Wall Street stock market crash of October 1929, and the accompanying national economic slide into depression, drew scant notice in the Country Life Commission's deliberations. According to an old joke, "Vermonters were already so used to poverty that they barely noticed the Depression." The decade-long national economic collapse, however, hit every segment of the state's life, farming and commerce as well as industry, and Vermonters struggled along with the nation.

The state's most productive economic sectors, manufacturing and dairy farming, both of which were tied to out-of-state markets, felt the depression's impact earliest, and suffered most severely from it. The value of Green Mountain industrial products dropped from $142,522,547 in 1928, to $80,602,968 in 1931, and to $56,623,538 by 1933. In the same period, the number of industrial wage earners statewide fell from 27,421 to 15,083, total wages from $33,809,987 to $12,456,113, and the number of manufacturing plants from 927 to 530.

Sales of the state's most important agricultural product, fluid milk, also dropped precipitously: more than one-half below 1929 levels by 1932—and, in some places, to 2.67 cents per quart—while the cost to the dairy farmer of feed and equipment remained high. In previous periods of economic downturn, farmers had been able to supplement their incomes with products other than milk, such as timbering or poultry. But the demand for these products declined as well. By 1933, Vermont farm laborers' purchasing power slipped to its lowest point since 1877.

With incomes low, many farmers for whom borrowing became difficult or impossible and paying property taxes out of the question, sold out and left farming altogether. In the ten years after 1930, the total number of Vermont farms dropped from 24,898 to 23,582. During the same period,

An abandoned farmhouse near Newport, August 1936. *Courtesy of Library of Congress.*

agricultural workers slipped from 27 percent of the state's employed to 22 percent. Much land went out of cultivation; by the end of the decade, the proportion of unimproved farmland had risen to 60 percent. By that time, as well, the state's population as a whole had suffered a net loss (-0.1 percent), for only the second time in its history. In contrast, during the same period, the New England region experienced a net population gain of 3.3 percent, and the nation as a whole increased by 7.3 percent.[26]

Vermonters of almost every stratum experienced a shortage of cash on hand. In October 1932, former Governor Franklin S. Billings turned down a political solicitation, explaining his need to "cut out all additional expenses" because of "the present conditions of my finances."[27] In that same year, Ernest W. Gibson, Jr., failed to provide a thirty-dollar loan to help out a friend in West Haven facing eviction: "One of our banks is closed, and what money I have is tied up there. Consequently, I have been living hand to mouth. I have three children to feed and I just haven't the cash."[28]

Payment in-kind for services became an important part of doing business. At Northfield, an employee of a local bank recalled, "We took cows, lumber, shingles, hay or anything we could trade."[29] In Morrisville the newly opened Copley Hospital acquired most of the wood for its furnace "on bills, where we have been unable to collect in any other way."[30] Hard-pressed citizens sometimes paid local taxes in similar fashion. In one town, "the agreement was that if you owed your taxes you could work on the road [and] they'd give you a dollar; if you worked five days you'd get five dollars that week, and eighty cents of it would go to your taxes."[31]

Farm wife Grace Hutchinson exemplified the ingenuity required of many rural families in order to survive. "From [1930] on, for a few years, nobody had any money, you know," she recalled; "It was very, very scarce." She then described one of her family's methods of "making-do": "All during the Depression grain came in cotton bags. The first ones were unbleached white cotton; light weight. Of course, they were printed with the grain company's name but if you soaked them in bleach long enough you could get those letters out and I used the bags for all kinds of things. Pillow cases. Four of them made a sheet. Dye them and make play suits for the children. Dresses and aprons. Even dish towels."[32]

The Depression made a visible imprint on the land. Officials in Newbury, St. Johnsbury, and Barre complained of the increased numbers of "tramps" and strangers in their midst, looking for work or hand-outs. Barre mayor William Lapoint, sounding like the mayor of any large industrial city, declared in 1932 that "our mechanics are idle; our engines silent; industrial plants closed; shops of trade depleted; general activities curtailed."[33] Even the smallest communities experienced severe pressure. The budget surplus enjoyed by tiny Peacham in 1929 had become an almost $10,000 deficit by 1939, its tax rolls showing fifty-five delinquencies and almost a dozen people living at town expense. The Depression's downward pull on people's spirits led staff workers of the Agricultural Extension Service and 4-H Clubs to shift the focus of their efforts in farm communities toward singing events and entertainment, "to sustain the morale."[34]

In Vermont, providing relief for unemployed citizens remained a town responsibility. The Depression, however, rapidly overwhelmed the simple town-by-town system. Two years after the Wall Street crash communities across the state confronted swollen lists of needy citizens, declining tax payments, and uncollected tax debts. Barre's mayor described a situation shared by many local officials: "On the one hand the people insisted that local and other government units assume the burden of unemployment relief. On the other hand they demanded greater economy in government and reduced taxes."[35] Towns instituted rigid economies and curtailed or eliminated all but the most essential municipal services, but costs continued to rise and the number of towns unable to meet the escalating expenses without borrowing grew.

St. Johnsbury's efforts typified the experience of many communities. "By late summer and fall of 1931, there was a rash of business failures" in town. And in that year, its budget for care of the poor made "by far the biggest jump ever," as did demands on private charities. In the month of January, the Family Welfare Society, a local private relief agency, reported "serving 69 families with clothing and 45 with food"; nine months later the society claimed that more than 20 percent of the town's population was "being kept alive" by its organization. By February 1932, the number of welfare families in town increased by four or five per day, and the town auditor's report for 1931 revealed that eighty families—and a total of 415 persons—had received poor-relief aid during the year. In addition, 695 citizens lost their eligibility to vote at town meeting because of nonpayment of their flood tax and poll tax.

The town tried diligently to provide for its needy. Private groups staged food and clothing drives; the Kiwanis and Rotary Clubs and a local milk dealer supported milk and food funds; and Cross Bakery provided forty loaves of bread each morning to hungry children and their families. Charity "food shows" brought in donations of everything from "a can of food to 200 bushels of potatoes or a ton of coal." Sponsors staged "charity balls," with proceeds to the Welfare Society, and placed food barrels in prominent downtown locations. In the spring, vacant lots on the village periphery were made available for garden plots for struggling families.

St. Johnsbury officials maintained a "constant search for ways to provide some employment at the least cost to the town." Local unemployed men were put to work graveling roadways, cutting wood (to be given to families on welfare), replacing an old covered bridge, and, by season, doing farm work. The crisis became more acute after several prominent stores in town filed for bankruptcy and Cross Bakery reduced its operations. Selectmen responded by cutting back the 1933 budget allocations for the fire and police departments and the skating rink, and eliminating the annual appropriation for town band concerts. Still, the plight of St. Johnsbury's needy exceeded the community's capacity to respond.[36]

In 1933, many towns reached the nadir of their Depression difficulties.

On November 3, the Barre city treasurer announced his inability to meet his payroll for the rest of the year. Barre figuratively had "gone broke," brought on by demands on the charity department, which, according to the *City Report*, "reached a figure that we thought a few years ago would never become possible." The charity-driven financial shortage occurred despite "the services and generosity of various local organizations, committees, Unions, Clubs, Churches and individuals" in the city.[37]

How much could reasonably be expected from town governments in the crisis? In January 1933, the question drew fresh scrutiny from two speakers at a meeting of the Vermont Institute on Municipal and State Affairs. Both called for drastic change in the state's system of local governments. Emphasizing the importance of greater efficiency, State Auditor Benjamin Gates urged a radical reduction in the number of municipalities from 248 to 80 or 90, and wholesale reorganization of state government. Henry F. Perkins, secretary of the Vermont Commission on Country Life, also emphasized the need for readjustment of town boundaries. Perkins asserted that "for administrative purposes," it had "long been recognized, albeit with much timidity by some, that the age-old town boundaries have ceased to satisfy. . . . Economy as well as efficiency demand the consideration of every thoughtful legislator of the question: 'Is it not the time to set in motion a readjustment of the present scheme of divisions and to begin to plan larger and more logical units of government, at least for purposes of poor relief administration, schools, libraries, and the protection of health?'. . . The town is too small a unit to function independently and effectively. It is inefficient, if it is time-honored."[38]

Although nothing came of Gates's and Perkins's proposals, Vermont's state government nevertheless did gradually begin to take on a stronger role in providing relief aid. In 1932 and 1933, hoping to "put as many people at work as possible, consistent with efficiency," Governor Stanley C. Wilson ordered an intensified program of state road construction. He employed several hundred additional men cutting wood and logs in state forests, and organized meetings of public and private welfare officials to coordinate relief preparations for the winter months. The governor, however, also warned town officials against "the practice of unloading town paupers on the state" by committing them to the state hospital for the insane at Waterbury.[39]

In 1932, modest assistance also began to come from Washington, D.C. Earlier in the depression, President Hoover had rigidly opposed a substantial relief program and counseled the American people to have patience for a "natural" economic recovery. In February 1932, however, he signed legislation creating the Reconstruction Finance Corporation (RFC). Although not addressing the issue of relief, the law empowered the RFC to make long-term loans to banks, railroads, and insurance companies to bolster the nation's faltering credit system. During the next five months, Vermont bankers borrowed $5 million under the program. In July, with the economy continuing its descent, Congress passed the Emergency Relief and Construction Act, enlarging the RFC's lending authority to $3.3 billion and permitting loans to state and local authorities, to supplement their relief efforts; for federal highway assistance; and for an agrarian branch of RFC.

After a few weeks, Vermont officials from several larger towns met and submitted a successful application for some of the new RFC funds, earmarked for road construction projects. Vermont Commissioner of Agriculture Edward H. Jones also acquired funds to disburse low-interest loans to needy farmers for the purpose of refinancing mortgages at favorable interest rates. These modest actions helped prepare the way for the state's involvement in the more ambitious subsequent relief and recovery experiments of Franklin D. Roosevelt.

Roosevelt became president on March 4, 1933, and two days later proclaimed a national "bank holiday." Although a majority of Vermont voters had not supported him, many appeared ready for his New Deal experimentation. The state's bankers ran full-page newspaper advertisements proclaiming "Hail to the Chief!" and "We're with you, Mr. President!"[40]

Vermont also responded quickly to the first New Deal relief legislation, an act signed by Roosevelt on April 5, 1933, creating the Civilian Conservation Corps (CCC). The program aimed at putting unemployed young people to the work of soil conservation and reforestation in the nation's woods and mountains. Perry Merrill, an ambitious planner, had become Vermont's forest service commissioner in 1929. (He eventually served in state government with nineteen governors, during a forty-seven-year span, as state forester and commissioner of forests and parks.) Having already drafted a number of projects suitable for federal programs, he reacted promptly to the CCC initiative. Within a week of its passage, he gained authorization for several camps to be located in the state.

Merrill eventually operated more than thirty CCC camps, employing 11,243 Vermonters, and involving almost forty-one thousand men, including

Civilian Conservation Corps workers at Mount Mansfield State Forest, July 1933. *Vermont Historical Society.*

enrollees from Massachusetts, Rhode Island, New York, and other states. The program allowed participation by young men between the ages of eighteen and twenty-five (after 1935, seventeen to twenty-eight), unmarried, out of school, and from families on relief. In exchange for their work, corpsmen received job training, room and board, and a salary of $30 a month, $25 of which was sent home to families. They also received medical examinations, and the "emaciated and underfed" conditions of many of the Vermont enrollees surprised Director Merrill.[41]

The camps' program of placing young men in tasks improving and managing the state and municipal forests resonated positively with Vermonters. During its ten-year existence, the CCC constructed 110 miles of forest roads, including ten miles of roadway connecting U.S. Route 2 and Route 302 through Groton State Forest, and roads on Burke Mountain, Mount Ascutney, and Mount Philo. "Why, we had more bulldozers than the Highway Department had," Merrill recalled.[42] The new roadways opened previously inaccessible areas to fire protection, scientific forest management and conservation, and recreation. Other projects involved planting trees, constructing shelters, cutting miles of hiking and skiing trails, flood-control efforts, and building about half of Vermont's forty-five state parks. After years of state parks being underfunded, the corpsmen's work, according to Merrill, "put Vermont's state recreational development ahead by 50 years."[43] The CCC drew more praise from Vermont newspapers than any other New Deal relief agency. The *Brattleboro Reformer* editorialized a widely shared appreciation: "The boys have done such creditable public service that we are hard put to remember where we looked for aid before there was any CCC."[44]

Through Merrill's CCC work with local overseers of the poor, the state acquired its first firm data concerning the number and distribution of Vermont's unemployed workers. Because the state deemed unemployment a local concern, town overseers of the poor held the figures. While working with these town officers in gathering CCC recruits, Merrill assembled records indicating that on May 1, 1933, Vermont's welfare list totaled approximately twenty-three thousand persons. That estimate almost certainly was low, however, because jobless Vermonters who were homeowners or landholders often refused to turn for help to the local overseer of the poor because, in many instances, it required surrender of property and demonstration of pauper status. Historian Richard Judd estimated that, if including undeclared paupers, jobless Vermonters totaled approximately fifty thousand in the spring of 1933.

In May, consequently, when Congress created the Federal Emergency Relief Administration (FERA), Vermonters again embraced federal help. FERA provided grants for unemployment relief on a roughly matching basis with recipient states. Within three months, 172 Vermont towns had submitted requests for a total of $121,000 in work relief funds. In June, Governor Wilson established the Vermont Emergency Relief Administration (VERA) to coordinate the program. Responsibility for the unemployed remained at the local level, however, and the legislature granted almost no state funds for FERA use. Of more than $6 million disbursed for towns' emergency relief work over the next two years, 56.6 percent came from Washington, 42.7 percent from the towns, and only 0.7 percent from the state. In 1933 and 1935, Civil Works Administration (CWA), Works Progress Administration (WPA), and National Youth Administration (NYA) programs also came into the state.

Just as after the flood of 1927, the towns' urgent need for relief assistance facilitated this acceptance of federal aid. Vermonters' acquiescence was eased also, however, by federal willingness to allow many relief programs in the state to be supervised primarily through local institutions rather than through state administration, and by Republican Party loyalists, thus undercutting Vermonters' ingrained distrust of government interference. Especially effective in this role, as a program manager, was Mary Jean Simpson, who went to work in 1933 as the first director of VERA's Women's and Professional Division. Simpson, a Republican from East Craftsbury, eventually served as a consultant to the WPA in Washington, D.C. (and later, for many years, as dean of women at the University of Vermont).

A third factor influencing Vermonters' willingness to cooperate with large parts of the New Deal welfare agenda was the generally nonpartisan, tactful, and competent character of the programs' state-level management, which yielded a cooperative spirit among local, state, and federal officials. Harry W. Witters, a Democrat and St. Johnsbury lawyer, exemplified that leadership as director of the Vermont WPA through most of its years in the state. A nationwide poll, conducted in April 1936, found that in Vermont federal relief aid received one of the highest favorable ratings of any state, with specific approval of the WPA for its freedom from political influence. The *Brattleboro Reformer* observed, "there may be a great deal more New Deal sympathy in Vermont than most people realize."[45]

WPA activities spanned the state, with Witters at one point managing projects in 126 of the 247 towns. Most of the money went for community service projects and construction, with local needs determining the specific undertakings. The WPA's Final Report, compiled in 1943, reflected the diversity of the Vermont program:

*814,740 garments for relief families produced in WPA sewing rooms.
*2,258,291 school lunches served.
*3,798 persons instructed in WPA-taught adult education classes.
*1,628 miles of highway built or improved.
*584 bridges constructed or rebuilt.
*3,803 culverts built or rebuilt.
*11 new schools constructed; 107 schools remodeled or improved.
*40 new public buildings (other than schools) constructed.
*221 public buildings remodeled or improved.
*15 parks, 30 playgrounds and 3 swimming pools constructed.[46]

Beyond these "brick and mortar" projects, other WPA programs had unquantifiable lasting effects in the state. The WPA provided registered and practical nurses to rural communities; school programs and teachers to prison inmates; music and art instructors to public schools; and adult education classes on a range of topics practical and theoretical. WPA workers provided free books, sheet music, art exhibits, and public concerts; they also surveyed the state's historical records, and prepared a guidebook, *Vermont, A Guide to the Green Mountain State*. Vermonters in the Federal Writers' Project produced a mimeographed magazine, *The Catamount*, which published four stories that subsequently earned "distinctive" citations in the publication *Best Short Stories of 1938*.

A small group of Vermont artists received support under the Federal Art Project and the related Treasury Relief Art Program. WPA artists painted murals on the walls of post offices at Northfield, Rutland, St. Albans, White River Junction, and Woodstock. The Vermont Symphony Orchestra came into existence in 1934 as a project growing out of the WPA music program. In 1939, the legislature voted the orchestra an appropriation, and it thereafter acquired a regular line in the legislative budget, becoming the first state-funded symphony orchestra in the United States, and the nation's only rural symphony ensemble.

In 1935 and 1936, state legislators continued to demonstrate a cooperative spirit toward specific New Deal programs. In response to Roosevelt's emphasis on planning, they established a five-member State Planning Board, and in anticipation of national legislation they adopted an old-age pension plan that opened the way for cooperation with the soon-to-be-enacted federal Social Security Act.[47] After Congress passed that historic bill, on August 14, 1935, Montpelier lawmakers produced additional enabling legislation that made Vermont "one of the first States of the Union to cooperate with every agency of the Social Security Act."[48] On January 31, 1940, Ida M. Fuller, of Ludlow, gained distinction as the nation's first beneficiary of monthly Social Security payments, receiving a check numbered 00–000–001, for $22.54.

Despite federal and state relief efforts, however, many Vermonters remained in desperate straits. In interviews at the time, struggling individuals described their circumstances in extreme terms. A woman in Barre, whose husband toiled "on the WPA," reported, "We never been so bad off. . . . I don't know what's going to become of us . . . we got nothing anymore."[49] An unemployed Barre man described his situation: "All you do is hang around and drink too much, and wise-crack and laugh at everything because you feel licked and empty inside."⁵⁰ The hardships were clear in a letter written by a Fair Haven woman to President Roosevelt in June 1934: "We have certainly seen some hard days. [W]e have been to bed a good many night with out nothing to eat. [S]ome days all we would have is blackberries. I would go and pick Black Berries last summer and we would eat them for dinner then my oldest boy 9 years old would take care of the smallest children while I and the next one to him eight years old would go and pitch on hay for [M]r. Ferguson. When my baby girl was born last December I didn't have a thing to put on her I wropt her up in one of my dresses until the Doctor got a few things for her. [T]hat is the way we are getting use. We didn't get only two quilts and one blanket that you sent out for the poor. [A]nd there is one person not far from here has got so many blankets she has got them stored away. . . . I am not complainin for it don't do any good, but it makes me feel bad. [W]hen some gets all they want and others can't. I know a party that has got a radio and spends some of his money for beer. We don't have no pleasure of any kind . . . and also tell us what we will do about the house I hate to lose it when I have seven little children and no place to go."⁵¹

A tense relationship prevailed between Vermonters and New Deal officials, despite the many areas of significant cooperation. Two issues in 1935, involving a proposed Green Mountain Parkway and a plan by the federal Resettlement Administration to retire submarginal hillside farmland, illustrate the point. The most riveting of these was the parkway proposal, which triggered one of the state's most bitter public controversies.

The parkway idea came from Col. William J. Wilgus, of Ascutney, the retired chief engineer of the New York Central Railroad. Wilgus advanced his proposal in June 1933, after passage of the National Industrial Recovery Act (NIRA), hoping to attract federal funds for its construction. He envisioned clearing a one-thousand-foot-wide swath along the spine of the Green Mountains, 260 miles in length, which would create a highway extending from Massachusetts to Canada. The project would encompass fifty thousand acres of land, with a million-acre state park at its northern end. Wilgus claimed his plan could fix some of the state's most pressing problems:

> Along this lofty scenic route I envisioned year-round cultural, recreational and spiritual centers, akin to those of ancient Greece, in

which attractive occupations thereby offered young Vermonters would hold them to their native heath. Coupled with this transformation of Vermont from a static to a dynamic region, pulsating with renewed vigor, would go healthful opportunities for the general public, near and far, to spend their increasingly available leisure time wisely.[52]

Governor Wilson endorsed Wilgus's plan, anticipating, in Richard Judd's words, that the road would be "an imaginative solution to the state's apparent need for a big project which would employ many people, stimulate the Vermont economy, and confer lasting benefits on everyone concerned."[53]

Both Wilgus and Wilson lobbied Washington for federal funds for the roadway. The Roosevelt Administration responded by making available $50,000 for an initial survey. By January 1935, the National Park Service and the U.S. Bureau of Public Roads, working with the Vermont Bureau of Public Works, completed a preliminary plan, using Virginia's Skyline Drive as a model. The plan placed the estimated cost at about $18,000,000, to be paid from NRA relief assistance funds. Vermont's only financial obligation would be to spend $500,000 for acquisition of the fifty thousand acres of land needed for the right-of-way, the money to come through a proposed tax on gasoline. The land itself would be deeded to the federal government.

The issue ignited a heated intrastate debate. The General Assembly undertook a series of public hearings. Supporters and opponents also pressed their views through the new medium of radio, utilizing the services of Waterbury's station WDEV, which had established a transmitting office next door to the Capitol in the Pavilion Hotel. Among the parkway's strongest advocates were Vermont Chamber of Commerce director James P. Taylor and *Burlington Free Press* publisher David Willard Howe. Both men favored a policy of vigorous economic development for the state, with an emphasis on commercial tourism that exploited the advantages of Vermont's scenic and outdoor attractions. An expanded road access for autos, such as the parkway, easily meshed with this focus. The completed parkway would be a sign of Vermont's "progress"—an opening to the outside world. Other supporters emphasized the immediate effect its construction would have on reducing unemployment, as well as the long-term boost it would give to Vermont's economy. *Bennington Banner* editor Frank E. Howe (no relation to David Willard Howe), an early advocate of a state

Map detailing the route of the proposed Green Mountain Parkway, prepared in 1934 by parkway supporters. *Vermont Historical Society.*

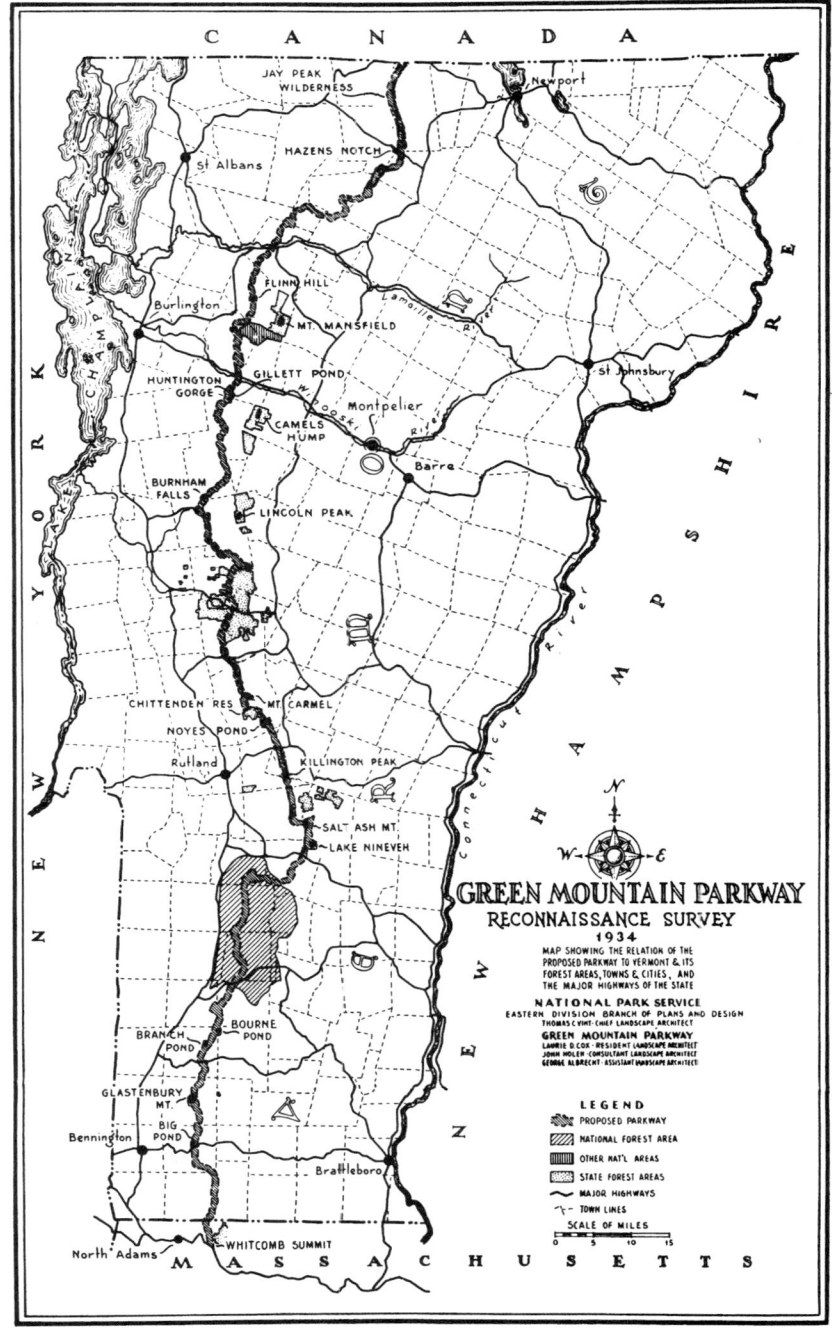

system of hard-surface roads, also supported the parkway, as did the State Planning Board and its chairman, Ralph Flanders, and the writer Dorothy Canfield Fisher.

Opponents argued, in various ways, that the parkway would "spoil" Vermont by scarring its natural beauty. The Green Mountain Club charged it would bring undesirable commercialization to unspoiled areas that were already accessible in their natural state to travelers by way of the Long Trail. Three influential Vermont opinion shapers, poet Walter Hard, Vermont Historical Society president John Spargo, and writer-publisher Vrest Orton, all condemned the parkway on environmental grounds, with the latter warning that the project would turn Vermont into a "Coney Island."[54] The *Rutland Herald*, expressing similar reservations, pushed a campaign against the Parkway described as "probably the most vigorous ever mounted by a Vermont newspaper."[55]

Other resisters opposed for reasons unrelated to the environment. They worried that the project would lead to further intrusions of federal control over the state's lands; that the road's upkeep would become a huge financial burden to future taxpayers; that the money it would cost the state in land acquisitions would be better spent on more pressing matters; or that it was likely to unwisely shift the state's economic destiny from agriculture and local industry to tourism dependent on scenery, weather, and other unpredictable, uncontrollable factors.

Lacking a clear mandate, the legislature equivocated. In March 1935, the senate approved an act permitting acquisition of land for the parkway; but the house defeated it, concluding essentially that the issue "was too hot to handle."[56] In the fall Governor Charles M. Smith, who did not take a public stand on the issue, called a special legislative session to deal with the parkway. This time the funding bill succeeded: Both houses acted positively on legislation allowing the state to incur bonded debt for the acquisition of parkway rights-of-way up to $500,000 and including a requirement calling for endorsement of their decision by the state's voters in a referendum on Town Meeting Day the following March. When that day arrived, March 3, 1936, opponents carried the vote by 43,176 to 31,101, ending the Green Mountain Parkway dream. Only five of the fourteen counties—Chittenden, Washington, Lamoille, Franklin, and Grand Isle—supported the question.

The parkway controversy overlapped with debate over another New Deal initiative for Vermont, this one put forward in the spring of 1934. It involved participation by FERA's Rural Rehabilitation Program (predecessor of the Resettlement Administration) and Land Program, and the Land Policy Section of the Agricultural Adjustment Administration. The proposal called for retirement of poor or so-called submarginal farmlands in southern and central Vermont by having the federal government buy the lands in question, move the farm families involved to more productive acreage, and then restore the land and lease it back to the state with restrictions against its future inhabitation. The federal government would retain subsoil rights. The plan envisioned eventual retirement of almost five hundred thousand acres of land, and the resettlement of thirteen thousand Vermonters. By participating in the program, the state had the opportunity to gain substantial amounts of federal funds.

Governor Wilson backed the plan and designated a committee to begin selecting acreage for land retirement, declaring that the federal program simply made less painful a process that had already been underway in the state for almost a century. The long-time commissioner of agriculture, Edward H. Jones, supported it, too. The state Chamber of Commerce and several newspapers, including the *Burlington Free Press*, the *Burlington Daily News*, and the *Brattleboro Reformer*, also endorsed the plan. A 1933 study by the Vermont Agricultural Experiment Station of farm abandonment and unprofitable land use in several hill towns provided additional support, concluding that state and federal planning was needed to improve the towns' management of land and population distribution, and that the "physical and economic handicaps to farming in the locality apparently made extensive farm abandonment inevitable."[57] By late summer 1934, residents of many hillside farms, anticipating the state's participation in the resettlement program, began preparing their land for sale to the federal government.

Speaker of the House George D. Aiken, however, opposed the land retirement program. Aiken, who had remained neutral on the parkway issue, argued that the federal government should be working to sustain and revivify Vermont's hill towns, not dismantle them. In addition, he reasoned that the hillside farmhouses were likely to be increasingly in demand, in the future, as year-round or summer homes by new residents in the state. Further, Aiken made clear that he resented this additional intrusion of the federal government, and the loss of control over state resources and state affairs that it embodied. The submarginal land controversy fed the anxieties of parkway opponents who already were fearful of the large amounts of acreage expected to be taken and the numbers of people anticipated to be moved from their land in that project.

In 1935, the General Assembly established a joint committee to study the issue. Aiken, by then the state's lieutenant governor, was designated chairman. His committee turned in a negative report that killed the plan.

The Rise of George D. Aiken

Historians Samuel B. Hand and Paul Searls have described George Aiken as "a different politician from his predecessors."[58] The difference derived, to a large extent, from Aiken's background and orientation that set him apart from the bankers, lawyers, and industrialists who traditionally composed the state's political elite. Aiken was a horticulturist and nurseryman who operated a five-hundred-acre hillside farm near Putney. Prior to entering politics, he had earned a reputation across the Connecticut River valley for his illustrated talks on wildflowers, and in 1933 he authored *Pioneering with Wildflowers*, a labor of love on his favorite topic. Aiken prided himself in being a working farmer, "one of the people," who thought and spoke as they did. After winning election to his first term as governor he often commented, to good effect, that the $5,000 salary that accompanied the office was the most money he ever earned. Historians Hand and Michael Sherman singled out Aiken's "uncanny gift to personify qualities Vermont rhetoric acclaimed as virtues. He embodied precisely those traditions the state most liked about itself."[59]

With the Depression as backdrop, Aiken made a rapid political ascent, one that led eventually to a position of leadership unmatched in twentieth-century state politics. In 1932, after a single term in the legislature, representing the 835 residents of Putney, he challenged and defeated the incumbent speaker of the house, and two years later won election as lieutenant governor. At age forty-four, in 1936, the slightly built, unassuming, and prematurely white-haired Aiken entered the race for governor. In the Republican primary, relying on a "war chest" of $969.35, he defeated three other candidates in a close race that included the publisher of the *Burlington Daily News* and a former speaker of the house. Then in the general election he defeated a popular Democrat from Burlington, Alfred Heininger, carrying 230 of Vermont's 248 towns and winning 60 percent of the votes.

Independent in temperament, Aiken had grown up in the progressive wing of the state Republican Party, his father E. W. Aiken having been a Theodore Roosevelt activist in 1912. George Aiken once recalled, "Teddy Roosevelt was a rebel and I think my father had it in his blood somewhat. And it had come down from generation to generation."[60] In his 1936 gubernatorial campaign, Aiken's primary opponent had railed against the New Deal; but Aiken had been less critical. "I have never opposed and never expect to oppose any measure calculated to relieve human distress, or to provide a more equitable opportunity for those equally deserving," Aiken said, solely on the basis that "those measures are endorsed by an opposing party or its candidates."[61]

A cautious politician in many respects, he avoided taking public stands on some of the decade's most volatile state issues, such as the Twenty-first Amendment repealing Prohibition (ratified by the Vermont legislature on September 26, 1933) and the Green Mountain Parkway proposal. He told an official of Friends of the Parkway in February 1936, "I cannot get excited enough about the Parkway to let either side use my name in any propaganda. I am sure it would not do the harm its opponents claim it would, nor would it do as much good as its proponents claim."[62] Many years later, however, Aiken characterized the parkway initiative as "one of President Roosevelt's ideas that I didn't go along with."[63]

As a legislator in the Depression's early years, Aiken backed a number of progressive initiatives. In 1931, he aided a successful drive led by the Vermont Farm Bureau for legislation that shifted the state's major source of revenue from the land tax, a significant burden to farmers, to a statewide income tax. (With this bill, the state also abolished the highway and education taxes, the intangibles tax, and the general statewide property tax.) In 1933, he helped enact the state's "worthy debtor" law, which extended to farmers, laborers, and small businessmen the same right to temporary receivership enjoyed by public utilities, banks, and large corporations.[64] In addition, he supported the state's newly enacted old-age pension bill while also criticizing it as being inadequately funded and calling for the federal government to bear a "much larger proportion" of the legislation's expense.[65]

Regarding the New Deal, Aiken pursued a carefully calibrated course. He often condemned its "paternalism" and "big government" policies, at one point describing it as "that visible and invisible government in Washington, whose thoughts and actions are so alien to the free-thinking people of Vermont and of the nation; whose policy for the last four years has been one of debt and destruction."⁶⁶ He denounced "undue regulation," proposed "cooperation" as a better way for broadening individual opportunity, and rejected deficit spending in favor of a pay-as-you-go approach, asserting that because "Vermont does it," the federal government should also be able to do it.⁶⁷ These views led him to engage in several highly visible battles with Roosevelt that contributed to his political popularity.

Nevertheless, he backed many federal relief and reform programs, and as governor led the state toward acceptance of larger responsibility for its needy citizens. He supported the CCC, federal farm subsidies, conservation efforts, unemployment relief, Social Security, and state planning, a record that prompted one national publication to characterize him "as liberal as any New Dealer."⁶⁸

Aiken took a leading role in promoting efforts to expand electric service in the state, which in the 1930s suffered from high rates and the least rural electrification in New England. In May 1935, President Roosevelt signed legislation creating the Rural Electrification Administration (REA), which, according to historian William E. Leuchtenburg, "changed more directly the way people lived" than any other single act of the Roosevelt years.⁶⁹ REA enabled farmers, working through nonprofit cooperatives, to get low-cost federal loans and do what private power companies refused to do: extend power lines into the countryside and bring electric power and lights to rural and farm homes.

While lieutenant governor, Aiken had shepherded a bill through the General Assembly that gave the REA its start in Vermont. Unlike his party's Old Guard who favored private power strategies, he led a group of self-styled progressives backing public power development. Aiken claimed the private "power companies were refusing to serve the rural areas, [to] run their lines there,"⁷⁰ and in fact were selling much of Vermont's ample hydroelectric power out of state to large users at higher profits. He characterized the utilities' attitude as "We'll serve whom we damn please—whom we can make the most money on."⁷¹

As governor, Aiken worked closely with the REA and citizens' cooperatives to expand rural electrification services. Between 1938 and 1940, the state's first two REA nonprofit cooperatives began operations: Washington Electric Cooperative, of East Montpelier; and Vermont Electric Cooperative, of Johnson. The cooperatives' emergence forced the private power companies to expand and upgrade their own service to rural

Vermonters, so that by 1945 almost 70 percent of Vermont farms were wired for electricity.

To protect these rural electrification gains, Aiken appointed commissioners to the Public Service Commission who were sympathetic to farmers. Most notably, he named as chairman Ellsworth B. Cornwall, the Vermont Farm Bureau's first president. Cornwall was a leading advocate of rural electrification and proponent of a "public ownership point of view."[72] Under his leadership, the commission forced down private power company rates, made electric lights more affordable for thousands of Vermonters, and put in place the elements of a public power tradition for the state.

Aiken's most important battles while governor concerned dam construction and protection of state control of water resources against the interests of both private utility companies and the federal government. At stake, he repeatedly told Vermonters, was nothing less than the state's capacity to manage its own land in its own interest. In addition, he described these battles as part of a larger struggle to protect Vermonters' "right to breathe and think and act freely and naturally."[73]

These had been central issues for Aiken from an early point in his career. In 1927, Congress had passed the Rivers and Harbors Act, recommending surveys of the nation's major river valleys for the purpose of planning for flood control and related activities. The 1927 floods in the Mississippi Valley and New England had produced federal legislation in May 1928 that gave responsibility for flood control to the Army Corps of Engineers. Soon thereafter, the Corps and engineers from the state and public utilities companies undertook a lengthy study of flood control throughout the Green Mountains. Out of this study came a proposal for construction of more than eighty dams and reservoirs on five flood-prone Vermont rivers. The federal proposal was drafted as a bill sponsored by the Vermont speaker of the house, a move intended to aid the power companies. The bill would have permitted a group of private utilities, largely controlled by out-of-state holding companies, to build storage reservoirs and produce hydroelectric power at dam sites in the state. As a freshman member of the House Conservation and Development Committee in 1931–1932, Aiken had been instrumental in defeating the bill, which failed by one vote.

By 1937, when Aiken became governor, Montpelier and Washington had been working efficiently together for several years on a number of water-management issues. In 1933, with Vermont's cooperation, the Corps began constructing retention dams at Winooski River tributaries in East Barre and Wrightsville, making channel improvements upstream from Middlesex village, and reconstructing the clothes-pin factory dam in Montpelier. Funds for the projects, and a supply of approximately five thousand workers, including an all-black unit assigned at East Barre, came from the Civilian Conservation Corps.

The workers at these several flood-control projects were largely unconventional CCC enlistees. Most had once been members of the so-called Bonus Expeditionary Force, the famous ragtag "Bonus Army" of World War I veterans who had marched on Washington, D.C., in 1932, demanding early payments of war bonuses that had been promised them by Congress. President Hoover's response had been to use U.S. Army troops to drive them from their makeshift capital camps. After the inauguration of Roosevelt, however, many Bonus marchers regrouped on the edge of Washington. In May 1933, Roosevelt offered the veterans a chance to work in the CCC at one dollar per day plus the Corps' regular stipend of food, clothing, and lodging. By summer, the first CCC Bonus Army contingent had arrived in Vermont, and this group eventually provided the bulk of workers not only for the Wrightsville and East Barre projects but also the Waterbury dam.

Construction on the largest of these undertakings, a dam on the Little River above Waterbury, began in spring 1935 (the state had purchased about ten thousand acres of land in the area). In keeping with CCC methods, workers accomplished their task mainly by hand. As evidence of the project's predilection for reliance on manpower rather than machines, several freight cars "stacked high with nothing but wheelbarrows" arrived at the Waterbury railroad station as the project commenced. When completed in 1938, the structure stood 175 feet in height and a half-mile in width—the largest earth-filled dam east of the Mississippi River, and the largest CCC flood-control project in the nation. It created a six-mile long lake. At a midpoint in the work, in summer 1936, President Roosevelt came to Montpelier and Barre, on a return trip from Québec City. The president traveled to the new Wrightsville Dam north of the capital, and then by rail to Waterbury to observe construction there. Bystanders reported that he pronounced it "a great sight—a great sight."[74]

In March 1936, another flood hit New England. This time, most of the damage occurred in Massachusetts and Connecticut, the southern portion of the Connecticut River watershed, where the deluge registered as the most destructive in those states' history. The new disaster prompted calls for a set of protective flood-control measures in the Connecticut River valley that would be modeled after the Tennessee Valley Authority. Congress responded with passage of the Omnibus Flood Control Act of 1936, authorizing states to enter joint agreements or "compacts" involving flood control. Soon thereafter, the states of New Hampshire, Massachusetts, Connecticut, and Vermont formed the Connecticut River Valley Flood Control Commission. In March 1937, shortly after Aiken became governor, the commission drew up a series of compacts among the four states for acquiring sites and planning construction of federally funded flood-control dams and reservoirs. Costs for engineering and construction would be federally funded and land acquisition and relocation costs would be state funded. Under the plans, construction by the Army Corps of Engineers would occur at eight sites, principally on tributaries of the upper Connecticut River, including three dams in Vermont.

Aiken, however, believed the plans presented major difficulties for Vermont and New Hampshire. The proposed dams would cause the fertile lands of several narrow valleys in the state to be submerged under water, taking away not only farmland but also local tax bases. He wanted clear agreement with the federal government on financing and compensation issues. Of most importance, he wanted to settle satisfactorily the question of who would control the dams and the hydroelectric power that might be generated by them.

The commission agreed, at Aiken's prodding, that the purpose of these dams ought to be limited to flood control, and that each state should retain title to land acquired for dam construction and "all benefit or advantage of water conservation, power storage or power development."[75] The Omnibus Flood Control Act required congressional ratification of the commission's agreements, however, and it never came. The way was blocked by legislative allies of Roosevelt who insisted on federal control of the dams and the power rights, including control of all the tributaries in the area that drained into the Connecticut River, clear up to their sources. Roosevelt sought this control primarily because of his distrust of private utility companies, whose access to the sites he wanted barred in order to protect other New Deal initiatives for lowering the nation's power and light costs.

Aiken's highly public struggle to maintain Vermont control over

Vermont lands led many observers beyond New England to mistakenly perceive the Green Mountain governor as an agent of the private utilities. In fact, Aiken's own state-level crusade for inexpensive rural electrification had permanently alienated him from those interests years before. "I was having a ruckus with Roosevelt and the utility boys at the same time," Aiken later said.[76] At a meeting of eastern governors in 1937, Aiken concisely stated his view of the central issue: "Shall the federal government have the authority to take from a state without its consent and with or without recompense the natural resources upon which the industry, the income and the welfare of the people may depend?"[77] Aiken's struggle attracted the strong support of Vermont's congressional delegation, especially Senator Warren R. Austin, who saw a moral issue in the federal government's assertion of a right to take land without Vermont's consent. Austin also shared Aiken's opposition to power development under federal auspices, in the Connecticut River valley; unlike Aiken, however, he preferred that it be left in the hands of private utilities.

In June 1938, Congress gave Roosevelt a new bill requiring the federal government to pay all costs of construction of flood-control dams and reservoirs, and also specifically allowing the government to take land for dams and reservoirs, build the dams, and control the generated power without formal agreement of the states involved. The federal plans included early construction of a dam in Vermont at Union Village, in the Ompompanoosuc River valley. Aiken challenged the law's constitutionality, insisting the state legislature would have to formally agree to acquisition of any Vermont land by the federal government. He charged that the bill demonstrated Roosevelt's intention "to abolish State lines and State existence as political units."[78] On January 12, 1939, Aiken took his fight to a joint session of the General Assembly. He told legislators the issue was not "not flood control . . . .The issue is simply and solely the insistence of the Federal government that it can take from us what it chooses, when it chooses without any regard at all for our wishes or our rights."[79] According to Green Mountain National Forest Supervisor Otto Koenig, "little Vermont felt that it was about to be swallowed by the federal government," and Aiken was trying to save it.[80]

At Aiken's request, the General Assembly voted a defense fund of $67,500 to challenge the constitutionality of the 1938 act through the courts. Two days later, however, the White House made clear that if Vermont opposed a federal dam, the state should not be forced to accept one. The president's secretary, Steven Early, announced: "If Vermont doesn't want the [flood-control] protection it doesn't have to have it. Other states want and can use the money."[81] In 1940, the U.S. Supreme Court upheld the 1938 law, but Aiken remained unyielding. When he left the governorship in 1941, to take a seat in the United States Senate, he had thwarted the federal effort for four years.

During the 1940s, at least two other Corps proposals for construction of multiple Vermont dams were also turned back. Governor William Wills (1941–1945) led these fights utilizing a $10,000 defense fund made available by the state emergency board; Aiken and Austin provided resistance in the Senate. In 1944, Congress removed Vermont's principal objection to the flood-control law, concerning state consultation, and in 1946 work began on a dam at Union Village. However, further dam construction in the state, and in New Hampshire, stalled over the issue of reimbursement of taxes lost to towns where dams and reservoirs would be located. In 1951, negotiators resolved this issue, and the four New England states finally agreed to the long-awaited flood-control plan for the Connecticut River basin. Congress enacted it into law in 1953. The compact included an agreement by Connecticut and Massachusetts to refund to Vermont and New Hampshire 90 percent of taxes lost to their towns through federal ownership of reservoir lands, and to make additional payments for other lost income and expenses. The agreement led to construction of dams by the Corps of Engineers on West River at Ball Mountain (1957) and West Townshend (1959); on the Black River at North Springfield (1960); and on the Ottauquechee River at North Hartland (1961).

The Vermont flood-control battle finally had reached an end. In this long struggle, the state sought to maintain the substance of local control and state's rights—that is, veto rights over flood-control proposals—and consequently limit as strictly as possible the amount of flood-control aid it would provide to its beleaguered southern New England neighbors. Vermont's stance appeared highly principled to some observers, especially in the Green Mountains, but in the eyes of some others it left impressions of Vermont, with its rigid "state's rights" claims, reluctant to acknowledge regional interdependence. And its meager counterproposals for resolving the conflict were viewed as compassionless and indifferent to the serious flood problems of its southern New England neighbors, Connecticut and Massachusetts.

More than anything else, however, the flood-control fight illuminated the continuing distrust held by many Vermonters for so-called "big business" and "big government." As in Vermonters' late-eighteenth-century resistance to claims of landlords and the power of government, so had Aiken led resistance to conceivably similar claims by similar forces one hundred and fifty years later. Aiken's role in the flood-control fight dramatically fused his name and the phrase "independent Vermont" in the public mind, enlarged his political popularity in the state, improved his electability, and strongly informed the attitude of great distrust for Franklin Roosevelt that Aiken exhibited in later skirmishes, on matters domestic and foreign, with the Democratic president.

Economic Struggles

The Depression brought hardship to Vermont's manufacturing and industrial workers and, according to the Vermont Commissioner of Industries, "a crop of labor difficulties" for Montpelier.[82] The first significant labor conflict occurred in the Barre granite district, which had experienced a drop in the demand for stone and a succession of layoffs and lowered wages. On April 1, 1933, the granite workers' unions responded by going on strike. Labor organizer John C. Lawson called it a "straight out union fight for survival."[83] More than three thousand people paraded through Barre streets, led by mayor William W. Lapoint and a brass band, in support of the workers.

The strike shut down six of the area's seven major companies. When owners sought to reopen, using strikebreakers, violence flared. The state responded on May 6 by sending more than a hundred deputies and several units of the Vermont National Guard, led by Leonard Wing, the Guard's regimental commander, to keep order in Barre. Other guardsmen were dispatched to the stone sheds in Northfield. Governor Stanley Wilson refused requests by Barre's merchants, city council, and mayor to withdraw the troops who, according to Company B's Major William G. Barrett, had gone "into action clearing the streets in a very workmanlike manner" and had occasionally resorted to the use of gas in dispensing the crowds. Heber G. England, manager of the Jones Brothers Company, largest of the area's granite firms, sent a letter of warm praise to Wilson for his "forcefulness" in preserving "law and order."[84]

In late May, the groups involved—the granite cutters' union, and open- and closed-shop manufacturers—agreed to arbitration by a special three-member board headed by President Ernest M. Hopkins of Dartmouth College. In August, they reached a settlement affecting about fifteen hundred workers, in which nonunion firms agreed to pay union-scale wages, and granite cutters held onto their prestrike minimum pay rates of $1.00 per hour, but with tool sharpeners and polishers receiving only 87 cents per hour. The union had asked for a return to the $1.12 per hour rate that existed in a previous contract, but nevertheless claimed a qualified victory.

In 1934, trouble surfaced at Vermont Marble Company. Workers in the company's quarries and sheds had recently established unions and affiliated with the American Federation of Labor (AFL). They sought formal recognition, establishment of a closed shop, and commencement of collective bargaining with an agenda calling for an increase in wages, which stood substantially lower than in the unionized Barre granite district. A thousand workers had been laid off since the beginning of the Depression, and those who remained faced significant hardship. Employee-residents of the company town of Proctor complained of excessive deductions from their pay for rent, electricity, water, insurance, and hospitalization. A contemporary account described the situation in Proctor: "Men had received weekly pay checks of two cents, twenty cents, sixty-eight cents. Many had received pink vouchers marked in ink 'no check.' Many who were in debt for rent in company-owned houses were working but a few hours per week."[85]

Management, however, refused to have any dealings with the unions or otherwise negotiate, insisting on absolute control over wages and hours. This stance placed the company at odds with federal legislation under Section 7(a) of the National Industrial Recovery Act (June 1933) and, after that law's revocation by the United States Supreme Court (1935), with the National Labor Relations Act (July 1935). Although both acts obliged employers to recognize workers' unions as bargaining agents, federal enforcement efforts in Vermont proved lax. By November 1935, a majority of the eleven hundred remaining Vermont Marble Company employees at its mills, shops, and quarries in Danby, West and Center Rutland, and Proctor went on strike. At issue was the company's refusal to confer with workers' representatives concerning wages and working conditions.

The strike lasted nine months. Company president Frank C. Partridge, who for several months in early 1931 had served an interim appointment in the U.S. Senate, kept the quarries and sheds operating on a reduced schedule by inducing nonunion workers to cross picket lines. As in Barre, however, the efforts triggered mass protests and sporadic violent incidents.

In West and Central Rutland and Danby, groups of strike sympathizers, sometimes seven hundred strong—composed of women, teenage boys and girls, and children—participated in regular street marches and other demonstrations of their support. In a march involving a thousand participants at West Rutland, participants' "yells, whistles and beating of pails, cans and wash tubs, could be heard echoing from hillside to hillside." According to newspaper accounts, older women wielding broomsticks brought up the rear in these demonstrations, "their heads wrapped in black shawls" and "talking heatedly in their native tongue."[86]

The demonstrations prompted Governor Charles M. Smith to dispatch sheriffs' deputies to the scene. Smith defended his decision, which cost Vermont taxpayers $1,200 a week, as an alternative to calling out the National Guard, aware that events in the earlier Barre strike had resulted in "very strong" public sentiment against the Guard's further use.[87] The armed deputies' principal task in the marble district involved escorting non-striking workers safely across picket lines to and from work.

On Thanksgiving Day 1935, despite sleet and rain, strikers and their supporters launched one of their largest marches. A participant recalled the dramatic day: "Some of the men and women wanted to go out to Proctor while the Proctors were enjoying their big [Thanksgiving] dinner, and show them how little their workers had to be thankful for . . . So hundreds of us landed into Proctor. The sheriffs and deputies tried to stop us, and we got the bunch of them and locked them up and took the town over. Then we paraded all afternoon through the streets. The next day the company unloaded a gang of deputies into Proctor and from then on nobody could stand on the [street] corner, or collect in even twos or threes, without being busted up."[88]

The workers' campaign drew support from beyond the marble district, though little from within the state. AFL union members in Barre, Graniteville, Websterville, Burlington, and Winooski sent weekly relief contributions; student and faculty sympathizers at Dartmouth College organized a support committee; students on other campuses, as far away as Wisconsin, aided the cause. From New York City came publicity and funds for the campaign through an organization called the United Committee to Aid the Vermont Marble Workers. The United Committee sponsored a mass meeting in New York to support the strike.

The New York event was publicized through a widely circulated poster drawn by the artist and Vermont summer resident Rockwell Kent. Kent's poster depicted a wintry scene in which a striking marble worker's family was being evicted from their home. The poster's caption read, "1775 to 1936," and cited Ethan Allen's eviction of the British from their stronghold at Ticonderoga "in the name of the Great Jehovah and the Continental Congress." It warned of an anticipated attempt by "the Proctors with the aid of the armed forces of their State, and, no doubt, in

Artist Rockwell Kent prepared this poster to advertise a New York City rally supporting the 1935–1936 Vermont Marble workers' strike. Here it is reused as the cover for a report of testimony given at a strikers' meeting at West Rutland. *Vermont Historical Society.*

the name of the Great Jehovah of the marble church at Proctor ... [to] evict some hundreds of defenceless human beings from their homes. If Ethan Allen lived today, where would he stand? Perhaps ... he'd say again: 'Women sobbing and lamenting, Children crying, and Men pierced to the heart with sorrow and indignation at the approaching tyranny of—Law.' The first Vermont eviction brought about a war; what will this one do?"[89]

On February 29, 1936, the United Committee sponsored a public hearing at the town hall in West Rutland, chaired by Kent, which provided information about the economic basis of the strike.[90] Soon afterward, articles backing the strikers appeared in the *Nation* and *New Republic* magazines, and nationally prominent individuals in art and theater circles endorsed the marble workers' cause. A play entitled *Vermont Rebels Again* opened on a New York stage.

These developments failed to intimidate the Vermont Marble Company.[91] In May 1936, company officials began evicting all strikers living in company housing. As the weeks passed, some workers returned to the quarries and sheds. A resolution of the conflict finally came in July 1936, through the efforts of a special commissioner from the United States Conciliation Service. Under the settlement agreement, strikers did not achieve union recognition, however, and made only minor pay gains. The two-and-a-half-cent-per-hour raise in wages awarded to most marble workers left their pay rates 50 to 35 percent less than for similar occupations in Vermont's unionized granite districts. In addition, many of the strike leaders were not hired back. The owners won this struggle and ten more years passed before the United Stone Workers finally achieved formal recognition in the marble industry and a union contract with the Vermont Marble Company.

Other labor organizing activities in the state brought mixed results. In the summer of 1934, brief strikes failed at two Burlington-area plants, the Queen City Cotton Company and the American Woolen Company, and unsuccessful union-organizing efforts occurred during the decade at several of Vermont's two dozen smaller textile mills, many of them owned by bitter opponents of organized labor. By 1937, however, organizing drives backed by the Congress of Industrial Organizations (CIO) succeeded in manufacturing plants in Bennington, Cavendish, and Ludlow. These relatively peaceful union gains in the late 1930s signaled the beginning of a moderation in the Green Mountains' traditional hostility toward unionism, a trend facilitated by federal encouragement of unionization efforts, but also by a friendlier outlook toward workingmen's problems by state government officials, led by Governor George Aiken, and continued by his successor, William Wills.

Aiken acted vigorously to open his administration to the state's industrial workers. Unlike any previous governor, he actively sought the views of union leaders and made regular speaking appearances before state labor groups. In three strikes that occurred during his governorship, he took on the role of informal mediator. According to Ernest Gibson, Jr., in each instance Aiken "called the strikers into his office" and "explained to them that he wanted fairness on both sides and asked them to see that order was kept and that no damage was done." Gibson believed that, largely because of Aiken's contributions in these interventions, "all three strikes were settled peaceably, and with no damage or bitterness."[92]

In the more labor-friendly atmosphere of Aiken's governorship, the 1939 legislature created a separate Department of Industrial Relations and passed a Mediation and Arbitration Act that provided for a three-member board to settle labor disputes. Despite these advances, however, the legislature continued to be an entity unfriendly to union interests. When it enacted a bill making sit-down strikes illegal, Aiken denounced it but signed the legislation into law. As the period came to an end, the state's labor forces nevertheless showed few signs of discouragement; by 1940, they comprised approximately 40 percent of the work force, a gain of almost 10 percent since 1930, and their growing numbers provided hope for an improved future.

Aiken's chief economic concern—and that of a majority of legislators—lay not with labor but with the well-being of the state's farmers. Struggling in the aftermath of the 1927 flood—described by the commissioner of agriculture as the most "staggering blow" that Vermont's "agricultural interests" had ever received—and the Great Depression, farmers absorbed another blow in the ferocious hurricane of September 1938.[93] This unusual New England tropical storm hit off the Florida shore, then traveled up the Atlantic coast from the Carolinas. Instead of veering out to sea, however, as hurricanes customarily do, it slammed into Long Island, then surged up the Connecticut River valley and through the center of Vermont, resulting in heavy damage at Brattleboro, Bellows Falls, Montpelier, and Burlington. The storm killed seven people in the state (almost seven hundred died in the New England region) and caused $12,000,000 in losses, including the destruction of thousands of trees. Farmers' sugar bushes and apple orchards suffered especially severely, with damages at a farm in Walden amounting to four-fifths of a five-thousand-tree sugar bush, and losses at a Cabot farm of twenty-four hundred of its thirty-five hundred trees. At the legislature's directive, Aiken borrowed $2,000,000 as a supplement to federal relief funds, to facilitate recovery from the hurricane's destruction.

Somewhat more manageable than natural catastrophe were dairy farmers' difficulties in getting fair treatment from Boston milk dealers and other out-of-state milk merchandisers. During the 1930s, Vermont dairymen supplied approximately 85 percent of their daily fluid milk production to markets in Boston and elsewhere beyond Vermont, but they faced several worsening problems. Overproduction, declining consumer demand, and inefficient systems of milk collection and transportation had eliminated or strongly cut into profits. The low prices hurt dairymen's ability to purchase needed farm equipment, seed, and grain, and to hire farm labor. These problems, in turn, increased their vulnerability to the machinations of distributors in the Boston and New York City markets.

Farm leaders sought to establish a more stable milk-marketing program. As a legislator, Aiken had been among those championing the farmers' use of milk-marketing cooperatives to accomplish their ends. These bargaining associations could act as sales agents for their members, negotiating better prices and conditions with the dealers, and as lobbyists for supportive legislation and improved transportation rates. If the Boston market cooperatives came together under one organization, farmers might be able to gain equal bargaining power with dealers. In the early 1930s, however, the numerous independent-minded cooperatives and individual proprietors remained reluctant, and dairymen had been unable to unite under a single banner.

A workable mechanism for stabilization did not emerge until after cooperative leaders had been "driven to desperate realization that no voluntary agreement plan could suffice."[94] That mechanism became available in May 1933 with passage of the New Deal's Agricultural Adjustment Act (AAA), as amended by the Marketing Agreement Act of 1935. Under the Act's auspices, on November 3, 1933, following months of elaborate negotiation, and with the support of most of the Boston milk shed's organized dairymen, the Boston Milk Marketing Agreement took effect. Even U. S. Senator Warren R. Austin, ardent anti-New Dealer, did not oppose regulation of the Boston milk market.

The agreement established a milk-price control system backed by federal enforcement. According to H. A. Dwinell, of the State Agriculture Department's marketing division, it had the effect of saving the market "from chaos and panic."[95] The system enabled producers to agree on prices to be charged in the "milk sheds," established marketing quotas for individual producers, discouraged the dumping of surplus milk from one area into another, and provided for an equitable distribution of the proceeds among the producers. In the next four years the system of federal regulation survived constitutional challenges and episodes of farmer restiveness to become a settled structure for the region's dairymen.

Vermont farmers reached agreements on stabilization for milk markets within the state, as well. The General Assembly enacted a State Milk Control Law in July 1933 to accomplish that goal, and in 1939 Governor Aiken signed into law the Uniform Milk Inspection Act, which brought a halt to the sale within Vermont of milk that could not pass requirements in other states. While strongly supporting federal and state assistance plans for dairy farmers, the ambivalent Aiken continued to insist that Vermont's agricultural problems "in the long run must be solved more by cooperation than by legislation."[96]

Delivering Vermont's milk to market by horse-and-buggy and rail. *National Archives, courtesy of Billings Farm and Museum.*

Vermont's economy enjoyed a modest upswing at the end of the 1930s, boosted by an increase in tourism made possible by the growth in ownership of motor vehicles in the previous decade and expansion of the state's hard-surfaced highways. The Green Mountains' on-going reputation for bad roads, however, continued to discourage many travelers. In the 1920s, the *Official Automobile Blue Book* had cautioned drivers who might venture into Vermont in the months of April and May: "Some sort of emergency tire chains should always be carried, whether your tires are anti-skid or not. For heavy deep mud heavy single chains or mud hooks fastened over the tire and around one spoke of the wheel will ensure a prompt getaway from the worst mud hole."[97]

Although main highways had improved by the late 1930s, the skepticism of many Vermonters about tourism's blessings presented another kind of impediment to its promotion. Vermont-born writer Vrest Orton put the case against tourist "development" most acerbically in 1929: "There are, we are ashamed to say, . . . facets to Vermont's character . . . which ought obviously to be stamped out. I refer to the influx of the wrong kind of tourists who rush through the state, scattering refuse, pulling up flowers, tearing down fences, and poking their noses into one's privacy. I refer to the present-day Babbitt element, chiefly concerned with increasing this horde of fly-by-night sojourners (and often urging them to buy land and stop) by methods of advertizing and publicity. I further refer to all others, in and out of Vermont, who keep on trying their level best to promote Vermont as Florida was promoted, so that in a few years there will be nothing but Jerry-built roadside shacks, summer camps, hot dog stands, sub-divisions of towns never to be completed, crazy realtor offices, a crowd of widows and orphans fleeced by promoters, inflated banks whose paper is worthless and whose money is invested in Missouri, amusement parks, cable railways to mountain tops, wide, horribly straight cement trunk highways, towns of cheap-john houses alike as so many peas, factories belching smoke, crushing the workers and breaking their souls—the list could easily go on—ad nauseum. And I refer to national advertizers, who have an urge to plaster all the roads retaining the least vestige of adjacent beauty, with massive, gaudy and hideous sign-boards, so that it might truly be said, 'Behind the signboard lies Vermont.' All these things are basically un-Vermonterish."[98]

State officials and business enterprisers maintained a hard push for tourism, nevertheless. In 1931, the Vermont Commission on Country Life had promoted the idea of Vermont "as a summer playground for eastern America," and predicted that "development as a recreational region affords the most promising opportunity for business growth in the state at the present time, and so far as can be foreseen, for a considerable period in the future."[99] In that spirit, the state bureau of publicity circulated brochures describing picturesque trips along the state's "back-roads" and mountains, highlighting its "lake-strewn hilly beauty."[100] The bureau also focused attention, with some success, on appealing to affluent out-of-staters to purchase abandoned hillside farms as summer homes. By the 1930s a few towns, such as Fairlee on the Connecticut River in central Vermont, received almost half their town taxes from out-of-state summer property owners.

This desire to enhance the flow of tourist dollars, combined with the continuing economic doldrums and the tireless efforts of dedicated conservationists, helped build support for a national forest in Vermont. The financial aspects alone seemed sufficient justification for its creation; according to the commissioner of forestry, a national forest could serve as an important recreation area for "over thirty million people within a radius of two hundred miles."[101] In 1928, President Coolidge agreed to an initial plan for a Green Mountain national forest, setting the boundaries for federal acquisition in the state at 370,000 acres. Under Hoover's presidency in 1932, the proposed area grew to 580,000 acres, and the National Forest Reservation Commission authorized the initial purchase of 31,228 acres of land in Windsor, Windham, Rutland, and Bennington counties.

Residents of the affected areas responded ambivalently. Many small timber companies and upland farmers who had been struggling for years with delinquent taxes and declining land values were eager to sell out, making it an opportune time for federal land purchases. Public officials and business leaders also viewed the purchases enthusiastically as a way to infuse additional federal dollars into the state's moribund economy. Some local inhabitants, however, were troubled by the expanded federal presence in the state. They warned also about the reduced tax dollars from lands lost from town control. Anticipating such concerns, the federal Weeks Act (1911) had mandated that towns within national forest boundaries be paid 25 percent of gross receipts from recreation, logging, and grazing fees, but Vermont's depressed economic conditions during the national forest's early years resulted in payments to towns that were disappointingly small. The dissatisfaction prompted creation in 1935 of a State

Land Use Board and requirements that town selectboards approve federal land purchases.[102] Although the new procedures significantly slowed federal acquisition efforts, by 1940 land acquisitions for the Green Mountain National Forest had grown to approximately 161,000 acres. Twenty thousand of those acres came in 1936 when Middlebury College sold the government two-thirds of the vast forestlands left to it by Joseph Battell at his death in 1915.

The depressed economy and the state's commitment to tourism also spurred the development of a winter sports industry centered on skiing that would extend tourism to the winter season. Although relatively unknown in New England before the 1890s, the sport of skiing had grown steadily in popularity in the early twentieth century, partly influenced by Swedish and Norwegian immigrants in the vicinities of Hanover, New Hampshire, and Stowe, Vermont. In 1910, Dartmouth College student Fred Harris, a Brattleboro native, emerged as an evangelist for the growing sport. Harris asserted, "If snowshoeing be the prose, then skiing is the poetry of winter sports."[103] He founded the Dartmouth Outing Club to encourage ski racing, ski jumping, and cross-country skiing; and brought his enthusiasms back to his home state. At about the same time, James Taylor, who in 1910 had established the Green Mountain Club, began organizing boys' skiing and annual boys' winter carnivals at Vermont Academy in Saxton's River.

In the 1920s, although snowshoeing continued to be Vermonters' main winter sport, ski meets and winter carnivals spread to the state's college campuses. The Winter Olympic Games, held at nearby Lake Placid, New York, in 1932, brought unprecedented new attention to the sport, and soon after, a downhill skiing craze took the mountains of New England by storm. Annual visits to Stowe in the early 1930s by the Amateur Ski Club of New York City led Vermonters to begin plowing mountain roads and insulating mountain lodges to accommodate the growing new winter clientele.

In 1934, a group of ski enthusiasts constructed a ski tow on a pasture hill at Clint Gilbert's farm north of Woodstock, thus eliminating the necessity of having first to climb the hill before skiing down it. Although various lift machines were already being used in California to service snowshoers and tobogganists as well as skiers, the Woodstock contraption "originated the rope-tow era in the United States." Similar to a rig established at Shawbridge, Québec, a year earlier, it utilized eighteen hundred feet of "endless rope" that ran "over pulley wheels attached to a timber horse

Skiers wait in line to ride the Model T-powered tow-line up Clinton Gilbert's hill, near Woodstock, in 1934. *Courtesy of the Woodstock Historical Society.*

guyed to a tree at the top of the hill." A Ford Model T engine powered the system, which lifted four or five skiers up the nine-hundred-foot slope at a speed of five to ten miles per hour. One early user claimed to have gotten "almost as much of a thrill going up as coming down."[104] A year later, the "Ski Way," as it was called, became capable of transporting three hundred skiers per hour up the low hill. During the decade, slopes outfitted with tows grew rapidly in popularity, spreading to ski areas at East Corinth, at Hogback Mountain in Marlboro, Shrewsbury Peak, and at Mount Prospect near Bennington.

Aid from federal and state governments hastened development of Vermont's nascent ski industry. Perry Merrill, the state's chief forester, had learned about downhill and cross-country skiing in 1920–1921, as a student at the Royal College of Forestry in Stockholm, Sweden. In the 1930s, utilizing workers from a CCC subcamp at Stowe, Merrill directed the cutting of Vermont's first trails specifically for skiing, and built a parking site and warming shelter at Mount Mansfield's Smugglers' Notch area. New

Hampshire preceded Vermont in using CCC labor for ski trail construction, and the neighboring state's model heavily influenced Merrill's design in the state forest at Mount Mansfield.

In 1939, Governor Aiken authorized at Mount Mansfield the first lease of state-owned land to private developers for ski area use. By the winter of 1940–1941, the leaseholders had constructed on the mountain the longest (one mile) and highest aerial chair lift in the world. Aiken deflected criticism of this commercial development of public land, asserting the state's need to maintain a balance between environmental preservation and economic growth. Under a system devised by Merrill, income from the leases funded a large part of each year's annual state parks' budget.

During the late 1930s and early 1940s, Stowe's winter sports popularity experienced a rapid growth. It became possible for wealthy New Yorkers, such as the members of the Amateur Ski Club of New York City, to catch special trains at Grand Central Station on Friday evening, arrive in Waterbury on Saturday morning, ski at Stowe all weekend and take the return train on Sunday night, arriving back in New York in time for work on Monday morning. The emergence into "fashionable favor" of skiing, other winter sports, and accompanying social activities centering on stylishness and youth, contributed to the gradual development, in subsequent years, of a new popular identity for Vermont that prospered uneasily alongside the more traditional one as the "place where your grandparents lived." A nationally favorite song of 1944, "Moonlight in Vermont," captured that unfolding new image of the state.[105] In the imagination of a growing number of Americans, according to art historian William C. Lipke, Vermont had begun to take on the aura of "a romantic all-season dreamland."[106]

Material and lifestyle changes vivid in tourist communities such as Stowe occurred more subtly in other towns, as "modernity" gradually crept into Vermont. One sign of the shifting times came in 1939 when the citizens of Waterbury voted a resolution approving Sunday baseball, movies, and concerts. Barre's citizens, meanwhile, already enjoyed the opportunities afforded by three movie houses with showings every night of the week; seven local bands and orchestras with nightly live music and dancing; and three bowling allies. Men from Barre's nearby CCC subcamps joined with local residents and area granite workers embracing the town's quickened tempo. Other Vermonters viewed the changes of the 1920s and 1930s more warily. Alienated by Barre's "rushin' and crowdin'," one hillside farmer above the town opted simply to stay away.

His explanation amounted to a rejection of urbanizing trends underway in many locations across the state:

"We don't go down to the City [Barre] much anymore. Used to go when we was younger and the kids was home. Now maybe we go down Saturday nights. But I don't like it. Too much traffic and noise, too many people, all strangers seems like; all hurryin' and rushin' and crowdin' like sheep. The lights hurt my eyes and the noise hurts my ears. It makes me feel old and tired-out. . . . No, I feel like a stranger down in the city. Maybe it ain't big but it seems big. I'd rather set home and listen to the radio. Or I'd rather go down here to the store and sat around talk'in with men I know. There's a friendly kind of feelin' you don't get down in the city. Up here people get time enough to set easy and talk and smoke and enjoy things. Down in the city they ain't. Seems crazy to me the way they rush around."[107]

Shifting Political Patterns

The 1930s economic collapse did not turn Vermonters against the party of Calvin Coolidge and Herbert Hoover, as it did in many parts of the country. Instead, during the decade Vermont gained a national reputation as perhaps the most adamant of all state foes of Franklin Roosevelt. That reputation, however, owed much to the 1936 presidential election returns in which only Vermont and Maine stayed in the Republican column. In fact, behind its national image during the decade the state began to experience a fundamental shift in political patterns. As has been seen, Vermont actually embraced large parts of the New Deal agenda. The election returns reflected the alteration, with Roosevelt in 1932 and 1936 claiming the highest presidential vote totals (more than 40 percent each year) ever achieved in the state by a Democrat. Furthermore, without much skill or effort, Roosevelt's party made sizable inroads on Republican strongholds in the legislature. And in the 1934 United States Senate contest, incumbent Warren R. Austin, the outspoken anti-New Deal stalwart and leader among the Senate Republican minority in Washington, won reelection by only 3,514 votes over Democrat Fred C. Martin in the closest finish of a statewide race since before the Civil War. By the end of the turbulent 1930s, Green Mountain Republicans, still comfortably in command of the state, had acknowledged the changing times by setting their electoral sails—in statewide contests, at least—on a general course of political moderation.

Political banners for the presidential campaign in Hardwick, September 1936. *Courtesy of the Library of Congress.*

George Aiken's strong 1936 gubernatorial victory provided the catalyst for a progressive perspective among state Republicans. His winning total of more than eighty-three thousand votes had given him a commanding victory margin of thirty thousand over his Democratic opponent. In the short term Aiken's election also pushed him briefly to the forefront of his party nationally. As one of only two Republicans to win governorships during that year's Democratic landslide, the newly elected Vermonter became "something of a national novelty," and, with his new stature, he allied himself unambiguously with the national party's small progressive wing searching for ways to change traditional Republican policies and widen the party's appeal.[108]

Aiken emerged as a major voice in national Republican ranks as a result of a Lincoln Day speech he gave on February 12, 1938. The address, delivered before a gathering of the New York Lincoln Club at the Waldorf Astoria Hotel in New York City, was transmitted by radio to a nationwide audience. In it Aiken expressed concern for Republicanism's future and called for new party leadership, asserting that in order to survive,

Governor George Aiken delivering his nationally broadcast Lincoln Day speech in New York City, February 1938. *Vermont Historical Society.*

Republicans needed to stand for more than simply the good old days. "The self-satisfied smugness of Old Guard Republicanism" would not suffice, he warned. Aiken told his Lincoln Club audience that the Republican Party's leadership no longer represented the nation's working people. "Today, the Republican party attracts neither the farmer nor the industrial worker. Why not? To represent the people one must know them. Lincoln did. The Republican national leadership today does not. The greatest praise I can give to Lincoln on this his anniversary is to say that he would be ashamed of his party's leadership today."[109]

Aiken's Lincoln Day speech infuriated the party's Old Guard. It also thrust the Vermont governor into the bright glare of the national spotlight and stirred excitement among Republican moderates, some of whom urged him to become a candidate for the party's 1940 presidential nomination. Aiken apparently did not seriously consider such a move; he nevertheless kept the presidential boomlet alive for a while—and inflated the pride of many Vermonters—by accepting invitations to speak before Republican groups in Illinois, Massachusetts, New Jersey, and elsewhere. Aiken understood that by keeping open the option of a presidential bid, he not only strengthened the drive to broaden his party's base, but also bolstered his ongoing fight against Roosevelt over flood control. As a part of this dual effort, he published a book, *Speaking From Vermont*, which compiled a number of his speeches during this period, intended as a comprehensive statement of a progressive Republican alternative to his party's traditional path.[110]

Consistent with his Lincoln Club themes, Aiken sought progressive allies within his own state's "ranks of labor and agriculture." In the 1936 election, he had done well in farm communities but had run poorly among urban and labor constituencies. As governor, in reaching out to industrial workers, he began characterizing the unions' goal of collective bargaining as "the same thing in labor relations as cooperatives in farming."[111] Aiken's efforts attracted the support of stone workers' leader John C. Lawson, who had by then concluded that the state Democratic Party's weakness and the absence of viable third-party options left him to search only among Republicans for allies.

Aiken also drew the interest of Arthur Packard of the Vermont Farm Bureau. Packard, of Jericho, had become the Bureau's president in 1928 and speedily shaped the fast-growing farm group into Vermont's "most powerful political organization,"[112] while earning for himself a reputation as "perhaps the single most powerful political figure in the state."[113] As with labor, the Depression's hard times provided the catalyst for the farmers' new activism, although the Bureau's political strength had been building since the early 1920s. Edwin C. Rozwenc wrote that under Packard's leadership the Bureau in Vermont gained a reputation of being "motivated by a kind of agrarian radicalism obnoxious to business interests and to the more conservative-minded farmers."[114] Although "radical," the Farm Bureau distrusted third-party politics. In 1935, when union leaders at the annual convention of the Vermont Federation of Labor proposed a resolution to form a new farm-labor party in the state, the idea went nowhere.[115]

Instead of a new third party, Aiken promoted the concept of informal alliance building. Speaking at the State Federation of Labor meeting in 1939, the governor urged Vermont's industrial workers and farmers to find ways to work together in pursuit of common interests. Not long afterwards, the Vermont Farm-Labor Council took form, led by Goddard College President Royce S. Pitkin, stone workers' leader Lawson, and Washington County Agent W. Gordon Loveless, representing the Farm Bureau. Aiken had encouraged this "working partnership between agriculture and labor," and the council became, for several years, an influential force for its constituencies in state politics.[116] His own connection to it, however, further estranged Aiken from his party's Old Guard.

Aiken's experience as a political candidate in the election of 1940 dramatized his alienation from state Republican leaders. Angered by his vigorous support for public power, by the Lincoln Day speech, by a lengthy letter he wrote to the Republican Party telling its leadership "if they didn't want to die they had to wake up and represent the people,"[117] and by his independent political course in general, they encouraged him not to seek a third term as governor. In an unprecedented move almost a year before the Republican primary, without waiting for Aiken to make known his political intentions for 1940, the Republican State Committee announced its unanimous endorsement of Lieutenant Governor William Wills, an insurance salesman from Bennington, for governor.

The resultant awkward political situation continued until after U.S. Senator Ernest W. Gibson, Sr., died unexpectedly on June 20, 1940. Aiken quickly appointed Ernest W. Gibson, Jr., a former Windham County state's attorney, and secretary of the Vermont state senate, to serve in his father's seat until an interim election could be held on Primary Day, September 10. A few weeks later, Gibson, Jr., one of Aiken's closest political allies, declared he would not be a candidate in the special election. When the governor announced his own Senate candidacy soon afterward, Republican Party stalwarts hastily recruited the highly respected Ralph E. Flanders to oppose him. The fact that Flanders agreed with Aiken on most issues proved to be no bar to the party's pledging him its full support.

Candidate Flanders presented a formidable challenge to Aiken. A poor boy from Barnet who made his way to the top, he had begun his practical education at age sixteen as an indentured apprentice at a machine-tool shop in Rhode Island. Returning to Vermont in 1910, he took a job in Springfield at the Fellows Gear Shaper Company, and subsequently joined James Hartness at Jones & Lamson. In 1911, Flanders married Hartness's daughter, Helen, helping his rise to the head of Jones & Lamson, and in the following years he became an unquestioned leader in the machine-tool industry. In 1940, as a Senate candidate, the fifty-nine-year-old Flanders had never held public office, but he had earned a national reputation for achievement as a machine-tool inventor, engineer, and progressive businessman. An individual of unusual integrity and ability, he had been a frequent participant on national and international advisory boards, including the Business Advisory Council of Franklin D. Roosevelt's Department of Commerce, and enjoyed the confidence of the rich and powerful.

Ralph Flanders poses with a red pig during his 1940 Republican primary race for the United States Senate against George Aiken. *Vermont Historical Society.*

The 1940 Aiken-Flanders primary campaign has been described as setting "the Vermont standard for bitterness, rancor and divisiveness."[118] The state's private power utilities; banking, insurance, and railroad companies; and granite and marble firms all backed Flanders, the primary issue for many of them being Aiken's struggles over utility regulation and rural electrification. Only two of the state's newspapers supported Aiken. Even the governor's old friend, journalist Dorothy Thompson, endorsed Flanders in her nationally syndicated column.

Against this formidable opponent, Aiken and his campaign manager, an Addison County farmer named Ed Peet, adopted a populist-style election strategy. Aiken claimed "the interests" were out to get him, he charged the state's newspapers with collusion, and he flailed his industrialist opponent and supporters as the "big boys." He described the campaign as a battle of "certain corporate interests against the common folks."[119]

Surrogates for the two candidates exchanged heated, although vague, charges. The political veteran Aiken, however, managed to hold the advantage throughout. In one devastatingly effective thrust, Aiken's backers turned a Flanders campaign photograph into a statewide joke. The picture showed the candidate holding a red pig in his arms. Allies of Aiken gleefully pointed out the industrialist's wardrobe, observing that it was unusual in Vermont to be handling a pig while wearing an expensive suit, a stiff-collared white shirt, and a necktie.

Aiken won the primary election by a surprisingly easy 55.4 percent of the votes, although Flanders outspent him $18,698 to $3,219. Most of Aiken's votes came from farmers and from the state's rural areas and smaller towns, with strong support from Arthur Packard's Vermont Farm Bureau. Although he ran far behind Flanders in Burlington, St. Johnsbury, St. Albans, Montpelier, and Rutland, he won overwhelmingly in Barre City and Barre Town, the locations of the state's most highly unionized work force and traditional allies of the Democrats. In November, Aiken also swept the general election, which brought a remarkably high voter turnout. Of the state's 191,273 registered voters, 141,413 cast ballots, and 87,150 of these (62 percent) went to Aiken.

Aiken's Senate success signaled the disarray of the old Proctor political "organization." The 1940 win, Aiken's third successive statewide victory, commenced a political half-century in which statewide electoral success tended to go to candidates of "moderation," even as they often marched under "conservative" banners. "The Old Guard is still operating, but I think weaker than ever," Aiken wrote to Ernest Gibson, Jr., in 1942.[120] Political reporter Robert W. Mitchell, of Rutland, agreed: "The party is under such loose control from the top that it is wide open for any newcomer. . . . The party has no boss, unofficial or otherwise."[121]

Although Vermonters reelected Aiken to the Senate five times, rewarding him with a career of thirty-four years in Washington, the anti-Aiken feelings among his party's traditionalists faded slowly. One account of this awkward relationship concluded that it was only late in Aiken's tenure that the *Burlington Free Press* "reached the point of admitting that he was an acceptable member of the Republican Party and the U.S. Senate."[122] Twenty years after he left the governorship for Washington, the *Free Press* continued calling on Aiken to either join the Democratic Party or form a "semi-socialist" party of his own.[123]

When Aiken moved to Washington following his 1940 election, he left behind a notable legacy. In the legislature, as lieutenant governor, and during two terms as governor, he had significantly influenced state developments in such areas as land use planning, energy and rural electrification, agricultural organization, and labor relations. In displaying unparalleled vote-getting skills, he established a model of independent politics that continued to be influential through the end of the century. By selectively welcoming New Deal programs in the state, and simultaneously engaging in high-profile struggles to keep Vermont's "destiny" out of reach of equally greedy "big government" and "big business," he won the hearts of many Vermonters. Finally, his reform advocacy placed him within a progressive Green Mountain heritage alongside the early-twentieth-century Progressive Era activists, the revivalistic crusaders of the 1830s and 1840s, and the political and social innovators of the initial period of statehood itself. To many in Vermont, Aiken stood as the "quintessential Vermonter."[124]

Perhaps indicative of the increasingly visible counterpoints evident in the political landscape in Vermont by the 1940s were the Washington, D.C., careers of two Northfield natives, Charles A. Plumley and William D. Hassett. Five years apart in age, the two were childhood friends despite differing family backgrounds: Plumley, the son of a distinguished lawyer and three-term member of the U.S. House of Representatives, and Hassett, the grandson of Irish immigrants and son of a railroad worker. The two Northfield boys maintained their acquaintance as they grew older. After completing his degree at the local college, Norwich University, young Plumley became principal of Northfield High School, where he selected Hassett, a member of the class of 1900, as editor of the student newspaper.

Hassett's interest in journalism, begun under Plumley's guidance, continued after high school. Lacking funds for college tuition, Hassett dropped out of Clark University in 1904 and launched a career as a newspaper reporter that led him eventually to a position with the Associated Press in Washington, D.C. In 1935, Hassett accepted an invitation to join the White House staff as a secretary to Franklin D. Roosevelt, with the principal duties of writing speeches and "ghosting" letters over the president's signature. The Irish railroad worker's son became a trusted Roosevelt aide, traveling regularly with the president, who enjoyed his company and his skill as a raconteur. One of Roosevelt's first biographers, Robert E. Sherwood, described Hassett in the White House as "a man of great gentleness; he was scholarly and devoted and a good, quiet companion for Roosevelt when he wanted to get away from the hurly-burly of Washington."[125] In April 1945 he accompanied Roosevelt on a trip to Warm Springs, Georgia; a cerebral hemorrhage killed the president there, and it was Hassett who informed the world of his death.

A year before Hassett came to the White House, Plumley, following his father's example, arrived in Washington as Vermont's only member of the House of Representatives. Plumley had left his high school principal's job to practice law in his father's Northfield firm, and in 1919 had taken a position as general counsel for the Firestone Tire and Rubber Company in Cleveland, Ohio. In 1920 he returned home to accept the presidency of Norwich University, where he remained until his election to Congress.

Situated in Washington at opposite ends of Pennsylvania Avenue, and harboring polar opposite political views, the two Northfielders indirectly dueled, with words as their weapons. Hassett, the ardent New Dealer, provided eloquent language for the president, and Plumley, the "dyed-in-the-wool" Republican, earned a reputation in Washington, and popularity in Vermont, for a florid, flamboyant oratorical style in the service of a strident opposition to the New Deal.

The two men shared an extraordinary durability in their Washington roles. Plumley won reelection to his House seat eight consecutive times, more than any other representative in the state's history; Hassett worked at the White House for seventeen years, continuing after Roosevelt's death as an aide to President Harry S. Truman. Plumley finally retired from Congress in 1950, Hassett two years later from the White House. Both men returned to Vermont and lived out their lives as genial Northfield neighbors—Plumley dying in 1964 at age eighty-nine, Hassett a year later at eighty-five, demonstrating in their friendship that a diverse political landscape need not result in civic disaster.

Vermont in World War II

In September 1939 full-scale warfare erupted again in Europe. Many Vermonters supported President Roosevelt's cautious policy of aiding the British and French Allies while attempting to avoid direct confrontation with Germany. After France fell to Hitler in June 1940, that support grew, prompted in part by fears in Newport and other northern Vermont communities that if Britain (and Canada) should also be toppled, a German invasion of the United States through the Champlain Valley might follow.

The war acquired new immediacy in September 1940 when the Secretary of War ordered units of the Vermont National Guard into active duty and Congress enacted a Selective Service Act creating the first peacetime draft in the nation's history, with a call-up of 1.2 million men. By October, young Vermonters began receiving draft notices, and over the winter of 1940–1941 Fort Ethan Allen underwent rapid expansion, with construction of ninety-one wooden buildings in a four-month period. In February 1941, the entire seventeen-hundred-man Vermont National Guard, including the 172nd Regiment of Infantry and other units, was inducted into federal service, and within weeks had departed the state. By April, Governor William Wills organized a State Guard, supplied by volunteers, to replace the missing 172nd on the home front.

Several of Vermont's political leaders took prominent roles in the national debate over the proper United States response to Europe's unfolding events. George Aiken had been vague on the war issue during his Senate campaign, in part because he lacked familiarity with foreign policy matters. Aiken nevertheless became embroiled in the national war debate almost immediately after the election. A Lend-Lease bill, pending before Congress, permitted the embattled British forces to receive from the United States aid otherwise barred by provisions of the Neutrality Acts. Aiken opposed the bill and questioned the motives of both the European Allies and President Roosevelt. Claiming he spoke for the "common people," Aiken characterized Lend-Lease as a vote for war and asserted that American boys should not be asked to die in order "to define the boundaries of [Europe's] African colonies," or to defend the interests of "dollar patriots." His position aligned in some respects with views of the Congressional Nye Committee that, after public hearings earlier in the decade, concluded "greedy businessmen" had caused United States intervention in World War I. Aiken's stance on Lend-Lease, however, also reflected his great distrust of Roosevelt: He repeatedly asserted that the bill would give the president unprecedented power and move the United States toward not only war in Europe but a domestic dictatorship.[126]

By the early months of 1941, with a Gallup Poll showing over 50 percent of Americans in favor of all-out aid to the Allies short of war, and many others ready to risk direct involvement, Aiken emerged among the noninterventionist leadership in Washington. The isolationist America First Committee's liaison with the Senate described Aiken as "one of the four most able non-interventionist senators."[127] As late as one month before Pearl Harbor, Aiken continued to give speeches declaring that a "war party" composed of international money lenders and private corporate overseas investors desiring protection for their speculations sought to drive the country to intervention, and that the big danger to the United States originated not abroad but from the Roosevelt Administration, at home. Aiken acknowledged that Hitler should be stopped, but by Europe, not the United States.[128]

Many prominent Vermonters did not share Aiken's views on Europe's war. Four influential newspapers, the *Burlington Free Press*, *Rutland Herald*, *Brattleboro Reformer*, and *Bennington Evening Banner*, gave editorial support to the Lend-Lease bill, as did the Vermont Chamber of Commerce and even the staunchly conservative *Vermonter* magazine. Membership in a Vermont organization called Fight for Freedom, an offshoot of the Committee to Defend America by Aiding the Allies, "read like 'the entire society of Vermont,'" including "'anybody who was anybody in the state.'" Middlebury Professor of History Waldo H. Heinrichs took a leading role, traveling throughout the state to deliver over a dozen speeches in support of Lend-Lease and trying to muster popular support that would convince Aiken to shift his position to support the bill.[129]

The state's Republican leadership, including National Committeeman Harold W. Mason and Governor Wills, although outspoken opponents of the New Deal, strongly backed both Roosevelt's Lend-Lease bill and repeal of the Neutrality Acts, as necessary to defeat Germany. And even New Deal nemesis Congressman Charles Plumley cast his vote for Lend-Lease, one of only twenty-three House Republicans (out of 159) to do so. Plumley also voted for extension of the Selective Service Act, which drew only twenty other Republican supporters. That act passed the House by a vote of 203 to 202.

During this period, another Vermonter, Ernest W. Gibson, Jr., Aiken's personal friend and political ally, became an outspoken national leader in rallying support for Roosevelt's policy of aid to the Allies. In a 1940 speech, typical of many he gave that year, Gibson argued: "If Hitler knows we propose to send ships and then more ships, to send planes and then more planes, to send all manner of material of war in great quantities to England," then Hitler will "not be so sure of himself. Peace may come the sooner."[130] In January 1941, shortly after leaving the Senate, Gibson accepted the high-profile national chairmanship of the Committee to Defend America by Aiding the Allies. The Committee, a private organization with seven chapters in Vermont and six hundred nationwide, heavily Republican in composition, had been organized by the Kansas journalist William Allen White, with Roosevelt's encouragement, to combat isolationist sentiment and rally support for England and France. Gibson's commitment to United States preparedness eventually led him to a more personal military involvement; in May 1941 he resigned from the Committee and, at age forty, entered the army, as a captain in the 43rd Division.

The most influential Vermont voice for aid to the Allies in 1940 and 1941, however, belonged to Senator Warren R. Austin. Austin's backing of the administration's war policy came as he occupied the key position of Assistant Senate Minority Leader and ranking Republican on the Senate Military Affairs Committee. His interest in international relations had begun when he spent a year in China early in his law career. He had opposed the national mood of isolationism of the 1920s and early 1930s and traced the current world troubles partly to the United States's failure to enter the League of Nations in 1919. Faced with Germany's military resurgence in the mid-1930s, he had rejected "neutrality" as a means of providing safety for the United States. Austin consequently became a strong supporter of Roosevelt's foreign policy as early as 1937, and had proposed repeal of the neutrality legislation, stronger armaments, and a conscription bill in advance of the president. Historian Kenneth S. Davis described Austin as "virtually alone among congressional leaders of his party in a fervent commitment to collective security."[131]

That most Vermonters supported Austin's views on world affairs became apparent in his 1940 reelection bid. He had almost lost to a Democratic challenger in his 1934 Senate election, but in 1940 this outspoken Roosevelt-backer in international affairs faced no primary opposition and only a token Democratic challenger. In 1941, when Congress finally revised the Neutrality Law, Austin, with a fresh election mandate, continued at odds with his national party, as one of only six Republican senators casting a supporting vote. The Republican internationalist Austin emerged as a notable figure in Democratic Washington during the war years, and served on Secretary of State Cordell Hull's elite, semisecret Committee of Eight which prepared the way for a postwar international organization. In 1946, President Harry S. Truman demonstrated his appreciation for Austin by naming him the United States's first ambassador to the United Nations.

In late 1941, with the views of Gibson and Austin dominant in state discussions, Vermonters braced for the war that seemed, by then, inevitable. In fact, Vermont did not wait for federal action. On September 16, Montpelier lawmakers decreed the nation to be in a state of "armed conflict" with Germany.[132] They enacted this remarkable resolution after concluding that, four days earlier, a "shoot on sight" order by Roosevelt, relating to Hitler's belligerent actions against American ships in the North Atlantic, had placed the United States on a war footing. The practical reason for the legislators' action was their desire to trigger a state law allowing bonus payments to Vermont troops in federal service during "armed conflict." As with a similar "early" war declaration by the legislature in 1917, the act drew considerable, if short-lived, national attention, and provoked references to the new "London-Moscow-Montpelier Axis."[133]

After the Japanese attack at Pearl Harbor on December 7 brought the United States directly into the fighting, George Aiken joined the state's other leaders in pledging complete support, and Vermonters joined in the national rush to enlist for military service. In the first year of American involvement only Texas, of all the states, had a higher percentage of volunteers than Vermont. By war's end, almost fifty thousand from the state, including about fourteen hundred women, had served in uniform, of whom 1,233 lost their lives. (One family in Burlington contributed six sons and a husband to the war effort.) As in World War I, however, the military rejected an unusually high number of Vermonters for service because of disabilities, many for malnutrition.

On the home front, Vermonters also did their duty. They bought $263,500,000 worth of war bonds by 1945. They practiced air raid maneuvers, acted as plane spotters, attended Red Cross training classes, and knitted sweaters and socks. Conscientious objectors to the war found alternative service at the private Brattleboro Retreat, a hospital specializing in treatment of the mentally ill. Vermonters participated in drives to collect scrap aluminum, paper, and rubber. The war plants' great need for scrap iron led to the dismantling of the ornate iron fence in front of the Motor Vehicle Department on State Street in Montpelier, the old trolley rails from the streets of Barre, and all but one of Burlington's Battery Park cannons. In the second half of 1943, Vermont led the nation in volunteer salvage collection, with a per capita rate of 162.9 pounds per person.

This home-front patriotism came to the attention of the nation through the remarkable artwork of Norman Rockwell, a painter and illustrator who lived in the southern Vermont town of Arlington from 1939 to 1952. His endearing, optimistic depictions of the lives of small-town people during the war years appeared in national magazines and publications, most notably on the covers of the *Saturday Evening Post*, and were received as evocations of the finest expression of the American spirit. Rockwell relied on his Vermont neighbors as inspiration—and as models—for his work,

Citizens at a Burlington department store line up to buy war bonds in the winter of 1944. *Courtesy of Special Collections, Bailey/Howe Library, University of Vermont.*

which included his famous "Four Freedoms" paintings. They depicted some of the most vivid American home-front images of the war years while also projecting for a national audience an unusually attractive and flattering impression of Vermont and its citizenry (see color plate III).

The war briefly invigorated Vermont's economy. The Springfield-Windsor area felt the impact earliest and most directly. Between 1929 and 1937, machine-tool crews at Springfield had been reduced to skeleton staffs of engineers and foremen. In the late 1930s, however, the Japanese government became a significant purchaser of Precision Valley tool-making products, gradually helping pull the area out of the Depression's doldrums. The Roosevelt Administration embargoed trade with Japan in 1940, but orders from United States government and civilian contractors sustained the local expansion.

From 1939 to late 1941, employment at Precision Valley shops climbed rapidly in response to war orders from Europe and Washington, turning

Springfield and Windsor into boom towns. After Pearl Harbor, the three Springfield machine-tool companies moved to twelve-hour shifts, despite a shortage of workers, turning out machine tools, and parts for airplanes, radar equipment, tanks, and guns for the war effort. Shop personnel at Jones & Lamson grew from 750 employees in 1939 to 3,200 by December 1942, with an increase in plant output of 600 percent. In the same period, Bryant's employment rose from 300 to 1,350. During the course of the war, the four Precision Valley plants became responsible for more than one-fifth of the nation's machine-tool production and earned a rank, according to historian W. Storrs Lee, of "seventh in importance among U.S. bombing targets" by the Axis powers.[134]

Woolen manufacturing also surged. In 1942, the state's sixteen mills (nine of them in Windsor County) produced the equivalent of five million coats, with many on-order for the United States military. Textile mills in Winooski operated on a schedule of three shifts per day, seven days a week. And a woolen mill in Northfield manufactured white navy blankets, providing employment for 125 people while driving the town to renewed prosperity.

Other state manufacturers adroitly adjusted to the demands of a wartime economy. In Burlington, Bell Aircraft took over the facilities of the defunct Queen City Cotton Company, and began producing gun mounts, B-29 parts, and bomb parts. The Vermont Marble Company sheds converted from marble finishing to the manufacture of machine products, mica radio and wooden aircraft parts, and wooden packing boxes. And the company allowed female workers in its sheds for the first time, as its employment rolls climbed from 850 in 1941 to 1,250 in 1943. Granite firms in Barre retooled to make anchor chains and wood-sheathed bumpers for United States Navy ships. In Rutland, the Howe Scales Company shifted to the manufacture of scales capable of weighing large aircraft. Workers in Vergennes produced aircraft spark plugs; in Bellows Falls, insect netting for tropical tents; in Rutland, reactor parts for the atomic bomb.

Shipbuilding gained renewed life. The small Shelburne Shipyards, near Burlington, switched over to building PT boats, small tugs, and submarine chasers, the first United States Navy ships built on Lake Champlain since the War of 1812. The shipyard's Navy contracts lifted spirits in Depression-dogged Burlington. "You will be surprised at the hope we Burlington-people sustain in that it may be a new City-building industry to us," a

Burlington contractor wrote to a friend.[135] The Shelburne Yards completed work on three subchasers, the last of its wartime construction, in late 1944. Built for delivery to the Soviet Union under the Lend-Lease program, all three were lost in a hurricane while being convoyed to Murmansk.

Farmers also enjoyed a wartime boost. From 1939 to 1944, the stimulus of military demands caused cash receipts from agriculture to go up 103 percent. The Agricultural Extension Service reported that Vermont farmers produced, over a four-year period, 4.3 percent more milk, 39.9 percent more eggs, 16.4 percent more chickens, 19.2 percent more turkeys, and 15.8 percent more maple products. Governor Wills told legislators in January 1945 that Vermont's agriculture had responded to the war with "the greatest production in her history," despite shortages in labor, farm equipment, grain, feed, and building materials.[136]

The agricultural labor shortage, in fact, continued throughout the war and was larger than occurred in the 1917–1918 period, a consequence of military enlistment, the draft, and the exodus of two out of three farm workers to higher-paying defense industry jobs, mostly outside the state. In the first quarter of 1944, the shortages were such that total employment in the state stood at about 125,000, a drop from 131,000 in 1940.

The farm labor shortfalls persisted despite energetic efforts to remedy the problem. One such attempt was led by the writer Dorothy Thompson, who in late 1941 began recruiting sponsors and money to establish a Volunteer Land Corps. She envisioned filling its ranks with pre-draft age city boys and girls who could provide annual summer volunteer replacement workers for the nation's missing farm hands. She planned that in the first summer, 1942, the program would be limited to Vermont.

A desire to aid the war effort motivated Thompson, but she also feared that the war's agricultural labor drainage threatened the long-term future of small family farms in Vermont and across the country. Concerned by what she saw happening "to the social structure of America as a result of the war," Thompson hoped that recruiting a "Land Corps" could assist not only in providing food for the war effort, but also in preserving the family farm and slowing the momentum toward farms becoming large-scale, centralized "agricultural factories." Thompson's project started encouragingly. In summer 1942, more than six hundred young volunteers joined her "Land Army"; she wrote a friend, "We had more applicants than we had places."[137]

After 1942, Governor Wills and the Vermont Farm Labor Committee, responding to an initiative from Thompson, absorbed the Land Corps into the state's ongoing farm labor program. In 1943, the legislature voted an appropriation of $25,000 for agricultural labor assistance, and the state Agricultural Extension Service was utilized as a farm labor recruiting agency for the 1943 and 1944 summer seasons. In January 1945 Governor Wills reported to the legislature that under the program, "1,070 regular farm workers were placed and 5,211 seasonal placements made, [and] ... a total of 5,915 workers were ordered." In addition, more than nine thousand boys had been deferred by Selective Service for farm work, providing, according to Wills, "food for freedom."[138]

Thompson's Land Corps concept clearly owed its origins to Roosevelt's CCC experiments of the 1930s. In 1940 and 1941, prior to Pearl Harbor, the CCC inspired another offshoot experiment known as Camp William James, located at the former site of a CCC camp in the Downer State Forest in the hills between Sharon and Strafford. The camp's name derived from the famous Harvard philosopher who penned a treatise on "The Moral Equivalent of War." A camp participant described "the heart" of James's idea as an advocacy "that every able-bodied young man should give some small part of his life to the service of his country, working with other young men of different backgrounds on projects of value to the nation, the region, and the local community."[139]

The camp existed as the brainchild of idealistic students at Dartmouth College and Harvard University, who had served apprenticeships in CCC camps after Corps requirements changed in 1940 to eliminate economic status as a consideration for enrollment. The changes redefined the Corps' mission to include a goal of preparing "young men for citizenship."[140] Enthusiastic about these modifications of the Corps, the college students now hoped to make Camp William James a model that could be used to shift the CCC even more directly from a relief agency into a permanent program of national service for young Americans. While providing instructions in democratic leadership principles, they planned that an integral part of the new program would involve Corpsmen engaging in activities to "reclaim, rebuild, and restore to usefulness abandoned farms, houses, and industries" in nearby rural communities.[141]

President Roosevelt gave Camp William James his enthusiastic support and in October 1940 directed his secretary of agriculture to establish it as quickly as possible. The camp also attracted local backing from Governor Aiken, Ralph Flanders, Dorothy Canfield Fisher, Dorothy Thompson, and other prominent Vermonters. Governor Aiken boosted the venture by authorizing the use of state buildings at Downer State Forest, enabling Camp William James to begin operating in January 1941. A group of college students made up the initial enrollment. Aiken, by then a United States senator, praised the project in a speech on the floor of the Senate: "If this camp fulfills its purposes satisfactorily, America needs a thousand more camps like it. I hope to see the time when every boy in America, be he rich or poor, will have the opportunity to spend a full year working in our forests or on our farms."[142]

Camp William James ran into significant problems, however. In Washington, several congressmen opposed the additional tampering with the CCC's basic relief mission. In addition, the background of the camp's administrator, Eugene Rosenstock-Hussey, a Dartmouth College professor and recently arrived refugee from Germany, further undermined the experiment's support in Congress. By March 1941, the Roosevelt Administration, fearing the project might trigger a broad political attack on the CCC, ended its support. Camp William James continued briefly as a private nonprofit entity, operating from a local farm purchased through a private gift. Despite encouragement from Eleanor Roosevelt, who made a visit to the camp, it ceased operations a few days after the attack on Pearl Harbor. Even in failure, however, the project provided evidence that after more than a century and a half of settlement, the Green Mountains remained an alluring ground for imaginative and idealistic social experimentation.[143]

The war-stimulated labor shortage emboldened union organizing efforts in the state's industrial sector and ushered in an era of sizable labor gains. The largest wartime union victory came at the Champlain Mills of the American Woolen Company in Winooski, the largest woolen mill in the state, where employees in 1943 turned back a bitter opposition campaign by the mill's management and local officials, and voted to form a union affiliated with the Textile Workers Union of America-CIO. Harold Daust, the union's state president, directed the campaign, which drew strong support from Vermont's unionized granite workers and from the Burlington area's Catholic clergy, one of whom, Father William Tennien, declared in a radio sermon that the "low wages in Burlington" amounted to "nothing more than slavery."[144] The Catholic Church's strongly prounion stance influenced a positive shift in local views about unions, undermining traditional charges that outsiders, communists, and "radicals" controlled the organizing efforts.

The victory at Champlain Mills ignited union drives across the state, under a "Spirit of '43" slogan. In January 1944, the United Electrical Workers of America succeeded in organizing Jones & Lamson, and Bryant, in Springfield; and in October, state government workers, spurred by notoriously low salary and benefit schedules, formed the Vermont State Employees Association, immediately becoming Vermont's largest union. By late 1944, the ranks of organized labor in the state numbered approximately twenty-five thousand, an increase of ten thousand over a ten-year period.

Even Vermont's farmers became targets of organizing activity. In the spring of 1942, representatives of John L. Lewis's United Mine Workers briefly attempted to affiliate dairy farmers into their union, but withdrew after confronting an overwhelmingly hostile reaction from farm groups and local newspapers. Unions organized by farmers themselves, however, experienced somewhat better success, and sometimes matched their industrial labor counterparts in union militancy. The Dairy Farmers' Union included dairymen in Addison and Rutland counties and twenty-six counties in New York State who marketed milk through New York City milk dealers. The union went on strike in the summer of 1941, demanding a raise in the uniform milk price. At a meeting attended by a thousand dairy farmers in the New Haven Town Hall on June 30, 1941, only twenty-three farmers voted against the strike.

The union suspended the "milk holiday," however, following the death of a Vergennes deputy sheriff in a fracas involving the dumping of milk belonging to a non-striking dairyman. A grand jury indicted four local farmers for manslaughter in the deputy's death. In the emotional trial that followed, a jury of their neighbors "resisted the temptation to acquit" and found the defendants guilty, but also took the unusual step of requesting that the four be treated with mercy. The judge responded by sentencing each of the men to pay fines, none exceeding $400, or spend two days in jail for each dollar not paid. The farmers paid the fines.[145]

The war's manpower needs struck a hard blow at college enrollments in the state. The University of Vermont, Middlebury College, and Norwich University all experienced heavy losses of male students. Enrollment dropped by one-half at the University of Vermont, and the number of male undergraduates at Middlebury fell from 352 in September 1942, to 74 by July 1943. Both schools remained financially stable, however, by admitting increased numbers of women and by bringing onto campus federally funded U.S. Army Air Cadets and military officer candidates for coursework and training. The University of Vermont's officer candidates provided sufficient income also to offset embarrassing financial losses the school had suffered as a consequence of mismanagement by its president dating from the early 1930s, and which by 1941 had reached a brief "acute stage."[146]

Norwich University, an all-male military college in Northfield, absorbed the most crippling student losses. In 1943, the school held its spring commencement exercises ten weeks early, after which its seventy-member graduating class, and all its juniors, sophomores, and freshmen—to a man—were called to active duty. For the duration of the war, the school operated as "an academic training center for student soldiers in the aviation and engineering branches of the army," with instruction provided by the regular Norwich professors.[147] Three other institutions, the Bennington College for Women (1932), Goddard College (1938) in Plainfield, and Lyndon State College (1944), came into existence in this era, managed to survive the hardships of depression and war, and prospered along with their older university counterparts in the broad national expansion of higher education that followed the war.

Other institutions temporarily took on new appearances and shapes as a result of the war. In 1936, women members of the Vermont legislature gathered at the Fletcher farm in Proctor for a two-day meeting at which they organized the Vermont chapter of the Order of Women Legislators (OWLs). Through 1941, an average of about fifteen women managed to gain election at each of the six legislative sessions. However, in the two wartime sessions, OWL membership jumped dramatically. In 1943, thirty-two women gained seats, all in the house; and in 1945, women claimed forty-six house seats and one in the senate. By 1943, legislative action, endorsed by a statewide referendum, had given women the right to serve on Vermont juries for the first time. In addition to the legislature and the jury box, women entered the wartime work force in large numbers, most notably at Springfield's machine shops, many of them traveling daily to their jobs from towns as far away as Northfield. The burden of wartime farm work, as well, shifted heavily to women. Agriculture Commissioner Edward H. Jones reported in 1944, "Never before since the pioneer days" had farm women "taken so active a part in the fields and in the care of dairy cattle."[148]

If the war altered some institutions, it halted others completely. The state's semi-professional baseball Northern League had been enjoying resurgent popularity in the late 1930s, after being largely dormant in Vermont for almost a decade following the flood of 1927. During that deluge approximately half the baseball diamonds in the state had been washed away, many of them situated on riverfront lowlands. Of all the Northern League and Green Mountain League playing fields, only Centennial Field, located on a hill in Burlington, had survived, and during the 1936 season the Queen City had rebounded by setting a Northern League attendance record. After the 1941 season, however, the league suspended operations for the war's duration.

In January 1945, with the war in its last months, Governor Wills announced that he had brought the state home with the largest income in its history. Vermont possessed reserves, he reported to the legislature, that would "stand us in good stead in the postwar era."[149] Moreover, Wills proudly reported that he had steered the state through the war and other demands on a pay-as-you-go basis.

While Wills tended the pay-as-you-go icon, Vermonters' grip in 1945 on other favorite Green Mountain ways nevertheless continued a century-long loosening. The long world war, the global depression, and the Great Flood accelerated the transformation of the state. Responsibilities once the domain of towns continued a shift to state and federal provinces. Gains in transportation, tourism, and communications technology further penetrated the isolation of back-road homes and communities. Green Mountain agriculture and industry occupied larger roles in regional and national enterprises. Many Vermonters, while remaining serious about long-held ideals, confronted the realization that faithfulness to the principles of local control, the Yankee Kingdom, and an agricultural future might require new forms of thinking and acting.

9
Vermont Transformed
1945–1969

More than forty-nine thousand Vermonters left the state to participate in World War II. Thirty-eight thousand men and women served on active duty, and an estimated eleven thousand went out of state to work in war-related jobs. Although most of those who stayed behind shared the common burden of wartime shortages and rationing, the demand for goods and recreation, which persisted throughout the war years, had an overall beneficial effect on the Vermont economy. "War and careful management in husbanding resources," wrote Hazel McLoed Wills in her memoir of her husband's years as governor, "brought substantial surpluses for those days." The legislature set aside most of the windfall to meet its obligation of the "Soldiers Bonus"—$10 a month additional pay for twelve months, if a veteran returned to Vermont after completion of active service. At the same time, Governor William H. Wills established a commission for postwar planning in June 1943 to map strategies for pursuing delayed projects and programs, and planning for "a possible slack in employment when peace should be declared."[1] Confident that most of the Vermont veterans and workers would return home—a statement of optimism that stood in sharp contrast with laments about emigration in previous generations—and assuming that they would become a powerful factor in Vermont's postwar economy, the commission set as it goals to "foster the maximum extension of employment opportunities in private industry and business for returning Vermonters from the war fronts [and] gear the state's educational facilities to the national program for the rehabilitation and readjustment of servicemen and women."[2] Confronted with a long list of postponed projects affecting infrastructure, economic development, and social welfare, the state government department heads who comprised the commission assembled recommendations affecting agriculture, education, labor, manufacturing industries, promotion of business, public works, recreational development, transportation, and communication. This response to the state's postwar needs suggested a shift from the traditional view of the state as home to a small, homogeneous population, rugged individualism, self-reliance, and local community control of local institutions, to one that envisioned a continuing and central role for state government in economic planning and in promoting the health and welfare of its citizens. The commission thereby prepared the way for Vermonters to embrace—sometimes cautiously and sometimes with enthusiasm—a wide range of new ideas and institutions in the postwar years and to explore ways to fit a cherished heritage into a new context.

Politics in a New Key

Observers of politics in Vermont anticipated that in addition to their impact on the economy, veterans and others returning to the state after the war would also have an impact on Vermont's political direction in the postwar era. The first clear sign of the accuracy of those predictions came in the Republican gubernatorial primary of 1946, when incumbent Mortimer D. Proctor faced a challenge from Ernest W. Gibson, Jr.

Proctor's ascent to the governorship in 1945 followed in many ways the predictable and established pattern of Vermont Republican politics. The fourth member of his family to serve as chief executive, Proctor climbed the political ladder through the Vermont House of Representatives, where he served as speaker in 1937, moved to the Senate in 1939, where he was president pro tempore, and then served as lieutenant governor under Bennington native William Wills from 1941 to 1945 and by doing so broke the "Mountain Rule" balance of having the governor and lieutenant governor come from different sides of the state. Wills himself, anticipating during his administration no interruption of the traditional ladder of succession, concluded that Proctor "must be as conversant as possible with everything pending, and to this end . . . either included him in conference or where that was not possible, sent him a copy of proceedings."[3] In the 1944 primary, Republican candidate W. Arthur Simpson unsuccessfully attempted to derail Proctor's rise by appealing to the last shred of the Mountain Rule: east-west rotation of the governorship. The argument failed to impress voters and Proctor swamped Simpson with a majority of almost ten thousand votes, winning in every part of the state except Caledonia County, Simpson's home. "Once celebrated by party managers as the foundation of Republican success," comments historian Samuel B. Hand, "the rule now seemed extraneous. Sectional rotation was abandoned with hardly a whimper."[4]

During his first term Proctor used the Wills Commission reports to propose and to some extent implement a progressive agenda. This included benefits and assistance to veterans; a modest increase in state aid to education and small increases in teacher salaries; capital improvements for the state's welfare institutions; expanding workmen's compensation and unemployment compensation laws; increasing and expanding old-age assistance; the creation of a development commission to promote business, industry, and agriculture; and modest increases "to prewar levels" of highway appropriations and grants to towns for town highways. But in 1946 much of what Proctor had proposed in his 1944 inaugural address and much of what remained outlined in the Wills Commission reports remained unfulfilled or stalled in study and planning committees. A fiscal conservative, Proctor, like many of his predecessors, tended to favor industrial interests and insisted that any increases in state expenditures would have to follow increases in revenues, but he failed to devise ways to increase those revenues. Gibson's supporters ridiculed Proctor's administration as "a study in still life."

Like Proctor, Ernest W. Gibson, Jr., had both an impressive political pedigree and wide political experience in Vermont. The son of U.S. Senator Ernest W. Gibson, Sr., Ernest, Jr., was a respected lawyer, had served as state's attorney for Windham County, and as assistant secretary and then secretary of the Vermont Senate, before his friend and neighbor Governor George D. Aiken appointed him to fill the U.S. Senate seat left vacant by his father's death in 1940. By then Gibson and Aiken knew and trusted each other well and shared a growing frustration with what they came to call the "Old Guard" Republican Party leadership in the state.

Gibson, whether from restlessness, discontent with life in Washington, or to fulfill an understanding with Aiken, gave up his Senate seat in 1940, opening the way for Aiken, who was completing his second term as governor, to run in the special election that year. In January 1941 Gibson succeeded William Allen White as chairman of the Committee to Defend America by Aiding the Allies, where he gained national exposure as a leading spokesman in support of Lend-Lease. Proud of the military tradition in his family and himself a graduate of Norwich University and a captain in the National Guard, he requested assignment to active duty. In May he joined his unit, now federalized, as an intelligence officer in the 43rd Division under the command of Vermont's popular military leader, Leonard "Red" Wing. Stationed on Rendova Island in New Georgia

(Solomon Islands), Gibson once again received national attention when a photograph, showing him wincing as a medic bound a shrapnel wound to his head, appeared prominently in several major newspapers. By the time the war ended he was a decorated hero, deputy director of War Department Intelligence, not yet forty-five years old, restless, and poised to make a bid for public office. His opportunity came when General Wing, presumed to be the leading candidate to succeed Proctor, died suddenly of a heart attack in December 1945. Proctor had expressed his intention to step aside after one term as governor, but revised his plan and announced his intention to run for a second term. Gibson assembled a coalition of veterans, agricultural interests, and labor with the encouragement and quiet assistance of his political ally George Aiken, who calculated that the large bloc of war veterans would prove effective in tipping the political balance for only a short time,[5] and who saw an opportunity to continue his attack on the Old Guard. Gibson entered the 1946 gubernatorial primary with energy, charm, an appetite for politics, and enthusiasm for an activist government, unusual in Vermont politics and in stark contrast with the more staid, conservative incumbent governor. He portrayed his primary campaign as an attack on the Republican rule of succession, which he characterized as "outmoded," "unwholesome," and a barrier that prevented "able men at the height of their ability" from seeking high public office.[6] In the September primary, Gibson defeated Proctor by a substantial eight thousand votes, the only time an incumbent governor has lost a primary challenge.

The *Rutland Herald,* which supported Gibson, saw the primary fight as "further evidence of the extent to which the disturbing effects of the war and of the following period have given Vermonters a new outlook on the old political order of things, symbolized by the Proctor regime."[7] The *Burlington Free Press* saw the results as less a rejection of Proctor than a vote "to support a war veteran who put on a vigorous campaign." The *Bennington Banner* interpreted the primary as a show of strength by veterans who "can and probably will control state elections in the future," and portrayed Proctor as "a victim of the situation."[8]

Proctor himself later wrote that his defeat resulted from his feud with Arthur Packard, president of the Vermont Farm Bureau, which had a long history of opposition to the industrialist leadership of the Republican Party and frustration with its resistance to change or inclusiveness in policy making. Packard had also been Aiken's ally in opposition to big private utility interests in the late 1930s. "As soon as I announced for a second term," Proctor wrote in his political memoirs, "Packard at once tried to find a candidate to oppose me.... Gibson was a bold talker, a veteran, and very personable. He spent a year campaigning relentlessly. So did Packard."[9] Proctor's comment ignores the strong support Gibson received from Aiken and the divisions within his own party represented by the strength of the coalition that defeated him. The primary fight suggested, however, that a substantial number of Vermonters emerging from an era of depression and wartime constraints now wanted more change and at a faster pace than the Old Guard offered. The *Rutland Herald* wrote, "It was a surprising departure for Vermont to repudiate an administration which, like some others in the past, was distinguished for lack of progressive policy rather than for any outstanding sins of commission."[10]

Gibson's primary victory opened a way for a shift in Vermont politics, but to a large extent it reflected his personal attractiveness and the strong fellow-feeling of veterans for one of their own more than a major reorientation in Vermonters' political outlook. Although they occasionally appeared together, Gibson and the other primary challengers to the Old Guard for statewide election did not run a coordinated campaign, and none of the others won their bids for nomination. Long-time Aiken friend and political advisor Sterry Waterman lost to former Aiken opponent Ralph Flanders for the U.S. Senate seat vacated by Warren E. Austin, about to be appointed the United States ambassador to the United Nations. Andrew Nuquist, a professor of political science at the University of Vermont, with roots in midwestern progressivism, an outspoken advocate for reciprocal trade with Canada, and critic of U.S. Representative Martin Dies's House Un-American Activities Committee, lost to the conservative incumbent U.S. Representative Charles Plumley. Foreshadowing things to come, Congressman Plumley branded Nuquist an ex-Roosevelt supporter and claimed that he had the support of the Communist Party.

The anticlimactic general election swept Gibson into office with an ambitious program of reform. In his inaugural address he proposed a wide-ranging agenda of programs to improve public education, health, welfare, and safety; conservation; and economic development; along with restructuring some state government offices to improve oversight and increase revenues. Among his most controversial recommendations were a call for more, better-paid teachers, a better retirement plan to retain them,

Republican Party primary campaign forum, June 26, 1946. *Vermont Historical Society.*

ATTENTION! PLEASE!
PRE-PRIMARY RALLY

Chandler Music Hall, Randolph, Vt.

June 26, 1946 ❖ ❖ 8 P. M., E. D. S. T.

SPEAKERS

Candidates

For U. S. Senator

Ralph E. Flanders
Springfield

Sterry R. Waterman
St. Johnsbury

For Congress

Charles A. Plumley
Northfield

Andrew E. Nuquist
Burlington

For Governor

Mortimer R. Proctor
Proctor

Ernest W. Gibson
Brattleboro

For County Senator

Harold H. White
W. Topsham

Earl L. Flanders
Orange

Music by Green Mountain Band

This is your chance to see and hear both sides.

Held under the auspices of the Town and County Republican Committee.

a plan to increase the state subsidy to towns for pupil transportation beyond eighth grade so that more students in rural areas could complete high school (about one-third of Vermont youth, he pointed out, did not go beyond eighth-grade education), and "equalized educational opportunity and distributing the costs as equally as possible among the towns and school districts of the State."[11] In the area of public health, noting that in World War I and again in World War II nearly half the Vermont youths called for service were rejected because of physical or mental health problems, he advocated for annual physical and dental health exams for every schoolchild and mobile health units, such as he had seen in the armed forces, equipped with modern laboratory facilities and staffed by resident physicians and public health nurses.

Another proposal announced in the inaugural speech was the creation of a Department of Public Safety. The automobile had already dramatically changed patterns of travel, commerce, and tourism, and Gibson proclaimed Vermont ill-prepared to cope with the increased traffic and its attendant problems. Referring to the unsolved disappearance of a Bennington College student in the fall of 1946, Gibson called for creation of a state police force, motor vehicle unit, detective force, fire marshal, and records section. Careful to define the limits of state police authority and insist that sheriffs would continue to have local authority on roads and in civil processes, the proposal nonetheless offended sheriffs, who opposed the plan.

Gibson also used his address to restate a major theme from his campaign: his unequivocal opposition to any plan that would "use fertile farm lands of Vermont as flood reservoirs for the protection of . . . Connecticut and Massachusetts." Both Aiken and Gibson had made a cornerstone of their political agendas opposition to the big utility companies whom they characterized as willing to sacrifice farm lands for hydroelectric power dams that would serve interests downriver and profit companies out of state. Throughout the primary campaign Gibson had attacked Proctor for his lukewarm resistance to dam construction. In addition to cementing his relationship with the Vermont Farm Bureau, this position earned Gibson the support of many consumers who agreed with the argument that the big electric utility companies took advantage of Vermont's resource potential for generating power sold downriver or to Vermonters at exorbitant prices. In his inaugural address, Gibson declared his opposition to flooding "another acre of fertile farm land for any purpose whatsoever," and challenged the Public Service Commission to undertake a new investigation of the electricity rate structure using independent expert witnesses rather than those provided by the utility companies.

For the veterans who had helped him win the governorship, Gibson offered a program of subsidized housing, preference in state employment, a fund to stimulate private business hiring of disabled veterans, the extension of unemployment compensation benefits for veterans, and a stronger Veterans Board. To labor he offered increased amounts, broader coverage, and a longer benefit period for workmen's compensation, unemployment compensation, increased funding for the state apprenticeship program, and jobs through $2.6 million of new state building construction and $4 million in state matching for federal highway construction funds.

To pay for these proposals Gibson offered suggestions for enhancing state income from fees for recreation and a plan of tax reform, including a tax withholding plan, and most important, creating a graduated tax scale that, he claimed, would not greatly increase the tax burden on the most wealthy, but also relieve the burden on the least wealthy. He recommended changes in corporate and business taxes to boost state revenues, while offering specific exemptions and allowances to aid small businesses, with estimated net proceeds of $400,000.

Although he arrived at the governor's office with a sizable majority of the popular vote, Gibson anticipated resistance in the legislature. He therefore broke with tradition and began accepting speaking engagements around the state and, following the example of Franklin D. Roosevelt, went on radio to promote and defend his agenda. For the most part the General Assembly followed Gibson's lead, the house more willingly and enthusiastically than the senate. All of his proposals for education reform passed except free transportation for high school pupils; all his health care proposals passed except for his treasured idea of mobile health units, which went down to defeat when Lieutenant Governor Lee Emerson broke a tie in the senate and voted against it. The unsolved Bennington College student case provided the political momentum that overcame the resistance of the county sheriffs and other local law enforcement officers to establishing a Public Safety Department. Gibson also won approval for most of his other proposals for administrative reorganization.

Major defeats came in the area of tax reform, where Gibson squared off against the Associated Industries of Vermont. Eventually the senate struck out some provisions from his tax reform package, including setting up a tax withholding system, and the plan for an unincorporated business tax. But

Two mobile units with crime scene search and photographic equipment of State Police Crime Lab at Redstone, Montpelier, 1957. Left to right: Sgt. Ronald Woodward, Commissioner William H. Baumann, Lieut. Andrew A.H. Monti. *Courtesy of the Vermont State Archives.*

Gibson won concessions on the corporation tax that brought in $1 million to the General Fund, and convinced the legislature to use state money to match federal funds for highway construction and welfare programs. Here, Gibson's personal appeal to Vermonters overcame resistance in the legislature and opened the way for federal-state cooperation that characterized much of the subsequent efforts to expand state road building and welfare programs.

In 1948, at odds with his own party, Gibson narrowly beat back a primary challenge by his conservative lieutenant governor, Lee Emerson, but lost a platform fight at the state convention, when his demand for a statement pledging no more dams on the Connecticut River went down to defeat two to one. Rebuffed in his efforts to nominate candidates who would support him in the legislature, he ran for a second term with yet another conservative lieutenant governor, Harold Arthur, a former grand master of the Vermont State Grange and, like Gibson himself, a war veteran.

More popular with voters than with party leaders, Gibson easily won the general election with a 72 percent majority and entered his second term determined to fill in the details of his agenda. He sent the 1949 legislature the largest number of proposals for a single session since 1912. In a special message to the General Assembly, Gibson proposed the creation of a Vermont power authority to transmit electricity from the St. Lawrence Seaway and to generate power to sell to Vermonters, in direct competition with the big utility companies, which he claimed continued to gouge Vermont customers. He followed this with another special message on public health, proposing a new health commission, expanding public health services, and a scaled-back plan for mobile health units on a trial basis.

Again, Gibson used his personal approach to politics and his coalition of farm, labor, and veteran interests to pressure the legislature. His state power company proposal, however, met strong resistance within his own party and lobbying by the utility companies and the Associated Industries of Vermont. Most of Vermont's newspapers attacked the power program as "socialist" and out of step with Vermont's traditions of individual and local government autonomy, and they editorialized against the proliferation of commissions and the ballooning state budget.

Gibson's meteoric rise attracted the attention of the press, with one national magazine characterizing him as "Vermont's New Dealing Yankee" and another declaring that his revolution in government and Vermont politics amounted to "Vermont Goes Radical," which stood in sharp contrast with the state's reputation for conservatism, earned in part by its stubborn and lonely refusal to award FDR its electoral votes in all four presidential

Governor Ernest Gibson, Jr. (right), Royce Pitkin, president of Goddard College (center), and Harris Soule, director of personnel, State of Vermont (left), at the Vermont Citizens' Conference on "Prospects for Industrial Development." January 23, 1948, Goddard College, Plainfield. *Royce Pitkin Papers, DOC 354, Folder 21. Vermont Historical Society.*

elections.[12] However, Vermont's long tradition of expecting its governors to serve no more than two terms in office, Gibson's fight with his own party, and the minority of "Aiken-Gibson wing" Republicans in the legislature limited his opportunities to implement more initiatives. He proclaimed himself satisfied that he had accomplished many of his goals, and in January 1950 stepped down as governor to accept appointment by Democratic President Harry S. Truman as the U.S. district judge in Vermont.

Writing in 1979, historian Richard Judd concluded that "with the inauguration of Governor Ernest W. Gibson in 1947, the social revolution launched by Franklin D. Roosevelt's New Deal came to full flower in the provincial Republican stronghold of Vermont,"[13] but with his departure, Gibson's revolution in state government went into temporary eclipse. Harold Arthur, who succeeded Gibson, did not share his predecessor's enthusiasm for progressive politics, and when he, in turn, chose to run for Congress rather than a term of office as governor, Lee Emerson reemerged as the Old Guard candidate. However, the Aiken-Gibson challenge did provide a seedbed for the emergence of new voices in Vermont politics, and the return of an Old Guard Republican to office did not altogether signal the return of the party to its old ways. Emerson devoted much of his 1953 inaugural address to a call for rooting out communism. But he conceded that education, welfare reform, highway construction, and business and tourism development "over a period of years have apparently become fixed in the people's minds as responsibilities with which to be dealt."[14]

Emerson had, in fact, inherited a divided Republican Party, barely managing to win the 1952 primary in a three-way race, and winning reelection in 1952 by one of the slimmest majorities in Vermont Republican Party history. The strong showing that year of Democrat Robert Larrow, who garnered sixty thousand votes in the general election, again revealed shifts in voter loyalties and suggested a somewhat revitalized Democratic Party, itself chastened and changed by the successes of progressive Republicanism. Moreover, the 1953 legislature, still solidly Republican, moved far beyond Emerson's fiscal conservatism by adding generously to highway construction and education funding budgets. That legislature also elected Republican legislator Consuelo Northrup Bailey as Vermont's first woman speaker of the house.

In 1954 Republican Joseph B. Johnson defeated Democratic candidate E. Frank Brannon by only five thousand votes in the race for governor, far behind the nearly eight-thousand-vote lead Consuelo Bailey accumulated to become the first woman in the United States elected a lieutenant governor. Inheriting a $4 million deficit, Johnson nonetheless committed his administration to increased spending for public school construction and increased support of the University of Vermont to boost attendance and stanch the flow of students to institutions in neighboring states. Like his predecessors, Johnson acknowledged and regretted the increasing tendency of towns to surrender their privileges and obligations to support schools, road building, care for the aged, disabled, indigent, and mentally ill, and other services. As a result, between 1947 and 1958, while the population size remained unchanged, the state's operating expenses jumped from $27.5 million to $75 million, and the number of full-time state employees increased from 1,537 to 3,321. Increases in road construction, promised by every administration since the end of the war, became a high priority in Johnson's. In his four years as governor he convinced the legislature to abandon the pay-as-you-go approach and authorize almost $40 million in bonds to pay for state roads, fill in the "gravel gaps," and begin construction of the federal Interstate highways in Vermont.

As he left office in 1959, Johnson acknowledged the changes taking place in the state. He saw in the greatly increased expenditures by state government over the previous fifteen years not only a sign of expectations among more and more Vermonters that government should provide a wider range of services, but also "a definite trend in Vermont, as elsewhere, to shift the payments of services from local government to State Government. This was to be expected," he stated, "from the change in our manner of living, especially in transportation, and in shifting from a rural economy to one where more and more people are supported through industry of one kind or another."[15]

Some of those changes showed up in the close race to succeed Johnson. Robert T. Stafford, who moved steadily up the rungs of state government from attorney general of Vermont to lieutenant governor, barely squeaked by his Democratic opponent, Bernard J. Leddy of Burlington, with a mere 719 votes after the only recount of a vote for governor in the state's history. In that election, Democrat William Meyer of West Rupert won election as Vermont's representative in Congress, the first member of his party to win statewide election since 1853.

Stafford, a moderate Republican, held off efforts within his party to pass an antiunion "right to work" law and a sales tax to bolster revenues. Taking advantage of an upswing in the economy, he convinced the legislature to increase welfare assistance to the elderly and disabled, and to dependent children. He won increased funding for community mental health and unemployment compensation, and added $1 million to support joint state-private partnerships in recreation and tourism, which he, like others, saw as an expanding market with strong revenue potential for the state. After serving a single term as governor, Stafford ran against William Meyer for Vermont's lone House seat in 1960.

The Republican primary contest for governor that year revealed once again the divisions within the party. F. Ray Keyser, Jr., speaker of the Vermont House of Representatives, and at thirty-four the youngest candidate ever to run for governor, represented the remnant of Old Guard Republicanism. He faced three rivals for the nomination: Lieutenant Governor and former legislator Robert Babcock; A. Luke Crispe, Gibson's former law partner and political lieutenant; and W. Arthur Simpson, a perennial candidate for governor and long-time state social welfare administrator. All three stood left of the Eisenhower center of Republican politics. Babcock, considered the front-runner, argued that Vermont had to anticipate additional spending for highway patrols, expanded medical benefits, increased legal services for the indigent, and swelling school enrollments. The towns, he argued, could no longer support these costs from property taxes, and he proposed instituting a sales tax to raise new revenues. He thereby alienated some Democratic voters who might have crossed over in the open primary to help him win the nomination.

The three progressive Republicans garnered over 70 percent of the primary votes, but the split gave Keyser the nomination. In the November election he swept past Democrat Russell Niquette of Winooski, an experienced legislator, the preeminent leader of the French-Canadian constituency in Vermont, a hard-working political organizer, a strong supporter of John F. Kennedy in the 1960 presidential election, but not a dynamic figure who could rally Democrats elsewhere in the state or lure disaffected Republicans away from their party. The Republicans swept the statewide elections, including sending Robert Stafford to Congress to replace William Meyer, whose advocacy of admitting Communist China to the United Nations, ending the draft, and promoting nuclear disarmament made him controversial even within his own party. Democrats, however, won more seats in the Vermont house than at any time since the New Deal, demonstrating their growing influence in state politics and building a broad constituency over their base of ethnic and racial minorities.

Almost from the beginning of his term, Governor Keyser faced problems of internal division within the legislature and his party. Unable to exercise leadership, he had to watch the 1961 legislative session fight its way through a record 209 days, during which it failed to enact any significant programs. Some of his own proposals—to repeal an electric energy tax, which would benefit the power companies, to abandon the bankrupt Rutland Railroad, to sell Lyndon State College, and to support a budget that exceeded any on record—alienated several constituencies in his party. The following year, the General Assembly stalled over the state constitution's mandate to reapportion the senate following the 1960 census. After the Vermont Supreme Court handed down its decision in *Mikell* v *Rousseau* in July 1962, refusing to do the legislature's work but threatening judicial interference if the legislators themselves did not complete the task, Keyser called a special session where he ran into opposition from Asa Bloomer and several independent and long-term legislators.[16] An experienced politician from West Rutland, who had long opposed the Proctor wing of his party, Bloomer fought hard to retain the four senate seats held by Rutland County despite Keyser's support of a plan that followed census results more closely by transferring one of them to Chittenden County. Although the governor won that skirmish in the bill that finally passed, it earned him further enmity within his own party.

In the house a group of ten freshman legislators, frustrated by the lack of leadership and quarrelsome environment, formed a study group that they called "the Young Turks." Initially meeting to review bills, the seven Republicans and three Democrats gradually developed policy positions and supported each other to devise new legislation. They included Franklin Billings, Jr., and Ernest Gibson III, both sons of governors; Richard Mallary, the son of Gertrude Mallary, a Republican leader in the house and senate in the 1950s and still an important figure in the Republican Party; Sanborn Partridge, whose father, Frank, had been president of Vermont Marble Company and an interim United States senator; John Downs, a lawyer who had served as a delegate to the 1960 Republican National Convention and chairman of the state platform committee; and Philip Hoff, one of the three Democrats in the group, and in those days of one town-one vote, the sole representative for the City of Burlington.

The Young Turks soon caught the attention of the press and by the end of the 1961 legislative session Hoff was being touted as the likely

Democratic candidate for governor. The party organization recognized an opportunity to present a young, energetic candidate; one, moreover, who as a Protestant would break the association of Democrats as the "Catholic Party." In 1962 Democratic Party leaders carefully maneuvered to eliminate Niquette as a potential Democratic candidate without having to endure a disruptive and potentially divisive primary, and hoping to keep Republican voters apathetic, pushed aside the controversial William Meyer by putting him up as a candidate for the U.S. Senate against the popular George Aiken.

Hoff adopted as his campaign slogan the call to "end a century of one-party rule," and he charged the Republicans with administering "a sleeping pill to the people." Early in the campaign Hoff won important support from disaffected Republicans, including A. Luke Crispe and T. Garry Buckley of Bennington, who formed the Vermont Independent Party (VIP) with the express purpose of giving anti-Keyser Republicans an opportunity to vote for Hoff without having to cast a Democratic ballot.

Keyser struggled to hold together a divided Republican Party, with little loyalty to him personally, and little to show for his two years in office. Late in the campaign, Hoff called Keyser's announcement of a $900,000 surplus bogus because, according to the Republican auditor of accounts, it did not include payments for outstanding bills in the current fiscal year. Keyser attempted to counter that charge with a report from a team of auditors he hired himself, but that misfired when they declared either method of accounting acceptable.

As towns began to report election returns, it became clear that the vote would be close. Hoff ran well in rural districts considered solidly Republican. By midnight Keyser's early lead had dwindled to fewer than one thousand votes. Winooski, a strongly Democratic, working-class city, held back its results, then announced 1,768 for Hoff and 188 for Keyser, making Hoff the first Democratic governor of Vermont since 1853, and the first one ever elected at the polls.

A jubilant Philip Hoff rode through the streets of Winooski at 1 a.m. proclaiming "A hundred years of bondage—broken." One enthusiastic member of the crowd handed him a tin crown and proclaimed him "King of Winooski." In the final count, Hoff won the governorship by only 1,348 votes of 121,389 votes cast. Keyser had garnered 49.5 percent of the vote; Hoff, running as a Democrat, got 46.3 percent of the vote, but the makeshift Vermont Independent Party brought him 3,282 votes (2.7 percent) and he received 1,872 votes (1.5 percent) as an Independent Democrat.

Philip Hoff, "King of Winooski" on election night, November 1962. *Photo by George Grimard, courtesy of the Philip Hoff family.*

Hoff did not have electoral coattails long enough to carry into office a Democratic lieutenant governor or any other Democrat in a statewide contest, and Republicans held secure majorities in both houses of the legislature. Thus, Hoff's election inaugurated a period of coalition politics, the first step toward creating a competitive two-party system. When the legislature reconvened, several of the Young Turks moved into important places: Billings as speaker of the house; Mallary as chairman of the Appropriations Committee; Downs as chairman of Ways and Means; and Gibson at the head of the Judiciary Committee. Hoff and his former colleagues saw each other as allies ready to cooperate to preside over another period of dramatic policy initiatives.

Two years later, when Hoff ran for a second term, the Democrats made a clean sweep, electing their candidates to all statewide offices. In the presidential election that year Vermont broke another long political tradition when it rejected conservative Republican Barry Goldwater and cast its presidential electoral votes for Democrat Lyndon Johnson. When Hoff beat Republican businessman Richard Snelling to win a third term as governor in 1966, the last vestiges of the political system that prevailed in Vermont since the Civil War disappeared.

Reflecting many years later on the dramatic changes in Vermont's political landscape, A. Luke Crispe, who had participated in and helped bring about some of those changes, commented, "I don't think Ernest Gibson changed it; I don't think George Aiken changed it; I don't think Phil Hoff really changed it. I think what happened was that the war changed it. . . . I think that people just flew their colors and before they wouldn't do that."[17]

A Revolution in Government: The Hoff Years, 1963-1969

Philip Hoff campaigned for governor in 1962 on the promise of "a bold new approach" to government and derided his opponent and the Republican Party in general for having administered a "sleeping pill" to Vermont voters. Just as Ernest Gibson, Jr., had pressed Vermonters to adopt—somewhat belatedly—New Deal solutions to solve Vermont problems, so Hoff now proposed to adopt the philosophy and programs of John F. Kennedy's New Frontier to help solve some of the problems he perceived in the operation of Vermont state government.

In his inaugural address in January 1963 Hoff proclaimed, "I am here today because the people of Vermont have clearly voiced a desire for a bold departure in meeting the pressing problems that face our state," and he interpreted his narrow victory as symbolic of "the subtle workings of a society in transition . . . [that] finally broke 109 years of tradition and habit."[18] In language that challenged the contented image of "Vermont as America as it used to be," Hoff declared, "The crisis we face today is one of obsolescence. Many of our old ways of doing things no longer serve as useful and valuable tools in the efficient handling of our public affairs. In fact, they thwart and hold us back in our search for a better future."[19] With no program of his own to propose, however, he announced his intention of taking a year to study the operation of state government and current needs, and proposed a modest budget that "will permit our State to move ahead to the very limits of its current ability." He urged bipartisan cooperation, and exhorted the legislature to "conserve our energies and our innovations" until he reconvened a special session to set in motion his proposals for reform.[20]

Hoff's announcement that he planned to take a year to study Vermont's problems stunned and disappointed his political allies and delighted his political opponents. But as the euphoria of his election subsided, the new governor discovered that he had to clear three basic roadblocks before he could propose, much less accomplish, anything approximating the "bold new approach" to state government that he promised: the decentralized executive branch of state government; a large, unwieldy, and malapportioned legislature with a one-town, one-vote system of representation in the house; and a long, weakened, but still rhetorically powerful tradition of local control in several crucial areas of government including education, roads, welfare, and planning for development, which together combined to frustrate any hopes of immediate action. In addition, Hoff came into the governor's office with only a small team of advisors, without members of his own party in other key elected positions, and with a minority Democratic Party in the legislature. When critics complained that Hoff moved too slowly in his first year he shot back, with only slight exaggeration, "I'm the only Democrat in my administration, you know."[21]

Despite his own experience in the legislature and warnings from experienced observers that he faced these problems, Hoff seemed totally unprepared for what awaited him. When he stepped into the governor's office in the State House for the first time after his election he was stunned to find all the file cabinets empty; he couldn't even locate the "black book" that kept track of all the crank callers. The next surprise—and disappointment—came when he held preliminary budget hearings prior to his inauguration. "I went into the hearing," he recalled, "and asked for a ten-year projection and they looked at me in complete bafflement and said that they didn't have that. So I said I'd like a five-year projection, and they looked at me in absolute bafflement again. Finally I said, 'Well how about a projection for this coming year?' and they said they didn't have that, either. I was flabbergasted. I didn't know what in hell I was going to do."[22] One of the things he did was secure $250,000 from the U.S. Urban Renewal Administration to support a planning effort that involved several hundred task forces and as many as five hundred individuals in and outside of government to propose programs and funding options for each of the problem areas he identified in his inaugural speech. The first of many infusions of federal money that followed during Hoff's administration, it signaled one of his new approaches to state government. Hoff proved to be both aggressive and highly successful at securing federal assistance from a sympathetic Democratic administration in Washington, D.C., eventually implementing over eighty federally funded projects during his six years in office.

The task forces helped Hoff get around some of the personnel problems he inherited. The new governor confronted a decentralized administrative system largely beyond his control and lacking both the means and the will to coordinate planning and policy. Despite repeated efforts to reorganize and simplify the structure of state government, the General Assembly's tendency to approach problem solving piecemeal resulted in the gradual proliferation of agencies, governing boards, and commissions, many of which reported to the legislature rather than to the governor. As a result, according to Andrew and Edith Nuquist in their 1966 book on Vermont state government, "through the years there was no cohesive administrative system in Vermont. There was nothing approaching a cabinet of department heads, and there was no formal method for regularly getting or giving advice."[23]

Following the lead of several other states, the General Assembly had tried to reorganize the executive branch in 1957 by authorizing a Commission to Study State Government. The Vermont task force, known generally as the "Little Hoover Commission," because it sought to emulate a similar effort at the federal level in 1947–1949 under the leadership of former President Herbert Hoover, was headed by Deane C. Davis, at the time president of the National Life Insurance Company and a prominent figure in the Republican Party. The commission worked for two years and produced a report with 135 recommendations. These included the creation of a Department of Administration that would consolidate eight existing agencies, the creation of a cabinet system of executive management, restructuring major departments and agencies to reduce their number and overlapping of authority, and overhaul of the state's budget and management system.[24]

Implementation of the Little Hoover Commission recommendations began in 1960 but proceeded slowly. By the time Hoff entered office he had to deal with only twenty administrative heads instead of the hundred or more in previous years. However, many of these remained beyond his direct control: Some were appointed for fixed terms by the governor with advice and consent of the senate; some were appointed by the boards they served, in several cases without the governor's approval. Most of the veteran agency heads had no allegiance to Hoff, anticipated outlasting him in government service, and exercised a great deal of independence. Commissioner of Forests and Parks Perry Merrill exemplified this group. In state government since 1919, he had developed his own power base, independent of governors and legislators who came and went while he stayed on and on. The Nuquists described him, somewhat tongue in cheek, as "one of the most effective politicians in the state," with an ability to secure regular appropriations "in more adequate amounts than many of his colleagues. His long-range plans for forestry have been known only to himself, and at each session of the legislature, he has unveiled a little more of his program, project by project, as he asked for and got funds."[25] Others spoke with blunt admiration: "Pretty damn near a czar," said Deane Davis; "The leaves don't turn red until Perry gives them the word," quipped one of his fellow commissioners, clearly in awe of Merrill's power and influence.[26]

A governor needed to win over this cadre of long-term, independent commissioners and agency heads to make policy. Moreover, the tendency of agency heads to avoid communicating with each other or with the governor doomed most efforts at coordinating policies, practices, and procedures, and failed to meet the needs of increasingly complicated social, economic, or political environments.

Although he never gained full control of this unwieldy administrative system, Hoff used the ad hoc task forces to bring in new constituencies—women, younger colleagues who had not yet gained experience in electoral politics or appointed government, and Democrats, until now all but shut out of most state and local government boards and departments—and he used their recommendations to circumvent entrenched agency heads or put pressure on them to institute new policies and procedures. He also created some interagency committees and in 1965 he created by executive order a Central Planning Office in the Department of Development, using more federal funds to expand the office until he convinced the legislature in 1967 to create the Vermont Planning Council, with the governor as chairman. This later became the State Planning Office, which took on increasingly important, far-reaching, and complicated projects in succeeding decades.[27]

In 1962 the General Assembly still labored under a structure guaranteed to frustrate any governor with a reformist agenda. The Vermont Constitution of 1777 established a system of representation based on the geographical unit of the town. A concession to the larger towns—over eighty taxable inhabitants—gave them a second representative for the first seven years of the state's history under its constitution. Thereafter, the legislature operated on the principle of one town-one vote.[28] The defects of this system became plain as early as 1785, when the first Council of Censors proposed both a smaller legislature and representation based on population. Both proposals, continually renewed over the next 180 years, continually failed in constitutional conventions dominated by the small towns. The sole concession came in 1836 with the addition of a thirty-member senate, where each county claimed one seat, the remaining sixteen apportioned by population, to be adjusted every ten years following the federal census.

By 1962 the Vermont House, with its 246 members, remained one of the largest legislative bodies among the fifty states, despite Vermont's small population of 389,000. William Jay Smith represented the town of Pownal (population 1,500) in the 1960–1961 legislative session. One of only forty-six Democrats, he sat next to freshman legislator Philip Hoff, who represented Burlington (population 35,351). Behind them sat Ethel Eddy, representing the town of Stratton (population 24). Each had a single vote in the house. Some commentators applauded this system for its localism. Representatives often knew most if not all of their constituents personally, they argued, and could therefore better represent their community's interests and opinions. Others, like Smith, decried the inequality of representation. "What we have in Vermont," he wrote, in his witty but bitter reflection on his two years in the legislature, "is not just the struggle between rural and urban populations. What we have is not a rural dictatorship, but a rural aristocracy. Being in the Vermont house was for me like a journey back into the eighteenth century, when one had to own land to vote.... The Vermont house is our House of Lords."[29] In the 1960 legislative session the twenty-five largest cities and towns constituted 55 percent of Vermont's population, paid 60 to 68 percent of state revenues, but had only 10 percent of the total votes in the house. "The inhabitants of the 221 smaller towns in Vermont very well understood their advantageous legislative situation," wrote Andrew and Edith Nuquist, "and the majority were against changing it."[30]

Change came nonetheless. After the United States Supreme Court ruled in 1962 (*Baker* v. *Carr*) that representation in state legislatures based on any criterion other than population violated the Fourteenth Amendment to the U.S. Constitution, maverick Republican T. Garry

Buckley of Bennington filed suit in federal district court demanding reapportionment of the Vermont House of Representatives. While that case made its way through the courts, a companion Supreme Court ruling in 1964 (*Reynolds* v. *Sims*) expanded the principle of one person-one vote by requiring representation by population in both houses of the state legislatures. A panel of federal judges finally ruled in July 1964 that "both Houses of the Vermont General Assembly are malapportioned." The court refrained from imposing a remedy of its own devising and allowed elections for the Vermont House of Representatives to proceed as usual on November 6, 1964, but restricted the term of election to one year instead of the usual two and ordered the General Assembly to produce a plan for population-based representation.[31]

Debate over reapportionment during the legendary session in 1965 became heated and emotional. Representative W. Clark Hutchinson of Rochester threatened to chain himself to his seat and declared, "We know that there is such a thing as honor and the sanctity of an oath, and that we intend to preserve it. We know that forced reapportionment is loss of self-government, and we intend to fight, and we intend to vote against it now and forever." Some legislators, such as Samuel A. Parsons of Hubbardton, feared that reapportionment would mean the death of small towns. "Cities aren't healthy minded," he said; in them "you lose sight of what is honorable and dishonorable." Representative Frank Hutchins of Stannard, population 113, spoke with tears of frustration rolling down his cheeks. "When outsiders come into this parlor and tear us to pieces, I regret it," he declared, and fearing that his small town would never again send a representative to the General Assembly, he concluded, "Don't forget Stannard."[32]

Hoff worked with Speaker Franklin S. Billings and his other former colleagues in the house to build a coalition of liberal and moderate Republicans and Democrats who shaped the legislative response to the court order. Late in the afternoon of May 14, 1965, as Hoff made an unprecedented appearance to look on from the balcony, Speaker Billings announced the result of the vote on a bill—163 in favor, 62 opposed—to reduce the size of the house to 150 members, elected on the basis of the population of registered voters. Although the final stage of this fundamental change in Vermont government had to await amendment to the state constitution in 1975, three additional bills passed on June 17, 1965, effectively ended the town-based system of representation. One reapportioned the senate by modifying the county-and-population system to use a population basis exclusively; one created a procedure for periodic reapportionment of both houses; and one established a procedure for new elections to a reapportioned house.

The new basis for representation had the immediate effect of creating a legislature dominated for the first time by representatives of the large cities and towns, who were generally amenable to Hoff's programs and philosophy of government. Even with these changes, however, Hoff still had to contend with the well-entrenched system of local control. He complained to a *New York Times* reporter in May 1963 that "with a population of less than 400,000 persons, Vermont has 800 school directors, 246 road commissioners, and 246 overseers of the poor. It's ludicrous, utterly ridiculous, and wasteful. It may be political suicide, but I am determined to end this sort of provincialism."[33] Although not suicidal, Hoff's attempts in the 1964 legislative session to replace local school taxing and administration, property tax assessment, and road building with regional structures met with failure.

By far the most controversial of Hoff's proposals for regional governance was his plan to replace the autonomous local school boards with twelve districts, each with its own regional board, taxing power, and school superintendent who would supervise a K–12 system of schools. The proposal emerged from one of Hoff's 1963 task forces, but also responded to continuing anxiety about the nation's educational system in the wake of the 1957 launch of Sputnik by the Soviet Union, the civil rights movement's call for equal educational opportunity, and President Lyndon Johnson's initial success in implementing some of John F. Kennedy's New Frontier proposals under the new name, the "Great Society." Closer to home, Vermont's veteran Commissioner of Education, John Holden, championed the consolidation of school districts, but the plan encountered tough resistance to relinquishing local control and failed to pass in 1964 and again in 1965. Meanwhile, Holden continued to advocate voluntary consolidation, and using laws enacted in the 1940s and 1950s, achieved some success in creating two dozen union high school districts before he retired in 1965. Several years later, Holden reflected on his role in promoting union high schools, their effectiveness, and the continuing dilemma of consolidation to achieve enhanced educational opportunities in a humane setting. "Sometimes," he wrote, "I wonder if they brought us what we wanted . . . Could they? . . . When a school or any other organization gets big, it tends to get impersonal, even sometimes inhumane. But inhumanity is not confined to the big ones."[34]

Hoff achieved more success in his effort to reform the welfare system. The welfare reform act passed in the 1967 legislature did away with the remnants of the old, often inequitable and abusive town-based system of overseers of the poor and poor farms. Many Vermont towns had already abandoned this system during the Great Depression. The larger towns continued to operate poor farms into the 1950s, but as federal and state welfare programs expanded, these, too, gradually closed: Brattleboro in 1951; Bennington in 1952–1953; Montpelier in 1956; St. Johnsbury and Burlington in 1958; Middlebury in 1959; Rutland in 1966.[35] During Hoff's second term, Social Welfare Commissioner John J. Wackerman, appointed by Governor Robert T. Stafford in 1959, used the report of Hoff's task force on social welfare to build a strong case for having the state take over the remnants of local authority for poor relief. The 1967 welfare reform bill had strong bipartisan support in the legislature and in the small towns eager to get rid of the financial burden of poor relief. A guarantee that anyone employed full time as a town or city overseer of the poor would have a state job in the new welfare program helped overcome whatever remained of local resistance. The new law created a state-funded and state-operated program to administer federal welfare funds to families with dependent children, the blind, elderly, and permanently disabled, and to determine in a uniform manner eligibility for distribution of state funds to those in need of short-term assistance.[36]

Hoff's skill at building coalitions in his first two terms resulted in several other achievements. In addition to fair employment and fair housing acts, the legislature approved bills creating the Vermont Council on the Arts (now known as the Vermont Arts Council), and the Vermont Student Assistance Corporation to give scholarships and loans for postsecondary education. New legislation made it easier for cities to start urban renewal projects and eased the way for several small-town projects; overhauled the state's penal system, placing more emphasis on rehabilitation than incarceration; and authorized the establishment of Vermont's educational television network. To the amazement of many, the legislature even relinquished its jealously guarded management of the deer herd to the Fish and Game Board.

Even at the height of his popularity and influence, however, Hoff suffered some major legislative defeats. In addition to the failure of most of his plans for regional government, one of his most bitter disappointments came in 1966 when the legislature defeated his plan to import hydroelectric power from Canada at a fixed rate under a long-term contract with the Canadian utility company Hydro-Québec. Hoff's administration negotiated the contract but needed enabling legislation to set up a nonprofit corporation to import the power and secure bonding for payments to a foreign company. The bill encountered an enormous lobbying effort, led by Albert Cree, Gibson's old adversary, former president of Central Vermont Public Service, now representing the local electric power industry in securing permits to build a nuclear power plant in Vermont. The authorizing legislation passed the senate but stalled in the house, which sent it to a study committee that killed it. Hoff considered this one of his biggest defeats and most bitter disappointments. To his surprise, he even failed to win support for the plan from U.S. Senator George Aiken, who had so often in the past opposed the interests of big power companies.[37] Two years later Cree won his battle to build a nuclear power plant with a one-vote margin in the house. Although later generations of Vermonters have fought over the environmental impact of both nuclear and Canadian hydro power, the issues discussed in 1966, according to William K. Porter and Stephen C. Terry—both working as journalists at that time—were economics, geography, and sovereignty. "The environmental constituency was not a player in the major public affairs debates in 1966."[38]

The environment, however, did emerge as both a political and policy issue in the later years of Hoff's administration. Responding to new problems created by rapid growth in population, industry, and tourism—spurred in part by the success of "The Beckoning Country" publicity and development campaign devised on his watch—Hoff's administration created the Interagency Committee on Natural Resources in 1964, the Scenery Preservation Council in 1966, proposed legislation screening junkyards and regulating dumps, promoted recreational planning, and secured more federal funds to help purchase additional park and forest land.

The biggest fight in this area, however, came over legislation to ban billboards from Vermont's roads and highways. The issue had been raised as early as 1937, when seven billboards went up in Springfield. A citizen's committee wrote letters to the advertisers arguing that the signs harmed local business. Within eighteen months all the signs had been removed and the Vermont Association for Billboard Restriction had been formed. In 1943 the Vermont Supreme Court ruled that property owners had no inherent rights as regards advertising billboards adjacent to public roads, and thus gave Vermont state government as well as cities, towns, and villages the option to ban billboards.[39] Most towns seemed quite happy to keep advertising off their roads. In 1957 the legislature passed a law eliminating advertising along limited-access roads.

By 1960, however, the booming tourism industry gave roadside advertising greater economic significance. Although an attempt that year to repeal the 1957 law failed, local merchants had become far more sympathetic to billboards and dependent on them to lure visiting motorists off the road and into their shops and facilities. At the same time, federal policy, such as the highway beautification campaign led by First Lady Ladybird Johnson, took aim at billboards built adjacent to interstate roads and other federal highways. The contest had been quietly festering at the local level, pitting garden clubs and local interests against the increasingly powerful billboard lobbyists. It broke into the open when freshman Republican Representative Ted Riehle from South Burlington introduced legislation in 1967 to ban billboards from the interstate roads and restrict advertising to small, licensed, directional signs elsewhere over Vermont's state road system, and to on-premises signs with limitations on size and mode of display.[40] Supported by Hoff, the press, and an emerging environmentalist constituency, Riehle shepherded his bill to a narrow victory over the hard-fought resistance of property-rights advocates and the national billboard industry. Democrats, who did not share Hoff's enthusiasm for environmental protection laws, abandoned him on this bill.

The billboard, quite literally a sign of changing times and values in Vermont society and politics, proved a harbinger of larger struggles over environmental issues and how Vermonters would deal with the consequences of an effective campaign to promote tourism, economic growth, and development, struggles that intensified over the final three decades of the twentieth century. In the wake of almost unprecedented immigration and prosperity in Vermont, new ideas, new values, and new divisions increasingly appeared on the formerly quiet landscape.

Governor Hoff had eagerly embraced and become an advocate for environmental protection laws early in his administration. By the time he entered his third term—a tenure in office unprecedented for over one hundred years of Vermont politics—they too, had become divisive issues undermining his prestige and authority. When Hoff broke with President Johnson over the Vietnam War in 1968, he divided Vermont Democrats and introduced in Vermont politics a new element of disagreement and distrust of government. By the time he left office in 1969, Hoff's once high level of popularity was shredded. The governorship went to Republican Deane C. Davis and Hoff himself suffered an overwhelming defeat at the polls in his 1970 run for the U.S. Senate against Republican Winston L. Prouty.

Whatever personal defeats marked the end of "the Hoff years," as journalist Stephen C. Terry dubbed them in his seven-part series written in late 1968 for the *Rutland Herald*, the period of his governorship did see some remarkable and irreversible changes in Vermont. Not all of them rested entirely on Hoff's leadership. In many ways he reflected, benefited, and occasionally suffered from larger changes taking place in the nation and in Vermont. If Hoff did not always deliver the "bold new approach" to government that he promised, he did at least renew and enhance the progressive tradition of an active executive and activist state government, and he introduced a broader perspective on state-federal cooperation in providing government programs and services. By winning his first election for governor and winning again with substantial majority votes in his two subsequent elections (64.9 percent in 1964, at the height of his popularity, and 57.7 percent in 1966), Hoff could justly claim to have initiated the era of two-party politics that has characterized Vermont ever since his departure from the governor's office. During Hoff's years in office Vermont drifted in many ways ever closer to the mainstream of American politics, society, and economy. This shift had both benefits and perils, as subsequent governors and successive generations of Vermonters were to discover.

The New Vermont Economy

In contrast to the optimism of Governor Wills's postwar planning commission, the 1950 census counted 377,747 Vermonters, a modest growth of just over 5 percent from the previous decade. This lagged far behind the 14.5 percent national growth rate and even the 10.5 percent population growth for New England. An even slower rate of population increase showed up in the next census, with Vermont gaining just over 3 percent compared with a national growth of 18.5 percent and regional growth of almost 13 percent. Not until the 1970 census did Vermont record a significant leap in its population, up 14 percent to 444,330, the largest increase since 1830.

Although Vermont had been discovered by tourists and those seeking recreation during the Depression and war years, it had not yet developed either the infrastructure or the foundation for economic growth that would later encourage new immigration. Commenting wryly on this situation, George Aiken is said to have quipped that everyone in Connecticut would move to Vermont if they could figure out a way to make a living here. Prospects for making a living began to change immediately following the war and gained momentum during the 1950s. Some of those who came to Vermont to play in the postwar years decided to stay, providing additional impetus to change in rural areas as the newcomers bought some of the less productive or abandoned uphill farms.

Within Vermont, the movement of people from rural to urban areas continued into the 1960s, exhibiting a peak in the 1960 census, when the ten largest towns accounted for 34 percent of the state's population, while the 124 smallest towns held less than 12 percent. Behind these numbers lies a story of change in the economic life of the state. Both agriculture and the long-established textile and machine-tool industries declined steadily, sometimes rapidly in the postwar period, while tourism and electronics played increasingly significant roles in the state's economy.

Agriculture served as a bellwether of change for the postwar years, which became a period of flux and often turmoil for Vermont's entire economy. By 1950 Vermont had just over half the number of farms counted in 1890, the late-nineteenth-century high point. Dairy farming, generally perceived as the centerpiece of Vermont agriculture, was in the midst of some important transitions. The emphasis on pure-breed herds raised the start-up costs for farmers, but increased the productivity of herds. A gradual shift from Jerseys, which produce richer milk, to Holsteins, which produce greater quantities of milk, also increased productivity. The introduction of stainless steel bulk tanks also significantly raised the costs to farmers and affected their allocation of resources.

Bulk tanks first appeared in the state in 1952. John Page, Bennington County agent for the Agricultural Extension Service, recalled that "in the early 1950s bulk tanks were a novelty and farmers were up in arms about their appearance." The conversion costs for the average farmer, however, presented a formidable obstacle to their acceptance. In the June 1955 edition of *Vermont Farm and Home Science*, the author of "Should You Buy a Bulk Tank?" placed the start-up costs at between $1,200 and $4,500, or 11 cents on the hundredweight of milk to purchase and maintain a bulk tank, compared to 5 cents handling milk "the old-fashioned way." The author concluded that "It is fairly safe to assume eventually almost all dairy farmers in Vermont will have to cool their milk in bulk," but cautioned farmers with fewer than fifty cows and not on a route serviced by a tank truck against taking the plunge.[41]

The Department of Agriculture and many creameries, concerned about both the health and marketability of milk, promoted the conversion from twenty-gallon milk cans to bulk tanks, which held about 355 gallons and were emptied every other day. Many creameries initially offered premium prices to farmers who converted. As a result, bulk-tank farming made rapid inroads in Vermont's dairy community by 1962, when the *Biennial Report of the Commissioner of Agriculture, 1961-62* counted forty-six hundred bulk-tank installations on the approximately sixty-nine hundred dairy farms in the state, with new tanks appearing at a rate of six to eight hundred per year.[42] Eventually, the creameries won total compliance by refusing to accept milk from those farmers who did not install the tanks. This contributed to the decision by many dairy farmers, already struggling to sustain their operations, to give up.

In Woodstock, according to town historian Peter S. Jennison, "many of the smaller farms which survived the Depression 'failed up' when bulk tank milk coolers were required . . . And for the next thirty years, further attrition occurred as the costs of other equipment and labor rose." In 1900, Jennison reports, 185 men were engaged in farming in Woodstock. By 1980 the number had dwindled to 69, including those engaged in forestry and fisheries.[43] Down the road in West Windsor the number of herds fell from 73 in 1942 to 18 in 1967. By the early 1970s only 4,153 dairy farms remained in business in Vermont. Governor Johnson noted the trend in his 1959 farewell address, but interpreted it as the price to be paid for modernization and overall prosperity for the dairy industry. "Many country milk plants are being closed," he conceded. "This is part of the great mechanical revolution in agriculture which in common with all revolutions creates hardships for some people, but if wisely handled can reduce the cost of assembling and transporting milk and keep Vermont competitive in our great milk markets."[44]

The bulk tank issue had other consequences. The larger herds required to justify and pay for the new equipment meant that many farmers gave up what was left of diversified farming to feed their herds. Wheat, buckwheat, and oats all but disappeared as cash crops for regional or national markets while farmers focused on raising hay, field corn, and other silage crops. By 1960, an article in *Food Marketing in New England* ranked Vermont as the leading hay-producing state in the region, at 1,159,000 tons—more than half a ton of hay per acre under cultivation. This development meant that most farmers gave up working their land in time-honored fashion, abandoning horses or oxen to purchase tractors and expensive machinery—yet another capital investment to increase the costs of operation. For some recent critics, the eighteen-year period of conversion to bulk tanks marks the end of the era of the small family farm in Vermont, followed by gentrification of rural areas, conversion of farm land to second-home development, and the rise of agribusiness. On the other hand, others argue that a constellation of factors, such as tractors, hybrid seeds, synthetic fertilizers, milking machines, and artificial insemination combined to undermine small hill farms.[45]

Like farming, the textile industry, a mainstay of the Vermont industrial economy since the 1840s, struggled to maintain itself in the post-World War II era. The loss of government contracts for wartime needs exposed a multitude of problems, including aging equipment, an aging and diminished rail system, inadequate roads, the growing popularity of synthetic fabrics, competition from cloth manufacturing in Japan and India—promoted by the United States government as a postwar recovery strategy and as a Cold War economic strategy to challenge communism in Asia—and lower labor costs in the South.

In 1948 Windsor County, once home to twenty-two woolen mills, had only nine still in operation. Three years later Harris Emery Company, occupying one of the oldest mills in the state, closed its Vermont operations and moved to Penacook, New Hampshire. Calling its Champlain Mills in Winooski "the most antiquated and inefficient" of any of its facilities, and with access to inexpensive power from the Tennessee Valley Authority for its other mills, the American Woolen Company closed the Winooski facility, the largest textile mill in the state, in September 1954, just three months before the company itself was purchased by Textron. The Winooski closing put hundreds of people out of work, and sent the entire city into an economic tailspin. Younger textile workers sold their homes at low prices and left the area in search of jobs in other fields or to follow the textile industry to the South.[46] The A. G. Dewey Company, founded in 1836, left Vermont in 1956 when construction of a power dam at Hartland forced the company to abandon its complex of sixty-three industrial buildings and workers' housing on the Otauquechee River. Wimbley Woolen Company and Jewell Brook Woolen Company in

Ludlow, and mills in Bennington, hung on for another generation, but by the early 1970s, large-scale textile manufacture had become largely a memory in Vermont.

The machine-tool industry in Springfield's "Precision Valley" also suffered in the first wave of reconversion from war production. Early in June 1945 the three major companies in the area—Jones & Lamson Machine Company, Fellows Gear Shaper Company, and Bryant Chucking Grinder Company—began cutbacks from wartime levels of employment by not making new hires and eliminating night shifts. By that November over one hundred workers in the three shops had lost their jobs. The companies all used seniority as a criterion, which meant that many women were the first laid off. Even with a pared-down work force and reduced hours, however, the industry continued to falter as the federal government terminated wartime contracts and began dumping surplus tools.

The United Electrical Workers (UE) of the CIO tried to protect workers at the Jones & Lamson and Bryant shops by pressing for a 30 percent wage increase to compensate for reduced hours. Bryant challenged the UE's authority to represent workers in its plant, and after considering an appeal to the National Labor Relations Board, the UE decided to pull out. The three companies then offered workers new contracts of 11- to 15-percent wage increases, followed by 10-percent increases in May 1946 and again in August 1947 and 1948. But with many American industries reluctant to make large capital investments in equipment, the Springfield companies struggled. Each company posted at least one year-end loss during the period 1945 to 1949, and each continued to reduce the size of its work force.

The Korean War, which erupted in 1950, created new uncertainties for the machine-tool industry. Anticipating a short war, the military held back on purchases of new materiel until China entered the war in late 1950. A brief spurt of activity in 1951 revived the industry and the region's economy until the war ended in 1953, but a nationwide economic slump in 1954 and a full recession in 1957 once again brought layoffs to Springfield's workers. By then the top management in all three companies had begun to explore opportunities for automation, international mergers, and diversification, all of which promised fewer jobs for Vermonters.[47]

Vermont's governors resorted to two major strategies in the postwar period to recover from the downward spirals of agriculture and industry. They increased attention and appropriations to planning and development, and increased spending on roads. Vermonters did not easily swallow the bitter pill of state coordination of planning and development. In the postwar and Cold War eras of the 1950s and 1960s the terms sounded too much like socialism and communism. But faced with a desperate situation, the legislature grudgingly passed new legislation in 1951 creating the Vermont Development Commission. With encouragement from the state, several regional semiprivate industrial development organizations began their own efforts to recruit new businesses. The Greater Burlington Industrial Corporation scored the greatest single success by convincing International Business Machines (IBM) to locate a plant in Essex Junction in 1957.

The legislature gave more substantial assistance to development efforts in 1953 when it authorized the creation of local Development Credit Corporations, which, by selling stock and accepting private contributions, raised money to build industrial plants for prospective users, then rented or sold them to companies to recoup the investment. IBM located its first plant in Vermont in one such building. The 1961 legislature followed up this experiment with the Vermont Industrial Building Authority, which promoted and helped finance speculative business ventures that benefited the state by insuring mortgages for start-up company buildings.

IBM employees at the corporation's new plant in Essex Junction, 1961. *Courtesy of the IBM Corporate Archives.*

Vermont Life, volume 1, number 1 (Fall 1946). *Courtesy of* Vermont Life *magazine.*

Ski country. The intersection of Vermont routes 100 and 9 in Wilmington (no date). *Vermont Travel Division collection, Vermont Historical Society.*

The state's major effort, however, went into promoting the tourism industry. Vermont state government had taken an active role in promoting tourism since the 1890s, when it created the nation's first tourism board. The 1931 report of the Vermont Commission on Country Life had included a long section endorsing tourism and efforts to attract summer residents and purchases of second homes in abandoned upland farms. It made several recommendations for promotion, including the publication of a magazine to stimulate tourism. In 1946 that recommendation bore fruit when *Vermont Life* appeared under the auspices of the Vermont Development Commission. Writing in the first issue, the editorial team of Earle Newton, Walter Hard, and Vrest Orton promised articles on Vermont history, educational institutions, agriculture, art and architecture, distinguished Vermonters, travel and recreation facilities, and other features "designed to interest and inform both residents and non-residents of the state."[48] Technological advances in color printing and photography allowed *Vermont Life* to portray the state as a rural, unspoiled paradise, using an abundance of lush, full-color images. From its very beginnings, *Vermont Life*, with a larger out-of-state than in-state subscription list, appealed to an urban, mobile, and modestly prosperous audience, and served as an attractive, effective promotional tool for the Development Department.

While summer tourism remained a major focus of promotional efforts, skiing rapidly became an important new element in the state's development plan. From its modest beginnings in the 1930s, skiing became an industry in Vermont in the 1950s, with major recreation facilities at Mt. Snow (1954), Ascutney (1956), Jay Peak (1958), and Killington (1958) among many others. John Howland and Robert Ely bought the Ascutney Mountain Resort, with three rope tows and a warming house, for $2,000. They sold season passes for $40 and offered ski lessons for 75 cents. In 1957 Ascutney became the first ski area to experiment with making snow.

Secondary industries—hotels, restaurants, tourist services, and construction—benefited from the ski industry and grew rapidly. In 1964 the *Rutland Herald* reported that gross receipts for Killington alone exceed $1 million, producing tax revenues to the state of over $68,000, spurring construction of more than a hundred new buildings, and doubling the value of land and property in Sherburne over a period of five years.

By 1965 a combination of winter skiing, summer camps, second homes, hiking, fishing, summer resorts, and autumn foliage touring had transformed Vermont into a three-season resort and recreation area. The state tourism board changed its welcome signs at the border from "The last stand of the Yankees" to "The Beckoning County," the motto of Governor Hoff's all-out, sophisticated, multimedia advertising campaign. Tourism and recreation became the second largest industry in the state, generating annual gross revenue of over $130 million.[49] With environmental and conservation issues not yet prominent in public consciousness or high on the political agenda, Vermont had found a way out of some of its economic problems by marketing as tourist attractions its agricultural landscape, forests, parks, wilderness areas, and abandoned rural homesteads that became available as second homes for escaping urbanites in coastal New England and the Middle Atlantic states.

Investment in roads made the new Vermont economy possible. In his 1953 inaugural address, Governor Emerson pledged his administration "to a policy of matching all available Federal funds" for constructing roads. The initial effort went to meet local needs of Vermont travelers and businesses: filling in the "gravel gaps" that connected Vermont's urban centers and paving roads to villages. Only scant attention or resources went to encouraging out-of-state traffic. Two years later, a plan for an interstate highway system began to take shape in Congress, and incoming governor Joseph B. Johnson, urging the legislature to appropriate increased spending for roads, asserted that Vermont's economic survival now depended on having more and better roads. Johnson therefore announced "the backing of this administration . . . to all efforts to furnish access roads to developments in which people, both from within Vermont and from outside the state, have invested their money."[50] The Interstate Highway Act, passed in 1954, provided a generous share of federal funds for the construction of four-lane roads to and through Vermont, and Johnson urged the legislature to take advantage of this unprecedented opportunity. The required 10-percent match, however, still exceeded any amount Vermont could spend using its traditional pay-as-you-go practice, and

Johnson proposed borrowing money to meet the state's obligation for what he considered an essential road-building project. He justified the expense and the indebtedness by arguing that "our highway network is a sound investment in the future of our State. It is one of our greatest selling points in our efforts to bring industry and tourists into the State and to transport our valuable agricultural products where they can be sold."[51]

Construction of the interstate highways in Vermont began in 1957 at the state's southeastern border. On December 6, 1961, U.S. Senator George Aiken helped open the first eleven miles of completed road, part of which passed on top of what had been his own boyhood home. "It is not given to everyone in his lifetime to help dedicate a monument over his own birthplace," he began, but he took consolation in the prospect that "we're on the verge of the greatest development Vermont has ever seen."[52]

By 1967, workers had completed more than one hundred twenty miles of two of the interstate roads, about one-third of the eventual total. Route I-89, open between the Mallett's Bay area and Montpelier, reduced driving time by about half. Interstate 91, running alongside the Connecticut River from the Massachusetts line to White River Junction, connected east-side Vermont commercial and industrial markets with population centers in central Massachusetts, central and northern Connecticut, and the New York City area. *Vermont Life* gushed in 1966 that the interstates provided "a new sense of spaciousness and freedom—freedom to move, freedom to see," and added enthusiastically that the highways "are not only freeing motor vehicles to serve their full economic and social potential, but are also the inevitable consequence, expected to influence the development of the state no less significantly than the coming of the railroad."[53] Even incomplete, the interstate roads put many more communities within reach of each other, and by making the state capital at Montpelier more accessible, extended the influence of state government.

The final product, 381 miles of four-lane highways, built at a cost of about $1 million a mile, ranks as the largest single public works project in the state's history. Only the southwest quarter of the state failed to benefit directly from the new roads, getting instead a long delayed and still mostly unfulfilled promise from several governors to upgrade Route 7 to a comparable highway. For most other areas of the state, however, the interstate roads connected Vermont internally, to its region, and to the nation.

Not everyone greeted the interstate roads with enthusiasm. As upland farms on the east side of the state disappeared under the new highway,

Building Interstate highway I-89, near Middlesex (1960). *Courtesy of the Vermont State Archives.*

some observers noted the irony of having Senator Aiken extol the project barely twenty years after he had vehemently opposed a federal plan to resettle farmers from "submarginal land," and recalled Governor Gibson's pledge not to sacrifice one acre of good farmland for power dams. One farmer, Romaine Tenney of Weathersfield, refused to go quietly and in September 1964 set fire to his 150-year-old homestead, with himself inside, rather than surrender the land to the bulldozers and pavers. Some critics argued that Vermont acquired the interstate highways at the expense of developing an adequate system of roads for local travel and an adequate public transportation system for connecting its dozen or so population centers. The success of the interstate roads, however, provided the final push needed to stimulate building more state and trunk roads, which connected more communities to each other and to the major new transportation corridors. As a result, the interstate roads in Vermont transformed more than the economy of the state. As the numbers of second-home owners, tourists, and other escapees from urban areas swelled and as many visitors took up permanent residence in Vermont, the state's institutions, and some argued, its very character, came under new pressures.

Shadows in the Mountains: The Red Scare, Race Relations, Summer People, and Other New Vermonters

"The fifties," wrote David Halberstam in his 1993 book on the decade, "appear to be an orderly era, one with a minimum of social dissent.... In that era of general good will and expanding affluence, few Americans doubted the essential goodness of their society." Especially when seen from the perspective of the activist 1960s and 1970s, the postwar era "seemed slower, almost languid."[54] For most observers inside and outside the state, Vermont provided no exception to that generalization. Vermonters took pride in the continuity of their institutions, their small-scale economy, and rural society. Using what became almost a cliché of the period, political scientist Duane Lockard wrote in his 1966 book, *New England State Politics*, that "Vermont is a kind of capsule of the American past. It is relatively isolated and it has retained many of the virtues of a simpler past era."[55] As in the rest of the nation, however, social ferment lay just below the calm surface, and Vermonters in the 1950s and 1960s found those virtues extolled by writers and commentators severely tested.

One major national controversy, the "Red Scare" of the 1950s, took some surprising turns in Vermont. No sooner had World War II ended than national attention turned toward trying to understand and respond to the emerging rivalry between the United States and the Soviet Union. The 1948 presidential election brought that issue into high relief when former Vice President Henry Wallace ran on a Progressive Party ticket, backed by a loose coalition of liberals, progressives, and communists. In the struggle over the foreign policy plank of the Wallace campaign platform, the Vermont delegation to the party's national convention, led by poet and farmer James Hayford, proposed a resolution that stated, "although we are critical of the present foreign policy of the United States, it is not our intention to give blanket endorsement to the foreign policy of any nation." Defeat of the resolution after a thirty-minute floor debate brought down on the entire convention the condemnation of the national press, waiting for "the opportunity to scream 'Red.'"[56] The Vermont delegation—Hayford, Martha Kennedy, and Luther K. MacNair, dean of Lyndon State Teachers College—returned to the state humiliated and under a cloud of suspicion as communists. The *Burlington Free Press* hounded MacNair, until he resigned from the school.

By 1951 the United States had become deeply embroiled in both the Cold War with the Soviet Union and the shooting war with North Korea and eventually the People's Republic of China, known popularly as "Red China." Moreover, the national tension and uneasiness over internal security created in the late 1940s by the House Un-American Activities Committee and the Internal Security Subcommittee of the U.S. Senate Judiciary Committee boiled over with the emergence in early 1950 of Wisconsin Senator Joseph R. McCarthy as the most vocal and visible public figure in the politics of anticommunism.

Vermont attracted Senator McCarthy's attention when he learned that former State Department official Alger Hiss, convicted in 1950 of perjury in a highly publicized spy case, owned property in Peacham; and that Owen Lattimore of the State Department, under a cloud of suspicion for his alleged role in "losing China," owned property in Bethel with Ordway Southard, who had run for governor of Alabama on the Communist Party ticket. For McCarthy, Vermont had become a communist hotbed.

McCarthy got his information from conservative columnist Westbrook Pegler writing for the Hearst syndicate, who had received letters from Bethel resident Lucille Miller, informing him of what she called a communist enclave in the Randolph-Bethel area. Although local and statewide newspapers dismissed the charges, this did not quiet anticommunist controversy. Lucille and Manuel Miller continued their own anticommunist campaigns in a newsletter, *The Green Mountain Rifleman*, which they sent to a few hundred people nationwide. They accused public figures from Vermont Superintendent of Schools John Holden and federal Judge Ernest Gibson, Jr., all the way up to President Dwight D. Eisenhower of either being communists themselves or under communist sway.

When Lucille Miller began counseling young men to resist the draft in order not to serve in United Nations peace-keeping actions—what she called "blue flag communism"—she received a subpoena to appear before Judge Gibson on an eighteen-count indictment of violating Selective Service laws. Gibson, proud of his military career, ordered Mrs. Miller to undergo six weeks of psychological testing at the Brattleboro Retreat, then had her sent to St. Elizabeth's mental hospital in Washington, D.C. When federal marshals arrived at the Millers' Bethel home on May 2, 1955, to take her away, Manuel Miller held them off with his rifle. The marshals used tear gas to disarm Manuel, who eventually served time in federal prison at Danbury, Connecticut, for his resistance, and packed Lucille off to Washington. A year later the Millers resumed publication of their newsletter, in which they condemned an odd mix of issues, including communist influence in the U.S.

government, U.S. support of Israel, desegregation of public schools, the peace-time military draft, the development of nuclear power, and eventually U.S. involvement in Southeast Asia. Right-wing newspapers, columnists, and commentators around the country championed the Millers but most Vermont newspapers denounced them. Their Bethel neighbors considered them harmless and elected Manuel town moderator from 1965 to 1985.[57]

A slightly more serious outburst of anticommunist hysteria began on September 29, 1950, when Vermont's Congressman Charles A. Plumley addressed the state Republican Party convention and called for investigation and removal of "Communists, fellow travelers, and sympathizers and their influence from the state's schools and colleges." Claiming that Vermont had been chosen as a testing ground for communist infiltration and that Vermonters "were chosen as a bunch of guinea pigs on which to experiment," Plumley called for close scrutiny of textbooks and warned the legislature against "those busy groups there in Vermont which disclaim any connection with Socialism but nevertheless work toward those ends."[58] The speech drew a sharp response from the Vermont Education Association, whose Representative Assembly challenged Plumley to name specific cases or publicly withdraw his statement; and the editorial writer for the *Free Press* took umbrage at the idea of Vermonters being guinea pigs.

With the election of Lee Emerson as governor, anticommunism moved up a notch on the official agenda. In his 1951 inaugural address, Emerson called on the legislature to amend the state's World War I-era Sabotage Prevention Act, applicable only in times of declared war, "to make it applicable under present day conditions." He also requested the legislature to clarify and enlarge the powers of a public safety council, designed to coordinate civil defense functions in the state. Alluding to a threatened strike of electrical workers in Newport in 1949, the new governor urged the legislature to reenact the 1943 State Emergency War Powers Act to give the governor authority to seize and take over the property of a utility threatened by labor action.[59]

The legislature sidestepped Emerson's request to amend the sabotage laws, but did pass a Civil Defense Act authorizing the governor "with concurrence of a majority of the civil defense boards ... [to] seize, take, or condemn property for the protection of the public."[60] This addition to the existing civil defense statute followed the overall pattern of civil defense preparedness sweeping the nation as part of the fear of atomic warfare, and did not aim specifically at crushing labor actions.

With the Wallace Progressive Party still on the ballot in Vermont, Emerson's insistence that "any party" advocating the overthrow of the government by force "should be outlawed in Vermont" also received legislative attention. Anticipating the presidential election of 1952, the legislature debated an act "to prohibit the qualification of groups or organizations engaged in subversive activities as a political party." The bill passed the house in April 1951 but the senate voted it down 28-0.

Charles Plumley, who retired from Congress in 1950, renewed his attack on textbooks in February 1953 when he addressed the Montpelier Rotary Club and recommended that the governor appoint a board to review school textbooks upon receipt of a written complaint from any individual. Plumley convinced a neighbor, Rep. Charles N. Barber of Northfield, to introduce a bill "to establish a board of review to investigate and examine text books used in the public schools for the purpose of determining whether such text books contain seditious or disloyal matters," and Plumley himself both offered to testify on behalf of the bill and requested an opportunity to address a joint session of the General Assembly on the topic of communists in Vermont. The house agreed to hear Plumley, but only a few hours before his scheduled appearance, the senate balked and changed the time—a thinly disguised tactic for rejecting the resolution to hold the joint meeting. The House Education Committee reported Plumley's bill without a recommendation, the Appropriations Committee voted 14-1 "not to put the stamp of approval on $1,000 for this witch hunt," and the house voted it down, 202-11.[61]

For a while it looked as if Vermont would escape the worst effects of McCarthyism. Writing in early 1953, Dorothy Canfield Fisher concluded her book, *Vermont Tradition*, by extolling Vermonters' calm preservation of free speech and civil liberties. She quoted the resolution of the Champlain Valley Teachers Association opposing the establishment of a code of orthodox doctrine and censorship. Recounting the Millers' anticommunist activities in Randolph and Bethel and the press response, Fisher quoted at length from Judge Gibson's charge to a grand jury investigating communist activity in Vermont and the panel's report that "no evidence was presented which seemed to require further investigation by us." She cited the defeat of the 1951 house bill outlawing some political parties and celebrated the defeat of the 1953 house bill proposing a state board to review textbooks. The happy conclusion to these threats to individual liberties and communal trust, Fisher thought, spoke for themselves concerning the durability and impermeability of Vermont traditions.[62]

Fisher's optimism proved premature. The most noteworthy episode of McCarthyism in Vermont would soon unfold as the University of Vermont struggled through the dismissal of biochemist Alex B. Novikoff for refusing to testify before a U.S. Senate subcommittee about his political activities before 1948.

Novikoff, a Jewish, Ukrainian-born scientist, joined the Communist Party in the 1930s while a graduate student in biology at Columbia University and a part-time instructor at the newly created Brooklyn College, already notorious for the left-wing activities of its faculty and students. Disillusioned with Soviet politics and concerned about possible exposure, Novikoff drifted away from his former associates by the time he left New York in 1946. In 1948 the University of Vermont College of Medicine hired him as a cancer researcher in the medical school. His work soon achieved wide recognition and the university rewarded him with tenure. Then, in March 1953, Novikoff received a subpoena from U.S. Senator William Jenner's subcommittee on internal security. Appearing before the subcommittee in April, Novikoff agreed to talk about his activities and associations since coming to Vermont in 1948, when he had taken the loyalty oath required of all faculty. He refused, however, to answer questions about or name his earlier associates, and he invoked his Fifth Amendment rights against self-incrimination.

Under pressure from Governor Emerson, and citing a university policy hastily put in place shortly before Novikoff appeared before the Jenner committee, UVM President Carl Borgmann convened a six-member committee of trustees and faculty to look into Novikoff's case and determine appropriate action. While the committee conducted its hearings the Vermont press took editorial positions ranging from cautious concern to outright disapproval of Novikoff's actions. Only the *Swanton Courier*, edited by Bernard ("Bun") O'Shea, unequivocally supported Novikoff, stating that "Senator Jenner has no right to inquire into your beliefs or ours; into anyone's politics."[63]

The six-member committee, chaired by Rev. Robert Joyce, a UVM graduate and pastor at St. Peter's Church in Rutland, who later became bishop of the Roman Catholic Diocese in Burlington, voted 5-1 to recommend that the university retain Novikoff, arguing that he had never been a "real communist," had not participated in Communist Party activities in any way since coming to UVM, had responded openly and cooperatively to the Senate subcommittee concerning his own past and present, and had demonstrated his loyalty by taking the university's required oath and registering with the draft. The university board of trustees reviewed the report at its June 1953 meeting. For the first time since coming to office, Governor Emerson exercised his authority as an *ex officio* member of the board to attend the meeting, where he made a motion to have Novikoff suspended without pay unless or until he agreed to appear before the Jenner committee and answer "fully and freely any questions that the committee may see fit to put to him."[64] On a 11–5 vote the trustees accepted the motion, which had the effect of dismissal.

Dissenters, including a small group of clergy led by Episcopal Bishop Vedder Van Dyck, Methodist minister Harold Bucklin, and Rabbi Max Wall, along with members of the UVM faculty and other institutions, accused the trustees of attacking democratic traditions; and UVM's chapter of the American Association of University Professors succeeded in August in convincing President Borgmann that the university had violated its own bylaws by not giving Novikoff a public hearing. The trustees hastily arranged such a hearing before a twenty-three-member board of review, consisting of Governor Emerson, thirteen university trustees, and nine faculty members.

In that hearing attorney Francis Peisch argued that dismissing Novikoff would violate the terms of tenure. Louis Lisman, attorney for the university, countered that invoking the Fifth Amendment constituted "moral turpitude" under the university's new policy and therefore became grounds for dismissal of a tenured member of the faculty. The board of review voted 14–8 to recommend that Novikoff be dismissed, and a week later the board of trustees reconvened to confirm the recommendation, with only Rev. Joyce voting against the motion, arguing that Novikoff broke no law by refusing to testify before the Jenner Committee.

Two years after his dismissal by UVM, Novikoff secured a position at the new Albert Einstein Medical School in New York City, with Einstein's assistance. Years later, Carl Borgmann admitted to Novikoff that "I have lost more than you"; and in 1983 UVM publicly acknowledged its mistake by awarding Novikoff an honorary degree, which he accepted in person at the commencement exercises, commenting that it "redresses an old grievance."[65]

A few months after the Novikoff case concluded the nation got to see more of McCarthy. A series of charges and countercharges on whether communists had infiltrated and influenced the U.S. Army culminated in the Senate's Army-McCarthy hearings, in which McCarthy became both the accuser and the accused. The hearings, broadcast live on national television from April to June 1954, gave many people their first close and sustained look at the senator and his methods. Most Vermonters, however, missed this spectacle, because the first TV transmission tower in the state went up in September 1954. So they continued to formulate their opinions of McCarthy from newspaper reports and radio coverage.

Shortly before the hearings began, Martin Trow, a graduate student in political science at Columbia University, conducted field research in Bennington for his doctoral dissertation in right-wing radicalism and political intolerance. Trow's team of field workers interviewed 771 Bennington men, representing several job categories and income levels, to test support for McCarthy in general, support for his methods of investigation and interrogation, and levels of political tolerance, which he described as "attitudes toward unpopular political minorities and views and their right to be heard."[66] Trow found that "a solid majority" of his sample approved of McCarthy's activities in general and that over 40 percent approved of his investigative methods, which by 1954 had come under attack in the press. In contrast with those results, however, 61 percent of Trow's sample demonstrated high political tolerance. The data revealed greatest support for McCarthy among individuals with fewer years of formal education. The study also found greatest overall support for McCarthy among small-business owners, shopkeepers, and merchants. Trow concluded that these Vermonters did not perceive McCarthy as launching an attack on freedom of speech, but instead as speaking up for the lower classes in defiance of "bureaucrats, stuffed-shirts, and big shots." Although Trow's sample did not include farmers, unemployed workers, retired men, or any women, it revealed a dimension of Vermonters' response to McCarthy and McCarthyism that both confirmed and modified Dorothy Canfield Fisher's description from 1953.

While Trow conducted his survey, yet another chapter in the McCarthy era of significance for Vermont began to unfold in Washington, D.C. On March 9, 1953, with McCarthy still at the height of his influence, Vermont's junior senator, Ralph Flanders, denounced him on the floor of the U.S. Senate, arguing that he had gone beyond any useful investigation of communist influence in the United States. Flanders had entered the Senate at age 66, after a long career in the machine-tool business, and a slow start in politics. Ideologically not a New Dealer, Flanders saw himself as a devoutly Christian, pragmatic, conservative businessman defending both free enterprise and moral order. Elected to the Senate in 1946, he concentrated on domestic and foreign economic issues. Frequently at odds with the Republican Party leadership, Flanders delivered a speech on March 9 warning the Senate that McCarthy's noisy and largely unproductive "housekeeping" diverted attention from what he considered to be the real threat of communism abroad. He warned his colleagues that "In very truth the world seems to be mobilizing for the great battle of Armageddon. Now is a crisis in the agelong warfare between God and the Devil for the souls of men.... [As for McCarthy,] if he cannot view the larger scene and the real danger, let him return to his housecleaning."[67]

Flanders renewed his attack on McCarthy in a Senate speech on June 1, 1954. Complaining that "he spreads division and confusion wherever he goes," he compared McCarthy to the cartoon character Dennis the Menace and, more bitterly, to Adolph Hitler—a comment he later regretted. Flanders made his next move on June 11. In a dramatic appearance with television cameras switched on, he entered the Army-McCarthy hearings and handed McCarthy a note inviting him to be present when Flanders would again address the Senate. In this speech, Flanders introduced a resolution to remove McCarthy as chairman of the Senate Government Operations Committee. This put Flanders into the center of a battle not only with McCarthy, but with the Republican Party leadership, embarrassed by the senator from Wisconsin but concerned about the impact and implications of punishing him in the way proposed by the senator from Vermont.

On July 16, Flanders addressed the Senate again and on the advice of Senators John Sherman Cooper of Kentucky and J. William Fulbright of Arkansas, changed his original motion to a motion of censure. The battle continued for the next five months, with Flanders under almost continual pressure from the leadership in his own party as well as the White House to withdraw his motion. On December 2, 1954, following a national election in which the Republican Party lost control of the U.S. Senate, Flanders won partial vindication when the Senate passed, on a 67–22 vote, a resolution condemning McCarthy's behavior as "contrary to senatorial traditions ... and ethics and [tending] to bring the Senate into dishonor and disrepute, to obstruct the constitutional processes of the Senate, and to impair its dignity."[68]

Recalling these events in his 1961 autobiography, Flanders described taking on McCarthy as "something which needed to be done when no one else had offered himself." He expressed disappointment that the Senate did not vote on the resolution of censure that he submitted, noting that "the case was not decided at all on the harm done to the country, or on the loss of respect for us in the world at large. It was a just sentence against malfeasance in the restricted area of relations between fellow Senators. But that was enough."[69] Indeed, it was, for, like a fever break, the Senate resolution of condemnation ended public awe of McCarthy and hastened the end of the McCarthy era.

Simultaneously with the Red Scare, the United States in the 1950s and 1960s experienced what became a transformative period in civil and human rights. Vermont, with a population of African Americans, Native Americans, and other "nonwhite" ethnic and racial groups counting less than 1 percent of the total population, perceived itself as remote from the center of controversy and insulated from the violence of conflicts taking place in the South. Vermonters expressed pride in their state constitution, which was the first to prohibit adult slavery and to guarantee universal male suffrage. They looked back also to the state's role in the antislavery debates of the 1840s and 1850s and its contribution to the Civil War. Such pride could not obscure the fact, however, that Vermont had its own difficult experiences with race and ethnic minority relations.

The rise of the tourist industry played a curious role in delineating race relations and prejudices. Jewish travelers frequently found themselves excluded from hotels and guest houses, and Dorothy Canfield Fisher's play, *Tourists Accommodated* (1934), made it clear that French Canadians did not always receive a warm welcome at guest houses. While some native people achieved recognition and earned seasonal livings as basket makers selling their handiwork to summer visitors, most native people were, or in order to spare themselves the pain of prejudice, chose to remain, invisible to their white neighbors.[70] Similarly, a small population of African Americans, dispersed throughout the state, rarely received acknowledgment in town histories, though some found employment in Vermont's growing tourism industry at hotels and resort areas. In the 1950s the Trakensee Hotel at Lake Bomoseen hired Jamaicans who moved up from Florida from July 4 to Labor Day. Other hotels in the area also hired African Americans, most often as kitchen staff. They lived in separate quarters from other staff and did not mix with the guests, although one observer reported that "there was never any tension between them and the local help."[71] African Americans also worked as migrant fruit pickers, especially in the apple orchards of Addison County.

Church program for Harlem youngsters, 1946. Vermont Life *(Spring 1949)*.

Few items in newspapers and magazines offer evidence of the lives and impact of African Americans in Vermont until the post-World War II period. The Fresh Air Fund program had been bringing African-American children from New York City to spend summers in rural Vermont communities since 1877. In 1945 Bruce R. Buchanan of Brattleboro wrote an article for *The Vermonter* describing "an interesting experiment in racial and international goodwill" at Windham County's 4-H camp that began in 1941, when its directors invited war refugees, including two Jewish children, to the summer program. In 1943 the directors "felt the need for better understanding of the color problem" and invited two children from New York City.[72] In 1946 the Alpha Xi Delta sorority at the University of Vermont pledged Crystal Malone, one of only two African-American students enrolled at the time. When admonished by the national sorority organization to withdraw its offer, the sorority sisters refused, burned their charter, and thus put themselves out of business.[73] In the absence of a sizeable population of African Americans, however, overt racial prejudice against them in the 1950s did not rise to the level of severity or frequency to constitute what most Vermonters might recognize as a social problem or political issue. When controversy did arise in the 1960s, therefore, it took many Vermonters by surprise.

At the University of Vermont, "Kake Walk" was a highlight of the social calendar. Established as a university event in 1893, Kake Walk became the centerpiece of the Winter Carnival in the postwar years. It drew large audiences of university students, faculty, and staff, and members of the Burlington community. Pairs of male dancers in dazzling costumes, "black face" makeup, and kinky-haired wigs performed this relic of nineteenth-century minstrel shows. In the 1950s Kake Walk received coverage in national newspapers and magazines. In the 1960s, however, the racial stereotyping that permeated the performances began to draw criticism and protest from some members of the university community and beyond, although some UVM students, faculty, and administrators continued to defend Kake Walk as nothing sinister and a venerable tradition.

As the national civil rights movement gained ground and attracted wider circles of support, Kake Walk came under increasing attack. Efforts to disentangle the event from its racist stereotypes, such as performing in "green face" or without any makeup at all and eliminating the kinky wigs, failed to satisfy critics or win student cooperation, and in 1969 the student directors of Kake Walk and the UVM Student Association finally voted to end it.[74]

One highly publicized incident associated with Kake Walk helped galvanize civil rights activists in Vermont and turned the event into a political issue. In 1957, Leroy Williams, Jr., an African-American student at UVM and captain of the school's football team, reserved a room for his Kake Walk date at a Burlington motel. The motel refused to accommodate her and informed her that "there was an arrangement on Williston Road among motel operators to take no Negroes."[75] The campus newspaper, *Vermont Cynic*, denounced the "small-minded inn-keeper" and called for a state civil rights bill "so that a public licensed institution such as a motel shall not be able to legally bar anyone from use of their facilities because of race, creed, or religion."[76] The legislature responded with unusual rapidity by passing a public accommodations bill that year.[77]

In 1961 Representative Philip Hoff introduced a bill "to provide freedom from discrimination in employment." The bill encountered strong resistance from labor groups, generally not friendly to civil rights legislation in the early 1960s and concerned that the legislation would interfere with their independence and the system of favoritism in the union halls. Organized labor also expressed fears that amendments tacked onto the bill would transform it into a right-to-work law. Hoff worked hard to fend off such amendments, but the bill nonetheless went down to defeat. The following year, after he became governor, Hoff backed a similar bill, which passed the house with labor support, survived a senate vote, even with an amendment to prohibit "discrimination in rates of pay by reason of sex" that appeared to be a maneuver to defeat it, and became law a year before Congress passed the Civil Rights Act of 1964.

Senator Aiken played a crucial role in the shaping and passage of that landmark federal legislation. Proposed by President John F. Kennedy, the omnibus bill languished in Congress until Lyndon Johnson made it a high-priority item shortly after Kennedy's assassination. It stalled in the Senate Judiciary Committee, opposed by a coalition of Southern Democrats and Republicans. The public accommodations sections of the bill in particular created a major stumbling block. Many lawmakers regarded it as an inappropriate federal intrusion into rights of private property and association. Aiken, who often before had opposed expanding the powers of the federal government, and now had concerns about the fate of Vermont's tourism industry, proposed making a distinction in the bill between a private home and a public facility. To illustrate his point he spoke of a fictional "Mrs. Murphy" who ran a boarding house in her home. "I don't think it would be safe to force Mrs. Murphy, who took tourists down a country road, to accept anyone who comes along and says, 'Under the law, we have a right to stay with you.' I think she should have the right to select the people who she is willing to take into her house and rent rooms to them, or give them board."[78] In its final form, Aiken's compromise exempted from federal oversight Mrs. Murphy's small business, defined as "not more than five rooms for rent or hire and which is actually occupied by the proprietor of such establishment as his residence."[79] Aiken's compromise broke the logjam in the Senate Judiciary Committee and paved the way for debate in the Senate, where he further defined and explained his idea, making "Mrs. Murphy" a widely recognized symbol of the public accommodations dispute.

In Vermont, Aiken received wide support for his proposal from small-business owners, who praised him for preserving the sanctity of private property and defending rights of privacy and association from what they considered "communistic" legislation. But Aiken also received some criticism for providing blacks and other minority groups only partial protection against discrimination. Journalist Vic Maerki, writing in the *Burlington Free Press*, noted that Vermont's 1957 public accommodations laws contained no such exemptions and argued that "private property rights are stretched thin when they are applied to public facilities."[80] Aiken nonetheless continued to defend his compromise in the Senate, in the press, and in correspondence with constituents as a pragmatic solution to the deadlock, and crucial for obtaining passage of the most comprehensive civil rights legislation since Reconstruction.

With civil rights now a national issue, Governor Hoff moved again to expand both the scope of and specific protections provided by Vermont law. Responding to a growing parallel movement for full civil rights for women, and following the example of his hero John F. Kennedy, who in December had created a President's Commission on the Status of Women, Hoff appointed a Governor's Commission on the Status of Women in November 1964, authorized to study and advise the governor on policy issues and needs related to discrimination and the changing roles of women in the workplace and in public life. With no appropriation of state funds and no staff, the commission conducted studies in the areas of education, employment (including a study on wages), home and community, and law. Members of the commission included Madeleine M. Kunin, later to become a legislator and then governor of Vermont, and Barbara Snelling, later a lieutenant governor and state senator.[81]

Passage of the 1964 federal Civil Rights Act also prompted individuals and groups in northern and southern states to turn their attention to social and economic conditions that in their view kept African Americans from achieving equality and security promised by the law. In Vermont several groups, including the Rutland-based Human Rights Council of Vermont, the Rutland chapter of the National Conference of Christians and Jews, the Burlington chapter of the National Association for the Advancement of Colored People (NAACP), and individuals from towns around the state organized in 1964 under the name the Vermont Civil Rights Union (VCRU). By January 1965, the VCRU had written a constitution, elected a Roman Catholic priest, Rev. Edward Fitzsimons, as president, and a Jewish businessman, Paul Hackel, as secretary/treasurer, and adopted the "Vermont in Mississippi" project as its first signature effort.

Ted and Carole Seaver, a young couple recently arrived from Wisconsin and living in Calais, proposed the project in 1964. Ted Seaver, who taught

English at Montpelier High School, had run a "freedom school" in Mississippi during the summer of 1964 and wanted to return and expand on his work. He proposed that he and Carole, a nursery school teacher in Adamant, spend a year in Jackson, Mississippi, developing a community center and day care program as a way to help promote community-based black leadership in the South. VCRU pledged $7,600 and received public support as well as contributions from prominent political figures such as Governor Hoff, Lieutenant Governor John Daley, Speaker of the Vermont House Franklin Billings, Robert Ryan, president of the Vermont Bar Association, and Ralph Williams, president of the Vermont Labor Council.

The Vermont in Mississippi project also drew a measure of criticism, and controversy reached a peak in February 1965 when the Montpelier School District canceled Ted Seaver's teaching contract. The Seavers headed off to Mississippi that summer and remained there two years with support from the VCRU. At the end of that period the Seavers, now without employment in Vermont, returned to Wisconsin and the VCRU turned its attention and energies to support the passage of fair-housing legislation in the state.[82]

In September 1965 Governor Hoff announced his intention to introduce a bill to prohibit racial discrimination in the sale and rental of property for homes. Hoff's announcement immediately raised a storm of controversy. Asserting that Vermont had no racial discrimination, opponents of the proposed bill argued that it would restrict property rights and accord special privileges to one sector of the population. The VCRU moved to help win support for the bill by encouraging its members to write letters to the editors of Vermont newspapers and holding public meetings around the state where African Americans, Jews, and other ethnic or minority groups discussed their personal experiences with housing discrimination. Once the General Assembly convened in January 1966, opposition, led by the Vermont Association of Realtor Boards, argued that Hoff's proposal introduced social warfare and discrimination against property owners and real-estate dealers. The bill failed in the house on a close vote of 69 to 72.

When the bill came back to the legislature in 1967, Representative John Alden of Woodstock, a successful real-estate dealer, who had led the opposition in the previous session, offered a compromise measure, substituting a Human Rights Commission to investigate complaints and try to resolve them without resort to fines or litigation. Alden's amendment failed and the original bill narrowly passed the house, only to be defeated by one vote in the senate. The next day, however, President Pro Tempore of the Senate George Cook, who had voted against the bill, introduced an amended version that included Alden's proposal for a Human Rights Commission. This version passed the senate with a unanimous vote and the house passed the new version on a vote of 95–38.

The law prohibited discrimination in the sale, lease, or transfer of real estate on the basis of race, religion, creed, or national origin, but included a version of the "Mrs. Murphy clause," exempting owner-occupied property of up to two units and owner-occupied properties with fewer than four rental units. In addition, the bill gave a Human Rights Commission, appointed by the governor, authority to investigate complaints, attempt to mediate agreements by conciliation, and in extreme cases to seek enforcement through court order, but without criminal prosecution. The commission could appoint a director, attorneys, hearing examiners, and other staff, but had no office and received no state appropriation. These limitations left the commission weak and largely ineffective for its first few years of existence.

The VCRU, which had steadfastly supported a fair-housing law, quietly disbanded following the compromise victory. Some of its members continued to be active in civil rights issues, however, and Hoff appointed three of them—Rev. Edward Fitzsimons, Paul Hackel, and Rev. Roger Albright—to the new Human Rights Commission, along with Margaret Lucenti, who kept the commission alive and working, often out of her kitchen in Montpelier in later years, when it received less attention from governors and the legislature.

By the end of 1967 the national civil rights movement had undergone several important, and for many whites, alarming changes. More radical leaders such as Malcolm X and Stokely Carmichael, as well as the Black Panthers and Student Nonviolent Coordinating Committee (SNCC), challenged Dr. Martin Luther King, Jr.'s leadership and dedication to nonviolent action. Impatience with the lack of economic and social improvements to accompany the legal remedies to injustice and inequality won through the Civil Rights Act of 1964 and the Voting Rights Act of 1965 resulted in urban riots in the Watts neighborhood of Los Angeles in 1965; in Chicago, San Francisco, and Atlanta in 1966; and in Newark and New Brunswick, New Jersey, and Detroit in 1967. In 1967 President Lyndon Johnson appointed a National Advisory Commission on Civil Disorders, chaired by former Illinois Governor Otto Kerner, to examine the causes of the urban riots of the past two years. The Riot Commission or Kerner Commission, as it came to be known, issued its report in 1968. While it characterized the riots as the culmination of "unresolved grievances by ghetto residents against local authorities," the report also pointed to persistent and underlying racism in American society as the root cause of urban unrest.

Governor Hoff read the newly released Kerner Commission report on a plane ride from Washington, D.C., to Burlington and accepted the commission's major premise. Determined that Vermont, which he believed shared in this racist attitude, could also play a part in meliorating it, Hoff assigned Ben Collins from his staff to work with New York City Mayor John Lindsay's office to devise the New York-Vermont Summer Youth Project. Based at the University of Vermont and St. Michael's College in Burlington, Johnson State College, Lyndon State College, the Ripton Job Corps Center, and the St. Johnsbury Academy, the program brought several hundred African-American and Hispanic high school students from New York City ghetto areas together with Vermont teenagers for six weeks during the summer of 1968. Participants worked on educational and recreational projects; but mostly they hung out together—a reflection of Hoff's optimism that familiarity could help overcome deep-seated racial prejudice. In a public statement issued from his office, Hoff declared that "no Vermonter can evade responsibility for the indictment of our society included in the [Kerner Commission] report. We know that the seeds of the conditions which have led to explosions in the cities exist in Vermont. As Americans and Vermonters, we have a responsibility for the safety and welfare of this country's citizens."[83]

Hoff's statement and the program as a whole generated immediate controversy. Perhaps frightened by the recent urban riots and resentful of ubiquitous social inequities, the criticism ranged from skepticism and mild disapproval to virulently racist hostility. An anonymous letter sent to Hoff's office reflected all these attitudes:

> Now Hoff wants to help all out of state niggers
> The World owes them a living he figures.
> But in rural Vermont is a horrible sight,
> Cause 75% of the Nation's poor is still white.

> So Hoff claims Vermont responsibility,
> For riots that happen down country.
> But he and Lindsay overlook one trifle,
> Every Vermont farmer owns a 30-30 rifle.[84]

The program ran for two years, always with underlying tension both internally and with the communities where it operated.

The racial hostility that Hoff predicted and invoked as the rationale for his youth program erupted in an event that had a tangential relationship to the program. Around midnight on July 18–19, 1968, an automobile passed through the village of Irasburg. Multiple shotgun blasts raked the home of Reverend David Lee Johnson, an African-American minister who had moved into town from California on July 4 with his family and a white female friend, Barbara Lawrence, and her two children. The car turned around and two more shotgun blasts were fired from it as it passed Johnson's house again. Johnson returned the fire with his own pistol as the car made its second pass.

Vermont Attorney General James Oakes visited Johnson the next day, expressed concern for his safety, and promised a swift and thorough investigation. State police, dispatched to protect Johnson, quickly located a suspect, Larry Conely of Glover, home on leave from the army, who had been arrested two weeks earlier for harassing students in the New York-Vermont Youth Project at Barton State Park. The incident took a strange turn when, rather than arrest Conely right away, police waited fourteen days while they conducted a background check on Johnson. It became even more controversial when one of the troopers assigned to guard Johnson's house reported that Johnson and Lawrence had sexual intercourse three days after the shotgun attack and state police arrested the couple at gunpoint in Bethel on August 9 on charges of adultery, a seldom-invoked statutory offence. Lawrence, interrogated for several hours, entered a plea of *nolo contendere*, paid a fine, and returned to California, where she maintained that authorities coerced her statement. Under cross-examination, the trooper later admitted that he could not be positive about the accuracy of his report.

Despite prodding from Attorney General Oakes, Orleans County State's Attorney Leonard Pearson delayed the arrest of Conely, then charged him with the minor offense of breach of the peace. Conely admitted racial motives for the assault, but upon conviction received a relatively light $500 fine and a suspended six-month jail sentence.

By contrast, Pearson charged Johnson with adultery, which Johnson denied. During the investigation, Johnson received several more threats and some verbal abuse by several men in Irasburg, and became the target of unfriendly editorials in several Vermont newspapers. In September, after state police and the state's attorney had spent 2,256 hours, and traveled 20,943 miles, including a trip to California to collect evidence and to try to extradite Barbara Lawrence, Pearson gave up the case.

The Irasburg Affair, as it soon came to be called, had wide ramifications. When Public Safety Commissioner Erwin Alexander publicly expressed doubts about the racial motivations of the midnight attack and related events, Governor Hoff reprimanded him, then appointed a special commission headed by U.S. District Judge Ernest W. Gibson, Jr., to investigate the entire affair, including the actions of the state police. The commission also reprimanded Alexander, and added Pearson, other law officers in Orleans County, and the Vermont press to the list of those it considered derelict in their duty to defend human and civil rights. Far from vindicating those who came to Johnson's defense, however, the results of the Irasburg Affair damaged several political careers. Oakes, associated with the Gibson-Aiken wing of the Republican Party, suffered a nearly two-to-one defeat in the primary election for governor. His opponent, Deane C. Davis, refrained from commenting on the event itself but remarked in a June press release that "I hope Vermonters will understand that when Governor Hoff uses the term racist to describe anyone who happens to be confused about his NY-Vt program, he is acting neither in the best interest of the negro community nor of the people of Vermont."[85] Hoff, too, claimed in later years that the Youth Project and Vermonters' reactions to it, including Irasburg, ruined any hopes he had for winning election to the U.S. Senate in 1970. Contrary to his hopes when he became governor, Vermont did not become a leader in conquering white racism; and when he left office at the end of 1968, civil rights faded as a prominent public policy issue for several years. The state's commitment faltered, wrote historian Stephen M. Wrinn, "when faced with the reality of blacks moving into the state."[86]

Racism was not the only, nor perhaps even the major cause, of tension and anxiety in Vermont communities in the 1950s and 1960s. Other groups of newcomers flocking into the state during this period had an impact on community life and ways of doing business.

"In 1929," wrote Shepard B. Clough and Lorna Quimby in their 1983 study of Peacham, the town "had many of the characteristics typical of a

Vermont farming community. It was a homogeneous community whose citizens generally shared common values and similar experiences. Only a few Catholics diluted the solid Protestant majority. Most of the inhabitants lived on or near the place of their birth. The small transient population consisted mostly of seasonal workers in the woods, farm laborers, and summer visitors."[87] The community educated its own children, met all its own expenses, took care of its elderly and poor, had a low crime rate, supported five general stores, and took in strangers and visitors at two inns.

By the end of the 1930s many farmers, burdened by technological and economic changes, had sold out and moved on. The new owners of those properties "mostly came from the academic segment of society, with secure, tenured positions . . . primarily from Columbia and Harvard Universities," attracted to Peacham by its good summer climate, declining prices for land, and houses in good condition. The summer pioneers brought their friends and soon Peacham residents joked that they had a higher proportion of their population in *Who's Who in America* than any town in the nation. While they gave a summertime boost to the economy and their property taxes helped keep the town afloat, the first wave of summer people in Peacham rarely integrated into the community, socially or politically. They initiated lecture series and discussion groups that mostly they attended, urged the hiring of seminary-trained ministers for the churches they rarely attended, and urged a higher level of training for teachers at the Peacham Academy, where only the local pupils went to school. But when the old town library burned in 1959, the summer people contributed generously to help build a new one.

As land became less of a resource and more of an investment, the number of farms in Peacham fell from fifty-three in 1929 to thirteen in 1980; the number of land transfers in a year rose from thirty-six in 1950 to forty-nine in 1979. By 1980 nonresidents paid 75 percent of Peacham's taxes on property. The new landowners included many summer residents, but also "a more heterogeneous group" of professionals who worked elsewhere in the region or state and commuted daily to St. Johnsbury, Morrisville, Montpelier, or even Burlington. Peacham, like many other small towns in Vermont, became a bedroom community.

The new residents insisted on what they believed to be improvements and made their way onto the selectboard and school board to implement those changes. In 1970 Peacham adopted its first zoning code, in a controversy that pitted residents concerned about uncoordinated growth that they thought threatened the character of the town against those who believed that "a man's home is his castle."[88] As demands for a wider range of goods increased, residents did more of their major shopping in the larger towns. Four of the five general stores had closed by 1979 and one had transformed itself into a specialty shop with catering service.

Venerable Peacham Academy became another victim of the change when, in the 1950s, it tried to meet the financial challenges of competing with union school districts by taking boarding students, offering college preparatory programs, and starting costly vocational education. The Academy folded in 1969, and became an "alternative" school known as the Peacham School in 1971. The building burned in 1976, and closed for good in 1979.

What happened to Peacham occurred in dozens of rural Vermont towns throughout the state. Summer tourism, evolving into second-home colonies, and the influx of commuters escaping the growing urban centers, created bedroom communities, preserved many splendid Vermont homesteads and farm buildings, but transformed the way Vermonters had lived for generations up to the 1960s. Writing about the "decline and growth" of tiny Calais, Vermont, Weston A. Cate, Jr., pointed to "the back-to-the-land movement arising out of the sixties, increased employment opportunities in Montpelier with the growth of insurance companies as well as state government, [and] better roads making commuting faster and more comfortable," as factors that created the need and demand for "a new central elementary school as well as access to a new regional high school, and a general improvement in the variety and number of services available to residents of rural areas from nearby larger population centers."[89] A parallel pattern emerged in towns near ski resorts and along the Interstate highways. Developers, second-home buyers eager for land near recreation areas, and city dwellers eager for a taste of country life snapped up failing farms and rural village dwellings where property taxes had already started to rise to pay for better schools and improved roads.[90]

Along with tourism, recreation, and the urban migration of the mid- to late 1960s, a business boom, helped along by state government initiatives, had a profound effect on Vermont's landscape, population, economy, and society. Dozens of corporations, many of them "white collar" business such as insurance, banking, and architecture, that had operated in Vermont in the late nineteenth and early twentieth centuries, diversified or expanded in the 1950s and early 1960s, providing new jobs and often attracting workers and executives from other states. In Montpelier, Union Mutual Insurance Company built new headquarters in 1959 and National Life Insurance Company followed in 1960 with its sixth new building as its employee roster approached one thousand. Burlington's Chittenden Bank, which barely survived the Great Depression, began to expand in 1947 with acquisition of the Swanton Savings Bank and Trust, then acquired two banks in the early 1950s, and four more in the early 1960s.[91]

The archetype of Vermont's new businesses, IBM, arrived in 1957 and hired 445 workers to produce parts for its giant computers. As the computer industry itself expanded and changed, so did IBM. After it began making miniature chips for smaller computers, IBM employed thirty-nine hundred people by 1969 and planned for continued expansion to forty-two hundred in the 1970s. While it created new jobs for Vermonters, claiming in 1969 that it hired 70 percent of its employees from the local work force, IBM and the high-tech companies that followed it into the area also brought in young executives, engineers, and other white-collar employees through nationwide recruiting efforts. The comparatively high wages and benefits package for all workers offered by the high-tech companies, and their employment of women and minorities in well-paying jobs, forced other businesses and industries to adopt similar employment practices and policies.[92] By 1969 IBM had become the state's largest industrial employer and helped attract other new businesses and services to northwestern Vermont. As a result, Chittenden County outstripped all other areas in population and population growth and by 1970 accounted for almost a quarter of those living in the state.

The new population of young, well-paid, and well-educated workers, professionals, and executives moved to outlying towns such as Underhill, Jericho, Milton, Williston, and Colchester, which after generations of little or no growth and relative isolation suddenly had to build new schools, pave roads, and improve infrastructure with only property taxes to support these expenses. As tract homes and suburban developments began to spring up, as towns debated budget items and school boards discussed new curricular, extracurricular, and facilities needs, Vermonters began facing and making some difficult choices that would affect the shape and operation of familiar institutions. For some, these new issues and newfangled institutions compromised traditional and historical values. Some long-time residents and newcomers alike made choices designed to preserve what they considered unique and valuable about the state's social, cultural, and natural environment.

Rediscovering Vermont's Culture and History

The population boom and growing prosperity of Vermont in the postwar years had a ripple effect on cultural life, simultaneously stimulating the creation of new institutions, renewed interest in Vermont history, and concern for preserving its culture. A complex relationship emerged in writing about Vermont between promoting its new era of prosperity, primarily in the tourism industry, and celebrating the characteristics of independence, thrift, restraint, stability, and rural caution about embracing change. Allen Foley, a retired professor of American history at Dartmouth College and a member of the Vermont General Assembly, captured the lighter side of this tension in his 1971 collection of Vermont wit, *What the Old-Timer Said*. About half of the book contained anecdotes that pitted "old-time" Vermonters against arrogant or greenhorn tourists and summer people struggling to find their way around mountains and over poor roads, negotiating for help, advice, goods, and services. The other half of Foley's collection poked gentle and admiring fun at the characteristics that seemed to set Vermonters apart from the mainstream of a fast-paced, fast-changing America. Foley's story of an elderly man "from up Strafford way" summed up the image of Vermonters as they saw themselves or wished to be seen by others. To his neighbor's question, "How are things?" the old Vermonter with a "tall, spare frame [and] craggy face with just a faint trace of a smile" gives a sly, terse, stoical reply: "No worse."

Foley considered that story "the essence of Vermont-ness."[93] The three writers who founded *Vermont Life* magazine in 1946—Walter Hard, Vrest Orton, and Earle Newton—understood this idea of "Vermont-ness," refined it, used it to promote Vermont's cultural differences and uniqueness, and built upon it to popularize and proselytize for Vermont's history and cultural life.

Walter Hard wrote stories in the form of free-verse poems about small-town and rural Vermont. Born in 1882 and raised in Manchester, he attended Williams College, and returned home to run the family drug store. A dedicated writer, he began producing editorials for the *Manchester Journal* and *Rutland Herald* in the 1920s and appended to these articles his own short poems. In 1928 he published *Some Vermonters*, the first of nine collections of his poetry. Encouraged by his success with critics, poets, and a wide reading audience throughout New England and the nation, Hard continued to use his hometown and neighbors as both the inspiration for and subject matter of his poetry. He portrayed them with a clear-eyed vision of their charm and virtues, but also with honest, sympathetic insight into their limitations and foibles. In the contrast between an exterior simplicity of life barely affected by the changes of a wider world, and an interior complexity of shadows and closed, intimate communities, Hard presented a picture of Vermont's past and present both attractive and unsettling. "The Village," published in his 1933 collection, *A Mountain Township*, suggests the overarching theme of his poetry:

> A sleepy village in a peaceful valley
> Yet, friend, there life stages its drama.
> Tragedy, comedy; nobility beside self-seeking;
> Petty crimes against the spirit;
> The wise serenity of old age;
> The rebellious passion of youth.
> There the whole of life unfolds
> From childhood's carefree days
> To that hillside with the white stones.
> Fifty houses offering the life of the race.[94]

Hard's book, *The Connecticut*, published in 1947 as part of the Rivers of America series, included large doses of Vermont history. He devoted one of the longest chapters to telling the story of Vermont's struggle for independence and statehood, and another entire chapter to the history of the publication of Ethan Allen's *Reason the Only Oracle of Man* and the scandalized reaction to it from divines downriver in Hartford and New Haven, Connecticut. He also included as many references as he could manage to Vermont river towns, even though he had to acknowledge that New Hampshire owned the river up to Vermont's shoreline.

As an editor of *Vermont Life*, Hard contributed regularly to the magazine with his column, "The Green Mountain Post Boy," a miscellany of observations and reflections on Vermont people and places. Not simply an observer and commentator, he took an active role in Vermont by helping form the Historic Sites Commission, and serving in the legislature and as a trustee of the Vermont Historical Society in the 1940s to early 1950s.

Like Walter Hard, Vrest Orton started his career as a journalist. Born in Hardwick in 1897, Orton spent his boyhood in East Calais, where his family ran a gristmill, sawmill, and country store that later served as the inspiration for his most famous and lucrative enterprise. The family moved to Massachusetts around 1909, and in 1925, after service in World War I, education at Harvard and Brown universities, some time with the U.S. consular service in Mexico, and working in an advertising agency in Los Angeles, Orton moved to New York City. There he worked for H. L. Mencken's *American Mercury* magazine, did freelance writing that brought him into contact with some of the important literary and publishing figures of the day, and founded *The Colophon*, an international magazine for typographers, book collectors, and connoisseurs of typography. Orton returned to Vermont in 1934, settled in Weston (then a village of 475 people), and continued working as a journalist, freelance writer, and entrepreneur. He helped established the Stephen Daye Press in Brattleboro, and Countryman Press in Weston. In 1946 he opened the Vermont Country Store with a small inventory of "old-fashioned items" that he found or had produced for his exclusive retail use. Orton relied on a descriptive mail-order catalog, peppered with carefully crafted folksy language, to reach and expand his clientele and to entice customers to the remote village of Weston. By 1952 the store and catalog had achieved nationwide fame, thanks in part to an article in the *Saturday Evening Post* and in part to Orton's ability to trade on good-quality items that appealed to American nostalgia for good old times. He made his catalog, now called "The Voice of the Green Mountains," a powerful marketing tool and, increasingly, a vehicle for his "Miscellany of Philippics, Vision, Admonitions [and] Imponderables" that over the years expressed his brand of political and cultural conservatism: diatribes on telephones, plastic, planned obsolescence, the fashion for "skinny female models." Orton's vision of Vermont corresponded with and shaped his marketing plan and he became a frank and eloquent spokesman for nostalgia. "Of course," he wrote for the Christmas 1953 issue of the catalog, "we have, in Vermont, the latest and most advanced . . . just like every other state. But we also have something the others don't have. This something is *nostalgia* . . . pure, genuine, and undefiled. And this nostalgia is the prodigious feeling that when you hear about Vermont you get homesick. It's the wonderful feeling that when you get here you're home."[95] As the United States moved into the troubled times of the 1960s, Orton's vision of Vermont became more combative and in 1968 he published a "warning" to "left-wing liberals and Socialists, do-gooders and (in a few cases Communists)" in Vermont: "Vermont is a genuine American state of loyal patriotic Americans. Vermont has many virtues and features that other states once had. Vermont is the last frontier of the American dream and the American spirit. It will not be destroyed by liberals because we will not let that happen. This is a message of warning to these persons and it is a message of hope to Americans."[96]

In addition to managing his store, and writing and editing his catalogue, Orton produced nineteen books of prose and poetry and countless articles for *Vermont Life*, *Vermont History* (the Vermont Historical Society's journal), other magazines, and newspapers.

The village of Weston itself also became the focus of Orton's engagement with an emerging historic preservation movement. Soon after his arrival he joined the small group who had already begun to restore the Farrar Mansur House on the village green and open it as the Old Tavern Museum. They transformed the Gothic Revival church on the green into the Greek Revival Weston Playhouse and in 1936 founded the Vermont Guild of Oldtime Crafts and Industries. By 1946, when Orton wrote about the "Weston Revival" for the first issue of *Vermont Life*, the village had become a mecca for tourists and a model of a new kind of historic preservation, "an experiment in achieving self-sufficiency." Rather than isolating old buildings on museum grounds, he argued, "Weston wants to prod Vermont into living up to its high reputation. The Weston group believe that it can be done by developing successful village and domestic industries, where people can make not only a good living for themselves, but also products that are good, for others."[97]

Youngest of the three founders of *Vermont Life*, Earle Williams Newton came to Vermont in 1942 to become director of the Vermont Historical Society. With a strong background in scholarly editing and publishing, Newton convinced the VHS trustees to adopt an ambitious plan to resume publication of documents from the VHS manuscripts, transform the annual "proceedings" into a quarterly journal that included accessible articles and a regular feature of Vermont folklore, and publish "The Growth of Vermont," a series of ten volumes to cover the entire span of Vermont history. While only five books in the series appeared, three of them have become classics in Vermont historiography: Harold Fisher Wilson's *The Hill Country of Northern New England* (originally published in 1936); David Ludlum's *Social Ferment in Vermont, 1791–1850* (originally published in 1939), and Lewis Stilwell's *Migration from Vermont* (published in 1946). These books gave new stimulus and renewed vigor to scholarship on Vermont history.

Newton also had a keen sense of marketing and promotion which he used to become the driving force in the creation of *Vermont Life*. Drawing inspiration from the success of *Life* and *Look* magazines, he urged the other founding editors to adopt the lavish visual format that set *Vermont Life* apart from its more staid predecessor, *The Vermonter*, which until its demise in 1945 had boasted of being "the state magazine." Moreover, the highly visual, upbeat, intelligent but intentionally accessible articles in *Vermont Life*, meant to appeal to outsiders, became the promotional vehicle and medium for portraying Vermont as a special world—a lost-and-found America—that the magazine's founders intended.

Newton collaborated with Hard, Orton, and Ralph Nading Hill in reviving interest in historic preservation and forming the Historic Sites Commission in 1947. Two years later the commissioners published *Historic Vermont: A Guide to Some Historic Sites and Roadside Markers*, an attractive, four-color booklet meant to help visitors and interested Vermonters find their way to buildings and places significant for their contributions to Vermont history. That same year Newton brought out *The Vermont Story: A History of the People of the Green Mountain State*, a folio-size volume that adopted the visual and literary format of *Vermont Life* to survey Vermont's most important events, individuals, industries, arts, and crafts. Active in the American Association for State and Local History, Newton convinced the organization to use his experience devising a format for popularizing history to publish *American Heritage* magazine, which he edited before going on to become the director of Old Sturbridge Village in Massachusetts, a living history museum representing New England in the 1840s.

A generation younger than Hard and Orton, Burlington native Ralph Nading Hill shared not only their life-long affection for Vermont, but also a dedication to writing about it. Hailed at his death in 1987, at the age of 70, as "the memory of the state," Hill produced seventeen books, beginning in 1949 with publication of *The Winooski: Heartway of Vermont*, which like Hard's *The Connecticut*, appeared as a volume in the American Rivers series. As a writer Hill looked for the drama of Vermont history; and like many writers and historians before him, he found it in the story of the Allen family, which occupies almost a third of his book on the Winooski.

Late in his life Hill located what he believed to be the site of Ethan Allen's homestead on the Winooski intervale, north of downtown Burlington. He developed the plans and began raising the money to construct a colonial-era-style log house incorporating what he insisted were the foundation and some material from the original structure, and to develop the site to include a museum and education center.

Hill's long fascination with the history of the Lake Champlain area became another focus of his writing. Six books, including a novel, *The Adventures of Brian Seaworthy*, and his own favorite, *Lake Champlain: Key to Liberty*, explore the history of the lake and its long tradition of ferry and steamboat transportation. This work also led him into both historical preservation and commercial ventures involving tourism and history. In 1950 Hill created the Shelburne Steamboat Company to own and operate the *Ticonderoga*, the last steamship on the lake. For three years Hill ran the aged side-wheeler as a tourist attraction until the boat could no longer pass safety inspections and the costs of fuel and repairs made continuing the operation financially impossible. He convinced Electra Webb, who founded the Shelburne Museum in 1949, to accept the *Ticonderoga* as an artifact for exhibit among her own collections of New England antiquities, and raised the money to haul the ship two miles overland to its final berth on the museum grounds. Hill's enthusiasm for Vermont's past and his vision of the economic possibilities for tourism based on historical sites steered him toward other efforts to popularize and publicize Vermont history and heritage. In 1951 he became senior editor of *Vermont Life*, a position he retained to the end of his days. He served as a trustee of the Shelburne Museum, Vermont Historical Society, and Vermont Archaeological Society (founded in 1968) and became interested in media by serving as a member of the Vermont Educational Television Broadcast Council, founded in 1967, and the board of Vermont Public Radio, founded in 1975.

An array of old and new institutions contributed to the cultural renaissance of the postwar period. The University of Vermont benefited from the GI Bill, then from the national trend that sent increasing numbers of high school graduates on to college, and finally from the coming of age of the postwar baby-boom generation. The university bounced back from an enrollment of fewer than nine hundred students in 1944–1945 (not including military students enrolled in special programs to equip them for service) to just over two thousand in 1946–1947, then kept growing until

President Edward Andrews imposed a cap on total enrollment in the early 1970s, when the number approached ten thousand. Along with students came more faculty and staff, new dormitories and academic facilities, and new academic programs and initiatives, including the Maple Research Farm in Underhill—a gift from Governor Mortimer Proctor in 1945—and a Special Collections division of the library in 1962. The arrival on campus of Thomas Day Seymour Bassett as librarian stimulated new enthusiasm for Vermont history and research. A native of Burlington, Bassett came to the university in 1958 with degrees from Yale and Harvard, an encyclopedic doctoral dissertation on Vermont in the mid-nineteenth century, broad knowledge of other eras of Vermont history, and an ambitious plan for collecting Vermontiana to add to the library's collections. At a time when scholars considered state and local history a barely reputable field of academic pursuit, Bassett eagerly volunteered to teach the Vermont history course listed in the UVM catalog but shunned by faculty. His enthusiasm for collecting documents and manuscripts that told the story of everyday lives of common citizens as well as the acknowledged heroes of the past opened new possibilities for research and writing. He did much of that writing himself, publishing numerous articles and reviews in regional and national professional journals and in *Vermont History*. By the end of the 1960s Bassett's work had lured new faculty members H. Nicholas Muller III and Samuel B. Hand into what was now a promising field of Vermont historical studies. Elsewhere in the university, political scientist Andrew Nuquist and his wife Edith undertook the formidable task of summarizing the history and operation of state government in their book, *Vermont State Government and Administration*, published in 1966. John C. Huden in the Education Department published *Indian Place Names in Vermont* (1957) and articles in *Vermont History* and other journals challenging the long-established traditional historical assertion that before European settlement in the seventeenth century, Vermont had been a no-man's land, with only transient native inhabitants. This work opened the way for fuller revision of the history of the Abenakis in Vermont by Barre native Gordon Day, formerly a forester, then working as an anthropologist in Canada, whose 1965 article in *Vermont History*, "The Indian Occupation of Vermont," established a new historiography for the native people.

Beyond the university, higher education flourished in Vermont with Royce "Tim" Pitkin's revival of John Dewey's progressive tradition at

Goddard College, the founding of Marlboro College in 1946, the union of Castleton State, Johnson State, Lyndon State, and Vermont Technical colleges in 1961 to form the Vermont State College system, and the establishment of the Community College of Vermont in 1970.

The calm pastoralism of Vermont, and its increasingly sophisticated, comparatively wealthy summer-visitor, second-home, and professional populations helped invigorate and expand audiences for the fine arts. The University of Vermont received a substantial gift to set up a performance series and in 1945 established the George Bishop Lane Series. In 1948 David Gil founded Bennington Potters, a cooperative that revived the commercial pottery tradition in Bennington by producing kitchenware in traditional styles and designs as well as original designs and works that earned numerous awards and exhibitions in fine arts galleries and museums. The Southern Vermont Artists association, founded in 1933 by a group that had been exhibiting together for four years at the Dorset Town Hall, purchased a mansion on the slope of Mt. Equinox that became its permanent home in 1951, adding a pavilion for theatre and music performances in 1956. Across the mountains, Marlboro attracted a group of musicians including violinist Adolph Busch, pianist Rudolph Serkin, flutist Marcel Moyse, his son Louis, and daughter-in-law Blanche Honneger Moyse, who together founded the Marlboro Music Festival in 1951. In 1969 Blanche Moyse founded the New England Bach Festival. That year, cellist David Wells and pianist Janet Wells established the Yellow Barn Music School and Festival in Putney. The dramatic growth of activity in the arts got additional help in 1964 when Governor Philip Hoff invited a group of citizens to form the Vermont Council on the Arts to encourage and coordinate cultural activities in the state. Vermont became one of the first states to create an arts council the next year when the legislature approved formal recognition and the promise of an appropriation as well as designation as "the state agency to formulate and apply for grants in aid under the national arts and cultural development act of 1964," which created the National Foundation for the Arts and Humanities and its spin-off federal agencies, the National Endowment for the Arts (NEA) and the National Endowment for the Humanities (NEH).

Vermont lagged behind the nation in the field of mass communications, but began to catch up in the 1950s. While the state had a thriving newspaper community, neither of the two major papers, the *Rutland Herald* and *Burlington Free Press*, produced a Sunday edition until 1975. Radio had played an important part in the lives of Vermonters since 1919, when WVMT began broadcasting from the campus of the University of Vermont. By 1954 thirteen radio stations operated in the state. That year television came to Vermont, the last state to have its own station, on September 22, when WCAX, an affiliate of the Columbia Broadcasting System, broadcast its first commercial signal from a transmitter at the summit of Mt. Mansfield. It had no local competitors until 1968, when Channel 22, an affiliate of the American Broadcasting Corporation, began service, followed in 1979 by WNNE-Channel 31 out of White River Junction, and in 1981 by WPTZ, a National Broadcasting Company affiliate based in Plattsburgh, New York, which began covering Vermont news.

By then the image of Vermont both within and outside the state as an isolated, rural, museumlike, homogeneous, and unchanging society was becoming increasingly difficult to maintain. At the same time, efforts to hold onto the unique and valuable heritage of Vermont's rural, small-town history and traditions, while simultaneously keeping pace with an expanding economy and accommodating a diverse society, had become both increasingly complicated and increasingly controversial.

10
"Another 250,000 People"
1969–2003

The Challenge of Growth

In his autobiography, published in 1991, former Governor Deane C. Davis reflected on a speech from the 1950s in which State Senator Harry Daniels of East Montpelier asserted that "All we need is to bring in another 250,000 people into Vermont, and our troubles would be over." Conceding that Daniels articulated the majority view at that time, Davis commented that "Since then we have learned better. Vermont now has the extra 250,000 people, and its problems have multiplied many times over."[1]

The trickle of new Vermonters that began in the post-World War II period continued for the remainder of the century, with the largest percentage of increases beginning after 1960. Vermont's population grew 14 percent in the 1960s and over 15 percent in the 1970s, when the population passed the half-million mark, then more slowly with an 11 percent increase in the 1980s and just over 8 percent in the next decade, for a count of 608,827 in the 2000 census. By 1970 Chittenden County had far outstripped every other area in the size of its population, with almost a quarter of the people in the state residing within its borders. Burlington alone in 1970 was home to almost 9 percent of all Vermonters. Even with this spurt of growth, Burlington remained the smallest on the list of each state's largest cities, and Vermont continued to rank among the least populous states in the nation.

The completion of the interstate roads and the in-fill road building and improvement that followed over the next several years facilitated shifts in population growth centers. Urban population in the state on the whole either declined or stalled in the decade 1990 to 2000, whereas the rural areas around the largest cities grew. Burlington's population declined slightly in the 2000 census count, while the numbers increased in surrounding communities, such as Essex, Colchester, South Burlington, and Shelburne, as did the populations in more distant towns of Georgia,

Milton, Fairfax, and South Hero. Grand Isle County alone grew by sixteen hundred people, almost 30 percent. In Washington County the population in Montpelier and Barre City declined through the 1990s while the towns of Berlin, East Montpelier, and Middlesex, and the Mad River Valley towns of Fayston, Moretown, Waitsfield, and Warren, close to recreation areas, grew. Other manufacturing and commercial centers including Bennington, Rutland, Springfield, Windsor, and St. Johnsbury lost population as their traditional economic bases collapsed and they struggled to develop new ones. Increasingly, Vermonters lived in different communities from where they worked. While this had been the case for many Americans since the growth of suburbia in the 1950s, it was something new in Vermont.

The changes that accompanied rapid and sustained growth did, as Senator Daniels anticipated, solve some problems for the state, but also, as Davis noted, created new ones. These problems in many ways dominated and defined the period 1969 to 2002. During these years Vermonters undertook a sustained effort to assess, meliorate, and plan for the impact of population growth, development, and tourism. As the state and federal governments assumed wider authority in activities traditionally set aside for local control, such as education, planning, health, and welfare, Vermonters found themselves engaged in troubling debates over the changing relationship between state government and the towns and cities, as well as fair and effective ways to accumulate and spend funds to meet these needs. As Vermont became a more populous and more diverse state, with a larger, more active state government, and with stronger, more persistent, and more pervasive ties to its region and the nation, Vermonters pondered the effects on their social, cultural, and political institutions, their identity as citizens of the state, and their priorities. The new Vermonters, who helped bring new levels of prosperity to the state, simultaneously adopted and challenged long-standing political habits and practices, social and political institutions, and cultural patterns. Solving these problems, resolving differences, and adapting to changes occasionally thrust the state into a position of leadership and innovation, often to the surprise, and sometimes to the consternation of many Vermonters. One remarkable consequence was the emergence of a more varied, sometimes unpredictable range of political choices and electoral results than Vermonters had seen for several generations.

The Economy: Doing Business and Saving the Farms

To many casual observers, and indeed to many governors as they launched their administrations with inaugural speeches, much of Vermont's economic prosperity in the last three decades of the twentieth century rested on the growth of tourism, recreation, and hospitality industries. While the emphasis on recreation and tourism was sometimes overstated, it was nonetheless the case that by the year 2000 the network of primary and secondary businesses involved in entertaining, feeding, housing, and selling necessary and luxury items to visitors had become one of Vermont's largest economic sectors.[2] This fact proved to have mixed benefits for Vermonters. Most often, tourism and recreation brought steady and substantial revenues to businesses, communities, and the state coffers through the sales and meals and rooms taxes that first went into effect in 1969. However, these industries left many workers vulnerable to low-paying, seasonal employment, usually without health insurance or other benefits, and left many small-business owners at the mercy of unpredictable and uncontrollable factors in the larger economy as well as occasional stretches of poor winter or summer weather. In 1974 Vermont had an unusually low snow fall, which, in addition to the energy crisis that kept gasoline supplies low and prices high, caused a drop in skier days in excess of 20 percent. The resulting loss of over $10 million in direct revenues, eight hundred jobs, $1.4 million in payroll, and $500,000 in tourist-related taxes, drove up welfare costs that year, and helped drive the state from a surplus into a $3 million deficit. In 1986 an unusually damp spring created a plague of mosquitoes. When network television broadcast nationwide news footage of Governor Madeleine May Kunin retreating from an insect-infested site, tourists cancelled summer reservations and the state agency charged with promoting tourism had to work hard to recapture business for scores of inns and bed-and-breakfast establishments. In the years following 1990 the ski industry, hard pressed to meet the challenge of Western competitors, saw several enterprises come and go in rapid succession as Pico, Bolton, Ascutney, Burke Mountain, and Sugarbush resorts, among others, changed hands or went out of business.

Governors and policy advisors, keenly aware of the uncertainties of the tourist and recreation economy, consistently called for efforts to diversify economic activity and encourage new businesses. As long-established manufacturing such as the machine-tool and textile industries disappeared

The original Ben & Jerry's Homemade ice cream production center and scoop shop opened in 1978 in this converted gas station in Burlington. *Vermont Historical Society postcard collection.*

from Vermont, state and local public officials cast about for ways to encourage new industries. Early in his administration Deane Davis called for the establishment of an agency that could assist start-up manufacturing through loans, tax-exempt bonds, and other financial assistance. Governor Thomas Salmon, who succeeded Davis in 1973, finally won approval of the plan the following year when the legislature created the Vermont Industrial Development Authority (VIDA, renamed the Vermont Economic Development Authority in 1993), which initially aimed at attracting new manufacturing businesses to the state. Later, as public attention focused increasingly on the preservation of open land and forests and the declining number of family farms, VIDA offered loans to farms, other resource-based industries, and recreation industries.

Among the most successful loans VIDA authorized was $2.1 million in Industrial Revenue Bonds to Ben and Jerry's Homemade, Inc. in 1984 to build and equip its ice cream factory in Waterbury Center. Started in 1977 in an abandoned gas station in downtown Burlington, Ben & Jerry's quickly won local fame, confounded big brand marketers, and became a Vermont icon. The business shrewdly and idiosyncratically combined high-end product manufacturing, some innovative marketing, and counterculture ideology. Owners Ben Cohen and Jerry Greenfield called their brand of enterprise "capitalism with conscience." They promised to buy milk only from Vermont dairies and later pledged not to use milk from herds treated with the controversial growth hormone, recombinant bovine somatotrophin (rBST). Their initial management plan included giving 7 percent of all profits to charity and a pledge that no employee would make more than five times the salary of the lowest-paid worker. By the 1990s Ben & Jerry's had become both a celebrated manufacturing venture and the most popular tourist attraction in the state. However, stagnant growth, increased competition in the premium ice cream market, and demands by its stockholders for profits over "conscience," led Cohen and Greenfield to put the company up for sale in 2000. Despite Governor Howard Dean's suggestion that the state might intervene to keep ownership in Vermont, the two founders sold their ice cream company to Unilever, a multinational corporation based in London and the Netherlands, which promised to keep jobs in Vermont and continue some of the charitable and "socially responsible" policies that Cohen and Greenfield had instituted.

Like his predecessors, Governor Richard Snelling, who succeeded Salmon in 1977, hoped to attract new businesses and commercial enterprises to Vermont. A year after taking office Snelling reported to the legislature that more than twenty new businesses had located in Vermont and that employment had increased by about five thousand jobs. Manufacturing jobs continued to rise, reaching a high point of fifty-one thousand workers in 1980. Technology and secondary defense contracts accounted for many of these, and when the next nationwide recessions hit, in the middle 1980s and again at the end of that decade, some of those industries proved vulnerable. A few manufacturing companies responded to opportunities and emerging industries. Vermont Castings began making cast-iron wood-burning stoves in Randolph in 1975, when fuel became scarce and expensive. Mack Molding, a New Jersey-based company that opened a plant in Arlington in 1940 that molded automobile parts and then converted to wartime production of military items, switched to producing computer housings in the mid-1970s. Simmonds Precision in Vergennes, which began in 1906 making screw-machine products and converted to manufacturing spark plugs during World War II, moved into manufacturing fuel instruments for the aerospace industry.[3]

The number of jobs in manufacturing declined to forty-eight thousand in the mid-1980s and remained about the same for the next two decades, so that in 2001 workers employed in manufacturing accounted for only

16.5 percent of the total work force. As elsewhere in the United States, the economy in Vermont continued the shift through the 1980s to service, small retailing, crafts, and specialty products. Vermonters' preference for "clean industries" imposed another barrier to increasing the number of manufacturing companies and Vermont had to work hard to lure the few start-up industries available. In 1997 the state served as a broker to convince a Canadian firm, Husky Injection Molding, to build a plant in Milton, and Governor Dean helped negotiate a package of tax incentives with the town. Such victories became increasingly rare, however, and in 2001, as the economic boom of the previous decade began to collapse, the state stood by helplessly as out-of-state companies closed plants or reduced their work force in Vermont and as some companies that started up in the state moved elsewhere. As had been the case in previous generations, manufacturing in Vermont proved especially sensitive to national economic trends.

At the turn of the twenty-first century, the economy shifted again. "Big-box" retailing, and the rise of information technology, with its commercial offshoots, Internet retailing and "dot-com" companies providing communications and Internet support services, helped spur the economy. While Vermonters demonstrated their adaptability once again, they remained cautious in their reception of these new marketing strategies, technologies, and their economic possibilities. Organizations such as the Preservation Trust of Vermont and the Vermont Forum on Sprawl worked hard and enlisted the aid of Governor Dean to save and revive commercial centers in small towns and cities. At the same time, mass-market corporations such as Wal-Mart, Home Depot, and Hannaford's made concerted efforts to establish stores in suburban or rural megamalls. Williston, which had fought off an early mall development plan, again became a focus of statewide attention when it became the home of the first Wal-Mart in the last state to accept the Arkansas-based corporation. But citizens in Bennington, St. Albans, and St. Johnsbury rejected proposals for the big-box stores on the periphery of their communities. Having come late to both the communications and commercial revolutions that swept the nation beginning in the 1980s, Vermont felt both the positive and negative impacts of their economic influence later and somewhat less dramatically than its neighbor states. In the first few months of 2001, however, the economic boom of the 1990s evaporated, exacerbated by a decline in the stock market that began in late summer and became a free fall following terrorist attacks on

Cows at the Howard Bank Building, Williston Road, c. 1989. Photograph by Dennis Bates. *Courtesy of Banknorth Vermont, Williston Branch.*

September 11, 2001, at the World Trade Center in New York City and the Pentagon in Washington, D.C. The state and nation now faced great uncertainties in political and economic life. With some industries and businesses in Vermont already contracting, others, including tourism and recreation, suddenly faced threatening changes brought about by world and national affairs. Governor Dean, responding to the end of a ten-year period of economic prosperity, imposed recisions in the budget for fiscal year 2002, then struggled with the legislature to produce what he believed to be an acceptably modest budget for fiscal year 2003, his last year in office. James Douglas, taking office as governor in January 2003, announced his intention to continue the belt-tightening strategy for the state budget in the face of a persistently sluggish economy.

In 1990 the U.S. Census Bureau classified Vermont as one of the most rural states in the nation, with almost 68 percent of its population living in open countryside or in communities with fewer than 2,500 individuals.[4] Vermont's rural character had persisted throughout its history. But the use of the land had changed significantly over the past half-century. In 1959 three million acres were farmland, already a significant retreat from the high point in the 1890s. By 1999 the amount of land in farms had dropped to 1.34 million acres, including woodlands, which accounted for about 37 percent of that total. At the turn of the twentieth century, approximately one-quarter of Vermont's landscape was wooded, with most of the remainder open fields dotted by villages and a few urban areas. At the turn of the twenty-first century the proportions of forest to cleared areas in that landscape had reversed, with about 75 percent forested. Moreover, dairy farming, the dominant image of Vermont and still the dominant agricultural activity in the state, continued to experience decline. Of the 11,000 dairy farms in the state in 1950 only 1,525 remained operating at the end of 2002, slightly more than half of them located in Franklin, Addison, and Orleans counties. Statistics do not tell the full story, as consolidation of land to make larger farms, and larger, more productive herds provide a counterpoint to the annual 4 percent decrease in farmsteads recorded by the Department of Agriculture. In 1967, 292,000 dairy cows in the state produced 1.8 billion pounds of milk. In 2002, a total of 152,000 dairy cows produced 2.6 billion pounds of milk.

Those farmers who survived the previous generation's technological revolution of bulk tanks, refrigerated milk storage, and machine milking, with their daunting capital costs, faced a new crisis of rising property values and rising property taxes in the years after 1960. In the mid-1970s a new round of farm failures alarmed policy makers, and in 1974 Governor Salmon appointed a Governor's Commission on Food that warned about the effects of a declining farm population for the state's economy and landscape and the increasing dependence on food production from outside the state. The commission recommended agricultural diversification, new attention to promotion, consumer education, and developing farmers' markets and cooperatives. It also recommended the purchase of land-development rights from farmers to provide income to them and to save farms and open-field landscape.[5]

The fuel shortages of the 1970s created by the Organization of Petroleum Exporting Countries (OPEC) also hit farmers with sharply increased costs for operating farm machinery, purchasing petroleum-based fertilizers and herbicides, and transporting milk to processing plants and commercial markets. The next crisis for dairy farming came in the 1980s, when increased milk production and decreased consumption nationally put a strain on the federal price-support system. As the prices paid to farmers declined, farmers found that it cost them more to produce milk

Dairy farmers from West Haven and Cornwall dumped milk to protest falling milk prices, September 1986. Photo by Vyto Starinskas, *Rutland Herald*. *Courtesy of the* Rutland Herald.

than they could fetch at markets. Nationwide, farmers began dumping milk and in some places slaughtering calves. The federal government first responded with the Milk Diversion Program, which paid farmers to produce less milk. Then, in 1985, the government put in place the Dairy Termination Program, known as the "whole herd buyout," which paid farmers to stop all milk production for five years. In Vermont 197 farmers sold their herds, and most of them never resumed dairy farming after the five-year moratorium. Although dramatic, these measures failed to solve the problem for remaining farmers, and by 1988 a combination of high production, high debt, low market prices, and a declining number of people willing to work in agriculture drove another 7 percent of the state's dairy farmers out of business.[6]

That year Governor Kunin's Commission on Vermont's Future made several recommendations to aid agriculture. In their public hearings the commission received testimony reiterating the theme of the economic, environmental, and historical importance of farming for Vermont. The commission's report included a dozen recommendations for state government action, many of which echoed Governor Salmon's Commission on Food over a decade earlier. Most important, it endorsed efforts to achieve regional milk pricing, an expansion of the Vermont Industrial Development Authority to include loans for farms and agriculture-related businesses, continuation of the "current use tax" program that reduced the tax burden on working farm properties, and a large increase of funds to the Housing and Conservation Trust Fund to help purchase development rights on farms and keep farms in the family.[7]

Efforts to control regional prices suffered a setback when the Regional Collective Marketing Agency, a 22,000-member cooperative organization designed to collect premiums from New England milk handlers and distribute them to farmers, collapsed in 1989. In the meantime, however, negotiations among New England's agriculture commissioners, dairy industry representatives, and congressional delegations eventually resulted in the creation of the Northeast Dairy Compact, signed into law as part of the federal farm bill in 1996. The compact allowed the six New England states to set minimum prices for fluid milk and paid premiums to farmers based on a complicated formula of base price and component price. In its first years of operation the compact increased farm income an average of $1,500 a month. The compact survived a challenge in federal court by the Milk Industry Foundation, and managed to squeak through renewal in 2000 after heavy lobbying by Vermont's Governor Dean with the governors of the other New England states and even more intense lobbying in Congress by Vermont's U.S. Senators Patrick Leahy and James Jeffords and Representative Bernie Sanders. Opposed by Midwestern and Western states, the compact faced another formidable challenge in the 2001 Congress, where the political changes brought about by the previous year's presidential and congressional elections, and Jeffords's move to an Independent position in the Senate, complicated the task of winning another renewal. Congress refused to renew the compact, but in April 2002 replaced it with a guaranteed minimum price to all dairy farmers when the market price for milk sold as a beverage in the Boston market falls below $16.94 per hundredweight (approximately twelve gallons).

The dairy industry took another systemic shock with federal approval in the early 1990s of a controversial growth hormone, rBST. Despite federal assurances of safety, many Vermont consumers remained wary of the hormone and the state legislature approved a law requiring labeling milk from herds treated with it. When a federal court struck down the labeling law some Vermont dairies adopted a voluntary labeling practice, assuring consumers that their milk or milk products were "rBST free." A few influential producers—like Ben & Jerry's ice cream, already paying premium prices to its milk suppliers—insisted on rBST-free milk. Consumer caution also encouraged the growth of organic dairy operations.

Diversification in farming emerged as another strategy for preserving agriculture. Some traditional crops and products such as apples and maple syrup, each representing about 2 to 3 percent of total agricultural receipts, continued to play a significant role in defining the state's agriculture. But in addition to the variability of yield because of climate and weather conditions these, too, suffered episodes of crisis. In the late 1980s health dangers associated with the use of Alar to regulate the growth of apples depressed the market. When the pesticide was banned in 1989 Vermont growers had to destroy a portion of their crop. Poor weather affected growing conditions through much of the 1990s and income from the apple crop declined significantly from a peak of $10.4 million in 1991 to a low of $5.5 million in 1993. Expansion of European markets for Vermont apples, however, helped support prices, which rebounded later in the decade.

The maple syrup industry, more sensitive to weather than many crops and already facing a challenge from Canadian producers, suffered a setback following an infestation of pear thrips in 1988. Unknown before it made its appearance that year, the insect weakened or damaged maple trees, which affected the sap yield for the next two years. Production fell from 570,000 gallons in 1992 to 310,000 gallons in 1993, resulting in a $5 million decline in receipts for maple syrup that year. Another crisis came in 1994, when high levels of lead, introduced from evaporator equipment, appeared in some samples of syrup. The newly renamed Vermont Department of Agriculture, Foods, and Markets worked with producers to identify the sources of the lead and kept contaminated syrup off the market. It then worked with producers of syrup-processing equipment to eliminate lead from the solder. In 1997 problems with plastic tubing to collect sap resulted in off-flavor syrup and the legislature adopted standards for plastic equipment and containers.[8]

The growth of markets for nontraditional agricultural goods, the possibilities of niche marketing, and general prosperity in the nation in the 1990s that could support high prices for exotic foods had the effect of partially offsetting the declines in the traditional areas. In the 1980s Vermont farmers began experimenting with a wider variety of crops, animals, and agricultural produce. Sheep returned to Vermont, now raised for meat as well as wool. Less-familiar animals, such as alpacas, llamas, and emus, began to appear in fields and at farm shows. And despite the popularity of a satirical book on Vermont in the 1980s, *Real Vermonters Don't Milk Goats*, some Vermont farmers earned a good living selling goats'-milk cheese, yogurt, and other products. In response to health and environmental concerns, organic farming became increasingly common, with new standards for defining organic practices and a regional organization, the Northeast Organic Farming Association (NOFA), to certify organic farms and food processing. When the federal government attempted to develop national standards for labeling food "organic," state and regional organizations took an active role in opposing what they considered weak and unenforceable criteria that appeared to favor agribusiness over small-scale farmers. In Vermont, farmers saw a steady increase of outlets for organic produce in farmers' markets, food cooperatives, community supported agriculture—in which farmers sell directly to consumers on an annual subscription basis—and in chain stores and conventional markets. Organic farming, once a fringe movement, became the fastest-growing sector of U.S. agriculture in the 1980s, with an estimated $25 million in sales in Vermont in 1988. By 2000, NOFA had certified 214 Vermont farms, working 16,000 acres, including 93 vegetable and fruit farms, 55 dairies, 18 livestock operations, and 10 herb growers.[9]

The Vermont Department of Agriculture's Seal of Quality Program, started in 1975, encouraged new products and used the cachet of Vermont's rural tradition to market a wide variety of Vermont products, including exotic items such as ginseng root, salsa, and oriental sauces, along with more familiar cheeses, honey, small fruits, jams, and jellies. The burgeoning tourism and entertainment industries also provided new opportunities for Vermont farmers. In 1997 the New England Culinary

Institute, a teaching and restaurant organization founded in 1980 in Montpelier, collaborated with the Vermont Department of Agriculture to create the Vermont Fresh Network, linking fifty farms with sixty restaurants. Chefs from the restaurants developed working relationships with their farmer-suppliers, and the farmers receive a percentage of restaurant sales each month in addition to having reliable local outlets for sale of their products. By 2000 the program had grown to include sixty-three farmers and ninety-seven restaurants. Building on the state government's discovery of "heritage" and "cultural" tourism, the Department of Agriculture instituted in 1998 the "Vermont Farms!" program to attract tourists to historic and working farms. Reminiscent of late-nineteenth- and early-twentieth-century tourism initiatives, the Vermont Farms! program enlisted the cooperation of farmers, agricultural processors, and rural bed-and-breakfast hosts to establish a network of sites where tourists could visit working farms, watch production methods, participate in some rural activities, and have "farm vacations" by staying in guest houses on working farms. Although catering primarily to well-heeled visitors, the department ostensibly designed the program to promote wider knowledge and appreciation of Vermont's agriculture, both historically and as it currently exists, and to expand the market for the state's agricultural products.

A few historic farm museums had already become major tourist attractions when the Vermont Farms! program began. These include Rokeby, the Robinson family farm and homestead in Ferrisburgh; the Justin Smith Morrill homestead in Strafford; Shelburne Farms, a gentleman farm designed by Frederick Law Olmsted for William Seward Webb and Elizabeth Vanderbilt Webb in the late nineteenth century; and Billings Farm and Museum in Woodstock, founded in 1983 on the site of an experimental farm established in 1871 by Frederick Billings. Both Shelburne Farms and Billings Farm and Museum, conceived as demonstration farms by their wealthy patrons, served in their day as extraordinary examples of agricultural experimentation and farm building. Both continued to operate scaled-back working farms and added educational or recreational facilities when heirs of the founding families gave up full-time, large-scale farming.

While Vermont in the 1990s witnessed a growth in high-tech and large-scale farming, such as an egg farm in Highgate, and large-herd dairy operations where cows remain exclusively in barns and are milked in shifts around the clock, most of Vermont's agriculture continued to be the work of families with a few employees. For these people, farming still reflected their love of the land, family tradition, and commitment, despite the difficulties they face. In 1995 the Vermont Folklife Center published *Families on the Land*, a collection of interviews with families on ten farms around the state. Some had sold off parts of their farms, some had stopped farming but still lived on the land, and some continued to farm, determined to stay at it, despite the changes and challenges present-day farmers face.

One of those interviewed, Ben Hulett, was the grandson of one of two brothers who purchased and increased the size of a farm in Shaftsbury. He lived on one of the lots that remained after the family sold the farm and divided the land in the 1930s. By the 1990s, the farm and the entire farming community around Shaftsbury had disappeared, and as Ben Hulett looked out on the valley that had once held his family's extensive farm he saw the following scene:

> There's only the house and probably 35 acres that are left. The rest of it . . . is now being developed, putting lots in. . . . The old sugar wood and back toward the mountain has to go into ten-acre lots. And then the lower portion will go into two-acre lots. The meadows have been bought by somebody else, and there's already a house in there. And I notice in the last few years they've drawn a little line down through there, so they must have subdivided what we called the three-corner lot.[10]

Another farmer interviewed for the book, Bob Graf, retired owner of Southwind Farm in Rupert, discussed changes from the time he started farming in the 1940s: "[T]hose days you didn't have any tractors, didn't have any equipment. Used to milk 30 cows. Now we're milking 150 cows on the same amount of land because you can use it, you got tractors, you got everything to work with. And you got to be big. Got to have cash flow to keep going."

Graf's grandson, Joel, recalled the decision to sell the development rights in order to have the land taxed for farm use and keep the farm going after Graf could no longer do farming himself. "I remember when we were selling our cows, the auctioneer . . . offered him I think one or two million dollars for the whole place. Obviously he decided not to do that. That's pretty tempting though, when you've been working for 40 years, 14 hours a day, and have someone come along and say I'll take it all off your back. But he didn't do it." Then, reflecting on why he has returned to the farm to work, Joel commented, "I wouldn't do it just to make money. You can't. . . . I would do it more just to preserve what we have, to work the land and you're providing food too. That's real important to me. . . . I think it's important to remember that farms aren't here to make Vermont look beautiful, they're here to provide food also."[11]

Symbols the state adopted in the last decades of the twentieth century make clear the continuing role of agriculture in Vermont as a productive sector of the economy, a traditional and revered part of the landscape, and a functional element in Vermont culture. When Governor Kunin's Commission on Vermont's Future published its report in 1988, it put on the cover a landscape by popular graphic artist Sabra Field. The print depicted a snug farm with trim buildings, plowed fields, and a herd of Holstein cows in the shadow of gently rolling hills (see color plate IV). When the state chose a design for a United States postage stamp celebrating the bicentennial of statehood in 1991, it again selected a rural design by Sabra Field, featuring plowed fields, the corner of a red barn, and a mountain in the background. And when the U.S. mint issued a new series of quarter dollars with a unique reverse design for each state, the Vermont coin, which began circulating in 2001, featured a farmer tapping maple trees in the foreground with Camel's Hump mountain looming behind.

"Champlain Valley" (1984) by Sabra Field. Woodcut, 11.5 x 19.5 inches. Used for the cover of the *Report of the Governor's Commission on Vermont's Future: Guidelines for Growth (1988)*. Courtesy of Sabra Field.

Vermonters in an Age of Social Change

Amidst the political and economic changes that defined much of the history of Vermont from 1969 to 2002, and sometimes influencing those changes, the state witnessed a number of dramatic episodes of social change. Often these mirrored trends and movements throughout the nation, but in Vermont they also reflected and sometimes challenged its history, traditions, cherished values, and institutions.

From 1967 to 1973 thousands of young people, a yeasty mix of college dropouts and young urbanites alienated from mainstream American commerce and disaffected by politics, especially the protracted war in Vietnam, rolled into or passed through Vermont. Lumped together under the term "hippies," they claimed to embrace the simplicity of the back-to-the-land ethos, found abundant unused and inexpensive land, and established more than a hundred communes and other experiments in communal living throughout the state.[12]

The influx received mixed reactions. Many Vermont towns watched in stunned amazement as flexible, informal, collective living arrangements grew up in their midst or on their periphery. Along with predictable distrust and misunderstanding, even some episodes of vigilante-like tactics to intimidate or drive them away, the hippies also found some tolerance for their ideas and the culture they were attempting to create. In the Brattleboro area, where sixteen to twenty communes operated at the height of the movement, hippies bought land, farmed, apprenticed as carpenters, and ran arts and crafts shops, macrobiotic food shops and restaurants, and "head shops" that sold apparatus related to the drug culture that was ubiquitous in the communes.

The communes varied as much as the people who lived in or passed through them. Members of New Hamburger in Plainfield, formed in 1970, raised fruits and vegetables on the commune's eighty-five acres, cooked and catered vegetarian meals, set up a cannery, and taught a course on "the politics of food" at Goddard College, itself a mecca for counterculture educational experimentation during the 1960s and early 1970s. Total Loss Farm in Guilford, established in 1968, survived the difficult early years with money earned from writing. Raymond Mungo's books, *Famous Long Ago* (1970) and *Total Loss Farm: A Year in the Life* (1970), enjoyed commercial success, followed by *Home Comfort: Stories, Scenes, and Life on Total Loss Farm* (1973) and *The Body's Symmetry* (1974), a book of poetry by Verandah Porche. Prickly Mountain commune in Warren specialized in architectural and alternative-energy experiments. A home-study course at Quarry Hill in Rochester, one of the first communes in the state, became a prototype for other alternative schools. Tail of the Tiger Commune in Barnet, established as a Tibetan Buddhist community, ran itself according to the teachings of Chogyam Trungpa, known as "Rinpoche," or "precious jewel," who had escaped from Tibet shortly before the invasion by China. The commune advocated nonviolence, did not allows drugs, raised its own food, and ran a study center, retreat, craft business, and therapeutic center for people with mental illness.

The most controversial experiment of the time took place at Earth People's Park in Norton, on the Canadian border in far northeast Vermont. Established in 1971 by Hog Farm Commune in California, which raised the money for a down payment on 550 acres at the edge of town, the Earth People's Park charter stipulated that no individual would own it, anyone could camp or settle on the land, and no one would be permitted to make rules or police the behavior of its residents. Unusual even by the standards of the 1970s, the park aroused curiosity and concern in about equal measure. Each resident or family lived independently of all others, with no pooled resources, no source of income, and no plan for developing one. During its first year of operation in 1971, Governor Davis toured the park, expressed some concern about the poor sanitary conditions, and stayed for tea with some of the residents. After Hog Farm Commune pulled out at the end of 1971, divisions between homesteaders and transients in the park intensified and relations with residents of the town of Norton deteriorated to the point that in 1975 an armed confrontation required the intervention of state police.

Most of the communes disbanded in the mid-1970s, reflecting changes among young people nationwide. With the end of the Vietnam War, the focal point for much radical dissent disintegrated and people began drifting back to the urban life most had abandoned during the years 1965 to 1975. About a dozen communes still operated by the late 1970s; perhaps fewer than ten a decade later. Although most commune residents left Vermont, many stayed to become active in politics, the arts, and small businesses. The communes also left behind a legacy of commitments to renewable energy, alternative schools, art collectives, community gardens, farmers' markets, food coops, day care centers, and women's networks that became part of the mainstream culture and economy of Vermont in the 1980s and 1990s.

The liberation politics and civil rights movements of the 1960s and 1970s also helped stimulate new interests in assuring equal rights for women, and this, too, had its effect in Vermont. While increasing numbers of women entered business and the professions during these years, many women entered the job market in low-paying jobs. In 1971 the legislature adopted a recommendation of the Governor's Commission on the Status of Women to expand legislation prohibiting discrimination in rates of pay based on gender to include prohibiting discrimination in hiring based on gender. As increasing numbers of young women sought entry into the job market with incomplete or inadequate training, state and federal job-training and apprenticeship programs focused on their needs. And as larger numbers of women became working mothers, day care, preschool, and after-school programs proliferated, with state government taking on increasing responsibility for licensing and setting standards for care and safety.

Despite such gains, leaders for women's rights and equality in Vermont failed to win an Equal Rights Amendment to the Vermont Constitution. The proposed amendment passed the legislature, supported in 1983 by Governor Snelling and in 1985 by Governor Kunin, but after an intense publicity campaign funded on both sides by national organizations, voters narrowly defeated it in the required popular referendum in 1986.

The number of women in state and local government began to increase in the mid-1940s and in 1953 the house had a record number of fifty-four female members. Following the reapportionment in 1965, that number declined to fourteen in 1973, then slowly rose to fifty-three in the 1993–1994 legislature, the same year the senate had eleven woman members. Governor Snelling brought several women into the executive branch, notably Sister Elizabeth Candon as secretary of human services in 1977 and V. Louise McCarren as chair of the Public Service Board in 1981. The election of Madeleine Kunin as Vermont's first Jewish and first woman governor in 1985 broke down two additional political barriers and had a dramatic effect on women in government when she brought many women onto her personal staff and appointed women to almost one-third of all state agency secretary and commissioner posts. "Women were present in significant numbers during my governorship," Kunin wrote in her political memoirs, "and in positions where they did not have to accommodate themselves to the existing power structure, but could, in fact, establish a new tone, new values and priorities, because women themselves were at the center."[13] In 1990, Governor Kunin nominated Denise Johnson as the

Equal Rights Amendment (ERA) rally, July 1, 1993. The press reported that about one hundred people showed up for this event, designed to start a new effort to ratify the proposed equal rights amendment to the U.S. Constitution. *Photo courtesy of United Press International, Vermont Historical Society.*

first woman to serve on the state Supreme Court and appointed women as the first judges in the newly created family and environmental courts. The momentum of Kunin's administration in this aspect of state government continued after she left office. Governors Snelling, in his brief return to office, and Dean, in his eleven years in office, continued to appoint women to judgeships, state agency and department heads, and many of the state's one hundred fifty commissions, boards, and advisory boards. In 1997 the General Assembly elected Martha T. Rainville the first woman adjutant general of the Vermont National Guard and the first woman to serve as the head of a state National Guard; and in subsequent years women won statewide elections as secretary of state and state auditor of accounts. Nonetheless, the Governor's Commission on Women remained a vulnerable and often-attacked target for budget cuts by the legislature. In general women remain underrepresented in the state legislature and, as historian Marilyn Blackwell noted, women's participation in party politics has not yet won them commensurate political advancement.[14]

Although Vermont's population had long included large ethnic groups such as French Canadians, Irish, and Italians, and many other smaller, less visible European ethnic groups, data in each of the three census periods from 1980 to 2000 revealed a small but steady increase of the state's non-white populations, reaching approximately 3.2 percent of the total at the 2000 count. This figure included 0.9 percent Hispanics or Latinos, 0.9 percent Asians and Pacific Islanders, 0.5 percent African Americans, and 0.4 percent Native Americans.[15]

The Native American population is made up largely of Abenaki Indians. Vermont historical tradition since the time of Ira Allen had argued that the Abenakis had no permanent and fixed settlement within the borders of the state and that bands of native people had simply hunted and fished on a transient, seasonal basis. Although town histories in the late nineteenth century contained occasional mention of Indians, these reinforced the impression of a transient and dispersed population rather than a community. By contrast, Abenaki and Anglo researchers point to evidence including oral histories, census data, town histories, scattered documents, and material culture that indicate the survival of a community of several hundred Abenakis throughout the nineteenth century and into the twentieth century. "This community was not a single unit with one physical residence," concludes historian Colin Calloway; "it was a fluid network of family bands, of which only the edges were visible to non-Indian

License plate issued by the Abenaki Nation, Missisquoi Band, 1990. *Vermont Historical Society.*

observers."[16] Abenaki scholar Frederick Wiseman states that native people adopted five strategies to endure in the nineteenth and most of the twentieth centuries: "exile; fade into the forest and marshes; live the 'Gypsies'/ 'Pirates'/ 'River Rat' life between Native and European culture; merge with the French community; 'pass' into English-American society."[17] Some evidence seems to support the assertion that Abenakis did indeed live transient lives, following hunting, fishing, and economic opportunities in a regular, predictable, and seasonal cycle. Other Abenaki families adopted a "settled" life, residing primarily in the northwestern Vermont towns of Swanton, Highgate, St. Albans, Grand Isle, and Milton, as far south as Charlotte, and in towns along the Connecticut River near Newbury and Bradford. And the case for "invisibility," with small family groups literally hidden in forests, wetlands, and other inaccessible areas, is supported by examples such as the federal government moving some Abenakis living deep in the wetlands when it created the Missisquoi National Wildlife Refuge in 1941. According to some scholars, writers, and Abenaki spokespersons, Abenakis living any or all of these lifestyles knew each other and maintained contacts down through generations, thereby preserving their history and traditions while keeping a low profile in the white communities where they lived or passed through.[18]

In the early 1970s cultural and political conditions for American Indians throughout the United States began to change. The American Indian Movement became a focal point for the reassertion of Native

American identity and claims to political, social, and economic rights. Abenakis in the Missisquoi area, many of whom had settled in Swanton's "back bay," elected a new chief, Homer St. Francis, in 1974, organized the Abenaki Self-Help Association, Inc. (ASHAI), and established a tribal office in the old railroad depot building. In July 1976 members of the Missisquoi Band circulated a petition to Governor Thomas Salmon, the legislature, and the Fish and Game Commission requesting that the state "recognize the rights of the people of the Abenaki Nation to fish and hunt on all lands and waterways throughout the state . . . without restriction as to season, size of catch, or state licensing."[19] Almost four hundred people, many of them non-Indian, signed the petition, which raised concerns about the impact of unrestricted hunting and fishing on tourism, sport hunting and fishing, fish and game management, and grants of special exemptions to groups. Moreover, the petition surprised many Vermonters in and outside state government, who had little awareness of the presence of Abenakis or their history in the state.

Governor Salmon asked Attorney General M. Jerome Diamond for a legal evaluation of the petition, then commissioned anthropologist Jane Baker of Berlin, Vermont, to prepare a research paper about the Abenakis. Baker's findings, based on interviews with Abenakis and tribal officials, ethnographic and historical materials collected by researcher John Moody and others, and state government documents, pointed to the depressed social and economic conditions in northwest Vermont, especially among those claiming Abenaki descent, and the adverse impact of the state's more rigorous enforcement of fish and game laws on traditional Abenaki patterns of hunting, fishing, and trapping for subsistence. Baker also discussed the tension between Abenakis and the non-Indian populations in the regions, commenting, by contrast, on "the developing profile of Indians with an accompanying sense of dignity and pride replacing the invisible, unmentionable sense of the last two hundred years."[20] In the meantime, the Odanak and Becancour Bands of Abenakis in Canada passed a joint resolution in August 1976 recognizing Vermont Abenakis and calling upon the State of Vermont to do the same by recognizing Abenaki land claims and hunting and fishing rights.

Salmon responded to these developments by issuing Executive Order Number 36 on Thanksgiving Day, 1976, just six weeks before he left office, granting official recognition of the Abenakis of Vermont. The order also established a Governor's Commission on Indian Affairs to examine several social and economic issues, assist in gathering materials to support a petition for recognition by the federal government, and study and report on the Abenakis' request for hunting and fishing exemptions, guardianship of the Missisquoi Wildlife Preserve, and transfer of title to the monument of St. Francis in Swanton. The proclamation was one of Salmon's last official actions as governor and when he delivered his farewell address he took credit for giving "modest recognition to a minority group with the highest unemployment rate in the state."[21]

His successor, Richard A. Snelling, had a different view and in one of his first acts as governor issued Executive Order Number 3 on January 28, 1977, revoking Salmon's recognition proclamation. With no specific reference to the Abenakis, Snelling recreated and restructured the Commission on Indian Affairs, assigned it to investigate "problems common to persons of American Indian heritage who are residents of this state," and authorized it to provide assistance to Indian organizations and individuals in their dealings with state, local, and federal government to gain access to social welfare, educational and health services, civil rights, housing, and employment opportunities.

In response to this setback the Abenakis, now led by a new chief, Leonard ("Blackie") Lampman, began the process of preparing a petition to the Bureau of Indian Affairs (BIA) of the United States government for federal recognition, which they finally submitted in 1982. Homer St. Francis, who favored direct action, led a group of Abenakis in asserting their fishing rights by holding "fish-ins" in 1979, 1983, and 1987. Re-elected chief in a controversial and bitterly contested election in 1987, then made chief for life in 1989, St. Francis resumed his assertive tactics for bringing issues of tribal sovereignty before the public by encouraging members of the tribal organization to replace their state automobile license plates with ones bearing a new Abenaki design.

Governor Kunin avoided the issue of state recognition during her years in office. However, acknowledging the growing body of historical and archaeological research published in the 1980s that argued the case for the continuous presence and cultural continuity of Abenakis in Vermont, she revived and renamed the Governor's Advisory Commission on Native American Affairs in 1990. In 1989 Vermont Judge Joseph Wolchik, in a decision concerning cases related to the 1987 fish-in, ruled that the Abenakis had retained aboriginal rights to hunt and fish on traditional lands. The Vermont Supreme Court, however, overturned that judgment in a 1993 decision on appeal from the state, ruling that "by the year 1791, aboriginal rights to the area now known as St. Albans, Highgate, and Swanton had been extinguished."[22]

Governor Dean tried quietly to set aside the question of recognition, which in any case was in abeyance because the Abenakis decided in 1989 to withdraw their petition to the federal government for tribal recognition. In an effort to ease some of the tension between the Abenakis and the state government, Dean proclaimed May 2–8, 1993, Abenaki Heritage Week and reconfirmed the Governor's Advisory Commission on Native American Affairs.

In 1995 the Abenakis resubmitted their petition for federal recognition, and the slow process of considering their claims began again. Meanwhile, although divided and weakened by splinter group challenges, the tribal organization continued concentrating on improving conditions within the native community by addressing social, economic, and cultural needs. Homer St. Francis resigned as chief in 1996 because of ill health and handed over tribal affairs to his daughter, April Rushlow. Assisted by federal laws mandating repatriation of Native American artifacts and remains, the Abenaki tribal organization worked with museums and cultural institutions to reclaim remains and artifacts and to increase awareness of Abenaki history and contemporary culture. The tribal government also worked with the Vermont Division for Historic Preservation to regain some traditional burial grounds, although others remained in dispute with non-Abenaki property owners. Still intent on winning ownership of these parcels, guardianship of the Missisquoi Preserve, unrestricted fishing and hunting, and other unresolved issues of sovereignty, the Abenaki Tribal Council in 2002 sought to achieve state recognition of "the tribal status of the Abenaki people" through a joint resolution of the legislature. Although the resolution included a disclaimer that "this recognition is not intended to confer any special rights upon the Abenaki people such as claims to Vermont lands or privileges not extended to other minority groups," the effort failed to win approval in either chamber after highly publicized hearings.[23]

Meanwhile, the attorney general's office, responding to the Abenaki petition to the BIA, issued a report refuting claims made by the tribal government. The report focused on the absence of documentation or, at best, the ambiguous documentation presented by Abenakis to demonstrate that they meet the federal criteria of comprising "a distinct community [that] has existed as a community from historical times until the present" and that the tribal organization in some recognizable manner has "maintained political influence or authority over its members [as] an autonomous entity from historical times until the present."[24] The final report's controversial findings, issued in December 2002, challenged Abenaki claims on four of the six federal critera.[25] The Abenaki petition and attorney general's response bring into focus conflicts over the interpretation of census and genealogical documentation. On another level, the Abenaki claims of continuity and sovereignty and the attorney general's refutation of those claims highlight differences over the use and relative authority of documents and rules of evidence by government agencies as opposed to tradition, material culture, and oral history by Abenakis. Resolution of these procedural and cultural conflicts, and consequently a final determination of the eligibility of the Abenakis for federal recognition, appears to remain a long way in the future.

As the twentieth century came to a close Vermonters confronted yet another challenge to what many considered "traditional" values and institutions. Across the nation an increasing number of gay and lesbian individuals, following in the footsteps of the modern civil rights and liberation movements, founded activist organizations to press for legal protections of their civil rights as well. A worldwide epidemic of auto immune deficiency syndrome (AIDS), while not confined to the gay and lesbian population in the United States, affected them in disproportionately large numbers, and contributed to making several issues related to sexual identity matters for public discussion and public policy. In 1987 and 1988 the Vermont House of Representatives debated and voted down bills to proscribe discrimination on the basis of sexual orientation and to prohibit discrimination in employment, schooling, and health care based on positive HIV-related blood tests. In 1990 the legislature passed a "hate crimes" bill that allowed judges to mete out stiffer than usual penalties for a crime motivated by animus toward a member of a minority group, defined to include sexual orientation. The General Assembly passed "An Act Relating to Discrimination on the Basis of Sexual Orientation" in 1992,[26] but controversy and anger over the law persisted beyond the close of that legislative session. The *Burlington Free Press* called the vote on the bill "Perhaps the bravest . . . any legislator cast this year" and attributed to this issue the defeat of some legislators in the November 1992 elections. One defeated incumbent was David Wolk, a Democratic state senator from Rutland County who led the floor fight for passage and who lost his bid for lieutenant governor in a race against Republican candidate Barbara Snelling.

Signs of the times: "Take Back Vermont" (2000), photograph by Amy Cunningham, Vermont Historical Society; "Vermont: Keep it Civil" (2000) referring to the proposed "Civil Unions" bill debated in the legislature during the 2000 session. *Bumper sticker, Vermont Historical Society.*

The fight over the nondiscrimination bill paled in comparison with the one that emerged from a 1997 court case concerning the rights of gay and lesbian couples. Although the civil rights bill of 1992 defined household members as "persons living together or sharing occupancy and persons who have lived together in a sexual relationship,"[27] it stopped short of defining the rights of gay and lesbian couples to secure some legal, medical, and property protections and privileges enjoyed by married heterosexual couples. Three same-sex couples, denied by town clerks their request for marriage licenses, sued the State of Vermont and the towns, claiming that the refusal violated state constitutional and legal guarantees under the "common benefits" clause. The state Supreme Court's ruling in *Baker et al.* v. *State of Vermont*, issued in December 1999, on the eve of a new legislative session, concluded that "the state is constitutionally required to extend to same-sex couples the common benefits and protections that flow from marriage under Vermont law." The court left it to the legislature to "craft an appropriate means of addressing this constitutional mandate," to establish "an alternative legal status to marriage for same-sex couples, impose similar formal requirements and limitations, create a parallel licensing or registration scheme, and extend all or most of the same rights and obligations provided by the law to married partners."[28]

A storm of controversy, similar to the one generated by the Equal Rights Amendment in 1986 and the gay rights bill in 1992, erupted in response to the court's decision and mandate to the legislature. A few towns

**VERMONT
KEEP IT CIVIL**

included opinion polls on the question of marriage rights and civil unions for gay and lesbian couples at the March 2000 town meeting and city elections. Organized groups supporting and opposing legislation to respond to the court order held rallies at the State House and inundated the news media with letters and opinion pieces.

The legislature proceeded cautiously to devise a solution, with most Democrats, supported by Governor Dean, in favor of granting some rights to same-sex couples, and most Republicans opposed. The House and Senate Judiciary committees held separate public hearings, closely followed by the press and public. Each committee drafted legislation that, while continuing to define marriage as the union of a man and a woman, provided for a "civil union" of same-sex couples, legally valid only within Vermont, that would fulfill the Supreme Court's requirements. In the final voting, some legislators crossed party lines to vote for or against the bill creating civil unions, which passed late in the legislative session. After the law became effective on July 1, 2000, a few town clerks resigned rather than issue licenses for civil unions and some others appointed assistant town clerks to fulfill the obligation. Most, however, quietly complied with the new law. In the September 2000 primaries for state elections, five Republican house members who had voted for the civil union bill lost to challengers within their own party and one Democrat who had voted against the bill was defeated. In the November 2000 elections for governor, lieutenant governor, and house and senate seats, civil unions became the dominant issue, with several candidates making repeal of the law and defeat of those who voted for it the cornerstone, if not the exclusive issue, of their campaign.

Seen by its supporters as consistent with Vermont traditions of tolerance for radical social reform, the civil union law became for its opponents a disturbing symbol of the changes that had disrupted Vermont society, culture, and politics in the past three decades. Almost as soon as the law passed, signs began to appear throughout the state admonishing voters to "Remember in November" and urging them to "Take Back Vermont." Claiming to speak for Vermonters with multigeneration roots in the state, some supporters of the "Take Back Vermont" agenda vowed to elect candidates who would repeal not only the civil union law but also education funding, land use, and land planning laws (known respectively as Act 60, Act 250, and Act 200), and other recent laws that they interpreted as infringements on property rights or restrictions of customary activities. Each of these laws, opponents complained, had been foisted upon Vermonters by people who had only recently come to the state. The campaign to "take back Vermont" exploited the rhetorical tradition of tension between "real Vermonters" and "flatlanders," but it also revealed the real resentment that some "native Vermonters" felt for those who had come to the state within the last three decades.

In the November 2000 elections, Republicans won a majority in the house and gained some seats in the senate, where Democrats retained their majority. Some of the new legislators came to Montpelier committed to enacting the changes they promised as part of the "Take Back Vermont" campaign, but found themselves unable to accomplish that task. A year after the civil union law went into effect, newspaper polls indicated that a slender majority of Vermonters still opposed it, but the strength and determination of opposition became increasingly difficult to gauge. *Rutland Herald* writer David Moats, who won a Pulitzer Prize for his series of editorials in April 2000 on the controversy and debates, commented that civil unions "have just become part of the landscape . . . It's part of everyday life."[29]

The laws targeted for repeal by dissatisfied Vermonters had emerged over the thirty years from 1970 to 2000. In some ways these laws responded to the pressures of population increase and growing prosperity in some sectors of the population and economy. For some critics, the new laws and new approach to law making failed to respond adequately or sympathetically to difficulties associated with Vermont's agricultural economy and rural society or to traditional Vermont institutions. Defenders of those laws argued that they brought resolution to long-standing problems, deeply embedded in the fabric of Vermont history and culture, and that they reflected the changes taking place not only in Vermont, but throughout the nation. Among those changes in Vermont were the end of Republican hegemony in electoral politics, the emergence of a two-party system and a seesaw of party success in both the governor's office and the legislature, and, closely related to those two political realities, new attitudes and beliefs about the role of government.

Politics

In January 1969 Deane C. Davis, 68 years old, a lawyer, former superior court judge, retired president of National Life Insurance Company, chairman of the "Little Hoover Commission" that a decade earlier had charted the reorganization of state government, and an influential member of the conservative wing of the Republican Party, succeeded the liberal, youthful, three-term governor, Philip Hoff. The Vermont press corps, somewhat disillusioned with Hoff although still charmed by him, initially derided Davis during the campaign for his age. Unperturbed by that criticism, Davis eventually won over reporters and the public with his wit, energetic campaigning, and caginess on some of the most controversial issues of the campaign. Democrats, divided in their loyalties after Hoff split with President Johnson over the Vietnam War, showed lukewarm support for John Daley of Rutland, lieutenant governor in Hoff's third term and widely viewed as a less aggressive torchbearer of his liberal politics and political philosophy. Many Vermonters, unsettled by racial and political unrest in the state and nation, as well as the rising costs of state government programs as federal funding shifted to support the war in Vietnam, saw Davis as a representative of traditional Vermont values and gave him a substantial victory in November 1968.

Davis entered office with solid Republican majorities in both houses and close ties to many in his party. These assets helped him win support for a controversial sales tax that he requested in his inaugural address. Throughout his campaign he had called a sales tax "the last resort" for increasing state revenues to pay for programs implemented during the Hoff administrations, and his request drew ridicule in the press. Davis compromised with Democrats, who disliked the tax as regressive but were eager to preserve the new directions of state government, by including a provision for a rebate to low-income taxpayers.

Governing in turbulent times, when the Vietnam War divided the nation and generations, and when social protest disrupted the operations of many institutions, Davis brought a calm good humor and avuncular mien to some

Deane Davis's famous "Vermont boat" ad was created for his second gubernatorial campaign (1970). In his autobiography, Davis noted that the ad "was an instant success and has since been called the most effective television ad in the history of Vermont politics" (*Autobiography*, follows page 242). *Vermont Historical Society.*

of the confrontations he faced in the state. The antiwar movement had gathered strength on Vermont campuses after the disastrous confrontations at the 1968 Democratic National Convention in Chicago and the narrow victory by Richard Nixon over Hubert Humphrey for the presidency. By 1969 protests at Middlebury College and the University of Vermont focused on eliminating the requirement of participation in Reserve Officer Training Corps (ROTC) programs. On October 15, 1969, several hundred students and other protesters held a rally in Burlington as part of the national "Moratorium Day," with Lieutenant Governor Thomas Hayes as one of the keynote speakers. Governor Davis, not sympathetic with the antiwar position, saw the protest movement on college campuses as a potential threat to public safety. Rather than taking a confrontational position, however, Davis appointed a special assistant to serve as a liaison to college groups, personally attended several meetings with opponents of the war on campuses and in communities around the state, and called a meeting at the State House for college presidents and student representatives.

The crisis year for the Vietnam War protest movement came in 1970. In March several town meetings passed resolutions condemning federal government policy to pursue the war. On May 5, when a protest rally at Kent State University in Ohio resulted in the shooting deaths by Ohio National Guard of four students and the wounding of eleven others, pandemonium broke loose on college campuses nationwide. In Vermont, students at UVM, Middlebury, Trinity College, and St. Michael's College boycotted classes and held rallies. A protest vigil at UVM drew several hundred students, the faculty voted to cancel final exams, and a group of students and faculty occupied the ROTC offices. At Middlebury, Lieutenant Governor Hayes spoke at a student gathering. When protest groups marched to the State House, Hayes, as acting governor while Davis attended a meeting of the National Governors' Conference in New Mexico, ordered the American flag flown at half-staff. Responding to reports and complaints about Hayes's action, Davis immediately flew back to Vermont and ordered the flag raised. Later that year Hayes challenged Davis in the gubernatorial primary, and after suffering an overwhelming defeat, left the Republican Party. (In 1985 Democratic Governor Madeleine Kunin elevated Hayes, then a superior court judge, to an associate justice of the Vermont Supreme Court.)

Protest movements and grassroots political organizations continued to expand into the mid-1980s, widening the agenda of political and social issues to be discussed and solved at the local as well as state level. The proliferation of splinter groups and informal political alliances, reminiscent of Vermont politics in the 1850s, opened the political process to new constituencies and created a counterpoint (some argued that it was a confusing cacophony) to traditional party politics. In perhaps the most notable example of this trend, in March 1982, 163 town meetings voted to endorse a resolution to end the production and deployment of nuclear weapons.

Not one to shy away from controversial issues, but careful to maage them, Davis ran a vigorous campaign for reelection in 1970 and with the help of his famous "Vermont boat" ad, won with an even larger majority than he attained in his first contest. After four turbulent years in office that included difficult battles with the legislature to pass a land-use bill regulating development (known as Act 250) and a water quality bill (known as Act 254) that later became the hallmarks of his administration, and presiding over the restructuring and remarkable expansion of the scope of state government, Davis declined to run for a third term. In the 1972 Republican Party primary he backed Luther F. "Fred" Hackett, a former legislator and chairman of the

House Appropriations Committee, against the more liberal Attorney General James Jeffords. Jeffords, who had won a high-profile case against Ticonderoga Mills that forced the paper company to clean up some of its environmental damage to Lake Champlain, attracted the moderates in his party. His defeat in the primary, followed by his failure to win approval as chair of the State Republican Committee, gave Democratic candidate Thomas Salmon an opportunity to court a bloc of disaffected Republicans.

Salmon, an attorney from Rockingham and a member of the legislature, campaigned energetically on the enigmatic promise to "Keep Vermont for Vermonters." The third-party candidate in that race, Bernard Sanders, running on the Liberty Union ticket, participated in television debates with the two major party candidates for governor. While he drew only slightly over 1 percent of the vote, his effectiveness in baiting Hackett further assisted Salmon in racking up a substantial upset victory.

Salmon came to the governor's office in 1973 prepared to expand on the social programs of his Democratic predecessor, Philip Hoff, and the land-use and environmental initiatives of his Republican predecessor, Deane Davis. In his first months in office Salmon continued the work of streamlining and thereby consolidating power in state government, and convinced the legislature to pass a property tax relief bill and a dental care plan for children from low-income families, called The Tooth Fairy program. A combination of local, national, and international events, however, embroiled Salmon in controversy and derailed his agenda early in his first term. A strike by union carpenters in 1972, brought about by a decline in heavy construction and resistance by eight of the largest Burlington-area contractors to negotiate new contracts with the International Brotherhood of Carpenters and Joiners, remained unresolved when Salmon took office. Elected with the help of organized labor in Vermont, Salmon attempted to intervene to help settle the strike after taking office by getting the union and contractors to agree to binding arbitration. The contractors refused and Salmon then appointed a fact-finding panel chaired by Lieutenant Governor John A. Burgess. The report of the panel in December 1973 unambiguously accused the contractors of failing "to bargain in good faith or enter into a contract with any of the unions" and concluded that "it was the intention of certain of the construction companies to destroy the organized labor union movement in the construction industry in the State of Vermont."[30] The panel noted that the strike had left two hundred to two hundred fifty men unemployed and had forced many to go out of state to find jobs; others had left the construction industry altogether. The panel also noted that eight construction firms against whom the strike was aimed, in what it identified as a clear effort at breaking the strength of the union, had employed out-of-state, nonunion workers.

Salmon briefly considered the option of disqualifying contractors involved in labor disputes from bidding on state construction projects, including a new state office building project approved in 1973. He retreated from taking that action on his own authority, however, after receiving an advisory opinion in November 1973 from Assistant Attorney General Louis Peck, and commented that "this might have been a popular step by a strong Governor in a heavily pro-union state, but as only the second Democrat elected in the history of Vermont where labor's influence is weak, and the prospect is the Republicans will continue to dominate the scene with periodic breakthroughs by Democrats, the move could very well set a precedent for future Governors to impose right-to-work or similar unacceptable conditions on contracts."[31] Union members complained that "Salmon sold us down the river," their frustration compounded when the Pizzagalli company, one of the eight firms that had refused to negotiate a new contract with the union, won the state contract to construct the Chittenden County Correctional Center.[32] Union membership declined sharply as a result of the strike and those who remained in the union found it difficult to get work on large construction projects.

The labor union movement in Vermont, already weakened by declining membership in the postwar years, and a general public attitude of "coolness . . . and even a great deal of opposition,"[33] had begun to revive with passage of the State Labor Relations Act in the 1967 session, which established a Labor Relations Board with authority to prevent unfair labor practices, supervise union elections, hear grievances, serve as a mediator, and resolve collective bargaining issues. This episode with the construction unions damaged the trade unions, however, and even the Vermont State Employees' Association (VSEA), founded in 1944, which had continued to thrive through the next several decades, suffered a temporary setback when State College workers left the association in 1973, and membership remained stagnant or declined slightly in 1974 and 1975.[34]

The next crisis to affect Salmon's administration was precipitated by a combination of the oil shortage created by the OPEC embargo in retaliation for U.S. support of Israel in the 1973 Yom Kippur War, followed by inflation that drove interest rates into double digits, and an abnormally low winter snowfall that further discouraged tourism and recreation. With revenues plummeting, expenses for fuel soaring, and the construction industry prostrated by high interest rates, Salmon made deep cuts wherever he could in state government. A sustained recession and inflation throughout the remainder of his two terms forced Salmon to continue reducing government expenses, even to the point of refusing to light the State House Christmas tree, which contributed to a widespread mood of gloom and led one financial analyst to conclude that "if statistics alone were used to measure political sentiment [Salmon] would go down in the books as the most conservative governor in modern Vermont history."[35]

Passing up the opportunity to run for the U.S. Senate seat being vacated by George Aiken, and despite the crises that beset his first term, Salmon easily won election to a second term as governor in 1974. Patrick Leahy, Democratic states attorney for Chittenden County, accepted the challenge to win Aiken's Senate seat for his party and after an aggressive campaign scored an upset victory over veteran legislator and former "Young Turk," Richard Mallary, who gave up his seat in the U.S. House of Representatives after one term to run for the Senate. Making his own political comeback in 1974, James Jeffords won the House seat vacated by Mallary. In 1976 Salmon challenged Robert Stafford for the U.S. Senate seat to which he had been appointed in 1971 upon the death of Winston Prouty. In a hard-fought election, Salmon lost by a narrow margin.

The seesaw of party dominance during this period when Vermont developed a multiparty political system also showed up in the legislature. In 1975 Timothy O'Connor of Brattleboro became the first Democrat elected speaker of the house and in 1976 the Democrats won a majority in the house for the first time.

Salmon's successor as governor, Republican Richard A. Snelling, won office after a three-term career in the Vermont House and an unsuccessful run for governor against Philip Hoff in 1966. A successful industrialist, Snelling arrived in the governor's office at a time when a sluggish economy had thrown state finances into debt. He imposed austerity budgets and tighter management of government agencies, promoted jobs and business initiatives to boost state revenues and productivity, and negotiated a contract with Hydro-Québec that brought inexpensive power to the state to offset the energy disaster caused by the OPEC embargo and its aftermath. As a national spokesman for President Richard Nixon's "new federalism" that let state governments develop details for administering federal funds released to them as block grants under broad policy guidelines and standards, Snelling walked a fine line between socially liberal policies and fiscal conservatism. He resisted proposals to expand the scope of state government by adding programs, and focused on administrative reform and internal efficiencies. His proposals for welfare reform created a system more responsive to a wide range of needs by both the recipients and administrators of welfare programs and proved less costly to the state. His cabinet appointments, which included a mix of veterans of government service and newcomers, Democrats and Republicans, and several women, demonstrated his skill at coalition building. Despite a sometimes imperious, thin-skinned public personality, he enjoyed wide support among voters, who elected him governor for an unprecedented four two-year terms from 1977 to 1985, when he temporarily retired from public office.

The election of 1984 proved to be another turning point in Vermont politics. Madeleine May Kunin, Swiss born, Jewish, a former journalist, had worked her way up the political ladder from the Burlington School Board to the Vermont House of Representatives, where she served as chair of the powerful Appropriations Committee, won election as lieutenant governor for one term under Snelling, and challenged him in the 1982 gubernatorial election. Temporarily forced out of public office, Kunin made her comeback in 1984 when she narrowly defeated Republican Attorney General John Easton to become Vermont's first woman governor. Benefiting from a revived economy, Kunin's administration eliminated the deficit inherited from Snelling's last year in office and eagerly set to work instituting a liberal agenda to expand education, welfare, and land-use planning programs.

Kunin accomplished much of this with the help of Democrat Ralph Wright, elected speaker of the house in 1985. A controversial but skillful legislative leader, Wright shared Kunin's commitment to an activist role for government, even though he disagreed with her and even opposed her on some issues, such as property tax reform. He did not hesitate to use the power of the speaker to keep his allies in line, pressure his opponents to fall in line, and work hard to recruit and elect Democrats to the house. Often blamed for elevating the partisan tone of debate in the house (probably as much a byproduct of the mature two-party system as his rough-and-tumble approach to politics), Wright commented unapologetically in his political memoirs that he intended "to send a clear signal to all who would listen that we had power and were not afraid to use it."[36] He held the speaker's position for a record ten years, until his defeat for reelection from his Bennington district in 1994.

The same year that Kunin won her first term, Vermont voters elected a majority of Democrats to the state senate, giving the Democrats unprecedented leadership simultaneously in the executive and legislative branches.

Another economic downturn in Kunin's third term again threw the state budget into deficit, forced her to impose unpopular recisions, and prompted retreat from some programs dear to liberals in the legislature and among voters. Kunin chose not to run for a fourth term, and in the election of 1990 voters returned Richard Snelling to the governorship.

With a promise once again to put Vermont state government on a "sustainable" level of spending, Snelling cut budgets in most agencies by as much as 20 percent, demanded cuts in the number of state employees, and imposed greater economy in the operation of state government. He barely had time to implement his policies, however, before he died suddenly of a heart attack in August 1991, on the eve of a celebration in Montpelier of Vermont's two hundred years as a state.

Democrat Howard Dean, who had served as lieutenant governor since 1986, succeeded Snelling. With his swearing in as governor by state Supreme Court Chief Justice Frederick Allen, Dean settled the constitutional question of whether the successor of a governor who dies in office serves as governor in his own right or as "acting governor."

Dean declared himself a social liberal and fiscal conservative, adopted Snelling's austerity budget, and promised to continue the late governor's fiscal policies of achieving and maintaining "sustainable levels" of spending. He retained many of Snelling's cabinet members through the remainder of his 1991–1993 term, making changes only after he began his next term following the 1992 elections. A medical doctor who had maintained a practice throughout his years in the state senate and as lieutenant governor, Dean gave high priority to expanding medical care for low-income children and adults, promoting the Dr. Dynasaur program of health insurance for children. His other priorities in his first years in office, early education and welfare reform, reflected emerging national trends, and received support in the legislature and among voters, who returned him to office with enormous majorities—as much as 70 percent of votes cast—in 1994 and 1996. Aided in implementing his social and fiscal policies by a sustained period of economic prosperity, Dean fought off attempts within his own party, which held majorities in both houses of the legislature, to increase spending beyond the modest levels he proposed. As a consequence, the state accumulated sizeable revenue surpluses through the year 2000. In 1998, facing an electorate divided on the controversial education funding law known as Act 60, and again in 2000, when many voters showed their anger at Dean's support of the civil union law, he faced strong challenges from conservative Republican candidate Ruth Dwyer. He narrowly won reelection to a fifth term in 2000, then announced in late summer 2001 that he would not seek reelection in 2002. He spent his final year in office coping with a precipitous downturn in the economy, which forced him, like his three predecessors, to slash budgets, cut programs, and impose layoffs of state employees. At the same time Dean began an aggressive, initially modestly funded, campaign to seek the Democratic Party nomination for president of the United States in the 2004 national election.

In 2002 Republican James Douglas, a former legislator, secretary of state, and state treasurer, scored what some observers considered an upset victory in the race for governor against Lieutenant Governor Douglas Racine. In a close election, which included an independent candidate, Douglas won 42 percent of the popular vote, short of the majority needed to win the general election, but with a 6,000-vote lead that made a floor fight unlikely when the legislature met to decide the election. The first Republican to hold the governorship in over a decade, Douglas entered office—as did his two Republican predecessors—during a period of dramatic economic downturn and declining state revenues. Also, like his predecessors, he focused his campaign and early budget messages on economic stimulus, attracting new industries and businesses to Vermont while promising to respect a tradition and legislative history of environmental protection, and cutting both the size and budget of state government while responding to a wide array of social welfare problems, including rising medical care costs, drug treatment, and prevention.

This election history suggests that in the almost forty years from the time Philip Hoff won election to the end of Howard Dean's fifth term, Vermont developed a two-party system of politics and governing. The story is more complicated, however, because the proliferation of third and fourth parties, along with a significant number of independent candidates, consistently played an important role in determining the outcome of elections for statewide and congressional offices.

The Liberty Union party, formed by Peter Diamondstone and former Democratic Congressman William Meyer in 1970, first appeared on a statewide ballot in 1972. In 1976, Bernard Sanders, a native of Brooklyn, New York, and a veteran of the commune movement of the late 1960s and early 1970s, ran for governor as the Liberty Union candidate and garnered over 6 percent of the vote. Other alternative and interest-group parties—Citizens, Libertarian, Small is Beautiful, New Alliance, Natural Law, Vermont Grassroots—maintained a persistent presence in statewide elections, rarely, however, having much influence on the outcomes. But in 1986, Sanders, now a seasoned political figure after three terms as mayor of Burlington, again ran for governor, this time as an independent, and took over 14 percent of the vote. That was enough to deny Madeleine Kunin the majority she needed to win at the polls and throw the election into the joint assembly. In the hotly contested election of 2000, Anthony Pollina, formerly a Democrat, a founder of Rural Vermont (a nonpartisan study and advocacy group), and a policy adviser to the Vermont Public Interest Research Group (a liberal political advocacy organization), ran for governor as a Progressive Party candidate and captured 9.5 percent of the vote. Dean, with only a 50.4 percent majority, barely escaped having the contest resolved in the legislature, which that year included many Republicans voted into office to "Take Back Vermont" by repealing laws that Dean had supported or initiated. In the 2002 election, independent candidate Cornelius Hogan won 10 percent of the vote, and no candidate emerged with the required constitutional majority. In that same election Pollina ran again, this time as the Progressive Party's candidate for lieutenant governor, and captured 25 percent of the popular vote, which probably made the difference in electing Republican Brian Dubie, who won only 41.2 percent of the popular vote. The Democratic candidates for governor and lieutenant governor conceded the election, thereby reducing the likelihood of a contest in the legislature and strengthening the practice of having the legislature elect the plurality winners when no candidate won the required majority. The results of the 2002 polling, however, revived discussion of amending the state constitution to eliminate the majority requirement itself, or to institute an "instant run-off" provision on the ballot.

Vermont voters consistently showed their independence from party affiliations in other contests. Six times between 1970 and 2002 they elected lieutenant governors from the opposite party of the governor they sent into office, and often crossed party lines to elect attorneys general, secretaries of state, treasurers, and auditors of accounts from opposite parties or who ran as candidates for both major parties. In 2002, while Republicans won the two top positions on the ticket, Democrats won all the remaining statewide elections, increased their majority in the senate, and won back some seats in the house, where the election of four Progressives and one Independent weakened the Republican majority, recaptured only two years earlier.

In elections for congressional seats, Vermont voters, who gave Snelling a 55 percent majority vote for his fourth term as governor in 1982, voted against him two-to-one when he ran against Patrick Leahy for the U.S. Senate in 1986. In 1990 they sent Bernard Sanders to the House of Representatives as an Independent, rejecting Republican Peter Smith, whom they had sent to Congress two years earlier in his first contest against Sanders for that position. In the next six elections, voters returned Sanders to the House with substantial majorities. After succeeding Robert Stafford in the Senate in 1988, James Jeffords consistently outstripped his Democratic opponents by drawing votes from independent moderates along with party regulars and some Democrats.

Two conclusions may be drawn from these results. First, as several historians have noted about recent political trends, strict allegiance and adherence to party has declined as a factor in American elections in general. In Vermont, as Samuel B. Hand emphasizes in his book on the Republican Party, neither party in the last half-century has proven capable of consistently assembling or sustaining a majority vote in general elections. What some observers might consider "inconsistencies" in voting habits—winning the governorship and losing elsewhere on the statewide ticket or in the legislature—is evidence of the emerging weaknesses in party politics that had periodically popped into view earlier in primary fights.[37] Second, in a small state like Vermont, even after the demise of one town-one vote representation in the house, politics is still personal and local. Coattails are short or irrelevant and single issues can determine elections at the local level while having less effect in choices for statewide office. Most political commentators and even many candidates agree that as many as one-third of Vermont voters cast their ballots independently of any party affiliation.

Like the voters, Vermont politicians in the decades from 1970 to 2000 exercised a high degree of independence in office. A self-proclaimed conservative, Governor Deane Davis promoted a land-use and conservation bill that defied deeply revered traditions of property rights. Richard Snelling worked hard to push through the legislature an amendment to the state constitution guaranteeing equal rights for women that the voters rejected at the polls in November 1986, and in 1991 he reluctantly accepted an increase in the rate of the sales tax. Howard Dean consistently proposed conservative budgets, even during times of great prosperity. And although he considered himself an enthusiastic supporter of environmental conservation, which he demonstrated through dramatic land acquisitions, such as the purchase of twenty-six thousand acres of forest lands in the Northeast Kingdom from the Champion International company in 1999, he demonstrated less enthusiasm for environmental planning, which caused chagrin among conservation and environmental activists.[38] Republican U.S. Senator Robert Stafford defied his party and President Ronald Reagan on environmental and education policies. Early in his U.S. Senate career, James Jeffords broke ranks with his party in his support of environmental protection, education funding, and the National Endowment for the Arts.

In a surprising but important shift in political allegiance, Jeffords, reelected to the Senate in November 2000, bolted the Republican Party and on May 25, 2001, declared himself an Independent, caucusing with the Senate Democrats. He based his decision, he said in his formal announcement, on disagreements with President George W. Bush and the Republican Party leadership over "very fundamental issues: the issues of [reproductive] choice, the direction of the judiciary, tax and spending decisions, missile defense, energy and the environment, and a host of other issues, large and small." His action had enormous if only temporary consequences for national politics, as it shifted the leadership in what had been an equally divided U.S. Senate for one year, until Republicans regained the majority in the November 2002 national elections. His decision had additional significance for Vermont, which for the first time since 1855 had no Republican in Congress. In his statement announcing his abandonment of the GOP, Jeffords invoked several legendary figures in the Vermont Republican Party pantheon: George Aiken, Ernest Gibson, Jr., Ralph Flanders, and Robert Stafford. They were all Republicans, Jeffords argued, "but they were Vermonters first. They spoke their minds—often to the dismay of their party leaders—and did their best to guide the party in the direction of our fundamental principles."[39] He failed to mention that even those highly respected mavericks never left the GOP fold.

Republican Party faithfuls within the state divided in reaction to Jeffords's move. Some believed that Jeffords's abandonment represented a self-serving action to gain more influence in Congress, while others saw it as a call for reform of the party and a move to the center following its drift to the right in the 2000 state and national elections. Perhaps, in this regard, the most pertinent reference in Jeffords's catalogue of Republican saints was Justin Smith Morrill, who, elected to the U.S. House of Representatives as a Whig in 1854—when the party was in decline—with his first vote in Congress switched his allegiance to the emerging Republican Party, which, as a fusion party, welcomed a wide range of dissident and disaffected voters and candidates from Whig, Free Soil, and Democratic parties under its broad banner. It was the loss of this inclusionary character of Vermont Republicanism, Jeffords claimed, and its failure to seek consensus among dissenting voices, that he lamented in his departure speech; and his move to the category of "Independent" seemed to bring the history of the Republican Party in Vermont full circle. Long before Jeffords bolted the party, however, Vermont Republicanism had lost its ability to contain divergent political viewpoints and forge them into a voting majority. This weakness was at least in part a reflection of the changing demographics of the state that began to have an effect on politics in the post-World War II era. Since the mid-1940s, as Samuel B. Hand notes, "The steady decline in family farms weakened a traditional GOP base, while the explosion of urbanites migrating to Vermont in the 1960s and 1970s included many who valued alternative life-styles and government-based solutions over rugged individualism."[40] Ironically, therefore, as the nation was arguably drifting to the right, Vermont at the turn of the twenty-first century had set its political anchor somewhere on the political left.

Government and "What Vermonters Want"

On the morning of January 9, 1969, Philip Hoff delivered his farewell speech as governor to the General Assembly. An advocate for activist government, who had overseen the biggest expansion of state government in Vermont's history, he looked ahead at unmet needs. By 1975, he said, the state would need almost five thousand new public school classrooms, six hundred new hospital beds, and thirteen thousand new housing units—exclusive of housing for the poor, elderly, and handicapped. It needed new roads to link the growing population centers not served directly or in some cases not even indirectly by the interstate system. Although discouraged by the dismantling of federal programs to support the expanding war in Southeast Asia, Hoff remained optimistic about the ability of state government to meliorate the conditions of the least fortunate and least well-off citizens.[41]

That afternoon, Deane Davis delivered his inaugural address, sounding a different theme. In these times, he began, people see "much that we do not like": an unending war in Southeast Asia "with which many have grown weary"; increases in crime, racial and class tension, and organized protest; international trade imbalance and rampant inflation that threatened to unravel the economy. In Vermont Davis saw "increasing affluence in the midst of increasing poverty, with the highest unemployment level in state history, the largest number of people on welfare, a housing shortage, firms rapidly going out of business, real-estate taxes climbing, towns unable to fund education and other services." Vermont, Davis pointed out, currently participated in eighty-two programs funded in part or in full by the federal government, but faced a serious financial problem comprised of declining revenues, declining federal underwriting, and expanding use of programs to which the state had committed itself. Davis then ran down a list of "what Vermonters want," including public safety, good elementary and secondary schools, wider access to higher education, welfare "for those who need it," preservation and protection of the environment, clean air and clean water, more job opportunities through industrial development, and "the cost of government distributed fairly."[42] Meeting these needs, Davis implied, meant drawing new boundaries between a cherished, if somewhat exaggerated tradition of local autonomy and a centralized administration.

Davis also discussed at length ways to rectify a staggering imbalance between obligations the state had assumed and the resources available to support them. These fell into the two categories of money and people. Davis, like many of his successors, reluctantly but insistently made the case for a sales tax, but also proposed continuing the reform of state government structures to meet more adequately and efficiently its expanding list of functions. In pointing out that imbalance Davis practically defined the dilemmas of state government for the next three decades. Year after year, the Vermont governors who followed him mounted the speaker's podium in the house and in their inaugural or state-of-the-state addresses offered variations of Davis's dichotomy. In an occasional year of prosperity, a governor would offer some new proposals to attack the wish list; in the more frequent years of tight finances until the sustained economic boom of the 1990s, the message centered on austerity and new schemes for increasing revenues through new or modified tax programs and reforming the structure of state government to make it more efficient and economical to run, if not always smaller.

As a businessman, and even more as chairman of the "Little Hoover Commission" that had recommended reorganization of state government in 1959, Davis was keenly aware of the structural problems that made management of the expanded roles he saw government called upon to play both costly and inefficient. Early in his administration, therefore, he continued to implement recommendations of his commission that had been set aside or ignored by the legislature after it created the Agency of Administration. In 1969 he appointed a Committee on Administrative Coordination to make specific recommendations for implementing the next stage of administrative reorganization. In the third of his four messages to the General Assembly in January 1970, Davis addressed this topic exclusively, proposing to sort out the 275 programs operating in state government among eight agencies with a secretary at the head of each. Together the secretaries would constitute the governor's cabinet. This arrangement, Davis argued, "would provide a clear line of authority and responsibility running from the governor down through each of the component parts . . . [and] narrow the span of control to approximately eight people."[43] The legislature complied with this plan by adding to the already functioning Agency of Administration the agencies for Environmental Conservation, Human Services, Natural Resources, and Development and Community Affairs. In 1975, at the urging of Governor Salmon, the legislature added the Agency of Transportation, thereby completing the reshaping of state government that started with the Little Hoover Commission almost twenty years earlier and was implemented piece by piece by several governors.

During Salmon's first term Vermont citizens had an unusual opportunity to participate in determining the structure of state government. Having rejected in 1969 the option of holding a constitutional convention to amend the constitution as an alternative to the prescribed ten-year time lock, voters in 1974 approved five of the six proposals for amendments to the state constitution that survived the legislative winnowing process. Vermonters now affirmed at the polls what had been in place for almost a decade to conform to federally mandated reapportionment methods: the reduction of the house to 150 members (implicitly ending representation by town and confirming apportionment by population-based districts);

eliminating the county-plus-population formula for apportionment of the senate; and requiring reapportionment of both houses "following every second presidential election" (changed again by voters in 1986 to reapportionment "following each federal decennial census").[44] Voters also approved amendments creating "a unified judicial system . . . composed of a Supreme Court, a Superior Court, and such other subordinate courts as the General Assembly may from time to time ordain and establish." For the first time, the constitution now defined the structure and jurisdiction (original or appellate) of the supreme court and lower courts; made all judges and justices except probate and assistant judges gubernatorial appointments with six-year renewable terms and prescribed the procedure for their appointment; gave the supreme court administrative, rule-making, and disciplinary authority within the entire judicial system; and imposed a mandatory retirement age of 70 on all judges and justices.[45] Another amendment, concerned with voter eligibility, gave eighteen-year-olds the right to vote, bringing the state constitution into conformity with Amendment 26 (1971) of the U.S. Constitution, and eliminated a one-year residency requirement, which courts had declared unconstitutional. Finally, voters approved reducing the ten-year time lock on amending the state constitution to four years.

In the same referendum, Vermonters rejected a proposal that included extending the terms of the governor and other constitutional officers to four years and a provision for a run-off election in case no candidate for statewide office received a majority of votes in the general election.[46] Proponents of the four-year term argued its importance as a way to give continuity to state government and facilitate effective planning and budgeting in a two-year fiscal cycle. Voters dismissed these arguments and, doubtless influenced in part by the recent Watergate scandals that had resulted in the resignation of President Richard M. Nixon, cast ballots to keep the executive on a short leash. Subsequent proposals to extend the terms of executive offices, even when supported by popular governors and ex-governors from both parties, failed to emerge from the state legislature to be put to the test by Vermont voters. Thus in the year 2004, Vermont and New Hampshire were the only states that continued to have two-year terms for governor.

With the superstructure of a modern state government in place, the priorities and interests of successive governors, the cycles of prosperous and lean times, actions of the federal government, and sometimes external forces or opportunities have all played parts in determining the initiatives and emphases in state government. Governor Snelling, committed to streamlining the operation and size of state government, proclaimed in his second inaugural address that "At this moment in history we are asked to provide a leadership which recognizes that Vermont is neither so rich nor so poor that it can avoid the anguish of choice. We will find some programs worthy, but must risk the criticism of their proponents by admitting we find them less worthy than others. We must agree that some programs would benefit Vermont, yet announce our sincere conviction that others are more timely because they will strengthen our future capacity to finance social accomplishment."[47] In his own administration and those that followed, welfare and education proved to be among the most controversial and difficult arenas of reform, which revealed the changing balance of responsibilities between state and local government.

Welfare reform, which Snelling discussed at length in his 1979 inaugural address, presented challenges of fiscal limitations, overlapping jurisdictions, and a multiplicity of programs. Snelling proposed to meet those challenges by enunciating four policy principles: helping welfare recipients toward independence; meeting "demonstrable needs, objectively determined"; gauging the limit of individual support against the level of income earned by a fully taxed citizen; and establishing priorities for state spending aimed at "improving mental health, alleviating drug abuse, reliev[ing] handicaps, and removing barriers to employment."[48] He supported these principles with programs that provided job training, education, partnerships with business and industry, and efforts to address drug and alcohol abuse. At the same time he insisted on administrative reform of the welfare system and pressed for the application of computer technology—still in a relatively immature stage of development—for gathering and consolidating information to determine the needs and benefits of each aid recipient. Snelling's successor, Madeleine Kunin, augmented his efforts with the "Reach Up" job-training program in 1986, which added higher education to existing training opportunities, increased subsidies for child care, and expanded medical benefits to those in the program. In 1989 she convinced the legislature to create the Dr. Dynasaur program to provide health insurance for pregnant women and children through age 6 who did not have any and who did not qualify for traditional Medicaid. When Howard Dean, a medical doctor, succeeded Snelling in 1991, he made providing health insurance for all Vermonters one of his highest priorities. He succeeded in expanding Dr. Dynasaur to cover needy children through age 17, then in 1998 broadening the coverage to include children in families with incomes up to 300 percent of the Federal Poverty Level.

The organization and funding of public education, a controversial issue in Vermont since the beginning of statehood, became at the end of the twentieth century an arena where state government took an increasingly active role, with leadership passing among all three branches of state government. In his 1979 inaugural Snelling noted that of "a dozen problems [that] have claimed the attention of my predecessors and yours endlessly over these last two centuries, none have been more frequently mentioned with frustration and anxiety . . . than those dealing with taxation and with support of the public schools." He hoped to win approval for a uniform property appraisal system "as the one indispensable foundation of a program aimed at equalizing educational opportunity and providing tax equity," but that goal eluded him.[49] When Madeleine Kunin succeeded him in 1985, she made education funding one of her top priorities. Entering office at the tail end of another economic downturn, Kunin had to wait for a more secure economic environment before she could address the full range of education issues, but as soon as she balanced the budget, she began to attack fiscal problems facing elementary and secondary education.

Twice in the previous two decades the legislature passed funding formulas for state supplementary support of public education. In 1969 the legislature adopted the "Miller Formula," named for consultant William Miller. This plan committed the state to a 40 percent funding share for a town of average wealth, calculated entirely on the basis of property values. While it had the effect of boosting state funding in 1970, the worsening economy in the following years and the sharp rise in property values as some towns experienced second-home development had the overall effect of reducing the state's level of support. In 1982 the General Assembly adopted a new formula, known as "Morse-Giuliani" for house members Gretchen Morse and Peter Giuliani, who drafted the bill and shepherded it through the legislature. It altered the Miller Formula by adding personal income to property in calculating a town's wealth and creating a sliding scale of state aid to towns. With the state enjoying relative prosperity, Vermont boosted education spending in the initial years of application of the formula. When the economy dipped again in the mid-1980s, state support declined as well, generating widespread dissatisfaction and calls for yet another funding scheme.

Governor Kunin inherited this concern as she came to office. Stymied in her plans for reforming the administration of schools, she convinced the legislature to implement a statewide requirement for kindergarten programs. In 1988, after three years of advocating for a new state aid formula and property tax reform, she won approval of a "foundation plan." Under this scheme the state gave each school district funds to meet requirements defined in the Public School Approval Standards (PSA), with the commissioner of education recommending a per-pupil cost to meet minimum requirements under PSA. As with the two previous formulas, the foundation plan initially resulted in a dramatic increase in state aid to schools. Another dip in the economy in the later years of Kunin's three-term governorship, however, torpedoed the plan, so state aid actually declined from 1991, when Kunin left office, to 1995. Towns continued to rely on property taxes to fund most of their school costs, and once again critics argued that the quality of education offered to children was demonstrably and unfairly linked to a town's willingness and ability to pay for programs, facilities, personnel, and materials.

Every governor from Deane Davis to Madeleine Kunin had urged the legislature to take up the controversial and contentious issue of property tax reform, either by instituting a statewide assessment, or a statewide property tax. In 1992 the House Education Committee crafted a bill to shift some of the property tax burden on to other broad-based taxes and a statewide property tax on businesses and second homes, and to create a statewide teachers' contract that would have brought all teachers up to the same level of pay in ten years. The bill met stiff opposition and failed to pass in the full house. Although legislative committees continued to explore alternative schemes, progress on solving the problems of property taxation and school funding came to a halt until 1996, when Amanda Brigham, an elementary school pupil from Whiting, along with the school districts in Brandon and Worcester, brought suit against the state, arguing that

Governor Howard Dean signing the Equal Educational Opportunity Act of 1997, known as "Act 60," in Whiting, Vermont, on June 26, 1997. Seated next to him (left) is Amanda Brigham, the pupil from Whiting in whose name a suit was filed that precipitated a state Supreme Court ruling requiring a new funding formula for public education. Photo by Vyto Starinskas, *Rutland Herald*. *Courtesy of the Barre-Montpelier Times Argus.*

reliance on the property tax violated the state's guarantee of equal educational opportunity under the Common Benefits clauses of the Vermont Constitution (Chapter I, article 7, and Chapter II, section 68). The Vermont Supreme Court, in a unanimous, highly controversial decision handed down in February 1997, argued that "in Vermont the right to education is so integral to our constitutional form of government, and its guarantees of political and civil rights, that any statutory framework that infringes upon the equal enjoyment of that right bears a commensurate heavy burden of justification." The court cited the example of Stannard and Sherburne, two towns with nearly identical per-pupil spending, to illustrate the inequities in the tax rate—the tax on an $85,000 home in Sherburne was $247; in Stannard, it was $2,040—and agreed with the plaintiffs that "comparatively low expenditures for education cause comparatively diminished educational opportunities for the students attending the affected schools." It concluded that "the current system ... denies equal educational opportunities, [and] is constitutionally deficient."[50] The court ruled that the state as a whole bore responsibility for funding education and charged the legislature with devising a way to remedy the situation.

The decision itself raised a storm of criticism, and three of the justices were challenged in their reappointment hearings in 1998. In the meantime, however, the 1997 legislature put aside renewed efforts to tackle property tax reform and institute a statewide teachers' contract, and instead began drafting a bill that met the court's requirements for equal education opportunities. In June 1997 Governor Dean signed into law the legislation that emerged from this contentious process.

The Equal Educational Opportunity Act of 1997, known as Act 60, created yet another new funding system, based on a $5,000-per-pupil block grant from the state paid from a combination of a statewide property tax of $1.10 on $100 of valuation (with a cap for taxpayers reporting less than $75,000 income), an appropriation from the general fund, and revenues from the Vermont State Lottery. To achieve this goal of per-pupil equal support, some towns became "receiving" and some became "sending" towns for state funds.

The law also provided for an equalized "sharing pool" of funds for education. For every one-cent increase on the local property tax rate approved by voters in a school district, the state committed itself to pay an additional $43 per pupil. If the local tax failed to raise an amount adequate to cover the additional block grant, the sharing pool would pay out the difference. If the local increase yielded more than the $43-per-pupil block grant, the town would contribute to the sharing pool. Called by its critics the "shark pool," this equalized fund amount soon became a major target of opponents of Act 60.

In addition to creating the new funding formula, Act 60 acknowledged a national debate on standards and accountability in education by requiring the state Board of Education to establish "rigorous, challenging standards for student performance in content areas, a means for assessing student performance and progress, an annual report to the legislature on a school-by-school basis of the condition of education, and a five-year report to evaluate the equalizing effects of Vermont's educational finance and school quality standards."[51]

Opponents immediately challenged Act 60 in court and in practice. It survived the court challenge and the state government faced down an incipient "tax revolt" in 1999, when several towns that refused to meet deadlines for payment into the education fund finally complied under threat of suits from the attorney general's office. Some communities, angered by the sharing pool and frustrated in their efforts to increase their own spending on schools without seeing part of the self-imposed tax increase leave their district, created nonprofit foundations to receive and transfer private contributions to their schools. For two years the Freeman Foundation of Stowe supported these efforts by giving matching grants to towns that sought alternatives to the sharing pool. The state tax department, in an effort to win wide support for the Act 60 funding formula, began the practice of sending "prebate" checks to Vermont taxpayers to help them pay their property tax bills. Efforts in the 1999 legislative session to repeal Act 60 failed, although some "repair" legislation did get approved.

Facing a tough reelection campaign in 2000, Governor Dean asserted that Act 60 had "largely met its goals" of equalizing educational opportunity by equalizing funding regardless of individual town property wealth. He conceded, however, that the sharing pool remained unacceptable to many Vermont taxpayers and that the time had come to consider some alternative while maintaining the general intent of the legislation. Dean's conservative Republican opponent, Ruth Dwyer, vowed to repeal Act 60, offering to replace it with a gross receipts tax on all goods and services. The Progressive Party candidate, Anthony Pollina, also attacked Act 60, arguing that Vermont should base funding for education only in part on a statewide property tax that assessed current land use rather than best possible use, and that an increase in the state income tax provided the only progressive alternative. Dean's victory assured the survival of Act 60. However, his own comments during the campaign and Republican Party gains in the legislature, where it regained control of the house and narrowed the Democratic majority in the senate, appeared to put the law on course for some modification. The 2000–2002 session of the General Assembly wrestled with plans for modifying Act 60, but when the house and senate proved unable to agree on a compromise to modify the law, the legislature adjourned without making any changes.

Encouraged by Governor James Douglas, the 2003 General Assembly did alter the law, providing some property tax relief by increasing the sales tax from 5 percent to 6 percent, extending it to telephone bills, soft drinks, and beer, and increasing the property transfer tax to help support education funding. The 2003 revisions also established a two-tiered statewide property tax whereby homeowners would pay a "floating" tax rate, starting at $1.10 per $100 of assessed value, based on local decisions about how much to spend on schools, and second-home owners and businesses would pay a higher fixed rate. These changes allowed the legislature to eliminate the most controversial feature of Act 60, the "sharing pool," and simplify the rules for income sensitivity. Finally, the legislation raised the amount of the per-pupil block grant to $5,810 and built in a schedule of continued increases in the per-pupil block grant for two additional years. After the house and senate conferees sealed their compromise deal on revision, one optimistic legislator commented, "We have, I think, put the Act 60 wars behind us."[52]

Vermont Environmentalism

The success of Vermont's post–World War II emphasis on recreation and tourism as key elements of its economic progress, and of the interstate roads in making the state accessible to southern New England, New York, New Jersey, and Canada, propelled Vermont into a new era of population growth and economic prosperity. At the same time, however, that very success created new dilemmas for preserving the landscape and environment, valued alike by citizens and visitors. Protecting the natural and built environment while continuing to promote economic growth and diversity forced political leaders to examine options for regulating growth and asking citizens to reexamine cherished values of self-reliance and independent choice in matters of economics and use of the land.

The problems and dilemmas that had been lurking in the background since the late 1950s burst into the open during Deane Davis's first term in office. In southern Vermont, ski resorts attracted developers who began to acquire large tracts of land for vacation homes for out-of-state buyers, sacrificing site planning, lot size, and adequate sewer systems to quick profits. In 1968 only 75 of the state's 237 towns had zoning regulations, and only 20 had subdivision rules or planning controls. Rapid growth overwhelmed some towns, even as the potential income from property taxes on developments and new jobs attracted them. Land prices skyrocketed: Property that sold for $50 per acre in 1960 brought $500 per acre by the early 1970s, and $2,000 or more per acre near ski areas and along Lake Champlain. These price increases made it impossible for many young Vermont families to purchase homes, often forcing them to leave family homesteads or live in substandard housing. Property taxes soared as communities struggled to pay for larger schools, increased road maintenance, more police and fire protection, and garbage disposal. Farmers unable to shoulder the burden of rising property taxes and attracted by offers of high prices for their land, sold out, often to developers who then turned more land into subdivision. In many places open land began shrinking rapidly as fields returned to forests or were turned into new housing developments, which in turn altered or posed new threats to wildlife habitats and fragile mountain soils. While the second-home boom bypassed many towns, it dramatically altered the look and economy of others, especially in Windham and Windsor counties, which had the largest concentration of ski resorts. In 1969, according to reporter Rob Eley, seventy-three developers had projects planned or underway in Wilmington and Dover—one for every twenty-five residents.[53]

As a youth, Deane Davis had spent summers on a farm in Barre and he brought to the problem of land use both sympathy for small farm operations and an appreciation for Vermonters' attitudes that they could do as they pleased with their land. His conservatism made him at first reluctant to resort to legislation to resolve these emerging problems. In 1969, when the International Paper Company (IPC) started to clear part of its tree farm in the town of Stratton to construct fourteen hundred recreation homes, Davis responded cautiously. He sent his special assistant, Elbert G. (Al) Moulton, to look at IPC's subdivision in Tamworth, New Hampshire. When Moulton reported that a development like the one in New Hampshire "certainly would not be in the best interests of the state of Vermont and the state cannot allow this to be done,"⁵⁴ Davis took the next measured step. "I called Ed Hinman, president of IPC," he recalled in his autobiography, "and asked him to come to Montpelier with such number of his associates as he cared to bring for the purpose of discussing the development." At that meeting the governor told Hinman "as courteously as is possible but in no uncertain terms that Vermont would not stand for a development of this size and in such a small town because of the effect upon the environment and the quality of life in the state." Hinman and his associates agreed to halt work on the development until they could devise a plan acceptable to the State of Vermont. IPC eventually abandoned its plans for building in Stratton. Officials in some towns where development appeared likely to increase property taxes objected to Davis's jawboning and, arguing that they were capable of handling town affairs on their own, decried state interference. The episode with IPC convinced Davis, however, "that speed was essential if we were to prevent large-scale, improper, poorly planned development."⁵⁵

Davis then conducted a highly publicized tour of the area around Wilmington and Dover, where he saw roads too steep to plow, expensive houses built into the mountainside dumping raw sewage into a nearby stream, and one-acre lots cleared of trees and already showing signs of erosion. Determined now to solve the problem with legislation, Davis moved cautiously to gain broad political support. In addition to announcing to the legislature his wish to have their help in attacking this problem, Davis used citizen groups to build a constituency for planning. He organized a widely publicized statewide Vermont Conference on Natural Resources, disarming potential opponents of his plan by inviting as keynote speaker environmental activist Barry Commoner, an ally most people would not have associated with Davis. The conference ended with participants calling on the governor to set up a special commission to gather more information and make recommendations to the governor to help craft a bill for the consideration of the legislature. Davis responded to this welcome and well-choreographed call for action on May 18, 1969, issuing Executive Order No. 7, creating the Governor's Commission on Environmental Control. Representative Arthur Gibb of Weybridge served as chairman of the seventeen-member commission, which included a wide range of expertise, professions, and political viewpoints, and studied the problem with the assistance of a twenty-nine-member advisory board. The commission's recommendations included the outlines of land-development and water-quality bills; recommendations for state regulation of land at high elevation, pesticides, and water resources; preservation of open spaces; and controls on electric power generation. Still careful to pave the way for what he knew would be controversial and bitterly contested legislation, Davis told the General Assembly, "the time has come to take responsible action to prevent further massive pollution of our land, water, and air, and to step up the pace of our efforts to eliminate many forms of pollution already existing."[56]

Developers and the construction industry helped organize the opposition, which included those who, as Davis anticipated, considered property rights sacred and inviolable and viewed the bill as tantamount to statewide zoning. As the end of the legislative session approached, the opposition had stalled progress on both the land-development and the water-quality bills, which Davis regarded as the cornerstones of his environmental package. He then put the weight of his office and his personal prestige within the Republican Party into breaking the roadblocks when he threatened to extend the session and, if necessary, call a special session of the legislature to secure passage.

The land-use bill that finally emerged from the legislature, known as Act 250, accomplished three things. First, it established an Environmental Board of nine members and nine district environmental commissions. Second, it established procedures and criteria whereby the district commissions on a regional basis would review and permit or deny proposals for development. The commissions' authority extended to the commercial or industrial uses of tracts of land greater than ten acres, developments of ten or more residential units, subdivisions of land for sale in parcels of ten acres or less, state or municipal construction on more than ten acres, or any commercial, industrial, or residential uses of land above 2,500 feet elevation. The law excluded from the permit process construction for farming, logging, or forestry purposes on land below 2,500 feet elevation. The ten criteria for permitting decisions included assessing the impact of the proposed development on air and water pollution, water supply, soil erosion, highway congestion, municipal services and public education, scenic, historic, cultural, and natural resources, and conformity with local and regional development plans.

The third part of Act 250 called for the development of three statewide plans. First came an interim land-capability plan that described present use and defined in broad categories the best possible uses for land based on ecological considerations. Next, a long-term capability and development plan was to use the interim plan, adding to the ecological factors social and economic considerations to guide and accomplish "a coordinated efficient, and economic development of the state." Finally, Act 250 called for a land-use plan, a map and text based on the capability and development plans, which could designate lands best suited for agriculture, forestry, recreation, and urban development throughout the state and which would provide guidance at the local level for creating land-use controls and rules.

The legislature adopted the Interim Capability Plan in 1972. Urged on by Davis's successor, Thomas Salmon, who ran a campaign with the slogan, "Vermont is not for sale," the legislature amended and clarified permit criteria, and approved the Land Capability and Development Plan in 1973.

The last part of the planning requirement of Act 250 encountered the strongest opposition. Some landowners, responding to a poorly printed and widely distributed draft of the land-use plan, expressed fears that their properties would lose value. Others found the wording vague, and still others argued that the plan deprived landowners and local communities of authority to establish their own criteria for development and land-use regulation. A bitter and widely reported dispute between the Environmental Board and the State Planning Office over limiting the state to designating only broad categories of elevation, flood plains, agricultural lands, and significant natural and historic areas, fed the growing unease with the land-use plan.

By the time the legislature took up adoption of a land-use plan in the 1974 session, opposition had crystallized in organizations with the names "Common Sense," "Landowners Steering Committee" in the Northeast Kingdom, "Balanced View" in the northwest section of the state, and "Green Mountain Boys" in southern Vermont, which campaigned against specific legislators who had supported Act 250. By that time, too, the OPEC oil embargo of 1973 had stalled the growth of the national economy and with it many development plans. The passing of the development crisis, in the view of some, obviated the need to pursue the planning provision of Act 250. The legislature therefore took no action on the land-use plans submitted in 1974, 1975, and 1976, and in 1984 removed the provision for a land-use plan from Act 250. At the same time, however, the legislature plugged the "ten-acre loophole" that had originally exempted from Act 250 permit reviews subdivisions that created tracts over ten acres and thereby had allowed thousands of acres of agricultural and forest land to be carved up into large-lot developments. After 1984, therefore, all subdivisions of ten or more units came under Act 250 permit review.

In interviews later in his life, Davis continued to defend Act 250, asserting in 1988 that it did not intend "to stop growth . . . [but] to introduce some sensible planning." In response to the complaint that it attacked local and individual property rights, Davis said that it "clearly brought into the picture the idea that the state itself, the people in the state, have an interest that has to be protected in the use of land."[57] In his autobiography, Davis stated that his greatest disappointment as governor was "my inability to complete the passage of the statewide Land Use Plan. . . . It would have given a sense of direction to the district environmental boards . . . It would have made decisions more uniform across the state. And, I believe it would have given legal stability to the whole of Act 250. The disappointment was mine, but the loss, I believe, was the entire state's."[58]

Nonetheless, the regulatory aspects of Act 250 held up under a series of early permit controversies and challenges. Among the earliest contests between developers and district environmental boards that tested the procedures and strength of Act 250 were proposals for a 2,200-home development, hotel, and golf course at Haystack Mountain; a housing development planned on Ryder Pond in Wilmington; a large campground on Summerset Pond in Dover; a 1,320-home development on 1,930 acres proposed by Green Mountain Meadows in Westford; an animal park called Wildlife Wonderland in Mount Holly; and 262 homes planned for Hawk Mountain in Pittsfield. Each proposal was rejected or abondoned.

A long fight over plans for a megamall at Tafts Corners, where I-89 and routes 2, 2A, and 116 converged in Williston, became a major test of the procedures and effectiveness of Act 250. The project called for creating an enclosed mall with two department stores, eighty shops, twenty fast-food outlets, and twenty-six hundred parking places on an eighty-acre hayfield. First proposed in 1976 by the Pyramid Corporation, which already owned twenty-six malls in New York State, the Williston project posed a threat to Burlington's downtown, just six miles away. Burlington Mayor Gordon Paquette had embarked on his own plans for urban renewal and downtown revitalization that included transforming Church Street into an urban marketplace with a connector from the interstate highway that would bring cars into the city's downtown. Opposition to Pyramid Mall coalesced almost immediately and the local press scrupulously examined every detail of the project. After two years of hearings, the District 4 Environmental Commission finally rejected the permit application in October 1978, citing criteria from Act 250 including traffic congestion and the potential burden on Williston municipal services, sewage disposal facilities, and highways.

The Pyramid Corporation challenged this decision in the courts, and the controversy and legal maneuvering dragged on for several years. In 1988, Pyramid returned with a new application, which it defended until 1999, when it finally gave up. By that time, however, other projects in Williston had transformed the Tafts Corners area into a big-box shopping area, similar to the one originally proposed by Pyramid, and malls in Burlington, South Burlington, and Winooski had transformed commercial and residential patterns in and around the western side of Chittenden County.

Despite charges that Act 250 suppressed development, stalled economic growth, and promoted an antibusiness climate in Vermont, the nine district commissions acted on nearly fifteen thousand applications in the twenty-five years following implementation. In the first ten years the commissions denied only 92 of 3,363 applications, and in 1987, a peak year of prosperity, "district commissions reviewed 876 applications with an estimated construction cost of $392 million."[59]

Every governor following Davis supported the principles and intent of Act 250. Thomas Salmon made implementation of Act 250 a high priority, using the law to slow development and as a way to back up his campaign slogan that "Vermont is not for sale." He pursued additional measures to protect the environment, urging the legislature to approve the controversial capabilities and land-use plans prescribed by Act 250, as well as implementation and expansion of the 1972 bottle law that required beverage manufacturers to impose and accept a deposit fee on returned glass and aluminum soft drink and beer containers. He also supported a ban on the use of phosphates that were choking Vermont's rivers and lakes with algae.

As an industrialist, Richard Snelling tried to create a more friendly relationship between government and business and, typical of his approach to government, he urged administrative streamlining of the Act 250 permit process. One of the members of the commission appointed by Davis to draft the law, Snelling supported it in principle and on occasion urged the Environmental Board to intervene when he saw threats to the state's interests. The Pyramid Mall controversy came to a head under his administration and once he satisfied himself that the procedures used by the district commission and Environmental Board conformed to those prescribed by the law, he refrained from any intervention or expression of opinion and backed the board.[60]

Madeleine Kunin made environmental issues one of the cornerstones of her administration and expended political capital in her effort to revive the statewide land-use planning part of Act 250 that had proven so controversial. The period of economic prosperity that stimulated development activity in the mid-1980s revealed the negative consequences of allowing small projects and incremental development to escape Act 250 jurisdiction. In promoting her interest in land-use planning, Kunin followed the pattern laid down by Davis almost twenty years earlier. In 1987 she created the Governor's Commission on Vermont's Future. She charged it to submit a report that would provide an "overview of growth patterns in Vermont and an assessment of the effectiveness of existing laws and practices in managing that growth; . . . a statement of goals and principles for the preservation of Vermont's character . . . [including] resource conservation, the preservation of agricultural land, the availability of housing for all Vermonters, the social diversity and vitality of all communities, the availability of good jobs for all Vermonters and the economic strength of communities . . . [and] recommendations on how to use the goals and principles to guide state, regional, and local decisions."[61]

The twelve-member commission, chaired by Dean of the Vermont Law School Douglas M. Costle, represented a range of interested professional and advocacy groups and included Arthur Gibb, who had chaired Davis's commission two decades earlier. Kunin's commission held eleven public meetings attended by over two thousand Vermonters, compiled hundreds of pages of written and oral testimony presented by three hundred individuals, and reviewed hundreds of letters, before publishing its report in January 1988. Recommendations fell into five broad categories: creating or improving the process of planning; encouraging economic development consistent with high environmental standards; protecting natural resources; protecting and strengthening agriculture; and providing affordable housing for all Vermonters.

The commission's report became the basis for legislation introduced in 1988. The Growth and Management bill of 1988 combined incentives with mandates to promote consistent and widespread planning at the local, regional, and state levels. In effect, it held out the carrots of funding, technical assistance, and data from the Geographical Information System (GIS) to encourage bottom-up planning by towns and cooperation with regional planning commissions. The law also wielded a stick by requiring all regional plans to conform with goals and principles enumerated in the act itself, and requiring review of regional plans by a Council of Regional Commissions, composed of regional representatives, three state officials, and two appointees of the governor.

The council and review functions of the regional planning commissions immediately became lightning rods for opposition to the bill. Opponents argued that these review and conformity requirements struck at the heart of individual property rights and local control of land-use planning. Supporters saved the bill from going down to defeat by adding a $7.5 million milk price subsidy, a one-year property tax abatement for farms other than dairy farms, the promise of tax abatement for all farms in Fiscal Year 1989, and exemption of farm properties from a proposed increase in the property transfer tax. In addition, supporters of the bill proposed to divert all the revenues of the property transfer tax increase to the Vermont Housing and Conservation Trust Fund, established in 1987 to support the creation of affordable housing and the preservation of agricultural land and natural resources. The package of compromises helped gather sufficient legislative support to get the bill passed in the closing days of the 1988 legislative session. Known as Act 200, the "Growth and Management" law restored the planning functions written into Act 250, but on a voluntary basis. While all but a handful of towns, cities, and incorporated villages developed town plans after 1998, only 137 of the state's 247 inhabited towns and cities had gone through the regional review process by 1999.

Resistance to Act 250 and Act 200 stiffened again in the early 1990s as the state struggled through yet another economic slump. Developers argued that the costs and procedural delays of review under the two laws prevented start-up projects that promised economic benefits to towns. A call for repeal of both laws became one of the important issues of the 1992 gubernatorial and legislative elections. It emerged as a major issue again in 1994, when the Senate Natural Resources and Energy Committee refused to confirm Governor Howard Dean's appointments to the Environmental Board. Dean acquiesced to the changes in board membership, but vetoed bills designed to limit the power of regional boards in dealing with town plans. The Environmental Board itself, however, revised some of its procedures and proposed some changes in administrative rules that the legislature adopted in 1996.

Acts 250 and 200 continued to draw fire from property-owners associations, and promises to pull the laws' regulatory teeth or repeal them remained core issues for conservative candidates for governor and the legislature. But the laws also continued to enjoy wide popular support and Act 250 has been credited not only with averting a crisis in 1970 but also with continuing to serve as a brake or corrective against opportunistic and ill-considered development plans. Defenders argued that rather than being antibusiness and antidevelopment, the laws helped create a healthier environment for both by assuring careful planning that minimizes adverse effects on the land.

The ink had barely dried on Act 250 and Act 252, the water-quality bill, when Governor Davis picked up another accolade as an environmentalist with the well-planned, well-publicized, and well-coordinated Green-Up Day, conceived by *Burlington Free Press* reporter Robert Babcock. After a year of planning, on April 18, 1970, seventy thousand volunteers picked up trash along Vermont's interstate highways, state highways, and town roads. Coopting the counterculture, which by 1970 had made environmental awareness one of its touchstone issues, Green-Up Day helped make environmentalism a popular tradition, which includes the participation of governors clad in work clothes stuffing roadside trash into specially printed bags. Its popularity as a civic ritual has contributed to Vermont's reputation as one of the leading states in environmental conservation and natural resources protection.

Yet the direction of the state's environmental course remains controversial, in part because it reflects fundamental tensions and contradictions in contemporary American life. Vermonters struggle over the best and most appropriate ways to protect forests and farms; how to preserve the open landscape of rural and agricultural society where agriculture no longer ranks as the dominant occupation or the engine of the economy; how to protect small downtown centers in a commercial environment in which consumers themselves clamor for shopping malls, big-box stores, and adequate parking space, which have become the commonplace symbols of progress and prosperity in America; and how to promote clustered dwellings near town centers in a cultural environment that places increasing value on suburban living, privacy, and individual property rights.

In the late 1990s, the struggle over housing development that thirty years earlier moved Governor Davis to promote Act 250 transmuted into a debate about the economic, social, and environmental effects of sprawl. In June 1993 the National Trust for Historic Preservation placed the entire state of Vermont on its well-known annual list of the eleven most endangered places in America. In 1998 the newly formed Orton Family

Foundation helped establish a Vermont Forum on Sprawl, which sponsored a statewide conference, "Sprawl in Vermont: How Is It Affected by State Policy and Public Funding?" Governor Dean, who participated in the conference, later negotiated with the Wal-Mart Corporation on the size and placement of stores it wished to open in Vermont after several communities rejected overtures from the Arkansas-based merchandizing company. That year Dean also put himself in the middle of negotiations with the Champion International Corporation over the price and conditions of sale of 133,000 acres of forest in the Northeast Kingdom. While critics of Act 250 and Act 200 continued to decry their invasion of individual and community autonomy, supporters of the laws worried that Vermont remained in danger of losing by degrees long-honored and highly cherished characteristics of an uncluttered landscape and small close-knit communities.

Imagining Vermont

A visitor to the Vermont State House encounters eight marble plaques in the "Hall of Inscriptions." The inscriptions, selected initially in the 1940s with some additions in 1998, tell visitors something about how Vermont citizens and those elected and appointed to represent their neighbors characterize themselves and their state.

> That frequent recurrence to fundamental Principles, and a firm adherence to Justice, Moderation, Temperance, Industry, and Frugality are absolutely necessary to preserve the blessings of Liberty, and keep Government free.
> *Vermont Constitution, 1777*

> I am as resolutely determined to Defend the Independence of Vermont as Congress are that of the United States and Rather than fail I will Return with hardy Green Mountain Boys into the Desolate Caverns of the mountains and wage war with human Nature at large.
> *Ethan Allen, 1781*

> Born of a resistance to arbitrary power—her first voice a declaration of equal rights of man—how could her people be other than haters of slavery—how can they do less than sympathize with every

human being and every community which asserts the rights of all men to blessings like their own?
Vermont State Report, 1855

They hewed this state out of the wilderness, they held it against a foreign foe, they laid deep and stable the foundation of our state life, because they sought not the life of ease, but the life of effort for a worthy end.
Theodore Roosevelt, 1902

The record of Vermont as a resolute champion of individual freedom, as a true interpreter of our fundamental law, as a defender of religious faith, as an unselfish but independent and uncompromising commonwealth of liberty-loving patriots, is not only unsurpassed, but unmatched by any other state in the Union.
George Harvey, 1921
United States Ambassador to Great Britain

If the spirit of liberty should perish in other parts of the Union and support of our institutions should languish, it could all be replenished from the generous store held by the people of this brave little state of Vermont.
Calvin Coolidge, 1928

Vermonters for 200 years have handed down certain attitudes of mind from generation to generation. Some folks call us old-fashioned and backward-looking for adhering to the ideals and principles characteristic of the people who settled our State. We value our heritage of ideals.
George D. Aiken, 1938

The Vermont tradition grapples energetically with the basic problem of human conduct . . . how to reconcile the needs of the group, of which every man or woman is a member, . . . with the craving for individual freedom to be what he really is.
Dorothy Canfield Fisher, 1953

These quotations consistently return to the touchstones of independence, justice, and equal rights, the freedom of individuals, the hard work of making and keeping communities. Writing in the Works Progress Administration American Guidebook Series on Vermont, Dorothy Canfield Fisher acknowledged that this way of imagining Vermont also embodies an American ideal that is both treasured and fragile. "What ought to be done with the old state," she quoted her godfather saying, "is to turn it into a National Park of a new kind—keep it just as it is, with Vermonters managing just as they do—so the rest of the country could come in to see how their grandparents lived."[62] In some respects, this prescient remark understood that Vermont represents itself to the rest of the nation as just such a theme park, even though Vermonters as they live their daily lives both honor the traditions and heritage of the state's history and have ventured off in new directions.

The idea of Vermont as a living reminder of American frontier society, where individuals and institutions continually reinvent themselves and renew or reembody treasured American institutions and attitudes, is integral to the fabric of the state's history and continues to influence its present. The issues Vermonters debated and resolved in the thirty years from 1970 to 2000, such as the proper role and limits of government; individual privileges and society's needs in land use and planning; society's role in caring for people in need; how to define the responsibility for educating children; and matters of personal, group, and community identity, led them to consider and debate competing versions of their social and political traditions. Critics of Vermont politics at the beginning of the twenty-first century decried the decline of effective local government and the concomitant increase of the role of state government in areas once—perhaps longer ago than they dared admit—under the authority of the "little republics." "Vermont can't save the world," Frank Bryan and John McClaughry wrote in their 1988 book, *The Vermont Papers*, "but it can save itself and by its example show America how to get its democracy back. . . . For Vermont, with its tiny state capital . . . with its town meetings, its citizen legislature, its two-year term for governor, has preserved the institutions of liberty and community."[63]

Every two years, Vermonters elect all their legislators and all their constitutional and statewide officers, including their governor. They are unusual in the frequency with which they decide who speaks for Vermont.

Asking who speaks for Vermont raises the question of who are

Vermonters. Any newcomer to the state quickly becomes familiar with two crucial cultural terms: "real Vermonters" and "flatlanders." Often the premise for a brand of Vermont humor that pokes fun at the inadequate preparation of city folks for the rigors and customs of Vermont's rural communities, this duality has more recently taken on the trappings of serious social and political divisions within Vermont.

"Real Vermonters don't milk goats," satirists Bill Mares and Frank Bryan insisted in their 1983 book of that title; and by reminding their readers of the foibles and *faux pas* of newcomers to the state (defined in Vermont folklore as those with fewer than three generations born and bred in the state), they pointed out equally those of rural backcountry folk. Howard Frank Mosher, who set many of his novels and short stories in rural northeast Vermont during the first half of the twentieth century, portrays both the safety and insularity of small rural communities. His "Kingdom Common" is notable for its ability and willingness to tolerate rugged individualism; to nurture unpretentious, earthy, sometimes even bizarre and antisocial behavior; to insist on practicality, regularity, and predictability; and to resist, sometimes violently, change and innovation.

Other writers and social commentators, such as Noel Perrin in his four books of essays on rural life in Thetford, David Budbill in his cycle of poems, *Judevine*, Norman Lewis in his persona as "Danny Gore," and Rusty DeWees as "The Logger," have probed the ambivalence that Vermonters feel about simultaneously maintaining their rural traditions and history on the one hand, and pursuing the amenities, comforts, and conveniences of high-tech, urbane, and urban American life on the other hand. The dialogue and tension that have resulted not only from sometimes having to choose between these two ways of imagining Vermont but also as a result of trying to preserve both and live in both at the same time, have become fixtures of Vermont's popular culture and political life.

In 1998 the humor of "real Vermonters versus flatlanders" merged with politics when retired farmer Fred Tuttle of Tunbridge defeated "newcomer" Jack McMullen, who had lived in Vermont only one year, in the Republican primary for a U.S. Senate seat. In a radio debate that almost replicated his role in *Man with a Plan*, a low-budget, locally popular film about a retired farmer who defeats a slick city incumbent in a race for the House of Representatives, Tuttle challenged McMullen on the pronunciation of Vermont town names and the number of teats on a cow. After winning the nomination, Tuttle all but handed the election to incumbent

Senator Patrick Leahy, but in the process also became an icon of the "real Vermonter" who seems to some to be disappearing from the cultural and political landscapes of the state and the nation.

The humorous symbolism of the Tuttle-McMullen primary race turned serious in the 2000 contests for governor and the legislature. The slogan "Take Back Vermont" became a catalyst for bitter exchanges of letters to the editor, characterized as "real Vermonters" chastising "flatlanders" for imposing their "downcountry" values on the state, and newcomers decrying the prejudices and small-mindedness of backcountry folks. The election swept eighteen legislators out of office, some veterans and some with shorter terms of service, whose votes on the civil union bill, either for or against, offended their constituents. The vote became more than a referendum on several controversial pieces of legislation from 1970 to 2000. It represented a culture war, a struggle over who claims traditional Vermont, what constitutes the Vermont tradition, how Vermonters imagine themselves and their history, and how they will carry it forward into the future.

In 1987 the Windham Foundation sponsored a conference titled, "Vermont: Who Are We Becoming?" Conferees expressed concern that the Vermont self-image as an agrarian society, watchful of its environment, where "Government has been conducted primarily at the local level with decisions made by citizen volunteers," had become merely an illusion. Vermont, the report concluded, stood poised on the verge of a crisis: endangered by a growing division between "a mobile, well-trained, and sophisticated segment of the population with a common perspective on the world [and] those Vermonters in isolated areas of the state and with limited opportunities to share the diversity of experience enjoyed by the mobile crowd."[64] Historian Allen F. Davis, writing in the Foreword to *Vermont Voices, 1609 Through the 1990s*, an anthology of primary sources for Vermont history, commented on an emerging Vermont underclass of "poor families living in 'mobile homes,' or the rundown farmhouses on land that could no longer support a dairy herd . . . which the tourist brochures denied, [and which] was becoming further marginalized by the technological and communication revolution that was transforming the rest of the state."[65] And in a survey of opinions and commentaries on twentieth-century Vermont, historian Richard Hathaway elaborated on Davis's observation to express great concern over "the tendency over the most recent decades to create two Vermonts, separate but unequal. The first Vermont is relatively prosperous, enjoys upward mobility, and is connected to the sophisticated apparatus of the ever-burgeoning Internet. The second 'other Vermont,' is an underclass population, literally as well as functionally 'out of sight.'"[66] Rural poverty has long been a theme in Vermont politics, social reform, and literature. Newer to Vermont are the urban poverty that accompanied the steady decline of the agricultural economy and migration to the cities, the fluctuating industrial and service economy, and the drug culture of contemporary America. Food pantries and homeless shelters have become part of the Vermont urban scene, hidden away from the bistros and boutiques. The two Vermonts that Hathaway discusses have started to emerge in fiction as well as reality. Writer Archer Mayor sets his police mystery books in the underbelly of Vermont life, portraying urban and rural poverty, drugs, crime, the workaday Vermont, and back streets of small towns, rarely seen by tourists or mentioned in the promotional brochures.

The list of what Vermonters respect and have worked hard to maintain in their lives and their history is an important complement and contrast to the problems they face. Despite their disagreements about how to express these values in their institutions, Vermonters continue to share many ideals about what is valuable and important about life in the state. Most would agree that they value the land on which they live, work, and find their recreation. The landscape of mountains, narrow valleys, and lakes is what has held Vermonters to their homes for generations and lured many to the state. Few places in Vermont are far from an open view or access to the ever-present features of the land, and few Vermonters fail to integrate them into their lives, whether in work or recreation. This may account for the large number of artists who continue to explore the landscape tradition in their work, whether it be the calm, neo-Renaissance, almost photorealist style of Kathleen Kolb, the softer, almost impressionistic vision of Wolf Kahn, or the more severe and abstract, and evocative land- and skyscapes of Eric Aho. Woodcut artist Mary Azarian, in a style closer to folk art and early-sixteenth-century printmakers, goes beyond landscape to portray in simple, bold vignettes the rugged but comfortable regularity of rural life (see color plates V to VIII).

Most places in Vermont continue to maintain an intimacy of communal and civic life, and this, too, remains one of the prized features of Vermont's history and society. In her nine books of essays and sketches of life on her Jericho, Vermont, homestead, published between 1965 and 1998, Marguerite Hurrey Wolf has portrayed some of the regularity and continuity that characterizes many of Vermont's towns and villages. "What still happens in Vermont is Town Meeting on the first Tuesday in March, where anyone can speak his mind and the same few usually do, Bennington Battle Day, on August 16, and the first day of hunting in November, are holidays, and there are chicken pie suppers in almost every village in September. . . . There are still country fairs and quilt shows, pig races and strawberry festivals—and where else could a moose fall in love with a cow? The Champlain monster surfaces periodically if not photogenically, and the flatlander tourist is still outwitted by the descendants of the Green Mountain Boys."[67] And when Grace Paley, born and bred in New York City, a political activist and feminist, and resident of Thetford, responded to a city friend who asked if life in the country is boring, she reeled off the dozens of personal and social activities that shape the day, mark the season, and provide a context for personal commitment and action. She tends her garden; goes to meetings of town zoning, water, or selectboards, food co-op, local historical, improvement, or Ladies Benevolent societies; attends local theater or choral group presentations, church suppers, fairs, and high school basketball games. The rituals and requirements of "ordinary life" include "keeping mud and hay out of the house, and stacking wood in the woodshed . . . stuffing newspapers and rags into the cracks and chinks that each new descent of temperature exposes." And she completed her portrait of life in small-town Vermont by listing the activities that make living in Vermont's landscape unique: "skiing across shining fields and through dangerous woods full of trees one must avoid. And of course there is standing in the front yard (or back) staring at the work time has accomplished in crumpling the hills into mountains, then stretching them out again only a few miles away into broad river plains."[68]

Vermonters continue to value the human scale of politics and problem solving. The fights sometimes have been bitter and long, but in most cases, they have managed to avoid personal enmity because the opponents so often know each other and know that they have to live with each other on a day-to-day basis. Reflecting the debates nationally about the role of government, the issues in Vermont have increasingly focused on maintaining and recalibrating the difficult balance between individual liberties, local control, and the common good. In Vermont, the debating and recalibrating go on face-to-face, among people who know each other and know that they will have to continue to live in the same village, town, or small city once the debates end and the decisions have been made.

Every place and the history of every place contain contradictions and paradoxes. In Vermont, the growing urban centers that define modern society sit within view and within walking distance of the pastoral landscape that has long served as the symbol of the state. While urban and suburban sprawl threaten to move out onto that landscape, following the demand for housing and shopping that come with prosperity, private and public funds support conservation and land trust efforts that try to preserve the rural landscape and small communities that persist as part of the mental and cultural ideals in the state.

Part of the experience of Vermont at the turn of the twenty-first century is the continuing and difficult balancing act going on throughout the state between responding to the needs and opportunities of large-scale modern economic development and commerce, mass culture, and mass politics, and making commitments to preserve and nurture small-scale economic, social, and political life. The options, present and in competition throughout Vermont history, have become part of how the state and its people imagine themselves through their past and into their future. Confronted with these difficult and often divisive choices, it is sometimes comforting, sometimes puzzling to ponder the assertion and the challenge contained in the motto adopted by Vermonters over two centuries ago: "Freedom and Unity." But Vermonters today, as the successors of generations of people who have come and gone or come and stayed in this place, can also interpret their state motto as an invitation to examine once again—and continuously—the boundaries and intersections, tension and balance, of interests and obligations implied in the state's motto. As in the past, so in the present, Vermonters enjoy the opportunity and privilege of making important choices for themselves and their communities. Through these choices they continue to explore what it means to be and act as an individual and a citizen in the contemporary world.

Appendix A

POPULATION OF VERMONT BY COUNTY, 1791–2000

COUNTY	1791	1800	1810	1820	1830	1840
Addison	6,420	13,417	19,993	20,469	24,940	23,583
Bennington	12,206	14,617	15,893	16,125	17,468	16,872
Caledonia	2,277	9,377	18,730	16,669	20,967	21,891
Chittenden	4,718	12,778	18,120	16,272	21,765	22,977
Essex	567	1,479	3,087	3,284	3,981	4,226
Franklin	2,454	8,782	16,427	17,192	24,525	24,531
Grand Isle	—	—	3,445	3,527	3,696	3,883
Lamoille	—	—	—	—	—	10,475
Orange	7,663	18,238	25,247	24,681	27,285	27,873
Orleans	134	1,439	5,830	6,976	13,980	13,634
Rutland	15,590	23,813	29,486	29,975	31,294	30,699
Washington	—	—	—	14,106	21,378	23,506
Windham	17,572	23,581	26,760	28,457	28,748	27,442
Windsor	15,740	26,944	34,877	38,233	40,625	40,356
TOTALS	85,341	154,465	217,895	235,966	280,652	291,948

COUNTY	1850	1860	1870	1880	1890	1900
Addison	26,549	24,010	23,484	24,173	22,277	21,912
Bennington	18,589	19,436	21,325	21,950	20,448	21,705
Caledonia	23,595	21,698	22,235	23,607	23,436	24,381
Chittenden	29,036	28,171	36,480	32,792	35,389	39,600
Essex	4,650	5,786	6,811	7,931	9,511	8,056
Franklin	28,586	27,231	30,291	30,225	29,755	30,198
Grand Isle	4,145	4,276	4,082	4,124	3,843	4,462
Lamoille	10,872	12,311	12,448	12,684	12,831	12,289
Orange	27,296	25,455	23,090	23,525	19,575	19,313
Orleans	15,707	18,981	21,035	22,083	22,101	22,024
Rutland	33,059	35,946	40,651	41,829	45,397	44,209
Washington	24,654	27,612	26,520	25,404	29,591	36,607
Windham	29,062	26,982	26,036	26,763	26,547	26,660
Windsor	38,320	37,193	36,063	35,196	31,706	32,225
TOTALS	314,120	315,088	330,551	332,286	332,407	343,641

POPULATION OF VERMONT BY COUNTIES, 1791–2000 *(continued)*

COUNTY	1910	1920	1930	1940	1950	1960
Addison	20,010	18,666	17,952	17,944	19,442	20,076
Bennington	21,378	21,577	21,655	22,286	24,115	25,088
Caledonia	26,031	25,762	27,253	24,320	24,049	22,786
Chittenden	42,447	43,708	47,471	52,098	62,570	74,425
Essex	7,384	7,364	7,067	6,490	6,257	6,083
Franklin	29,866	30,026	29,975	29,601	29,894	29,474
Grand Isle	3,761	3,784	3,944	3,802	3,406	2,927
Lamoille	12,585	11,858	10,947	11,028	11,388	11,027
Orange	18,703	17,279	16,694	17,048	17,027	16,014
Orleans	23,337	23,913	23,036	21,718	21,190	20,143
Rutland	48,139	46,213	48,453	45,638	45,905	46,719
Washington	41,702	38,921	41,733	41,546	42,870	42,860
Windham	26,932	26,373	26,015	27,850	28,749	29,776
Windsor	33,681	36,984	37,416	37,862	40,885	42,483
TOTALS	355,956	352,428	359,611	359,231	377,747	389,881

COUNTY	1970	1980	1990	2000
Addison	24,266	29,420	32,953	35,974
Bennington	29,282	33,307	35,845	36,994
Caledonia	22,789	25,814	27,846	29,702
Chittenden	99,131	115,588	131,761	146,571
Essex	5,416	6,300	6,405	6,459
Franklin	31,282	34,800	39,980	45,417
Grand Isle	3,574	4,593	5,318	6,901
Lamoille	13,309	16,769	19,735	23,233
Orange	17,676	22,763	26,149	28,226
Orleans	20,153	23,455	24,053	26,277
Rutland	52,637	58,332	62,142	63,400
Washington	47,659	52,371	54,928	58,039
Windham	33,074	36,878	41,588	44,216
Windsor	44,082	50,832	54,055	57,718
TOTALS	444,330	511,272	562,758	609,127
official census figures	444,732	511,456	566,615	608,827

Adapted, with permission, from H. Nicholas Muller III and Samuel B. Hand, eds., *In a State of Nature: Readings in Vermont History*, second ed. (Montpelier: Vermont Historical Society, 1985), Appendix A: 401–402.

Appendix B

FIVE LARGEST POPULATION CENTERS, 1791–2000

Rank		1791	1800	1810	1820	1830	1840
1st		Guilford	Guilford	Windsor	Windsor	Burlington	Burlington
	town population	2,422	2,256	2,757	2,956	3,526	4,271
	% of total state population	2.83%	1.16%	1.26%	1.25%	1.25%	1.46%
2nd		Bennington	Bennington	Woodstock	Springfield	Middlebury	Montpelier
	town population	2,350	2,243	2,672	2,702	3,468	3,725
	% of total state population	2.75%	1.45%	1.23%	1.14%	1.23%	1.27%
3rd		Shaftsbury	Windsor	Springfield	Rutland	Bennington	Bennington
	town population	1,990	2,211	2,556	2,669	3,419	3,429
	% of total state population	2.32%	1.43%	1.17%	1.13%	1.22%	1.17%
4th		Putney	Woodstock	Bennington	Woodstock	Windsor	Woodstock
	town population	1,848	2,132	2,524	2,610	3,134	3,315
	% of total state population	2.16%	1.38%	1.15%	1.11%	1.12%	1.14%
5th		Pownal	Rutland	Rutland	Hartland	Woodstock	Middlebury
	town population	1,732	2,125	2,379	2,553	3,044	3,162
	% of total state population	2.02%	1.37%	1.09%	1.08%	1.08%	1.08%
TOTAL		12.1%	7.1%	5.9%	5.7%	5.9%	6.1%

Rank		1850	1860	1870	1880	1890
1st		Burlington	Burlington	Burlington	Rutland	Burlington
	town population	7,585	7,713	13,596	12,149	14,590
	% of total state population	2.41%	2.44%	4.11%	3.65%	4.38%
2nd		Bennington	Rutland	Rutland	Burlington	Rutland
	town population	3,923	7,577	9,834	11,365	11,760
	% of total state population	1.25%	2.40%	2.97%	3.42%	3.53%
3rd		Brattleboro	Bennington	St. Albans	St. Albans	St. Albans
	town population	3,816	4,389	7,014	7,193	7,771
	% of total state population	1.21%	1.39%	2.12%	2.16%	2.33%
4th		Rutland	Northfield	Bennington	Bennington	Brattleboro
	town population	3,715	4,329	5,670	6,333	6,862
	% of total state population	1.18%	1.37%	1.71%	1.91%	2.06%
5th		St. Albans	Brattleboro	Brattleboro	Brattleboro	Barre
	town population	3,567	3,855	4,933	5,880	6,812
	% of total state population	1.14%	1.22%	1.49%	1.77%	2.05%
TOTAL		7.2%	8.8%	12.4%	12.9%	14.35%

FIVE LARGEST POPULATION CENTERS, 1791–2000 *(continued)*

Rank		1900	1910	1920	1930	1940	1950
1st		Burlington	Burlington	Burlington	Burlington	Burlington	Burlington
	town population	18,640	20,468	22,779	24,789	27,686	33,155
	% of total state population	5.42%	5.75%	6.46%	6.89%	7.70%	8.77%
2nd		Rutland#	Rutland	Rutland	Rutland	Rutland	Rutland
	town population	11,499	18,546	14,954	17,315	17,082	17,659
	% of total state population	3.34%	5.21%	4.24%	4.81%	4.75%	4.67%
3rd		Barre*	Barre	Barre	Barre	Bennington	Bennington
	town population	8,488	10,734	10,008	11,307	11,257	12,411
	% of total state population	2.47%	3.02%	2.83%	3.14%	3.13%	3.29%
4th		Bennington	Bennington	Bennington	Bennington	Brattleboro	Brattleboro
	town population	8,033	8,698	9,982	10,628	10,983	11,522
	% of total state population	2.34%	2.44%	2.83%	2.95%	3.05%	3.05%
5th		St. Johnsbury	St. Johnsbury	St. Johnsbury	St. Johnsbury	Barre	Barre
	town population	7,010	8,098	8,708	9,816	10,904	10,922
	% of total state population	2.04%	2.28%	2.47%	2.73%	3.04%	2.89%
TOTAL		15.61%	18.70%	18.83%	20.52%	21.67%	22.67%

Rank		1960	1970	1980	1990	2000
1st		Burlington	Burlington	Burlington	Burlington	Burlington
	town population	35,531	38,633	37,721	39,127	38,889
	% of total state population	9.11%	8.62%	7.37%	6.90%	6.40%
2nd		Rutland	Rutland	Rutland	Rutland	Essex
	town population	18,325	19,293	18,427	18,230	18,626
	% of total state population	4.70%	4.30%	3.60%	3.20%	3.00%
3rd		Bennington	Bennington	Bennington	Essex, Essex Jct.	Rutland
	town population	13,002	14,586	15,772	16,498	17,292
	% of total state population	3.33%	3.26%	3.08%	2.90%	2.80%
4th		Brattleboro	Brattleboro	Essex	Bennington	Colchester
	town population	11,734	12,239	14,418	16,451	16,986
	% of total state population	3.01%	2.73%	2.82%	2.90%	2.80%
5th		Barre	Essex	Colchester	Colchester	So. Burlington
	town population	10,387	10,951	12,624	14,731	15,814
	% of total state population	2.66%	2.45%	2.46%	2.60%	2.60%
TOTAL		22.81%	21.36%	19.35%	18.50%	17.60%

Rutland City incorporated 1892; first appears as a separate entity in the census of 1900.

* Barre City incorporated in 1894; first appears as a separate entity in the census of 1900.

Adapted, with permission, from H. Nicholas Muller III and Samuel B. Hand, eds., *In a State of Nature: Readings in Vermont History*, second ed., (Montpelier: Vermont Historical Society, 1985), Appendix B: 403.

Appendix C

GOVERNORS

Name	Years in Office	Political Party
Thomas Chittenden	1778–1789[1]	
Moses Robinson*	1789–1790	
Thomas Chittenden[2]	1790–1797	
Paul Brigham[3]	1797	
Isaac Tichenor*	1797–1807	Federalist
Israel Smith	1807–1808	Democratic-Republican
Isaac Tichenor	1808–1809	Federalist
Jonas Galusha	1809–1813	Federalist
Martin Chittenden*	1813–1815	Federalist
Jonas Galusha	1815–1820	Democratic-Republican
Richard Skinner	1820–1823	Democratic-Republican
Cornelius P. Van Ness	1823–1826	Democratic-Republican
Ezra Butler	1826–1828	Democratic-Republican
Samuel C. Crafts*	1828–1831	National Republican
William A. Palmer*	1831–1835	Anti-Mason
Silas H. Jenison*[4]	1835–1836	Anti-Mason/Whig
Silas H. Jenison	1836–1841	Whig
Charles Paine*	1841–1843	Whig
John Mattocks*	1843–1844	Whig
William Slade*	1844–1846	Whig
Horace Eaton*	1846–1848	Whig
Carlos Coolidge*	1848–1850	Whig
Charles K. Williams	1850–1852	Whig
Erastus Fairbanks*	1852–1853	Whig
John S. Robinson*	1853–1854	Democratic
Stephen Royce	1854–1856	Whig/Republican
Ryland Fletcher	1856–1858	Republican[5]
Hiland Hall	1858–1860	Republican
Erastus Fairbanks	1860–1861	Republican
Frederick Holbrook	1861–1863	Republican
J. Gregory Smith	1863–1865	Republican
Paul Dillingham	1865–1867	Republican
John B. Page	1867–1869	Republican
Peter T. Washburn[6]	1869–1870	Republican
George W. Hendee[7]	1870	Republican
John W. Stewart	1870–1872	Republican
Julius Converse	1872–1874	Republican
Asahel Peck	1874–1876	Republican

GOVERNORS *(continued)*

Name	Years in Office	Political Party
Horace Fairbanks	1876–1878	Republican
Redfield Proctor	1878–1880	Republican
Roswell Farnham	1880–1882	Republican
John L. Barstow	1882–1884	Republican
Samuel E. Pingree	1884–1886	Republican
Ebenezer J. Ormsbee	1886–1888	Republican
William P. Dillingham	1888–1890	Republican
Carroll S. Page	1890–1892	Republican
Levi K. Fuller	1892–1894	Republican
Urban A. Woodbury	1894–1896	Republican
Josiah Grout	1896–1898	Republican
Edward C. Smith	1898–1900	Republican
William W. Stickney	1900–1902	Republican
John G. McCullough*	1902–1904	Republican
Charles J. Bell	1904–1906	Republican
Fletcher D. Proctor	1906–1908	Republican
George H. Prouty	1908–1910	Republican
John A. Mead	1910–1912	Republican
Allen M. Fletcher*	1912–1915	Republican
Charles W. Gates	1915–1917	Republican
Horace F. Graham	1917–1919	Republican
Percival W. Clement	1919–1921	Republican
James Hartness	1921–1923	Republican
Redfield Proctor	1923–1925	Republican
Franklin S. Billings	1925–1927	Republican
John E. Weeks	1927–1931	Republican
Stanley C. Wilson	1931–1935	Republican
Charles M. Smith	1935–1937	Republican
George D. Aiken	1937–1941	Republican
William H. Wills	1941–1945	Republican
Mortimer R. Proctor	1945–1947	Republican
Ernest W. Gibson[8]	1947–1950	Republican
Harold J. Arthur[9]	1950–1951	Republican
Lee E. Emerson	1951–1955	Republican
Joseph B. Johnson	1955–1959	Republican
Robert T. Stafford	1959–1961	Republican
F. Ray Keyser, Jr.	1961–1963	Republican

GOVERNORS *(continued)*

Name	Years in Office	Political Party
Philip H. Hoff	1963–1969	Democrat
Deane C. Davis	1969–1973	Republican
Thomas P. Salmon	1973–1977	Democrat
Richard A. Snelling	1977–1985	Republican
Madeleine May Kunin*	1985–1991	Democrat
Richard A. Snelling[10]	1991	Republican
Howard Dean[11]	1991–2003	Democrat
James Douglas*	2003–	Republican

*Elected by the legislature due to the failure of any candidate to receive a majority of the popular vote. The legislative elections were held in the year indicated:

Moses Robinson (1789)	Charles Paine (1841)	John S. Robinson (1853)
Isaac Tichenor (1797)	John Mattocks (1843)	John G. McCullough (1902)
Martin Chittenden (1813, 1814)	William Slade (1845)	Allen M. Fletcher (1912)
Samuel C. Crafts (1830)	Horace Eaton (1846, 1847)	Madeleine May Kunin (1987)
William A. Palmer (1831, 1832, 1834)	Carlos Coolidge (1848, 1849)	James Douglas (2003)
Silas H. Jenison (1835)	Erastus Fairbanks (1852)	

Adapted, with permission, from H. Nicholas Muller III and Samuel B. Hand, eds., *In A State of Nature: Readings in Vermont History*, second ed. (Montpelier: Vermont Historical Society, 1985), Appendix E: 407–410.

Notes:

[1] The governor's term was for one year from 1778 to 1870, and has been two years from 1870 to the present. Until 1912, general elections were held in September and governors were inaugurated in October. After 1912, governors were elected in November and inaugurated in January.

[2] Died in office, August 25, 1797.

[3] Lieutenant governor; acting governor on the death of Governor Chittenden. Served August 25 to October 16, 1797.

[4] Lieutenant governor; governor by reason of no election of governor by the people.

[5] Affiliated with the American Party ("Know Nothing"), elected as a Republican.

[6] Died in office, February 7, 1870.

[7] Lieutenant governor; governor by reason of the death of Governor Washburn.

[8] Resigned and appointed U.S. District Judge by President Truman, January 16, 1950.

[9] Lieutenant governor; became governor when Governor Gibson resigned, January 15, 1950.

[10] Died in office, August 14, 1991.

[11] Lieutenant governor; became governor when Governor Snelling died in office, August 14, 1991.

Appendix D

UNITED STATES REPRESENTATIVES

DATE[1]	DISTRICT	REPRESENTATIVE	HOME TOWN
1791	2 districts	Nathaniel Niles Israel Smith	West Fairlee Rutland
1792	2 districts	Nathaniel Niles Israel Smith	West Fairlee Rutland
1794	2 districts	Daniel Buck Israel Smith	Norwich Rutland
1796	2 districts	Lewis R. Morris Matthew Lyon	Springfield Fair Haven
1798	2 districts	Lewis R. Morris Matthew Lyon	Springfield Fair Haven
1800	2 districts	Lewis R. Morris Israel Smith	Springfield Rutland
1802	4 districts	William Chamberlain Martin Chittenden James Elliot Gideon Olin	Peacham Jericho Brattleboro Shaftsbury
1804	4 districts	James Fisk Martin Chittenden James Elliot Gideon Olin	Barre Jericho Brattleboro Shaftsbury
1806	4 districts	James Fisk Martin Chittenden James Elliot James Witherell[2]	Barre Jericho Brattleboro Fair Haven
1808	4 districts	William Chamberlain Martin Chittenden Jonathan H. Hubbard Samuel Shaw	Peacham Jericho Windsor Castleton
1810	4 districts	James Fisk Martin Chittenden William Strong Samuel Shaw	Barre Jericho Hartford Castleton
1812	6 at large	William Bradley Ezra Butler James Fisk Charles Rich Richard Skinner William Strong	Westminster Waterbury Barre Shoreham Manchester Hartford

APPENDIX D 633

UNITED STATES REPRESENTATIVES *(continued)*

DATE	DISTRICT	REPRESENTATIVE	HOME TOWN
1814	6 at large	Daniel Chipman	Middlebury
		Luther Jewett	St. Johnsbury
		Chauncey Langdon	Castleton
		Asa Lyon	Grand Isle
		Charles Marsh	Woodstock
		John Noyes	Brattleboro
1816	6 at large	Heman Allen	Colchester
		Samuel C. Crafts	Craftsbury
		William Hunter	Windsor
		Orsamus C. Merrill	Bennington
		Charles Rich	Shoreham
		Mark Richards	Westminster
1818	6 districts	Orsamus C. Merrill[3]	Bennington
		Mark Richards	Westminster
		Charles Rich	Shoreham
		William Strong	Hartford
		Ezra Meech	Shelburne
		Samuel C. Crafts	Craftsbury
1820	6 districts	Rollin C. Mallary	Poultney
		Phineas White	Putney
		Charles Rich	Shoreham
		Elias Keyes	Stockbridge
		John Mattocks	Peacham
		Samuel C. Crafts	Craftsbury
1822	5 districts	William C. Bradley	Westminster
		Rollin C. Mallary	Poultney
		Charles Rich[4]	Shoreham
		Samuel C. Crafts	Craftsbury
		D. Azro A. Buck	Chelsea
1824	5 districts	William C. Bradley	Westminster
		Rollin C. Mallary	Poultney
		George E. Wales	Hartford
		Ezra Meech	Shelburne
		John Mattocks	Peacham
1826	5 districts	Jonathan Hunt	Brattleboro
		Rollin C. Mallary	Poultney
		George E. Wales	Hartford
		Benjamin Swift	St. Albans
		D. Azro A. Buck	Chelsea

UNITED STATES REPRESENTATIVES *(continued)*

DATE	DISTRICT	REPRESENTATIVE	HOME TOWN
1828	5 districts	Jonathan Hunt	Brattleboro
		Rollin C. Mallary	Poultney
		Horace Everett	Windsor
		Benjamin Swift	St. Albans
		William Cahoon	Lyndon
1830	5 districts	Jonathan Hunt[5]	Brattleboro
		Rollin C. Mallary[6]	Poultney
		Horace Everett	Windsor
		Heman Allen	Burlington
		William Cahoon[7]	Lyndon
1832	5 districts (redefined)	Hiland Hall	Bennington
		William Slade	Middlebury
		Horace Everett	Windsor
		Heman Allen	Burlington
		Benjamin F. Deming[8]	Danville
1834	5 districts	Hiland Hall	Bennington
		William Slade	Middlebury
		Horace Everett	Windsor
		Heman Allen	Burlington
		Henry F. Janes	Waterbury
1836	5 districts	Hiland Hall	Bennington
		William Slade	Middlebury
		Horace Everett	Windsor
		Heman Allen	Burlington
		Isaac Fletcher	Lyndon
1838	5 districts	Hiland Hall	Bennington
		William Slade	Middlebury
		Horace Everett	Windsor
		John Smith	St. Albans
		Isaac Fletcher	Lyndon
1840	5 districts	Hiland Hall	Bennington
		William Slade	Middlebury
		Horace Everett	Windsor
		Augustus Young	Craftsbury
		John Mattocks	Peacham
1842	4 districts	Solomon Foot	Rutland
		Jacob Collamer	Woodstock
		George P. Marsh	Burlington
		Paul Dillingham	Waterbury

UNITED STATES REPRESENTATIVES *(continued)*

DATE	DISTRICT	REPRESENTATIVE	HOME TOWN
1844	4 districts	Solomon Foot	Rutland
		Jacob Collamer	Woodstock
		George P. Marsh	Burlington
		Paul Dillingham	Waterbury
1846	4 districts	William Henry	Rockingham
		Jacob Collamer	Woodstock
		George P. Marsh	Burlington
		Lucius B. Peck	Montpelier
1848	4 districts	William Henry	Rockingham
		William Hebard	Chelsea
		George P. Marsh[9]	Burlington
		Lucius B. Peck	Montpelier
1850	4 districts	Ahiman L. Miner	Manchester
		William Hebard	Chelsea
		James Meacham	Middlebury
		Thomas Bartlett, Jr.	Lyndon
1852	3 districts	James Meacham	Middlebury
		Andrew Tracy	Woodstock
		Alvah Sabin	Georgia
1854	3 districts	James Meacham[10]	Middlebury
		Justin S. Morrill	Strafford
		Alvah Sabin	Georgia
1856	3 districts	Eliakim P. Walton	Montpelier
		Justin S. Morrill	Strafford
		Homer E. Royce	St. Albans
1858	3 districts	Eliakim P. Walton	Montpelier
		Justin S. Morrill	Strafford
		Homer E. Royce	St. Albans
1860	3 districts	Eliakim P. Walton	Montpelier
		Justin S. Morrill	Strafford
		Portus Baxter	Derby
1862	3 districts	Frederick E. Woodbridge	Vergennes
		Justin S. Morrill	Strafford
		Portus Baxter	Derby
1864	3 districts	Frederick E. Woodbridge	Vergennes
		Justin S. Morrill	Strafford
		Portus Baxter	Derby

UNITED STATES REPRESENTATIVES *(continued)*

DATE	DISTRICT	REPRESENTATIVE	HOME TOWN
1866	3 districts	Frederick E. Woodbridge Luke P. Poland Worthington C. Smith	Vergennes St. Johnsbury St. Albans
1868	3 districts	Charles W. Willard Luke P. Poland Worthington C. Smith	Montpelier St. Johnsbury St. Albans
1870	3 districts	Charles W. Willard Luke P. Poland Worthington C. Smith	Montpelier St. Johnsbury St. Albans
1872	3 districts	Charles W. Willard Luke P. Poland George W. Hendee	Montpelier St. Johnsbury Morristown
1874	3 districts	Charles H. Joyce Dudley C. Dennison George W. Hendee	Rutland Royalton Morristown
1876	3 districts	Charles H. Joyce Dudley C. Dennison George W. Hendee	Rutland Royalton Morristown
1878	3 districts	Charles H. Joyce James M. Tyler Bradley Barlow	Rutland Brattleboro St. Albans
1880	3 districts	Charles H. Joyce James M. Tyler William W. Grout	Rutland Brattleboro Barton
1882	2 districts	John W. Stewart Luke P. Poland	Middlebury St. Johnsbury
1884	2 districts	John W. Stewart William W. Grout	Middlebury Barton
1886	2 districts	John W. Stewart William W. Grout	Middlebury Barton
1888	2 districts	John W. Stewart William W. Grout	Middlebury Barton
1890	2 districts	H. Henry Powers William W. Grout	Morristown Barton
1892	2 districts	H. Henry Powers William W. Grout	Morristown Barton

APPENDIX D 637

UNITED STATES REPRESENTATIVES *(continued)*

DATE	DISTRICT	REPRESENTATIVE	HOME TOWN
1894	2 districts	H. Henry Powers William W. Grout	Morristown Barton
1896	2 districts	H. Henry Powers William W. Grout	Morristown Barton
1898	2 districts	H. Henry Powers William W. Grout	Morristown Barton
1900	2 districts	David J. Foster Kittredge Haskins	Burlington Brattleboro
1902	2 districts	David J. Foster Kittredge Haskins	Burlington Brattleboro
1904	2 districts	David J. Foster Kittredge Haskins	Burlington Brattleboro
1906	2 districts	David J. Foster Kittredge Haskins	Burlington Brattleboro
1908	2 districts	David J. Foster Frank Plumley	Burlington Northfield
1910	2 districts	David J. Foster[11] Frank Plumley	Burlington Northfield
1912	2 districts	Frank L. Greene Frank Plumley	St. Albans Northfield
1914	2 districts	Frank L. Greene Porter H. Dale	St. Albans Island Pond
1916	2 districts	Frank L. Greene Porter H. Dale	St. Albans Island Pond
1918	2 districts	Frank L. Greene Porter H. Dale	St. Albans Island Pond
1920	2 districts	Frank L. Greene Porter H. Dale	St. Albans Island Pond
1922	2 districts	Frederick Fleetwood Porter H. Dale[12]	Morrisville Island Pond
1924	2 districts	Elbert S. Brigham Ernest W. Gibson, Sr.	St. Albans Brattleboro
1926	2 districts	Elbert S. Brigham Ernest W. Gibson, Sr.	St. Albans Brattleboro

UNITED STATES REPRESENTATIVES *(continued)*

DATE	DISTRICT	REPRESENTATIVE	HOME TOWN
1928	2 districts	Elbert S. Brigham	St. Albans
		Ernest W. Gibson, Sr.	Brattleboro
1930	2 districts	John E. Weeks	Middlebury
		Ernest W. Gibson, Sr.	Brattleboro
1932	1 district	Ernest W. Gibson, Sr.[13]	Brattleboro
1934–1950		Charles A. Plumley	Northfield
1950–1958		Winston L. Prouty	Newport City
1958–1960		William H. Meyer	West Rupert
1960–1971		Robert T. Stafford[14]	Rutland
1972–1974		Richard T. Mallary[15]	Fairlee
1974–1988		James M. Jeffords	Rutland
1988–1990		Peter P. Smith	Middlesex
1990–		Bernard Sanders	Burlington

Adapted, with permission, from H. Nicholas Muller III and Samuel B. Hand, eds., *In a State of Nature: Readings in Vermont History*, second ed. (Montpelier: Vermont Historical Society, 1985), Appendix G: 414–419.

Notes:

[1] Year of election.
[2] Resigned in 1808; replaced by Samuel Shaw, Castleton.
[3] Seat contested and awarded January 13, 1829, to Rollin C. Mallary, Poultney.
[4] Died October 15, 1824; seat filled by Henry Olin, Leicester.
[5] Died May 14, 1832; replaced by Hiland Hall, Bennington.
[6] Died April 15, 1831; replaced by William Slade, Middlebury.
[7] Died May 30, 1833; replaced by Benjamin F. Deming, Danville.
[8] Died July 11, 1834; replaced by Henry F. Janes, Waterbury.
[9] Appointed U. S. Minister to Turkey, 1849; replaced by James Meacham, Middlebury.
[10] Died August 23, 1856; replaced by George T. Hodges, Rutland.
[11] Died March 21, 1912; replaced by Frank L. Greene, St. Albans.
[12] Resigned 1923 to become U.S. Senator; replaced by Ernest W. Gibson, Sr., Brattleboro.
[13] Elected U.S. Senator in 1934; replaced by Charles A. Plumley, Northfield.
[14] Appointed U.S. Senator upon the death of Winston Prouty, September 16, 1971; seat left vacant until special election of January 7, 1972.
[15] Elected in a special election, January 7, 1972, to replace Robert T. Stafford.

Appendix E

UNITED STATES SENATORS (since 1791)*

Class 1	Class 3
1791–1797 Moses R. Robinson[1] Isaac Tichenor [1]	1791–1795 Stephen R. Bradley
1797–1803 Nathaniel Chipman[1]	1795–1801 Elijah Paine
1803–1809 Israel Smith[3] Jonathan Robinson[3]	1801–1807 Elijah Paine[2] Stephen R. Bradley[2]
1809–1815 Jonathan Robinson	1807–1813 Stephen R. Bradley
1815–1821 Isaac Tichenor	1813–1819 Dudley Chase[4] James Fish[4,5] William A. Palmer[5]
1821–1827 Horatio Seymour	1819–1825 William A. Palmer
1827–1833 Horatio Seymour	1825–1831 Dudley Chase
1833–1839 Benjamin Swift	1831–1837 Samuel Prentiss
1839–1845 Samuel S. Phelps	1837–1843 Samuel Prentiss[6] Samuel C. Crafts[6]
1845-1851 Samuel S. Phelps	1843–1849 William Upham
1851–1857 Solomon Foot	1849–1855 William Upham[7] Samuel S. Phelps[7] Lawrence Brainerd[7]
1857–1863 Solomon Foot	1855–1861 Jacob Collamer
1863–1869 Solomon Foot[9] George F. Edmunds[9]	1861–1867 Jacob Collamer[8] Luke P. Poland[8]

*Article 1, section 3, paragraph 2 of the U.S. Constitution provides a mechanism for dividing the members of the U.S. Senate into three groups, which it calls "classes," to accommodate the requirement that one-third of the Senate shall be elected every two years. The two senators from each state are assigned to different classes so that their terms will stagger rather than ending simultaneously. Vermont's two senators belong to Class 1 and Class 3.

UNITED STATES SENATORS (since 1791) *(continued)*

Class 1	Class 3
1869–1875 George F. Edmunds	1867–1873 Justin S. Morrill
1875–1881 George F. Edmunds	1873–1879 Justin S. Morrill
1881–1887 George F. Edmunds	1879–1885 Justin S. Morrill
1887–1893 George F. Edmunds[10] Redfield Proctor[10]	1885–1891 Justin S. Morrill
1893–1899 Redfield Proctor	1891–1897 Justin S. Morrill
1899–1905 Redfield Proctor	1897–1903 Justin S. Morrill[11] Jonathan Ross[11] William P. Dillingham[11]
1905–1911 Redfield Proctor[12] John W. Stewart[12] Carroll S. Page[12]	1903–1909 William P. Dillingham
1911–1917 Carroll S. Page	1909–1915 William P. Dillingham
1917–1923 Carroll S. Page	1915–1921 William P. Dillingham[13]
1923–1929 Frank L. Greene	1921–1927 William P. Dillingham[14] Porter H. Dale[14]
1929–1935 Frank L. Greene[15] Frank C. Partridge[15] Warren R. Austin[15]	1927–1933 Porter H. Dale
1935–1941 Warren R. Austin	1933–1939 Porter H. Dale[16] Ernest W. Gibson[16]
1941–1947 Warren R. Austin	1939–1945 Ernest W. Gibson[17] Ernest W. Gibson, Jr.[17] George D. Aiken[17]

UNITED STATES SENATORS (since 1791) *(continued)*

Class 1	Class 3
1947–1953 Ralph E. Flanders	1945–1951 George D. Aiken
1953–1959 Ralph E. Flanders	1951–1957 George D. Aiken
1959–1965 Winston L. Prouty	1957–1963 George D. Aiken
1965–1971 Winston L. Prouty	1963–1969 George D. Aiken
1971–1977 Winston L. Prouty[18] Robert T. Stafford	1969–1975 George D. Aiken
1977–1983 Robert T. Stafford	1975–1981 Patrick J. Leahy
1983–1989 Robert T. Stafford	1981–1987 Patrick J. Leahy
1989–1995 James M. Jeffords	1987–1993 Patrick J. Leahy
1995–2001 James M. Jeffords	1993–1999 Patrick J. Leahy
2001– James M. Jeffords	1999– Patrick J. Leahy

Adapted, with permission, from H. Nicholas Muller III and Samuel B. Hand, eds., *In a State of Nature: Readings in Vermont History*, second ed. (Montpelier: Vermont Historical Society, 1985), Appendix H: 420–423.

Notes:

[1] Robinson resigned on October 15, 1796. Tichenor was elected on October 18, 1796, for the balance of the term, but resigned in 1797 to become governor of Vermont; Chipman was elected to fill the vacancy.

[2] Paine resigned to become U.S. District Judge for the District of Vermont; Bradley was elected in 1801 to fill the vacancy.

[3] Smith resigned to become governor in 1807; Robinson was elected October 10, 1807.

[4] Chase resigned in 1817 to become Chief Judge of the Vermont Supreme Court; Fish was elected November 4, 1817.

[5] Fish resigned January 29, 1818, to be Collector of Customs for Vermont; Palmer was elected October 20, 1818, for the balance of the term.

[6] Prentiss resigned April 11, 1842, to become U.S. Judge for the District of Vermont; Crafts was appointed pending an election, and was elected October 26, 1842, for the balance of the term.

[7] Upham died January 14, 1853; Phelps was appointed on a temporary basis. After twenty-two inconclusive ballots, the legislature could not elect a successor and resolved to wait until the following session to fill the vacancy; Brainerd was elected October 14, 1854.

[8] Collamer died November 9, 1865; Poland was appointed November 21, 1865, and elected October 23, 1866, for the balance of the term.

[9] Foot died March 28, 1866; Edmunds was appointed April 5, 1866, and elected October 23, 1866, for the balance of the term.

[10] Edmunds resigned in November 1891; Proctor was appointed pending an election and was elected October 18, 1892, for the balance of the term.

[11] Morrill died December 28, 1898; Ross was appointed January 16, 1899, pending an election; Dillingham was elected October 18, 1900, for the balance of the term.

[12] Proctor died March 4, 1908; Stewart was appointed March 24, 1908, pending an election; Page was elected October 20, 1908, for the balance of the term.

[13] Last Senate election by the legislature; first Senator elected in a popular election, following ratification of Amendment XVII to the U.S. Constitution (1913).

[14] Dillingham died July 12, 1923; Dale was elected November 6, 1923.

[15] Greene died December 17, 1930; Partridge was appointed pending an election; Austin was elected March 31, 1931, for the balance of the term.

[16] Dale died October 6, 1933; Gibson was elected January 16, 1934.

[17] Gibson died June 20, 1940. Gibson, Jr., was appointed pending an election. Aiken was elected November 5, 1940.

[18] Prouty died September 10, 1971; Stafford was appointed September 16, 1971, pending a special election. Stafford was elected January 7, 1971, to fill the unexpired term.

Notes

Introduction

1 Thomas Day Seymour Bassett, *Vermont: A Bibliography of Its History*, volume four of *Bibliography of New England History* (Boston: G. K. Hall, 1981; reprint, Hanover, N.H.: University Press of New England, 1983), xix.

2 Peter S. Onuf, "Vermont and the Union," in Michael Sherman, ed., *A More Perfect Union: Vermont Becomes a State, 1777–1816* (Montpelier: Vermont Historical Society, 1991), 150–169.

3 See Michael Sherman and Jennie Versteeg, "The Character of Vermont, Then and Now," in Center for Research on Vermont, *The Character of Vermont: Twentieth-Anniversary Reflections*, Occasional Paper no.19 (Burlington: Center for Research on Vermont, University of Vermont, 1996), 1–44.

4 See press report clippings in the "Bicentennial debates" folder, records of the Vermont Statehood Bicentennial Commission, Vermont State Archives, Montpelier, Vermont.

5 Dorothy Canfield Fisher, "Vermonters," in *Vermont: A Guide to the Green Mountain State*, American Guide Series (Boston: Houghton Mifflin Company, 1937), 9.

6 Joyce Appleby, "Recovering America's Historic Diversity: Beyond Exceptionalism," *Journal of American History* 79 (September 1992): 430.

7 Alexis de Tocqueville, *Democracy in America*, trans. George Lawrence, ed. J. P. Mayer (Garden City, N.Y.: Doubleday, 1969) 1: 61.

Chapter 1
Footprints: Prehistory to 1609

1 For a more detailed discussion of these land-forming events, see Charles W. Johnson, *The Nature of Vermont: Introduction and Guide to a New England Environment* (Hanover, N.H.: University Press of New England, 1980), 5–38; Harold A. Meeks, *Vermont's Land and Resources* (Shelburne, Vt.: New England Press, 1986), 3–70; Bradford B. Van Diver, *Roadside Geology of Vermont and New Hampshire* (Missoula, Mont.: Mountain Press Publishing Company, 1987), 1–49 et passim.

2 See Philip Johnson, "The Bones with No Name," *Vermont History News* 44 (March–April 1993): 21–26.

3 Because the focus here is on native people, we use the abbreviations B.C.E. (before the common era) and C.E. (common era) for prehistoric, precontact, and postcontact dates. Beginning with the subsequent section, the reader can assume that the dating system is the more familiar A.D. On systems for archaeological dating, radiocarbon dating, and terminology, see William A. Haviland and Marjory W. Power, *The Original Vermonters: Native Inhabitants, Past and Present*, revised and expended edition (Hanover, N.H.: University Press of New England, 1994), 11–14; Peter A.

Thomas, "Vermont's Prehistoric Cultural Heritage," in *Vermont Historic Preservation Plan* (Montpelier: Division for Historic Preservation, 1991), 1.4–1.5.

4   Haviland and Power, *The Original Vermonters*, 125.

5   Ibid., 144–145; William A. Haviland, note to author, 1998.

6   William Cronon, *Changes in the Land: Indians, Colonists, and the Ecology of New England* (New York: Hill and Wang, 1983), 41–42.

7   Jared Diamond, *Guns, Germs, and Steel: The Fates of Human Societies* (New York: W. W. Norton, 1997), 83–113.

8   See Cronon, *Changes in the Land*, 34–53.

9   William A. Haviland and Marjory W. Power, "A New Look at Vermont's Oldest Art: Understanding the Bellows Falls Petroglyphs," *Vermont History* 62 (Fall 1994): 197–213.

10 For a more detailed description of the cycle, see Haviland and Power, *The Original Vermonters*, 159–168; Cronon, *Changes in the Land*, 39–40; Gordon M. Day, "The Western Abenaki," in Bruce G. Trigger, ed., *Northeast. Handbook of North American Indians*, ed. William C. Sturtevant, vol. 15 (Washington, D.C.: Smithsonian Institution, 1978), 153–154. Cronon concentrates on the coastal Indians, but his account traces a cycle of food gathering similar to the inland pattern described by Haviland and Power. For a story about maple sugar making see "Gluskabe and the Maple Trees," in Joseph Bruchac, *The Faithful Hunter: Abenaki Stories* (Greenfield Center, N.Y.: Greenfield Review Press, 1988), 15–17.

11 For Indian place names see John C. Huden, *Indian Place Names in Vermont* (Burlington, Vt.: n.p., 1957); Day, "The Western Abenaki"; Cronon, *Changes in the Land*, 65–66; Gordon M. Day, "Abenaki Place Names in the Champlain Valley," *International Journal of American Linguistics* 47 (1981): 143–171, reprinted in Gordon M. Day, *In Search of New England's Native Past: Essays by Gordon M. Day*, ed. Michael K. Foster and William Cowan (Amherst: University of Massachusetts Press, 1998), 229–262. Cronon explains that most Indian place names in New England "related not to possession but to use.... The purpose of such names was to turn the landscape into a map, which, if studied carefully, literally gave a village's inhabitants the information they needed to sustain themselves."

12 See Haviland and Power, *The Original Vermonters*, 159. Colin G. Calloway reports current reasonable guesses of the precontact population of Western Abenaki in Vermont and New Hampshire as "at least 10,000 people": 2,000 in the upper Merrimack drainage, 3,800 in the upper Connecticut River valley, and 4,200 in the Champlain Valley. Colin G. Calloway, *The Western Abenakis of Vermont, 1600–1800: War, Migration, and the Survival of an Indian People* (Norman: University of Oklahoma Press, 1990), 39.

13 For summaries of the early European voyages to North America, see Samuel Eliot Morison, *The European Discovery of America: The Northern Voyages, A.D. 500–1600* (New York: Oxford University Press, 1971), and David B. Quinn, *North America from Earliest Discovery to First Settlements: The Norse Voyages to 1612* (New York: Harper & Row, 1977). Many of the earliest accounts of European voyages were collected and published by Richard Hakluyt (1552–1616) under the title *The Principal Navigations, Voyages, Traffiques & Discoveries of the English Nation* (first edition, 1589; second edition 1598–1560). Although focused on English exploits, Hakluyt

includes many accounts written by French, Spanish, and Dutch explorers. See James F. Pendergast, "Native Encounters with Europeans in the Sixteenth Century in the Region Now Known as Vermont," *Vermont History* 58 (Spring 1990): 103-107.

14 For the identity of the Stadacona Indians see Bruce G. Trigger and James F. Pendergast, "Saint Lawrence Iroquoians," in *Handbook of North American Indians*, 15: 357-361.

15 Marcel Trudell, *The Beginnings of New France* (Toronto: University of Toronto Press, 1973), 98-99.

16 The North American fur trade was in important respects an extension of a much older feature of European and Asian economic life. In ancient Rome and as late as the eighteenth century Scandinavian furs moved across the continent and east into Russia and the Islamic Levant. North American furs, especially beaver, offered France, England, and Holland opportunities to break the monopoly of Scandinavian suppliers. Beaver hats became increasingly popular during the sixteenth century—replacing wool caps in England, Spain, and the Netherlands—and demand for beaver fur soon led to the near extinction of the animals in Europe. See Eric R. Wolf, *Europe and the People without History* (Berkeley: University of California Press, 1982), 158-194. The literature on the effects of Amerindian contact with Europeans is enormous and growing. For an excellent summary, with emphasis on the changes brought about by the fur trade, see T. J. Brasser, "Early Indian-European Contact," in Trigger, ed., *Northeast Handbook of North American Indians*, 15: 78-88.

17 Samuel de Champlain, *The Works of Samuel de Champlain in Six Volumes*, ed. H. P. Biggar (Toronto: Champlain Society, 1922-1936), 2: 90-93; also in T. D. Seymour Bassett, ed., *Outsiders Inside Vermont: Three Centuries of Visitors' Viewpoints on the Green Mountain State* (Canaan, N.H.: Phoenix Publishing, 1967), 3-7.

18 See Haviland and Power, *The Original Vermonters*, 1.

19 See Gordon M. Day, "Abenakis in the Lake Champlain Valley," in Jennie Versteeg, ed., *Lake Champlain: Reflections on Our Past* (Burlington: University of Vermont, 1987), 277-288; Trigger and Pendergast, "Saint Lawrence Iroquoians"; Haviland and Power, *The Original Vermonters*, 152; Calloway, *Western Abenakis of Vermont*, 57.

20 See Calloway, *Western Abenakis of Vermont*, 57; Quinn, *North America from Earliest Discovery to First Settlement*, 476-477.

21 Haviland and Power, *The Original Vermonters*, 181-182; Alan Nelson, *American Colonies* (New York: Viking, 2001), 102.

22 See the following articles in Trigger, ed., *Handbook of North American Indians*, vol. 15: Brasser, "Early Indian-European Contact"; Bruce G. Trigger, "Early Iroquoian Contact with Europeans," 344-356; see also Trigger and Pendergast, "Saint Lawrence Iroquoians."

23 See George I. Quimby, *Indian Culture and European Trade Goods* (Madison: University of Wisconsin Press, 1966); Bruce G. Trigger, "Early Native North American Responses to European Contact: Romantic versus Rationalistic Interpretations," *The Journal of American History* 77 (March 1991): 1195-1215; Brasser, "Early Indian-European Contact," 86-88.

24 Wolf, *Europe and the People without History*, 193.

25 For a summary of the arguments linking present-day Abenaki to the Vergennes Archaic people, see Haviland and Power, *The Original Vermonters*, 203; Day, "Abenakis in the Lake Champlain Valley."

Chapter 2
Struggle for Empire, the Vermont Crossroad: 1609-1763

1. Samuel de Champlain, *The Works of Samuel de Champlain in Six Volumes*, ed. H. P. Biggar (Toronto: Champlain Society, 1922-1936) 2: 91-93.
2. See *Works of Champlain*, volume 1.
3. Ibid., 2: 71.
4. Ibid., 2: 100.
5. Francis Jennings, *The Invasion of America: Indians, Colonialism, and the Cant of Conquest* (Chapel Hill: University of North Carolina Press, 1975), 97.
6. William Bradford, *Of Plymouth Plantation*, ed. Harvey Wish (New York: Capricorn Books, 1962), 64.
7. Reuben Gold Thwaites, ed.. *The Jesuit Relations and Allied Documents: Travels and Explorations of the Jesuit Missionaries in New France, 1610-1791* (Cleveland: The Burrows Brothers Company, 1896-1901), 33: 68-69.
8. Guy Omeron Coolidge, *The French Occupation of the Champlain Valley from 1609 to 1759* (1938; second ed., Mamaroneck, N.Y.: Harbor Hill Books, 1989), 17-18.
9. James Axtell, *The Invasion Within: The Contest of Cultures in Colonial North America* (New York: Oxford University Press, 1985), 86.
10. Thwaites, ed., *Jesuit Relations*, 24: 295.
11. Ibid., 24: 297.
12. Marcel Trudel, *The Beginnings of New France, 1524-1663*, trans. Patricia Claxton (Toronto: McClennand and Stewart, 1973), 220-221.
13. Colin Calloway, *The Western Abenakis of Vermont, 1600-1800: War, Migration, and the Survival of an Indian People* (Norman: University of Oklahoma Press, 1990), 68.
14. Francis Parkman, *The Old Regime in Canada* (Boston: Little, Brown, and Company, 1874), 186.
15. Thwaites, ed., *Jesuit Relations*, 50: 131.
16. Jill Lepore, *The Name of War: King Philip's War and the Origins of American Identity* (New York: Alfred A. Knopf, 1998), 118.
17. Ibid., 167.
18. Calloway, *Western Abenakis of Vermont*, 79.
19. Alden T. Vaughan and Edward W. Clark, eds., *Puritans among the Indians: Accounts of Captivity and Redemption, 1676-1724* (Cambridge: Harvard University Press, 1981), 1.
20. Charles H. Lincoln, ed., *Narratives of the Indian Wars, 1675-1699* (New York: Charles Scribner's Sons, 1913), 116.
21. James D. Drake, *King Philip's War: Civil War in New England, 1675-1676* (Amherst: University of Massachusetts Press, 1999), 134.
22. Barbara E. Austen, "Captured, Never Came Back: Social Networks among New England Female Captives in Canada, 1689-1763," in Peter Benes, ed., *New England/New France, 1600-1850*, Dublin Seminar for New England Folklife, vol. 14 (Boston: Boston University Press, 1992), 29.
23. Colonel John Schuyler's 1713 encounter with Eunice Williams quoted in Emma Lewis Coleman, *New England Captives Carried to Canada* (Portland, Maine: Southworth Press, 1925), 2: 56-57. For a recent and imaginative retelling of Eunice Williams's story see John Demos, *The Unredeemed Captive: A Family Story from Early America* (New York: Alfred A. Knopf, 1994).

24 Francis Parkman, *Count Frontenac and New France under Louis XIV* (Boston: Little, Brown and Company, 1913), 224.
25 John Williams, *The Redeemed Captive*, ed. Edward W. Clark (Amherst: The University of Massachusetts Press, 1976), 44-52.
26 Benjamin H. Hall, *History of Eastern Vermont, from its Early Settlement to the Close of the Eighteenth Century* (New York: D. Appleton & Co., 1858), 15.
27 Calloway, *Western Abenakis of Vermont*, 131.
28 Hall, *History of Eastern Vermont*, 23, 18.
29 For most of the information about the habitation at Fort St. Frédéric, the authors are indebted to Joseph-André Senécal, who has examined official records of the fort, census and parish records, and death inventories to acquire detailed knowledge of the material life of the seigneurie and who generously shared that information in conversation. Professor Senécal is currently working on a monograph about the fort and *habitation*.
30 Peter Kalm, *Peter Kalm's Travels in North America. From the English Version of 1770*, ed. Adolph B. Benson (Mineola, N.Y.: Dover, 1987; reprint of 2 vol. ed., 1937), 379-380. Senécal reports that the records of the King's store include an inventory of 2,000 panes of glass in the 1740s.
31 Ibid., 395.
32 Coolidge, *French Occupation of the Champlain Valley*, 132-133.
33 Kalm, *Peter Kalm's Travels*, 395. For details of the grants and summaries of the history of each of the Lake Champlain *seigneuries* see Coolidge, *French Occupation of the Champlain Valley*, 85-115.
34 For detailed accounts of this period see the classic work of Francis Parkman, *France and England in North America. A Series of Historical Narratives* (Boston: Little, Brown), Part 6: *A Half Century of Conflict* (1892) and Part 7: *Montcalme and Wolfe* (1884); abridged in Samuel Eliot Morison, ed., *The Francis Parkman Reader* (New York: DaCapo Press, 1998). W.J. Eccles, *France in America* (revised ed., Markham, Ont.: Fitzhenry & Whiteside, 1990), 125-156 and 188-222 offers a Canadian perspective and one more sympathetic to the French. Fred Anderson, *The Crucible War: The Seven Years War and the Fate of Empire in British North America, 1754-1766* (New York: Alfred A. Knopf, 2001), examines the war from an American perspective.
35 Calloway, *Western Abenakis of Vermont*, 163.
36 Ibid., 171.
37 Arthur Quinn, *A New World: An Epic of Colonial America from the Founding of Jamestown to the Fall of Quebec* (New York: Berkley Books, 1995), 493.
38 "To Major Hawk of the Massachusett's Forces and Coll. Ruggle's first Battalion," quoted in Flora B. Weeks, "Crown Point Road History: In 1759 a 'New Road,'" in Crown Point Road Association, *Historical Markers on the Crown Point Road, Vermont's First Road*, rev. ed. (Rutland, Vt.: Crown Point Road Association, 1992), 5.
39 *Journals of Major Robert Rogers* (1765), excerpt in J. Kevin Graffagnino, Samuel B. Hand, and Gene Sessions, eds., *Vermont Voices, 1609 Through the 1990s: A Documentary History of the Green Mountain State* (Montpelier: Vermont Historical Society, 1999), 24.
40 Gordon M. Day, "Oral Tradition as Complement [1962]," in Day, *In Search of New England's Native Past: Essays by Gordon M. Day*, ed. Michael K. Foster and William Cowan (Amherst: University of Massachusetts Press, 1998), 127-135.
41 Calloway, *Western Abenakis of Vermont*, 175-177.

Chapter 3
The Lure of the Land: 1763-1807

1 E. B. O'Callaghan, ed., *The Documentary History of the State of New-York* (Albany, N.Y.: Charles Van Benthuysen, 1851), 4: 574-575. See also J. Kevin Graffagnino, Samuel B. Hand, and Gene Sessions, eds., *Vermont Voices, 1609 Through the 1990s A Documentary History of the Green Mountain State* (Montpelier: Vermont Historical Society, 1999), 35-37; Michael A. Bellesiles, *Revolutionary Outlaws: Ethan Allen and the Struggle for Independence on the Early American Frontier* (Charlottesville: University Press of Virginia, 1993): 31-32.

2 J. Kevin Graffagnino, "The Vermont 'Story': Continuity and Change in Vermont Historiography," *Vermont History* 46 (Spring 1978): 95.

3 See Charles A. Jellison, *Ethan Allen: Frontier Rebel* (Syracuse, N.Y.: Syracuse University Press, 1969), vii. See also Bellesiles, *Revolutionary Outlaws*.

4 T. D. Seymour Bassett, ed., *Vermont: A Bibliography of Its History*, volume 4 of *Bibliographies of New England History* (Boston: G. K. Hall, 1981; reprint, Hanover, N.H.: University Press of New England, 1983), "Foreword," xix. For additional comments on this concept, see Michael Sherman, "Brickyards and Frameworks: A Retrospectus and Prospectus on Vermont History Writing," *Vermont History* 71 (Winter/Spring 2003): 11-45, esp. 12-14.

5 Irving Mark, *Agrarian Conflicts in Colonial New York, 1711-1775* (1940; 2nd ed., Port Washington, N.Y.: Ira J. Friedman, Inc., 1965), 99.

6 Patricia U. Bonomi, *A Factious People: Politics and Society in Colonial New York* (New York: Columbia University Press, 1971), 203.

7 Mark, *Agrarian Conflicts in Colonial New York*, 66, 104.

8 See Walter Hill Crockett, *Vermont, The Green Mountain State,* (New York: The Century History Co., 1921-1923), 1: 293-297.

9 Report of Board of Trade, 24 July 1767, in O'Callaghan, ed., *Documentary History of New-York*, 4: 609-611.

10 Matt B. Jones, *Vermont in the Making, 1750-1777* (Cambridge, Mass.: Harvard University Press, 1939) and Chilton Williamson, *Vermont in Quandary: 1763-1825* (Montpelier: Vermont Historical Society, 1949) provide the most detailed information on early population. Williamson (p. 14) mentions that in 1762 there were roughly 70 families in 12 towns east of the Green Mountains and 50 west. Jones cites a letter from Gov. Sir Henry Moore to Lord Hillsborough, dated July 6, 1768, in which he sent an agent to count people in 1767, indicating there were 366 resident families in the east and 205 in the west (for a total of 571 families); in 1768, the numbers were 323 in the west, 476 in the east (799 families). Jones goes on to speculate, working backward to 1765, that there may have been between 425 and 475 families total in the Grants in 1765 (p. 87). For the 1771 figure, see Lewis D. Stilwell, *Migration from Vermont* (Montpelier: Vermont Historical Society, 1948; reprint Montpelier and Rutland, Vt.: Academy Books, 1983), 70, fn 31. Stilwell cites a source with a 1771 census count of 4,300 east of the mountains and arrives at an estimate of 7,000 for the whole state. Genieve Lamson, *Geographic Influences in the Early History of Vermont* (Montpelier: Vermont Historical Society, 1922), p. 97, refers to either 4,667 or 4,669 (that's Williamson's number, p. 14) that were actually counted by New York in a survey done on the eastern side of the state in 1771. Lamson reports that "early historians estimate that about two-thirds of the people

living in the state were in those (Gloucester and Cumberland) counties" and set the whole population at about 7,000. She uses Samuel Williams, *History of Vermont*, (1794), 410–411, as her source for this estimate.
11 Jellison, *Ethan Allen*, 7.
12 Bellesiles, *Revolutionary Outlaws*, 86, 87.
13 Benjamin H. Hall, *History of Eastern Vermont, From its Earliest Settlement to the Close of the Eighteenth Century* (New York: D. Appleton & Co., 1858), 169.
14 "Petition of the Inhabitants of Gloucester and Cumberland," 26 January 1773, O'Callaghan, ed., *Documentary History of the State of New-York*, 4: 821–824.
15 Edwin A. Bayley, "An Address Commemorative of the Life and Public Services of Brig. Gen. Jacob Bayley," *Proceedings of the Vermont Historical Society, 1917–1918* (Montpelier, Vt., 1920): 62, 67.
16 See Donald Alan Smith, "Legacy of Dissent: Religion and Politics in Revolutionary Vermont" (Ph.D. diss., Clark University, 1980); Smith, "Green Mountain Insurgency: Transformation of New York's Forty-Year Land War," *Vermont History* 64 (Fall, 1996): 197–235.
17 Mark, *Agrarian Conflicts in Colonial New York*, 124.
18 Jones, *Vermont in the Making*, 287.
19 O'Callaghan, ed., *Documentary History of New-York*, 4: 792–793.
20 Cockburn letter to James Duane, quoted in Hiland Hall, *The History of Vermont From Its Discovery to Its Admission into the Union in 1791* (Albany, N.Y.: Joel Munsell, 1868), 130.
21 Edwin P. Hoyt, *The Damndest Yankees: Ethan Allen and His Clan* (Brattleboro, Vt.: The Stephen Greene Press, 1976), 76.
22 O'Callaghan, ed., *Documentary History of New-York*, 4: 897.
23 "New York's 'Bloody Act'" (1774), in Graffagnino et al., *Vermont Voices*, 43–44.
24 Ethan Allen, et al., "Yankee Response to the 'Bloody Act'" (1774), ibid., 44–47.
25 Jellison, *Ethan Allen*, 91–92, 94.
26 Reuben Jones, "A Relation of the Proceedings of the People of the County of Cumberland, and Province of New York," 25 March 1775, in Graffagnino, et al., *Vermont Voices*, 47–49.
27 Ibid., 49; Hall, *History of Eastern Vermont*, 222.
28 Hall, History of Eastern Vermont, 239–240.
29 Ethan Allen, *A Narrative of Colonel Ethan Allen's Captivity, Containing His Voyages & Travels* [1779] (1930; reprint, Rutland, Vt.: Vermont Heritage Press, 1988), 5.
30 Ibid., 8. For the "damned British rat" quotation, see Bellesiles, *Revolutionary Outlaws*, 118. Also, see Bellesiles's footnote 16, p. 325, for discussion of the confusion over what Allen actually said. The Allens make no mention of this. The Rev. Josiah F. Goodhue, in his *History of the Town of Shoreham, Vermont* (Middlebury, Vt.: A. H. Copeland, 1861), p. 14, asserts that Allen's actual statement was: "What shall I do with the damned rascal? Shall I put him under guard?"
31 Willard Sterne Randall, *Benedict Arnold: Patriot and Traitor* (New York: William Morrow, 1990), 105.
32 Jellison, *Ethan Allen*, 160.
33 Washington quoted in Washington Irving, *Life of George Washington*, ed. Allen Guttmann and James A. Sappenfield (Boston: Twayne Publishers, 1982), 2: 322.
34 Hall, *History of Eastern Vermont*, 246–247.

35 Jones, *Vermont in the Making*, 364.
36 Cynthia A. Kierner, *Traders and Gentlefolk: The Livingstons of New York, 1675–1790* (Ithaca, N.Y.: Cornell University Press, 1992), 208.
37 Eliakim P. Walton, ed., *Records of the Governor and Council of Vermont*, 8 vols. (Montpelier: J. & J. M. Poland, 1873–1800), 1: 30–31, 375.
38 Ira Allen, "Some Miscellaneous Remarks," reprinted in ibid., 1: 388–389.
39 See "In Congress," 15 May 1776, in Michael Sherman, ed., *A More Perfect Union: Vermont Becomes a State, 1777–1816* (Montpelier: Vermont Historical Society and Vermont Statehood Bicentennial Commission, 1991), 188.
40 Thomas Young, "To the Inhabitants of Vermont, a Free and Independent State, bounding on the River Connecticut and Lake Champlain" (Philadelphia, 11 April 1777), in ibid., 189.
41 Ibid., 190. Concerning states that had written constitutions before Vermont, Gordon S. Wood writes: "By the end of 1776, New Jersey, Delaware, Pennsylvania, Maryland, and North Carolina had adopted new constitutions. Because they were corporate chartered colonies, Rhode Island and Connecticut were already republics in fact, and thus they simply confined themselves to eliminating all mention of royal authority in their charters. War conditions forced Georgia and New York to delay their constitution-making until 1777. Massachusetts had recovered its old charter, which the British had abolished in 1774, and was busy preparing to write a more permanent constitution." Gordon S. Wood, *The American Revolution: A History* (New York: Modern Library, 2002), 65–66.
42 *Vermont Constitution* (1777), [Preamble]. The preamble is no longer printed as part of the Vermont Constitution. It was eliminated from the text in 1786.
43 Bernard Bailyn, *The Ideological Origins of the American Revolution* (Cambridge, Mass.: Harvard University Press, 1967), 197.
44 Wood, *The American Revolution*, 128. Wood writes that "[B]y 1804 every northern state had committed itself to emancipation in one form or another," and historian Eric Foner notes that "during the 1780s in the North, every state from New Hampshire to Pennsylvania took steps toward emancipation." Eric Foner, *The Story of American Freedom* (New York: Norton, 1998), 35.
45 See Andrew E. Nuquist and Edith W. Nuquist, *Vermont State Government and Administration: An Historical and Descriptive Study of the Living Past* (Burlington: Government Research Center, University of Vermont, 1966), 29.
46 *Vermont Constitution* (1777), Chapter II, Section XLIV.
47 H. Nicholas Muller III, "Early Vermont State Government: Oligarchy or Democracy?, 1778–1815," in H. Nicholas Muller III and Samuel B. Hand, eds., *In a State of Nature: Readings in Vermont History* (Montpelier: Vermont Historical Society, 1982), 80–81; John N. Shaeffer, "A Comparison of the First Constitutions of Vermont and Pennsylvania," *Vermont History* 43 (Winter 1975): 37; Gary Aichele, "Making the Vermont Constitution, 1777–1824," in Sherman, ed., *A More Perfect Union*, 15–17.
48 Chapter I, Article 3. This limitation was removed in the revision of 1793. The Vermont Constitution has been amended on sixteen occasions. The first two of those, in 1786 and 1793, resulted in what legislators called new versions. Thus writers on Vermont's constitutional history refer to the "constitutions" of 1777, 1786, and 1793, when the preamble was removed by omission. Beginning in 1828,

changes in the 1793 version of the constitution have been recorded as amendments.
49 Andrew E. Nuquist, *Town Government in Vermont or "Making Democracy 'Democ'"* (Burlington: Government Research Center, University of Vermont, 1964), 4; John Fairfield Shy, *Town Government in Massachusetts, 1620-1930* (Cambridge, Mass.: Harvard University Press, 1930), 28-31.
50 See James H. Douglas and Paul S. Gillies, *A Book of Opinions*, 2 vols. (Montpelier: Office of the Secretary of State, 1992), 2: 673-674.
51 Nuquist, *Town Government in Vermont*, 6-7.
52 See Jack N. Rakove, *Original Meanings: Politics and Ideas in the Making of the Constitution* (New York: Knopf, 1997), 97.
53 Irving, *Life of George Washington*, 3: 59.
54 Richard M. Ketchum, *Saratoga: Turning Point of America's Revolutionary War* (New York: Henry Holt and Company, 1997), 330.
55 Chilton Williamson, *Vermont in Quandary, 1763-1825* (Montpelier: Vermont Historical Society, 1949), 69.
56 Ibid., 72.
57 *New Hampshire Provincial and State Papers* (Concord, N.H.: Edward A. Jenks, 1874), 8: 424.
58 *Records of the Governor and Council of Vermont*, 1: 426, 415-416.
59 William Doyle, *The Vermont Political Tradition and Those Who Helped Make It* (Barre, Vt.: The Author, 1984), 35.
60 O'Callaghan, ed., *Documentary History of New-York*, 4: 965-966.
61 Jellison, *Ethan Allen*, 224, 225.
62 *Records of the Governor and Council of Vermont*, 1: 524.
63 William Slade, ed., *Vermont State Papers* (Middlebury, Vt.: J. W. Copeland, 1823), 120.
64 Henry Steele Wardner, "The Haldimand Negotiations," *Proceedings of the Vermont Historical Society* 2 (1931): 16.
65 "Journal of Captain Justus Sherwood," *Vermont History* 24 (April 1956): 102.
66 *Records of the Governor and Council of Vermont*, 2: 91.
67 Ibid., 2: 407.
68 Jellison, *Ethan Allen*, 257.
69 Williamson, *Vermont in Quandary*, 104-105.
70 Wardner, "The Haldimand Negotiations," 22.
71 *Collections of the Vermont Historical Society* (Montpelier: Vermont Historical Society, 1871), 2: 228, 269.
72 John Page, "The Economic Structure of Society in Revolutionary Bennington," *Vermont History* 49 (Spring 1981): 72, 75.
73 T. D. Seymour Bassett, ed., *Outsiders Inside Vermont: Travelers' Tales Over 358 Years* (Brattleboro, Vt.: The Stephen Greene Press, 1967), 35, 39.
74 Seth Hubbell, *A Narrative of the Sufferings of Seth Hubbell & Family* (1824; reprint, Bennington, Vt.: Vermont Heritage Press, 1986), 4, 7, 8, 10, 25, 24.
75 Miriam Herwig and Wes Herwig, eds., *Jonathan Carpenter's Journal. Being the Diary of a Revolutionary War Soldier and Pioneer Settler of Vermont* (Randolph Center, Vt.: Greenhill Books, 1994), 84-107; quotation at 99.
76 Rev. Nathan Perkins, *A Narrative of a Tour through the State of Vermont from April 27 to June 12, 1789* (Rutland, Vt.: Charles E. Tuttle, 1964), 18-19, 24, 23, 33, 37.

77 Frank Smallwood, *Thomas Chittenden: Vermont's First Statesman* (Shelburne, Vt.: The New England Press, Inc., 1997), 127.
78 Aleine Austin, *Matthew Lyon: "New Man" of the Democratic Revolution, 1749-1822* (University Park: The Pennsylvania State University Press, 1981), 53.
79 Hall, *History of Eastern Vermont*, 548-549.
80 Ibid., 551.
81 Samuel B. Hand and P. Jeffrey Potash, "Nathaniel Chipman: Vermont's Forgotten Founder," in Sherman, ed., *A More Perfect Union*, 58-59.
82 Peter S. Onuf, "Vermont and the Union," in ibid., 150-169.
83 *Records of the Governor and Council of Vermont*, 3: 441-443.
84 Daniel Chipman, *The Life of Hon. Nathaniel Chipman* (Boston: Charles C. Little and James Brown, 1846), 88.
85 *Records of the Governor and Council of Vermont*, 3: 488.
86 Hand and Potash, "Nathaniel Chipman," 52.
87 Austin, *Matthew Lyon*, 79, 98, 100.
88 Ibid., 108.
89 Peter S. Jennison, *Roadside History of Vermont* (Missoula, Mont.: Mountain Press Publishing Company, 1989), 199.
90 Williamson, *Vermont in Quandary*, 148.
91 J. Kevin Graffagnino, "Revolution and Empire on the Northern Frontier: Ira Allen of Vermont, 1751-1814" (Ph.D. diss., University of Massachusetts, 1993), 333; Graffagnino, "'Twenty Thousand Muskets!!!': Ira Allen and the *Olive Branch* Affair," *William & Mary Quarterly*, 3rd ser., 48 (July 1991): 409-431.
92 See P. Jeffrey Potash, *Vermont's Burned-Over District: Patterns of Community Development and Religious Activity, 1761-1850* (Brooklyn, N.Y.: Carlson Publishing, 1991), 46.
93 Samuel Williams, *The Natural and Civil History of Vermont* (Walpole, N.H.: Isaiah Thomas and David Carlisle, 1794), 312.
94 Timothy Dwight, *Travels In New England and New York*, (New Haven, Conn.: T. Dwight, 1821-1822), 2: 288.
95 Robert Malvern, "Of Money Needs and Family News: Brigham Family Letters, 1800-1820," *Vermont History* 41 (Summer 1973): 115, 116.
96 Ira Allen, *The Natural and Political History of the State of Vermont* (1798; reprint, Rutland, Vt.: Charles E. Tuttle Co., 1969), 156.
97 Malvern, "Of Money Needs and Family News," 115.
98 Arthur W. Biddle and Paul A. Eschholz, eds., *The Literature of Vermont: A Sampler* (Hanover, N.H.: The University Press of New England, 1973), 145-146.
99 See Potash, *Vermont's Burned-Over District*, sections II and III, for analysis of agricultural records.
100 Edward A. Hoyt, ed., *State Papers of Vermont, General Petitions, 1788-1792* (Montpelier, Vt.: Lane Press, 1955), 9: 143-144.
101 These quotations come from a variety of petitions submitted in support of Middlebury's request to become the shiretown of Addison County. See Potash, *Vermont's Burned-Over District*, 42; also footnotes 120 and 121, on p. 208.
102 Hoyt, "General Petitions," in *State Papers of Vermont*, 9: 245.
103 Painter's role in the establishment of Middlebury College has been, perhaps, exaggerated. Equally important was the role of Seth Storrs in helping to fulfill the desire of

Congregationalists for a college. See Robert L. Ferm, "Seth Storrs, Congregationalism, and the Founding of Middlebury College," *Vermont History* 69 (Summer/Fall, 2001): 256-266.

104 John Lambert, *Travels Through Canada, and the United States of North America in the Years 1806, 1807, & 1808* (London: Baldwin, Cradock, and Joy, 1816), 2: 509.

105 William J. Gilmore, *Reading Becomes a Necessity of Life: Material and Cultural Life in Rural New England, 1780-1835* (Knoxville: The University of Tennessee Press, 1989).

106 Perkins, *A Narrative of a Tour through the State of Vermont*, 32. On the religious landscape of late-eighteenth- and early-nineteenth-century Vermont, see T. D. Seymour Bassett, *The Gods of the Hills: Piety and Society in Nineteenth-Century Vermont* (Montpelier: Vermont Historical Society, 2000), chapters 1-4.

107 Quoted in Robert E. Shalhope, *Bennington and the Green Mountain Boys: The Emergence of Liberal Democracy in Vermont, 1760-1850* (Baltimore: Johns Hopkins University Press, 1996), 212.

108 Allen, *The Natural and Political History of the State of Vermont*, 166.

Chapter 4
Years of Optimism and Anxiety: 1807-1850

1 Randolph A. Roth, *The Democratic Dilemma: Religion, Reform, and the Social Order in the Connecticut River Valley of Vermont, 1791-1850* (Cambridge: Cambridge University Press, 1987), 55.

2 William Slade, ed., *Vermont State Papers* (Middlebury, Vt.: J. W. Copeland, 1823), 472.

3 *Acts and Laws Passed by the Legislature of the State of Vermont, 1807*, 22. Also, see E. P. Walton, ed., *Records of the Governor and Council of the State of Vermont* (Montpelier, Vt.: J. & J. M. Poland, 1873-1880), 1: 400-402.

4 *Records of the Governor and Council*, 5: 395.

5 Ibid., 5: 394.

6 *Acts and Laws . . . of Vermont, 1807*, 94-96.

7 *Constitution of the State of Vermont* [1777], Chapter II, Section XL. Allen Soule, ed., *Laws of Vermont, 1777-1780*, in *State Papers of Vermont* (Montpelier, Vt.: 1964), 12: 20.

8 John A. Williams, ed., *Laws of Vermont, 1791-1795*, in *State Papers of Vermont* (Montpelier, Vt., 1967) 15: 32-35.

9 T. D. Seymour Bassett, "The Origins of UVM, 1791-1833: Overview," in Robert V. Daniels, ed., *The University of Vermont: The First Two Hundred Years* (Hanover, N.H.: University Press of New England, 1991), 10; P. Jeffrey Potash, "Years of Trial: Religion, Money, War, Fire, and the Competition with Middlebury," in Daniels, ibid., 35.

10 Samuel Morey, an Orford, New Hampshire, farmer and inventor who maintained a workshop in Fairlee, Vermont, claimed that he, not Fulton, had designed and built the first steamboat at the Connecticut River in 1793, and that Fulton, in fact, had stolen the invention from him. On Morey, see Alice Doan Hodgson, *Samuel Morey: Inventor Extraordinary* (Orford, N.H.: Historical Fact Publications, 1961).

11 *The History of the Town of Montpelier, Including the Town of East Montpelier, for the*

NOTES TO PAGES 151–64

First One Hundred and Two Years (Montpelier, Vt.: Miss A. M. Hemenway, 1882), 283–85; *Acts and Laws Passed by the Legislature of the State of Vermont at the Session at Danville, on the Second Thursday of October, 1805* (Windsor, Vt.: Alden Spooner, 1805), 215–16. See also, Walter Hill Crockett, *Vermont, The Green Mountain State* (New York: The Century History Company, 1921–1923) 2: 599–605.

12 Lewis D. Stilwell, *Migration From Vermont* (Montpelier: Vermont Historical Society, 1948), 124.
13 H. Nicholas Muller III, "Smuggling into Canada: How the Champlain Valley Defied Jefferson's Embargo," *Vermont History* 38 (Winter 1970): 9.
14 Ibid., 7.
15 Ibid., 9.
16 Ibid., 11.
17 The broadside appears in John J. Duffy, "Broadside Illustrations of the Jeffersonian-Federalist Conflict in Vermont, 1809–1816," *Vermont History* 49 (Fall 1981): 213.
18 Ralph Nading Hill, *Lake Champlain: Key to Liberty* (Taftsville, Vt.: Countryman Press, 1977), 169.
19 The Highgate quotation is in Abby Maria Hemenway, ed., *The Vermont Historical Gazetteer* (Burlington, Vt.: A. M. Hemenway, 1867–1891), 2: 266.
20 Muller, "Smuggling into Canada," 16. For Muller's study of Canadian customs records, see "The Commercial History of the Lake Champlain-Richelieu River Route, 1760–1815" (Ph.D. diss., University of Rochester, 1968).
21 P. Jeffrey Potash, *Vermont's Burned-Over District: Patterns of Community Development and Religious Activity, 1761–1850* (Brooklyn, N.Y.: Carlson Publishing Inc., 1991), 90–91.
22 Crockett, *Vermont, the Green Mountain State,* 3: 55–56.
23 Karen Stites Campbell, "Propaganda, Pestilence, and Prosperity: Burlington's Camptown Days During the War of 1812," *Vermont History* 64 (Summer 1996): 139, 140.
24 Ibid., 143.
25 Ibid., 141.
26 Ibid., 147.
27 Ibid., 149.
28 Ibid., 150.
29 *Records of the Governor and Council*, 6: 421.
30 Duffy, "Broadside Illustrations," 219.
31 *Records of the Governor and Council*, 6: 493–494.
32 Duffy, "Broadside Illustrations," 210.
33 *Records of the Governor and Council*, 5: 382–383.
34 H. Nicholas Muller III, "A 'Traitorous and Diabolical Traffic': The Commerce of the Champlain-Richelieu Corridor During the War of 1812," *Vermont History* 44 (Spring 1976): 86–87.
35 Ibid., 91.
36 P. Jeffrey Potash, "Years of Trial," in Daniels, ed., *The University of Vermont*, 39–40.
37 Hemenway, ed., *Vermont Historical Gazetteer*, 2: 266.
38 Ibid.
39 For Galusha's speech, see *Records of the Governor and Council*, 6: 427. Monroe's speech is in *Inaugural Addresses of the Presidents of the United States, from George*

Washington 1789 to Richard Milhous Nixon 1973 (Washington, D.C.: U.S. Government Printing Office, 1974), 29–36.

40 Potash, *Vermont's Burned-Over District*, 93.
41 Ibid., 93–94.
42 David M. Ludlum, *The Vermont Weather Book* (Montpelier: Vermont Historical Society, 1985), 91–92.
43 *Records of Governor and Council*, 6: 431.
44 T. D. Seymour Bassett, "Fitch against Emigration: Hyde Park, Vermont, 1816," *New York Folklore Quarterly*, 28 (March 1972): 39.
45 Edward Conant, *Geography, History and Civil Government of Vermont* (Rutland, Vt.: The Tuttle Company, 1890), 151.
46 See Hill, *Lake Champlain*, 208.
47 Potash, *Vermont's Burned-Over District*, 101.
48 David Demeritt, "Climate, Cropping, and Society in Vermont, 1820–1850," *Vermont History* 59 (Summer 1991): 141–142. The quotation is from Vermont Commission on Country Life, *Rural Vermont: A Program for the Future* (Burlington: Vermont Commission on Country Life, 1931), 61.
49 Stilwell, *Migration From Vermont*, 157.
50 Potash, *Vermont's Burned-Over District*, 103.
51 Ibid., 102.
52 On Vermont's experience with sheep raising, see Harold F. Wilson, *The Hill Country of Northern New England: Its Social and Economic History, 1790–1830* (New York: Columbia University Press, 1936; reprint, New York: AMS Press, Inc., 1967), 75–94.
53 Nathan Hoskins, *A History of the State of Vermont* (Vergennes, Vt.: J. Shedd, 1831), 268.
54 Wilson, *Hill Country of Northern New England*, 77.
55 Hoskins, *A History of the State of Vermont*, 269.
56 Wilson, *Hill Country of Northern New England*, 79.
57 Ernest L. Bogart, *Peacham: the Story of a Vermont Hill Town* (Montpelier: Vermont Historical Society, 1948), 303–305.
58 Charles Paine, "Memoires," typescript carbon copy, pp. 19–20, in Vermont Historical Society.
59 Hemenway, ed., *Vermont Historical Gazetteer*, 3: 837.
60 Historian T. D. Seymour Bassett suggests that many Vermonters who lived at a distance from established institutions may not, in fact, have been so distant from religion. He concludes that many who lacked church affiliation in these years nevertheless worshipped regularly in their own fashion, in family or community groups, and that less than half of Vermonters claimed formal affiliation with any church until the twentieth century. See Bassett, *The Gods of the Hills: Piety and Society in Nineteenth-Century Vermont* (Montpelier: Vermont Historical Society, 2000), 261–262.
61 On Haynes, see John D. Saillant, "Lemuel Haynes's Black Republicanism and the American Republican Tradition, 1775–1820," *Journal of the Early Republic* 14 (Fall 1994): 293–324; John D. Saillant, "'A Doctrinal Controversy Between the Hopkintonian and the Universalist': Religion, Race, and Ideology in Postrevolutionary Vermont," *Vermont History* 61 (Fall 1993): 197–216.
62 Hemenway, ed., *Vermont Historical Gazetteer*, 3: 1,044.
63 See David M. Ludlum, *Social Ferment in Vermont, 1791–1850* (1939; reprint, New York: AMS Press, Inc., 1966), 25–62. The quotation concerning Methodist belief is

in Winthrop S. Hudson, *American Protestantism* (Chicago: The University of Chicago Press, 1961), 101.
64 Ludlum, *Social Ferment in Vermont*, 51.
65 Roth, *The Democratic Dilemma*, 104.
66 See Hudson, *American Protestantism*, 101.
67 Potash, *Vermont's Burned-Over District*, 159.
68 Roth, *The Democratic Dilemma*, 189.
69 Potash, *Vermont's Burned-Over District*, 156.
70 Ludlum, *Social Ferment in Vermont*, 28; Potash, "Years of Trial," in Daniels, ed., *The University of Vermont*, 35.
71 Potash, *Vermont's Burned-Over District*, 180.
72 "Rutland Association (Congregational Churches) Protest against (Burchardism) the system of exciting and promoting revivals of religion known to have been in operation during the year past in Vermont," February 2, 1836; manuscript in Vermont Historical Society.
73 Roth, *The Democratic Dilemma*, 105.
74 Ludlum, *Social Ferment in Vermont*, 64.
75 Roth, *The Democratic Dilemma*, 105.
76 Ludlum, *Social Ferment in Vermont*, 68.
77 Roth, *The Democratic Dilemma*, 169.
78 Hemenway, ed., *Vermont Historical Gazetteer*, 2: 348.
79 Bogart, *Peacham*, 214.
80 Ludlum, *Social Ferment in Vermont*, 69-70.
81 Ibid., 74-75.
82 David Freeman Hawke, *Everyday Life in Early America* (New York: Harper & Row, 1988), 80.
83 Paine, "Memoires," 19.
84 Edward Pessen, *Jacksonian America: Society, Personality, and Politics* (revised edition; Urbana, Ill.: University of Illinois Press, 1985), 269; Hal S. Barron, *Those Who Stayed Behind: Rural Society in Nineteenth-Century New England* (Cambridge: Cambridge University Press, 1984), 25; Robert E. Shalhope, *Bennington and the Green Mountain Boys: The Emergence of Liberal Democracy in Vermont, 1760-1850* (Baltimore: Johns Hopkins University Press, 1996), 320; Paul Goodman, *Towards a Christian Republic: Antimasonry and the Great Transition in New England, 1826-1836* (New York: Oxford University Press, 1988), 122-129.
85 Shalhope, *Bennington and the Green Mountain Boys*, 320.
86 Ibid., 321.
87 Pessen, *Jacksonian America*, 263.
88 Vermont political parties customarily used legislative caucuses to select candidates for statewide office, but the new Antimason Party had no legislators. To resolve this dilemma, Vermont's first nominating convention emerged. Eighty-one Antimason delegates attended the 1829 Montpelier meeting, representing eleven of the state's thirteen counties.
89 Ludlum, *Social Ferment in Vermont*, 128-131.
90 Ibid., 130-131.
91 See Wilbur H. Siebert, *Vermont's Anti-Slavery and Underground Railroad Record* (1937; reprint, New York: Negro Universities Press, 1969), 23.

92 On slavery and race in early Vermont, see Roth, *The Democratic Dilemma*, 23-24; Elise A. Guyette, "The Working Lives of African Vermonters in Census and Literature, 1790-1870," *Vermont History* 61 (Spring 1993): 69-84; J. Kevin Graffagnino, "Vermont Attitudes Toward Slavery: The Need For A Closer Look," *Vermont History* 45 (Winter 1977): 31-34; Marshall M. True, "Slavery in Burlington? An Historical Note," *Vermont History* 50 (Fall 1982): 227-230; Siebert, *Vermont's Anti-Slavery and Underground Railroad Record*; Saillant, "'A Doctrinal Controversy Between the Hopkintonian and the Universalist'"; John M. Lovejoy, "Racism in Antebellum Vermont," *Vermont History* 69, supplement (Winter 2001): 48-65; Arthur O. White, "Prince Saunders: An Instance of Social Mobility among Antibellum New England Blacks," *Journal of Negro History* 60 (October 1975): 532.

93 *Records of the Governor and Council*, 6: 542-543.

94 J. K. Converse, *A Discourse on the Moral, Legal and Domestic Condition of Our Colored Population, Preached Before the Vermont Colonization Society, at Montpelier, October 17, 1832* (Burlington, Vt.: Edward Smith, 1832), 23.

95 T. D. Seymour Bassett, ed., "A Letter by William Lloyd Garrison, Written from Bennington, Vermont, on March 30, 1829," *Vermont History* 37 (Autumn 1969): 257-258.

96 Ibid., 261.

97 John Myers, "The Beginning of Antislavery Agencies in Vermont, 1832-1836," *Vermont History* 36 (Summer 1968): 132.

98 Ludlum, *Social Ferment in Vermont*, 144.

99 Paine, "Memoires," 27-28.

100 See Jane Williamson, "Rowland T. Robinson, Rokeby, and the Underground Railroad in Vermont," *Vermont History* 69, supplement (Winter 2001): 19-31; Ronald Salomon, "Being Good: An Abolitionist Family Attempts to Live Up to Its Own Standards," *Vermont History* 69, supplement (Winter 2001): 32-47; Raymond Paul Zirblis, "Friends of Freedom: The Vermont Underground Railroad Survey Report," (Montpelier: State of Vermont Division of Historic Preservation, 1996).

101 Ludlum, *Social Ferment in Vermont*, 147.

102 *Laws of Vermont, 1837*, 60, 105-108; *Congressional Globe, 25th Congress, 2nd Session*, VI (1838), 34, 39, 41; Crockett, *Vermont, The Green Mountain State*, 3: 290-294.

103 Ludlum, *Social Ferment in Vermont*, 149.

104 Lovejoy, "Racism in Antebellum Vermont," 59, 61.

105 Stephen Kenny, "The Canadian Rebellions and the Limits of Historical Perspective," *Vermont History* 58 (Summer 1990): 186.

106 The quotation is translated from the French: "qui represente au voyageur un de ces sites pittoresques et remarquables de la Suisse," in Stephen Kenny, "Duvernay's Exile in 'Balenton' [Burlington]: The Vermont Interlude of a Canadian Patriot," *Vermont History* 52 (Spring 1984): 110. See also, "The Great Wolf Hunt," in John J. Duffy and H. Nicholas Muller III, *An Anxious Democracy: Aspects of the 1830s* (Westport, Conn.: Greenwood Press, 1982), 57-77.

107 Hemenway, ed., *Vermont Historical Gazetteer*, 3: 595, 837; H. P. Smith and W. S. Rann, eds., *History of Rutland County, Vermont* (Syracuse, N.Y.: D. Mason & Co., 1886), 352; Shalhope, *Bennington and the Green Mountain Boys*, 323; T. D. Seymour Bassett, "The Classical College, 1833-1895: Growth and Stability: Overview," in Daniels, ed., *The University of Vermont*, 80; Stilwell, *Migration From Vermont*, 178-179.

108 Wilson, *Hill Country of Northern New England*, 80.

109 Nathaniel Hawthorne, "An Inland Port," in T. D. Seymour Bassett, ed., *Outsiders Inside Vermont: Travelers' Tales Over 358 Years,* (Brattleboro, Vt.: The Stephen Greene Press, 1967), 63.
110 Roth, *The Democratic Dilemma*, 274.
111 On converts to Catholicism in Vermont in the antebellum period, see Deborah P. Clifford, "Abby Hemenway's Road to Rome," *Vermont History* 63 (Fall 1995): 197–213.
112 Richard P. McCormick, *The Second American Party System: Party Formation in the Jacksonian Era* (Chapel Hill: The University of North Carolina Press, 1966), 349–350.
113 T. D. Seymour Bassett, "Vermont Politics and the Press in the 1840s," *Vermont History* 47 (Summer 1979): 209.
114 Roth, *The Democratic Dilemma*, 143.
115 The Clarke discussion is based on unpublished ms., "DeWitt Clinton Clarke," by Gene Sessions, in possession of the author.
116 Abby Maria Hemenway, ed., *Clarke Papers, Mrs. Meech and Her Family* (Burlington, Vt., 1878), 194.
117 Bassett, "Vermont Politics and the Press in the 1840s," 196.
118 Paine, "Memoires," 8.
119 Crockett, *Vermont, the Green Mountain State*, 3: 307–308.
120 Claude Moore Fuess, *Daniel Webster* (Boston: Little, Brown, and Company, 1930) 2:85.
121 E. S. Marsh, "High Spots in Brandon's History," *The Vermonter* (July 1932): 145.
122 J. E. Dow to Charles G. Eastman, 21 March 1844, Eastman papers, box 41, "1844" folder, Vermont Historical Society.
123 J. Kevin Graffagnino, Samuel B. Hand, and Gene Sessions, eds., *Vermont Voices, 1609 Through the 1990s: A Documentary History of the Green Mountain State* (Montpelier: The Vermont Historical Society, 1999), 153.
124 Ludlum, *Social Ferment in Vermont*, 271.
125 *Journal of the Senate of . . . Vermont, 1848*, 32.
126 Ludlum, *Social Ferment in Vermont*, 245; Vernon Louis Parrington, *Main Currents in American Thought: An Interpretation of American Literature from the Beginning to 1920* (New York: Harcourt, Brace, & World, 1958), vol. 3, *The Beginnings of Critical Realism*, 74.
127 On Noyes, see Robert Davis Thomas, *The Man Who Would Be Perfect: John Humphrey Noyes and the Utopian Impulse* (Philadelphia: University of Pennsylvania Press, 1977).
128 Ludlum, *Social Ferment in Vermont*, 252.
129 Paine, "Memoires," 70.
130 Ibid.
131 On Miller and Millerism, see Ronald L. Numbers and Jonathan M. Butler, eds., *The Disappointed: Millerism and Millenarianism in the Nineteenth Century* (Knoxville: The University of Tennessee Press, 1993).
132 Ludlum, *Social Ferment in Vermont*, 76.
133 On Alexander Twilight, see Gregory Hileman, "The Iron-Willed Black Schoolteacher and his Granite Academy," *Middlebury* 48 (Spring 1974): 6–14. Also, see Hemenway, ed., *Vermont Historical Gazetteer*, 3: 101–104.
134 *Records of Governor and Council*, 7: 448.
135 Ludlum, *Social Ferment in Vermont*, 225–226.
136 *The Acts and Resolves . . . of Vermont, 1845*, 25–29.

137 Ludlum, *Social Ferment in Vermont*, 237, 231.
138 See James D. Butler, *Deficiencies in Our History: An Address Delivered Before the Vermont Historical and Antiquarian Society at Montpelier, October 16, 1846* (Montpelier: Eastman and Danforth, 1846).
139 On Stevens and Vermont "tradition," see David E. Narrett, "'I must remind you that you are a Vermonter': Henry Stevens, Historical Tradition, and Green Mountain State Patriotism in the 1840s," *Vermont History* 66 (Summer/Fall 1998): 69-101. On the founding of the Vermont Historical Society see Weston A. Cate, Jr., *Up and Doing: The Vermont Historical Society, 1838-1970* (Montpelier: Vermont Historical Society, 1988), 1-21.
140 In this period, two other Green Mountain medical schools competed with the University of Vermont for students: Castleton Medical College (1818-1859) and the Clinical School of Medicine (1827-1856), at Woodstock. See Martin Kaufman, *University of Vermont College of Medicine* (Hanover, N. H.: University Press of New England, 1979); Frederick Clayton Waite, *The First Medical College in Vermont: Castleton, 1818-1862* (Montpelier: Vermont Historical Society, 1949); Waite, *The Story of a Country Medical College: A History of the Clinical School of Medicine and the Vermont Medical College, Woodstock, Vermont, 1827-1856* (Montpelier: Vermont Historical Society, 1945); Crockett, *Vermont, The Green Mountain State*, 5: 609-622.

Chapter 5
Links to the Nation: 1850-1870

1 Addison Bancroft to his mother. Philadelphia, 25 August 1847. Vermont Historical Society manuscript collection, MSC 209, folder 38.
2 *Acts and Resolves of the State of Vermont*, 1843 (Montpelier: E. P. Walton & Sons, 1843), 50-56. No. 54, "An Act to Incorporate the Champlain and Connecticut River Rail Road Company." For a summary of the provisions in the act see William E. Navin, "The Founding of the Rutland Railroad," *Vermont Quarterly*, n.s. 14 (July 1946): 87-94. Navin, a trustee of the Rutland Railroad Company, gives an imaginative and notably biased account of the signing of the bill by Governor John Mattocks; nonetheless, the article includes long quotations from Act No. 54. For general histories of Vermont railroads see T. D. Seymour Bassett, "500 Miles of Trouble and Excitement: Vermont Railroads, 1848-1861," *Vermont History* 49 (Summer 1981): 133-154; Bassett, *The Growing Edge: Vermont Villages 1840-1880* (Montpelier: Vermont Historical Society, 1992), 51-54 et passim; Walter Hill Crockett, *Vermont, The Green Mountain State*, (New York: Century History Company, 1921-1923), 5: 577-587; Robert C. Jones, *Railroads of Vermont*, 2 vols. (Shelburne, Vt.: The New England Press, 1993); Harold A. Meeks, *Time and Change in Vermont: A Human Geography* (Chester, Conn.: Globe Pequot Press, 1986), 105-139; William J. Wilgus, *The Role of Transportation in the Development of Vermont* (Montpelier: Vermont Historical Society, 1945).
3 [DeWitt Clinton Clarke], "Disturbance on the Railroad," *Burlington Free Press*, 10 July 1846, in J. Kevin Graffagnino, Samuel B. Hand, and Gene Sessions, eds., *Vermont Voices, 1609 Through the 1990s: A Documentary History of the Green Mountain State* (Montpelier: Vermont Historical Society, 1999), 155.
4 From *Vermont Journal* (Windsor) reprinted in *Vermont Watchman*, 6 July 1848, in "Some Railroad 'Firsts' in Vermont As Observed by the Press," *Vermont Quarterly*, n.s. 14 (July 1946): 115-116.

5 "The Journal of Jonas Wilder, Railroader" with introduction by William J. Wilgus, *Vermont Quarterly*, n.s. 14 (July 1946): 121-134.
6 Meeks, *Time and Change in Vermont*, 115.
7 See ibid., Figure 5.2 (p. 120), which shows twenty-four railroads, including some electric railways, built in Vermont after June 1869.
8 Alfred D. Chandler, "The Railroads: Pioneers in Modern Corporate Management," in Thomas K. McCraw, ed., *The Essential Alfred Chandler: Essays toward a Historical Theory of Big Business* (Boston: Harvard Business School Press, 1988), 179-201.
9 Robin W. Winks, *Frederick Billings: A Life* (New York: Oxford University Press, 1991), 187-189, 241-242.
10 Wilgus, ed., "The Journal of Jonas Wilder."
11 Gene Sessions, "Years of Struggle: The Irish in the Village of Northfield, 1845-1900," *Vermont History* 55 (Spring 1987): 69-96.
12 Gene Sessions, "Vermont's Nineteenth-Century Railroad Workers," in Michael Sherman and Jennie Versteeg, eds., *We Vermonters: Perspectives on the Past* (Montpelier: Vermont Historical Society, 1992), 239-248.
13 Ralph Nading Hill, *Lake Champlain: Key to Liberty* (Woodstock, Vt.: Countryman Press, 1987), 233-234.
14 See Meeks, *Time and Change in Vermont*, 140-156; Louise Roomet, "Vermont as a Resort Area in the Nineteenth Century," *Vermont History* 44 (Winter 1976): 1-13
15 George Perkins Marsh, *Third Report of the Railroad Commissioner* (1858), 3-15. See David Lowenthal, *George Perkins Marsh: Prophet of Conservation* (Seattle: University of Washington Press, 2000), 191-195.
16 George Perkins Marsh, *Man and Nature, Or Physical Geography as Modified by Human Actions* (1864), ed. with an introduction by David Lowenthal (Cambridge, Mass.: Harvard University Press, 1965), 36 and 51, fn. 53.
17 Edward J. Phelps, "The Lay of the Lost Traveler," in H. Nicholas Muller III and Samuel B. Hand, eds., *In A State of Nature: Readings in Vermont History* (Montpelier: Vermont Historical Society, 1982), 206-207.
18 "Farming in Vermont," *The Cultivator*, n.s. 2 (1845): 219-221, 257-258.
19 Much of the information on agricultural production that follows comes from Howard S. Russell, *A Long Deep Furrow: Three Centuries of Farming in New England* (Hanover, N.H.: University Press of New England, 1976).
20 "Husbandry of Vermont," *The Cultivator*, n.s. 6 (August 1849): 233-234.
21 See David A. Donath, "Agriculture and the Good Society: The Image of Rural Vermont," in Sherman and Versteeg, eds. *We Vermonters*, 213-218; Sally McMurry, *Transforming Rural Life: Dairying Families and Agricultural Change, 1820-1885* (Baltimore: Johns Hopkins University Press, 1995).
22 J. S. Pettibone, "Profits of Sheep Husbandry," *The Cultivator*, n.s. 6 (April 1849): 110; Abby Maria Hemenway, ed., *Vermont Historical Gazetteer* (Claremont, N.H.: The Claremont Manufacturing Company, 1877), 2: 44.
23 Harold L. Bailey, *Vermont's Potato Story* (Montpelier, Vt.: The George W. Merck Fund, 1955); Bailey, "Vermont in the Potato Lineage Book," *Vermont History* 22 (April 1955): 188-223; Hemenway, *Vermont Historical Gazetteer*, 3: 45.
24 The railroad continued to play an important role in the strawberry trade into the middle of the twentieth century. See Margaret Jenkins Pratt, "The Strawberry King of Bradford," *Vermont History News*, 44 (July-August 1993), 55-60.

25 Thomas Rumney, "The Hops Boom in Nineteenth-Century Vermont," *Vermont History* 56 (Winter 1988): 36–41.
26 Daisy Dopp, *Daisy Dopp's Vermont*, ed. Elka Schumann (Brownington: Orleans County Historical Society, 1983), 29.
27 *The Cultivator*, third series, 7 (March 1859): 98.
28 *The Cultivator*, n.s. 8 (November 1851); see Bassett, *The Growing Edge*, 1–12; Brenda Bullion, "The Agricultural Press: 'To Improve the Soil and Mind,'" in Peter Benes, ed., *The Farm,* Dublin Seminar for New England Folklife, volume 11 (Boston: Boston University Press, 1987): 74–94; Edwin Rozwenc, *Agricultural Policies in Vermont, 1860–1945* (Montpelier: Vermont Historical Society, 1981), chapters 1–3.
29 J. L. Hills, *The Vermont Dairymen's Association, A History, 1869–1947* (n.p.: 1948).
30 Barry Salussolia, "The City of Burlington and Municipal Incorporation in Vermont," *Vermont History* 54 (Winter 1986): 5–19; see also Bassett, *The Growing Edge*, chapters 2, 10, 11. Bassett argues throughout this important book that the period 1840-1880 saw the fundamental reshaping of Vermont society by what he called the "urban penetration of rural Vermont."
31 Lewis Stilwell, *Migration from Vermont* (Montpelier and Rutland: Vermont Historical Society and Academy Books, 1948), 214–229.
32 Harold F. Wilson, *The Hill Country of Northern New England: Its Social and Economic History, 1790–1930* (New York: Columbia University Press, 1936), 67 fn. 53; Mary Paul to Bela Paul, 13 September 1845 and 21 December 1845, in Thomas Dublin, ed., *Farm to Factory: Women's Letters, 1830–1860* (New York: Columbia University Press, 1981), 100, 104.
33 Bassett, *The Growing Edge,* 59–60. His chart of Vermont woolen mills, 1850–1860, shows 1,213 male workers and 1,317 female workers. The Burlington Mill Company in Winooski in 1850 employed 150 males and 300 females; H. E. Bradford Company in Bennington employed 30 men and 60 women in 1860. In most of the other mills, men and women were employed in about equal numbers.
34 See Stilwell's map, "Changes in Population, 1850–1860," in *Migration from Vermont*, facing p. 217; Bassett, *The Growing Edge*, 58–60; Victor R. Rolando, *200 Years of Soot and Sweat: The History and Archaeology of Vermont's Iron, Charcoal, and Lime Industries* (Manchester Center, Vt.: Vermont Archaeological Society, 1992), 107–128.
35 Wilson, *Hill Country of Northern New England,* 74. See McMurry, *Transforming Rural Life.* McMurry's study of the changes in dairying, especially cheese making, in Oneida County, New York, is equally applicable to Vermont. She identifies several elements that signal a major shift in dairy farms: the use of agents to market cheese to distant points of sale; the rise of the factory as the location for cheese making, which had the accompanying result of removing cheese making from women's work to men's work; and the introduction of pure breeds of dairy herds to increase the butterfat content of milk for the butter and cheese market.
36 *Laws of Vermont, 1850*, No. 16, "An Act Relating to the Writ of Habeas Corpus to Persons Claimed as Fugitive Slaves and the Right of Trial by Jury," 9–10; Joint Resolution No. 78, "Resolution on so Much of the Governor's Message as Relates to Slavery, &c.," 53–54.
37 Crockett, *Vermont, The Green Mountain State*, 3: 421.
38 Ibid., 3: 425.
39 *Rutland Herald*, 16 June 1854, quoted in T. D. Seymour Bassett, "Urban Penetration

of Rural Vermont, 1840-1880" (Ph.D. diss., Harvard University, 1952), 2: 438; and Edward P. Brynn, "Vermont's Political Vacuum of 1845-1856 and the Emergence of the Republican Party," *Vermont History* 38 (Spring 1970): 113-123. See also, Bassett, *The Growing Edge*, 124-125; Samuel B. Hand, *The Star That Set: The Vermont Republican Party, 1854-1974* (Lanham, Md.: Lexington Books, 2002), 5-7.

40 T. D. Seymour Bassett, "Nature's Nobleman: Justin Smith Morrill, A Victorian Politician," *Vermont History* 30 (January 1962); *Dictionary of American Biography*, 13: 198-199; Crockett, *Vermont, The Green Mountain State*, 3: 433-435, and et passim, also 4: 250-255 et passim.

41 See Christie Carter, ed. and comp., *Vermont Elections, 1789-1989*, State Papers of Vermont, vol. 21 (Montpelier: Secretary of State, 1989). In the contest for lieutenant governor, the Democrats ran two candidates, reflecting the split in the national ticket between supporters of Douglas and those of Breckenridge. The Republican candidate, Levi Underwood, received 68.1 percent of the vote.

42 George Perkins Marsh to Erastus Fairbanks, Burlington, 19 April 1855, Vermont Historical Society, Erastus Fairbanks Papers, Doc. Box 95.

43 For details of Vermonters' participation in the fighting see G. G. Benedict, *Vermont in the Civil War: A History of the Part Taken by the Vermont Soldiers and Sailors in the War for the Union, 1861-65*, 2 vol. (Burlington, Vt.: The Free Press Association, 1886); and Howard Coffin, *Full Duty: Vermonters in the Civil War* (Woodstock, Vt.: Countryman Press, 1993). Much of the information about military aspects of the war in this chapter has been adapted from these two thorough works.

44 *Journal of the House of Representatives of the State of Vermont, Extra Session, 1861*, 22.

45 See Bassett, *The Growing Edge*, 142-143; J. Kevin Graffagnino, "Vermont Attitudes Toward Slavery: The Need for a Closer Look," *Vermont History* 45 (Winter 1977): 31-34. In August 1863, Stephen Pingree of Hartford, Vermont, a lieutenant in the Fourth Vermont Regiment, wrote to his cousin, Augustus P. Hunton, from Rappahannock Station, Virginia. "I once doubted the policy of this war. I never doubted the right to maintain the Union, and no living man ever heard a word that could be so construed from me. Thousands who thought they foresaw a short struggle would have opposed the war as impolitic had they foreseen the half of what has occurred, and some who called me a traitor for doubting its practicability now shudder at the idea of being forced to do what I did voluntarily—and am still ready and anxious to do to the end, cost what it may." See Kelly Nolan, "The Civil War Letters of S. E. and S. M. Pingree, 1862-1864," *Vermont History* 63 (Spring 1995): 81-83.

46 The Morgan horse, a breed developed in Vermont, traced its origins to "Figure," a stallion traded in 1789 to itinerant music teacher Justin Morgan. Renamed "Justin Morgan" to honor its former owner, the stallion passed on its characteristic deep chest, small head, calm demeanor, and remarkable endurance to its offspring. The Morgans, already prized as work and pleasure horses by the 1850s, became famous during the Civil War for their strength and reliability in battle.

47 Coffin, *Full Duty*, 262.

48 See R. D. Harris, "The War Legislation of Vermont," *The Vermonter* 3 (November 1897): 87-92.

49 Lydia E. White, "The Record of a Day," *The Vermonter* 20 (January 1915): 4-17.

50 Abby Estey Fuller (Mrs. Levi K. Fuller), "Some Reminiscences of Brattleboro during the Civil War," in *Addresses Given by Mrs. Fuller before the Brattleboro Chapter of the Daughters of the American Revolution* (n.p., n.d. [Brattleboro, 1929?]), 18.

51 Lynn A. Bonfield and Mary C. Morrison, *Roxana's Children: The Biography of a Nineteenth-Century Vermont Family* (Amherst: University of Massachusetts Press, 1995), 182.

52 Huldah Morse to Franklin Morse, 9 December 1863, and 14 December 1863. Gale-Morse Family Papers, folder 17, Vermont Historical Society. For wages, see Thurston M. Adams, "Prices Paid by Vermont Farmers for Goods and Services and Received by Them for Farm Products, 1790–1940; Wages of Vermont Farm Labor, 1780–1940," University of Vermont and State Agricultural College, Vermont Agricultural Experiment Stations, Bulletin 507 (February 1944). See chart of farm wage rates, 1780–1940, p. 88.

53 "State of Vermont, by John Gregory Smith, Governor, A Proclamation," Montpelier, 28 October 1863. Broadside, Vermont Historical Society.

54 Harriet Lawson to Franklin Morse, 27 August 1862; George Morse to Franklin Morse, 2 August 1863. Gale-Morse Family Papers, folder 17.

55 Capt. C. R. Crane, provost-marshal, First District of Vermont to Brig. Gen. T. G. Pitcher, acting assistant provost-marshal-general, Rutland, 18 June 1863; Fred C. Ainsworth and Joseph W. Kirkley, eds., *The War of the Rebellion: A Compilation of the Official Records of the Union and Confederate Armies* (Washington, D.C.: Government Printing Office, 1899) series 3, 3: 384, 385.

56 James Fuller, *Men of Color, to Arms! Vermont African-Americans in the Civil War* (San Jose, Calif.: University Press, 2001).

57 Don Wickman, "Rutland Blacks in the 54th Massachusetts Regiments. Their Share of the Glory," Rutland Historical Society *Quarterly* 22:2 (1992).

58 Correspondence from Elise Guyette to Michael Sherman, 2 May 1997. In possession of the author.

59 Alice Watts Choate to Augusta Gregory Mills, Grass Lake County, Michigan, in Bonfield and Morrison, *Roxana's Children*, 243, n.; Fuller, "Reminiscences," 19.

60 Adams, "Prices Paid by Vermont Farmers," 20. Elsewhere in his study, Adams states that "farm and retail prices nearly doubled during the 4-year period" of the war, due in part to currency depreciation caused by the government's issue of $443 million in paper money, called "greenbacks." Ibid., 109.

61 Bassett, *The Growing Edge*, 145; Bassett, "For Freedom and Unity: Vermont's Civil War," *Vermont Life* 15 (Spring 1961): 36–37, 47–50.

62 Collamer M. Abbott, *Green Mountain Copper: The Story of Vermont's Red Metal* (Randolph, Vt.: The Herald Printery, 1973); see also Thomas Gardner, "Copper Mining during the Civil War: Reflections on the Origins of 520/521," (n.p., n.d. [1985?]); Rolando, *200 Years of Soot and Sweat*, 49, et passim.

63 Frederick Holbrook, "The Military Hospital," in *Picturesque Brattleboro*, ed. Frank T. Pomeroy (Northampton, Mass.: Picturesque Press, 1894), 40–44.

64 Hemenway, *Vermont Historical Gazetteer*, 1: 512; Bassett, *The Growing Edge*, 145.

65 On the architecture and operation of Vermont's three Civil War hospitals, see Nancy E. Boone and Michael Sherman, "Designed to Cure: Civil War Hospitals in Vermont," *Vermont History* 69 (Winter/Spring 2001): 173–200.

66 Reports on the number of Confederates involved in the raid vary. There may have been as many as twenty-five. See Robin W. Winks, *Canada and the United States: The Civil War Years* (Baltimore: Johns Hopkins University Press, 1960), 295-336. Howard Coffin states that the raiding party included Young and nineteen others. Coffin, *Full Duty*, 320. Crockett counted twenty-five in the raid but gives the names of only fourteen. Crockett, *Vermont, The Green Mountain State*, 3: 592.

67 Quoted in Crockett, *Vermont, The Green Mountain State*, 3: 622.

68 The pass is in the collections of the Vermont Historical Society, Barre, Vermont.

69 Benedict, *Vermont in the Civil War*, 2: 791-792, 799; Crockett, *Vermont, The Green Mountain State*, 3: 626-628.

70 Franklin Morse Diary. Gale-Morse Family papers, folder 17. See Daniel E. Sutherland, *The Expansion of Everyday Life, 1860-1876* (New York: Harper and Row, 1989), 106-109.

71 Faith L. Pepe, "The Shaping of An Artist: Larkin Mead and the Civil War," *Vermont History News* 37 (Sept.-Oct. 1986): 103-106.

72 *Vermont Phoenix*, 21 October 1862, 2; quoted in George R. Lindsey, "George Harper Houghton: The Civil War Photographer from Brattleboro, Vermont," *Vermont History News* 37 (Sept.-Oct. 1986): 106-108.

73 Anne Lawless, "Save Outdoor Sculpture! Records, 1992-1993," *Vermont History* 62 (Summer 1994): 166-182. The St. Johnsbury sculpture by Larkin Mead and the Swanton sculpture by town resident Daniel Perry are both classically draped female allegorical figures, meant to inspire citizens with the ideals of the republic. Monuments depicting the common soldier appeared in the twentieth century, often mass-produced by foundries and sold on order to communities.

74 Daniel Robbins, *The Vermont State House: A History and Guide* (Montpelier: Vermont Council on the Arts and Vermont State House Preservation Committee, 1980), 69-70, 119-122.

75 Paul S. Gillies and D. Gregory Sanford, eds., *Records of the Council of Censors of the State of Vermont* (Montpelier: Secretary of State, 1991), 517-609. On the significance of the 1855 Council of Censors and votes on the proposals to amend the constitution see Samuel B. Hand, Jeffrey D. Marshall, and D. Gregory Sanford, "'Little Republics': The Structure of State Politics in Vermont, 1854-1920," *Vermont History* 52 (Summer 1985): 141-166.

76 Rachel Cree Sherman, "Never Did Two Contending Armys," *Vermont History News* 39 (July-August 1988): 71-73; Bassett, *The Growing Edge*, 128.

77 See Hand, *The Star That Set*, 15-29, Gillies and Sanford, *Records of the Council of Censors*, 629-707; and the Vermont State Archives web site, <http://vermont-archives.org/governance/Constitution/amending.html#history>.

78 Madeleine M. Kunin, "Clarina Howard Nichols," *Vermont Life* 28 (Winter 1973): 14-17; Bassett, *The Growing Edge*, 98-99.

79 Gillies and Sanford, *Records of the Council of Censors*, 640.

80 T. D. Seymour Bassett, "The 1870 Campaign for Woman Suffrage in Vermont," *Vermont Quarterly*, n.s., 14:2 (April 1946): 47-61; Deborah P. Clifford, "An Invasion of Strong-Minded Women: The Newspapers and the Women Suffrage Campaign in Vermont in 1870," *Vermont History* 31 (Winter 1975):, 1-19; J. Kevin Graffagnino, *Vermont in the Victorian Age: Continuity and Change in the Green Mountain State, 1850-1900* (Rutland: Vermont Heritage Press, 1985), 51-53; Harvey Howes, "A Last Resort" (Fair Haven: D. Lyman Crandall, 1870).

81 Weston A. Cate, Jr., *Up & Doing: The Vermont Historical Society, 1838–1970* (Montpelier: Vermont Historical Society, 1988), 18, 84–86; Daniel A. Metraux, "Early Vermont Historiography: The Career of Pliny H. White," *Vermont History News* 43 (July–August 1992): 63–66.

82 Hemenway, *Vermont Historical Gazetteer*, 1: iii–iv; Cate, *Up & Doing*, 17–19; Deborah P. Clifford, "Abby Hemenway's Road to Rome," *Vermont History* 62 (Fall 1995): 197–213; Janet Greene, "To Meet Miss Abby Hemenway," in Abby M. Hemenway, *Abby Hemenway's Vermont: Unique Portrait of a State*, ed. Brenda C. Morrissey (Brattleboro, Vt.: Stephen Greene Press, 1972), 1–8.

83 Deborah Pickman Clifford, *The Passion of Abby Hemenway: Memory, Spirit, and the Making of History* (Montpelier: Vermont Historical Society, 2001), 303.

Chapter 6
The Reconfiguration of Vermont: 1870–1900

1 *Journal of the House of Representatives of the State of Vermont, 1870* (Montpelier: Freeman Steam Printing House, 1871), 25.

2 *Journal of the House of Representatives of the State of Vermont, 1882* (Rutland, Vt.: Tuttle & Co., 1883), 37.

3 *Journal of the Senate of the State of Vermont, 1890* (Burlington: Free Press Association), 306.

4 Ibid., 307.

5 "Pacific Coast Association Native Sons of Vermont, Constitution and Bylaws," (San Francisco, 1880), in Vermont Historical Society, pamphlet file.

6 "Daughters of Vermont, Constitution and Bylaws, 1896–97," (n.p. [Boston, Mass.], 1896), in Vermont Historical Society, pamphlet file.

7 Barry Salussolia, "The City of Burlington and Municipal Incorporation in Vermont," *Vermont History* 54 (Winter 1986): 5.

8 See Lilian Baker Carlisle, "Humanities' Needs Deserve Our Fortune: Mary Martha Fletcher and the Fletcher Family Benevolences," *Vermont History* 50 (Summer 1982): 133–42; George B. Bryan, "The Howard Opera House in Burlington," *Vermont History* 45 (Fall 1977): 197–220.

9 Marshall True, "Middle-Class Women and Civic Improvement in Burlington, 1865–1890," *Vermont History* 56 (Spring 1988): 116.

10 Victor R. Rolando, *200 Years of Soot and Sweat: The History and Archaeology of Vermont's Iron, Charcoal, and Lime Industries* (Manchester Center, Vt.: Vermont Archaeological Society, 1992), 15–16.

11 Leon Fink, *Workingmen's Democracy: The Knights of Labor and American Politics* (Urbana & Chicago: University of Illinois Press, 1983), 67. Fink's close study of the Knights of Labor and their role in the transformation of Rutland to a city with surrounding towns is the basis for the following account. See ibid., 66–111.

12 Hamilton Child, *Gazetteer and Business Directory of Rutland County, Vt., for 1881–82* (Syracuse, N.Y.: Journal Office, 1881), 195; see also Robert E. West, ed., *Rutland in Retrospect* (Rutland, Vt.: Academy Books, 1978), 30.

13 Hamilton Child, *Gazetteer and Business Directory of Bennington County, Vermont for 1880–81* (Syracuse, N.Y.: Journal Office, 1880).

14 Dennis G. Waring, *Manufacturing the Muse: Estey Organs and Consumer Culture in Victorian America* (Middletown, Conn.: Wesleyan University Press, 2002), 135.

15 Hamilton Child, *Gazetteer and Business Directory of Windham County, Vt., 1724–1884* (Syracuse, N.Y.: Journal Office, 1884), 87–88. For details of the Estey operations and its importance as a supplier of instruments that served as symbols of middle-class culture and prosperity, see Waring, *Manufacturing the Muse*.

16 Hamilton Child, *Historical Gazetteer of Caledonia and Essex Counties, Vt., 1764–1887* (Syracuse, N.Y.: Syracuse Journal Co., 1887), 312.

17 Charles Edward Russell, *Bare Hands and Stone Walls: Some Recollections of a Side-Line Reformer* (New York: Charles Scribner's Sons, 1933), 15.

18 Allen Rice Yale, Jr., "Ingenious & Enterprising Mechanics: A Case Study of Industrialization in Rural Vermont, 1815–1900" (Ph.D. diss., University of Connecticut, 1995), 258.

19 Hamilton Child, *Child's Gazetteer of Washington County, Vt., 1783–1889: Part Second* (Syracuse, N.Y.: Syracuse Journal Co., 1889), 246–247. See also J. Kevin Graffagnino, *Vermont in the Victorian Age: Continuity and Change in the Green Mountain State, 1850–1900* (Bennington and Shelburne, Vt.: Vermont Heritage Press and Shelburne Museum, 1985), 111–115.

20 Hamilton Child, *Gazetteer and Business Directory of Franklin and Grand Isle Counties, Vt. for 1882–83* (Syracuse, N.Y.: Journal Office, 1883), 162.

21 Lewis Cass Aldrich, *History of Franklin and Grand Isle Counties, Vermont* (Syracuse, N.Y.: D. Mason & Company, 1891), 381.

22 Ibid., 388.

23 Child, *Gazetteer of Franklin and Grand Isle Counties*, 162, 174.

24 Ibid., 166.

25 Hamilton Child, *Gazetteer of Washington County, Vermont*, 334.

26 For an account of the fires and their aftermath, see Abby Maria Hemenway, *Vermont Historical Gazetteer* (Burlington, Vt.: various publishers, 1867–1891), 4: 336–337; Reidun D. Nuquist, et al., *A Walk Through Montpelier* (Montpelier, Vt.: Montpelier Heritage Group, 1976), 3–5, 22, 28; Nuquist, et al., *A Second Walk through Montpelier* (Montpelier, Vt.: Montpelier Heritage Group, 1976), 6–7; Child, *Gazetteer of Washington County, Vermont, 1783–1889*, 326–337; Perry H. Merrill, *Montpelier: The Capital City's History, 1780–1976* (Montpelier: The Author, 1976), 63–65, 74–76.

27 Harold F. Wilson, *The Hill Country of Northern New England: Its Social and Economic History, 1790–1930* (New York: Columbia University Press, 1936), 95.

28 Albert Dwinell, "What Can Be Done to Keep Our Young Men in Vermont?" in Vermont State Board of Agriculture, *Manufactures and Mining, Second Biennial Report . . . 1873–74* (Montpelier, 1874), 681–682; see Graffagnino, *Vermont in the Victorian Age*, 80.

29 Zuar E. Jameson, "Vermont as a Home," in J. Kevin Graffagnino, Samuel B. Hand, and Gene Sessions, eds., *Vermont Voices, 1609 Through the 1990s: A Documentary History of the Green Mountain State* (Montpelier: Vermont Historical Society, 1999), 209–211.

30 Hal S. Barron, *Those Who Stayed Behind: Rural Society in Nineteenth-Century New England* (New York: Cambridge University Press, 1984), 59.

31 H. Nicholas Muller III, "From Ferment to Fatigue? 1870–1900: A New Look at the Neglected Winter of Vermont," Occasional Paper no. 7 (Burlington: Center for Research on Vermont, 1984), 4.

32 See, for example, Vermont Historical Society, Small Broadsides, Music, Cavendish, which includes eleven items advertising concerts, theater events, and other entertainment by local and itinerant talent, covering the years 1875 to 1900.
33 *Acts and Resolves of the State of Vermont, 1886* (Springfield, Mass.: Springfield Printing Co., 1887), no. 93.
34 *The Vermont League for Good Roads, Its Objects, Membership and Officers* (Montpelier, Vt.: Watchman Publishing Co., 1892), 4, quoted in Andrew E. Nuquist and Edith W. Nuquist, *Vermont State Government and Administration: An Historical and Descriptive Study of the Living Past* (Burlington: Government Research Center, University of Vermont, 1966), 384.
35 National Grange of the Patrons of Husbandry, *Proceedings, 1874*, 58, quoted in Lawrence A. Cremin, *The Transformation of the School: Progressivism in American Education, 1876-1957* (New York: Vintage Books, 1964), 42.
36 *School Report, 1869*, 4-8, quoted in John C. Huden, *Development of State School Administration in Vermont* (Montpelier: Vermont Historical Society, 1944), 166.
37 Marshall True, "Schools and Society in the Nineteenth Century," *Vermont History* 40 (Spring 1972): 87.
38 Huden, *School Administration in Vermont*, 173.
39 *Acts and Resolves of the State of Vermont, 1866*, no. 1. See Huden, *School Administration in Vermont*, 133.
40 In 1941 Mortimer R. Proctor, a west-sider, succeeded William H. Wills from Bennington as lieutenant governor, thus breaking the rule for that office; when Proctor succeeded Wills as governor in 1945, he broke the rule for that office as well. See chapter 9, below.
41 Samuel B. Hand, "The Mechanisms of Control: The Mountain Rule," *Vermont History* 48 (Fall 1980): 199-200; Lyman Jay Gould and Samuel B. Hand, "A View from the Mountain: Perspectives of Vermont's Political Geography," in Reginald L. Cook, ed., *Growth and Development of Government in Vermont*, The Vermont Academy of Arts and Sciences, Occasional Paper no. 5 (1970), 19-24, reprinted in H. Nicholas Muller III and Samuel B. Hand, eds., *In A State of Nature, Readings in Vermont History* (Montpelier: Vermont Historical Society, 1982),186-190; Samuel B. Hand, *The Star That Set: The Vermont Republican Party, 1854-1974* (Lanham, Md.: Lexington Books, 2002), 33-56, et passim; Samuel B. Hand, "Mountain Rule Revisited," *Vermont History* 71 (Summer/Fall 2003): 139-151.
42 Robin W. Winks, *Frederick Billings: A Life* (New York: Oxford University Press, 1991), 268-70.
43 Hand, *The Star That Set*, 40-41.
44 Samuel B. Hand, Jeffrey D. Marshall, and D. Gregory Sanford, "'Little Republics': The Structure of State Politics in Vermont, 1854-1920," *Vermont History* 53 (Summer 1985):144.
45 *Women's Journal*, 4 October 1879, 320, quoted in Deborah P. Clifford, "The Drive for Women's Municipal Suffrage in Vermont, 1883-1917," *Vermont History* 47 (Summer 1979): 175.
46 R. L. Duffus, *Williamstown Branch: Impersonal Memories of a Vermont Boyhood* (New York: W. W. Norton & Company, 1958), 67.
47 Hand, et al., "'Little Republics,'" 149.
48 Barron, *Those Who Stayed Behind*, 122.

49 See Graffagnino, *Vermont in the Victorian Age*, 98–101.
50 See George B. Bryan, "A Historical Who's Who of Vermont Theatre," Occasional Paper no. 13 (Burlington: Center for Research on Vermont, 1991), 15–16.
51 See Michael Sherman, "Art by the Yard: Vermont's Painted Theatre Curtains," *Vermont Life* 57 (Winter 2002-2003): 44–49; Ed Wells, "Curtain Call," *Preservation* 54 (May/June 2002): 66–70.
52 See Graffagnino, *Vermont in the Victorian Age*, ix–xxxii.
53 Harold A. Meeks, *Time and Change in Vermont: A Human Geography* (Chester, Conn.: Globe Pequot Press, 1986), 140–156.
54 See Dona Brown, *Inventing New England: Regional Tourism in the Nineteenth Century* (Washington, D.C.: Smithsonian Institution Press, 1995), 135–167.
55 Rowland E. Robinson, preface to *Danvis Folk* (1894), quoted in Hayden Carruth, "Vermont's Genius of the Folk, Rowland E. Robinson," in *Danvis Tales: Selected Stories by Rowland E. Robinson*, ed. David Budbill (Hanover, N.H.: University Press of New England, 1995), xxxi.
56 Rowland E. Robinson, "Author's Foreword," *Danvis Tales*, 3.
57 See William C. Lipke, "The Readable Image: Thomas Waterman Wood and Popular Genre," in *Thomas Waterman Wood, P.N.A, 1823-1903* (Montpelier, Vt.: Wood Art Gallery, 1972), 13–58.
58 Quoted in Walter Hill Crockett, *Vermont, The Green Mountain State* (New York: The Century History Company, 1921-1923), 4: 201–202.
59 For Harrison's itinerary and his comments along the route, see ibid., 4: 204–210.

Chapter 7
"Behind the Times": 1900-1927

1 Austin F. Hawes, "History of Forestry in Vermont," 3. Unpublished typescript copy in Vermont Historical Society.
2 Charles S. Forbes, *The Celebration of the Centennial of the Establishment of the Capital of Vermont at Montpelier, October 4, 1905* (St. Albans, Vt.: St. Albans Messenger Co., 1905), 27, 22, 29, 30.
3 *Journal of the Senate of the State of Vermont, Biennial Session 1906* (St. Albans, Vt.: St. Albans Messenger Company Print., 1907), 527.
4 See Gerard J. Brault, *The French-Canadian Heritage in New England* (Hanover, N.H.: University Press of New England, 1986); U.S. Commission on Civil Rights, Vermont Advisory Committee, *Franco-Americans in Vermont, A Civil Rights Perspective* (Washington, D.C.: U.S. Commission on Civil Rights, 1983); Lewis S. Feuer and Mervyn W. Perrine, "Religion in a Northern Vermont Town," *Journal for the Scientific Study of Religion* 5 (Fall 1966): 370; Gwilym R. Roberts, *New Lives in the Valley: Slate Quarries and Quarry Villages in North Wales, New York, and Vermont, 1850–1920* (Somersworth, N.H.: New Hampshire Printers, 1998); T. D. Seymour Bassett, *The Gods of the Hills: Piety and Society in Nineteenth-Century Vermont* (Montpelier: Vermont Historical Society, 2000), 223–235; Ronald C. Murphy and Jeffrey Potash, "'The Highgate Affair,' An Episode in Establishing the Authority of the Roman Catholic Diocese of Burlington," *Vermont History* 52 (Winter 1984): 33–43; William Wolkovich-Valkavicius, "The Lithuanians of Arlington," *Vermont History* 54 (Summer 1986): 164–174.
5 Forbes, *The Celebration of the Centennial*, 30.

6   Federal Writers' Project, Life History Narratives, Vermont, interview no. 103, Library of Congress.
7   Paul Demers, "Labor and the Social Relations of the Granite Industry in Barre" (B.A. thesis, Goddard College, 1974), 24, in Vermont Historical Society.
8   Deane C. Davis, with Nancy Price Graff, *Deane C. Davis: An Autobiography* (Shelburne, Vt.: The New England Press, 1991), 67.
9   Ibid.
10 *Burlington Free Press*, 7 March 1906.
11 Demers, "Labor and Social Relations," 35–36. The following discussion of local Barre politics is based on the author's examination of Barre City Records, 1898–1917, Barre City Clerk's office, including voter checklists, election returns, and lists of takers of the Freeman's Oath; Barre City Reports, 1898–1916; U.S. Census, schedule 1, Barre City, 1910.
12 Manuscript voting records, Barre City Clerk's office, Barre, Vermont.
13 Greg Guma, *The People's Republic: Vermont and the Sanders Revolution* (Shelburne, Vt.: The New England Press, 1989), 76.
14 Andrew E. Nuquist and Edith W. Nuquist, *Vermont State Government and Administration: An Historical and Descriptive Study of the Living Past* (Burlington: Government Research Center, University of Vermont, 1966): 74.
15 Earle S. Kinsley, *Recollections of Vermonters in State and National Affairs* (Rutland, Vt., 1946), 122.
16 Mason A. Green, *Nineteen-Two in Vermont: The Fight for Local Option* (Rutland, Vt.: The Marble City Press, c.1912), 51, 69; *Montpelier Evening Argus*, 4 October 1905; Arthur F. Stone, *The Vermont of Today: With Its Historical Backgrounds, Attractions, and People* (New York: Lewis Historical Publishing Company, 1929), 1: 109–110.
17 Green, *Nineteen-Two in Vermont*, 13.
18 Kinsley, *Recollections*, 92.
19 Green, *Nineteen-Two in Vermont*, 14, 95.
20 For the local option law, see *Acts and Resolves Passed by the General Assembly of the State of Vermont at the Seventeenth Biennial Session, 1902* (Burlington, Vt.: Free Press Association, 1902), 92–113; for the Corrupt Practices Act, see ibid., 5–6. For the caucus reform legislation, see *Acts and Resolve Passed by the General Assembly of the State of Vermont at the Eighteenth Biennial Session, 1904* (Burlington, Vt.: Free Press Association, 1904), 4–8. The *Free Press* quotation appeared on 1 December 1904.
21 R. L. Duffus, *The Waterbury Record* (New York: W. W. Norton & Company, 1959), 191.
22 Samuel B. Hand, Jeffrey D. Marshall, and D. Gregory Sanford, "'Little Republics': The Structure of State Politics in Vermont, 1854–1920," *Vermont History* 53 (Summer 1985): 158.
23 Hawes, "History of Forestry," 1.
24 For the judicial reform plan, see *Acts and Resolves Passed by the General Assembly of the State of Vermont at the Nineteenth Biennial Session, 1906* (Burlington, Vt.: Free Press Printing co., 1906), 67–74; for the bill on weekly wage payments, see ibid., 114.
25 Ibid., 138–146, 128–133, 35–37.
26 See *Acts and Resolves Passed by the General Assembly of the State of Vermont at the*

Twentieth Biennial Session, 1908 (Montpelier, Vt.: Capital City Press, Printers, 1908), 101–108.

27 Walter Hill Crockett, *Vermont, The Green Mountain State*, (New York: The Century History Co., 1921–1923), 4: 435.

28 "Platform of the Progressive Party of the State of Vermont, 1912," in Vermont Historical Society.

29 Winston Allen Flint, *The Progressive Movement in Vermont* (Washington, D.C.: American Council on Public Affairs, 1941), 75.

30 See *Acts and Resolves . . . of the State of Vermont, 1904*, 211–212; *Acts and Resolves . . . of the State of Vermont, 1906*, 54–56; and *Acts and Resolves Passed by the General Assembly of the State of Vermont at the Twenty-First Biennial Session, 1910* (Rutland, Vt.: The Tuttle Company, 1911), 79–82.

31 For the factory inspection enactment, see *Acts and Resolves Passed by the General Assembly of the State of Vermont at the Twenty-Second Biennial Session, 1912* (Montpelier, Vt.: Capital City Press, Printers, 1913), 241–243; for the "Act Relative to the Hours of Employment of Women and Children in Manufacturing and Mechanical Establishments," see ibid., 104–105. For the workmen's compensation law, see *Acts and Resolves Passed by the General Assembly of the State of Vermont at the Twenty-Third Biennial Session, 1915* (Concord, N.H.: Rumford Press, 1915), 275–292.

32 *Acts and Resolves Passed by the General Assembly of the State of Vermont at the Twelfth Biennial Session, 1892* (Burlington, Vt.: The Free Press Association, Printers and Binders, 1892), 24–32.

33 Arthur Wentworth Hewitt, *The Old Brick Manse* (New York: Harper & Row, 1966), 118.

34 David B. Danbom, *Born in the Country: A History of Rural America* (Baltimore: The Johns Hopkins University Press, 1995), 169.

35 See *Acts and Resolves . . . of the State of Vermont, 1906*, 47–49; *Acts and Resolves . . . of the State of Vermont, 1912*, 64–68.

36 See "A Joint Resolution Relating to a Commission to Investigate the Educational System and Conditions of Vermont," in *Acts and Resolves . . . of the State of Vermont, 1912*, 629–630.

37 Commission to Investigate the Educational System and Conditions of Vermont, *Report* (Brattleboro, Vt.: The Vermont Printing Company, 1914), 5. The Carnegie Foundation findings, "A Study of Education in Vermont," are included in this *Report*.

38 The school-related bills enacted by the 1915 legislature are in *Acts and Resolves . . . of the State of Vermont, 1915*, 124–171.

39 Hewitt, *Old Brick Manse*, 111–112, 118. The "Carnegie legislation" is in *Acts and Resolves . . . of the State of Vermont, 1915*, 124–161.

40 See Hand, Marshall, and Sanford, "'Little Republics,'" 156–157.

41 Edwin C. Rozwenc, *Agricultural Policies in Vermont: 1860–1945* (Montpelier: Vermont Historical Society, 1981), 79–80.

42 See Marshall M. True and Judith Cyronak, *Vermont Department of Education, 1900–1968* (Montpelier: Vermont Department of Education, 1968), 25.

43 Mason S. Stone, *History of Education: State of Vermont* (Montpelier, Vt.: Capital City Press, 1934), 327.

44 See *Acts and Resolves . . . of the State of Vermont, 1915*, 58–69.

45 "Report of the Commissioners on Forestry" [to the General Assembly], (Montpelier, Vt.), 31 October 1884.

46 Joseph Battell, "Our Forests; Necessity For Their Preservation" (reprint from *Middlebury Register*, 5 December 1890), 2, 4, 5.

47 John Aubrey Douglass, "Prospective for a National Forest: Economic Influences on Vermont's Efforts to Manage Forest Resources," *Vermont History* 54 (Spring 1986): 73-74.

48 Laura Waterman and Guy Waterman, *Forest and Crag: A History of Hiking, Trail Blazing, and Adventure in the Northeast Mountains* (Boston: Appalachian Mountain Club, 1989), 312.

49 Hawes, "History of Forestry," 18.

50 Ibid., 19.

51 Ibid., 13-14.

52 Perry H. Merrill, *History of Forestry in Vermont, 1909-1959* (Montpelier, Vt.: State Board of Forests and Parks, 1959), 11.

53 *Acts and Resolves . . . of the State of Vermont, 1912*, 26.

54 W. Storrs Lee, *The Green Mountains of Vermont* (New York: Henry Holt and Company, 1955), 199-200.

55 Waterman and Waterman, *Forest and Crag*, 355, 353, 252.

56 See ibid., 353-373, for a discussion of the beginnings of the Green Mountain Club. See also Hal Goldman, "'A Desirable Class of People': The Leadership of the Green Mountain Club and Social Exclusivity, 1920-1936," *Vermont History* 65 (Summer/Fall 1997): 131-152.

57 Howard L. Hindley, *The Gentleman From Hayville* (Rutland, Vt., 1909).

58 Ibid., 17, 32-33, 16.

59 Ibid., 71.

60 Ibid., 14-15, 19-20, 86-87.

61 Lorenzo D'Agostino, *The History of Public Welfare in Vermont* (Washington, D.C.: The Catholic University of America Press, 1948), 271.

62 *Acts and Resolves . . . of the State of Vermont, 1902*, 59-60.

63 Lee, *The Green Mountains*, 153.

64 *Acts and Resolves . . . of the State of Vermont, 1910*, 134.

65 Benjamin Gates, "Holding Hands With Speed," *The Vermonter* (November 1921): 219.

66 Allen A. Sher, "The Street Railways of Rutland," *Rutland Historical Society Quarterly* 10 (Winter 1980): 3.

67 "Rudyard Kipling Defends 'The Beauty For Which Brattleboro Is So Greatly Famous': An Unpublished Letter Written in 1895," *Vermont History* 37 (Spring 1969): 95.

68 A useful introduction to the impact of technological changes on domestic labor is Susan Strasser, *Never Done: A History of American Housework* (New York: Henry Holt, 2000).

69 Dorothy C. Walter, "Chautauqua Week in Lyndonville: A Description Written in 1915," *Vermont History* 38 (Summer 1970): 200-203.

70 Vermont Commission on Country Life, *Rural Vermont: A Program for the Future* (Burlington: Vermont Commission on Country Life, 1931), 179.

71 John T. Cushing and Arthur F. Stone, eds., *Vermont in the World War, 1917-1919*

(Burlington, Vt.: Free Press Printing Company, 1928), 453-455; *Acts and Resolves Passed by the General Assembly of the State of Vermont at the Twenty-Fourth Biennial Session, 1917* (Montpelier, Vt.: Capital City Press, 1917), 53.

72 Gene Sessions, "Espionage in Windsor: Clarence H. Waldron and Patriotism in World War I," *Vermont History* 61 (Summer 1993): 138.

73 See John Buechler, "Buffalo Soldiers in the Green Mountains," *Chittenden County Historical Society Bulletin* (November 1969); and Buechler, "Buffalo Soldiers in the Green Mountains, Part II," *Chittenden County Historical Society Bulletin* (April 1970).

74 *Acts and Resolves . . . of the State of Vermont, 1917*, 255-257.

75 Sessions, "Espionage in Windsor," 133-155.

76 Cushing and Stone, eds., *Vermont in the World War*, 740; *Journal of the Senate of the State of Vermont, Twenty-Fifth Biennial Session, 1919* (Montpelier, Vt.: Capital City Press, Printers, 1919), 671; *Acts and Resolves Passed by the General Assembly of the State of Vermont at the Twenty-Fifth Biennial Session, 1919* (Montpelier, Vt.: Capital City Press, 1919), 203-204.

77 An introduction to Vermont's influenza experience is in Michael Sherman, "Spanish Influenza in Vermont, 1918-1919," (unpublished typescript copy in possession of author), 5-6. A version of this manuscript is in *Historic Roots* 3 (April 1998): 11-17.

78 D. Gregory Sanford, "Redstone Reflections," *Vermont News & Notes* (State of Vermont Department of Personnel), February 1987, 5.

79 Vermont Commission on Country Life, *Rural Vermont*, 231. See also Marilyn S. Blackwell, "The Politics of Public Health: Medical Inspection and School Nursing in Vermont, 1910-1923," *Vermont History* 68 (Winter/Spring 2000): 76-79.

80 *Acts and Resolves of the State of Vermont, 1923* (n.p., n.d.), Act No. 7, p. 617.

81 Kinsley, *Recollections*, 62.

82 Mary Beardsley Fenn, "James Hartness and Lena Pond Hartness," unpublished typescript copy in Vermont Historical Society, 34. See also, John A. Neuenschwander, "An Engineer for Governor: James Hartness in 1920," *Vermont History* 38 (Spring 1970): 139-149.

83 J. Kevin Graffagnino, Samuel B. Hand, and Gene Sessions, eds., *Vermont Voices, 1609 Through the 1990s: A Documentary History of the Green Mountain State* (Montpelier: Vermont Historical Society, 1999), 289, 288.

84 Charles Edward Crane, *Let Me Show You Vermont* (New York: Alfred A. Knopf, 1937), 263.

85 Arthur Schlesinger, Jr., *The Crisis of the Old Order, 1919-1933* (Boston: Houghton Mifflin Company, 1957), 56.

86 *Journal of the Senate of the State of Vermont, 1919*, 723.

87 Ann Banks, ed., *First-Person America* (New York: Vintage Books, 1981), 106.

88 Scott E. Hastings, Jr., *Goodbye Highland Yankee: Stories of a North Country Boyhood* (Chelsea, Vt.: Chelsea Green Publishing, 1988), 129-130.

89 On Vermont's prohibition era, see also Scott Wheeler, *Rumrunners & Revenuers: Prohibition in Vermont* (Shelburne, Vt.: The New England Press, 2003), 168.

90 Burlington (Vt.) Bicentennial Committee, *Bygone Burlington* (Burlington, Vt.: Queen City Printers, 1976), 47.

91 *Journal of the Senate of the State of Vermont, 1921*, 668.

92 Northfield Town History Committee, *Green Mountain Heritage; the Chronicle of Northfield, Vermont* (Canaan, N. H.: Phoenix Publishing, 1974), 383.

93 See Maudean Neill, *Fiery Crosses in the Green Mountains: The Story of the Ku Klux Klan in Vermont* (Randolph Center, Vt.: Greenhills Books, 1989).

94 Kenneth T. Jackson, *The Ku Klux Klan in the City, 1915-1930* (New York: Oxford University Press, 1967), 237.

95 Neill, *Fiery Crosses in the Green Mountains*, 70.

96 St. Augustine Church (Montpelier, Vt.), *The Church of St. Augustine at Montpelier, Vermont: 1892-1992, A Century of Blessings* ([no imprint], 1992), 21.

97 On dairying and the rise of agricultural specialization, see Harold F. Wilson, *The Hill Country of Northern New England: Its Social and Economic History, 1790-1930* (New York: Columbia University Press, 1936; reprint, New York: AMS Press, 1967), 184-230.

98 For a discussion of fluid milk and cream marketing, see H. A. Dwinell, *Vermont's Dairy Industry, 1791-1941*, Bulletin No. 56 (Montpelier: Vermont Department of Agriculture, August 1941), 18-19.

99 Rozwenc, *Agricultural Policies in Vermont*, 139.

100 On the "Boston Milk War," see Wilson, *Hill Country of Northern New England*, 339-341.

101 Gregory Sharrow and Nancy Price Graff, *Measured Furrows: Vermont's Farming History* (Colchester: Vermont ETV, Middlebury: Vermont Folklife Center, 1996), 23.

102 Stone, *The Vermont of Today*, 2: 477, 483.

103 Dorman B. E. Kent, "Vermont in Agriculture and Industry," *Vermont Highways* (June 1930): 19-20.

104 Wilson, *The Hill Country of Northern New England*, 377.

105 Howard S. Russell, *A Long, Deep Furrow: Three Centuries of Farming in New England* (Hanover, N.H.: University Press of New England, 1976), 519.

106 Richard M. Judd, *The New Deal in Vermont: Its Impact and Aftermath* (New York: Garland Publishing Inc., 1979), 16.

107 *Journal of the Senate of the State of Vermont Biennial Session, 1921* (Montpelier, Vt.: Capital City Press, Printers, 1921), 684.

108 In 1929, Vermont's ten largest industries based on numbers of employees were:
granite/marble/stone—5,200
foundry and machine—4,000
lumber and timber—2,700
woolen goods—1,500
furniture —1,200
knit goods—1,100
paper and pulp—1,000
railroad car and shop—750
printing and publishing—500
dairy products—100
See *State Planning, Vermont 1936, Progress Report Submitted to The Vermont State Planning Board and the Natural Resources Committee* (Montpelier, Vt., 1936), 28-29.

109 New England Power Association, "Industrial Survey of Vermont, Summary Report, 1930," 25-26.

110 Roberts, *New Lives in the Valley,* 273–274.
111 Allison M. Deen, "The Story of the 1912 Strike against the International Paper Company in Bellows Falls, Vermont," 1983. Photocopy of transcript in Vermont Historical Society.
112 Federal Writers' Project, life history narratives, Vermont, interview no. 121, Library of Congress.
113 *They Came to Work: Oral Histories of the Vermont Granite Industry During the 1920s and 1930s,* interviews conducted by Marjorie Strong, Greg Sharrow; ed. Kim Chase (Middlesex, Vt.: Franglais Cultural Center, 1997), 5.
114 Banks, ed., *First-Person America,* 109.
115 See David Howard Bain and Mary Smyth Duffy, eds., *Whose Woods These Are: A History of the Bread Loaf Writers' Conference, 1926–1992* (Hopewell, N.J.: The Ecco Press, 1993).
116 Vermont Commission on Country Life, *Rural Vermont,* 371.
117 J. Kevin Graffagnino, "It Did Happen Here: Sinclair Lewis and the Image of Vermont," *Vermont History* 49 (Winter 1981): 32, 35.
118 Castleton State College History Students, *Beautiful Lake Bomoseen* (Castleton, Vt.: Castleton State College, 1999), 204.
119 "Episodes from *Herald* History," in *The Sunday Rutland Herald and the Sunday Times Argus,* 18 August 1991, 25.
120 Sinclair Lewis, "A Double Life for Writers," *The Readers' Digest* (October 1936): 72.
121 Walter J. Coates, "Rediscovering Vermont Literature," *The Driftwind* (June 1926): [17].

Chapter 8
Floods, Depression, and War: 1927–1945
1 *Burlington Free Press,* 14 November 1927.
2 Ralph Nading Hill, *Lake Champlain: Key to Liberty* (Taftsville, Vt.: The Countryman Press, 1976), 258.
3 *Journal of the Senate of the State of Vermont, Special Session, 1927; Biennial Session, 1929* (Montpelier, Vt.: Capital City Press, Printers, 1929), 34.
4 Charles S. Ferrin, "Military Reminiscences of the Flood of 1927," ed. Robert V. Daniels, *Vermont History* 43 (Spring 1975): 149.
5 Earle S. Kinsley, *Recollections of Vermonters in State and National Affairs* (Rutland, Vt., 1946), 140–141.
6 *Burlington Free Press,* 17 November 1927, 15 November 1927.
7 Ibid., 18 November 1927.
8 The governor's message and the flood legislation are in *Acts and Resolves Passed by the General Assembly of the State of Vermont at the Thirteenth Biennial Session, 1929; Special Session, November 30, 1927* (n.p., n.d.), 241–257.
9 *Congressional Record,* 70th Cong., 1st sess., 1928, 69, pt. 5: 4,880.
10 Ibid., pt. 3: 2,800.
11 *Thirty-Third Annual Report of the Officers of the City of Montpelier for the Year Ending January 31, 1928* (Montpelier, Vt.: Capital City Press, Printers, 1928), 60.
12 *The Vermonter* (September 1929): 129.
13 Otto T. Johnson, "The Spirit of Vermont," *The Vermonter* (October 1937): 190.

14 William H. Rice, "Vermont in Retrospect," *The Vermonter* (September 1942): 126.
15 *Burlington Free Press*, 10 June 1952.
16 Consuelo Bailey, *Leaves Before the Wind: The Autobiography of Vermont's Own Daughter* (Burlington, Vt.: George Little Press, 1976), 134.
17 Vermont Commission on Country Life, *Rural Vermont: A Program for the Future* (Burlington: Vermont Commission on Country Life, 1931), 2, iii.
18 On Perkins's Eugenics Survey, see Kevin Dann, "From Degeneration to Regeneration: The Eugenics Survey of Vermont, 1925-1936," *Vermont History* 59 (Winter 1991): 5-29; and Nancy L. Gallagher, *Breeding Better Vermonters: The Eugenics Project in the Green Mountain State* (Hanover, N.H.: University Press of New England, 1999).
19 Samuel A. McReynolds, "Eugenics and Rural Development: The Vermont Commission on Country Life's Program for the Future," *Agricultural History* 71 (Summer 1997): 311.
20 Ibid., 312.
21 Vermont Commission on Country Life, *Rural Vermont*, 31, 32.
22 Ibid., 300.
23 *Acts and Resolves Passed by the General Assembly of the State of Vermont at the Thirty-First Biennial Session, 1931* (n.p., n.d.), 194-195.
24 Richard M. Judd, *The New Deal in Vermont: Its Impact and Aftermath* (New York: Garland Publishing, 1979), 3.
25 Gallagher, *Breeding Better Vermonters*, 161.
26 U.S. Census, Biennial Census of Manufactures, cited in *Brattleboro Reformer*, 17 May 1935; *Brattleboro Reformer*, 24 May 1932; U.S. Census, 1940.
27 Franklin S. Billings to John P. Clement, 18 October 1932, John P. Clement Papers, Vermont Historical Society.
28 Ernest W. Gibson, Jr., to Floyd Johnson, 31 March 1933, Ernest W. Gibson, Jr. Papers, Bailey-Howe Library, University of Vermont.
29 Northfield Town History Committee, *Green Mountain Heritage: The Chronicle of Northfield, Vermont* (Canaan, N.H.: Phoenix Publishing, 1974), 418.
30 Anna L. Mower and Robert L. Hagerman, *Morristown Two Times* (Morrisville, Vt.: Morristown Historical Society, 1982), 476.
31 "Vermont in the Great Depression," audio tape no. 26 in "Green Mountain Chronicles, A Program of the Vermont Historical Society," Vermont Historical Society.
32 Scott E. Hastings, *Up in the Morning Early: Vermont Farm Families in the Thirties* (Hanover, N.H.: University Press of New England, 1992), 89.
33 *Thirty-eighth Annual Report of the City of Barre, Vermont for the Year Ending December 31, 1932* (Barre, Vt.: Granite City Press, Printers, 1933), 9.
34 *Eighteenth Annual Report of Cooperative Extension Work in Agriculture and Home Economics, State of Vermont, For Year 1932*, Extension Bulletin No. 18 (April 1933), 12.
35 *Fortieth Annual Report of the City of Barre, Vermont for the Year Ending December 31, 1934* (Barre, Vt.: Granite City Press, Printer, 1935), 10.
36 Claire Dunne Johnson, *"I See By the Paper—: An Informal History of St. Johnsbury, Vol. II, 1920-1960* (St. Johnsbury, Vt.: The Cowles Press, 1989), 126-149; and *Auditor's Report, Town of St. Johnsbury, Vt., Also report of Treasurer and Manager for the Year Ending January 19, 1932*, (St. Johnsbury, Vt.: The Cowles Press, 1932), 2: 10.

37 *Barre Times*, 3 November 1933; *Barre City Report*, 1933, 10, 90.
38 *Burlington Free Press*, 16 January 1933.
39 *Journal of the Senate of the State of Vermont, Biennial Session 1933* (Montpelier, Vt.: Capital City Press, Printers, 1933), 510, 500–501.
40 Judd, *New Deal in Vermont*, 35–36.
41 Perry H. Merrill, *Vermont Under Four Flags: A History of the Green Mountain State, 1635–1975* (Montpelier, Vt.: The Author, 1975), 210.
42 Frederick W. Stetson, "The Civilian Conservation Corps in Vermont," *Vermont History* 46 (Winter 1978): 37.
43 Perry H. Merrill, *History of Forestry in Vermont 1909–1959* (Montpelier, Vt.: State Board of Forests and Parks, 1959), 63.
44 Stetson, "The Civilian Conservation Corps," 26.
45 Judd, *New Deal in Vermont*, 212.
46 Ibid., 215.
47 *Acts and Resolves Passed by the General Assembly of the State of Vermont at the Thirty-Third Biennial Session, 1935* (n.p., n.d.), 93–100.
48 George D. Aiken, *Speaking From Vermont* (New York: Frederick A. Stokes Company, 1938), 113.
49 Federal Writers' Project, life history narratives, Vermont, interview no. 44, Library of Congress.
50 Ibid., interview no. 56.
51 Connell B. Gallagher, "Vermonters at Work and at Home," in Michael Sherman and Jennie Versteeg, eds., *We Vermonters: Perspectives on the Past* (Montpelier, Vt.: Capital City Press, 1992), 179.
52 Hannah Silverstein, "No Parking: Vermont Rejects the Green Mountain Parkway," *Vermont History* 63 (Summer 1995): 142.
53 Judd, *New Deal in Vermont*, 85.
54 Frank M. Bryan, *Yankee Politics in Rural Vermont* (Hanover, N.H.: The University Press of New England, 1974), 205.
55 "Episodes from *Herald* History," *The Sunday Rutland Herald* and the *Sunday Times-Argus*, 18 August 1991, 26.
56 Ibid.
57 Sara M. Gregg, "Can We 'Trust Uncle Sam'? Vermont and the Submarginal Lands Project, 1934–1936," *Vermont History* 69 (Winter/Spring 2001): 206.
58 Samuel B. Hand and Paul M. Searls, "Transition Politics: Vermont, 1940–1952," *Vermont History* 62 (Winter 1994): 9.
59 Samuel B. Hand and Michael Sherman, "Introduction," in Michael Sherman, ed., *The Political Legacy of George D. Aiken: Wise Old Owl of the U.S. Senate* (Montpelier: Vermont Historical Society, 1995), 16.
60 James Wright, "Growing Up Progressive," in ibid.
61 Samuel B. Hand and D. Gregory Sanford, "Carrying Water on Both Shoulders: George D. Aiken's 1936 Gubernatorial Campaign in Vermont," *Vermont History* 43 (Fall 1975): 304.
62 Ibid., 303.
63 "George D. Aiken Oral History Memoir," photocopy of transcript, Vermont Historical Society, 56.

64 *Acts and Resolves Passed by the General Assembly of the State of Vermont at the Thirty-Second Biennial Session, 1933* (n.p., n.d.), 49–53.
65 Hand and Sanford, "Carrying Water," 305.
66 Ibid.
67 Aiken, *Speaking From Vermont*, 117.
68 Michael John Jarvis, "The Senators from Vermont and Lend-Lease, 1939–1941" (M.A. thesis, University of Vermont, 1974), 41.
69 William E. Leuchtenburg, *Franklin D. Roosevelt and the New Deal* (New York: Harper and Row, 1963), 157.
70 Samuel B. Hand and D. Gregory Sanford, "'I Believe I Will Go': Organization Politics in Republican Vermont," *Vermont History News* 39 (January–February 1988): 11.
71 Neal R. Peirce, *The New England States: People, Politics, and Power in the Six New England States* (New York: W. W. Norton & Company, 1976), 266.
72 Edwin C. Rozwenc, "The Group Basis of Vermont Farm Politics, 1870–1945," *Vermont History* 25 (October 1957): 283.
73 Hand and Sherman, "Introduction," in Sherman, ed., *The Public Legacy of George D. Aiken*, 17.
74 Ralph Nading Hill, *The Winooski: Heartway of Vermont* (New York: Rinehart & Company, 1949), 194; also, see *Barre-Montpelier Times Argus*, 20 July 2000.
75 D. Gregory Sanford, "You Can't Get There From Here: The Presidential Boomlet for Governor George D. Aiken, 1937–1939," *Vermont History* 49 (Fall 1981): 200.
76 "George D. Aiken Oral History Memoir," 74.
77 Johnson, "The Spirit of Vermont," 191.
78 Aiken, *Speaking From Vermont*, 175.
79 *Journal of the Senate of the State of Vermont, 1939* (Montpelier, Vt.: Capital City Press, 1939), 824.
80 John Aubrey Douglass, "The Forest Service, the Depression, and Vermont Political Culture: Implementing New Deal Conservation and Relief Policy," *Forest and Conservation History* 34 (October 1990): 170.
81 Hill, *The Winooski*, 199.
82 Paul M. Searls, "Labor, Politics, and Republican Vermont" (M.A. thesis, University of Vermont, 1993), 10.
83 Roby Colodny, "Labor in Barre: 1900–1941," in *Vermont's Untold History* (Burlington, Vt.: Public Occurrence, 1976), 16.
84 Peter H. Haraty, ed., *Put the Vermonters Ahead: A History of the Vermont National Guard, 1764–1978* (Burlington, Vt.: Queen City Printers, 1982), 191; Heber G. England to Governor Stanley C. Wilson, 13 June 1933, Stanley Calef Wilson Papers (microfilm), Correspondence 1933, Vermont State Archives.
85 Federal Writers' Project, life history narratives, Vermont, interview no. 116, Library of Congress.
86 *Rutland Herald*, 23 November 1935.
87 Haraty, ed., *Put the Vermonters Ahead*, 192.
88 Federal Writers Project, life history narratives, Vermont, interview no. 48, Library of Congress.
89 Frances Pohl, "Rockwell Kent and the Marble Workers' Strike," *Archives of American Art Journal* 29 nos. 3–4 (1989): 54, 55.

90 "Strike, of Vermont Marble Company Workers, Verbatim Report of Public Hearing, Town Hall, West Rutland, Vt., Feb. 29, 1936," United Committee to Aid Vermont Marble Workers, New York City, in Vermont Historical Society.

91 Two months prior to the striking marble workers' public meeting at the West Rutland Town Hall, the Vermont Marble Company circulated an eight-page statement of its position. See "A Statement by the Vermont Marble Company," 21 December 1935, in Vermont State Library, Montpelier.

92 Searls, "Labor, Politics, and Republican Vermont," 35.

93 *Agriculture of Vermont: Fourteenth Biennial Report of the Commissioner of Agriculture, 1926-1928* (Montpelier, Vt.: Department of Agriculture), 5-6.

94 H. A. Dwinell, *Vermont's Dairy Industry, 1791-1941*, Bulletin no. 56, Vermont Department of Agriculture (Montpelier, Vt.: August 1941), 29

95 Ibid.

96 *Journal of the Senate of the State of Vermont; Special Sessions, 1935-1936, and Biennial Session, 1937* (Montpelier, Vt.: Capital City Press, Printers, 1937), 673.

97 Meeks, *Time and Change in Vermont*, 225.

98 Vrest Orton, "How to Make Vermont Free," *Driftwind* 3 (January 1929): 145-146.

99 Vermont Commission on Country Life, *Rural Vermont*, 118, 117.

100 *Brattleboro Reformer*, 4 November 1933.

101 John Aubrey Douglass, "Prospective for a National Forest: Economic Influences on Vermont's Efforts to Manage Forest Resources," *Vermont History* 54 (Spring 1986): 84.

102 *Acts and Resolves of the State of Vermont, 1935*, 4-5.

103 Laura Waterman and Guy Waterman, *Forest and Crag: A History of Hiking, Trail Blazing, and Adventure in the Northeast Mountains* (Boston: Appalachian Mountain Club, 1989), 334.

104 E. John B. Allen, *From Skisport to Skiing: One Hundred Years of an American Sport, 1840-1940* (Amherst: The University of Massachusetts Press, 1993), 109-111.

105 Lyrics for the song, "Moonlight in Vermont," by John Blackburn, are:

> Pennies in a stream
> Falling leaves, a Sycamore,
> Moonlight in Vermont.
>
> Icy finger waves
> Ski trails on a mountain-side,
> Snowlight in Vermont.
>
> Telegraph cables, they sing down the high-way
> And travel each bend in the road,
> People who meet in this romantic setting
> Are so hypnotized by the lovely . . .
>
> Ev'ning summer breeze
> Warbling of a meadowlark,
> Moonlight in Vermont
> You and I and Moonlight in Vermont.

106 William C. Lipke, "From Pastoralism to Progressivism: Myth and Reality in Twentieth-Century Vermont," in Nancy Price Graff, ed., *Celebrating Vermont: Myths and Realities* (Middlebury, Vt.: Christian A. Johnson Memorial Gallery and Middlebury College, 1991), 72-74.

107 Federal Writers' Project, life history narratives, Vermont, interview no. 45, Library of Congress.
108 Sanford, "You Can't Get There From Here," 198.
109 *New York Times*, 13 February 1938.
110 See "George D. Aiken Oral History Memoir," 83.
111 Hand and Searls, "Transition Politics," 10.
112 Searls, "Labor, Politics, and Republican Vermont," 39.
113 Deane C. Davis, with Nancy Price Graff, *Deane C. Davis: An Autobiography* (Shelburne, Vt.: The New England Press, 1991), 185.
114 Rozwenc, "The Group Basis of Vermont Farm Politics, 1870-1945," 284.
115 *Burlington Free Press*, 3 December 1935. See also, *Rutland Herald*, 6 November 1935.
116 Searls, "Labor, Politics, and Republican Vermont," 40.
117 See "George D. Aiken Oral History Memoir," 60.
118 Bill Porter and Stephen C. Terry, "Down and Dirty, the Aiken-Flanders Primary of 1940," *Rutland Herald*, 9 September 1990, *Vermont Sunday Magazine*.
119 *Brattleboro Reformer*, 18 July 1940.
120 Samuel B. Hand, "Friends, Neighbors, and Political Allies: Reflections on the Gibson-Aiken Connection," Occasional Paper no. 11, Center for Research on Vermont, University of Vermont (Burlington, Vt., 1986), 10.
121 Robert W. Mitchell, "Unique Vermont," *The American Mercury* (March 1945): 338.
122 "Episodes from *Herald* History," 27.
123 Herbert S. Parmet, "George Aiken: A Republican Senator and His Party," in Sherman, ed., *The Political Legacy of George D. Aiken*, 38.
124 James L. Oakes, "George D. Aiken: A Tribute," in ibid., 149.
125 Robert E. Sherwood, *Roosevelt and Hopkins: An Intimate History* (New York: Harper & Brothers, 1950), 208.
126 Jarvis, "The Senators from Vermont," 58.
127 Wayne S. Coles, *Roosevelt & the Isolationists, 1932-45* (Lincoln: University of Nebraska Press, 1983), 467.
128 Jarvis, "The Senators from Vermont," 62-63.
129 Waldo H. Heinrichs, Jr., "Waldo H. Heinrichs, George D. Aiken, and the Lend Lease Debate of 1941," *Vermont History* 69 (Summer/Fall 2001): 267-283.
130 Ernest W. Gibson, Jr., "America's Part in the Defense of Democracy," *The Vermonter* (December 1940): 279.
131 Kenneth S. Davis, *F.D.R.: Into the Storm, 1937-1940* (New York: Random House, 1993), 456.
132 J.R.H. 13, Special Session, 1941 ("Joint Resolution Relating to the Definition of 'Armed Conflict' and 'Resided'"), Vermont State Archives; *Acts and Resolves Passed by the General Assembly of the State of Vermont at the Thirty-Seventh Biennial Session, 1943; Special Session, September 10-16, 1941* (Burlington, Vt.: Free Press Printing Co., 1943), 298; *Burlington Free Press*, 17 September 1941.
133 *Middlebury College News Letter*, December 1941, 5.
134 W. Storrs Lee, *The Green Mountains of Vermont* (New York: Henry Holt and Company, 1955), 76.
135 Jerry Aske, Jr., and Gardiner Lane, *History of the Shelburne Shipyard, and Its Shipbuilding Activities during World War II and the Korean Conflict* (Essex Junction, Vt.: Chittenden County Regional Planning Commission, 1992), 17.

136 *Journal of the Senate of the State of Vermont, Biennial Session 1945* (Montpelier, Vt.: Capital City Press, 1945), 272.
137 Peter Kurth, *American Cassandra: The Life of Dorothy Thompson* (Boston: Little, Brown and Company, 1990), 347-348.
138 *Journal of the Senate of the State of Vermont, 1945*, 272.
139 Arnold Childs, "Working at Tunbridge; the Genesis of Camp William James," pamphlet of Harvard and Dartmouth American Defense Groups (Cambridge, Mass.: Harvard University Press, [1941]), 6.
140 John A. Salmond, *The Civilian Conservation Corps, 1933-1942: A New Deal Case Study* (Durham, N.C.: Duke University Press, 1967), 201.
141 *Congressional Record*, 77th Cong., 1st sess., 1941, 87, pt. 1: 467.
142 Ibid., 468.
143 See Jack J. Preiss, *Camp William James* (Norwich, Vt.: Argo Books, 1978).
144 Roberta Strauss, "Unionization Battle in Winooski: Fifty Year Anniversary," *Chittenden County Historical Society Bulletin* 27 (Spring 1993): 5. Also, see Searls, "Labor, Politics, and Republican Vermont," 61-66.
145 Peter Langrock, *Beyond the Courthouse: Tales of Lawyers and Lawyering* (Forest Dale, Vt.: Paul S. Eriksson, 1999), 20; also, see *Middlebury Register*, 4 July, 11 July 1941.
146 *Journal of the Senate of the State of Vermont, Special Session, September, 1941* (Burlington, Vt.: Free Press Printing Co.), 26.
147 *Norwich University Record*, 2 April 1943, 1.
148 *Agriculture of Vermont: 22nd Biennial Report of the Commissioner of Agriculture, 1943-1944* (Montpelier: Vermont Department of Agriculture, 1944), 3.
149 *Journal of the Senate of the State of Vermont, 1945*, 282.

Chapter 9
Vermont Transformed: 1945-1969

1 Hazel McLoed Wills, *Bill Wills and Company* (Burlington, Vt.: Lane Press, 1953), 45.
2 "The Republican Record: Postwar Planning" (n.p.: National Federation of Women's Republican Clubs, 1944), 17.
3 Wills, *Bill Wills and Company*, 45.
4 Samuel B. Hand, *The Star That Set: The Vermont Republican Party, 1854-1974* (Lanham, Md.: Lexington Books, 2002), 175.
5 See Samuel B. Hand, "Friends, Neighbors, and Political Allies: Reflections on the Gibson-Aiken Connection," Center for Research on Vermont, Occasional Paper No. 11 (Burlington: University of Vermont, 1986), 16-19.
6 Ibid., 20.
7 Robert Mitchell, "Gibson's Strength," editorial, 10 September 1946, in Tyler Resch, ed., *The Bob Mitchell Years: An Anthology of a Half Century of Editorial Writing by the Publisher of the Rutland Herald* (Rutland, Vt.: The Rutland Herald, 1994), 71.
8 Robert Mitchell, "Reaction to Primary Outcome," editorial, 17 September 1946, in ibid., 71-73.
9 Mortimer Robinson Proctor, *Pleasant Memories from Political Life, 1932-1952* (Proctor, Vt.: Privately printed [Edwin F. Sharp], 1950; third printing, 1964), 14.

10 Mitchell, "Reaction to Primary Outcome," 72-73. See also Richard M. Judd, *The New Deal in Vermont: Its Impact and Aftermath* (New York: Garland Publishing, 1979), 244.
11 For this and the following quotations from Gibson's speech see Ernest W. Gibson, Jr., Inaugural Address, 9 January 1947, *Journal of the Senate, 1947* (Montpelier, Vt.: Capital City Press, 1947), 709-730.
12 Melvin Waxman, "Vermont's New Dealing Yankee," *Nation* 168 (11 June 1949): 569-560; William Gilman, "Vermont Goes Radical," *Collier's* (19 April 1947): 12-14, 104-105 (reprinted in J. Kevin Graffagnino, Samuel B. Hand, and Gene Sessions, eds., *Vermont Voices, 1609 Through the 1990s: A Documentary History of the Green Mountain State* (Montpelier: Vermont Historical Society, 1999), 326-330.
13 Judd, *The New Deal in Vermont*, 246.
14 Lee Emerson, inaugural address, 4 January 1953, *Journal of the Senate, 1953* (Montpelier, Vt.: Capital City Press, 1953), 724.
15 Joseph B. Johnson, farewell address, 15 January 1959, *Journal of the Senate, 1959* (Montpelier, Vt.: Capital City Press, 1959), 687.
16 *William E. Mikell v. Robert J. Rousseau et als* [123 Vt. 139], 19 July 1962. In this decision, the court affirmed the principle that "The constitutional concern is representation in the Senate according to population," and that the Vermont Constitution "does not permit the legislature to let the question of apportionment drift and remain unanswered." The court refused to order a solution, as requested by the petitioners in the case, but concluded by noting that "this Court will retain jurisdiction to afford the parties such further relief as justice shall require" (147-148).
17 A. Luke Crispe, interview, 20 August 1981, pp. 19-20. Folklore and Oral History Collection, Special Collections, Bailey/Howe Library, University of Vermont; quoted in Samuel B. Hand and D. Gregory Sanford, "'I Believe I Will Go'": Organization Politics in Republican Vermont," *Vermont History News* 39, (January-February 1988): 10.
18 Philip H. Hoff, inaugural address, 17 January 1963, *Journal of the Senate, 1963* (Montpelier, Vt.: Capital City Press, 1963), 693.
19 Ibid., 694.
20 Ibid., 698.
21 Quoted in Joe Sherman, *Fast Lane on a Dirt Road: Vermont Transformed, 1945-1990* (Woodstock, Vt.: Countryman Press, 1991), 57.
22 Stephen C. Terry, "A History of the Hoff Years, 1963-1969" (hereafter cited as "The Hoff Years"), compiled from seven articles written for the *Rutland Herald*, 23 December 1968 to 1 January 1969, edited by Samuel B. Hand and Sally Johnson [Burlington, Vt.: privately printed], 1990; Vermont Historical Society, X Pam., 17 (*Rutland Herald*, part 3, 27 December 1968).
23 Andrew E. Nuquist and Edith W. Nuquist, *Vermont State Government and Administration: An Historical and Descriptive Study of the Living Past* (Burlington: Government Research Center, University of Vermont, 1966), 144.
24 See Deane C. Davis, with Nancy Price Graff, *Deane C. Davis: An Autobiography* (Shelburne, Vt.: The New England Press, 1991), 191-194; Nuquist and Nuquist, *Vermont State Government and Administration*, 144-148; John H. Fitzhugh, "The Executive," in Michael Sherman, ed., *Vermont State Government Since 1965* (Burlington, Vt.: Center for Research on Vermont and Snelling Center for Government, 1999), 93-99.

25 Nuquist and Nuquist, *Vermont State Government and Administration*, 352–353.
26 Sherman, *Fast Lane on a Dirt Road*, 57–58; Terry, "The Hoff Years," 27 (part 3, 27 December 1968).
27 Nuquist and Nuquist, *Vermont State Government and Administration*, 520–521; Fitzhugh, "The Executive," 97–99.
28 Constitution of Vermont, 1777, Chapter II, Section 16.
29 William Jay Smith, "My Poetic Career in Vermont Politics," in H. Nicholas Muller III and Samuel B. Hand, eds., *In a State of Nature: Readings in Vermont History* (Montpelier: Vermont Historical Society, 1982), 370. See Frank Bryan, *Yankee Politics in Rural Vermont* (Hanover, N.H.: University Press of New England, 1974), chapter 4: "The Rural Legislature," 125–201.
30 Nuquist and Nuquist, *Vermont State Government and Administration*, 89.
31 *Buckley v. Hoff* [234 F. Supp. 191 (1964)].
32 Terry, "The Hoff Years," 35–36 (part 5, 30 December 1968); Howard Ball, "From 'One Town, One [or Two] Vote[s]' to 'One person, One Vote': The Impact of Reapportionment on Vermont, 1777–1992," *Vermont History* 61 (Spring 1993): 85–99; Nuquist and Nuquist, *Vermont State Government and Administration*, 41–52; Paul S. Gillies, "'As Equally as May Be': The Maturation of Reapportionment," *Vermont History News* 38 (January–February 1987): 11–15; William C. Hill, "The Constitution," in Sherman, ed., *Vermont State Government Since 1965*, 20–24; D. Gregory Sanford and William Doyle, "The General Assembly," in Sherman, ed., ibid., 32–35.
33 Terry, "The Hoff Years," 19 (part 3, 27 December 1968).
34 Association of Retired Teachers of Vermont, *School Bells among Green Hills* (Essex Jct., Vt.: Essex Publishers, 1975), 17; quoted in Michele A. White [Cross], "Public School Education in Vermont: The 'Myth of Local Control'" (M.A. thesis, Graduate Program, Vermont College of Norwich University, 1992), 88.
35 See Steven R. Hoffbeck, "'Remember the Poor' (Galatians 2:10): Poor Farms in Vermont," *Vermont History* 57, (Fall 1989): 226–240.
36 See Judith Rosenstreich, "Public Welfare," in Sherman, ed., *Vermont State Government Since 1965*, 396–399.
37 Philip H. Hoff, "George D. Aiken: A Personal View from the State House," in Michael Sherman, ed., *The Political Legacy of George D. Aiken: Wise Old Owl of the U.S. Senate* (Montpelier and Taftsville, Vt.: Vermont Historical Society and Countryman Press, 1995), 138–139.
38 William K. Porter and Stephen C. Terry, "The Media," in Sherman, ed., *Vermont State Government Since 1965*, 131–132.
39 *Kelbro Inc. v. Myrick, Secretary of State*, 113 Vt. 64; 30 Atlantic Reporter (2nd series), 527 (Jan, 1943), quoted in Anonymous, "How Vermont Solves Its Billboard Problem on Planning and Civic Comment," *The Vermonter* 50 (January 1945): 12.
40 See Nuquist and Nuquist, *Vermont State Government and Administration*, 469; John H. Marshall, "Business, Labor, and Industry," in Sherman, ed., *Vermont State Government Since 1965*, 543–544; Porter and Terry, "The Media," in ibid., 130–131.
41 *Vermont Farm and Home Science* (Burlington, Vt.: University of Vermont, Extension Service and Experiment Station) 1 (1955): 3–4.

42 Commissioner of Agriculture, *Agriculture of Vermont: Thirty-First Biennial Report of the Commissioner of Agriculture of the State of Vermont, 1961-1962* (n.p. [Montpelier: State of Vermont], 1962), 40-41.
43 Peter S. Jennison, *The History of Woodstock, Vermont, 1890-1983* (Taftsville, Vt.: Countryman Press, 1985), 33.
44 Joseph B. Johnson, farewell address, 15 January 1959, *Journal of the Senate, 1959*, 690.
45 Daniel A. Neary, Jr., "When Did Bulk Tanks Arrive?" *Barre-Montpelier Times Argus*, 4 December 1977; Bruce P. Shields, "Bulk Tanks Didn't Eliminate Dairy Farms," *Barre-Montpelier Times Argus*, 3 March 1996, C3.
46 Douglas Slaybaugh, "Why the Mills Closed," in Laura Krawitt, ed., *The Mills at Winooski Falls: Illustrated Essays and Oral Histories* (Winooski, Vt.: Onion River Press, 2000), 178-183; Lilian Baker Carlisle, et al., *Look Around Winooski, Vermont* (Burlington, Vt.: Chittenden County Historical Society, 1972), iii.
47 See Wayne G. Broehl, Jr., *Precision Valley: The Machine Tool Companies of Springfield, Vermont* (Englewood Cliffs, N.J.: Prentice Hall, 1959), chapter 10.
48 *Vermont Life* 1 (Fall 1946): 2.
49 Nuquist and Nuquist, *Vermont State Government and Administration*, 513.
50 Joseph P. Johnson, inaugural address, 6, January 1955, *Journal of the Senate, 1955* (Montpelier, Vt.: Capital City Press, 1955), 823.
51 Joseph B. Johnson, farewell address, 15 January 1959, *Journal of the Senate, 1959*, 688-689.
52 Quoted in Kevin O'Connor, "25 Years Later: The Impact of the Interstate," *Vermont Sunday Magazine*, 2 December 1986, 4.
53 "Building Vermont's Highways," *Vermont Life* (Spring 1966); quoted in O'Connor, ibid., 5.
54 David Halberstam, *The Fifties* (New York: Villard Books, 1993), ix-x.
55 Duane Lockard, *New England State Politics* (Princeton, N.J.: Princeton University Press, 1966), 35-45.
56 Curtis MacDougall, *Gideon's Army*, (New York: Marzani and Munsell, 1965), 2: 574.
57 See biographical materials on the Millers and copies of *The Green Mountain Rifleman* in Vermont Historical Society, manuscript collection *X343.012 M615.
58 *Burlington Free Press*, 30 September 1950.
59 Lee Emerson, inaugural address, 1951, *Journal of the Senate, 1951*, 692-695.
60 See *Laws of Vermont, 1951*, Act 224, pp. 303-315; 20 V.S.A. 911.
61 *Burlington Free Press*, 11 March and 31 March 1953.
62 Dorothy Canfield Fisher, *Vermont Tradition: The Biography of an Outlook on Life* (Boston: Little, Brown and Company, 1953), 395-402.
63 Swanton Courier, 14 May 1953, quoted in David R. Holmes, *Stalking the Academic Communist: Intellectual Freedom and the Firing of Alex Novikoff* (Hanover, N.H.: University Press of New England, 1989), 151.
64 Quoted in ibid., 154.
65 Ibid., 247.
66 See Martin A. Trow, "Right-Wing Radicalism and Political Intolerance: A Study of Support for McCarthy in a New England Town," (Ph.D. diss., Columbia University, 1957), 12 n.1, 15 n.2. To test attitudes toward McCarthy, Trow posed three questions:

- How do you feel about Senator McCarthy's activities—do you strongly favor them, mildly favor them, mildly oppose them, or strongly support them?
- Just speaking of Senator McCarthy's methods of investigation, how do you feel about them? Do you strongly favor them, [etc.].
- On the whole, do you think his investigation committee accomplished more good than harm—or more harm than good?

To assess political tolerance, Trow asked another cluster of three questions:
- In peace time, do you think the Socialist Party should be allowed to publish newspapers in this country?
- Do you think newspapers should be allowed to criticize our form of government?
- Do you think members of the Communist party in this country should be allowed to speak on the radio?

67 *Congressional Record,* Senate, 9 March 1954, 2,286.
68 *Congressional Record,* Senate, 2 December 1954, 16,392.
69 Ralph E. Flanders, *Senator from Vermont* (Boston: Little, Brown and Company, 1961), 263, 267.
70 See Nancy Price Graff, ed., *Celebrating Vermont: Myths and Realities* (Middlebury, Vt.: Christian A. Johnson Memorial Gallery and Middlebury College, 1991), catalogue items 44–46, 57, 63 (pp. 178–183, 204–205, 216–217).
71 Castleton State College History Students, *Beautiful Lake Bomoseen* (Castleton, Vt.: Castleton State College, 1999), 38, 56, 65.
72 Bruce R. Buchanan, "An Experiment in Racial Appreciation," *The Vermonter* 50 (March 1945): 61–62.
73 Jules Older, "Jews, Blacks, and Catholics: UVM's Anomalous Minorities," in Robert V. Daniels, ed., *The University of Vermont: The First Two Hundred Years* (Hanover, N.H.: University Press of New England, 1991), 321–322.
74 See James W. Loewen, "Black Image in White Vermont: The Origin, Meaning, and Abolition of Kake Walk," in ibid., 333–369.
75 Quoted in Richard T. Cassidy, "Civil and Human Rights," in Sherman, ed., *Vermont State Government Since 1965,* 298.
76 "Segregation in Vermont," *Vermont Cynic,* 28 February 1957, 4; quoted in Older, "Jews, Blacks, and Catholics," 322.
77 Act 109, *Laws of Vermont, 1957;* See Older, "Jews, Blacks, and Catholics," 313–332; Stephen M. Wrinn, *Civil Rights in the Whitest State: Vermont Perceptions of Civil Rights, 1945–1968* (Lanham, Md.: University Press of America, 1998), 22–23.
78 "Opinion in the Capitol," WWTG-TV, Washington, D.C., interview with Mark Evans, 7 July 1963, quoted in Wrinn, *Civil Rights in the Whitest State,* 39.
79 Title II of the Civil Rights Act of 1964, sec 201 (b)(1). See Wrinn, *Civil Rights in the Whitest State,* Appendix A, 85–86.
80 Wrinn, *Civil Rights in the Whitest State,* 42–45.
81 See Cassidy, "Civil and Human Rights," in Sherman, ed., *Vermont State Government Since 1965,* 300; Rita Edwards and Lyn Heglund, "25 Years of Change for Women," in "Gala Celebration of the 25th Anniversary of the Governor's Commission on Women," (n.p., 5 April 1989).
82 See Michael Sherman, "Vermont in Mississippi," *Vermont History News* 37

(January–February 1986): 8–12; Wrinn, *Civil Rights in the Whitest State,* 52–53; Kevin J. Kelley, "The Mississippi Connection," *Vermont Times* 3 (25 February 1993), 1–2, 6.
83 Philip H. Hoff, "Vermont's Response: A Commitment to Full Citizenship for Every American" (statement from the Governor's Office, May 1968), quoted in Cassidy, "Civil and Human Rights," in Sherman, ed., *Vermont State Government Since 1965,* 303. See also Wrinn, *Civil Rights in the Whitest State,* 66–69.
84 Quoted in Wrinn, *Civil Rights in the Whitest State,* 69.
85 Quoted in Cassidy, "Civil and Human Rights," in Sherman, ed., *Vermont State Government Since 1965,* 315, n.66.
86 Wrinn, *Civil Rights in the Whitest State,* 75–76.
87 Shepard B. Clough and Lorna Quimby, "Peacham, Vermont: Fifty Years of Economic and Social Change, 1929–1979," *Vermont History* 51 (Winter 1983): 5–28.
88 Ibid., 24.
89 Weston A. Cate, Jr., *Forever Calais: A History of Calais, Vermont* (Calais, Vt.: Calais Historical Society, 1999), 180–203.
90 See Sherman, *Fast Lane on a Dirt Road,* 79–80.
91 See Alan J. Fortney and David E. Robinson, "Partners in Progress," in John Duffy and Faith Learned Pepe, eds., *Vermont: An Illustrated History* (Northridge, Calif.: Windsor Publications, 1985), 190–255.
92 Ruth Page, "IBM: Burden or Bonanza?" *Chittenden* 1 (December 1969): 10–15, reprinted in J. Kevin Graffagnino, Samuel B. Hand, and Gene Sessions, *Vermont Voices, 1609 Through the 1990s: A Documentary History of the Green Mountain State* (Montpelier: Vermont Historical Society, 1999), 355–358.
93 Allen R. Foley, *What the Old-Timer Said: To the Feller from Down-country—and even to His Neighbor when He Had It Coming* (Brattleboro, Vt.: Stephen Green Press, 1971), 34–35.
94 Walter Hard, "The Village," in *A Mountain Township* (1933), 3rd edition (Middlebury, Vt.: Vermont Books, 1963), 4.
95 Vrest Orton, "Nostalgia, undefiled," *The Voice of the Mountains* (Christmas 1953): 6.
96 Vrest Orton, "Vermont's Protective Coloration—A Warning," *Voice of the Mountains* (Fall 1968/Winter 1969): 43.
97 Vrest Orton, "The Weston Revival," *Vermont Life* 1 (Fall 1946): 19.

Chapter 10
"Another 250,000 People": 1969–2003
1 Deane C. Davis, with Nancy Price Graff, *Deane C. Davis: An Autobiography*, (Shelburne, Vt.: New England Press, 1991), 332.
2 Employment numbers, annual total wages, and annual average wages for those employed in the "Leisure and Hospitality" industries in Vermont are available by consulting the chart of "Covered Employment & Wages" at the Vermont Department of Employment and Training web site <http://www.vtlmi.info/indstatenaics.cfm>. The chart identifies thirteen industry groups. For the purpose of this analysis, "Manufacturing" is divided into two categories—durable goods and nondurable goods—and figures for "scenic and sightseeing transportation" (listed under "Transportation and Warehousing") have been added to "Leisure and Hospitality." The chart for 2001 shows that "Leisure and Hospitality" ranks fourth in the number of people employed (32,962 in a total work force of 249,927 in private, i.e., non-

government, jobs), seventh in total annual wages earned, and fourteenth in annual average wages ($14,214, compared with $29,920 for all workers in private ownership industries).

3 Alan Jon Fortney and David E. Robinson, "Partners in Progress," in John Duffy, *Vermont: An Illustrated History* (n.p.: Windsor Publications, 1985), 202-203, 210, 242-243. For informative snapshots of the business community in Vermont, see the "Partners in Progress" section in Duffy's book, pp. 190-255; and "Chronicles of Leadership," pp. 210-286, in John Duffy and Vincent Feeney, *Vermont: An Illustrated History,* [rev. ed.], (Sun Valley, Calif.: American Historical Press, 2000).

4 In 1990, 191 Vermont towns had a population of fewer than 2,500 and 177,100 people lived in those towns, 31.5 percent of the total population of the state. In 2000, 183 towns had population of fewer than 2,500, accounting for 178,796 individuals, or 29.4 percent of the total state population.

5 *Report of the Governor's Commission on Food* (1976), Thomas P. Salmon records, Box H, folder 92.3. Vermont State Archives, Montpelier.

6 *Agriculture of Vermont: 43rd Biennial Report, Vermont Department of Agriculture, 1985-1986* (Montpelier: Vermont Department of Agriculture, 1986), 1; *44th Biennial Report, 1987 and 1988* (1988), 1.

7 *Report of the Governor's Commission on Vermont's Future: Guidelines for Growth* (Montpelier: The Commission, 1988).

8 See *Agriculture of Vermont,* the biennial reports of the commissioner of agriculture of the State of Vermont. The reports contain both narrative summaries of events and trends and statistical tables of five-year production records.

9 Frederick Bever, "Growing Up. In late fall, fresh signs that the organic-farming movement is maturing," *Vermont Sunday Magazine*, 3 December 2000, 8-11; John Dillon, "Growing Organic: Farming without Chemicals Finds Fertile Ground," *Vermont Life* 55 (Summer 2000): 38-43.

10 Gregory Sharrow and Meg Ostrum, eds., *Families on the Land: Profiles of Vermont Farm Families* (Middlebury, Vt.: Vermont Folklife Center, 1995), 45.

11 Ibid., 32, 36-37.

12 Numbers are imprecise, a reflection of the fact that many in the counterculture were constantly on the move. Joe Sherman estimates 100,000 hippies who established more than 100 communes (*Fast Lane on a Dirt Road: Vermont Transformed, 1945-1990* [Woodstock, Vt.: Countryman Press, 1991], 82). Yvonne Daley, in "The Hippie Legacy," a retrospective article written for the *Sunday Rutland Herald-Times Argus* (10 October 1983), counted 75 communes. Journalist Richard Pollak, in a 1972 article in *Playboy* magazine, estimated 35,800 hippies, roughly one-third of the state's population of individuals between the ages of 18 and 34. (Richard Pollak, "Taking over Vermont," *Playboy* [April 1972], 147 *et seq.*). Anthropologist Barry Laffan reports that in 1971 a statewide conference of community leaders and law enforcement officers "anticipated . . . 100,000 freak visitors" and that he counted "at least sixty-two recognized communes" in the region, which he calls for research purposes "Provincia," although he adds that "an estimate of one hundred communes . . . in 1972 would be safe, even conservative." Barry Laffan, *Communal Organization and Social Transition: A Case Study from the Counterculture of the Sixties and Seventies* (New York: Peter Lang Publishing, 1997), 19.

13 Madeleine M. Kunin, *Leading a Political Life* (New York: Alfred A. Knopf, 1994), 10.

14 Marilyn S. Blackwell, "Gender and Vermont History: Moving Women from the Sidebars into the Text," *Vermont History* 71 (Winter/Spring 2003): 46–61.

15 "Vermont QuickStats," University of Vermont, Center for Rural Studies, web site: <http://geo-vt.uvm.edu/indicators/html/quickstats_population.html>, U.S. Census Bureau, 2001.

16 Colin Calloway, *The Western Abenakis of Vermont, 1600–1800: War, Migration, and the Survival of an Indian People* (Norman: University of Oklahoma Press, 1990), 240.

17 Frederick M. Wiseman, *Voice of the Dawn: An Autohistory* (Hanover N.H.: University Press of New England, 2001), 115.

18 See William A. Haviland and Marjory W. Power, *The Original Vermonters: Native Inhabitants, Past and Present*, rev. ed. (Hanover, N.H.: University Press of New England, 1994), 248–250; Calloway, *The Western Abenakis of Vermont*, 248; John Moody, "The Native American Legacy," in Jane Beck, ed., *Always In Season* (Montpelier: Vermont Council on the Arts, 1982), 59, 62; Wiseman, *Voice of the Dawn*, 114–150.

19 Quoted in Haviland and Power, *Original Vermonters*, 255.

20 Jane S. Baker, *Report to Governor Thomas R.[sic.] Salmon of the State of Vermont Regarding the Claims Presented by the Abenaki Nation* (Montpelier, Vt.: Office of the Governor, 1976), quoted in Haviland and Power, *Original Vermonters*, 257.

21 Thomas P. Salmon, retiring address, 6 January 1977, *Journal of the Senate, 1977* (Burlington: Queen City Printers, 1977), 539.

22 *State of Vermont* v. *Raleigh Elliott, et al.* (159 Vt. 102 [1993]), quoted in J. Kevin Graffagnino, Samuel B. Hand, and Gene Sessions, eds., *Vermont Voices, 1609 Through the 1990s: A Documentary History of the Green Mountain State* (Montpelier: Vermont Historical Society, 1999), 378.

23 Joint House Resolution, "Granting State Recognition to the Abenaki Indian Tribe" (JHR 183) and Joint Senate Resolution, "Recognizing the Tribal Status of the Abenaki Tribe" (JSR 010).

24 Bureau of Indian Affairs regulations, 25 C.F.R. 83.7, quoted in State of Vermont, Office of the Attorney General [William Griffin and Eve Jacobs-Carnahan], "Preliminary Report on Abenaki Petition for Tribal Recognition" (Montpelier, Vt.: Office of the Attorney General, 12 March 2002), 4.

25 Eve Jacobs-Carnahan, "State of Vermont's Response to Petition for Federal Acknowledgement of the St. Francis/Sokoki Band of the Abenaki Nation of Vermont" (Montpelier: Attorney General of Vermont, December 2002). Available online: <http://www.state.vt.us/atg/Abenaki%20Petition%20 for %20Tribal%20 Recognition.pdf>.

26 *Acts and Resolves of the State of Vermont, 1992* (Montpelier, Vt.: Secretary of State, 1992), No. 135, 27–32.

27 Ibid., , 1991, No. 135, §14.

28 *Baker et al.* v. *State of Vermont*, 170 Vt. 194, 744 A. 2d (1999), page 39.

29 Carey Goldberg, "Civil Unions are Blending In," *Barre-Montpelier Times Argus*, 31 July 2001, B4 (from the *New York Times*, 31 July 2001).

30 "Report of Fact Finding Panel re Construction Strike" (14 December 1973), 24, 29. Salmon Papers, Vermont State Archives, folder LL 444.1.

31 Governor Thomas P. Salmon to William Chapels, 30 September 1974, Salmon Papers, Vermont State Archives, Box VV, Folder WW 444 [now missing], quoted in Charles T. Morrissey, *The Men Who Made It: Vermont's Union Carpenters* (n.p.: United Brotherhood of Carpenters and Joiners, n.d. [1984]), 76.

32 Ibid., 77.

33 Andrew E. Nuquist and Edith W. Nuquist, *Vermont State Government and Administration: An Historical and Descriptive Study of the Living Past* (Burlington: Government Research Center, University of Vermont, 1966), 414.

34 VSEA History Committee, "Highlights: A Brief Chronology of the Vermont State Employees' Association, Inc., 1944–1984," (Brattleboro: VSEA, 1984), 10–11.

35 "The Vermont Business World," 1980, quoted in William Doyle, *The Vermont Political Tradition and Those Who Helped Make It* (Montpelier, Vt.: The Author, 1984), 215–216.

36 Ralph Wright, *All Politics is Personal* (Manchester Center, Vt.: Marshall Jones Company, 1996), 117.

37 See Michael Schudson, *The Good Citizen: A History of American Civic Life* (Cambridge, Mass.: Harvard University Press, 1998), 274–281; Samuel B. Hand, *The Star That Set: The Vermont Republican Party, 1854–1974* (Lanham, Md.: Lexington Books, 2002), 302.

38 Symbolic evidence of Dean's eagerness to associate himself with environmental conservation is his official portrait, unveiled shortly before his retirement from office in January 2003, which portrays him with a paddle in a canoe on Lake Champlain rather than the usual scene, seated in or near the State House. His critics argued, however, that while the governor was enthusiastic about acquiring land to place under protection, his administration failed to encourage or support environmental planning and enforcement. For example, the Vermont Natural Resources Council in January 2001 reported that "Over the past five years the Agency of Natural Resources' (ANR) budget has bottomed out at just over 1% of the General Fund compared to an average of around 2% during the 1980s and early 1990s. The amount of state general funds invested in environmental protection has dropped from $35 per year/per Vermonter in 1993 to $15.50 per year in 1998, and staffing has been reduced by almost 40 people." *VNRC Bulletin & Legislative Platform* (January 2001), 1.

39 James Jeffords, "Text of Sen. Jeffords' Announcement," *New York Times*, 24 May 2001.

40 Hand, *The Star That Set*, ix.

41 Philip H. Hoff, retiring address, 9 January 1969, *Journal of the Senate, 1969* (Montpelier, Vt.: Capital City Press), 604–609.

42 Deane C. Davis, inaugural address, 9 January 1969, ibid., 615.

43 Davis, *Deane C. Davis*, 225.

44 Vermont Constitution, Articles of Amendment 48 (1974) and 50 (1986).

45 Vermont Constitution, Article of Amendment 46 (1974). The provision for mandatory retirement was modified by voters in 2002, to give the legislature the option to continue judges in office beyond age 70. See Vermont Constitution, Chapter II, section 35.

46 Proposals for Amendment, 1971, Number 1. See Vermont State Archives Web site: <http://vermont-archives.org/governance/Constitution/proposals.html>. The Senate

in 1971 considered two similar proposals, each of which included a provision for a run-off election in lieu of legislative determination of the winner where neither candidate secured a majority. Proposal 1 emphasized the four-year term, with the run-off provision mentioned later in the text; proposal 2 emphasized the run-off provision first. Proposal 2 did not emerge from the senate and consequently was not an item on the popular referendum of 1974.

47 Richard A. Snelling, [Second] inaugural address, 4 January 1979, *Journal of the Senate, 1979* (Burlington, Vt.: Queen City Press, 1979) 588-589.
48 Ibid., 591.
49 Ibid., 589-590.
50 *Amanda Brigham, et al. v. State of Vermont* (166 Vt. 246); (692 A.2d 384).
51 *Laws of Vermont 1997*, No. 60, sec. 3 (Montpelier, Vt.: Secretary of State, 1997), 279.
52 *Barre-Montpelier Times Argus*, 23 May 2003, A1, A7.
53 Rob Eley, "Growth Sparked Birth of Act 250," *Burlington Free Press*, 2 June 1980, 1A, 14A.
54 Ibid., 1A.
55 Davis, *Deane C. Davis*, 250.
56 "Environmental Control Message," *Journal of the Joint Assembly, 1970* (Montpelier, Vt.: Capital City Press, 1970), 601; Eley, "Growth Sparked Birth of Act 250," 14A.
57 "Act 250," program number 39 of "The Green Mountain Chronicles," Woodsmoke Productions for the Vermont Historical Society, 1988.
58 Davis, *Deane C. Davis*, 312-313.
59 Leonard U. Wilson, "Land Use, and Environmental Protection," in Michael Sherman, ed., *Vermont State Government Since 1965* (Burlington, Vt.: Center for Research on Vermont and Snelling Center for Government, 1999), 461.
60 Vermont Public Radio, "Switchboard: The Richard Snelling Legacy," 14 August 2001.
61 State of Vermont, Executive Order, 22 September 1987, in Governor's Commission on Vermont's Future, *Report of the Governor's Commission on Vermont's Future: Guidelines for Growth* (Montpelier: The Commission, 1988), 31-32.
62 Dorothy Canfield Fisher, "Vermonters," in *Vermont: A Guide to the Green Mountain State*, American Guide Series (Boston: Houghton Mifflin Company, 1937), 3.
63 Frank Bryan and John McClaughry, *The Vermont Papers: Recreating Democracy on a Human Scale* (Chelsea, Vt.: Chelsea Green Publishing Company, 1988), 4.
64 *Vermont: Who Are We Becoming? Report of the Twelfth Grafton Conference, June 19-21, 1987* (Grafton, Vt.: Windham Foundation, 1987), 12, 15.
65 Allen F. Davis, "Foreword," in Graffagnino et al., *Vermont Voices*, xx.
66 Dick [Richard O.] Hathaway, "In Praise of the 'Little New Deal,'" *Sunday Rutland Herald and Sunday Times Argus*, 10 October 1999, F-3.
67 Marguerite Hurrey Wolf, *At Home in Vermont* (Shelburne, Vt.: New England Press, 1990), vi. The reference to a moose and cow is an allusion to an elaborate hoax, contrived by Vermont farmer Larry Carrara, who sprayed one of his cows, "Jessica," with moose musk that attracted a male moose, who visited the farm frequently, attracting as well a lot of reporters and tourists. The trick thus fooled the moose and earned for the perpetrator of the hoax a fair sum of money as well. See Pat A. Wakefield with Larry Carrara, *A Moose for Jessica* (New York : E.P. Dutton, 1987).
68 Grace Paley, "Life in the County: A City Friend Asks, 'Is It Boring?'" in *Just As I Thought* (New York: Farrar, Straus, Giroux, 1998), 300.

Selected Bibliography

The following items constitute a selected bibliography, drawn largely but not exclusively from the endnotes of the text. We have included here mostly books, with only a few articles that are most frequently cited in contemporary writing on Vermont history. With a few exceptions, we have listed items that concentrate on or are resources for Vermont history, therefore excluding most of the items that provide regional, national, or global contexts for events, ideas, and trends that we discuss in this book.

We therefore encourage readers to consult our footnotes for a more complete guide to the full range of resources and materials that we have used and that are available to researchers and writers in Vermont history. We recognize that even with such a list, we have missed some materials that readers may know of.

In addition to the specific items cited in our notes and in the selected bibliography we offer here, we have relied heavily on the following published resources in the preparation of this book:

Vermont History
Vermont History News/News & Notes
State Papers of Vermont (22 volumes)
Vermont Legislative Directories (published under several titles, 1837 to the present)
Journals of the Vermont General Assembly (House and Senate journals)
Acts and Resolves of the State of Vermont [Laws of Vermont]
Town histories. There are an enormous number of town histories. Many were written and published in the late nineteenth century; many were written or updated as "Bicentennial Projects" for the 1976 National Bicentennial; and many more were written or updated for the 1991 Vermont Statehood Bicentennial. Town histories and church histories continue to appear regularly.

The authors also made extensive use of manuscript, photograph, newspaper, microfilm, and ephemera collections at the following repositories:

Special Collections, Bailey/Howe Library, University of Vermont, Burlington.
Vermont Department of Libraries—Reference and Law Library, Montpelier.
Vermont Historical Society, Barre.
Vermont State Archives, Montpelier.

Abbott, Collamer M. *Green Mountain Copper: The Story of Vermont's Red Metal*. Randolph, Vt.: The Herald Printery, 1973.

Aiken, George D. *Speaking From Vermont*. New York: Frederick A. Stokes Company, 1938.

Albers, Jan. *Hands on the Land: A History of the Vermont Landscape*. Cambridge, Mass.: The MIT Press, 2000.

Allen, E. John B. *From Skisport to Skiing: One Hundred Years of an American Sport*. Amherst, Mass.: The University of Massachusetts Press, 1993.

Allen, Ira. *The Natural and Political History of the State of Vermont*. London: J. W. Myers, 1798; reprint, Rutland, Vt.: Charles E. Tuttle Co., 1969.

Aske, Jerry, Jr., and Gardiner Lane. *History of the Shelburne Shipyard, and Its Shipbuilding Activities during World War II and the Korean Conflict*. Essex Junction, Vt.: Chittenden County Regional Planning Commission, 1992.

Austin, Aleine. *Matthew Lyon: "New Man" of the Democratic Revolution, 1749–1822*. University Park, Pa.: The Pennsylvania State University Press, 1981.

Axtel, James. *The Invasion Within: The Contest of Cultures in Colonial North America*. New York: Oxford University Press, 1985.

Bailey, Consuelo. *Leaves Before the Wind: The Autobiography of Vermont's Own Daughter*. Burlington, Vt.: George Little Press, 1976.

Bain, David Howard, and Mary Smyth Duffy, eds. *Whose Woods These Are: A History of the Bread Loaf Writers' Conference, 1926–1992*. Hopewell, N.J.: The Ecco Press, 1993.

Banks, Ann, ed. *First-Person America*. New York: Vintage Books, 1981.

Barron, Hal S. *Those Who Stayed Behind: Rural Society in Nineteenth-Century New England*. Cambridge: Cambridge University Press, 1984.

Bassett, Thomas Day Seymour. *The Gods of the Hills: Piety and Society in Nineteenth-Century Vermont*. Montpelier, Vt.: Vermont Historical Society, 2000.

———. *The Growing Edge: Vermont Villages, 1840–1880*. Montpelier, Vt.: Vermont Historical Society, 1992.

———, ed. *Outsiders Inside Vermont: Travelers' Tales Over 358 Years*. Brattleboro, Vt.: The Stephen Greene Press, 1967.

———. "Urban Penetration of Rural Vermont, 1840–1880." Ph.D. diss., Harvard University, 1952.

———, ed. *Vermont: A Bibliography of Its History*. Volume 4 of Bibliographies of New England History. Boston: G. K. Hall & Co., 1981; reprint, Hanover, N.H.: University Press of New England, 1983.

Beck, Jane, ed. *Always in Season*. Montpelier, Vt.: Vermont Council on the Arts, 1982.

Bellesiles, Michael A. *Revolutionary Outlaws: Ethan Allen and the Struggle for Independence on the Early American Frontier*. Charlottesville: University Press of Virginia, 1993.

Benedict, George. G. *Vermont in the Civil War: A History of the Part Taken by the Vermont Soldiers and Sailors in the War for the Union, 1861–65*. 2 vols. Burlington, Vt.: The Free Press Association, 1886-1888.

Benes, Peter, ed. *The Farm*. Dublin Seminar for New England Folklife, vol. 11. Boston: Boston University Press, 1987.

———, ed. *New England/New France, 1600–1850*. Dublin Seminar for New England Folklife, vol. 14. Boston: Boston University Press, 1992.

Blackwell, Marilyn S., compiler. "Women in Vermont: A Bibliography." *Vermont History* 56 (Spring 1988): 84–101.

Bogart, Ernest L. *Peacham: The Story of a Vermont Hill Town*. Montpelier, Vt.: Vermont Historical Society, 1948.

Bonfield, Lynn A., and Mary C. Morrison. *Roxana's Children: The Biography of a Nineteenth-Century Vermont Family*. Amherst, Mass.: University of Massachusetts, Press, 1995.

Bonomi, Patricia U. *A Factious People: Politics and Society in Colonial New York*. New York: Columbia University Press, 1971.

Broehl, Wayne G., Jr. *Precision Valley: The Machine Tool Companies of Springfield, Vermont*. Englewood Cliffs, N.J.: Prentice Hall, 1959.

Brown, Dona. *Inventing New England: Regional Tourism in the Nineteenth Century*. Washington, D.C.: Smithsonian Institution Press, 1995.

Bruchac, Joseph. *The Faithful Hunter: Abenaki Stories*. Greenfield Center, N.Y.: Bowman Books, 1988.

———. *The Wind Eagle and Other Abenaki Stories*. Greenfield Center, N.Y.: Bowman Books, 1985.

Bryan, Frank M. *Yankee Politics in Rural Vermont*. Hanover, N.H.: The University Press of New England, 1974.

———, and John McClaughry. *The Vermont Papers: Recreating Democracy on a Human Scale*. Chelsea, Vt.: Chelsea Green Publishing Company, 1988.

Calloway, Colin. *The Western Abenakis of Vermont, 1600-1800: War, Migration, and the Survival of an Indian People*. Norman, Okla.: University of Oklahoma Press, 1990.

Carter, Christie, compiler and editor. *Vermont Elections, 1789-1989*. State Papers of Vermont, vol. 21. Montpelier, Vt.: Office of the Secretary of State, 1989.

Castleton State College History Students. *Beautiful Lake Bomoseen*. Castleton, Vt.: Castleton State College, 1999.

Cate, Weston A., Jr. *Up & Doing: The Vermont Historical Society, 1838-1970*. Montpelier, Vt.: Vermont Historical Society, 1988.

Champlain, Samuel de. *The Works of Samuel de Champlain in Six Volumes*. Edited by H. P. Biggar. Toronto: Champlain Society, 1922-1936.

Clifford, Deborah Pickman. "An Invasion of Strong-minded Women: The Newspapers and the Woman Suffrage Campaign in Vermont in 1870." *Vermont History* 43 (Winter 1975): 1-19.

———. "The Drive for Women's Municipal Suffrage in Vermont, 1883-1917." *Vermont History* 47 (Summer 1979): 173-190.

———. *The Passion of Abby Hemenway: Memory, Spirit, and the Making of History*. Montpelier, Vt.: Vermont Historical Society, 2001.

Coffin, Howard. *Full Duty: Vermonters in the Civil War*. Woodstock, Vt.: Countryman Press, 1993.

Coleman, Emma Lewis. *New England Captives Carried to Canada*. Portland, Maine: Southworth Press, 1925.

Conant, Edward. *Geography, History and Civil Government of Vermont*. Rutland, Vt.: The Tuttle Company, 1890.

Coolidge, Guy Omeron. *The French Occupation of the Champlain Valley from 1609 to 1759*. 2nd ed. Mamaroneck, N.Y.: Harbor Hill Books, 1989.

Crane, Charles Edward. *Let Me Show You Vermont*. New York: Alfred A. Knopf, 1937.

Crockett, Walter Hill. *Vermont, The Green Mountain State*. 5 vols. New York: The Century History Company, 1921-1923.

Cronon, William. *Changes in the Land: Indians, Colonists, and the Ecology of New England*. New York: Hill and Wang, 1983.

Crown Point Road Association. *Historical Markers on the Crown Point Road, Vermont's First Road*. Rev. ed. Rutland, Vt.: Crown Point Road Association, 1992.

Cushing, John T., and Arthur F. Stone, eds. *Vermont in the World War, 1917-1919*. Burlington, Vt.: Free Press Printing Co., 1928.

D'Agostino, Lorenzo. *The History of Public Welfare in Vermont*. Washington, D.C.: The Catholic University of America Press, 1948.

Danbom, David B. *Born in the Country: A History of Rural America*. Baltimore: The Johns Hopkins University Press, 1995.

Daniels, Robert V., ed. *The University of Vermont: The First Two Hundred Years*. Hanover, N.H.: University Press of New England, 1991.

Dann, Kevin. *Lewis Creek, Lost and Found*. Hanover, N.H.: University Press of New England, 2001.

Davis, Deane C., with Nancy Price Graff. *Deane C. Davis: An Autobiography*. Shelburne, Vt.: The New England Press. 1991.

Day, Gordon M. *In Search of New England's Native Past: Essays by Gordon M. Day*. Edited by Michael K. Foster and William Cowan. Amherst, Mass.: University of Massachusetts Press, 1998.

Demers, Paul. "Labor and the Social Relations of the Granite Industry in Barre." B.A. thesis, Goddard College, 1974.

Dopp, Daisy. *Daisy Dopp's Vermont*. Edited by Elka Schumann. Brownington, Vt.: Orleans County Historical Society, 1983.

Doyle, William. *The Vermont Political Tradition and Those Who Helped Make It*. Barre, Vt.: The Author, 1984.

Drake, James D. *King Philip's War: Civil War in New England, 1675-1676*. Amherst, Mass.: University of Massachusetts Press, 1999.

Dublin, Thomas, ed. *Farm to Factory: Women's Letters, 1830-1860*. New York: Columbia University Press, 1981.

Duffus, R. L. *The Waterbury Record*. New York: W. W. Norton & Company, Inc., 1959.

———. *Williamstown Branch: Impersonal Memories of a Vermont Boyhood*. New York: W. W. Norton & Company, 1958.

Duffy, John J., ed. *Ethan Allen and His Kin: Correspondence, 1772-1819*. 2 vols. Hanover, N.H.: University Press of New England, 1998.

———, and H. Nicholas Muller III. *An Anxious Democracy: Aspects of the 1830s*. Westport, Conn.: Greenwood Press, 1982.

———, and Faith Learned Pepe. *Vermont: An Illustrated History*. Northridge, Calif.: Windsor Publications, 1985; rev. ed. with Vincent Feeney. Sun Valley, Calif.: American Historical Press, 2000.

Dwinell, H. A. *Vermont's Dairy Industry, 1791-1941*. Bulletin no. 56, Vermont Department of Agriculture. Montpelier, Vt.: August 1941.

Eccles, W. J. *France in America*. Rev. ed. Markham, Ontario: Fitzhenry and Whiteside, 1990.

Everest, Allen S. *The War of 1812 in the Champlain Valley*. Syracuse, N.Y.: Syracuse University Press, 1981.

Fago, D'Ann Calhoun. *A Diversity of Gifts: Vermont Women at Work*. Woodstock, Vt.: Countryman Press, 1989.

Federal Writers' Project, Works Progress Administration. *Vermont: A Guide to the Green Mountain State*. American Guide Series. Boston: Houghton Mifflin Company, 1937.

Fink, Leon. *Workingmen's Democracy: The Knights of Labor and American Politics*. Urbana and Chicago: University of Illinois Press, 1983.

Fisher, Dorothy Canfield. *Vermont Tradition: The Biography of an Outlook on Life.* Boston: Little, Brown and Company, 1953.

Flanders, Ralph E. *Senator from Vermont.* Boston: Little, Brown and Company, 1961.

Flint, Winston Allen. *The Progressive Movement in Vermont.* Washington, D.C.: American Council on Public Affairs, 1941.

Gallagher, Nancy L. *Breeding Better Vermonters: The Eugenics Project in the Green Mountain State.* Hanover, N.H.: University Press of New England, 1999.

Gillies, Paul S., and D. Gregory Sanford, eds. *Records of the Council of Censors of the State of Vermont.* Montpelier, Vt.: Secretary of State, 1991.

Gilmore, William H. *Reading Becomes a Necessity of Life: Material and Cultural Life in Rural New England, 1780–1835.* Knoxville, Tenn.: The University of Tennessee Press, 1989.

Goodman, Paul. *Towards a Christian Republic: Antimasonry and the Great Transition in New England, 1826–1836.* New York: Oxford University Press, 1988.

Gould, Lyman J., and Samuel B. Hand. "A View from the Mountain: Perspectives of Vermont's Political Geography." In *Growth and Development of Government in Vermont*, Reginald L. Cook, ed. The Vermont Academy of Arts and Sciences, Occasional Paper no. 5 (1970), 19–24.

Graff, Nancy Price, ed. *Celebrating Vermont: Myths and Realities.* Middlebury, Vt.: Christian A. Johnson Memorial Gallery and Middlebury College, 1991.

———. *Looking Back at Vermont: Farm Security Administration Photographs, 1936–1942.* Middlebury, Vt.: Middlebury College Museum of Art, 2002.

Graffagnino, J. Kevin, ed. *Ethan and Ira Allen: Collected Works.* 3 vols. Benson, Vt.: Chalidze Publications, 1992.

———. *The Shaping of Vermont: From the Wilderness to the Centennial, 1749–1877.* Rutland, Vt.: Vermont Heritage Press and the Bennington Museum, 1983.

———. *Vermont in the Victorian Age: Continuity and Change in the Green Mountain State, 1850–1900.* Bennington and Shelburne, Vt.: Vermont Heritage Press and Shelburne Museum, 1985.

———, Samuel B. Hand, and Gene Sessions, eds. *Vermont Voices, 1609 Through the 1990s: A Documentary History of the Green Mountain State.* Montpelier, Vt.: Vermont Historical Society, 1999.

Graham, John A. *A Descriptive Sketch of the Present State of Vermont.* London: H. Frey, 1797; reprint, Bennington, Vt.: Vermont Heritage Press, 1987.

Green, Mason A. *Nineteen-Two in Vermont: The Fight for Local Option.* Rutland, Vt.: The Marble City Press, 1912.

Guma, Greg. *The People's Republic: Vermont and the Sanders Revolution.* Shelburne, Vt.: The New England Press, 1989.

Guyette, Elise. *Vermont: A Cultural Patchwork.* Peterborough, N.H.: Cobblestone Publishing, Inc., 1986.

Hall, Benjamin H. *History of Eastern Vermont, from Its Earliest Settlement to the Close of the Eighteenth Century.* New York: D. Appleton & Co., 1858.

Hall, Hiland. *The History of Vermont, from Its Discovery to Its Admission into the Union in 1791.* Albany, N.Y.: Joel Munsell, 1868.

Hand, Samuel B. "Friends, Neighbors, and Political Allies: Reflections on the Gibson-Aiken Connection." Occasional Paper no. 11. Burlington, Vt.: Center For Research on Vermont, University of Vermont, 1986.

———. "Mountain Rule Revisited." *Vermont History* 71 (Summer/Fall 2003): 139–151.

———. *The Star That Set: The Vermont Republican Party, 1854–1974.* Lanham, Md.:

Lexington Books, 2002.
———, Jeffrey D. Marshall, and D. Gregory Sanford. "'Little Republics': The Structure of State Politics in Vermont, 1854–1920. *Vermont History* 53 (Summer 1985): 141–166.
———, and Paul M. Searls. "Transition Politics: Vermont, 1940–1952." *Vermont History* 62 (Winter 1994): 5–25.
Haraty, Peter H., ed. *Put the Vermonters Ahead: A History of the Vermont National Guard, 1764–1978*. Burlington, Vt.: Queen City Printers, Inc., 1982.
Hard, Walter. *The Connecticut*. Rivers of America Series. New York: Rinehart & Company, Inc., 1947.
Hastings, Scott E., Jr. *Goodbye Highland Yankee: Stories of a North Country Boyhood*. Chelsea, Vt.: Chelsea Green Publishing Company, 1988.
———. *The Last Yankees: Folkways in Eastern Vermont and the Border Country*. Hanover, N.H.: University Press of New England, 1990.
———. *Up in the Morning Early: Vermont Farm Families in the Thirties*. Hanover, N.H.: University Press of New England, 1992.
———, and Geraldine S. Ames. *The Vermont Farm Year In 1890*. Woodstock, Vt.: Billings Farm and Museum, 1983.
Haviland, William A., and Marjory W. Power. *The Original Vermonters: Native Inhabitants, Past and Present*. Rev. ed. Hanover, N.H.: University Press of New England, 1994.
Hemenway, Abby Maria, ed. *The Vermont Historical Gazetteer*. 5 vols. Burlington, Vt.: various locations and printers, 1867–1891.
Hewitt, Arthur Wentworth. *The Old Brick Manse*. New York: Harper & Row, 1966.
Hill, Ralph Nading. *Lake Champlain: Key to Liberty*. Taftsville, Vt.: Countryman Press, 1977.
———. *The Winooski: Heartway of Vermont*. Rivers of America Series. New York: Rinehart & Company, Inc., 1949.
Hindley, Howard L. *The Gentleman from Hayville*. Rutland, Vt.: [n.p.] 1909.
Holbrook, Stewart Hall. *The Story of American Railroads*. New York: Crown Publishers, 1947.
Holmes, David R. *Stalking the Academic Communist: Intellectual Freedom and the Firing of Alex Novikoff*. Hanover, N.H.: University Press of New England, 1989.
Hoskins, Nathan. *A History of the State of Vermont*. Vergennes, Vt.: J. Shedd, 1831.
Hoyt, Edwin P. *The Damndest Yankees: Ethan Allen and His Clan*. Brattleboro, Vt.: The Stephen Greene Press, 1976.
Huden, John C. *Development of State School Administration in Vermont*. Montpelier, Vt.: Vermont Historical Society, 1944.
———. *Indian Place Names in Vermont*. Burlington, Vt.: n.p., 1957.
Jarvis, Michael John. "The Senators from Vermont and Lend-Lease, 1939–1941." M.A. thesis, University of Vermont, 1974.
Jellison, Charles A. *Ethan Allen: Frontier Rebel*. Syracuse, N.Y.: Syracuse University Press, 1969.
Jennings, Francis. *The Invasion of America: Indians, Colonialism, and the Cant of Conquest*. Chapel Hill, N.C.: University of North Carolina Press, 1975.
Jennison, Peter S. *The History of Woodstock, Vermont, 1890–1983*. Taftsville, Vt.: Countryman Press, 1985.
Johnson, Charles W. *The Nature of Vermont: Introduction and Guide to a New England Environment*. Rev. ed. Hanover, N.H.: University Press of New England, 1998.
Johnson, Claire Dunne. *"I See By the Paper": An Informal History of St. Johnsbury*. 2 vols. St. Johnsbury, Vt.: The Cowles Press, 1989.

Johnson, Otto T. *Nineteen-Six in Vermont.* n.p.: n.p., 1944.
Jones, Matt B. *Vermont in the Making, 1750–1777.* 1939; reprint, New York: AMS Press, 1968.
Jones, Robert C. *Railroads of Vermont.* 2 vols. Shelburne, Vt.: The New England Press, 1993.
Judd, Richard M. *The New Deal in Vermont: Its Impact and Aftermath.* New York: Garland Publishing Inc., 1979.
Kalm, Peter. *Peter Kalm's Travels in North America: From the English Version of 1770.* Edited by Adolph B. Benson. Reprint of 2 vol. edition, 1937. Mineola, N.Y.: Dover, 1987.
Kaufman, Martin. *University of Vermont College of Medicine.* Hanover, N.H.: University Press of New England, 1979.
Ketchum, Richard M. *Saratoga: Turning Point of America's Revolutionary War.* New York: Henry Holt and Company, 1997.
Kinsley, Earle S. *Recollections of Vermonters in State and National Affairs.* Rutland, Vt.: n.p., 1946.
Klyza, Christopher McGrory, and Stephen C. Trombulak. *The Story of Vermont: A Natural and Cultural History.* Hanover, N.H.: University Press of New England, 1999.
Krawitt, Laura, ed. *The Mills at Winooski Falls: Illustrated Essays and Oral Histories.* Winooski, Vt.: Onion River Press, 2000.
Kunin, Madeleine M. *Living a Political Life.* New York: Alfred A. Knopf, 1994.
Laffan, Barry. *Communal Organization and Social Transition: A Case Study from the Counter Culture of the Sixties and Seventies.* New York: Peter Lang Publishing, 1997.
Langrock, Peter. *Beyond the Courthouse: Tales of Lawyers and Lawyering.* Forest Dale, Vt.: Paul S. Eriksson, 1999.
Lee, W. Storrs. *The Green Mountains of Vermont.* New York: Henry Holt and Company, 1955.
Lepore, Jill. *The Name of War: King Philip's War and the Origins of American Identity.* New York: Alfred A. Knopf, 1998.
Lincoln, Charles H., ed. *Narratives of the Indian Wars, 1675–1699.* New York: Charles Scribner's Sons, 1913.
Lockard, Duane. *New England State Politics.* Princeton, N.J.: Princeton University Press, 1966.
Lowenthal, David. *George Perkins Marsh: Prophet of Conservation.* Seattle: University of Washington Press, 2000.
Ludlum David M. *Social Ferment in Vermont, 1791–1850.* New York: Columbia University Press, 1939; reprint, New York: AMS Press, Inc., 1966.
———. *The Vermont Weather Book.* Montpelier, Vt.: Vermont Historical Society, 1985.
McCormick, Richard P. *The Second American Party System: Party Formation in the Jacksonian Era.* Chapel Hill, N.C.: The University of North Carolina Press, 1966.
McMurry, Sally. *Transforming Rural Life: Dairying Families and Agricultural Change, 1820–1885.* Baltimore: Johns Hopkins University Press, 1995.
Mark, Irving. *Agrarian Conflicts in Colonial New York, 1711–1775.* 2nd. ed., 1940; Port Washington, N.Y.: Ira J. Friedman, Inc., 1965.
Marsh, George Perkins. *Man and Nature, Or Physical Geography as Modified by Human Actions* (1864). Edited with introduction by David Lowenthal. Cambridge, Mass.: Harvard University Press, 1965.
Marshall, Jeffrey D., ed. *A War of the People: Vermont Civil War Letters.* Hanover, N.H.: University Press of New England, 1999.

SELECTED BIBLIOGRAPHY

Meeks, Harold A. *Time and Change in Vermont: A Human Geography*. Chester, Conn.: Globe Pequot Press, 1986.

———. *Vermont's Land and Resources*. Shelburne, Vt.: New England Press, 1986.

Merrill, Perry H. *History of Forestry in Vermont, 1909-1959*. Montpelier, Vt.: State Board of Forests and Parks, 1959.

———. *Montpelier: The Capital City's History, 1780-1976*. Montpelier, Vt.: The Author, 1976.

———. *Roosevelt's Forest Army: A History of the Civilian Conservation Corps, 1933-1942*. Montpelier, Vt.: The Author, 1981.

Morison, Samuel Eliot. *The European Discovery of America: The Northern Voyages, A.D. 500-1600*. New York: Oxford University Press, 1971.

Morrissey, Charles T. *The Men Who Made It: Vermont's Union Carpenters*. United Brotherhod of Carpenters and Joiners, n.d. [1984].

———. *Vermont, A History*. New York: W. W. Norton & Company, Inc., 1981.

Mower, Anna L., and Robert L. Hagerman. *Morristown Two Times*. Morrisville, Vt.: Morristown Historical Society, 1982.

Muller, H. Nicholas III. "From Ferment to Fatigue? 1870-1900: A New Look at the Neglected Winter of Vermont." Occasional Paper no. 7. Burlington, Vt.: Center for Research on Vermont, University of Vermont, 1984.

———, and Samuel B. Hand, eds. *In A State of Nature: Readings in Vermont History*. Montpelier, Vt.: Vermont Historical Society, 1982.

Neill, Maudean. *Fiery Crosses in the Green Mountains: The Story of the Ku Klux Klan in Vermont*. Randolph Center, Vt.: Greenhills Books, 1989.

Nelson, Alan. *American Colonies*. New York: Viking, 2001.

Northfield Town History Committee. *Green Mountain Heritage: The Chronicle of Northfield, Vermont*. Canaan, N.H.: Phoenix Publishing, 1974.

Numbers, Ronald L., and Jonathan M. Butler, eds. *The Disappointed: Millerism and Millenarianism in the Nineteenth Century*. Knoxville, Tenn.: The University of Tennessee Press, 1993.

Nuquist, Andrew E. *Town Government in Vermont or "Making Democracy."* Burlington, Vt.: Government Research Center, University of Vermont, 1964.

———, and Edith W. Nuquist. *Vermont State Government and Administration: An Historical and Descriptive Study of the Living Past*. Burlington, Vt.: Government Research Center, University of Vermont, 1966.

O'Callaghan, E. B., ed. *The Documentary History of the State of New-York*. 4 vols. Albany, N.Y.: Charles Van Benthuysen, 1849-1851.

Parkman, Francis. *Count Frontenac and New France under Louis XIV*. Boston: Little, Brown and Company, 1913.

———. *The Old Regime in Canada*. Boston: Little, Brown, and Company, 1874.

Pepe, Faith L. *Vermont Workers, Vermont Resources: Clay, Wood, Metal, Stone*. Brattleboro, Vt.: Brattleboro Museum and Art Center, 1984.

———. "Toward a History of Women in Vermont: An Essay and Bibliography." *Vermont History* 45 (Spring 1977): 69-101.

Pierce, Neal R. *The New England States: People, Politics, and Power in the Six New England States*. New York: W. W. Norton & Company, 1976.

Potash, P. Jeffrey. *Vermont's Burned-Over District: Patterns of Community Development and Religious Activity, 1761-1850*. Brooklyn, N.Y.: Carlson Publishing, 1991.

Preiss, Jack J. *Camp William James*. Norwich, Vt.: Argo Books, 1978.

Proctor, Mortimer Robinson. *Pleasant Memories from Political Life, 1932-1952*. Proctor, Vt.: Privately printed [Edwin F. Sharp], 1950; third printing, 1964.

Quinn, Arthur. *A New World: An Epic of Colonial America from the Founding of Jamestown to the Fall of Quebec.* New York: Berkley Books, 1995.

Quinn, David B. *North America from Earliest Discovery to First Settlements: The Norse Voyages to 1612.* New York: Harper & Row, 1977.

Randall, Willard Sterne. *Benedict Arnold: Patriot and Traitor.* New York: William Morrow and Company, Inc., 1990.

Resch, Tyler, ed. *The Bob Mitchell Years: An Anthology of a Half Century of Editorial Writing by the Publisher of the Rutland Herald.* Rutland, Vt.: The Rutland Herald, 1994.

Roberts, Gwilym R. *New Lives in the Valley: Slate Quarries and Quarry Villages in North Wales, New York, and Vermont, 1850–1920.* Somersworth, N.H.: New Hampshire Printers, 1998.

Robinson, Rowland E. *Danvis Tales: Selected Stories.* David Budbill, ed., with an introduction by Hayden Carruth. Hanover, N.H.: University Press of New England, 1995.

Rolando, Victor R. *200 Years of Soot and Sweat: The History and Archaeology of Vermont's Iron, Charcoal, and Lime Industries.* Manchester Center, Vt.: Vermont Archaeological Society, 1992.

Roth, Randolph A. *The Democratic Dilemma: Religion, Reform, and the Social Order in the Connecticut River Valley of Vermont, 1791–1850.* Cambridge: Cambridge University Press, 1987.

Rozwenc, Edwin. *Agricultural Policies in Vermont, 1860–1945.* Montpelier, Vt.: Vermont Historical Society, 1981.

Russell, Charles Edward. *Bare Hands and Stone Walls: Some Recollections of a Side-Line Reformer.* New York: Charles Scribner's Sons, 1933.

Russell, Howard S. *A Long Deep Furrow: Three Centuries of Farming in New England.* Hanover, N.H.: University Press of New England, 1976.

Rutland Herald and *Barre-Montpelier Times Argus.* *A Vermont Century: Photographs and Essays from the Green Mountain State.* Rutland and Barre, Vt.: Rutland Herald and Barre-Montpelier Times Argus, 1999.

Salmond, John A. *The Civilian Conservation Corps, 1933–1942: A New Deal Case Study.* Durham, N.C.: Duke University Press, 1967.

Searls, Paul M. "Labor, Politics, and Republican Vermont." M.A. thesis, University of Vermont, 1993.

Sessions, Gene, ed. *Celebrating a Century of Granite Art.* Montpelier, Vt.: T. W. Wood Art Gallery, 1989.

———. "'Years of Struggle': The Irish in the Village of Northfield, 1845–1900." *Vermont History* 55 (Spring 1987): 69–95.

Shalhope, Robert E. *Bennington and the Green Mountain Boys: The Emergence of Liberal Democracy in Vermont, 1760–1850.* Baltimore: Johns Hopkins University Press, 1996.

Sharrow, Gregory, and Meg Ostrum, eds. *Families on the Land: Profiles of Vermont Farm Families.* Middlebury, Vt.: Vermont Folklife Center, 1995.

———, and Nancy Price Graff. *Measured Furrows: Vermont's Farming History.* Colchester, Vt.: Vermont ETV/Middlebury, Vt.: Vermont Folklife Center, 1996.

Sherman, Joe. *Fast Lane on a Dirt Road: Vermont Transformed, 1945-1990.* Woodstock, Vt.: Countryman Press, 1991; 2nd ed., White River Junction, Vt.: Chelsea Green Publishing Co., 2000.

Sherman, Michael, ed. *A More Perfect Union: Vermont Becomes a State, 1777–1816.* Montpelier, Vt.: Vermont Historical Society, 1991.

———, ed. *The Political Legacy of George D. Aiken: Wise Old Owl of the U.S. Senate.* Montpelier, Vt.: Vermont Historical Society and Countryman Press, 1995.

———, ed. *Vermont State Government Since 1965*. Burlington, Vt.: Center for Research on Vermont and Snelling Center for Government, 1999.

———, and Jennie Versteeg, eds. *We Vermonters: Perspectives on the Past*. Montpelier, Vt.: Vermont Historical Society, 1992.

Siebert, Wilbur H. *Vermont's Anti-Slavery and Underground Railroad Record*. Columbus, Ohio: 1937; reprint, New York: Negro Universities Press, 1969.

Slade, William, ed. *Vermont State Papers*. Middlebury, Vt.: J. W. Copeland, 1823.

Smallwood, Frank. *Thomas Chittenden: Vermont's First Statesman*. Shelburne, Vt.: The New England Press, Inc., 1997.

Smith, Donald Alan. "Legacy of Dissent: Religion and Politics in Revolutionary Vermont." Ph.D. diss., Clark University, 1980.

———. "Green Mountain Insurgency: Transformation of New York's Forty-Year Land War." *Vermont History* 64 (Fall 1996): 197–235.

Smith, Esther Munroe. *Vermont Place-names: Footprints of History*. 1977; reprint, Camden, Maine, 1996.

Stilwell, Lewis D. *Migration from Vermont*. Montpelier, Vt.: Vermont Historical Society, 1948; reprint, Montpelier and Rutland, Vt., Academy Books, 1983.

Stone, Arthur F. *The Vermont of Today, With Its Historical Background, Attractions, and People*. 4 vols. New York: Lewis Historical Publishing Company, Inc., 1929.

Stone, Mason. *History of Education: State of Vermont*. Montpelier, Vt.: Capital City Press, 1934.

Strickland, Ron. *Vermonters: Oral Histories from Down Country to the Northeast Kingdom*. Hanover, N.H.: University Press of New England, 1986.

They Came to Work: Oral Histories of the Vermont Granite Industry During the 1920s and 1930s. Interviews conducted by Marjorie Strong and Greg Sharrow, edited by Kim Chase. Middlesex, Vt.: Franglais Cultural Center, 1997.

Thomas, Robert Davis. *The Man Who Would Be Perfect: John Humphrey Noyes and the Utopian Impulse*. Philadelphia: University of Pennsylvania Press, Inc., 1977.

Thompson, Zadock. *History of Vermont: Natural, Civil, and Statistical*. Burlington, Vt.: C. Goodrich, 1842.

Thwaites, Reuben Gold, ed. *The Jesuit Relations and Allied Documents: Travels and Explorations of the Jesuit Missionaries in New France, 1610–1791*. 73 vols. Cleveland: The Burrows Brothers Company, 1896–1901.

Trigger, Bruce G., ed. *Northeast. Handbook of North American Indians*. Vol. 15. Gen. ed., William C. Sturtevant. Washington, D.C.: Smithsonian Institution, 1978.

Trow, Martin A. "Right-Wing Radicalism and Political Intolerance: A Study of Support for McCarthy in a New England Town." Ph.D. diss., Columbia University, 1957.

Trudell, Marcel. *The Beginnings of New France*. Toronto: University of Toronto Press, 1973.

True, Marshall M., and Judith Cyronak. *Vermont Department of Education, 1900–1968*. Montpelier, Vt.: Vermont Department of Education, 1968.

Van Diver, Bradford B. *Roadside Geology of Vermont and New Hampshire*. Missoula, Mont.: Mountain Press Publishing Company, 1987.

Vaughan, Alden T., and Edward W. Clark, eds. *Puritans Among the Indians: Accounts of Captivity and Redemption, 1676–1724*. Cambridge: Harvard University Press, 1981.

Vermont Commission on Country Life. *Rural Vermont: A Program for the Future*. Burlington, Vt.: Vermont Commission on Country Life, 1931.

Versteeg, Jennie, ed. *Lake Champlain: Reflections on Our Past*. Burlington, Vt.: University of Vermont, 1987.

Waite, Frederick Clayton. *The First Medical College in Vermont: Castleton, 1818-1862*. Montpelier, Vt.: Vermont Historical Society, 1949.

———. *The Story of a Country Medical College: A History of the Clinical School of Medicine and the Vermont Medical College, Woodstock, Vermont, 1827-1856*. Montpelier, Vt.: Vermont Historical Society, 1945.

Walton, Eliakim P., ed. *Records of the Governor and Council of the State of Vermont*. 8 vols. Montpelier, Vt.: J. & J. M. Poland, 1873-1880.

Waring, Dennis G. *Manufacturing the Muse: Estey Organs and Consumer Culture in Victorian America*. Middletown, Conn.: Wesleyan University Press, 2002.

Waterman, Laura, and Guy Waterman. *Forest and Crag: A History of Hiking, Trail Blazing, and Adventure in the Northeast Mountains*. Boston: Appalachian Mountain Club, 1989.

Wheeler, Scott. *Rumrunners & Revenuers: Prohibition in Vermont*. Shelburne, Vt.: The New England Press, 2003.

White [Cross], Michele A. "Public School Education in Vermont: The 'Myth of Local Control.'" M.A. thesis, Graduate Program, Vermont College of Norwich University, 1992.

Wilgus, William J. *The Role of Transportation in the Development of Vermont*. Montpelier, Vt.: Vermont Historical Society, 1945.

Williams, John. *The Redeemed Captive*. Edited by Edward W. Clark. Amherst, Mass.: The University of Massachusetts Press, 1976.

Williams, Samuel. *The Natural and Civil History of Vermont*. 2 vols. Walpole, N.H.: 1794; rev. ed., Burlington, Vt.: Samuel Mills, 1809.

Williamson, Chilton. *Vermont in Quandary: 1763-1825*. Montpelier, Vt.: Vermont Historical Society, 1949.

Wills, Hazel M. *Bill Wills and Company*. Burlington, Vt.: Lane Press, 1953.

Wilson, Harold F. *The Hill Country of Northern New England: Its Social and Economic History, 1790-1930*. New York: Columbia University Press, 1936; reprint, New York: AMS Press, Inc., 1967.

Winks, Robin W. *Frederick Billings: A Life*. New York: Oxford University Press, 1991.

Wiseman, Frederick M. *Voice of the Dawn: An Autohistory*. Hanover, N.H.: University Press of New England, 2001.

Wolf, Eric R. *Europe and the People Without History*. Berkeley: University of California Press, 1982.

Wolf, Marguerite Hurrey. *At Home in Vermont*. Shelburne, Vt.: New England Press, 1990.

Wright, Ralph. *All Politics is Personal*. Manchester Center, Vt.: Marshall Jones Company, 1996.

Wrinn, Stephen M. *Civil Rights in the Whitest State: Vermont Perceptions of Civil Rights, 1945-1968*. Lanham, Md.: University Press of America, 1998.

Yale, Allen Rice, Jr. "Ingenious & Enterprising Mechanics: A Case Study of Industrialization in Rural Vermont, 1815-1900." Ph.D. diss., University of Connecticut, 1995.

———. *While the Sun Shines: Making Hay in Vermont, 1789-1900*. Montpelier, Vt.: Vermont Historical Society, 1991.

Zirblis, Raymond Paul. *Friends of Freedom: The Vermont Underground Railway Survey Report*. Montpelier, Vt.: State of Vermont, Vermont Department of State Buildings and Vermont Division for Historic Preservation, 1996.

Index

Numbers in italics refer to illustrations.

Abenaki Indians: contact with Europeans, 30-31; disease, 40; eastern Abenaki, 42; and eugenics report, 430; flight north, 47-49; French and Indian War, 62-63; historiography of 553; invisible neighbors, 534; mythology, 30; population, 576; in Swanton, 60; tribal recognition, struggle for, 576-80; villages, 19-20, 60; in War of 1812, 161; warfare with other tribes, 20; Woodland period, 16, 17-18. *See also* St. Francis raid, 1759, *28*.
Abenaki Nation, *577*
Abercromby, James, 65
Abraham, Mount, 9, 381
Acadian Mountain Building Cycle, 2-4
Act 60, 1997, 593, *603,* 604-6
Act 200, 1988, 613-14, 616
Act 250, 1970, 587, 609-13, 614-15, 616
Act 252, 1970, 615
Act Relating to Discrimination on the Basis of Sexual Orientation, 1992, 581
Adams, John, 128-29
Adams, John Quincy, 185, 188
Adams, Samuel, *91*
Addison, Vt., 120, 201
Addison County, Vt.: land prices, 117; population, 310; probate records, 136; settlement patterns, 132; "sheep craze," 173, 194
Adirondack Mountains, 2
advertising, political, *586, 587*
African Americans: "Buffalo Soldiers," 393; CCC workers, 451; census, 576; in Civil War, 259-60; discrimination against, 535-36, 538, 539, 542-43; pre-World War II, 534. *See also* Fresh Air Fund; New York-Vermont Summer Youth Project; Vermont in Mississippi
Agaya, Dom, 22
Agricultural Adjustment Act, 1933, 461

agricultural colleges, 320-22
agricultural experiment station, 321-22, 410
agricultural extension work, 410-11, 434, 484
agricultural machinery, 173-75, 236
agricultural organizations, 237-38, 315-17
agriculture, 16; in 1845, 230-32; in 1859, 235-36; in 1929-1930, 412; diversification, 568-69; English field method, 56; French strip pattern, 60; on frontier, 134; fuel shortages affect, 564; government assistance, 316; grazing animals for commerce, 169-70; in post-World War II era, 516-18; recommendations from governor's commission, 566; symbolic of Vt., 571; wartime boosts, 261, 408-9; in World War II, 483-84. *See also* cooperatives; dairying; livestock; organic farming; soils; names of crops
agriculture commissioner, 410-11
Aho, Eric, 621
AIDS disease, 581
Aiken, E. W., 448
Aiken, George D.: on 1927 flood, 428; agriculture, support of, 460-61, 462, 471-72, 474; civil rights legislation, 537-38; congressional election, 472-74; Ernest Gibson, friendship with, 491, 492-93; farming background, 447; and flood control projects, 450-55, 495; and Green Mountain Parkway, 448; gubernatorial elections, 447, 469; Hydro-Québec deal, against, 513; Interstate highway, opens, 524, 525; labor, support of, 460, 471-72, 474; Lincoln Day speech, 1938, 469-71; on making a living in Vt., 516; model for Sen. Jeffords, 596; and New Deal, 446-47, 448-9; political legacy, 474-75; presidential boomlet, 471; retirement from U.S. Senate, 590; and rural electrification, 449-50; ski industry, leases

703

state land for, 467; tax legislation, 448; on Vermonters, 617; Vt. legislator, 447; World War II, positions on, 477-78, 480, 485
Albanel, Charles, 46
Albright, Roger, 540
Alburg, Vt., 60, 192-93
Alden, John, 539-40
Alexander, Erwin, 543
Algonquian Indians, 11-12, 36-37, 39. *See also* Abenaki Indians
Allen, Ethan: arrival in Vt., 83-84; Connecticut background, 83; in Continental Congress, 111; cow wars, 111-12; death of, 126; on defending Vt. independence, 616; Ejectment Trials, 83, 84; Fort Ticonderoga, taking of, 94-96; Green Mountain Boys leader, 84-85, 89-91, 94, 97; and Haldimand negotiations, 114; historiography of, 74-75, 548; homestead, 552; island named for, 113; judge, appointed, 110; land owner, 89; Montreal, attack on, 97; New York anti-rent riots, 88; religious views, 75, 141, 179; sculpture of, 271; symbol of Vt. independence, 458-59
Allen, Frederick, 592
Allen, Heman, 99, 131
Allen, Ira: canal scheme, 129; in Continental Congress, 113; death of, 131; downfall, 120-21; on farm families, 135; founder of Vt., 100-1, 103; Green Mountain Boy, 89; and Haldimand negotiations, 114-15, 120; loyalist seizures, 110; *Olive Branch* fiasco, *130*-31; state motto, xiii; state treasurer, 123; at statehood convention, 126; on Vermonters, 143; Woodbridge scandal, 125
Allen, Joseph, 83
Allen, Levi, 129
Allen, Mary (Brownson), 83
almanacs, *186*, 237
Alnobak, 20
Alpha Xi Delta, 535
American Antislavery Society, 190-91
American Colonization Society, 189, 190
American Federation of Labor, 356, 456
American Heritage, 551
American Historical Society, 208
American Party. *See* Know-Nothing Party
American Woman Suffrage Association, 328
American Woolen Company, 368, 459, 485, 518
Amherst, Jeffrey, Lord, 65-67, 68, 70
anarchists, *353*, 354
Andrews, Edward C., 553
Andros, Edmund, 47
Andrus, Charles Hardin, 273, *334*

Antietam, Battle of, 1862, 252
Antimasonic party, 185-88
Antimasonry, 183-87
antislavery. *See* slavery
Appelmann, Anton Hermann, 394
Appleby, Joyce, xviii
apples, 182-83, 234, 567
Archaic period, 9-12
Arlington, Vt., 78, 88-89, 480, 561
Arlington Junto, 112; authority challenged, 120; Haldimand negotiations, 114, 115; and Jacob Bayley, 110-11; leader of, 106; and loyalist issue, 121; Union, hesitant to join, 124. *See also* names of individuals
Armstrong, John, 116
Arnold, Benedict, 95-96, 97-99
art and artists, 417-18, 441, 554, 621. *See also* music and musicians; painting and painters; sculpture and sculptors
art galleries, 300, 334
Arthur, Chester Alan, 288
Arthur, Harold, 497, 499
Ascutney, Mount, 2, 438, 522
Asian Americans, 576
Associated Industries of Vermont, 496, 498
Astor, John Jacob, 159
Atkinson, Theodore, 78
Austin, Warren R.: agricultural policy, 461; ally of George Aiken, 453, 454; ambassador to UN, 493; election, 468; and electric utilities, 453; in World War II, 479
automobiles, 384-86, 463
Azarian, Mary, 621

Babcock, Robert, 615
Babcock, Robert S. (1915-1985), 501
back-to-the-land movement, 572
Bailey, Consuelo Northrop, 428, 499-500
Bailyn, Bernard, 104
Baker, Jane, 578
Baker, Remember, 84, 85, 88-90, 126
Baker et al. v. State of Vermont, 582
Bakersfield, Vt., 134-35
Baldwin, C. C. P., 251
Bancker, Gerard, 76
Bancroft, Addison, 213
banks, 122-23, 546
Banks, Ann, 417
Barber, Charles N., 529
Barnard, Vt., 418
Barnet, Vt., 196, *332*, 573

Barre City, Vt.: in 1927 flood, *422, 423;* Boutwell quarry, *351;* Gov. Davis's hometown, 607; granite industry, 301-3; labor strikes, 415, 416-17, 455-56; in Great Depression, 434-35, 436, 441-42; labor history of, 352-56; opera house, *334;* population, 301, 352, 558; prohibition rumrunning, 402-3; recreation, 467-68; Spanish Flu, 395-96; street trolley, *387;* Theodore Roosevelt in, *365;* in World War II, 480, 482

Barre Town, Vt.: East Barre dam, 451

Barrett, William G., 455

Barron, Hal S., 311-12, 331

Barstow, John L., 287, 294

baseball, 488

Bassett, T. D. Seymour: on antebellum politics, 198; on Civil War, 260-61; on state capital selection, 279; on urbanization of Vt., 284; UVM career, 553; on Vt. as border area, xvi, 75

Bates, Dennis, *563*

Bates, Henry, 249

Bates, Joshua, 178, 179, 181

Bathurst, Lord, 160

Battell, Joseph, 376-79, 381, 384-86, 417, 465

Battista, Giovanni, 22

Baum, Frederick, 109

Baumann, William H., *497*

Baxter, Portus, 263

Baxter General Hospital, 263, *264,* 265, 266

Bayley, Jacob, 86, 99, 100, 110-11, 115-16

Bean, Amos, 235

Bean, Cromwell, 235

Beard, Edna L., 404

bedroom communities. *See* rural communities

Belknap, Seward F., 215

Bell, Charles T., 385

Bell, John, 248

Bellows Falls, Vt. *See* Rockingham, Vt.

Ben & Jerry's Homemade, *560*-61, 567

Benchley, Robert, 418

Bennington, Battle of, 1777, 109, 208

Bennington, Vt.: 1789 description of, 120; 1816 in, 165-66; agriculture, 169-70; antislavery movement, 188-89, 190; big-box stores, rejects, 562; delegate to London, 81; industry, 296, 518-19; Jefferson and Madison in, 145; McCarthy era in, 532; N.H. charter, 73; N.Y. grants controversy in, 79, 82, 88, 89; panic of 1837, 193; poor farm, 512; population, 92, 132, 558; pottery, *209;* religion, 75, 87; taverns, 142; trade-union drive, 459; view of, *92;* Vt. centennial celebration, 341; War of 1812, opposition to, 157. *See also* Catamount Tavern

Bennington Battle Day, 336, 340-41

Bennington Battle monument, *340*-41

Bennington College, 487, 495, 496

Bennington convention, 1791, 126

Bennington County, Vt., 116-17, 167

Bennington Evening Banner, 478

Bennington Journal of the Times, 188-89

Bennington Potters, 554

Bennington Powder Company, 261

Bentinck, William H. C., 129

Berlin, Irving, 418

Berlin, Vt., 308, 394, 558

berries, 234

Bethel, Vt., 167, 258, 527-28, 529

Betterment Act, 1785, 121-22

Bianchi, Mrs., 329

bibliography, 284, 419

bicycling, 331

bilingualism, 350

billboards, 463, 513-14

Billings, Franklin S. (1862-1935), 400, 407, 433

Billings, Franklin S., (b. 1922), 502, 504, 510, 539

Billings, Frederick, 221, 324-25, 377, 569

Billings Farm and Museum, 569

Bingham, C. C., 388

bird's-eye views, 334-45

Black River, 454

Black Snake (ship), 153-54

Blackstone, William, Sir, 112

Blackwell, Henry, 328

Blackwell, Marilyn S., 576

Bloody Act, 1774, 90

Bloomer, Asa, 502

Blue laws. *See* Sunday legislation

Bolton, Vt., 422

Bolton War, 1846, 216

Bomoseen, Lake, 418, 534

Booth, John Wilkes, 269

Borgmann, Carl W., 530-31

Boston, 96

Boston Tea Party, 1773, 92

bottle law, 172, 612

Boucher cemetery, 12, 13

Bougainville, Louis Antoine de, 70

boundaries, 74, 78

Bourlamaque, François de, 66, 70

bovine growth hormone, 561, 567

Bowen, Dr., Rutland, Vt., 182

Braddock, Edward, 63

Bradford, Vt., 234, 577
Bradley, Henry, 237
Bradley, Stephen Rowe, 113
Brainerd, Lawrence, 244
Brandon, Vt., 197-98, 199, 341-42
Brandon Training School, 314, 375
Brannon, E. Frank, 499
Brattle, William, 54
Brattleboro, Vt., *195*; automobile ownership, 386; in Civil War, 254, 256, 260; communes in, 572; equivalent lands, 54; industry, 297-98; poor farm, 512; recreation, *331*; telephone exchange, 388; woman suffrage meeting, 283. *See also* Fort Dummer; Smith General Hospital
Brattleboro Reformer, 478
Brattleboro Retreat, 298, 314, 480
Bread Loaf Mountain, 376
Bread Loaf Writers Conference, 417-18
Breakenridge, James, 82-83, 88, 90, 116
Breckenridge, John C., 248
Breese, Albert, 234
breweries, 136
Brigham, Amanda, *603*
Brigham, Elbert, 410, 411-12, 426
Brigham, Uriah, 134-35
Brighton, Vt., 219, 226
Bromley Mountain, 379
Broun, Heywood, 418
Brown, Dona, 336
Browne, Preston, 424
Brownington, Vt., 206
Brownson, Mary. *See* Allen, Mary (Brownson)
Brush, Crean, 79
Bryan, Frank M., xvii, 618, 619
Bryan, William Jennings, 376
Bryant, W. J., 414
Bryant Chucking Grinder Company, 414, 482, 486, 519
Buchanan, Bruce R., 535
Buchanan, James, 247
Buckley, T. Garry, 503, 509-10
Bucklin, Harold, 531
Budbill, David, 619
Buddhism, 573
Bull Run, 1st Battle, 1861, 250, 251-52
Burchard, Jedediah, 179-80
Burgess, John A., 588
Burgoyne, John, 101, 108, 109, 110
burials, Indian, 11, 12
Burke, James E., 357, 364
Burke Mountain, 438

Burlington, Vt.: in 1840, 195-96; 1840 election in, 198-99; 1927 flood, 423; Allen homestead, 552; automobile ownership, 386; bird's-eye-view, *289*; charitable organizations, 291-92; child mill workers, 368-69; city incorporation, *239, 290*; electrification, 389; Embargo, effect upon, 153-54; Flynn Theater, 391; French Canadians in, *193*, 350; Ku Klux Klan in, 406-7; labor strike, 459; legislature at, 150; lumber port, 224, 290-91; manufacturing, 291, *560*; poor farm, 512; population, 167-68, 284, 290, 557; Pres. Harrison in, 342; and railroads, 217-18; recreation, 331, 488; religion in, 179-80; shipping, 138; shopping malls, 611-12; state capital, vies for, 279; street trolley, 387; in War of 1812, 156, 157-58, 159-60, 163; woman suffrage meeting, 283; workingman's mayor, 357-58; in World War II, 480, *481, 482-83*, 485. *See also* Baxter General Hospital
Burlington Free Press, 216, 474, 478, 554
Burlington *Northern Sentinel,* 160
Burton, Asa, 177
Busch, Adolph, 554
Bush, George W., 596
business enterprises, 260-61, 545-46, 559-60. *See also* industry
business tax, 496-97
Butler, Ezra, 189
Butler, James Davie, 207-8

Cabot, John, 21
Cabot, Vt., 461
Cabot Farmers' Cooperative Creamery, 410
Cahoon, William, 187
Calais, Vt., 257, 549
Calhoun, John C., 241-42
Calloway, Colin, 55, 576-77
Camel's Hump, 5, 9, 378, 379, 571
Camp William James, 484-85
Canada, 130, 148-49, 168, 267. *See also* Embargo, 1807-1809
canals, 129, 139, 168, 169. *See also* Champlain Canal
Candon, Elizabeth, Sister, 574
Canfield, Thomas H., *221-222*
capital. *See* state capital
capital punishment, *393*
Carder, Jack S., 357
Cardini, Frank, 402-3
Carleton, Guy, Sir, 99
Carmichael, Stokely, 540
Carnegie Foundation, 370-72, 373
Carpenter, Isaiah, 84

Carpenter, Jonathan, 118-19
Cartier, Jacques, 21-24
Castleton, Vt., 114, 320, 350
Castleton State College, 554
Catamount Tavern, *84, 91*
Catholic church: Klan demonstrations against, 405, 406-7; largest denomination in state, 350; pro-labor, 485-86; sentiment against, 196, 249
caucus. *See* political conventions
Cavendish, Vt., 312, *332,* 459
Cedar Creek, Battle of, 1864, 266, *275*
census. *See* population, state
Central Vermont Railroad, 307; Barre spur line, 352; critique of, 229-30; move to St. Albans, 303; and Rutland Railroad, 219; and St. Johnsbury Railroad, 220. *See also* Vermont Central Railroad
Centre Turnpike Company, 139
Chamberlain, William, 178
Champ, 34
Champion International Corporation, 596, 616
Champlain, Lake, 7, 34, *59,* 552. *See also* shipping; names of islands
Champlain, Samuel de, 25-26, 30, 34-38, 39, 42
Champlain & Connecticut River Railroad, 215
Champlain Canal, 168-70
Champlain Lowlands, 1
Champlain Sea, 7, 9
Champlain Valley, 101, *133, 571*
Chancellorsville, Battle of, 1863, 253
Chandler, Thomas, 93
Charlestown, N.H., 70
Charlotte, Vt., 243, 577
Chastes, Aymar de, 34
Chateaugay (ship), 423
Chautauquas, 390-91
Chelsea, Vt., *311*-12, 331
Chesapeake-Leopard Affair, 1807, 151-52
Chester, Vt., 85
child labor, *367*-68
child welfare, 396
Childs, Frank, *227*
Chimney Point, 56, 66
Chipman, Nathaniel, 121-26
Chittenden, Martin, 153, 156-57, 159
Chittenden, Thomas: Arlington Junto leader, 106, 110-11; arms purchase, 130, 131; correspondence of, 208; on Council of Safety, 108; cow wars, 112; against N.Y. jurisdiction, 113; state bank issue, 122-23; and statehood for Vt., 124, 125, 126; Williston farm, 120

Chittenden, Vt., 334
Chittenden Bank, 546
Chittenden County, Vt., 546, 557
Choate, Alice Watts, 256, 260
church and state, 145-46
church lands, 81
circus, *332*
cities and towns: automobiles, effect on, 386; consolidation proposal, 435; growth of, 137-38; incorporation of cities, 239, 290, 294, 295, 296; legislative representation, 106-7, 111; railroads determine location, 226. *See also* rural communities; urban sprawl; urbanization
Citizens Union Party of Order, 296
Civil Defense Act, 1951, 528
civil rights, 536-41, 543, 574, 581
civil union, 582-84, 620
Civil War, 1861-1865: African-Americans in, 259-60; beginning of, 249-50; cost to Vt., 250, 254, 269; dead and wounded, 254, 269; draft system, 256-59; economy, effect on, 260-61; end of, 267-69; home front, 254-70; hospitals, 254, 262-66; manufacturing, effect on, 241; opposition to, 255; regiments in, 250, 252-53; visual images of, 271-76. *See also* St. Albans raid, 1864; names of battles
Civilian Conservation Corps, 437-39, 451, 466-67, 484
Clarendon, Vt., 89-90
Clark, Charles E., 343
Clark, Isaac, 156
Clark, Roger, 65
Clarke, Dewitt Clinton, 197-98, 199, 216
Clay, Henry, 170, 241-42
Cleghorn, Sarah, 417
Clement, Percival W.: 1902 election campaign, 359-62; governor, 292, 398-99; pardon of Gov. Graham, 400; and prohibition, 401-2; railroad owner, 364; woman suffrage veto, 403-4
Clermont (ship), 148-49
Cleveland, George, 155
Clifford, Deborah P., 286
Clinton, DeWitt, 168
Clinton, George, 112
clothing factories, 296
Clough, Shepard B., 543-44
Coates, Walter John, 418-20
Coburn, Joseph, 237
Cochran, Robert, 89, 90, 94
Cockburn, William, 89
Cohen, Ben, 560-61
coins. *See* money

Colchester, Vt., 158-59, 546, 557
Colchester jar, *13*
Colden, Cadwallader, *74,* 79, 80, 94
Collamer, Jacob, 247, 260
Collins, Ben, 541
Colophon, 549
Columbia University, 544
Colver, Nathaniel, 185
Commoner, Barry, 608
communes, 572-73, 594
communism, 493, 499, 526-34
Community College of Vermont, 554
Compromise of 1850, 241-42
computer industry, 546
Conant, Edward, 319
Concord Academy, 206, 320
Conely, Larry, 542
Confiance (ship), 162-63
Conger, George, 266-67
Congregational church, 145, 176, 178, 182
Connecticut, 53-54, 105
Connecticut & Passumpsic Rivers Railroad, 196, 215, 220
Connecticut River: canal around, 139, 149, 168; creation of, 6; flood control, 452-54, 497; history of, 548
Connecticut Valley, 2, 16, 19, 133
constitutional conventions, 278, 280
construction industry, 588-89, 590
Continental Congress: 1776 resolution, 101; Eastern Union, reaction to, 111; and Vt. statehood, 99, 110, 112-13, 114, 116
Converse, John Kendrick, 189
Converse, Julius, *323,* 324-25
Cook, George, 540
Coolidge, Calvin, 401, 424, 464, 617
Coolidge, Carlos, 202
Coolidge, John, 401
Cooper, John Sherman, 533
cooperatives, 201, 410, 449, 461
Copley Hospital, 434
copper mining, 294
corn, 15, 82, 170, 194, 231
Cornwall, Ellsworth B., 450
Cornwall, Vt., 135-36, 137, 177, *565*
Cornwallis, Charles, 115
corporations, 364
correctional institutions, 314. *See also* Vermont. State Prison
Corrupt Practices Law, 1902, 361
corruption, 400-1

Corti, Elia, 354
Costle, Douglas M., 613
Cote, C. H. O., 192-93
counterculture. *See* hippies
Country Life Movement, 370
Countryman Press, 549
Courcelles, Daniel de Remy, sieur de, 45-46
courts, 600. *See also* Vermont. Supreme Court
cow wars, 112
Cowass, 31, 62
Cowasuck Indians, 18, 49
Crafts, Samuel, 190
Craftsbury, Vt., 166
Creamery Inspection Act, 1912, 412
Cree, Albert, 513
Cree, George W., 279
Cree, T. Jefferson, 279
Crispe, A. Luke, 501, 503, 505
Crockett, Walter Hill, 366
Cronon, William, 16
Crown Point, 56-57. *See also* Fort St. Frédéric
Crown Point Road, 67
culture conflict, 572, 573, 583-84, 620-21
Cumberland County, 85-86, 93, 99-100
Cummings, Charles R., 428
Cunningham, Amy, 582
Cushing, John T., 394-95

D'Agostino, Lorenzo, 383-84
dairying: bovine tuberculosis testing, 411-12; bulk tanks, transition to, 516-17; dairymen organize, 237-38; decline in farms, 564, 566; electrification, effect on, 389; follows sheep boom, 232-33; government assistance, 315-16; during Great Depression, 432; railroads expand market, 305, 408. *See also* milk
Dale, Porter H., 425
Daley, John, 539, 585
Danby, Vt., 193-94, 456-57
Daniels, Harry, 557, 558
Danville, Vt., 150
Darling, Alfred Burbank, 269
Dart, Calvin, 84
Dartt, Justus, 319
Daughters of Vermont, 289
Daunt, Harold, 485
Davis, Allen F., 620
Davis, Deane C.: administrative reorganization, 599; commune tour, 573; and economic development, 560; elections, 515, *586,* 587; and environmental conservation,

607-9, 611, 615; inaugural address, 598-99; lawyer in Klan case, 406; Little Hoover Commission chair, 507; on Perry Merrill, 508; on racism, 543; record as governor, 585-86, 595; on Vt.'s population, 557
Davis, Kenneth S., 479
Day, Gordon M., 68, 553
Dean, Cyrus, 154
Dean, Howard: 2000 gubernatorial election, 594; and Abenaki tribal recognition, 580; and Act 60, *603*, 604, 605-6; civil union, supports, 583; dairy compact, lobbies for, 566; and economic development, 561, 562; and environmental conservation, 596, 614, 616; fiscal policy, 463; health insurance policy, 601-2; preservation of downtowns, 562, 616; record as governor, 592-93; women, appointment of, 576
Dearborn, Henry, 157
DeBoer, Joseph A., 347-48, 351, 382, 420
Debs, Eugene V., 355, 356
debt, 93, 122-24, 131
Declaration of Independence, 103, 104
deer, 512
Deere, John, 236
Deerfield, Mass., 52-53
Defiance, Mount, 108, 109
Delaplace, William, 96
Democratic Party: 1970-1980s gains in Vt. legislature, 590, 592; first 20th-century statewide win, 500; Free Soil alliance, 202; and Kansas-Nebraska Act, 243-44; in retreat, 1870-1900, 323; revitalization of, 499, 501, 503-5; slavery, identified with, 278-79
Democratic-Republican Party: condemns Hartford Convention, 164; election of 1813, 158-59; and Embargo, 152, 153; favors James Madison, 154; governorship, 146; in legislature, 164, 185; in War of 1812, 163
deposit-refund system, 612
depressions: of 1785, 122; of 1837, 193-94; of 1920-21, 412-13, 415; Great Depression of 1929, 432-37. *See also* New Deal
Derby, Vt., 273, 334
DeWees, Rusty, 619
Dewey, Elijah, 92
Dewey, George, 342-45
Dewey, Jedediah, 89, 92, 116-17
Dewey, John, 553-54
Diamond, Jared, 16
Diamond, M. Jerome, 578
Diamondstone, Peter, 594
Dies, Martin, 493

Dietz, Howard, 418
Dillingham, Paul, 251
Dillingham, William P., 287-88
director of state institutions, 398
disease. *See* epidemics
distilleries, 136, 181
district environmental commissions, 609, 612
District of Columbia. *See* Washington, D.C.
Dix, Dorothea, 256
Dr. Dynasaur program, 592, 601, 602
Donahue site, 15
Donnaconna, 22, 23, 24
Dooley, John A., xvii
Doolittle, Amos, 118
Dopp, Daisy, 234-35
Dorset, Vt., *227*, 388, 554
Dorset Convention, 1776, 99, 100
Douglas, James H., 563, 593, 606
Douglas, Stephen A., 242-43, 248
Douglass, Frederick, 192
Dover, Vt., 607, 608, 611
Downer, Charles, 379
Downey, George, 163
Downs, John H., 502, 504
Driftwind Press, 419
Druillettes, Gabriel, Father, 43-44
Duane, James, 79, 83, 84, 89
Dubie, Brian, 594
Duffus, Robert L., 329, 362
Dummer, William, 54
Dummerston, Vt., 54, 387-88
Dunham, Josiah, 163, 164
Dutch East India Company, 38
Dwight, Timothy, 54, 56, 134
Dwinell, Albert, 309
Dwinell, Harold A., 462
Dwyer, Ruth, 593, 605

Earl, Ralph, 92
Early, Steven, 454
Earth People's Park, 573
East Montpelier, Vt., 305, 402, 418-19, 558
Eastern Union, 111, 113, 114-15, 116
Eastman, Charles G., 199
Easton, John, 591
Eaton, Horace, 207, 317-18
economic development, 559-62
Eddy, Ethel, 509
Eddy, Jacob, 320

Edmunds, George F., 294, 341, 342
education, higher, 319-22, 553-54. *See also* names of schools
education: funding, 372, 602-6; reform, 206-7, 317-19, 369-74, 511; Vt. constitution on, 107, 317, 604. *See also* Act 60, 1997; teachers; school buildings
education commissioner, 373
Eighteen-hundred-and-froze-to-death, 165-66
Ejectment Trials, 1770, 83
elections: of 1808, 154; of 1813, 158; of 1828, 185; of 1840, 198-99; of 1854, 245; of 1902, 359-61; of 1912, 356-66, 364-66; of 1920, 399; of 1934, 468; of 1936, 469; of 1940, 472-74, 479; of 1946, 490, 492-93, *494*; of 1948, 497; of 1962, 502-4; of 1970, *586*; of 1972, 587-88; of 1974, 590; of 1976, 594; of 1986, 594; of 1988, 595, 619-20; of 1990, 595; of 2000, 583, 594, 620; of 2002, 593, 594; decided by legislature, 196, 361, 366, 593, 594. *See also* primaries, direct; voting
electric power. *See* hydroelectric power
electric utilities, 449-50, 452-53, 495-96
electrification, 388-89, 390, 449-50
Eley, Rob, 607
Ely, Robert, 522
Embargo, 1807-1809, 152-56
Emergency Relief and Construction Act, 1932, 437
Emerson, Lee E.: anti-communist agenda, 499, 528-29, 530-31; governor, 499; gubernatorial aspiration, 497; health care proposal, against, 496; road construction under, 523
Emery, Edson, 252
emigration. *See* migration
endangered historic places, xviii, 615
England, Heber G., 455
Enterprise (ship), 96
environmental protection, 227-28, 375-80, 513-14, 596, 606-16
epidemics, 27, 29-30, 40-41, 158, 395-96
Episcopal church, 367-69
Equal Educational Opportunity Act, 1997, 604
Equal Rights Amendment, 574, *575*, 595-96
equivalent lands, 53-54
escape clause. *See* secession
eskers, 6
Espionage Act, 1917, 393-94
Essex, Vt., 226, 229-30, 422, 520, 557
Essex County Railroad, 220
Estey, Jacob, 297-98, 310
Estey Organ Company, 224, *297*-98

eugenics, 429, 430-31
exceptionalism. *See* Vermont exceptionalism

Fair Haven, Vt., 126, 241, 341-42, 350, 442
Fairbanks, Erastus: agriculture, promoter of, 237, 238; Civil War governor, 249-50, 252; declines governorship, 244; industrialist, 299; letter from G. P. Marsh, 248; temperance supporter, 205
Fairbanks, Franklin, 300, 342
Fairbanks, Horace, 220, 221, 299-300, 324
Fairbanks, Thaddeus, 299
Fairbanks (E. & T.) & Company, 240, 261, 298-301, 414
Fairfax, Vt., 557
Fairlee, Vt., 334, 464
fairs, agricultural, 237
farm buildings, 409
farm life, 134-36, 389-90
farmers, 382-83, 486, 570-71
farming. *See* agriculture
farms: abandoned farms, use for, 337, 464, 522; decline in: 1890-1950, 516; 1900-1930, 407-8; farmed land, 1900 and 2000, 564; Great Depression, reduction in, 432-*33*; land subdivisions of, 607; New Deal resettlement proposal, 445-47; number of, 310-11, 517; paying guests, 569; property tax abatement, 614; size of, 173, 194, 235
Farnham, Roswell, 269-70
Fay, Jonas, 89
Fay, Stephen, 89
Fayston, Vt., 379, 558
Federal Aid Road Act, 1916, 386
Federal Emergency Relief Administration, 439
Federal Writers' Project, 441
Federalist Party, 158, 163-64
Fellows, Edward R., 414
Fellows Gear Shaper Company, 414, 519
Feltham, Jocelyn, 96
fences, 231
Ferber, Edna, 418
Ferrin, Charles S., 424
Ferrisburgh, Vt., 190-91, 259, 338, 569
Field, Sabra, *571*
Fillmore, Millard, 218
films. *See* motion pictures
Fink, Leon, 292
Finney, Charles Grandison, 178
fire departments, 305
firsts in Vermont: automobile fatality, 385; bibliography, 284; birth, 56; mental hospital, 298; milestones for

women, 404, 500, 574, 575-76; permanent settlement, 55; political convention, 185-87; snowmaking, 522; state fair, 237; street trolley, 387; telephones, 388

fiscal paper. *See* money

Fisher, Dorothy Canfield: on anti-communism, 529-30, 532; Camp William James, supports, 485; on economic depression, 413; her play *Tourists Accommodated,* 534; parkway proposal, supports, 445; settles in Vt., 417; on Vermonters, xviii; on Vt. tradition, 617-18

fishing. *See* hunting and fishing

Fitch, Theophilus Wilson, 166

Fitzsimons, Edward, 538, 540

Flanders, Earl L., *494*

Flanders, Helen Hartness, 430, 472-73

Flanders, Ralph E.: Camp William James, supports, 485; elections, 472-74, 493, *494*; model for Sen. Jeffords, 596; for parkway proposal, 445; Sen. McCarthy, attacks, 532-34; on Springfield, 414

Fletcher, Allen M., 366, 369, 370-71, 380, 431

Fletcher, Mary L., 291

Fletcher, Mary Martha, 291

Fletcher, Ryland, 244-45, 249

flood, 1927: cleanup and restoration, 424-27; death toll, 422, 423; devastation from, 421-24; federal assistance, 424-26, 428; perceptions of, 427-28

flood control dams and reservoirs, 450-55, 495

Flower, J. Howard, 418-19

Fly (ship), 153

Foley, Allen R., 547

Follett, Timothy, 214-15, 218-19, 221

food crops, 564

food products, 568

Ford, Henry, 386

Forestry Association of Vermont, 379-80, 381

forestry commissioner, 378-79

forests and forestry, 375-80. *See also* Green Mountain National Forest; state forests

Fort Carillon, 64, 65-66. *See also* Fort Ticonderoga

Fort Dummer, 54-55, 56, 61, 78

Fort Ethan Allen, 392-93, 477

Fort Hill, 18, 19, 31, 44

Fort Number Four, 61, 62, 63, 67

Fort Number One, 61

Fort Number Two, 61

Fort Richelieu, 45

Fort St. Frédéric, 57-58, 61, 62, 63, 64, 66

Fort St. Jean, 45

Fort St. Louis de Chambly, 45

Fort Ste. Anne, 45-46, 53

Fort Ste. Therese, 45

Fort Ticonderoga, 66, 95-96, 99, 108-9. *See also* Fort Carillon

Fort Wentworth, 62

Fort William Henry, 64, *65*

fossils, 2. *See also* state fossil

4-H clubs, 411, 434, 535

Fourth of July, *225*

France, 21-25, 130-31. *See also* New France

Francis I (King of France), 24

Franklin, A. B., 321-22

Fraser, Simon, 108-9

Free Soil party, 201-2, 243, 245

"Freedom and Unity," xiii, 623

Freeman Foundation, 605

Freeman's Farm, Battle of, 1777, 110

Freeman's Oath, 105

Freemasons, 183-84, 187, 331. *See also* Antimasonry

freemen, 107

Frémont, John C., 247

French and Indian War, 1756-1763, 62-71. *See also* St. Francis raid, 1759

French Canadians: antipathy toward, 196; Barre strike breakers, 417; in Burlington, 193, 196; discrimination against, 534; and eugenics report, 430; in Fairbanks factory, 301; influx of, 349-50; in marble industry, 295, 296

Fresh Air Fund, 535

Frontenac, Louis de Beaude, Comte de, 51-52

frontier life. *See* pioneer life

frontier thesis, xv-xvi, xviii

Frost, Robert, 417

Fugitive Slave Act, 1850, 242, 259-60

Fulbright, J. William, 533

Fuller, Abby Estey, 256, 260

Fuller, Ida M., 441

Fuller, Levi K., 261

Fulton, Robert, 148, 149

fur trade: commercial value, 25; with Indians, 27-28, 38-39, 42; location for, 36; monopoly rights, 34, 35

Gallagher, Nancy L., 431

Galleani, Luigi, 353

Gallup, Joseph, 158

Galusha, Jonas, 158-59, 164, 166, 181

Garrison, William Lloyd, 188-90, 283

gasoline tax, 398

Gates, Benjamin, 436

Gates, Charles, 372

gays. *See* homosexuals
Gen. Greene (ship), *149*
general stores, 137, 549
George, Lake, 64, 65
George III (King of England), 74, 94, 103
Georgia, Vt., 557
Germain, George, Lord, 109, 113
German Americans, 298, 393-94
Germans, 109
Gettysburg, Battle of, 1863, 253, 275
Gibb, Arthur, 608, 613
Gibson, Ernest W. (1872-1940), 364, 426, 472
Gibson, Ernest W. (1901-1969): 1946 election, 490, 492-93, *494*; appointed to father's U.S. Senate seat, 472, 491; and communist scare, 527, 529; George Aiken, friendship with, 474, 491, 492-93; on Gov. Aiken and labor, 460; governor, record as, 496-99, 525; during Great Depression, 433; inaugural address, 493-96; Irasburg affair, investigates, 543; legal and military careers, 478-79, 491-92, 499; model for Sen. Jeffords, 596
Gibson, Ernest W. (b. 1927), 502, 504
Gil, David, 554
Gilbert, Clinton, 465-66
Gilman, James Franklin, *339*
Gilmore, William J., 141
Giuliani, Peter, 602
glaciation, 5-7
Glastenbury, Vt., 79
Gleaner (ship), 168
glebes. *See* church lands
globes, *151*
Gloucester County, 85-86, 99-100
Glover, Vt., 234-35
Goddard College, 487, 553-54, 572
Goddard Seminary, 303
Goffe, John, 67
Goldman, Emma, 355
Goldsbrow, Banyar, 79, 84
Goldwater, Barry, 505
golfing, *331*
Gompers, Samuel, 355
Goodrich, Charles A., 95
Goodrich, Chauncey, 180
Gordon, Robert, 355
government. *See* politics and government; state government; town meeting
governors: first 20th-century Democrat as, 503; and Mountain Rule, 323-24; only recount for, 500; terms and term limits, 324-26, 427, 600; woman, first, 574

Governor's Advisory Commission on Native American Affairs, 1976, 578-79, 580
Governor's Commission on Environmental Control, 1969, 608-9
Governor's Commission on Food, 1974, 564, 566
Governor's Commission on Vermont's Future, 1987, 566, 571, 613-14
Governor's Commission on Women, 1964, 538, 574, 576
Graf, Joel, 570-71
Graf, Robert, 570
Graffagnino, J. Kevin, 74-75, *335*
Graham, Horace F.: convicted for malfeasance, 400; government reform, 398; and Red Threat, 395; signs child welfare law, 375; wartime governor, 391-92, 393, 394
Graham, L. L., 334
Grand Army of the Republic (GAR), 270, 273, *331*
Grand Isle, Vt., 577
Grand Isle County, Vt., 557
Grange, 316-17, 321-22, *331*, 411
granite, 4
Granite Cutters Union, 352, 355
granite industry: in 1927 flood, 423; in Barre, 301-3, *351*-56; labor strikes, 415, 416-17, 455-56; Spanish Flu hits, 395; in World War II, 482
Grant, Anne, 80
Grant, Lewis A., 253
Granville, Vt., 379
Grasset, Jacques, 43
Great League of Peace and Power, 27
Green, Herman, 255
Green Mountain Boys, 84, 85, 86, 88-92, 94
Green Mountain Club, 381, 445
Green Mountain Guard, 393
Green Mountain National Forest, 379, 464-65
Green Mountain Parkway, 442-45, 448
Green Mountain Regiment, 97, 109
Green Mountain Rifleman, 527
Green Mountains, 1-5, 336, 378, 442-45
Green-Up Day, 615
Greenfield, Jerry, 560-61
Gregory, Thomas W., 394
Grenville event, 2
Grey Lock, 19, 54-55
Grey Lock's War, 1723-1727, 54-56
Griffith, Silas, 377
gristmills. *See* mills
Griswold, Roger, *128*
Groton State Forest, 438

Grout, John, 85
Grumlie, John, 135
Guilford, Vt., 92, 132, 572

Hackel, Paul, 538, 540
Hackett, Luther F., 587-88
Halberstam, David, 526
Haldimand, Frederick, 114, 129
Haldimand negotiations, 113-16
Hale, Dr., Rutland, Vt., 182
Hall, Hiland, 341
Hall, Samuel Read, 206, 320
Hamilton, Alexander, 125, 126
Hampton, Wade, 159
Hancock, Vt., 379
Hand, Samuel B.: arrival in Vt., 553; on Mountain Rule, 324, 326, 490; on prohibition, 330; on Republican Party, 595, 597
Hapgood, Marshall, 377, 379
Hard, Walter R. (1882-1966), 417, 445, 522, 547-48, 551
Harding, Warren, 401
Hardwick, Vt., *469*
Harper's Weekly, 271
Harris, Fred, 465
Harrison, Benjamin, 294, 341-42, 392
Harrison, William Henry, 198, 199, 270
Hart, George, 260
Hart, Moss, 418
Hartford, Vt., 201, 393, 403, 441
Hartford Convention, 1815, 163-64
Hartland, Vt., 518
Hartness, James, 398-400, 404, 413-14, 415, 416
Harvard University, 544
Harvey, George, 617
Harwood, Benjamin, 165-66
Harwood, Hiram, 169-70
Hassett, William D., 475-76
Haswell, Anthony, 142
hate crimes, 581
Hathaway, Richard O., 620-21
Haviland, William A., 14, 15, 19
Hawes, Austin F., 380
Hawks, John, 67
Hawthorne, Nathaniel, 196
hay and haying, *236,* 517-18
Hayes, Thomas L., 586, 587
Hayford, James, 526
Haynes, Lemuel, *176*
Haystack Mountain, 611

Haywood, William Dudley ("Big Bill"), 355
health. *See* public health
health insurance, 601-2
Healy, Ben F., 354, 356
Heath, Charles, 238
Heininger, Alfred, 447
Heinrich, Waldo H., 478
Hemenway, Abby Maria, *285-86,* 308
Henri IV (King of France), 34, 37
Henry, Charles A., *334*
Herrick, Samuel, 113
Hewitt, Arthur W., 372
Heyde, Charles L., 339
high schools, 206, 511
Highgate, Vt.: Abenakis in, 577, 580; egg farm, 569; Paleoindian site, 8; smuggling in, 155; in War of 1812, 161, 167
highways. *See* roads
hiking trails, 381. *See also* Long Trail
Hill, Ralph Nading, 224, 551-52
Hill, Titus, 135-36
Himes, Joshua V., 204
Hindley, H. L., 382-83
Hindman, Ed, 608
Hine, Lewis W., *367, 368*
Hinesburg, Vt., 260
Hinsdale, Ebenezer, 56
hippies, 572-73
Hispanic Americans, 541
Hiss, Alger, 527
historians, 284-86, 550-52, 553. *See also* names of historians
historic preservation, 550, 551, 562, 615-16
historiography, 74-75
history. *See* state and local history
Hitchcock, Lake, 6
Hochelaga, 22-24, 26, 27. *See also* Montreal
Hodgdon, Ian, 7
Hoff, Philip H.: administrative reform, 508; arts council, creation of, 554; challenges facing administration, 506-8; civil rights activist, 536-37, 538, 539-43; defeated for U.S. Senate, 515, 543; education reform, 511; environmental policy, 513-14; farewell speech, 597-98; gubernatorial elections, 502-5, 515; inaugural address, 505-6; member of Vt. House, 509; power policy, 512-13; and press corps, 585; and reapportionment, 510; Vietnam war, opposed to, 514-15; welfare policy, 512; Young Turk, 502
Hogan, Cornelius, 594

Holbrook, Frederick: agriculture, promoter of, 236, 237; Civil War governor, 252, 261, 262-63, 265-66
Holden, A. John, 511, 527
homosexuals, 581-84. *See also* civil union
Hooker, William, 155
Hoover, Herbert, 424-25, 436-37, 451, 464, 507
Hope, James, 252
Hopkins, Ernest M., 456
Hopkins, John Henry, 180, 206, 251
hops, 234
horses. *See* Morgan horse
horticulture, 14-17
Hoskins, Nathan, 172, 173
hospitals, 254, 262-66, 291, 294. *See also* psychiatric hospitals
hotels, 305, 335-36
Hough, Benjamin, 90
Houghton, George H., 271-73
housing, 297-98, 539-40
Howard, John Purple, 291
Howard, Louisa, 291
Howard Bank, *563*
Howe, David Willard, 443
Howe, Frank E., 443-44
Howe, George Augustus, Lord, 65, 101
Howe, Harland B., 366
Howe, Harvey, 283
Howe, Julia Ward, 283, 328
Howe Scale Company, 224, 293, 295, 482
Howland, Fred A., 424
Howland, John, 522
Hubbard, William, 50-51
Hubbardton, Battle of, 1777, 109
Hubbell, Seth, 117-*18*
Huden, John C., 319, 553
Hudson, Henry, 38
Hudson Valley, 80, 87
Huguenots, 40
Huiest, Mr., 334
Hulett, Ben, 570
Hull, Cordell, 479
humor, 382-83, 547, 568
Humphrey, Hubert, 586
Humphrey, Zephine, 417
Hunt, Jonathan, 189
hunting, in prehistoric times, 8-10, 11, 13-14, 15-16
hunting and fishing, 314, 378, 382
Huntington, Vt., 177, 260

Huron Indians, 23, 27, 36-37, 41, 42
hurricane, 1938, 460-61
Huskey Injection Molding, 562
Hutchins, Frank, 510
Hutchinson, Grace, 434
Hutchinson, W. Clark, 510
Hyde Park, Vt., 334
Hydro-Québec, 513, 590
hydroelectric power, 512-13, 518, 590
hydrotherapy, 226, 298, 335-36

Ice Age. *See* glaciation
immigration. *See* migration; names of ethnic groups
impressment, 151-52
income tax, 398, 448
Independence, Mount, 99, 108-9
Independence Day. *See* Fourth of July
Indian captivities, 49-51, 52-53, 63, 70
industry: 1850 manufacturing census, 208; adjustment to market forces, 561; Civil War, impact on, 241; decline, following WWI, 415; Great Depression downturn, 432; growth, 1900-1920, 413-14; job loss, 1980-2000, 561-62; post-World War II development, 520; railroad-related manufacturing, 304; railroads extend markets, 224; World War II upturn, 481-83. *See also* business enterprises; names of companies and types of industry
Inflexible (ship), 98
influenza. *See* Spanish Flu
Ingersoll, Jared, 83
insurance companies, 307, 546
intangibles tax, 398
International Business Machines (IBM), *520,* 546
International Order of Good Templars (IOOGT), 331
International Paper Company, 380, 415-16, 607-8
Interstate Commerce Act, 1887, 313-14
Interstate Highway System, 500, 523-*25*
Irasburg affair, 1968, 542-43
Irish Americans: antipathy toward, 196; Civil War draft, resist, 259; in Fairbanks factory, 301; in marble industry, 295, 296; party affiliation, 323; railroad workers, 216, 222-23
ironworks, 292
Iroquois Indians: attacks on Jesuits, 41-42, *43*-44; bounded by Lake Champlain, 11-12; encounter with Cartier, 21-23; encounter with Champlain, 25-27, *36,* 37-38; Five Nations, 36, 42, 52; in King George's War, 62; raids on Montreal, 51-52. *See also* Mohawk Indians
Iroquois Lake. *See* Champlain, Lake

Iroquois River. *See* Richelieu River
Island Pond, Vt. *See* Brighton, Vt.
Isle aux Noix, 66, 70
Isle La Motte, Vt., 2, 11, 45-46, 53, 210
Italian Americans, 329, 352, 353, 354-55

Jackson, Andrew, 163, 185
Jackson, Hollister, 422
Jackson, Horatio Nelson, 384
Jackson, Kenneth, 405
Jamaica, Vt., 167
Jamaicans, 534
Jameson, Zuar E., 233, 310
Janes, Henry, 265
Japan, 481
Jarvis, William, 170-71, 232
Jay Peak, 522
Jefferson, Thomas: Democratic Republican, 126; and Embargo Act, 152, 153, 155; his "Bill for the Diffusion of Knowledge," 107; in Vt., 145
Jeffords, James: dairy compact, lobbies for, 566-67; departure from Republican party, 596-97; elections, 588, 590, 595; record as U.S. senator, 596
Jeffreys, Thomas, 66, 76
Jenison, Silas, 169, 192
Jenner, William, 530-31
Jennison, Peter S., 517
Jericho, Vt., 158, 312, 546
Jesuits, 41-43, 46
Jews, 534, 535, 539
Jogues, Father Isaac, 41-42
Johnson, Capt., 13
Johnson, Captive, 63
Johnson, David Lee, 542-43
Johnson, Denise, 574-76
Johnson, Herbert T., 424
Johnson, James, 63
Johnson, Joseph B., 499-500, 517, 523-24
Johnson, Ladybird, 514
Johnson, Lyndon B., 505, 511, 514-15, 537, 540-41
Johnson, Oliver, 190
Johnson, Susannah, 63
Johnson, Vt., 320
Johnson State College, 541, 554
Joliet, Louis, 46
Jones, Edward H., 437, 446, 487
Jones, Epaphras, 165
Jones, L. R., 378, 379

Jones, Mary Harris ("Mother"), 355
Jones, Reuben, 93-94
Jones and Lamson Machine Company, 413-14, 472-73, 482, 486, 519
journals. *See* periodicals
Joyce, Charles H., 270
Joyce, Robert, 530, 531
Judd, Eben, 156, 165, 168
Judd, Richard M., 439, 499

Kahn, Wolf, 621
Kake Walk, 536
Kalm, Peter, 58, 59, 90
kames, 6
Kansas-Nebraska Act, 1854, 242-43
Kaufman, George S., 418
Kelly, Florence, 367-68
Kemp, John Tabor, 79, 83, 84
Kennedy, John F., 501, 505, 537, 538
Kennedy, Martha, 526
Kent, Dorman B. E., 412
Kent, Rockwell, 417, 457-59
Kent State University protest, 1970, 587
Kentucky, 124, 125
Kerner Commission, 1967, 541
Ketchum Island, 11
kettles (glacial), 6
Keyser, F. Ray, 501, 502, 503
Killington Peak, 522, 523
King, Gideon, 138, 159
King, Martin Luther, 540
King, Rufus, 164
King George's War, 1744-1748, 61-62
King Philip's War, 1675-1676, 47, 49
King William's War, 1689-1697, 51-52
Kipling, Rudyard, 387-88
Kirke, David, 39
Knights of Labor, 294-95, 296, 356-57
Know-Nothing Party, 248-49, 276-78
Koenig, Otto, 453
Kolb, Kathleen, 621
Korean War, 1950-1953, 519
Ku Klux Klan, 404-7
Kunin, Madeleine May: 1986 election, 594; and Abenaki tribal recognition, 579; commission on Vt.'s future, appoints, 566, 613-14; and education funding, 602-3; environmental policy, 612-13; ERA, support of, 574; member of commission on women, 538; mosquitoes

incident, 559; record as governor, 591-92, 601; Supreme Court nominations, 574-76, 587; women, appointment of, 574-76
Kurth, Hilda M., *381*

La Lande, M., 41
La Moss, Erwin, *334*
labor and laboring classes: and civil rights legislation, 536-37; in Fairbanks company town, 301; under Gov. Aiken, 460; in marble industry, 294-96; railroad workers, 222-23, 304; World War II labor shortfall, 483-84. *See also* Bolton War, 1846; child labor; strikes and lockouts; trade unions
labor laws, 369
Laird, Addie, *367*
Lake Dunmore Glass Works, 165
Lake Vermont, 6-7
Lambert, John, 139
Lamoille County, Vt., 310
Lampman, Leonard, 579
Lamson, Goodnow, and Yale, 261
Land Capability and Development Plan, 1973, 610
Land Grant Act, 1862, 237, 247, 320-22
land prices, 117
land settlement, 131, 445-47
land speculation, 73, 75, 78-79, 81
land use, 587, 607-13, 614-15. *See also* Act 250, 1970; urban sprawl
land use planning, 610-11, 612-14. *See also* Act 200, 1988
Landis, J. S. (?), 299
landscape, 227-29
Lane Manufacturing Company, 306
Lapoint, William W., 434, 455
Lardner, Ring, 418
Larocque, J., 43
Larrow, Robert, 499
Lattimore, Owen, 527
Lawrence, Abbott, 217
Lawrence, Barbara, 542-43
Lawson, Harriet, 257-58
Lawson, James, 356
Lawson, John C., 455, 471, 472
Lawson, Truman, 257
Le Mercier, Francis Joseph, 45
League of Nations, 479
League of Vermont Writers, 419
Leahy, Patrick J., 566, 590, 595, 619-20
Leddy, Bernard J., 500
Lee, Robert E., 253, 269

Lee, W. Storrs, 482
Lend-Lease operations, 477-78, 483, 491
Lepore, Jill, 47
lesbians, 581-84. *See also* civil union
Leuchtenburg, William E., 449
Lewis, John L., 486
Lewis, Norman, 619
Lewis, Sinclair, 418, 419-20
Lexington, Battle of, 1775, 94
Liberia, 189
Liberty Party, 201-2
Liberty Union Party, 594
libraries, 291, 294, *397*
license plates, *577,* 579
lieutenant governors, 323-24
Lincoln, Abraham: death of, 269; sculptures of, 271; signs Land Grant Act, 320; Vt. votes for, 248, 269; Vt. war support, 249, 257, 262
Lincoln Mountain, 378, 381
Lindsay, John, 541
Lipke, William C., 467
liquors, 136
Lisman, Louis, 531
literacy, 141
literature. *See* poetry; writers
"Little Hoover Commission," 507, 585, 599
Little River, 451
Livermore, Mary, 283
livestock, 234-35. *See also* species of animals
local government. *See* cities and towns; town meeting
local history. *See* state and local history
local option, 205, 330, 360, 361, 401-2, 404
Local Option League, 360
Lockard, Duane, 526
Londonderry, Vt., 167
Long Trail, 1-2, *381*-82, 445
lotteries, 136, 604
Louis XIV (King of France), 44
Louis XV (King of France), 59
Louisburg fortress, 53, 62, 64
Loveless, W. Gordon, 472
Lowell, Mass., 240
loyalists, 110-11, 121-22
Lucenti, Margaret, 540
Ludlow, Vt., 167, 332, 441, 459, 518-19
Ludlum, David M., 177, 550-51
lumbering and lumber trade, 224, 290-91, 376-77, 377-78, 415
Lyndon, Vt., 390-91

Lyndon State College, 487, 502, 541, 554
Lyon, Matthew, 121-22, 126-29, 131, 145

McCarren, V. Louise, 574
McCarthy, Joseph R., 527, 531-34
McCarthy era, 529-534
McClaughry, John, 618
Macdonough, Thomas, 161, 162-63
machine-tool industry, 413-4, 415, 481-82, 519
Mack Molding, 561
McKinley, William, 343
Mackley, Harold, 394
McMullen, Jack, 619-20
MacNair, Luther K., 526
Macomb, Alexander, 161
Madison, James, 116, 145, 154, 156
Maerki, Vic, 538
magazines. *See* periodicals
Mahican Indians, 38-39
mail service. *See* postal service
Malcolm X, 540
Mallary, Gertrude, 502
Mallary, Richard W., 502, 504, 590
Malone, Crystal, 535
mammoth, wooly, 8
Manchester, Vt.: arts center, 554; farming in, 233; poet portrays, 547-48; rebel convention, 91; recreation, 331; telephone exchange, 388
Mann, Horace, 207
Mann, James, 157
Mansfield, Mount, *1, 9,* 379, 466-67, 555
Mansur, George, 208
manufacturing. *See* industry
maple sugar industry, 461, 553, 567-68, 571
marble, 2
marble industry, 292-93, 356-57, 414, 456-59
Mares, Bill, 619
Marie de l'Incarnation, Sister, 42, 44
Mark, Irving, 80
Marketing Agreement Act, 1935, 461
Marlboro College, 554
Marlboro Music Festival, 554
Marquette, Jacques, 46
Marsh, Charles, 181, 325
Marsh, George Perkins, 227-30, 248-49, 325, 377
Marsh, James, 180
Marshfield, Vt., 257
Martin, Fred C., 468
Martineau, Harriet, 172-73

Marx, Harpo, 418
Mason, Harold W., 478
mass media. *See* newspapers; radio broadcasting; television broadcasting
Massachusetts Bay Colony, 40
Mattocks, Samuel, 123
Mayor, Archer, 621
McClellan, George, 269
McCullough, John G., 360, 361
McNeil, John, 158
Mead, Larkin G., 271, *272*
meals and rooms tax, 559
Meeks, Harold A., 3, 218, 335
Meilbek, E., *289*
Mencken, H. L., 549
mental hospitals. *See* psychiatric hospitals
mentally ill, 314
Merrill, Hazen, 179
Merrill, Perry H., 437-39, 466-67, 508
Merrill, Thomas, 179
Metacom. *See* Philip, King
Methodist church, 176-77
Metzger, Frazier, 365-66, 394
Mexican War, 1846-1848, 201
Meyer, William H., 500, 501, 503, 594
Micmac Indians, 21
Middlebury, Vt.: antislavery movement, 190-91, 192; Champlain Canal, benefits, 168; distillery, 136; Embargo, effect upon, 155, 156; legislature at, 150; marble quarry, 293; panic of 1837, 193; poor farm, 512; population, 167-68; Pres. Harrison in, 341-42; religion, 177, 179; schools, 206; state capital, vies for, 279; state fair at, 237; town's father, 138-39; trade war affects, 165
Middlebury College: chartered, 138; forest bequest, 379, 465; merger proposal, 210, 320-21; religious affiliation, 143, 179, 180; Vietnam War protest, 586-87; in World War II, 486-87. *See also* Bread Loaf Writers Conference
Middlebury Register, 376
Middlesex, Vt., 451, 525, 558
Middletown Springs, Vt., 174-75, 193
migration: after panic of 1837, 194-95; depression-era returnees, 412-13; in-state migration, 289-90, 310-12; number of Vermonters living out-of-state, 210, 288. *See also* names of ethnic groups; summer people; Vermont associations
Mikell v. Rousseau, 502
militia, 181-82, 256

milk: dumping and whole-herd buyout, 364-66; growth hormone controversy, 561, 567; marketing and price control, 461-62; Northeast Dairy Compact, 566-67; production increase, 408-10, 411-2, 564; strike for uniform pricing, 486
Miller, Lucille, 527-28, 529
Miller, Manuel, 527-28, 529
Miller, William, 202-3, 203-5, 602
"Miller Formula," 602
mills, 60, 136-37. *See also* windmills
Milton, Vt., 546, 557, 562, 577
mineral springs. *See* hydrotherapy
minorities, 534, 576. *See also* names of groups
missionaries, 141
Missisquoi Bay, 154
Missisquoi National Wildlife Refuge, 577, 579, 580
Missisquoi River, 19, 49
Missouri compromise, 1820, 188, 242-43, 244
Mrs. Murphy's boarding house, 537, 540
Mitchell, Robert W., 474
Moats, David, 584
Mohawk Indians: and Abenakis, 20; disease, 40; encounter with Champlain, 26, 36-37; English allies, 47, 52; and Sokokis, 44; trade with Europeans, 38-39; war with French, 45-46
money, *123*, 571
Monkton, Vt., 157
Monkton Iron Works, 165
Monroe, James, 164
Montagnais Indians: attack by Mohawks, 39; encounter with Cartier, 21; French allies, 26, 35, 36, 43
Montcalm, Louis Joseph Gozon de Véran, Marquis de, 64, 68
Montgomery, Richard, 97
Monti, Andrew A. H., *497*
Montpelier, Vt.: 1927 flood in, 421-*22*, 423, 426, 427; 1816 in, 166; Antimasonry in, 185-86; antislavery movement, 191-92, 243; business and manufacturing, 305-7, 546; canal convention, 169; capital, selection as, *150*-51, 279; centennial celebration, 347-48, 351; civil rights teacher loses job, 538-39; in Civil War, 251, 268; Dewey Day, 343-45; electrification, 389; ERA rally, 575; fires in, 307-8; incorporation as city, 305, 308; Interstate highway reaches, 524; Ku Klux Klan in, 405, *406-7*; *patriotes* honored, 193; poor farm, 512; population, 168, 195, 558, 306; in prohibition era, 402-3; and railroads, 215, 220, 307; Redstone, *497*; school, 568-69; Spanish Flu in, 395-96; T. W. Wood's hometown, 334, 339; telephone exchange, 388; Vietnam War protest, 587; War of 1812 demonstration, 157; woman suffrage convention, 283; in World War II, 480; Wrightsville dam, 451. *See also* Sloan General Hospital; Vermont State House

Montpelier & St. Johnsbury Railroad, 220
Montpelier & Wells River Railroad, 307
Montpelier Seminary, 266
Montreal, 97. *See also* Hochelaga
Monts, sieur de, 35
Moody, John, 578
Moonlight in Vermont, 467
Moore, Henry, 88
Moretown, Vt., 558
Morgan, William, 183, 184
Morgan horse, 253, 261, 384
Morrill, Justin Smith: at Bennington celebration, 341; Land Grant Act, 237, 320-22; political career, 245-47; portrait of, 340; Sen Jeffords, comparison with, 597; Strafford homestead, 569; war, opposed to, 342-43
Morris, Gouverneur, 79
Morris, Lewis, 79-80
Morrison, Robert, 122
Morristown, Vt., 405, 434
Morse, Franklin, 257, 258, 270
Morse, George, 258-59
Morse, Gretchen, 602
Morse, Huldah, 257
Morse, Orlando, 257
"Morse-Giuliani Formula," 602
Mosher, Howard Frank, 619
mosquitoes, 559
motion pictures, 391, 467, 619
Moulton, Elbert G., 607-8
Mount Holly, Vt., 8, 214, 611
Mountain Rule, 4, 323-26, 359, 490
Moyse, Blanche Honneger, 554
Moyse, Louis, 554
Moyse, Marcel, 554
Mudgett, Truman, 154
Muller, H. Nicholas, 155, 312, 553
Mungo, Raymond, 572
Munro, Hugh, 89
Munro, John, 88-89
Murray, Orson, 189-90
museums, 300, 569. *See also* art galleries
music and musicians, 331-33, 554. *See also* Vermont Symphony Orchestra

musical instruments, 297-98. *See also* Estey Organ
   Company
Mutch, John, 355

Napoleon I (Emperor of the French), 151
Napoleonic Wars, 1800-1814, 151-52
Nash, William, 237
National Child Labor Committee, 367, 368
National Life Insurance Company, 307, 546
National Republican Party, 185-87
National Trust for Historic Preservation, xviii, 615
Native Americans: Archaic period, 9-12; burial rituals,
   11, 12; disease, 27, 29-30; family units, 18; horticul-
   ture, 14-17, 26; hunting-gathering, 8-11, 13-16, 18, 28,
   29; Paleoindians, 8-9; trade with Europeans, 29; vil-
   lages, 18-19, 28; warfare, 25-27; witchcraft, 28;
   Woodland period, 12-18. *See also* names of tribes
Nelson, Robert, 192-93
New Amsterdam, 45
New Deal, 437-47, 448-49, 476. *See also* names of spe-
   cific programs, e.g. Civilian Conservation Corps
New England, 40, 44, 79-80, 143
New England Agricultural Society, 237
New England Antislavery Society, 189
New England Bach Festival, 554
New England Culinary Institute, 568-69
New England Milk Producers' Association, 409-10
New France, 33; fall of, 70; fur trade, 39; Huguenots
   prohibited, 40; Indian enemies, 38; population, 46, 60,
   63; royal colony, 44. *See also* seigneuries
New Hampshire. *See* Eastern Union
New Hampshire Grants: Fort Dummer precedent, 61,
   78; land grant controversy, 73-81, 82-83, 85-86, 89,
   90, 113; map, *76*
New Haven, Vt., 486
New Netherlands, 33, 38-39, 42
New Orleans, Battle of, 1815, 163
New York Anti-Rent Wars, 87- 88
New York (Colony): manorial system, 80, 87-88
New York land grants in Vermont: 1775 map, 77; con-
   troversy over, 79-94 *passim*, 99-100, 110, 112
New York (State): admission of Vt. into Union, 116, 124-
   25; 1777 constitution, 100, 105. *See also* Western Union
New York-Vermont Summer Youth Project, 541-42, 543
Newbury, Vt.: Abenakis in, 577; antislavery movement,
   192; Catholics, antipathy toward, 196; first settler, 86;
   legislature at, 150; Montebello resort, *335*. *See also*
   Cowass

Newport, Vt., 267, *433*, 528
newspapers, 141, 197, 226, 554. *See also* titles of
   newspapers
Newton, Earle Williams, 522, 547, 550-51
Nichols, Clarina Howard, 280-82
Nichols, George W., 281
Nichols, Mr., 329
Nightingale, Florence, 263
Niquette, Russell, 501, 503
Nixon, Richard M., 586, 590, 600
normal schools, 206, 320
Norris, George E., 302
Norris, Kathleen, *381*
North Hero, Vt., 113
North River (ship), 149
Northeast Dairy Compact, 566-67
Northeast Organic Farming Association, 568
Northfield, Vt.: Ku Klux Klan in, 406; labor strike, 455;
   railroad town, 215-16, 223, 303; state capital, vies for,
   279; textile industry, 156, 482; women voters, 404;
   WPA mural, 441
Northwest Passage, 21, 22, 24-25
Norton, Edward, *209*
Norton, Vt., 573
Norwich University, 210, 267, 320-21, 476, 486-87
nostalgia, for Vermont, 549-50, 618
Novikoff, Alex B., 530-31
Noyes, John Humphrey, 202-3
nuclear power plant, 513
numismatics. *See* money
Nuquist, Andrew E.: candidate for U.S. House, 493, *494*;
   on election process, 358, 359; on local government,
   107; on one town-one vote, 509; on Perry Merrill, 508;
   on state government, 507; state historian, 553
Nuquist, Edith W., 507, 508, 509, 553

Oakes, James L., 542-43
Oakes Ames (ship), 219
O'Connor, Timothy, 590
Odziozo, 30, *31*
oil embargo, 1973, 564, 589, 590, 610
Old Home Week, 336-37
Olive Branch (ship), 131
Olmsted, Frederick Law, 569
Omnibus Flood Control Act, 1936, 452
Ompompanoosuc River, 453
Oneida Community, 203
Onion River Land Company: break-up of, 129, 131;

formation of, 84; future of, 115; political representation, 111; Yorker encroachments on, 89, 120
Onuf, Peter S., xvi-xvii, 124
opera houses, 293, 308, *333-34*, 352
Orange County, Vt., 310
Order of Women Legislators, 487
organic farming, 568
Orleans County, Vt., 233, 234
orphanages, 305
Orton, Vrest: career, 549-50; cofounder of *Vermont Life*, 522, 547; historic preservationist, 551; parkway proposal, against, 445; on W. J. Coates, 419
Orton Family Foundation, 615-16
Orvis, John, 201
Orwell, Vt., 167
O'Shea, Bernard, 530
Ottauquechee River, 454
overseers of the poor, 439, 512
oxen, 386

pacifists, 393-94
Packard, Arthur, 411, 471, 474, 492-93
Page, Carroll S., 341
Page, David, 155
Page, John, 516
Page, John B., 219, 221, 292
Paine, Charles (1799-1853), 174, 198, 214-18, 221
Paine, Charles (b. 1830), 174, 183, 204
Paine, Elijah, 156, 174, 183, 190
Painter, Gamaliel, 138-39
painting and painters, 226-27, 252, 273-75, *333-34*. *See also* names of artists
Paleoindians, 8-9
Paley, Grace, 622
Palmer, A. Mitchell, 394-95
Palmer, Edward, 319
Palmer, William, 187
panics. *See* depressions
Panton, Vt., 89
paper industry, 380, 415, 416, 588, 607-8
Paquette, Gordon, 611
Parmelee, Annette W., *404*
Parrington, Vernon Louis, 203
Parsons, Samuel, 95
Parsons, Samuel A., 510
Partridge, Frank C., 456, 502
Partridge, Sanborn, 502
Passumpsic River Railroad, 299
Patriote War, 1837-1842, 192-93

Patrons of Husbandry. *See* Grange
Patterson, Eleazer, 112
Patterson, William, 93
Paul, Mary, 240
Pawlet, Vt., 350
Peach, Arthur Wallace, 419
Peacham, Vt.: Alger Hiss, landowner in, 527; in Civil War, 256; distilleries, 157; grand list, 173; Great Depression in, 434; religion, 178, 179; schoolhouse, *371*; summer people, influence on, 543-45; telephones, 388
pear thrips, 567
Pearson, Leonard, 542-43
Peck, Asahel, 323-24
Peck, Louis, 589
Peet, Ed, 473
Pegler, Westbrook, 527
Peisch, Francis, 531
Penniman, Jabez, 152, 153
Pennsylvania Constitution, 102-3, 104, 105, 106, 108
Perfectionism, 203
periodicals, 419-20. *See also* specific titles
Perkins, Henry F., 429, 430-31, 436
Perkins, Nathan, 120, 141-42, 179
Perkins Geology Museum, 7
Perrin, Noel, 619
Peru, Vt., *140*
petroglyphs, 17-18
Pettibone, J. S., 233
Phelps, Edward J., 230, 341, 377
Phelps, John Wolcott, 250
Philadelphia, 131
Philip, King, 47, 49
Philo, Mount, 7, 438
photography and photographers, 271-73. *See also* names of photographers
Pierce, Franklin, 243
Pike, Zebulon Montgomery, 160
Pilgrims, 40
Pinchot, Gifford, 378-79
Pingree, Samuel E., 269-70
pioneer life: 1789 description, 120, 141-42; end of, 143; on N.H. Grants, 82; in Randolph, 118-19; in Wolcott, *117-18*; in Woodstock, 117
Pitkin, Royce S., 472, *498*, 553-54
Pitt, William, 65
Pittsfield, Vt., 611
Pizzagalli Construction Company, 589
Plainfield, Vt., 379, 572
planning, state, 441, 506-7, 508

plate tectonics, 2-4
Plattsburgh, Battle of, 1814, 161-63
Plattsburgh, N.Y., 158, 159
Pleistocene period. *See* glaciation
Plumley, Charles A.: 1946 election campaign, 493, *494*; anti-Communist agenda, 528, 529; Lend-Lease, votes for, 478; Northfield background, 475-76
Plymouth, Vt., 167
Plymouth Colony, 40
poetry: Hard, *A Mountain Township,* 548; "John Grumlie," 135; Phelps, "The Lay of the Lost Traveler," 230; race discrimination verse, 541-42; Saxe, "The Whig's Lament," 200
poets. *See* writers
political conventions, 185-87, 360, 361-62, 374
politics and government: decline of party identities, 164; growing voter independence, 1970-2002, 594-95; in-migration's influence on, 597; party politics, 1830s, 196-97; two-party system, emergence of, 593. *See also* elections; state government; town meeting; names of political parties
poll tax, 107
Pollina, Anthony, 594, 605-6
Pomeroy, John, 158
Pomfret, Vt., 119
poor, 193-94, 436, 439, 620-21
Poor, John Alfred, 219
poor farms, 209, 512
population, state: 1840 census, 194-95; 1850 census, 210; 1870 census, 283-84; 1880 and 1890 census, 288; 1950 and 1970 census, 515; growth, impact of, 558; growth following statehood, 131; growth rates: 1960-2000, 557; early 1800s, 167; on N.H. Grants, 81, 92; rural and foreign-born, early 1900s, 348
Porche, Verandah, 572-73
Porter, William K., 513
Portland & Ogdensburg Railroad, 220
postage stamps, 571
postal service, 141, 388
potash, 82, 153
Potash, P. Jeffrey, 126
potatoes, 231, *233*-34
pottery, 12, 17, *209,* 554
Poultney, Vt., 157, 204, 350-51
powder horns, *65*
Power, Marjory W., 14, 15, 19
Powers, H. Henry, 282-83
Pownal, Vt., 79, 120, 367
Prendergast, William, 88

Preservation Trust of Vermont, 562
Prevost, George, Sir, 160, 161-63
prices and wages: granite industry wages, 456; marble industry wages, 456, 459; in St. Johnsbury, 301; weekly wages mandate, 363
primaries, direct, 374, 398, 399
Princetown, 79
printing and printers, 418-20
prisons. *See* correctional institutions; Vermont. State Prison
probate records, 116, 136
Proctor, Fletcher, 349, 358, 363-64, 380
Proctor, Mortimer D.: 1946 gubernatorial primary, 490, 492-93, *494,* 495; donor of maple research farm, 553; governor, 491
Proctor, Redfield (1831-1908): in Civil War, 270; on forestry commission, 377; Fort Ethan Allen, promotes, 392; marble industry magnate, 293-95, 310; political career, 293-*94,* 358; war supporter, 342-43
Proctor, Redfield (1879-1957), 400, 407
Proctor, Vt., 295-96, 456-59
Proctor Machine. *See* Republican Party
Progressive Party (founded 1912), 365-66, 374
Progressive Party (founded 1948), 526, 529
Progressive Party (founded 2000), 594
progressivism, 362-66, 383, 398
prohibition, 205-6, 330, 360, 361, 401-3. *See also* temperance
projectile points, 8-9, 10, 13-14
property rights, 104, 611, 609
property tax, 372, 427, 603-4, 606; abatement for farms, 614
Prouty, George H., 364, 380
Prouty, Winston L., 515, 590
psychiatric hospitals, 298, 314
public health, 314, 396-97
public utilities, 364. *See also* electric utilities
public welfare, 375, 383-84, 434-37, 512, 601-2
publishers, 549, 550-51
Putney, Vt.: cow wars, 112; equivalent lands, 54; George Aiken's hometown, 447; Great Meadows, 56; music in, 554; religion, 203
Pynchon, Thomas, 40
Pyramid Corporation, 611-12

Quarry Workers International Union, 352
Québec City, 35, 39, 67-68, 97
Queen Anne's War, 1702-1713, 52-53
Queen City Cotton Company, 459, 482

Quimby, Lorna, 543-44
quotations, in State House, 616-17

Racine, Douglas, 593
radio broadcasting, 443, 496, 552, 554-55
Ragueneau, Paul, Father, 41
railroads: 1927 flood, decline following, 427; building of, 213-30; Civil War use of, 261-62; government oversight, 313-14; regulation of, 364; St. Albans, significance to, 303-5; and tourism, 226, 305, 336. *See also* names of railroads; street railroads
Rainville, Martha T., 576
Rand, Jasper, 282-83
Randle, C., 98
Randolph, Vt.: Antimasonry in, 184; antislavery movement, 192; frontier life, 118-19; industry, 561; normal school, 320; political rally, *494*; suspicion of communism, 527, 529; woman suffrage rally, *404*
rBST, 567
"Reach Up" program, 601
Read, Charles, 282-83
reading. *See* literacy
Reagan, Ronald, 596
Reagan site, 8
real estate business, 539-40
reapportionment: 1962 special legislative session, 502; Buckley sues for, 509-10; Council of Censors proposals for, 276-79, 509; federal courts force 1965 reform, 510-11; to follow federal decennial census, 599-600
recreation, 331-34, 558. *See also* Chautauquas
red ochre, 11
Red Scare. *See* communism
Redemption Act, 1780, 121
regional planning commissions, 613-14
religion, 75, 86, 106, 141-43. *See also* revivals; names of denominations and sects
Remington Arms, 414
Republican Party: birth of, 244-45, 247-48, 249; hegemony: 1870-1900, 323-28; 1900-1927, 397-401; Old Guard, waning of, 492-93, 499, 501; Proctor Machine, 358-61, 399, 400, 474; progressive turn, 1930s, 468-75; Sen. Jeffords' leaving, 596-97. *See also* Mountain Rule
restaurants, 569
retail stores, 562, 611. *See also* general stores; shopping malls
Revere, Paul, 48
revivals, 175, 177-80
Revolutionary War, 1775-1783, 94-99, 101, 108-10. *See also* names of battles

Rice, William H., 428
Richardson, Harry W., 1
Richelieu River, 25, 36, 37, 41, 45, 129
Riedesel, Friedrich von, 109
Riehle, Theodore M., 514
Rinn, J. Phillip, 341
Ripley, Edward H., 293
Ripton, Vt., 376, 379, 417-18, 541
Riverton, Vt. *See* Berlin, Vt.
roads: 1927 flood repairs, 425, 426, 427; automobiles' demands on, 386, 463; CCC projects, 438; federal-state cooperation, 497; Fort Number Four to Cowass, 62; on frontier, 133-34; government oversight, 314-15. *See also* Crown Point Road; Green Mountain Parkway; Interstate Highway System; turnpikes
Robbins, Catherine, *381*
Roberval, Jean-François de la Roque, sieur de, 24
Robinson, John, 244
Robinson, Moses, 110-11
Robinson, Rachel Gilpin, 190-91, *337*
Robinson, Rowland Evans, 337-39
Robinson, Rowland Thomas, 190-91, *337*
Robinson, Samuel, 75, 81, 86-87, 116
Rochester, Vt., 573
Rock Dunder, *31*
Rockingham, Vt.: Bellows Falls: labor strike, 415, 416; petroglyphs, 17-18; in World War II, 482; first Protestant sermon in Vt., 53; French and Indians attack, 61; Saxton's River: winter carnival, 465; War of 1812, opposition to, 157; Westminister massacre, prelude to, 93
Rockwell, Norman, 480-81
Rogers, Robert, 68-70
Rollins, Frank, 336
Roosevelt, Eleanor, 485
Roosevelt, Franklin D.: Camp William James, supports, 484-85; George Aiken disagrees with, 449, 452-53, 455, 477-78; and New Deal, 437, 442, 451; Vt. opposition to, xvii; Vt. secretary to, 475; Vt. support for, 468, 476, 479
Roosevelt, Theodore: environmental conservationist, 375-76, 378, 379; Vt. supporter, 448; in Vt., *365*-66; on Vt., 617
Rosenstock-Hussey, Eugene, 485
Ross, Harold, 418
Roth, Randolph A., 188, 197
Rowlandson, Mary, 49-*50*
Royce, Stephen, 244-45, 247
Rozwenc, Edwin C., 471

Ruggles, Carl, 417
Rumney, Thomas, 234
rumrunning. *See* smuggling
Rupert, Vt., 89, 570-71
rural communities: 1990 census figures, 563; bedroom communities, becoming, 545, 546-47, 557-58; life in, 621-22; local services, support for, 383; national reform movement for, 370; political influence of, 375, 398; social change, 1870-1900, 309-13; state program for, 428-32
Rural Electrification Administration, 449
Rural Rehabilitation Program, 445-7
Rural Vermont, 594
Rushlow, April, 580
Russell, Charles Edward, 300
Russell, Howard S., 413
Rutherford, Walter, 79
Rutland, Vt.: antislavery sentiment, 243; automobile, arrival of, 384, 386; in Civil War, 250, 259, 260, 261; distillery, 136; early growth, 132; incorporation as city, 294, 295, 296; industrial history, 292-96; labor history, 356-57; labor strike, 456-57; legislature at, 150; panic of 1837, 193; poor farm, 512; population, 292, 558; Pres. Harrison in, 341-42; religion, 180, 205; state capital, vies for, 279; street trolley, 387; woman suffrage convention, 283; in World War II, 482; WPA mural, 441
Rutland & Burlington Railroad Company, 214, 215, 218-19, *225*
Rutland County, Vt., 240-41, 284, 502
Rutland County Temperance Society, 182
Rutland Herald, 359, 478, 554
Rutland Marble Company, 293
Rutland Railroad, 219, 229-30, 359, 364, 502
Ryan, Robert, 539

Saguenay, Kingdom of, 23, 24
St. Albans, Vt.: Abenakis in, 577, 580; big-box stores, rejects, 562; Embargo, opposition to, 153; intemperance in, 182; Pres. Harrison in, 341-42; railroad center, *303*-5; woman suffrage meeting, 283; WPA mural, 441
St. Albans raid, 1864, 266-67, *268*
St. Armand, Nicolas-René Levasseur, sieur de, 60
St. Clair, Arthur, 108-9
St. Denis, P.Q., 192
St. Francis, Homer, 578, 579, 580
St. Francis raid, 1759, 68-70
St. John, P.Q., 96, 155
St. Johnsbury, Vt.: Athenaeum, 300, 334; automobile ownership, 386; big-box stores, rejects, 562; Civil War memorial, 273; Fairbanks company town, 298-301; Great Depression in, 435; N.Y.-Vt. Summer Youth Project, 541; poor farm, 512; population decline, 558; pottery, 157; Pres. Harrison in, 341-42; recreation, 331; telephones, first, 388; woman suffrage meeting, 283, 328
St. Johnsbury Academy, 300, 301
St. Johnsbury & Lake Champlain Railroad, *213*
St. Leger, Barry, 101, 115
St. Michael's College, 350, 541, 587
sales tax, 585, 596, 606
Salisbury, Vt., 157
Salmon, Thomas P.: Abenaki tribal recognition, 578-79; administrative reorganization, 599; appoints commission on food, 564; environmental policy, 612; and industrial development, 560; record as governor, 588-90
Salussolia, Barry, 290
same-sex couples. *See* civil union
Sanders, Bernard, 566, 588, 594, 595
Saratoga, Battle of, 1777, 110
Saratoga (ship), 162-63
Sargent, John G., 425
sawmills. *See* mills
Saxe, John Godfrey, 200
Saxton's River, Vt. *See* Rockingham, Vt.
scales (weighing instruments). *See* Fairbanks (E. & T.) & Company; Howe Scale Company
Schenectady, N.Y., 45, 52
school buildings, 206, 318-19, *371*
schools. *See* high schools; normal schools; names of schools
Schuyler, John, 51, 52
Schuyler, Philip, 97
Scott, Julian, *275*
Scottish Americans, 353-54
sculpture and sculptors, 271, 273. *See also* names of artists
Seal of Quality, 568
Seaver, Carole, 538-39
Seaver, Ted, 538-39
secession, xvii
second homes. *See* vacation homes
Sedgwick, John, 253
Sedition Act, 1798, 128-29
seigneuries, 57-58, *59,* 60
Senécal, Joseph-André, 58-59
September 11 terrorist attacks, 2001, 562-63
Serkin, Rudolph, 554

Shafter, Oscar L., 244, 245
Shaftsbury, Vt., 79, 83, 334, 570
Sharon, Vt., 379, 484-85
Shays, Daniel, 124
Shays's Rebellion, 1786, 124-25
sheep: Civil War benefits sheep farmers, 261; merinos, 232; sheep craze: beginning of, 170-73; height of, 194; wool prices, fall of, 199-201. *See also* wool tariff
Shelburne, Vt., 138, 557
Shelburne, William Petty Fitzmaurice, Earl of, 81
Shelburne Farms, 569
Shelburne Museum, 552
Shelburne Shipyards, 482-83
Sherburne, Vt., 604
Sheridan, Philip, 266
Sherman, Michael, 447
Sherwood, Justus, 114
Sherwood, Robert (1896-1955), 418
Sherwood, Robert E., 475
shipping, 138, 148-49, 222
shopping malls, 611-12
Shoreham, Vt., 95-96, 132, 173, 167
Simmonds Precision, 561
Simon, William J., 404-5
Simpson, Mary Jean, 440
Simpson, W. Arthur, 490, 501
Skenesborough, N.Y., 98
skiing: early days of, 465-66; industry growth, *522-23*; resorts attract developers, 607; state promotion of, 522; trail building, 466-67; weather, effect on, 559
Skitchewaug site, 14-15
Slade, James L., 249
Slade, William, 187, 191, 207
slate, 2
slate industry, 306, 416
slavery: 1855 quotation on, 616-17; antislavery movement, 188-92, 201-2; Bennington Co. slave, 116; support for, 251; Thirteenth Amendment, 276, 278-79; Vt. constitution on, 104, 188. *See also* Fugitive Slave Act, 1850; Missouri Compromise, 1820
Sloan, W. J., 263
Sloan General Hospital, 263-65, 266
Small, Sam, 360
Small v. *Carpenter,* 84
Smalley, David, 263
Smith, Charles M., 445, 457
Smith, Donald Alan, 86
Smith, Edwin C., 343-45
Smith, Elias, 117

Smith, Israel, 146, 147
Smith, John Gregory: Civil War governor, 252, 257, 263; host to Pres. Harrison, 342; railroad entrepreneur, 218, 221, 303
Smith, John Gregory, Mrs., 267
Smith, Joseph, 202
Smith, Oramel H., 208
Smith, Peter, 595
Smith, William Farrar, 252, 271, 275
Smith, William Jay, 509
Smith General Hospital, 262-63, *264,* 265, 266
Smith-Lever Act, 1914, 411
Smugglers' Notch, 154-55
smuggling, 159-60, 402. *See also* Embargo, 1807-1809
Snake Mountain, 7
Snelling, Barbara Weil, 538, 581
Snelling, Richard A.: Abenaki recognition, denial of, 579; death of, 592; economic development, 561; and education funding, 602; elections lost, 505, 595; ERA supporter, 574; inaugural address, 601; record as governor, 590-91, 592, 595-96, 612; women, appointment of, 574
Snow, Mount, 522
snowshoeing, 45, 52, 465
social conflict, 572, 573, 583-84, 620-21
Social Security, 441
social welfare. *See* public welfare
Socialist Party of America, 355-56
Society for the Propagation of the Gospel (SPG), 81
soils, 132-33
Sokoki Indians, 18, 19, 43-44, 47, 49
Solitarian Press, 419
songs, 430, 467
Sons of Temperance, 331
Soule, Harris, *498*
South Burlington, Vt., 290, 557
South Hero, Vt., 113, 557
Southard, Ordway, 527
Southern Vermont Artists, 554
Soviet Union, 483
Spanish-American War, 1898, 342-43
Spanish Flu, 395-96
Spargo, John, 445
Spencer, Benjamin, 89-90
sports. *See* baseball; skiing
Spotsylvania, Battle of, 1864, 253-54
Springfield, Vt.: antislavery sentiment, 243; billboard controversy, 513; in Civil War, 261; Freemasons in, 183; immigrants to, 350; Indian site, 14-15; industry,

413-14, 481-82, 519; population, 168, 558; in World War II, 487
Squakheag, 47, 49
Stadacona, 21, 24, 26. *See also* Québec City
Stafford, Robert T.: elected to U.S. House, 501; for environment and education, 596; governor, 500-1, 512; succeeded by Sen. Jeffords, 595; wins U.S. Senate seat, 590
Stanford, Leland, 302
Stannard, George, 253, 267, 270
Stannard, Vt., 604
Stanton, Edwin, 262
Starinskas, Vyto, *565,* 603
Stark, John, 109, 110, 341
state and local history: collecting and teaching Vt. history, 553; founding of Vt. Historical Society, 207-8; pioneers in, 284-86; publications on Vt. history, 550-52, 553
state capital, 150-51, 279
State Emergency War Powers Act, 1943, 528
state forester, 380, 382
state forests, 379, 380, 484-85
state fossil, 7
state government: administrative reorganization, 398-400, 599-600; centralization of, 507; expansion of, 383, 500; planning, introduction of, 441, 506-7, 508. *See also* governors; names of governors; names of agencies, departments, etc.
state motto, xiii
state parks, 439, 467
Stebbins, Benjamin, 122
Stephen Daye Press, 549
sterilization, eugenic, 431
Stevens, Benjamin, 89
Stevens, Henry, 208, xiii
Stevens, Phineas, 62
Stewart, John W., 274-275, 287, *323,* 324-26
Stilwell, Lewis D., 551
Stoddard, Anthony, 54
Stoddard, John, 54
Stone, Lucy, 283, 328
Stone, Mason S., 319, 369, 373-74
Stone, Nathan, 85
stone boats, 6
stone walls, 5-6
stores. *See* general stores; retail stores; shopping malls
Storrs, Seth, 138
Stoughton, Charles B., 252
Stowe, Vt., 465
Strafford, Vt., 245, 569

Stratton, Vt., 607-8
Stratton Mountain, 199
street railroads, *306, 387*-88
Streeter, Russell, 180
strikes and lockouts: in construction industry, 588-89; in dairy industry, 486; Gov. Aiken settles, 460; in granite industry, 415, 416-17, 455-56; in marble industry, 456-59; in paper industry, 415, 416; in textile industry, 459
Strong, Samuel, 120
student protesters, 585-87
suffrage, 107. *See also* woman suffrage
Sugar Loaf Hill. *See* Defiance, Mount
Suitor, Fred, *356*
summer people, 544-45. *See also* vacation homes
Sunday legislation, 467
Sunderland, Vt., 79, 90
Sutherland Falls Marble Company, 293
Swanton, Vt.: Abenakis in, 577, 578, 579, 580; Boucher cemetery site, 12, 13, 60; Civil War memorial, 273; industry, 414; panic of 1837, 193
Swanton Courier, 530
Swedish Americans, 288, 295, 298, 310, 316
Swift, Benjamin, 191
Sylvester, Peter, 83

Taconic Range, 2, 6-7
Tadoussac, P.Q., 21, 22, 35, 39
Taft, William Howard, 365-66
Taignoagny, 22
"Take Back Vermont," *582,* 584, 594, 620
Talon, Jean Baptist, 46
tanning, 137
taverns, 142, 181, 182
taxation. *See* specific taxes, e.g. sales tax
Taylor, Henry C., 428-29
Taylor, James P., 381, 443, 465
Taylor, Zachary, 202
teachers, 206, 318, 319-20, 369-70
telegraph, 221
telephone, 298, 305, *388*
television broadcasting, 512, 552, 555
temperance, 181-83, 205, 300, 318, 327-30. *See also* prohibition
Ten Eyck, Henry, 88
Tenney, Romaine, 525
Tennien, William, Father, 485
term limits, 324-26, 427, 600
Terry, Stephen C., 513, 515
Texas, 201

textile industry: child labor, 368-69; Civil War, benefit from, 261; decline following World War II, 518-19; labor strikes, 459; Northfield woolen factory, 156; and "sheep craze," 172; Vt. women in Mass. mills, 240; during World War II, 482, 485-86

Thayer, S. W., 263

theater, 390

Thetford, Vt.: school system, 318, 319; Union Village dam, 453, 454; writers in, 619, 622

Thompson, Daniel Pierce, 208

Thompson, Dorothy, 418, 473, 483-85

Thompson, Zadock, 7

Three Rivers, P.Q., 39, 42

Thunderer (ship), 98

Tichenor, Isaac, 92, 121-22, 146, 154

Ticonderoga Mills, 588

Ticonderoga (ship), 552

Tinmouth, Vt., 121

tobacco, 14

tobogganing, 331

Tocqueville, Alexis de, xviii

Tomasi, Mari, 353

Tooth Fairy program, 588

Topsham, Vt., 254-55

tourism: artists, influx of, 417; and billboards, 514; economic dependency on, 559; farm vacations, 569; increase in, 1930s, 463-64; industry growth, 523; most popular attraction, 561; and parkway proposal, 443, 445; in post-Civil War era, 335-37; race discrimination in, 534, 536, 537; railroads increase, 226, 305; scenery-dependent, 377, 378; state promotion of, 386-87, 522; Vrest Orton skeptical of, 463. *See also* skiing; vacation homes

town charters, 73, 78

town health officer, 396-97

town meeting, 80, 107, 363, 587

towns. *See* cities and towns

Townshend, Vt., 167

Tracy, Alexandre de Prouville, seigneur de, 44, 45-46

trade unions: in Burlington, 357; in construction industry, 588-89; in granite industry, 352-56; in machine-tool industry, 519; in marble industry, 356-57; parody on union men, 382-83; resistance to, 415-16, 456-60; World War II drives for, 485-86

transportation. *See* automobiles; canals; railroads; roads; shipping; street railroads

travelogues: Addison Bancroft, 1847, 213; John Lambert, 1807, 139; Nathan Perkins, 1789, 120, 141-42; Nathaniel Hawthorne, 1835, 196; Timothy Dwight, 1798, 134

treaties: of Aix-la-Chapelle, 1748, 62; of Ghent, 1814, 163; of Paris, 1763, 71; of Ryswick, 1697, 52; of St. Germain en Laye, 39; of Utrecht, 1713, 53

Trinity College, 587

trolleys. *See* street railroads

Trow, Martin, 532

Troy Female Seminary, 206

True, Marshall M., 291

Truman, Harry S., 476, 479, 499

Tryon, William, 88, 89

tuberculosis, in cattle, 411-12

turkey drives, 234-35

Turner, Frederick Jackson, xv-xvi, xviii

turnpikes, 139, *140,* 314-15

Tuttle, Fred, 619-20

Twilight, Alexander, 206

Underground Railroad, 190-91

Underhill, Vt., 546

Underwood, Levi, 218

unemployed, in Great Depression, 434-35, 439

unicameral legislatures, 105, 196-97

Unilever, 561

Union Mutual Fire Insurance Company, 307, 546

Union Village, Vt. *See* Thetford, Vt.

United Columbia, 130-31

United Labor Party, 295

United Nations, 493, 527

United States Congress, 287, 323, 324

United States Constitution, 124

University of Vermont: African American students at, 535-36; agricultural college, establishment of, 320-22; decline of, 210; extension work, 410-11; founding, *148*; Lane Series, 554; nondenominational, 179-80; Novikoff firing, 530-31; N.Y.-Vt. Summer Youth Project, 541; in panic of 1837; post-World War II boom, 552-53; radio broadcasting from, 555; state funding, 500; state history, collecting and teaching of, 553; Vietnam War protest, 586-87; War of 1812 troops at, 160; in World War II, 486-87. *See also* Kake Walk

Upham Lake, 6

urban sprawl, 562, 611-12, 615-16

urbanization, 239-40, 284, 467-68, 516, 557

U.S. Pottery Company, *209*

utilities. *See* electric utilities; public utilities

vacation homes, 337, 446, 464, 545. *See also* summer people

Valcour Island, Battle of, 1776, *98*-99

INDEX

Valentine, Alonzo B., 310, 216
Valley of Vermont, 2
Van Buren, Martin, 198
van Corlaer, Arendt, 41
Van Dyck, Vedder, 531
Van Ness, Cornelius P., 156, 159-60, 169, 189, 206
Vaudreuil, Gov., 55
Veazey, Wheelock, 270
Vergennes, Vt.: first incorporated city, 239, 290; industry, 561; iron works, 157; legislature at, 150; Lyon in jail in, 129; Pres. Harrison visits, 341-42; shipbuilding at, 161; in World War II, 482
Vergennes people, 30
Vermont. Administration, Agency of, 507, 599
Vermont, admission into the Union, 99, 112-13, 115, 116, 123, 124-26, *127*
Vermont. Agriculture, Board of, 238, 316, 337, 380
Vermont. Agriculture, Department of, 411-12
Vermont. Censors, Council of: 1855 meeting, 276-77; 1869 meeting, 278-80; abolishment of, 280; Know-Nothing members of, 249; proposals for popular representation, 509; Vt. constitution on, 105
Vermont. Control, Board of, 398, 400
Vermont. Country Life, Commission on, 428-32, 463-64, 522
Vermont. Development and Community Affairs, Agency of, 599
Vermont. Development Commission, 520
Vermont. Economic Development Authority, 560
Vermont. Education, State Board of, 370, 372, 373
Vermont. Emergency Relief Administration, 439, 440
Vermont. Environmental Board, 609, 610, 614
Vermont. Environmental Conservation, Agency of, 599
Vermont. Forestry Commission, 377
Vermont. General Assembly: biennial sessions proposed, 278, 279-80; one town-one vote, 508-9; parody on farmer legislator, 382-83; permanent location for, 150; Senate established, 196-97; sessions, length of, 326-27, 502; terms, number of, 326; urban centers gain influence, 398; women in, 404, 487, 574. *See also* reapportionment
Vermont. Governor's Council, 196-97
Vermont. Historic Sites Commission, 548, 551
Vermont. Housing and Conservation Trust Fund, 614
Vermont. Human Rights Commission, 539-40
Vermont. Human Services, Agency of, 599
Vermont, ideas of, 616-23
Vermont. Industrial Building Authority, 520
Vermont. Industrial Development Authority, 560, 566
Vermont. Industrial Relations, Department of, 460

Vermont. Labor Relations Board, 589
Vermont. Lottery, State, 604
Vermont. National Guard: in 1927 flood, 423; called out to strike, 416, 455, 457; first woman adjutant, 576; at Fort Ethan Allen, 392; in World War II, 476-77
Vermont. Natural Resources, Agency of, 599
Vermont. Natural Resources, Interagency Committee on, 513
Vermont. Public Safety, Committee of, 393
Vermont. Public Safety, Department of, 495, 496, *497*
Vermont. Public Service Commission, 364, 450
Vermont. Public Welfare, Department of, 398
Vermont. Publicity, Bureau of, 386-87, 464
Vermont. Railroad Commission, 313-14, 364
Vermont, Republic of, 1777-1791. *See* Eastern Union; Haldimand negotiations; Vermont Constitution; Western Union
Vermont. Safety, Council of, 108, 110
Vermont. Scenery Preservation Council, 513
Vermont. State Colleges, 554, 589
Vermont. State Hospital, 314, 436
Vermont. State Land Use Board, 464-65
Vermont. State Library Commission, 368
Vermont. State Planning Board, 441
Vermont. State Planning Office, 508, 610
Vermont. State Prison, *146,* 147-48, 209-10, 314
Vermont. Student Assistance Corporation, 512
Vermont. Study State Government, Commission to. *See* "Little Hoover Commission"
Vermont. Supreme Court, 574-76, 587
Vermont. Transportation, Agency of, 599
Vermont & Canada Railroad, 218
Vermont & Massachusetts Railroad, 215
Vermont Antislavery Society, 190-91
Vermont Archaeological Society, 552
Vermont Arts Council, 512, 554
Vermont associations, 288-89, 309
Vermont Castings, 561
Vermont Central Railroad, 213-19, 222, 223-24. *See also* Central Vermont Railroad
Vermont Chamber of Commerce, 478
Vermont Children's Aid Society, 396
Vermont Civil Rights Union, 538-40
Vermont Colonization Society, 190
Vermont Conference of Charities and Corrections, 375
Vermont Conference of Social Work, 396
Vermont Constitution, *102*-8; amending process, 280, 600; amendments to, 599; on education, 107, 317, 604; on legislative representation, 508-9; on liberty and

free government, 616; on slavery, 188; on state university, 148. *See also* constitutional conventions
Vermont Cooperative Creameries, 410
Vermont Copper Mining Company, 294
Vermont Country Store, 549
Vermont Dairyman's Association, 237-38, 315, 321
Vermont Education Association, 528
Vermont Electric Cooperative, 449
Vermont exceptionalism, xvi-xviii
Vermont Farm Bureau: cooperation with Aiken, 471-72, 474; opposed to Republican leadership, 492-93; state federation, 411; supports Gov. Gibson, 495; and taxation, 448
Vermont Farms!, 569
Vermont Federation of Labor, 356, 471-72
Vermont Federation of Women's Clubs, 367-68, 369, *397*
Vermont Flood Credit Corporation, 425
Vermont Folklife Center, 570
Vermont Forum on Sprawl, 562, 615-16
Vermont Fresh Network, 569
Vermont Historical Society, 207-8, 286, 550-51
Vermont History, 550, 553
Vermont Horticultural Society, 316
Vermont in Mississippi, 538-39
Vermont Independent Party, 503
Vermont League for Good Roads, 315
Vermont Life: editors and contributors, 548, 550, 552; its portrayal of Vt., 547, 548; launching of, *521*-22, 551
Vermont Maple Sugar Makers Association, 316
Vermont Marble Company, 293, 296, 356, 456-59, 482
Vermont Mutual Life Insurance Company, 307
Vermont Piedmont, 2
Vermont Progressive Republican League, 365
Vermont Public Interest Research Group, 594
Vermont Public Radio, 552
Vermont (ship), 149
Vermont State Agricultural Society, 237
Vermont State Employees Association, 486, 589
Vermont State Fair, 237
Vermont State House: art in, 271, *275*; Christmas tree, 590; fire of 1857, 278; first capitol, *150*-51; Hall of Inscriptions, 616-17; marble floor, 2; second capitol, 277; third capitol, 307-8
Vermont statehood bicentennial, 1991, xvii
Vermont statehood centennial, 1891, 341-42
Vermont Symphony Orchestra, 441
Vermont Technical College, 554
Vermont Temperance Society, 181, 182, 205

Vermont Valley Railroad, 219
Vermont Woman Suffrage Association, 283, 328-29
Vermonters, 618-20
The Vermonter magazine, 289, 478, 551
Vernon, Vt. *See* Squakheag
Verrazzano, Giovanni, 21
veto power, 106
Vietnamese conflict, 1961-1975, 514-15, 572, 573, 585-87, 598
Volstead Act, 1919, 402
Volunteer Land Corps, 483-84
voting, 300, 600
voyages, European, 21-24, 38. *See also* names of explorerers

Wackerman, John J., 512
wages. *See* prices and wages
Waitsfield, Vt., *236, 558*
Wal-Mart Corporation, 562, 616
Walden, Vt., 461
Waldron, Clarence, 393-94
Wall, Max, 531
Wallace, Henry, 526
Walter, Dorothy C., 390-91
Walton, Eliakim P., 244
Walton, Ezekiel P., 244
Wampanoag Indians, 47
War of 1812, 156-63
Wardner, Henry Steele, 115
Warner, Chauncey, 305
Warner, Seth: death of, 126; on Ethan Allen's capture, 97; Green Mountain Boy, 85, 89, 90; Green Mountain Regt. leader, 97, 109; and Haldimand negotiations, 114
Warren, Vt., 379, 558
Washburn, Peter T., 250, 269-70, 325
Washington, D.C., 191, 242
Washington, George, 62, 63, 97, 109, 116
Washington County, Vt., 167, 558
Washington Electric Cooperative, 449
water cure. *See* hydrotherapy
water supply, 293, 308
Waterbury, Vt.: in 1927 flood, 422, 423; Little River dam, 451; recreation, 467; religion, 204; Waterbury Center: manufacturing, 560-61
Watergate affair, 1972-1974, 600
Waterman, Guy, 381
Waterman, Laura, 381
Waterman, Sterry R., 493, *494*

Watson, John H., 370-71
weather, 559. *See also* Eighteen-hundred-and-froze-to-death
Weathersfield, Vt., 136, 525
Weathersfield Telephone Company, 388
Webb, Electra Havemeyer, 552
Webb, Elizabeth Vanderbilt, 569
Webb, William Seward, 343-44, 377, 569
Webster, Daniel, 199, 241-42
Weeks, John E.: 1927 flood, deals with, 424, 425, 427, 428; and Commission on Country Life, 428; serves two 2-year terms, 326
Wells, David, 554
Wells, Janet, 554
Wells, William, 270
Welsh Americans, 350-51
Wentworth, Benning, 61, 73-74, 78-79
Wesselhoeft water cure, 298
West Haven, Vt., *565*
West River, 454
West Rutland, Vt., 176, 295, 296, 456-59
West Windsor, Vt., 517
Western Union, 115, 116
Westford, Vt., 611
Westminister, Vt., 61, 112, 150
Westminister massacre, 1775, 93-94
Weston, Vt., 310, *328,* 549
Weybridge, Vt., 384
whale, 7, 8-9
wheat, 133, 169-70, 172, 231
Wheeler, John, 194
Whig Party, 187-88, 201-2, 244, 245
White, John, 54
White, Lydia E., 254-55, 260
White, Pliny Holton, 284-*85*
White, William Allen, 400-1, 478, 491
White Harold H., *494*
White River Junction, Vt. *See* Hartford, Vt.
Whitefield, George, 87
Whitehall, N.Y., 152
Whitelaw, James, 118
Whiting, Henry, 270
Whiting, Vt., 603
whole-herd buyout, 566
Wilder, Jonas, 217-18, 222, 232
Wilgus, William J., 442-43
Willard, Emma Hart, 206, 320
Williams, Eunice, 51

Williams, John, 51, 52-53
Williams, Leroy, 536
Williams, Ralph, 539
Williams, Samuel, 133
Williamson, Chilton, 115
Williamstown, Vt., 174, 183, 273, 329
Williston, Vt., 120, 546, 562, 611-12
Wills, Hazel McLeod, 489
Wills, William: and agriculture, 483, 484; and flood control, 454; his lieutenant governor, 490; and labor, 460; Lend-Lease, favors, 478; nominated for lieutenant governor, 472; postwar planning, 489-90; State Guard, organizes, 477; on wartime Vt., 388
Wilmington, Vt.: land development, 607, 608, 611; ski areas sign, *522*; Swedes in, 310; in World War I, 394
Wilson, Harold Fisher, 241, 309, 550
Wilson, James, 151
Wilson, Stanley C., 436, 439, 446, 455
Wilson, Woodrow, 392, 393, 394
Winans, James, 149
Winans, John, 149
Windham County Democrat, 281
Windham Foundation, 620
windmills, 60
Windsor, Vt.: antislavery movement in, 192; canal convention, 169; early growth, 132; immigrants to, 350; industry, 413-14, 481-82; legislature at, 150; *patriotes* arrested, 192; population, 168, 558; in World War I, 393-94. *See also* Vermont. State Prison
Windsor Convention, 1777, 101-3, 108, 110
Windsor County, Vt., 284, 518
Windsor Tool Company, 414
Wing, Leonard, 455, 491-92
Winks, Robin W., 325-26
Winooski, Vt.: 1962 election in, 503, *504*; bird's-eye view, *289*; child mill workers, 368; immigrants, 350; textile industry, 518; in World War II, 482, 485
Winooski River: in 1927 flood, 421-22, *423*; flood control, 451; history of, 551; naming of, 18; smuggling on, 153
winter sports. *See* skiing; snowshoeing; tobogganing
Wirt, William, 187
Wiseman, Frederick, 577
Witters, Harry W., 440
Wolchik, Joseph, 579
Wolcott, Vt., 117-18
Wolf, Eric, 30
Wolf, Marguerite Hurrey, 621-22
Wolfe, James, 68

Wolk, David, 581

woman suffrage, 280-83, 327-28, 403-*4*

women: charitable organizations, support, 291-92; Civil War contributions, 282; commission to study rights of, 538; education of, 206; equal rights for, 574; farm work, 175; in state government, 574-76; in Vt. legislature, 404, 487, 574; World War I employment, 414; World War II employment, 482, 487. *See also* Equal Rights Amendment

Women's Christian Temperance Union (WCTU), 327-28, 329-30, 331

Wood, Gordon, 104

Wood, Leonard, 401

Wood, Thomas Waterman, *246,* 339-40, *343*

Woodbridge scandal, 125

Woodbury, Urban A., 269-70, 327, 378

Woodbury, Vt., 257, 258, 270

Woodland period, 12-18

Woodstock, Vt.: agriculture, 517; antislavery movement, 192; automobile, arrival of, 384; in Civil War, 259; early growth, 132; legislature at, 150; mail, quantity, 141; museum, 569; pioneer life in, 117; religion, 180; sheep raising, 172; ski tow, 465-*66*; WPA mural, 441

Woodward, Ronald, *497*

wool tariff, 170-72, 199-200

Woollcott, Alexander, 418

Worcester Mountains, 1

Works Progress Administration, 439, 440-41

World War I: agriculture, boost to, 408-9; Bonus Army veterans in Vt., 451; economy, impact on, 408-9, 414-15; home front, 393- 94; volunteers for, 392; Vt.'s war declaration, 391-92

World War II: draft, 476-77; home front, 480-88; numbers who served, 489; prelude to, 476-70; US entry into, 480; veterans of, 489, 496; volunteers for, 480; Vt.'s declaration of war, 479-80

World's Columbian Exposition, 1893, 340

Wright, Ralph G., 591-92

Wrightsville, Vt. *See* Montpelier, Vt.

Wrinn, Stephen M., 543

writers, 417-18, 572-73, 619. *See also* names of writers

Yale, Allen Rice, 300-1

Young, Ammi, 277, 278

Young, Bennett, 266-67

Young, Thomas, 101-3, 105

Young Turks, 502-3, 504, 590

About the Authors

P. Jeffrey Potash is co-director of the Center for System Dynamics at the Vermont Commons School in South Burlington, Vermont. A former college teacher, he is the author of *Vermont's Burned-Over District* (1991) and many articles on Vermont history.

Gene Sessions is professor emeritus of American history at Norwich University. He was co-editor of *Vermont Voices, 1609 Through the 1990s: A Documentary History of the Green Mountain State* (1999), has edited and contributed to many other publications on Vermont history, and was editor of *Vermont History*, the journal of the Vermont Historical Society.

Michael Sherman teaches at Vermont College of the Union Institute & University, in Montpelier, Vermont. He is the editor of *Vermont History*, has edited several books on Vermont history and government, and published many articles on Vermont and other topics.